Communications
in Computer and Information Science 1587

T0142045

More information about this series at https://link.springer.com/bookseries/7899

Xingming Sun · Xiaorui Zhang · Zhihua Xia ·
Elisa Bertino (Eds.)

Advances in Artificial Intelligence and Security

8th International Conference
on Artificial Intelligence and Security, ICAIS 2022
Qinghai, China, July 15–20, 2022
Proceedings, Part II

 Springer

Editors
Xingming Sun ⓘD
Nanjing University of Information Science
and Technology
Nanjing, China

Zhihua Xia ⓘD
Jinan University
Guangzhou, China

Xiaorui Zhang ⓘD
Nanjing University of Information Science
and Technology
Nanjing, China

Elisa Bertino ⓘD
Purdue University
West Lafayette, IN, USA

ISSN 1865-0929   ISSN 1865-0937 (electronic)
Communications in Computer and Information Science
ISBN 978-3-031-06760-0   ISBN 978-3-031-06761-7 (eBook)
https://doi.org/10.1007/978-3-031-06761-7

This Springer imprint is published by the registered company Springer Nature Switzerland AG
The registered company address is: Gewerbestrasse 11, 6330 Cham, Switzerland

Preface

The 8th International Conference on Artificial Intelligence and Security (ICAIS 2022), formerly called the International Conference on Cloud Computing and Security (ICCCS), was held during July 15–20, 2022, in Qinghai, China. Over the past seven years, ICAIS has become a leading conference for researchers and engineers to share their latest results of research, development, and applications in the fields of artificial intelligence and information security.

We used the Microsoft Conference Management Toolkit (CMT) system to manage the submission and review processes of ICAIS 2022. We received 1124 submissions from authors in 20 countries and regions, including the USA, Canada, the UK, Italy, Ireland, Japan, Russia, France, Australia, South Korea, South Africa, Iraq, Kazakhstan, Indonesia, Vietnam, Ghana, China, Taiwan, Macao, etc. The submissions cover the areas of artificial intelligence, big data, cloud computing and security, information hiding, IoT security, multimedia forensics, encryption and cybersecurity, and so on. We thank our Technical Program Committee (TPC) members and external reviewers for their efforts in reviewing papers and providing valuable comments to the authors. From the total of 1124 submissions, and based on at least three reviews per submission, the Program Chairs decided to accept 166 papers to be published in three LNCS volumes and 168 papers to be published in three CCIS volumes, yielding an acceptance rate of 30%. This volume of the conference proceedings contains all the regular, poster, and workshop papers.

The conference program was enriched by a series of keynote presentations, and the keynote speakers included Q.M. Jonathan Wu and Brij B. Gupta, amongst others. We thank them for their wonderful speeches.

There were 68 workshops organized in ICAIS 2022 which covered all the hot topics in artificial intelligence and security. We would like to take this moment to express our sincere appreciation for the contribution of all the workshop chairs and participants. We would like to extend our sincere thanks to all authors who submitted papers to ICAIS 2022 and to all TPC members. It was a truly great experience to work with such talented and hard-working researchers. We also appreciate the external reviewers for assisting the TPC members in their particular areas of expertise. Moreover, we want to thank our sponsors: ACM, ACM SIGWEB China, the University of Electronic Science and Technology of China, Qinghai Minzu University, Yuchi Blockchain Research Institute, Nanjing Normal University, Northeastern State University, New York University, Michigan State University, the University of Central Arkansas, Dublin City University,

Université Bretagne Sud, the National Nature Science Foundation of China, and Tech Science Press.

April 2022

Xingming Sun
Xiaorui Zhang
Zhihua Xia
Elisa Bertino

Organization

General Chairs

Yun Q. Shi	New Jersey Institute of Technology, USA
Weisheng Ma	Qinghai Minzu University, China
Mauro Barni	University of Siena, Italy
Ping Jiang	Southeast University, China
Elisa Bertino	Purdue University, USA
Xingming Sun	Nanjing University of Information Science and Technology, China

Technical Program Chairs

Aniello Castiglione	University of Salerno, Italy
Yunbiao Guo	China Information Technology Security Evaluation Center, China
Xiaorui Zhang	Engineering Research Center of Digital Forensics, Ministry of Education, China
Q. M. Jonathan Wu	University of Windsor, Canada
Shijie Zhou	University of Electronic Science and Technology of China, China

Publication Chair

Zhihua Xia	Jinan University, China

Publication Vice Chair

Ruohan Meng	Nanjing University of Information Science and Technology, China

Publicity Chair

Zhaoxia Yin	Anhui University, China

Workshop Chairs

Baowei Wang   Nanjing University of Information Science and
                                Technology, China
Lingyun Xiang   Changsha University of Science and Technology,
                                China

Organization Chairs

Genlin Ji   Nanjing Normal University, China
Jianguo Wei   Qinghai Minzu University and Tianjin University,
                                China
Xiaoyu Li   University of Electronic Science and Technology
                                of China, China
Zhangjie Fu   Nanjing University of Information Science and
                                Technology, China
Qilong Sun   Qinghai Minzu University, China

Technical Program Committee

Saeed Arif   University of Algeria, Algeria
Anthony Ayodele   University of Maryland Global Campus, USA
Zhifeng Bao   Royal Melbourne Institute of Technology,
                                Australia
Zhiping Cai   National University of Defense Technology,
                                China
Ning Cao   Qingdao Binhai University, China
Paolina Centonze   Iona College, USA
Chin-chen Chang   Feng Chia University, Taiwan
Han-Chieh Chao   National Dong Hwa University, Taiwan
Bing Chen   Nanjing University of Aeronautics and
                                Astronautics, China
Hanhua Chen   Huazhong University of Science and Technology,
                                China
Xiaofeng Chen   Xidian University, China
Jieren Cheng   Hainan University, China
Lianhua Chi   IBM Research Center, Australia
Kim-Kwang Raymond Choo   University of Texas at San Antonio, USA
Ilyong Chung   Chosun University, South Korea
Martin Collier   Dublin City University, Ireland
Qi Cui   Nanjing University of Information Science and
                                Technology, China
Robert H. Deng   Singapore Management University, Singapore
Jintai Ding   University of Cincinnati, USA

Xinwen Fu	University of Central Florida, USA
Zhangjie Fu	Nanjing University of Information Science and Technology, China
Moncef Gabbouj	Tampere University of Technology, Finland
Ruili Geng	Spectral MD, USA
Song Guo	Hong Kong Polytechnic University, Hong Kong
Mohammad Mehedi Hassan	King Saud University, Saudi Arabia
Russell Higgs	University College Dublin, Ireland
Dinh Thai Hoang	University of Technology Sydney, Australia
Wien Hong	Nanfang College of Sun Yat-Sen University, China
Chih-Hsien Hsia	National Ilan University, Taiwan
Robert Hsu	Chung Hua University, Taiwan
Xinyi Huang	Fujian Normal University, China
Yongfeng Huang	Tsinghua University, China
Zhiqiu Huang	Nanjing University of Aeronautics and Astronautics, China
Patrick C. K. Hung	University of Ontario Institute of Technology, Canada
Farookh Hussain	University of Technology Sydney, Australia
Genlin Ji	Nanjing Normal University, China
Hai Jin	Huazhong University of Science and Technology, China
Sam Tak Wu Kwong	City University of Hong Kong, China
Chin-Feng Lai	Taiwan Cheng Kung University, Taiwan
Loukas Lazos	University of Arizona, USA
Sungyoung Lee	Kyung Hee University, South Korea
Hang Lei	University of Electronic Science and Technology of China, China
Chengcheng Li	University of Cincinnati, USA
Xiaoyu Li	University of Electronic Science and Technology of China, China
Feifei Li	Utah State University, USA
Jin Li	Guangzhou University, China
Jing Li	Rutgers University, USA
Kuan-Ching Li	Providence University, Taiwan
Peng Li	University of Aizu, Japan
Yangming Li	University of Washington, USA
Luming Liang	Uber Technology, USA
Haixiang Lin	Leiden University, The Netherlands
Xiaodong Lin	University of Ontario Institute of Technology, Canada
Zhenyi Lin	Verizon Wireless, USA

Alex Liu	Michigan State University, USA
Guangchi Liu	Stratifyd Inc., USA
Guohua Liu	Donghua University, China
Joseph Liu	Monash University, Australia
Quansheng Liu	University of South Brittany, France
Xiaodong Liu	Edinburgh Napier University, UK
Yuling Liu	Hunan University, China
Zhe Liu	Nanjing University of Aeronautics and Astronautics, China
Daniel Xiapu Luo	Hong Kong Polytechnic University, Hong Kong
Xiangyang Luo	Zhengzhou Science and Technology Institute, China
Tom Masino	TradeWeb LLC, USA
Nasir Memon	New York University, USA
Noel Murphy	Dublin City University, Ireland
Sangman Moh	Chosun University, South Korea
Yi Mu	University of Wollongong, Australia
Elie Naufal	Applied Deep Learning LLC, USA
Jiangqun Ni	Sun Yat-sen University, China
Rafal Niemiec	University of Information Technology and Management, Poland
Zemin Ning	Wellcome Trust Sanger Institute, UK
Shaozhang Niu	Beijing University of Posts and Telecommunications, China
Srikant Ojha	Sharda University, India
Jeff Z. Pan	University of Aberdeen, UK
Wei Pang	University of Aberdeen, UK
Chen Qian	University of California, Santa Cruz, USA
Zhenxing Qian	Fudan University, China
Chuan Qin	University of Shanghai for Science and Technology, China
Jiaohua Qin	Central South University of Forestry and Technology, China
Yanzhen Qu	Colorado Technical University, USA
Zhiguo Qu	Nanjing University of Information Science and Technology, China
Yongjun Ren	Nanjing University of Information Science and Technology, China
Arun Kumar Sangaiah	VIT University, India
Di Shang	Long Island University, USA
Victor S. Sheng	Texas Tech University, USA
Zheng-guo Sheng	University of Sussex, UK
Robert Simon Sherratt	University of Reading, UK

Yun Q. Shi	New Jersey Institute of Technology, USA
Frank Y. Shih	New Jersey Institute of Technology, USA
Guang Sun	Hunan University of Finance and Economics, China
Jianguo Sun	Harbin University of Engineering, China
Krzysztof Szczypiorski	Warsaw University of Technology, Poland
Tsuyoshi Takagi	Kyushu University, Japan
Shanyu Tang	University of West London, UK
Jing Tian	National University of Singapore, Singapore
Yoshito Tobe	Aoyang University, Japan
Cezhong Tong	Washington University in St. Louis, USA
Pengjun Wan	Illinois Institute of Technology, USA
Cai-Zhuang Wang	Ames Laboratory, USA
Ding Wang	Peking University, China
Guiling Wang	New Jersey Institute of Technology, USA
Honggang Wang	University of Massachusetts-Dartmouth, USA
Jian Wang	Nanjing University of Aeronautics and Astronautics, China
Jie Wang	University of Massachusetts Lowell, USA
Jin Wang	Changsha University of Science and Technology, China
Liangmin Wang	Jiangsu University, China
Ruili Wang	Massey University, New Zealand
Xiaojun Wang	Dublin City University, Ireland
Xiaokang Wang	St. Francis Xavier University, Canada
Zhaoxia Wang	Singapore Management University, Singapore
Jianguo Wei	Qinghai Minzu University and Tianjin University, China
Sheng Wen	Swinburne University of Technology, Australia
Jian Weng	Jinan University, China
Edward Wong	New York University, USA
Eric Wong	University of Texas at Dallas, USA
Shaoen Wu	Ball State University, USA
Shuangkui Xia	Beijing Institute of Electronics Technology and Application, China
Lingyun Xiang	Changsha University of Science and Technology, China
Yang Xiang	Deakin University, Australia
Yang Xiao	University of Alabama, USA
Haoran Xie	Education University of Hong Kong, China
Naixue Xiong	Northeastern State University, USA
Wei Qi Yan	Auckland University of Technology, New Zealand

Aimin Yang	Guangdong University of Technology, China
Ching-Nung Yang	National Dong Hwa University, Taiwan
Chunfang Yang	Zhengzhou Science and Technology Institute, China
Fan Yang	University of Maryland, USA
Guomin Yang	University of Wollongong, Australia
Qing Yang	University of North Texas, USA
Yimin Yang	Lakehead University, Canada
Ming Yin	Purdue University, USA
Shaodi You	Australian National University, Australia
Kun-Ming Yu	Chung Hua University, Taiwan
Shibin Zhang	Chengdu University of Information Technology, China
Weiming Zhang	University of Science and Technology of China, China
Xinpeng Zhang	Fudan University, China
Yan Zhang	Simula Research Laboratory, Norway
Yanchun Zhang	Victoria University, Australia
Yao Zhao	Beijing Jiaotong University, China
Desheng Zheng	Southwest Petroleum University, China

Organization Committee

Xianyi Chen	Nanjing University of Information Science and Technology, China
Qi Cui	Nanjing University of Information Science and Technology, China
Zilong Jin	Nanjing University of Information Science and Technology, China
Yiwei Li	Columbia University, USA
Yuling Liu	Hunan University, China
Zhiguo Qu	Nanjing University of Information Science and Technology, China
Huiyu Sun	New York University, USA
Le Sun	Nanjing University of Information Science and Technology, China
Jian Su	Nanjing University of Information Science and Technology, China
Qing Tian	Nanjing University of Information Science and Technology, China
Qi Wang	Nanjing University of Information Science and Technology, China
Lingyun Xiang	Changsha University of Science and Technology, China

Zhihua Xia   Nanjing University of Information Science and
                                  Technology, China
Lizhi Xiong   Nanjing University of Information Science and
                                  Technology, China
Leiming Yan   Nanjing University of Information Science and
                                  Technology, China
Tao Ye   Qinghai Minzu University, China
Li Yu   Nanjing University of Information Science and
                                  Technology, China
Zhili Zhou   Nanjing University of Information Science and
                                  Technology, China

Contents – Part II

Big Data

Cloud Computing and Security

Multimedia Forensics

Artificial Intelligence

Crowd Anomaly Detection in Surveillance Video

Yunzuo Zhang[1(✉)], Kaina Guo[1], Zhaoquan Cai[2], and Tianshan Fu[1]

[1] School of Information Science and Technology, Shijiazhuang Tiedao
University, Shijiazhuang 050043, China
zhangyunzuo888@sina.com
[2] Shanwei Institute of Technology, Shanwei 516600, Guangdong, China

Abstract. With the advancement of technology, the analysis of crowd abnormal behavior has become a hot topic in the field of computer vision. The research not only includes the analysis of the abnormal behavior of a single pedestrian in a simple scene, but also includes the analysis of the overall abnormal behavior of the crowd in a complex scene. This paper research on the detection and alarm of abnormal crowd behavior in surveillance video. First, the moving target is detected by the background subtraction method. Secondly, the fall behavior in the video is detected through two-level SVM and human feature action recognition. At this stage, the human body features obtained in the target detection stage are analyzed, and the key point features of the human body are analyzed to determine whether the detection target has fallen behavior. Finally, a counting module is introduced to count the pedestrians on the basis of target detection in the current scene. We compare the changes in the number of people in the video frames at a set time interval in the same scene to determine whether a sudden crowd gathering occurred abnormal behavior.

Keywords: Crowd anomaly detection · Two-level SVM · GMM · Crowd counting

1 Introduction

In recent years, the recognition technology of crowd abnormal behavior has been widely used. Especially in the current epidemic era, pedestrians fall, and pedestrians suddenly gather and disperse are particularly concerned. Therefore, how to quickly and accurately perform target detection and abnormal behavior detection on pedestrians in surveillance video has become an urgent problem to be solved. Various detection methods that meet social needs have emerged as the times require, and have received extensive attention from the society [1–3].

At present, the behavior analysis technology based on single target has been relatively mature. The US Defense Advanced Research Projects Agency, Carnegie Mellon University, Massachusetts Institute of Technology and other universities jointly researched the major visual surveillance project VSAM, which realizes automatic video understanding technology for monitoring battlefields and ordinary civilian scenes. MIT's Pfinder system can track pedestrians in real time and recognize human behavior.

© The Author(s), under exclusive license to Springer Nature Switzerland AG 2022
X. Sun et al. (Eds.): ICAIS 2022, CCIS 1587, pp. 3–15, 2022.
https://doi.org/10.1007/978-3-031-06761-7_1

The system can adapt to different types of scenes, but it can only handle a single human behavior that is not blocked and requires a person to be standing. The W4 real-time visual monitoring system developed by Haritaolu and others can not only accurately locate people and segment the body parts of the human body, but also realize the tracking of multiple people, and can recognize simple behaviors such as standing, sitting, lying, and lying.

The existing group abnormal behavior detection and recognition technology can be divided into two categories according to the detection method: the first type is the traditional single-target-based behavior analysis method [4], which regards the group as composed of multiple single targets, respectively. The movement and behavior of a single target are analyzed and understood using target detection, segmentation, tracking, and recognition techniques. This type of method can achieve better results in simple scenes, but in complex and dense scenes, due to the diversity of group behaviors, mutual occlusion between individuals and other factors, the segmentation and tracking of moving targets are severely affected. The detection and identification of group abnormal behavior becomes very difficult. At the same time, because the calculation speed is affected by the number of targets, and the single-target-based analysis method ignores the interaction between people, the single-target-based behavior analysis method cannot efficiently and accurately detect and identify group abnormal behaviors. The second category is based on the behavior analysis method of the group as a whole [5]. At present, the behavior analysis method based on the group as a whole has been extensively studied because it is not affected by occlusion and shadow, and a variety of abnormal behavior detection and recognition methods based on the group as a whole have appeared. The most typical features are optical flow and space-time features [6]. Optical flow method is widely used in behavior analysis, and it is often used in moving object tracking and behavior recognition.

In the algorithm of group abnormal behavior detection and recognition based on the group as a whole, in addition to the feature description, abnormal detection is often achieved by training the behavior model and calculating the probability of the observation value under the model [7]. For example, HMM and LDA are probability-based models, which are divided into two stages: training and detection. In the training phase, the observation sequence samples in the normal scene are used for learning and training, and the group behavior model in the normal scene is established; in the detection phase, the observation features to be recognized are input into the model, and whether the input data is abnormal is judged according to its likelihood [8].

This paper mainly studies the detection and alarm of abnormal crowd behavior under surveillance video. There are many types of abnormal behavior in the crowd. This paper studies the behavior of pedestrians falling in various scenarios and the abnormal crowd suddenly gathering and dispersing in surveillance scenarios. behavior. Improved on the basis of "only recording but not judgment" in most surveillance systems at present, the detection and tracking of pedestrians appearing in surveillance videos, behavior analysis, and identification of abnormal behaviors can be used to detect sudden abnormal behaviors. The algorithm flow chart of this paper is shown in Fig. 1 below.

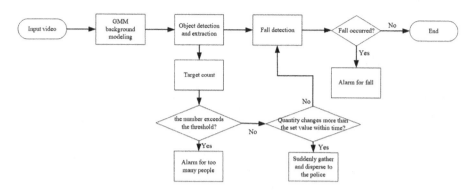

Fig. 1. Algorithm flow chart of this paper.

2 Background Modeling

Background and foreground are both relative concepts. Take a highway as an example: sometimes we are interested in cars coming and going on the highway. At this time, the car is the foreground, and the road and the surrounding environment are the background; sometimes we are only interested in breaking into Pedestrians on the highway are interested, at this time the intruder is the foreground, and other things including cars become the background. Using background modeling can identify moving pedestrian targets from real-time continuous video image frames, and perform detection and tracking to detect moving targets [9].

2.1 Frame Difference

The frame difference method [10] is to make difference between two or three adjacent frames of images in a video sequence. If the difference of a pixel at its corresponding position exceeds a set threshold, the pixel belongs to the foreground, otherwise it belongs to the background. The formula of the frame difference method is shown in formula (1).

$$g(x,y) = \begin{cases} 1, & |f_k(x,y) - f_{k-1}(x,y)| \geq T \\ 0, & |f_k(x,y) - f_{k-1}(x,y)| < T \end{cases} \tag{1}$$

Among them, $g(x,y)$ is the difference map of pixels (x,y) at frame k and frame $k-1$, and T is the preset threshold. If the T selection is too small, a lot of noise will be generated, and if the T selection is too large, larger holes may appear.

Although the frame difference method is simple in operation and easy to process in real time, it is sensitive to the movement of the target, cannot detect the complete target, and will produce a hole phenomenon [11].

2.2   ViBe Background Modeling

ViBe algorithm [12] is a background modeling algorithm based on random clustering of samples. The steps of the algorithm include background model initialization, pixel classification and background model update.

The ViBe algorithm uses the first frame of the video sequence to establish a background model, and the moving target can be detected from the second frame. The background model initialization is to select a pixel x value in the 8-neighborhood of the pixel as the background sample, and repeat it N times, as shown in formula (2).

$$ViBe \begin{cases} N_G(x) = \{x_1, x_2, \cdots, x_8\} \\ M(x) = \{v(y|y \in N_G(x))\} \end{cases} \tag{2}$$

where $v(x)$ is the pixel value of x and $M(x)$ is the background model. The Vibe algorithm calculates the Euclidean distance to classify pixels. $S_R(v(x))$ is a two-dimensional Euclidean space with a radius as the center point $v(x)$ to match the threshold R. If the number of elements in the intersection H of $S_R(v(x))$ and $M(x)$ is not less than the minimum matching number $\#min$, then pixel x is considered to be a background pixel, as shown in formula (3).

$$H\{S_R(v(x)) \cap \{v_1(x), v_2(x), \cdots, v_N(x)\}\} \tag{3}$$

The ViBe algorithm has a small amount of calculation and is fast and easy to implement. However, in the foreground segmentation stage, because the algorithm uses a fixed threshold, it will produce a large number of misjudgments under a dynamic background with interference such as water ripples and light, resulting in unsatisfactory detection results [13].

2.3   Mixed Gaussian Background Modeling

Gaussian mixture background modeling is a method based on pixel sample statistics. This method treats the pixel at each position of the video frame as an independent individual, and does not consider the relationship between the pixel and its surrounding neighboring pixels [14]. For the pixel at each position in the video frame, the probability of appearing in time sequence presents a Gaussian distribution. The implementation process of mixed Gaussian background modeling is as follows:

(1) Pixel description: describe each pixel $V(x, y, t)$ in the video with k single Gaussian background model, which can be expressed as

$$V(x,y,t) = \{w_i(x,y,t), \mu_i(x,y,t), \sigma_i^2(x,y,t)\}, i = 1,2,\ldots,k \tag{4}$$

Among them, $w_i(x,y,t)$, $\mu_i(x,y,t)$ and $\sigma_i^2(x,y,t)$ respectively represent the weight, mean and variance of the i-th single Gaussian model. The value of k is generally 3–5, and the weight of k single Gaussian model satisfies

$$\sum_{i=1}^{k} w_i(x,y,t) = 1 \qquad (5)$$

(2) Model matching: match the new input video frame with k single Gaussian model, and the matching condition is

$$|X_t - \mu_{i,t}| < 2.5\sigma_{i,t} \qquad (6)$$

Among them, X_t represents the pixel value of the new input video frame, $\mu_{i,t}$ and $\sigma_{i,t}$ represents the mean and standard deviation of the i-th Gaussian background model.

(3) Successful matching: If the pixel in the newly input video frame can be matched with at least one single Gaussian model, then the matching is successful, then the pixel is a background pixel. At this time, the weight of the successfully matched single Gaussian model Update with the parameters as follows:

$$\mu_i(x,y,t) = (1 - \alpha) \times \mu_i(x,y,t - 1) + \alpha \times I(x,y,t) \qquad (7)$$

$$\sigma_i^2(x,y,t) = (1 - \alpha) \times \sigma_i^2(x,y,t - 1) + \alpha \times [I(x,y,t) - \mu_i(x,y,t)]^2 \qquad (8)$$

$$\sigma_i(x,y,t) = \sqrt{\sigma_i^2(x,y,t)} \qquad (9)$$

$$dw = \alpha(1 - w_i(x,y,t - 1)) \qquad (10)$$

$$w_i(x,y,t) = w_i(x,y,t - 1) + dw \qquad (11)$$

Among them, $I(x,y,t)$ represents the current input frame, $\mu_i(x,y,t)$, $\sigma_i^2(x,y,t)$ and $w_i(x,y,t)$ represent the mean, variance and weight of the updated i-th single Gaussian model. $\mu_i(x,y,t - 1)$, $\sigma_i^2(x,y,t - 1)$ and $w_i(x,y,t - 1)$ represent the mean, variance and weight of the first single Gaussian model before updating. α represents the learning rate, usually 0.005.

(4) Matching failure: If the newly input video frame fails to match with any single Gaussian model, the pixel is judged as the foreground. At this time, a new Gaussian background model is established to replace the Gaussian model with the smallest weight in the previous background model. The mean value of the new Gaussian model is the newly input pixel value, the weight is a smaller value, and the variance is a larger value.

(5) Weight normalization: After updating the model parameters through the two steps (3) and (4), the model weights are further normalized, and the weight of the fourth cake model is normalized to

$$w_{newi}(x,y,t) = \frac{w_i(x,y,t)}{\sum_{j=1}^{k} w_j(x,y,t)} \tag{12}$$

Among them, $w_{newi}(x,y,t)$ is the weight of the standardized i-th Gaussian model.

(6) Model selection: sort the models according to their importance *key* from high to low, and select the first n Gaussian model as the background model, and the importance *key* and n should satisfy

$$key_i(x, y) = \frac{w_i(x,y,t)}{\sigma_i(x,y,t)} \tag{13}$$

$$\sum_{i=1}^{n} w_i(x,y,t) > T \tag{14}$$

The mixed Gaussian background model is k weighted sum of Gaussian functions. It can not only describe the multi-peak state of pixels, but also accurately model complex environments such as light gradients, weather changes, and leaf shaking. After continuous improvement by researchers, the method has become a more commonly used modeling method. In this paper, the Gaussian mixture model is used to extract moving targets [13]. This article uses GMM for target detection.

3   Fall Detection Based on Human Morphological Features and HOG Features

3.1   SVM Classifier

Support vector machine is a two-category model based on the theory of statistics for resumes. It can handle regression problems and pattern recognition and many other problems, and can be popularized in fields and disciplines such as prediction and comprehensive evaluation [15].

The basic idea of SVM learning is to solve the separation hyperplane that can correctly divide the training data set and have the largest geometric interval. In theory, support vector machines can achieve the optimal classification of linearly separable data.

For binary data, given a training sample set $(x_i, y_i), i = 1, 2, \cdots, l, x \in R^n$, $y \in \{\pm 1\}$, the hyperplane is denoted $(w \cdot x) + b = 0$ as the separating hyperplane. For a linearly separable data set, there are infinitely many such hyperplanes, but the separating hyperplane with the largest geometric interval is only one. So our goal is to find a segmentation plane that meets the classification requirements under the condition that the given sample point is separable, and make the given sample point as far as possible from the segmentation plane [16]. In order to make the classification face all samples correctly classified and have classification problems, it is required to meet the constraints

$$y_i[(w \cdot x) + b] \geq 1, i = 1, 2, \cdots, l \tag{15}$$

It can be calculated that the classification interval is $2/\|w\|$, so the problem of constructing the optimal hyperplane is transformed into finding

$$\min \Phi(w) = \frac{1}{2}\|w\|^2 = \frac{1}{2}(w' \cdot w) \tag{16}$$

In order to solve the constrained optimization problem, the Lagrange function is used

$$L(w, b, a) = \frac{1}{2}\|w\| - a(y((w \cdot x) + b) - 1) \tag{17}$$

where $a_i > 0$ is the Lagrange Multiplier. The solution of the constrained optimization problem is determined by the Lagrange function, and the solution of the optimization problem satisfies the partial derivative of w and b is 0. This QP problem is transformed into a corresponding dual problem:

$$\max Q(a) = \sum_{j=1}^{l} a_j - \frac{1}{2}\sum_{i=1}^{l}\sum_{j=1}^{l} a_i a_j y_i y_j(x_i, x_j), \quad s.t. \quad \sum_{j=1}^{l} a_j y_j = 0 \quad j = 1, 2, \cdots, l, a_j \geq 0 \tag{18}$$

Solve the optimal solution is $a^* = (a_1^*, a_2^*, \cdots, a_i^*)^{\mathrm{T}}$.

Calculate the optimal weight vector w^* and the optimal bias b^*, respectively

$$w^* = \sum_{j=1}^{l} a_j^* y_j x_j \tag{19}$$

$$b^* = y_i - \sum_{j=1}^{l} y_j a_j^* (x_j \cdot x_i) \tag{20}$$

In the formula, subscript $j \in \{j|a_j^* > 0\}$. Therefore, the optimal classification hyperplane $(w^* \cdot x) + b = 0$ is obtained, and the optimal classification function is

$$f(x) = sgn\{(w^* \cdot x) + b^*\} = sgn\{(\sum_{j=1}^{l} a_j^* y_j(x_j \cdot x_i)) + b^*\}, x \in R^n \qquad (21)$$

3.2   Fall Detection Combined with SVM and HOG Features

This paper uses two-level SVM classification and recognition. First, the first-level SVM classification and recognition uses the aspect ratio of the human body's circumscribed rectangle as the judgment feature and uses the sample data set to train the classifier to recognize the behavior of the current detection target:

The aspect ratio of the circumscribed rectangle of the human body, because the human body can be approximately equivalent to a rectangle, the human body bounding box obtained by the human body target detection at the previous stage is regarded as the minimum circumscribed rectangle of the human body, and the ratio of width to height of the circumscribed rectangle $X : Y = (X_{max} - X_{min})/(Y_{max} - Y_{min})$ is used as the judgment of falling characteristics. X_{max}, X_{min} are the maximum and minimum values of the abscissa of the minimum enclosing rectangle of the human body, respectively, and Y_{max}, Y_{min} are the maximum and minimum values of the ordinate of the minimum enclosing rectangle of the human body, respectively. When a person walks normally, the aspect ratio of the smallest enclosing rectangle of the human body will not change greatly, and when a fall occurs, the aspect ratio will change drastically.

The second-level SVM classification and recognition, extract the HOG features of the human target obtained in the target detection stage and input it into the trained second-level SVM classifier to determine whether the detection target has a fall behavior.

HOG feature extraction process:

(1) Use $[-1,0,1]$ and $[1,0,-1]^T$ as the horizontal and vertical edge operators to extract pixel gradient features.
(2) Define the horizontal gradient as $G_a(a,b) = H(a+1,b) - H(a-1,b)$ and the vertical gradient as $G_b(a,b) = H(a,b+1) - H(a,b-1)$, where a is the abscissa of the pixel in the image, b is the ordinate of the pixel in the image, and $H(a, b)$ is the pixel value of the corresponding pixel.
(3) The gradient amplitude of pixel (a, b) is $G(a,b) = \sqrt{G_a^2(a,b) + G_b^2(a,b)}$, direction is $\theta(a,b) = \arctan(Gb(a,b))/Ga(a,b))$.
(4) Take 6*6 pixel values as the height and width values of the divided cells, calculate the histogram of the cell gradient direction, and obtain a 9-dimensional feature vector of the cell.
(5) Finally, the final target area HOG feature vector is obtained by merging and normalizing cell vectors, and the SVM classification model is input to complete the training, and then a classification model that can be used for fall recognition is obtained.

This part of the process is shown in Fig. 2 below.

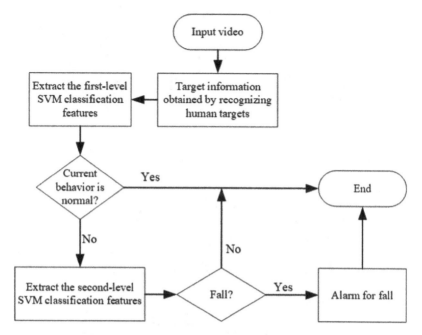

Fig. 2. Flow chart of two-stage SVM fall detection method.

4 Experiment Analysis

This article uses self-collected videos and public videos on the Internet to conduct experiments. The experimental environment is Windows 10 system, Intel(R) Core (TM) i5-8265U CPU quad-core processor, NVIDIA GeForce MX250 graphics card, and 8G memory.

Abnormal behavior detects the number of people in the video screen and the three types of abnormal behaviors that occur in the video: falls, abnormal gatherings, and abnormal discretes, and alarms when abnormal behaviors occur. After loading the video, click the detection button on the main interface to detect the abnormal behavior of the loaded video. When abnormal behavior occurs, the interface will have a red alert prompt box.

As shown in Fig. 3, clicking the detection button will first count the number of people in the video frame in the current video scene. The counting function is mainly used to detect two abnormal behaviors of abnormal crowd gathering and abnormal crowd dispersion in the future.

As shown in Fig. 4, after clicking the detection button, a fall is detected in the video. The system will mark the target of the fall with a red box. The system will alert the scene where the abnormality occurs and save a screenshot of the time when the abnormality occurs.

Fig. 3. People counting interface in video.

Fig. 4. Fall behavior detection interface.

As shown in Fig. 5, if the number of people in the current scene is suddenly reduced to half of the original within 5 video frames, the system will determine that there is an abnormal crowd behavior in the current scene, and the system will alert the scene where the abnormality occurs and save the abnormal occurrence. Screenshot of the moment.

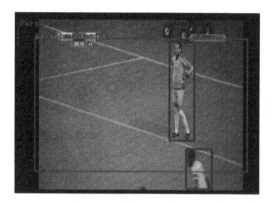

Fig. 5. Crowd abnormal discrete behavior detection interface.

As shown in Fig. 6, if the number of people in the current scene suddenly increases to half of the original number within 5 video frames or exceeds a preset threshold, the system will determine that there is an abnormal crowd behavior in the current scene, and the system will respond to abnormalities. The scene alarms and saves a screenshot of the moment when the abnormality occurs.

Fig. 6. Crowd abnormal gathering behavior detection interface.

5   Conclusion

This article mainly conducts experiments and research on abnormal crowd behavior detection and alarm, analyzes the key technical principles and framework of crowd abnormal behavior detection, realizes the detection of crowd abnormal behavior under surveillance video, and deeply analyzes the technical details and implementation of each part., Including background modeling, detection and extraction of moving objects, tracking of moving objects and sudden gathering of pedestrians in a crowd, sudden dispersal of pedestrians in a crowd, detection of 4 abnormal behaviors in a crowd, and a fall of pedestrians in the crowd. The feasibility of the algorithm. Based on the problems found in real applications and combined with the actual requirements of the abnormal behavior detection system, a new video summary framework was formulated, and the relevant modules involved in it were selected and the appropriate algorithm was improved to make it more compliant the need for abnormal behavior detection.

Funding Statement. This work was supported by the key-area and development program of Guangdong province (Grant No. 2019B010137002), National Nature Science Foundation of China (Grant No. 61702347), Natural Science Foundation of Hebei Province (Grant No. F2017210161), Science and Technology Research Project of Higher Education in Hebei Province (Grant No. ZD2022100).

Conflicts of Interest. The authors declare no conflicts of interest to report regarding the present study.

References

1. Khan, A.A., Khan, F.A.: A cost-efficient radiation monitoring system for nuclear sites: designing and implementation. Intell. Autom. Soft Comput. **32**(3), 1357–1367 (2022)
2. Dong, Y.C., Shan, Y.G., Yuan, J.: Pedestrian detection based on improved HOG. Comput. Eng. Design **41**(10), 2921–2926 (2020)
3. Lee, S.: A study on classification and detection of small moths using CNN model. Comput. Mater. Contin. **71**(1), 1987–1998 (2022)
4. Wang, Z., Jiao, R., Jiang, H.: Emotion recognition using wt-svm in human-computer interaction. J. New Media **2**(3), 121–130 (2020)
5. Liu, W., Hao, X.L., Lv, J.L.: Efficient moving targets detection based on adaptive Gaussian mixture modelling. J. Image Graph. **25**(01), 113–125 (2020)
6. Xia, S.W., Zhou, X.: Object tracking algorithm based on optical flow method and block training. Comput. Eng. Design **41**(07), 2063–2068 (2020)
7. Li, W.S., Han, Y., Ruan, M.H., Wang, Z.X.: Improved pedestrian detection method based on enhanced HOG. Comput. Syst. Appl. **29**(10), 199–204 (2020)
8. Guo, X.P., Du, J.S., Bai, J.J., Wang, W.: Fast human detection algorithm based on BING objectness. Appl. Res. Comput. **35**(11), 3458–3461 (2018)
9. Zhao, L., Zhao, M.: Feature-enhanced refinedet: fast detection of small objects. J. Inform. Hiding Privacy Protect. **3**(1), 1–8 (2021)
10. Xiao, B., Lu, C., Chen, H.: Moving object detection and recognition based on the frame difference algorithm and moment invariant features. In: 27th Chinese Control Conference, pp. 578–581 (2008)
11. Qu, J.J., Xin, Y.H.: Combined continuous frame difference with background difference method for moving object detection. Acta Photonica Sinica **43**(07), 219–226 (2018)
12. Barnich, O., Droogenbroeck, M.V.: ViBE: A powerful random technique to estimate the background in video sequences. In: IEEE International Conference on Acoustics, Speech and Signal Processing, pp. 945–948 (2009)

13. Zhang, Q.L., Qiu, J., Yang, X.L.: Improved vibe algorithm and its application in moving objects detection. J. Nanjing Norm. Univ. (Nat. Sci. Ed.) **43**(04), 104–112 (2020)
14. Shankar, K., Venkatraman, S.: A secure encrypted classified electronic healthcare data for public cloud environment. Intell. Autom. Soft Comput. **32**(2), 765–779 (2022)
15. Shankar, B.P., Chitra, S.: Optimal data placement and replication approach for siot with edge. Comput. Syst. Sci. Eng. **41**(2), 661–676 (2022)
16. Ding, S.F., Bing, B.J., Tan, H.Y.: An overview on theory and algorithm of support vector machines. J. Univ. Electron. Sci. Technol. China **40**(1), 2–10 (2011)

Improved Regularization of Convolutional Neural Networks with Point Mask

Li Xu, Yueqi Li, and Jin Li[(⊠)]

College of Computer Science and Technology, Harbin Engineering University,
Harbin 150001, China
lijinokok@hrbeu.edu.cn

Abstract. Image Data are critical data for computer vision. Above all, occluded Image Data is still challenging. This paper, introduces Point Mask, a new data augmentation method for training the convolutional neural network (CNN). In training, Point Mask selects some corners region in an image and erases its pixels with zero values. In this process, training images with various places of occlusion are generated, which reduces the risk of over-fitting and makes the model robust to occlusion. Point Mask is extremely easy to implement and can be integrated with most CNN-based recognition models. Point Mask is very effective and consistently improves over solid baselines in image classification, object detection, and person re-identification. The extensive experiments have demonstrated the new method's the generality and effectiveness.

Keywords: Data augmentation · Over-fitting · Occlusion

1 Introduction

In recent years, deep Convolutional Neural Networks (CNNs) have achieved state-of-the-art performance for computer vision tasks [1–4], including image classification [5, 6], object detection [7, 8], human pose estimation [9], and semantic segmentation [10]. Many CNN models are too complex have hundreds of millions of parameters, making training require a large amount of data. Otherwise, over-fitting severe problems can occur. Nevertheless, over-fitting is a common serious problem in this type of deep Convolutional Neural Networks (CNNs). Data augmentation can improve the robustness and overall performance of deep Convolutional Neural Networks (CNNs). Recently, Information deletion has been widely adopted for its effectiveness and efficiency. It includes Random Erasing [11], Cutout [12], Hide and Seek (HaS) [13], GridMask [14], Mixup [15], and Cutmix [16]. It is known that by removing a certain level of information from an image, a CNN can learn other less sensitive or important information and increase the perceptual domain, resulting in a more robust model. Deleting a certain degree of data from an image can make strong CNN's stronger and weak CNN's stronger.

© The Author(s), under exclusive license to Springer Nature Switzerland AG 2022
X. Sun et al. (Eds.): ICAIS 2022, CCIS 1587, pp. 16–25, 2022.
https://doi.org/10.1007/978-3-031-06761-7_2

2 Motivation

Interestingly, we found that deep Convolutional Neural Networks (CNNs) have excellent performance on various computer vision tasks. Still, it cannot classify similar things that are very different from the training set or occluded. The reason is that deep Convolutional Neural Networks (CNNs) learn the characteristics of the training set too well, causing over-fitting. A successful feature learning method should be robust. It should achieve invariance to various places of occlusion. When some parts of an object are occluded, a powerful classification model should recognize its category from the overall object structure. Due to the limited generalization ability of the CNN model, it may fail to identify objects which are very different from the training set or occluded. To address the occlusion problem and improve the generalization ability of CNNs, we found that removing a certain level of information from the training set data can prevent over-fitting. This paper introduces a new data augmentation approach, Point Mask. It can be easily implemented in most existing CNN models. In the training phase, an image within a mini-batch randomly undergoes either of the two operations: (1) The picture kept unchanged; (2) we choose some corners region of a fixed size and assign the pixels within the selected region with zero values. During (2), an image is partially occluded in some corners with a fixed-sized mask. In this manner, augmented images with various occlusion places can be generated. Examples of Point Mask are shown Fig. 1 below.

On the one hand, excessive removal of one or several regions may result in insufficient information for the complete object to be classified. On the other hand, excessive retention of areas does not prevent over-fitting. Therefore, it becomes essential to design a simple method to reduce the chances of causing these two problems. Existing information discarding algorithms are not well implemented to prevent over-deletion, over-retention, and invalid deletion. For example, both cutout and random erasing delete only one contiguous region of an image at random. Performing image enhancement may cause over-deletion and over-retention because the deleted region is a region. The approach of hide and seek (HaS) is to divide the image equally into small squares and randomly delete several small areas. Performing image enhancement may still result in over-deletion and over-preservation because there is still a chance to delete or retain regions consecutively.

Contrary to previous approaches, we were surprised to find that a straightforward strategy that statistically better balances these two conditions is to use image features extracted from image processing techniques. Point Mask can be easily applied to other CNN-based recognition tasks and still yields competitive accuracy. To summarize, Point Mask has the following advantages: Point Mask is very effective and delivers consistent improvement over solid baselines in image classification. The extensive experiments have demonstrated that the generality and effectiveness of the new method.

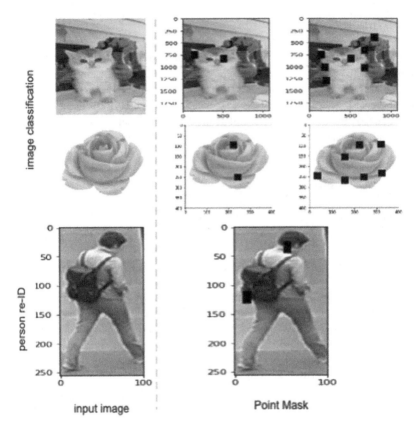

Fig. 1. Examples of Point Mask. In CNN training, we choose a corners region in the image and erase its pixels with zero values. Images with various places of occlusion are thus generated.

3 Related Work

Our work is most closely related to standard regularization techniques: data augmentation and Digital image processing. Here we examine the use of both methods in training convolutional neural networks. We also discuss denoising auto-encoders, corner detection, edge detection, and context encoders, similar to our work. Popular data augmentation techniques include random cropping, image resizing, image flipping, normalization, image transposition, dithering, and random image rotation. Data augmentation plays a crucial role in improving the performance of computer vision tasks, such as image classification, object detection, sentiment recognition, and person re-identification. Our Point Mask idea is to create new training data by selecting some corners region in an image and erasing its pixels with zero values for data augmentation. The network can be robust to occlusions by seeing training images with occluded images.

3.1   Data Augmentation

Data augmentation plays a crucial role in improving the performance of computer vision tasks, such as image classification, object detection, sentiment recognition, and person re-identification. Data augmentation is widely used in the training of deep CNNs. Its fundamental purpose is to artificially introduce a priori knowledge from human vision to improve the model. The more commonly used geometric transformation methods are mainly: flipping, rotation, cropping, scaling, translation, and dither. The most widely used pixel transformation methods are: adding pretzel noise, Gaussian noise, performing Gaussian blur, adjusting HSV contrast, adjusting brightness, saturation, histogram equalization, adjusting white balance. Our Point Mask idea is to create new training data by selecting some corners region in an image and erasing its pixels with zero values for data augmentation. The network can be robust to occlusions by seeing training images with occluded images. Random flipping is to flip the input image horizontally. Random Flip, while Random Cropping extracts a random subslice from the input image. Random Erasing may discard some parts of the object. For random cropping, it may cut off the image's corners, while Point Mask may obscure a tiny amount of some critical parts of the thing. Point Mask keeps the overall structure of the object. In addition, it can be seen as adding noise to the image. The combination of Point Mask and other data augmentation algorithms can generate more different training data. point mask can generate more different training data. Point mask generates a new image from the original image simulates where the original image is occluded.

3.2   Denoising Autoencoders and Context Encoders

Self-supervised learning to elicit useful feature representations of images is essential for denoising autoencoders and context encoders. Denoising autoencoders and context encoders determine how best to fill in the corrupted parts by corrupting the input images and asking the network to reconstruct them using the remaining pixels as context. The denoising autoencoder applies Bernoulli noise to randomly erase individual pixels in the input image, while the contextual encoder erases more significant spatial regions containing multiple pixels. Instead of simply learning the identity function, the autoencoder is forced to learn how to extract useful features from the image to fill in the missing information. Since contextual encoders need to fill more significant areas of the image, they need to understand the global content of the image better and, therefore, learn higher-level features than denoising autoencoders. These feature representations are helpful for pre-training classification, detection models.

3.3   Edge Detection and Corner Detection

A corner point is the most basic interest point in an image [17]. A point of interest is a point that is easily detected and represented in a picture. A corner point can be defined as the intersection of two edges in the image or a local extreme value point of curvature on the target contour line. The image has large gradient values in all directions at the intersection point and a significant rate of change in the direction of gradient change. On the other hand, the edges have large gradient values in one direction and flat gradient values in different directions. In other words, the corner points show the location of the image where the gray value changes dramatically in two dimensions, and there is a clear difference between the corner points and their surrounding neighbors.

4   Our Approach

Point Mask is very effective and consistently improves solid baselines in image classification, object detection, and person re-identification. The extensive experiments have demonstrated that the generality and effectiveness of the new method.

4.1   Point Mask

Point Mask is conducted with a certain probability. For an image I in a mini-batch, the likelihood of it undergoing Point Mask is p, and the probability of it being kept unchanged is $1 - p$. In this process, training images with various places of occlusion are generated. Random Erasing selects n of corners region I_C in an image, and erases its pixels with zero values. Assume that the size of the training image is W × H. The area of the image is S = W × H. We set the width of erasing corners part to $m_w = \frac{1}{12} \times W$, set the height of erasing corners region to $m_h = \frac{1}{12} \times H$. We randomly initialize the area of erasing corners region to $m_s = m_w \times m_h$. Then, we selected a point $P_1 = (x_1, y_1)$ in I. If P_1 is the largest gradient change in two orthogonal directions, we set the first region, $I_{C1} = \left(x_1, y_1, x_1 + \frac{1}{2} \times m_w, y_1 + \frac{1}{2} \times m_h\right)$, as the first selected rectangle region. Otherwise, repeat the above process until an appropriate I_{C1} is selected. Each pixel in I_{C1} is assigned to value 0 with the chosen erasing region I_{C1}, respectively. Then, we decided on a point $P_2 = (x_2, y_2)$ in I, repeating the above process until an appropriate P_n is selected. Repeat the above process until each pixel in I_{Cn} is assigned to value 0.

4.2   Corner Detection

First, we use a 3 × 3 Sobel kernel to calculate the horizontal and vertical gradients of the image I in a mini-batch.

$$f_x = \frac{\partial f}{\partial x} = f \otimes \begin{bmatrix} -1 & 0 & +1 \\ -2 & 0 & +2 \\ -1 & 0 & +1 \end{bmatrix} \tag{1}$$

$$f_y = \frac{\partial f}{\partial y} = f \otimes \begin{bmatrix} +1 & +2 & +1 \\ 0 & 0 & 0 \\ -1 & -2 & +1 \end{bmatrix} \tag{2}$$

f_x is the X-direction gradient of the image f, f_y is the Y-direction gradient of the image, $\otimes$ denotes the convolution calculation. The formulations of the horizontal and vertical gradients can be written as: $f_x f_y$, f_x^2 and f_y^2, and We use Gaussian filter G to weighting $f_x f_y$, f_x^2 and f_y^2 and generate the matrix M. We express our setting as:

$$G = \frac{1}{16} \otimes \begin{bmatrix} 1 & 2 & 1 \\ 2 & 4 & 2 \\ 1 & 2 & 1 \end{bmatrix} \tag{3}$$

$$A = f_x^2 \otimes G \tag{4}$$

$$B = f_y^2 \otimes G \tag{5}$$

$$C = f_x f_y \otimes G \tag{6}$$

$$M = \begin{bmatrix} A & C \\ C & B \end{bmatrix} \tag{7}$$

$$R = [\det(M) - k * (tra(M))^2] > 0 \tag{8}$$

k is generally taken as 0.04–0.06, is the value of the matrix row equation and is the trace of the matrix. If the of pixels satisfy greater than zero, it is considered a prepared corner point. Select the pixel from the set of prepared corners with R > 0 that has the largest R value and satisfies a distance greater than D from any of the elements in the corner set, and add it to the corner set. N times, the number of elements in the corner set at the end of the loop num(corner set) < n, set n = num(corner set) where n is the number of data The number of small areas to augmentation the occlusion. We express our setting as:

$$D = |s-x_c| + |t-y_c| > \lambda \times T \tag{9}$$

$$T = \min(W,H) \tag{10}$$

which (s, t) is the coordinate of the pre-selected corner point. λ is the distance factor and takes values in the range of $0.2 < \lambda < 0.5$, W is the image width, and H is the image height.

5   Experiments

5.1   Image Classification

In our experiment, we compare the CNN models trained with or without Point Mask. In all of our experiment, we compare the CNN models trained with Point Mask and trained with Existing information discarding algorithms. All the models are trained from the same weight initialization for the same deep architecture. We stop training by the 10th epoch on Gemstone and stop by the 90th epoch on CIFAR-10. Note that various data augmentations are employed. Classification accuracy on different datasets. The results of applying Point Mask on CIFAR-10 and Gemstone trained with or without Point Mask are shown in Table 1. We set n = 2. Results indicate that models trained with Point Mask have significant improvement, demonstrating that our method is applies to various CNN architectures. For CIFAR-10, Gemstone our method improves the accuracy by 0.41% and 0.38% using ResNet-50 and ResNet-20, respectively. Comparison with Dropout and random noise. We compare Point Mask with two variant methods applied on the image layer. (1) Dropout: we apply dropout on the image layer with probability. (2) Random noise: we add different noise regions on the input image by changing the pixel to value 0, with the center of the region being the corner. The probability of whether an image undergoes dropout is set to 0.5 as Point Mask. Comparing with data augmentation methods. A large number of experiments were designed and conducted, as shown in Table 1, to demonstrate the effectiveness of Point Mask. Point Mask can improve the accuracy of ResNet50 to 75.6% in an image classification task using the dataset Gemstones, which is much higher than the accuracy of Cutout and HaS, which reach 73.7% and 74.9%, respectively. We compare the test accuracy of our method with data augmentation methods shown in Fig. 2 below. We compare the training loss of our method with data augmentation methods. The result is summarized in Fig. 3 below. We compare the val accuracy of our method with data augmentation methods. The result is shown in Fig. 4 below.

Table 1. Test errors (%) with or without Point Mask on CIFAR-10 and Gemstone.

Model	CIFAR-10	Gemstones
	ResNet-20	ResNet-50
Baseline	8.68 ± 0.06	27.28 ± 0.05
Point mask	5.73 ± 0.08	23.42 ± 0.04

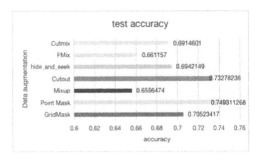

Fig. 2. Test accuracy (%) of our method with data augmentation methods on Gemstone.

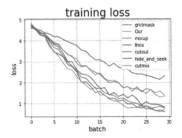

Fig. 3. Our method's training loss (%) with data augmentation methods on Gemstone.

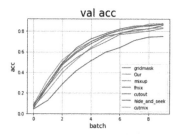

Fig. 4. Val accuracy (%) of our method with data augmentation methods on Gemstone.

5.2   Ablation Study

In this section, we train models with Point Mask under different parameters and show variations of Point Mask. Hyperparameter n: Examples of varying n are shown in Fig. 5 below. We experiment with setting n as 2, 3, 4, 6, 12, 13, 14,15 and 16 on Gemstone with ResNet50. We choose the most effective n = 2 as the choice of n for different models on the Gemstone dataset. The results of applying Point Mask on Gemstone trained with Point Mask under different parameters are shown in Table 2. We choose n = 2 as the choice of n on CIFAR10. Put differently, we should keep more information on datasets to avoid under-fitting. To reduce overfitting, we should keep more occultations on multiple objective datasets to avoid under-fitting and delete more on simple datasets. This finding is in obedience to our common sense.

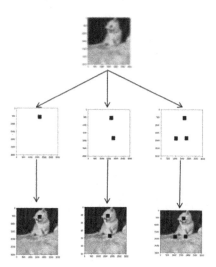

Fig. 5. Examples of different n. In Point Mask.

Table 2. Test accuracy (%) of our method under different parameters with data augmentation methods on Gemstone.

Model	Gemstones
	ResNet-50
Baseline + Point Mask + n = 2	74.93
Baseline + Point Mask + n = 3	75.51
Baseline + Point Mask + n = 4	73.30
Baseline + Point Mask + n = 6	71.93
Baseline + Point Mask + n = 12	73.03
Baseline + Point Mask + n = 13	72.51
Baseline + Point Mask + n = 14	71.93
Baseline + Point Mask + n = 15	71.65
Baseline + Point Mask + n = 16	70.55

To summarize, Point Mask has the following advantages: Point Mask is very effective and yields consistent improvement over solid baselines in image classification. The extensive experiments have demonstrated that the generality and effectiveness of the new method. To summarize, Point Mask has the following advantages: (1) Point Mask can be integrated with various CNN models without changing the learning strategy. (2) A complimentary method to existing data augmentation and regularization approaches. Point Mask further improves the recognition performance. (3) Improving the robustness of CNNs to partially occluded samples. (4) When we randomly add occlusion to the CIFAR-10 testing dataset, Point Mask significantly outperforms the baseline model. (5) Increase the training data to improve the model's generalization ability.

6 Discussion

This paper proposes a new data augmentation approach named "Point Mask" for training the CNN. It is easy to implemented: Point Mask occludes some corners regions of the input image during each training iteration. In an experiment conducted on CIFAR10, Gemstones with various architectures validate the effectiveness of our method. Moreover, we obtain reasonable improvement on object detection and person re-identification, demonstrating that our practices perform well on various recognition tasks. In future work, we will apply our approach to other CNN recognition tasks, such as image segmentation.

References

1. Qiang, X., Aamir, M., Naeem, M., Ali, S., Aslam, A., Shao, Z.: Analysis and forecasting covid-19 outbreak in Pakistan using decomposition and ensemble model. Comput. Mater. Continua **68**(1), 841–856 (2021)

2. Alsubie, A., Abdelhamid, M., Ahmed, A.H.N., Alqawba, M., Afify, A.Z.: Inference on generalized inverse-pareto distribution under complete and censored samples. Intell. Autom. Soft Comput **29**(1), 213–232 (2021)

3. Alharbi, A., et al.: Evaluating the impacts of security-durability characteristic: data science perspective. Comput. Syst. Sci. Eng. **41**(2), 557–567 (2022)

4. Guan, Y., Choi, B.J.: Design, Implementation and verification of topology network architecture of smart home tree. Comput. Mater. Contin. **68**(2), 2399–2411 (2021)

5. Ghaderizadeh, S., Abbasi-Moghadam, D., Sharifi, A., Zhao, N., Tariq, A.: Hyperspectral image classification using a hybrid 3D–2D convolutional neural networks. IEEE J. Sel. Top. Appl. Earth Obs. Remote Sens. **14**, 7570–7588 (2021)

6. Hirano, H., Minagi, A., Takemoto, K.: Universal adversarial attacks on deep neural networks for medical image classification. BMC Med. Imaging **21**(1), 1–13 (2021)

7. Khan, M.A., et al.: Machine learning-based detection and classification of walnut fungi diseases. Intell. Autom. Soft Comput. **30**(3), 771–785 (2021)

8. Zhou, T., Fan, D.-P., Cheng, M.-M., Shen, J., Shao, L.: RGB-D salient object detection: a survey. Comp. Visual Media **7**(1), 37–69 (2021)

9. Huang, X., Huang, J., Tang, Z.: 3D human pose estimation with spatial structure information. IEEE Access **9**, 35947–35956 (2021)

10. Kamann, C., Rother, C.: Benchmarking the robustness of semantic segmentation models with respect to common corruptions. Int. J. Comput. Vis. **129**(2), 462–483 (2021)

11. Zhong, Z., Zheng, L., Kang, G., Li, S., Yang, Y.: Random erasing data augmentation. In: Proceedings of the AAAI Conference on Artificial Intelligence, vol. 34(07), pp. 13001–13008 (2020)

12. DeVries, T., Taylor, G.W.: Improved regularization of convolutional neural networks with cutout. arXiv:1708.04552 (2017)

13. Singh, K.K., Yu, H., Sarmasi, A., Pradeep, G., Lee, Y.J.: Hide-and-seek: A data augmentation technique for weakly-supervised localization and beyond. arXiv:1811.02545 (2018)

14. Chen, P., Liu, S., Zhao, H., Jia, J.: Gridmask data augmentation. arXiv:2001.04086 (2020)

15. Zhang, H., Cisse, M., Dauphin, Y. N., Lopez-Paz, D.: Mixup: beyond empirical risk minimization. arXiv:1710.09412 (2017)

16. Yun, S., Han, D., Oh, S. J., Chun, S., Choe, J., Yoo, Y.: Cutmix: Regularization strategy to train strong classifiers with localizable features. In: Proceedings of the IEEE/CVF International Conference on Computer Vision, pp. 6023–6032. IEEE, Seoul, Korea (2019)

17. Wan, L., Yu, Z., Yang, Q.: Corner detection algorithm with improved harris. In: Tan, T., Ruan, Q., Wang, S., Ma, H., Di, K. (eds.) IGTA 2015. CCIS, vol. 525, pp. 260–271. Springer, Heidelberg (2015). https://doi.org/10.1007/978-3-662-47791-5_30

Research on Crack Detection Technology of Buildings After Earthquake Based on Structured Light

XiaoGang Zhang[1], Shao Cui[2], Sen Zhang[2], JingFang Su[2(✉)],
CaiXing Wang[2], and Derek Perakis[3]

[1] Hebei Seismological Bureau, Shijiazhuang 050000, China
[2] School of Information Science and Engineering, Hebei University of Science
and Technology, Shijiazhuang 050000, China
sujingfang1980@hebust.edu.cn
[3] Case Western Reserve University, Cleveland, USA

Abstract. The existing intelligent crack detection methods of buildings can not meet the needs of crack detection because the surface of buildings has the characteristics of multi-texture and multi-target after earthquake disaster and is interfered by other factors. A three-dimensional measurement technique based on structured light is proposed to detect cracks after earthquake in order to improve the detection rate. Firstly, a raster fringe image with a four-step phase shift is generated and calibrated by a projector connected to a computer. Then, the generated sinusoidal grating fringe image is projected onto the measured object and background, and the modulated grating fringe image of seismic crack surface is collected by a camera and transmitted to a computer. Next the algorithm combining four-step phase shift method and multi-frequency heterodyne method is used to carry out phase unwrapping, and the phase value and height conversion formula are combined to calculate the height to reconstruct the three-dimensional information of cracks generated in the earthquake. Finally, ICP algorithm is used to mosaic images, and the cracks generated after the earthquake are detected combined with the height difference. The experimental results show that the four-step phase shift method combined with multi-frequency heterodyne method is selected to achieve better phase unwrapping accuracy than other algorithms, and the reconstructed error is less than other algorithms. The method based on structured light can accurately detect the spliced fracture image without interference from other factors, which provides technical support for earthquake disaster investigation.

Keywords: Crack detection · Structured light · Four-step phase shift method · Multifrequency heterodyne method · ICP image mosaic

1 Introduction

After the earthquake, due to the strong ground vibration and the associated cracks and deformation of the ground, many buildings collapsed or damaged, will cause the loss of life and property [1]. The field team will carry out disaster investigation on the earthquake site, and the evaluation of house damage grade is one of the important work [2]. From the safety point of view, post-earthquake crack detection is of great significance to the sustainable development of the region, urban planning and construction and ecological development, and is conducive to the reconstruction and recovery of the earthquake area [3].

At present, there are many methods used to detect cracks [4]. Image processing technology [5, 6] has been used in seismic data processing for more than ten years, and many scholars have done a lot of research on the practical application of this technology. Non-contact radar detection method [7] has the advantage of not causing damage to cracks, but in the detection process, due to the influence of interference factors, the processing efficiency of target echo signal is reduced, once the crack depth is deep, there will be false detection phenomenon. Li et al. [8] used image edge detection technology to automatically detect the in-phase axis of seismic profile. Wang et al. [9] proposed to decompose seismic data into different levels of background and reservoir target reflection responses based on blind source separation technology, and then extract effective information that can reflect reservoir fracture characteristics to intuitively describe and predict fracture development zones. With the maturity of image detection technology [10], it is convenient to detect cracks in buildings after earthquake.

It cannot be ignored that building surface has the characteristics of multi-texture and multi-objective after the earthquake disaster, which affects the accuracy of detecting the crack depth information. Therefore, this paper proposes a three-dimensional measurement technology using structured light to detect the cracks on the ground after the earthquake, and achieve accurately crack detection by obtaining the three-dimensional information of the cracks, which can provide the basis for the damage grade evaluation in the field investigation of earthquake disaster in Fig. 1.

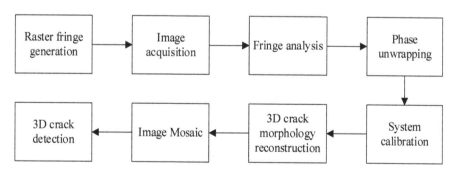

Fig. 1. Flow chart of 3D crack detection system.

2 Sine Grating Fringe Pattern Acquisition

Firstly, the camera and projector are connected by computer, then the raster fringe image is generated, and finally projected by the projector. This method has low cost, good flexibility and high precision of grating. The hardware system structure of 3D crack measurement is shown in Fig. 2.

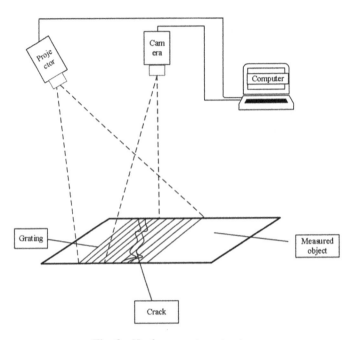

Fig. 2. Hardware system structure.

The digital projection device is connected to a computer, which generates sinusoidal grating fringe with different frequency and phase shift through software. The gray value of fringe generated in the computer is as follows:

$$I(x,y) = A(x,y) + B(x,y) * \cos\left[x\frac{2\pi}{P} + \varphi'\right] \tag{1}$$

$$P = \frac{1}{f} \tag{2}$$

where $A(x,y)$ is the background light intensity, $B(x,y)$ is the modulation factor, P is the carrier fringe spacing, f is the carrier frequency of grating fringe, and φ' is the phase shift amount.

By changing the frequency of the raster fringe, the pattern will have different widths. As shown in Fig. 3, grating fringes with different frequencies and the same phase are set to 32, 56, and 64. The gray values of the points on each row of each graph are the same, and the sampling points on the fringes of each column change according to the sinusoidal curve. Take any column, and the value changes are shown in Fig. 4.

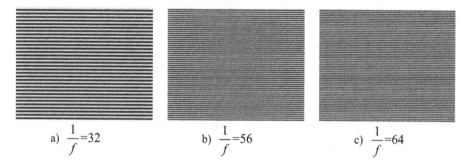

a) $\dfrac{1}{f}=32$ b) $\dfrac{1}{f}=56$ c) $\dfrac{1}{f}=64$

Fig. 3. Sinusoidal grating fringe at different frequencies.

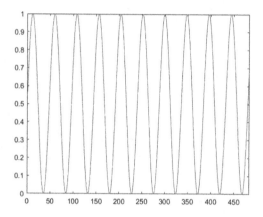

Fig. 4. Waveform diagram of grating fringe.

The computer needs to generate 12 raster fringe images and project three groups of sinusoidal fringe grating images with different frequencies (1/73, 1/64, 1/56), and each group contains four images with a phase Angle difference of 90°, a total of 12 images. The deformation raster fringe image captured by the camera is shown in the Fig. 5. The phases of the 4 images in each group were 0°, 90°, 180° and 270° respectively.

(a)   (b)   (c)

((a) Frequency is 56; Phase shift is 0 °, 90 °, 180 °, 270 ° (b) Frequency is 64; Phase shift is 0 °, 90 °, 180 °, 270 °(c) Frequency is 73; Phase shift is 0 °, 90 °, 180 °, 270 °))

Fig. 5. Images of crack after earthquake.

3 Crack Detection of Buildings After Earthquake Based on Structural Light

Structured light 3D detection technology is one of the non-contact measurement technologies. The sinusoidal grating fringe image generated above is projected onto the measured object and background, and the modulated grating fringe image of crack surface after earthquake is collected by a camera. Because the collected images are periodically distributed in the measurement range, phase unwrapping is required. In this paper, four-step phase shift method and multi-frequency heterodyne method are used to carry out phase unrolling, and the height is calculated by combining the phase value and height conversion formula, which can accurately reconstruct the three-dimensional information details of cracks generated in the earthquake. Finally, ICP algorithm is used for image Mosaic, and the height difference is used to detect cracks.

3.1 Phase Unwrapping Based on Four-Step Phase Shift Method and Multi-frequency Heterodyne Algorithm

Four-step Phase Shift Method. The basic principle of the method is to project more than three sinusoidal grating fringe patterns to the object in time sequence by controlling the projector. There is a fixed phase value difference between the two grating patterns. The camera collects the image of the measured object modulated by sinusoidal grating, extracts the phase information through arctangent processing, and calculates the depth information of the object according to the phase value.

Assume that the period of sinusoidal grating fringe is 2π and there are N grating fringe images, then the phase shift will differ by $2\pi/N$, and the phase machine will collect N modulated grating fringe images in a certain order. The gray distribution of each image is shown in the formula below:

$$I(x,y) = R(x,y)\{A(x,y) + B(x,y)\cos[\varphi(x,y) + \varphi']\} \tag{3}$$

where $A(x,y)$ indicates the gray value of the background environment, $B(x,y)/A(x,y)$ indicates the contrast of stripes, $\varphi(x,y)$ indicates the phase of the deformation fringe to be found, φ' the amount of phase shift, $R(x,y)$ indicates the uneven reflectivity of an object's surface.

It is easy to calculate the phase by using N multiple fringe images. When $N = 4$, it is the four-step phase shift method, and the phase shift quantity is $\varphi' = \frac{\pi}{2}$.

Phase $\varphi(x,y)$ can be obtained by solving the equation, that is, the wrapped phase is expressed in the equation:

$$\varphi(x,y) = \arctan\frac{-\sum_{n=1}^{N} I_n(x,y)\sin(\varphi')}{\sum_{n=1}^{N} I_n(x,y)\cos(\varphi')} \tag{4}$$

The four-step phase shift method is used to measure the enveloping phase, so the intensity distribution of four grating fringes with four-step phase-shift is shown in the following formulas:

$$I_1(x,y) = A(x,y) + B(x,y) \cos[\varphi(x,y)] \tag{5}$$

$$I_2(x,y) = A(x,y) + B(x,y) \cos[\varphi(x,y) + \frac{\pi}{2}] \tag{6}$$

$$I_3(x,y) = A(x,y) + B(x,y) \cos[\varphi(x,y) + \pi] \tag{7}$$

$$I_4(x,y) = A(x,y) + B(x,y) \cos[\varphi(x,y) + \frac{3\pi}{2}] \tag{8}$$

The phase distribution of the surface of the measured object can be found, and the distribution range is between $[-\pi, \pi]$:

$$\varphi(x,y) = \arctan \frac{I_4 - I_2}{I_1 - I_3} \tag{9}$$

Multifrequency Heterodyne Method. According to the above four-step phase shift method, the phase value of the package is obtained, and then the phase is unfolded by the multi-frequency heterodyne method. The principle of multi-frequency heterodyne is to transform the phase principal value of the small period into the phase difference of the large period through the phase difference of the sinusoidal grating of different frequencies or periods, so that the phase difference signal covers the whole field of view, and then the absolute phase value of the image is obtained according to the phase difference.

Three-frequency heterodyne is a phase unwrapping algorithm based on dual-frequency heterodyne. Its dual-frequency heterodyne schematic diagram is shown in the Fig. 6. The phase φ_1 and φ_2 corresponding to the two frequencies λ_1 and λ_2 are obtained by heterodyne method with the new frequency λ_{12} and the new phase φ_{12}.

The frequency is superimposed with the corresponding phases λ_1 and λ_2. A phase value can be obtained from the dual-frequency principle as shown in the formula:

$$\varphi_{12} = \begin{cases} 2\pi + \varphi_1 - \varphi & \varphi_1 < \varphi_2 \\ \varphi_1 - \varphi_2 & \varphi_1 \geq \varphi_2 \end{cases} \tag{10}$$

Its corresponding frequency λ_{12} can be expressed as

$$\lambda_{12} = \frac{\lambda_1 \lambda_2}{\lambda_1 - \lambda_2} \tag{11}$$

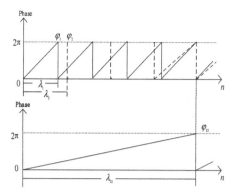

Fig. 6. Principle of dual frequency heterodyne method.

The value of λ_{12} is less than the value of λ_1 hand λ_2. In the case of multi-frequency heterodyne unwrapping, in order to be able to carry out phase unwrapping for all ranges of pixels, its phase needs to satisfy the equation:

$$V_0 < \frac{1}{2(\Delta\Phi + \Delta\phi)} \tag{12}$$

where V_0 represents the ratio of the initial principal frequency to the frequency after heterodyne calculation; $\Delta\phi$ represents the error of the phase principal value; $\Delta\Phi$ represents the phase error after heterodyne calculation.

If the frequency is 1/64, the error must be less than 1/384. However, it is difficult to realize in practice, so three frequency heterodyne is used to study. The principle of three-frequency heterodyne is based on dual-frequency heterodyne method, and its three sine grating frequencies are shown in formula:

$$\begin{cases} \lambda_1 = 1/73 \\ \lambda_2 = 1/64 \\ \lambda_3 = 1/56 \end{cases} \tag{13}$$

The wrap phase value of each frequency can be obtained by four-step phase shift method, and the corresponding two frequencies can be calculated:

$$\begin{cases} \lambda_{12} = 1/9 \\ \lambda_{23} = 1/8 \end{cases} \tag{14}$$

Finally, the heterodyne calculation of λ_{12} and λ_{23} can obtain the complete cycle covering all pixels, that is, $\lambda_{123} = 1$. The heterodyne calculation process is shown in Fig. 7.

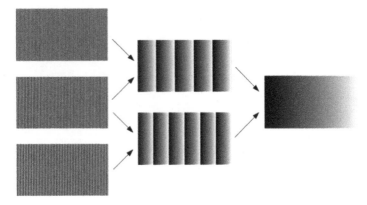

Fig. 7. Principle of multifrequency heterodyne.

3.2 Image Mosaic Based on ICP Algorithm

Iterated Closest Poin (ICP) algorithm [11, 12] is adopted in this paper. First, the algorithm roughly splices objects into the same coordinate system using the method of rough splicing. Then, b-spline surface fitting is used to fit the overlapping regions, and the initial corresponding point set was established. A constraint method is used to remove the wrong point pairs combined with curvature constraint. Finally, the least square method was used to solve the coordinate transformation iteratively. This algorithm is more accurate than the calibration splicing method, considering not only the registration of point set to point set, but also the registration of point set to model and model to model.

Minimizing an objective function is the core of ICP algorithm, and the formula is as follows:

$$E(R,t) = \frac{1}{n}\sum_{i=1}^{n} q_k - (Rp_k + t)^2 \tag{15}$$

The corresponding point sets P and Q are determined according to certain criteria, where the number of corresponding point pairs is n, and then the rotation matrix R and shift vector t are calculated iteratively by the least square method.

The basic steps of the algorithm are as follows:

Step1: Determine the initial set of corresponding points.
A point set A is taken from the point cloud with splicing at P, and a point set B is taken from the splicing point cloud to be spliced at Q.

Step2: Remove the error corresponding point pairs.
There will be wrong corresponding point pairs in the established corresponding point set, so it is necessary to introduce a constraint method to remove the wrong corresponding point pairs. An incorrect pair of corresponding points will directly affect the solution of the rigid body transformation matrix. Therefore, the maximum distance

threshold of corresponding points should be designed, and only the points whose distance is less than the threshold should be considered in the matching time.

Step3: Solution of coordinate change.

The least square method is used to solve the coordinate change matrix between the established corresponding point set and two point clouds.

3.3   Crack Detection of Buildings Based on Height Difference

In three dimensional images, the overall outline of crack after the earthquake is mainly concave, that is, the shape of high and low, so the height difference is used to detect cracks. According to this characteristic, a product operator is designed [13], which magnifies the difference between cracks and non-cracks.

The pixel height difference of the center to be tested is shown in the following formula:

$$\Delta L(x_i) = f(x_j) - f(x_i) \quad j\epsilon[i - r,i] \tag{16}$$

The height difference of pixels on both sides is shown in the following formula:

$$\Delta R(x_i) = f(x_j) - f(x_i) \quad j\epsilon[i,i+r] \tag{17}$$

where $\Delta L(x_i)$ in the formula represents the height difference between the center pixel x_i and one side of the pixel x_j, $\Delta R(x_i)$ refers to the change of the height difference with the point on the other side, r is the section radius, representing the calculated range.

The maximum height difference on both sides is taken as the product operator, and the height difference $\Delta(x_i)$ at the center pixel x_i is calculated by product:

$$\Delta(x_i) = \max_{j\epsilon[i-r,i]} (\Delta L(x_i)) \cdot \max_{j\epsilon[i,i+r]} (\Delta R(x_i)) \tag{18}$$

According to the observation and analysis of the fracture profile, the two sides of the fracture profile are relatively symmetric, so its product operator $\Delta(x_i)$ is larger than the asymmetric step profile.

4   Experimental Results and Analysis

4.1   Results of Crack Phase Unwrapping After Earthquake

In this paper, the four-step phase shift method and multi-frequency heterodyne method are used to unwrap the phase of crack image for buildings after earthquake and get the phase value of the parcel in Fig. 8.

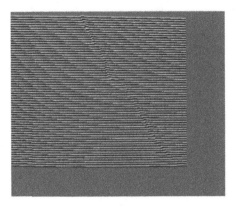

Fig. 8. Enveloping phase diagram.

In this paper, the phase unwrapping of crack images of buildings after earthquake is analyzed by combining four step phase shift method with branch cutting method, least square method and three frequency heterodyne method. The experimental effect diagram is shown in Fig. 9, which shows that the algorithm combining four-step phase shift and branch cutting has unsatisfactory unwrapping effect and low accuracy due to the influence of noise. According to Fig. 10, it can be concluded that the crack reconstruction accuracy of the algorithm adopted in this paper is better than the algorithm combined with four-step phase shift and least square method. It can be seen from Table 1 that the reconstruction error of the combined algorithm of four-step phase shift method and multi-frequency heterodyne method is much smaller than that of other algorithms. In summary, the algorithm presented in this paper has good unwrapping effect and ideal reconstruction accuracy.

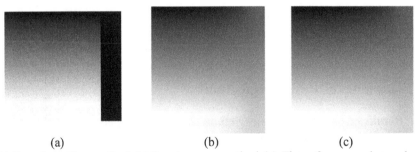

(a)   (b)   (c)

((a) Branch cutting method (b) Least square method (c) Three frequency heterodyne method)

Fig. 9. Phase unwrapping comparison of three algorithms.

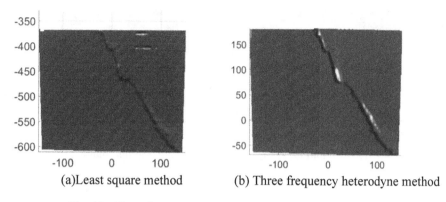

(a)Least square method   (b) Three frequency heterodyne method

Fig. 10. Three dimensional comparison diagram of reconstruction.

Table 1. Each algorithm reconstruction error.

Phase unwrapping	Reconstruction accuracy error (mm)
Four - step phase shift method combined with least square method	2.165
Four-step phase shift method combined with the branch cutting method	0.998
Four - step phase shift method combined with multi-frequency heterodyne method	0.468

4.2 Results of Crack Image Mosaic After Earthquake

After the structural light 3D detection technology, the contour of crack image for buildings after the earthquake is reconstructed to obtain the depth information of the crack. Then the ICP algorithm is used to splice the image, and the final splice map is generated as shown in the Fig. 11.

4.3 Crack Detection of Buildings After Earthquake

The crack detection of buildings after earthquake is based on height differences, However, the depth of the fracture varies at different locations. It can be seen from the comparison of effects in Fig. 12 that fine cracks cannot be detected by two-dimensional method in Fig. 12 (b), and oil stains can also be mistaken for cracks and detected, thus affecting the calculation of crack width. In Fig. 12 (c), three dimensional structural light detection technology can accurately obtain three dimensional data of post-earthquake buildings compared with two dimensional.

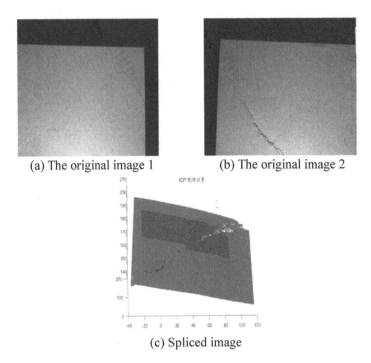

(a) The original image 1   (b) The original image 2

(c) Spliced image

Fig. 11. ICP image stitching diagram.

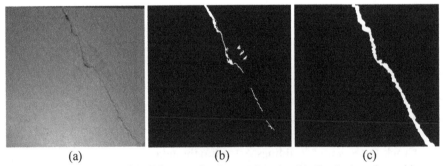

(a)   (b)   (c)

((a) Original view of building crack after earthquake (b) Crack detection with two-dimensional threshold (c) Crack detection based on height difference)

Fig. 12. Comparison diagram of crack detection.

5   Conclusion

In order to solve the problem of multi-texture features and interference factors in crack image after earthquake detection. A three-dimensional measurement technique based on structured light is proposed to detect cracks after earthquake. Firstly, a raster fringe image with a four-step phase shift is generated and calibrated by a projector connected to a computer. Then the algorithm combining four-step phase shift method and multi-frequency heterodyne method is used to carry out phase unwrapping, and the phase value and height conversion formula are combined to calculate the height to reconstruct the three-dimensional information of cracks generated in the earthquake. Finally, ICP algorithm is used to mosaic images, and the cracks generated after the earthquake are detected combined with the height difference. The experimental results show that the four-step phase shift method combined with multi-frequency heterodyne method is selected to achieve better phase unwrapping accuracy than other algorithms. The error of reconstruction precision is 0.468 mm, which is smaller than other algorithms The method based on structured light can accurately detect the spliced fracture image. Further, the crack parameters can be calculated, the length, width and depth of the crack can be calculated automatically, and the crack of buildings after earthquake level can be automatically classified.

Funding Statement. This research was funded by Special project for cultivating scientific and technological innovation ability of college and middle school students (Grant No. 2021H010206).

References

1. Jin, W., Iqbal, N., Kang, H., Kim, D.: Earthquake risk assessment approach using multiple spatial parameters for shelter demands. Comput. Mater. Contin. **70**(2), 3763–3780 (2022)
2. Han, Y., Sun, H., Li, L., Ma, G.X., You, S.D.: Design and implementation of rapid inspection system for building surface crack based on UAV. J. Civ. Eng. Manag. **36**(4), 60–65 (2019)
3. Chen, R., Zeng, G., Wang, K., Luo, L., Cai, Z.: A real time vision-based smoking detection framework on edge. J. Internet of Things **2**(2), 55–64 (2020)
4. Zhuang, X., Nguyen-Xuan, H., Zhou, S.: The interaction between microcapsules with different sizes and propagating cracks. Comput. Mater. Contin. **67**(1), 577–593 (2021)
5. Shaban, S.A., Elsheweikh, D.L.: Blood group classification system based on image processing techniques. Intell. Autom. Soft Comput. **31**(2), 817–834 (2022)
6. Zhou, L.J.: Low-contrast crack extraction method based on image enhancement and watershed segmentation. Comput. Sci. **45**(6), 259–261 (2018)
7. Karlovšek, J., Schuermann, A., Willimas, D.J.: Investigation of voids and cavities in bored tunnels using GPR. In: International Conference on Ground Penetrating Radar, pp. 496–501. IEEE (2012)
8. Li, H., Liu, C., Tao, C.H.: Image edge detection method in seismic profile in phase axis for the application of automatic detection. Prog. Geophys. **22**(5), 1607–1610 (2007)
9. Wang, Y.T., Gui, Z.X.: Application of ICA denoising based on blind source separation in fracture prediction. J. Data Acquisition Process. **34**(2), 288–296 (2018)
10. Liu, S., Cao, Y., Gao, L., Zeng, W.J.: Realization of mobile augmented reality system based on image recognition. J. Inform. Hiding Priv. Protect. **3**(2), 55–59 (2021)
11. Chen, S.L., Zhao, J.B., Xia, R.B.: Improvement of the phase unwrapping method based on multi-frequency heterodyne principle. Acta Optica Sinica **36**(4), 155–165 (2016)
12. Han, Y., Yang, Y.Z., Su, X.L.: A phase unwrapping method based on multifrequency heterodyne. J. Donghua Univ. (Nat. Sci.) **47**(5), 105–110 (2021)
13. Qiu, Y.J., Wang, G.L., Yang, E.H., Yu, X.L., Wang, C.P.: Crack detection of 3d asphalt pavement based on multi-feature test. J. Southwest Jiaotong Univ. **55**(3), 518–524 (2020)

Group-Attention Transformer
for Fine-Grained Image Recognition

Bo Yan[1]([✉]), Siwei Wang[1], En Zhu[1], Xinwang Liu[1], and Wei Chen[2]

[1] National University of Defense Technology, Changsha 410000, China
754004434@qq.com
[2] School of Computer Science, University of Birmingham, Birmingham, UK

Abstract. In the task of Fine-Grained Image Recognition (FGIR), the overall difference between different types of images is slight, so locating the representative local region in the image is the key to improving the classification accuracy. This idea of FGIR has been widely used in previous work, and has achieved good results on the benchmark dataset. Recently, the proposal of the Vision Transformer (ViT) method, provides a new method for the field of computer vision. Compared with the previous work based on Convolutional Neural Network (CNN), it has achieved better performance. ViT performs well in general image recognition tasks. However, when applied to FGIR tasks, it only pays attention to the global information and does not pay enough attention to the local features with discrimination. In order to make the model pay more attention to differentiated local regions, we propose an attention-based local region merging method Group Attention Transformer (GA-Trans), which evaluates the importance of each patch by using the self-attention weight inside the Transformer, and then aggregates adjacent high weight attention blocks into groups, then randomly select groups for image crop and drop. Through the weight sharing encoder, the global and local regions of the image are classified after obtaining the features respectively, which is convenient to realize the end-to-end training. Comprehensive experiments show that GA-Trans can achieve state-of-the-art performance on multiple benchmark datasets.

Keywords: Computer vision · FGIR · Transformer

1 Introduction

FGIR is a challenging task. Compared with the recognition of general objects, it has the characteristics of small intra-class differences and large inter-class differences. Therefore, how to locate and recognizing the local features with discrimination in the image is the key to the task of FGIR. In the past related research, a lot of work has been carried out based on CNN, and good results have been achieved. These methods focus on the local features of the image, such as the method of focusing on the target components proposed in the article [1–3].

X. Sun et al. (Eds.): ICAIS 2022, CCIS 1587, pp. 40–54, 2022.
https://doi.org/10.1007/978-3-031-06761-7_4

There are also some works that use bounding boxes or component annotation to improve the accuracy of classification, such as [4]. However, the number of labels required for fine-grained classified images is much more than that of general images. In order to improve the adaptability of practical applications, some works use only image-level category labels to represent the areas of network concern through the attention weight information of CNNs itself. How to effectively use the information provided by the model itself and reduce the annotation cost without losing accuracy is a problem that needs to be faced and solved in the task of FGIR.

Due to its translation invariance and local feature representation ability, CNNs has made good achievements in the field of image classification. CNNs continuously downsampling with the increase of network depth, and the receptive field increases. In this way, the global and local information of the feature map is used. For example, in VggNet [5] and ResNet [6] networks, the smaller the receptive field of the downsampled convolution neural network, the more local information, while the higher the convolution, the larger the receptive field and the more global information. In the task of FGIR, due to the small difference between different categories, in order to improve the accuracy of classification, the network needs to learn the discriminative features in the image.

In recent years, the research focus of Transformer has gradually changed from NLP (natural language processing) to computer vision tasks. The research on Transformer in the field of computer vision has become a research hotspot and is widely used in the fields of image recognition, target detection and image segmentation. Vision Transformer [7] brings new methods to the field of computer vision, in which self-attention mechanism and image serialization method have attracted extensive attention. Vision Transformer uses the attention mechanism to learn the key areas in the image by dividing the 2D image into multiple fixed-size and non-overlapping blocks and embedding them through convolution layers and then adding randomly initialized learnable positions to obtain 1D sequences. Good results have been achieved in the general image recognition dataset. However, due to the defects of native ViT itself, it can not directly play its advantages in FGIR. For example, the receptive field of ViT cannot be extended effectively because the length of the block token does not change with the increase of its encoder block. In addition, ViT focuses on global information and cannot effectively capture the local area information carried in the block token.

In order to solve the above problems, TransFG [8] proposes to use ViT's self-attention weight to filter the blocks entering the last transformer layer, and only retain the block tokens with the largest weight. However, when generating an attention graph for selecting tokens, TransFG cannot fully use all Transformer layer attention. The attention weight of each layer plays different roles in the final fused attention graph. The purpose of attention graph fusion is to correspond to the relative importance of input markers. In addition, TransFG pays too much attention to global loss, pays insufficient attention to local features, and lacks support for multi-scale.

In this paper, we propose a new ViT attention combination method, which forms groups of attention blocks to represent local attention regions, and applies this feature to FGIR. By aggregating the adjacent blocks into several groups by using the attention weight in the transformer, the corresponding groups are enlarged, cut and discarded, so that the network can learn the distinguishing features to improve the classification accuracy. We propose a new important block selection method, called Attention Group Module (AGM), which selects the blocks with high weight in the multi-head self-attention mechanism, forms the region of interest through the combination of adjacent positions, and is processed as the input of the next branch. In addition, we explore the performance of our method on four popular FGIR benchmark datasets to comprehensively verify the classification ability of our proposed GA-Trans. Finally, our work has three main contributions.

- We reconsider the FGIR problem from the perspective of image serialization and design a new vision transformer structure, namely Group Attention Transformer (GA-Trans). It combines the advantages of CNN in expanding receptive field and increasing local information and transformer's advantages in using global information.
- We use the multi-head self-attention weight in the Transformer to locate the region with high discrimination and promote the network to learn the characteristics of the effective region in the serialized image by cropping, enlarging, and dropping, so as to realize the feature representation through the serialized image.
- Comprehensive experiments show that compared with the traditional CNNs, our GA-Trans model can better learn the representative features in the image, and achieve SOTA performance on four FGIR benchmark datasets.

2 Related Works

2.1 Convolutional Neural Network

FGIR methods can be basically divided into the following two directions: feature-based coding methods and location-based methods.

The first method encodes the discriminative local features into high-order information based on feature coding or finds the relationship between contrast pairs to learn information features. For example, in [9], the bilinear model is used to learn the interactive features of two independent CNN, so as to improve the fine-grained recognition accuracy. However, due to the high computational cost of the bilinear model, it can not be popularized and applied in the real environment. Chen et al. [10] make the classification network learn discriminative local areas by destroying and reconstructing the raw image. However, from the perspective of the global view, these methods are difficult to pay attention to the distinguishing details in the FGIR task, and can not explain how the model distinguishes the subtle differences between sub-categories.

The second method is based on localization, which trains a detection network to localize the discriminative local region and uses it for classification tasks. In the task of FGIR, some datasets provide information such as bounding box, component annotation and so on. Part of the work [3][?] uses these annotations to strongly supervise the learning of local features. However, the labor cost of the bounding boxes and component labeling is too high to be popularized. On the other hand, the weakly supervised recognition method [12][?], which only uses image level annotation, uses the attention information inside the network to obtain the positioning components to solve the classification problem.

These methods use the attention mechanism to extract the differentiated local regions. However, they need to design a dedicated structure to extract potential discriminant regions and finally classify the selected regions through the backbone network again. Moreover, the extracted discriminant regions often rely heavily on the accuracy of attention, which affects performance improvement.

Similar to this work is WS-DAN [13], which divides the key areas according to the attention weight of the raw image in CNN, and carries out reinforcement learning for cropping, enlarging or partially dropping this area. Different from WS-DAN, our work uses the internal attention weight of the Transformer layer to aggregate adjacent patches into groups, randomly select groups for cropping and dropping, in order to learn the classification features from the local areas with certain discrimination.

2.2 Transformer

In recent years, the Transformer and self-attention models have achieved great success in the field of NLP [14–16]. Many researches have been inspired and tried to apply Transformer to the field of computer vision, such as image classification [7], object detection [17], image segmentation [18–20], object tracking [21], image super-resolution [22] and video detection [23].

ViT [7] is the first work to directly apply pure Transformer to multiple fixed-size image patches sequences and realize the latest performance of image classification. Although, there are few studies to explore the Vision Transformer in the task of FGIR. TransFG [8] is the first work to expand ViT to the field of FGIR. TransFG makes effective use of the attention of each Transformer layer, and fine-grained classifies the images by filtering the patch marks entering the last layer of the Transformer.

However, TransFG pays too much attention to global information, does not make full use of attention, and can not obtain enough discrimination information. The difference between our work and TransFG is that we aggregate according to the attention weight and spatial adjacency of each image patches to obtain multiple local regions of interest, and enlarge, crop or drop these local regions, so as to guide the network to learn the discriminant features from the local regions of interest, so as to obtain better classification performance. Compared with previous work, our model achieves better performance on multiple FGIR benchmark datasets.

3 Approach

Our proposed method takes the Vision Transformer as the feature extractor. In this chapter, we will first briefly introduce the vision transformer framework, Then we introduce how our method can learn the distinguishing features from fine-grained images and improve the classification performance.

3.1 Vision Transformer for Image Recognition

Vision Transformer successfully applies Transformer to the visual field by introducing patches embedding. The innovation and key is to process the 2D image into a 1D sequence of class strings. Specifically, the model divides the 2D image $X \in \mathbb{R}^{H \times W \times C}$ into N non-overlapping blocks X with a size of $P \times P$ patch $x_p \in \mathbb{R}^{N \times P \times P \times C}$. Then, each block is embedded through the convolution layer with the convolution kernel size of $P \times P$ and the randomly initialized learnable position to obtain the 1D sequence.

$$x_{embedded} = [x_{cls} \| (x_{p1}, x_{p2}, \ldots, x_{pN})PaE] + PosE \tag{1}$$

where N is the number of image blocks, similar to BERT, $x_{cls} \in \mathbb{R}^{1 \times D}$ is the initialized category tag, $PaE \in \mathbb{R}^{(P^2 \cdot C) * D}$ is the block embedding mapping, $E_{pos} \in \mathbb{R}^{(1+N) \times D}$ indicates location embedding that can be learned. Position embedding can bring the corresponding location information to the block without location information. Patches via Eq. 1 is mapped to the potential D dimensional embedding space, resulting in $X_{embedded}$ is used as the input of subsequent Transformer encoder modules.

Transformer encoder is composed of multi-head self-attention (MSA) and multi-layer perceptron (MLP) modules. The output of the k-th Transformer layer can be expressed in the following form:

$$x'_k = x_{k-1} + MSA(LN(x_{k-1})) \qquad k \in 1, 2, \cdots, L \tag{2}$$
$$x_k = x'_k + MLP(LN(x'_k)) \qquad k \in 1, 2, \cdots, L \tag{3}$$

where $LN(\cdot)$ represents the layer normalization operation. x'_k is the output of MSA, x_k is the output of k-th MLP layer. Vision Transformer selects the first output x_L^0 generated by the l-th Transformer layer as class token X_{cls} is input into the classification network to obtain the final classification result. This is because x_l^0 has richer global information than other block tags. The formula of classification network is as follows:

$$out = Softmax(x_{cls} \cdot W) \tag{4}$$

where out is the output of the classification network and W is the weight of the classification network.

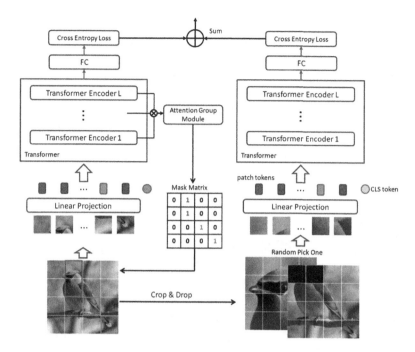

Fig. 1. The structure diagram of our proposed method GA-Trans. Raw image is split into small patches and projected into the embedding space through linear projection, and then input to the transformer. Our method uses the attention weight in the Transformer layer to propagate the attention of the input layer to a higher level through matrix multiplication. Finally, the generated attention weight matrix is filtered to form a mask matrix, and the adjacent patches are grouped to form multiple local regions. Use crop and drop for each region to enlarge region to the size of the raw image and classify it.

3.2 Proposed Network Architecture

As can be seen from Sect. 4.2, Vision Transformer can be applied to fine-grained classification and achieve better performance than most CNN based work. However, it can not capture the local information required by FGIR, which affects its effect to a certain extent. In order to solve the above problems, we propose splice attention blocks to form grouping regions for multi-scale image learning, and improve the classification performance by discarding some information to learn the transformer structure of secondary features in the image. The structure diagram of our proposed method is shown in Fig. 1.

Patches Attention Calculate. In order to divide patches with high discrimination from the original image, we first take the attention weight of each Transformer layer as:

$$A = softmax(\frac{QK^T}{D^{\frac{1}{2}}}) = [\mathbf{a}_0, \mathbf{a}_1, \ldots, \mathbf{a}_{L-1}] \tag{5}$$

$$\mathbf{a}_l = [a_l^1, a_l^2, \cdots, a_l^K] \qquad\qquad l \in 1, 2, \cdots, L \tag{6}$$

$$a_l^i = [a_l^{i_0}, a_l^{i_1}, a_l^{i_2}, \cdots, a_l^{i_N}] \qquad\qquad i \in 1, 2, \cdots, K \tag{7}$$

where Q and K represent the query and key vectors in the multi-head self-attention mechanism (MSA). Attention weight of previous layers $\mathbf{a}_l$ integrate through matrix multiplication to obtain the final attention matrix $\mathbf{a}_{final}$,

$$\mathbf{a}_{final} = \prod_{l=1}^{L} \mathbf{a}_l \tag{8}$$

By matrix multiplication the attention weight of each layer, the attention information of each patch is transmitted from the input layer to a higher layer. Therefore, compared with the attention weight of the last layer $\mathbf{a}_L$, $\mathbf{a}_{final}$ can better represent the discrimination of each patch. And then we're talking about $\mathbf{a}_{final}$ average the attention weights of multiple-head self-attention of:

$$G = \frac{\sum_{k=1}^{K} a_{final}^k}{K} \tag{9}$$

The attention weight vector $G \in \mathbb{R}^{(N^{\frac{1}{2}} \times N^{\frac{1}{2}})}$ can regarded as a 2D form $G(x, y)$, where (x, y) represents the relative position of the patch(x, y) in $N^{\frac{1}{2}} \times N^{\frac{1}{2}}$.

Group Attention Crop Module. In order to enhance the detail feature extraction of discrimination regions, the attention weight of the patch is processed. The patch whose weight exceeds the threshold is marked as 1, otherwise it is marked as 0. As shown in the Eq. 10, Where G_{max} is the max value of G.

$$M_c(x, y) = \begin{cases} 1, & \text{if } G(x, y) > \theta_c G_{max} \\ 0, & \text{otherwise} \end{cases} \tag{10}$$

The patches with 1 in M_c are adjacently merged to form multiple local regions. Randomly select one of the regions, including the region with a rectangular bounding box, cut the region in the bounding box and enlarge it to the size of the raw image. The new graph is used as the input data of the new scale and forward into the model with shared weights for training. Because the local area of the target with discrimination is enlarged, the model can extract more detailed features.

Group Attention Drop Module. When the information of a certain area is lost, we hope that the model can accurately judge the object category from the remaining features, so as to simulate the occlusion of common targets in practice. Filter the attention weight of the block, as shown in the Eq. 11.

$$M_d(x,y) = \begin{cases} 1, & \text{if } G(x,y) > \theta_d G_{max} \\ 0, & \text{otherwise} \end{cases} \tag{11}$$

The adjacent patches with 1 in M_d are combined to form multiple local regions. Randomly select few of the areas and drop the information to generate a new picture. The new picture is input into the weight sharing network as the graph that discards some details for training, so as to strengthen the learning of secondary features.

4 Experiments

In this section, we describe our experimental setup, discuss and analyze the experimental results and ablation experiments of each component. First, introduce the details of experimental setup in Sect. 4.1, including the basic introduction of dataset and the setting of training parameters. Then, it is compared with previous research work in Sect. 4.2. Conduct ablation research in Sect. 4.3 to compare the roles of various modules in the network. Finally, the visualization results of this work are analyzed in Sect. 4.4.

4.1 Experiments Setup

Datasets: We evaluated our approach on three popular benchmark datasets. Such as CUB200-2011, Stanford-Cars, and Stanford-Dogs. The statistics of each dataset are displayed in Table 1, such as the number of categories, training samples, and test samples.

Table 1. Statistic of fine-grained datasets used

Datasets	Category	Training	Testing
CUB-Birds	200	5994	5794
Stanford Dogs	120	12000	8580
Stanford Cars	196	8144	8041

Implement Details: We used Pytoch to complete the construction of the whole model. In all experiments, we used the official model ViT-B_16 pretrained on ImageNet21k as the backbone network. Like most SOTA FGIR methods, the size of the input image is set to 448 × 448. The data augmentation method used in our experiment: random clipping and horizontal flipping are used in the training stage, and only central cropping is used in the inference stage.

Cut the picture into small patches with a size of 16 × 16 as input to the ViT network. Model training uses random gradient descent with a batch size of 8 and momentum of 0.9. The initial learning rate is set to 0.01, and the learning rate adjustment method is the cosine decay function. The model trains a total of 40 epochs, two of which are warm-up. In the experiment, we used Top1 accuracy as the evaluation scale. To demonstrate the advantages of our model, we compared it with some previously published work.

4.2   Comparison with the SOTA

To further validate GA-Trans, we compared our method with the latest method on four publicly available datasets.

CUB200-2011. We compare the proposed method with the latest FGIR method on CUB200-2011, and the result is shown in the third column of Table 2. From the experimental results shown in the table, we can draw the following conclusions:

In general, from the experiment, we found that on the dataset CUB200-2011, our proposed method GA-Trans is better than all previous methods. It can be seen from the result that the accuracy of the network model based on Transformer is better than that based on CNN. The proposed method improves by 1.5% on the basis of ViT, which proves the effectiveness of multi-branch network structure. API-Net [24] and TransFG [8] use the comparative learning mechanism to improve the effect of the model. The method we propose can also use the comparative learning method to improve performance.

Table 2. Comparison of our method with existing SOTA methods on CUB-200-2011, Stanford Cars

Method	Backbone	CUB	Cars
NTS-Net [27]	ResNet-50	87.5	93.9
Cross-X [28]	ResNet-50	87.7	94.6
DCL [10]	ResNet-50	87.8	94.5
CIN [29]	ResNet-101	88.1	94.5
ACNet [31]	ResNet-50	88.1	94.6
S3N [32]	ResNet-50	88.5	94.7
FDL [33]	DenseNet-161	89.1	94.2
PMG [34]	ResNet-50	89.6	95.1
API-Net [24]	DenseNet-161	90.0	**95.3**
ViT [7]	ViT-B_16	90.6	93.5
TransFG [8]	ViT-B_16	90.9	94.2
GA-Trans (ours)	ViT-B_16	**91.5**	94.6

Stanford-Cars. The fourth column of Table 2 shows the experimental results of the latest FGIR model on the Stanford cars dataset. By comparing the experimental results, it can be found that the performance of our proposed method is better than most of the methods listed in the table and slightly worse than API-Net, PMG, and S3N methods. We believe that the image data in Stanford-Cars has the characteristics of prominent recognition subject and small background proportion, which weakens the need for accurate target positioning ability, so the advantages of our method are not prominent. Therefore, it can be seen that the results of many models are close on this dataset. Nevertheless, the accuracy of our proposed method is still 1.1% higher than that of the backbone network ViT.

Stanford-Dogs. As can be seen from Table 3, our method improves the performance more on the Stanford-Dogs dataset. API-Net [24] in the table constructs data batches through ingenious methods, learns the mutual feature vectors of two similar images, compares the fused feature vectors to learn subtle differences, and achieves SOTA performance. Compared with API-Net [24], our method still improves the accuracy by 2.0%. It is worth noting that the method based on the Transformer is generally better than the method based on CNN, which shows the effectiveness of Transformer structure in the FGIR task.

Table 3. Comparison of our Trans with existing state of the arts methods on Stanford Dogs.

Method	Backbone	Acc. (%)
FDL [33]	DenseNet-161	84.9
Cross-X [28]	ResNet-50	88.9
API-Net [24]	ResNet-101	90.3
ViT [7]	ViT-B_16	91.2
TransFG	ViT-B_16	90.4
GA-Trans (ours)	ViT-B_16	**92.3**

4.3 Ablation Experiments

In this section, we study the ablation of GA-Trans. Through experiments on the addition, deletion and parameter value adjustment of each module in the model, we analyze how our proposed method affects the classification accuracy of fine-grained images through the experimental results. All the ablation experiments below are conducted on the CUB200-2011 dataset, and common experimental phenomena can also be observed on other datasets. In order to evaluate the influence of each module and parameter in the proposed method, we designed the following experiments: the influence of image resolution, patch size, the influence of cropping and dropping modules. The influence of each set on the experimental results is described and analyzed below.

Influence of Image Resolution. The resolution of the input image is a key factor affecting the performance of image classification. High-resolution images can show clearer detailed features of objects, and low-resolution images can show insufficient local details, which often affect the classification performance, especially on fine-grained classification tasks. In order to study the classification accuracy of Vit, transfg and our proposed method based on transformer architecture under different image resolutions, we set a variety of different resolutions, 192 × 192, 224 × 224, 256 × 256, 288 × 288, 320 × 320 respectively. The above methods are tested under five resolution conditions. The results obtained are shown in Table 4. It can be seen from the table that the classification performance of each model is better with the improvement of image resolution. And our method GA-Trans exceeds the reference value at each resolution and achieves the best performance.

Table 4. Ablation experiments on CUB200 with different input resolutions

Resolution	192	224	256	288	320
ViT	81.5	85.3	87.4	88.3	88.9
TransFG	81.6	84.9	86.8	88.0	89.1
Ours	83.5	87.7	88.2	89.0	89.9

Influence of Crop and Drop Module: In order to analyze the impact of cropping and dropping modules on the performance of the overall model in our proposed method. We ran experiments on the CUB200-2011 dataset to show the effectiveness of each module on the accuracy of the overall model. The experimental results are shown in Table 5. It can be seen from the experimental results that both drop and crop modules contribute to the accuracy of our proposed method. Compared with drop, crop improves performance even more. When the two components act at the same time, the model can still improve performance. In the verification stage, we only use the localization and cropping method for the input data, which slightly improves the final performance.

Table 5. Contribution of proposed components and their combinations.

Group attention crop	Group attention drop	Accuracy (%)
		90.6
√		91.2
	√	91.0
√	√	91.5

Influence of Patch Size: Patch size is an important factor affecting the performance of the Transformer structure. In order to analyze the impact of different patch sizes on fine-grained classification tasks, we designed comparative experiments for different patch sizes, and the experimental results are shown in Table 6. In the Transformer, the larger the patch size, the larger the block size of the original image cut, and the fewer the number of input blocks. The less discriminative local information the network learns from the original graph. As can be seen from the table, the smaller the patch size, the higher the classification accuracy of the model. Compared with ViT and TransFG, our method is better than other methods under the same patch size.

Table 6. Ablation experiments on patch size.

Method	Patch size	Accuracy (%)
ViT	16 × 16	90.6
TransFG	16 × 16	90.9
Ours	16 × 16	91.5
ViT	32 × 32	88.4
TransFG	32 × 32	88.9
Ours	32 × 32	89.4

4.4   Visualization Analysis

Fig. 2. For attention-based object localization, cropping and dropping, the first row in the figure is the raw images. From the second row, we can see the method we proposed, extract the main part of the target object from the picture, and from the third row, we can see the local drop of the discrimination region of the object.

We randomly selected some images from CUB200-2011 and Stanford-Dogs datasets and compared the differences between the original image and the image after attention clipping and attention discarding in Fig. 2. In the figure, the first line is the raw image, the second row is the image after attention amplification and cropping, the third row is the image after attention dropping. From the second and third lines of the figure, we can see that our GA-Trans method is accurate in locating the key area of the target in the image. Our method successfully captures the highly differentiated areas of the target, such as the bird's head, wings, and tail; A dog's ears, eyes, legs. From the fourth and fifth lines of the figure, it can be seen that by cutting the key areas of the image, the attention map is more focused, the key areas are more concerned, and the accuracy is higher. It can be seen that by grouping and clipping the attention in the Transformer, our method accurately locates the target subject to be recognized from the image, and eliminates a large amount of background information and foreground information irrelevant to the target.

5   Conclusion

In this paper, we propose a multi-scale attention grouping method of FGIR to learn fine area attention, which makes up for the deficiency in ViT for the FGIR tasks. When there is no bounding box and component annotation and only image-level category annotation is used, the transformer's self-attention weight is used to evaluate the importance of the small blocks corresponding to the original image, merge the important blocks into groups, and conduct targeted learning for the new region after local clipping or discarding. Our proposed algorithm achieves SOTA performance on three public fine-grained benchmark datasets: CUB200-2011, Stanford-Dogs, and Stanford-Cars. The future work is to improve the location accuracy of regional attention and experiment on more complex datasets to further improve the classification performance of the model.

References

1. Wei, X., Xie, C., Wu, J.: Mask-CNN: localizing parts and selecting descriptors for fine-grained image recognition. arXiv:1605.06878 (2016)
2. Xie, L., et al.: Hierarchical part matching for fine-grained visual categorization. In: Proceedings of the IEEE International Conference on Computer Vision (2013)
3. Branson, S., et al.: Bird species categorization using pose normalized deep convolutional nets. arXiv:1406.2952 (2014)
4. Huang, S., et al.: Part-stacked CNN for fine-grained visual categorization. In: Proceedings of the IEEE Conference on Computer Vision and Pattern Recognition (2016)
5. Simonyan, K., Zisserman A.: Very deep convolutional networks for large-scale image recognition. arXiv:1409.1556 (2014)
6. He, K., et al.: Deep residual learning for image recognition. In: Proceedings of the IEEE Conference on Computer Vision and Pattern Recognition (2016)

7. Dosovitskiy, A., et al.: An image is worth 16x16 words: transformers for image recognition at scale. arXiv:2010.11929 (2020)
8. He, J., et al.: TransFG: a transformer architecture for fine-grained recognition. arXiv:2103.07976 (2021)
9. Lin, T., Aruni, R., Subhransu, M.: Bilinear CNN models for fine-grained visual recognition. In: Proceedings of the IEEE International Conference on Computer Vision (2015)
10. Chen, Y., et al.: Destruction and construction learning for fine-grained image recognition. In: Proceedings of the IEEE/CVF Conference on Computer Vision and Pattern Recognition (2019)
11. Jiang, S., et al.: Multi-scale multi-view deep feature aggregation for food recognition. IEEE Trans. Image Process. **29**, 265–276 (2019)
12. Ge, W., Lin, X., Yu, Y.: Weakly supervised complementary parts models for fine-grained image classification from the bottom up. In: Proceedings of the IEEE/CVF Conference on Computer Vision and Pattern Recognition, pp. 3034–3043 (2019)
13. Hu, T., et al.: See better before looking closer: weakly supervised data augmentation network for fine-grained visual classification. arXiv:1901.09891 (2019)
14. Vaswani, A., et al.: Attention is all you need. In: Advances in Neural Information Processing Systems (2017)
15. Devlin, J., et al.: BERT: pre-training of deep bidirectional transformers for language understanding. arXiv:1810.04805 (2018)
16. Yang, Z., et al.: XLNet: generalized autoregressive pretraining for language understanding. In: Advances in Neural Information Processing Systems (2019)
17. Carion, N., Massa, F., Synnaeve, G., Usunier, N., Kirillov, A., Zagoruyko, S.: End-to-end object detection with transformers. In: Vedaldi, A., Bischof, H., Brox, T., Frahm, J.-M. (eds.) ECCV 2020. LNCS, vol. 12346, pp. 213–229. Springer, Cham (2020). https://doi.org/10.1007/978-3-030-58452-8_13
18. Zheng, S., et al.: Rethinking semantic segmentation from a sequence-to-sequence perspective with transformers. In: Proceedings of the IEEE/CVF Conference on Computer Vision and Pattern Recognition (2021)
19. Chen, J., et al.: TransUNet: transformers make strong encoders for medical image segmentation. arXiv:2102.04306 (2021)
20. Xie, E., et al.: Trans2Seg: transparent object segmentation with transformer. arXiv:2101.08461 (2021)
21. Sun, P., et al.: TransTrack: multiple-object tracking with transformer. arXiv:2012.15460 (2020)
22. Yang, F., et al.: Learning texture transformer network for image super-resolution. In: Proceedings of the IEEE/CVF Conference on Computer Vision and Pattern Recognition (2020)
23. Girdhar, R., et al.: Video action transformer network. In: Proceedings of the IEEE/CVF Conference on Computer Vision and Pattern Recognition (2019)
24. Zhuang, P., Wang, Y., Qiao, Y.: Learning attentive pairwise interaction for fine-grained classification. In: Proceedings of the AAAI Conference on Artificial Intelligence, vol. 34, no. 07 (2020)
25. Dubey, A., et al.: Maximum-entropy fine-grained classification. arXiv:1809.05934 (2018)
26. Wang, Y., Vlad, I., Morariu, L., Davis, S.: Learning a discriminative filter bank within a CNN for fine-grained recognition. In: Proceedings of the IEEE Conference on Computer Vision and Pattern Recognition (2018)
27. Yang, Z., et al.: Learning to navigate for fine-grained classification. In: Proceedings of the European Conference on Computer Vision (ECCV) (2018)

28. Luo, W., et al.: Cross-X learning for fine-grained visual categorization. In: Proceedings of the IEEE/CVF International Conference on Computer Vision (2019)
29. Gao, Y., et al.: Channel interaction networks for fine-grained image categorization. In: Proceedings of the AAAI Conference on Artificial Intelligence, vol. 34, no. 07 (2020)
30. Zheng, H., et al.: Learning deep bilinear transformation for fine-grained image representation. arXiv:1911.03621 (2019)
31. Ji, R., et al.: Attention convolutional binary neural tree for fine-grained visual categorization. In: Proceedings of the IEEE/CVF Conference on Computer Vision and Pattern Recognition (2020)
32. Ding, Y., et al.: Selective sparse sampling for fine-grained image recognition. In: Proceedings of the IEEE/CVF International Conference on Computer Vision (2019)
33. Liu, C., et al.: Filtration and distillation: enhancing region attention for fine-grained visual categorization. In: Proceedings of the AAAI Conference on Artificial Intelligence, vol. 34, no. 07 (2020)
34. Du, R., et al.: Fine-grained visual classification via progressive multi-granularity training of jigsaw patches. In: Vedaldi, A., Bischof, H., Brox, T., Frahm, J.-M. (eds.) ECCV 2020. LNCS, vol. 12365, pp. 153–168. Springer, Cham (2020). https://doi.org/10.1007/978-3-030-58565-5_10

GCN-Based Text Classification Research

Chang Yin and Ming Yuan[✉]

Jiangsu Police Institute, Nanjing, China
yuanming@jspi.edu.cn

Abstract. With the development and popularity of the Internet, a huge amount of text data has emerged on the web, and how to accurately and quickly identify the categories of these text data has become a challenge in the field of text classification. To address this challenge, this paper aims to apply deep learning techniques to text classification and build a model that can classify text data in a batch manner and automatically. By studying the current state of the art in text classification needs, this paper proposes a TextGCN model, a text classification method that presents high robustness on small data sets, based on graph convolutional neural networks. This paper makes the model perform better by modifying the IDF formula.

Keywords: Graph convolutional neural network · Text classification · Deep learning

1 Introduction

1.1 Research Background

Between 1961 and 2021, the research on text classification has undergone a transition from shallow to deep learning. During the period from 1960 to 2010, text classification models were mainly based on shallow learning, such as Naive Bayesian and KNN, which were time-consuming and laborious, although they also had good accuracy and stability. Moreover, these classification methods usually do not take into account the order and structure of the text data, so the learning ability of the models is poor.

Since 2000, machine learning techniques have advanced dramatically, and the models used for text classification have begun to shift to a deep learning-based approach. Deep learning-based text classification models are more complex in structure and have improved performance significantly compared to shallow learning. Deep learning methods can autonomously uncover information from text and provide a deeper understanding of the content of text by analysing the contextual information and natural order structure in the text, thus significantly improving the efficiency of text classification.

© The Author(s), under exclusive license to Springer Nature Switzerland AG 2022
X. Sun et al. (Eds.): ICAIS 2022, CCIS 1587, pp. 55–66, 2022.
https://doi.org/10.1007/978-3-031-06761-7_5

1.2 Research Status

Traditional text classification focuses on feature functions and classification algorithms. For feature functions, the most commonly used is the bag-of-words function. With the advancement of technology, some more complex features have also been devised, such as Chinese language models [2] and entities in ontologies [3]. As research continues, some studies on converting text to graphics or performing feature engineering on graphics and subgraphs have also emerged [4, 5].

Deep learning-based text classification research has achieved remarkable results in recent years, and the research has taken two directions. One research direction is focused on word embedding-based models [6, 7]. Some recent studies have shown that the effectiveness of word embeddings becomes a criterion for judging the effectiveness of deep learning-based text classification models. Some authors have therefore aggregated unsupervised words as document embeddings and then fed these document embeddings into a classifier [8, 9], allowing the other parts to learn the word/document and document label embeddings together [10, 11].

Another research direction draws on deep neural networks. Two of the most representative models are convolutional neural networks and recurrent neural networks. CNNs are used in the literature [12] for sentence classification, and the architecture is a direct application of CNNs in computer vision. Character-level CNNs were designed in the literature [13] and effective results were obtained. The literature [14–16] used LSTM (a specific type of RNN) to learn textual representations. To further improve the flexibility of the model, the literature [17, 18] introduced an attention mechanism into the text classification model.

Recently, graph neural networks GNNs have received increasing attention in the field of text classification for deep learning. Kipf and Welling proposed a simplified graph neural network model, called the graph convolutional neural network GCN, which achieved excellent classification results on many benchmark graph datasets [19]. Recently, several studies are also attempting to apply graph convolutional neural networks to text classification.

2 Related Technologies

2.1 Neural Network Model

The structure of a neural network is shown in Fig. 1 and usually contains an input layer, a hidden layer and an output layer. Each layer has a number of neurons, and the neurons in the next layer are connected to all the neurons in the previous layer one by one, but the neurons in the same layer are not connected to each other.

Neural networks are very adaptable and can be fitted to essentially any function, but a large number of neurons are required to build a neural network, so the number of parameters contained in a neural network is huge, resulting in a neural network that

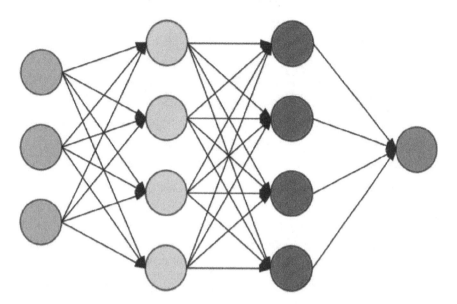

Fig. 1. The schematic of neural network model.

requires a staggering amount of computation for anything slightly more complex. Thus, fully connected neural networks are feasible for computationally extracting features from structurally simple data. However, to extract features from complex data sets with such a neural network would be computationally intensive in terms of time and effort. The introduction of convolutional neural networks can effectively limit the connections of neurons between layers, thus solving the problem of large number of parameters and large computational effort.

2.2   Convolutional Neural Networks

The earliest research on convolutional neural networks can be traced back to the 1980s and 1990s, when Japanese scholar Kunihiko Fukushima proposed a neural network model called "neocognitron" in his paper [19], which has the prototype of convolutional neural networks and can implement some of the functions of convolutional and pooling layers. This model is the prototype of a convolutional neural network and can implement some of the functions of the convolutional and pooling layers.

In 1989, LeCun constructed a convolutional neural network called LeNet [21], which was the first attempt to apply convolutional neural networks to computer vision problems. In 1989, LeCun constructed a convolutional neural network called LeNet [21], which was the first attempt to apply convolutional neural networks to computer vision problems, and in his paper, he introduced the term "convolution" for the first time, which gave convolutional neural networks their name.

A standard convolutional neural network model generally consists of an input layer, a convolutional layer, a pooling layer, a fully connected layer and an output layer, as shown in Fig. 2.

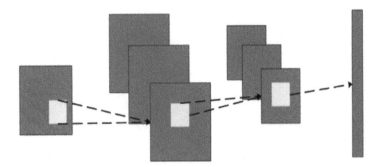

Fig. 2. The schematic of convolutional neural network model.

The role of the convolutional layer is to extract the features of the image; the role of the pooling layer is to reduce the dimensionality of the data. The fully-connected layer is generally the last layer of the convolutional neural network, and its function is to collate the output results into a one-dimensional data string, and then fully connect these one-dimensional data strings to produce the final classification results.

Convolutional Layer - Feature Extraction. The convolutional layer is a key part of a convolutional neural network, and most of the computations in a convolutional neural network model are in the convolutional layer. The convolutional layer solves a problem that exists with a fully connected layer.

Pooling Layer - Data Dimensionality Reduction. The pooling layer generally alternates with the convolution layer and is located behind the convolution layer. The pooling layer generally has three functions: Firstly, feature non-deformation; Secondly, feature dimensionality reduction; Thirdly, Avoid overfitting.

The common pooling methods are Mean pooling, Max Pooling and Stochastic Pooling. These three pooling methods have their own applications According to Boureau's theory [20], in the pooling operation, Mean pooling reduces the error caused by the large variance of the estimate and allows the image background information root to be retained more completely; Max pooling reduces the error caused by the offset of the estimated mean and more texture information is retained.

3   Graph Convolutional Neural Network

A graph convolutional neural network is a method capable of learning graph data in depth. Its main function is implemented on the basis of CNN. the definition of convolution in the GCN model can basically be divided into two categories, one is spectral based graph convolution and the other is spatial domain based graph convolution. The spatial domain-based convolution approach defines the convolution operation directly on the connection relation of each node, more similar to the convolution in a convolutional neural network. The spectral-based graph convolution method is more abstract in that it uses the Fourier transform to map the nodes from the irregular time domain to the regular frequency domain, then performs the convolution operation on the node data in the frequency domain, and finally maps the convolution result back to the time domain space through the Fourier inverse transform.

As the graph convolution based on the spectral domain is more used and the application is more extensive going forward, this paper introduces the graph convolution neural network based on the spectral method.

3.1 Fourier Transform of Graph Information

The Fourier Transform is a transformation that converts time-domain spatial data to frequency-domain spatial data, and the data before and after the transformation is equivalent. The time domain is the real time axis of the signal, representing the real world, while the frequency domain is a mathematical tool used for signal analysis.

To transfer the traditional Fourier transform and convolution to the GCN model, the central task is to transform the eigenfunctions of the Laplace operator into the eigenvectors of the corresponding Laplace matrix of the GCN.

Suppose a graph G, with n nodes, has a signal x on that graph, and each component represents the signal value of the corresponding node. The signal value of the first node is 2.

$$x = \begin{pmatrix} 2 \\ 3 \\ \dots \\ 1 \end{pmatrix} \tag{1}$$

Knowing that the Laplacian matrix L of a graph G, whose eigenvectors form an eigenmatrix U, then the signal x on the graph, which has a Fourier transform of:

$$\dot{x} = F(x) = U^T x \tag{2}$$

In the same way, the Fourier transform of a signal is known, then the original signal is x:

$$x = F^{-1}(\hat{x}) = U^T \hat{x} \tag{3}$$

3.2 Graph Convolution Operations

Convolution is essentially a weighted summation that uses a filter with shared parameters to compute a weighted sum of central pixel points and adjacent pixel points to form a feature map, thus enabling the extraction of spatial features. the convolution of the f and g functions can be written as $f * g$ and is mathematically defined as follows:

$$(f * g)(t) = \int_{-\infty}^{\infty} f(\tau)g(t - \tau) \tag{4}$$

$$(f * g)(t) = \sum_{\tau=-\infty}^{\infty} f(\tau)g(t - \tau) \tag{5}$$

The convolution operation in a convolutional neural network can only handle Euclidean space data, such as 2-dimensional images and 1-dimensional text. However, the convolution operation cannot handle non-Euclidean space data because the convolution operation cannot maintain translation invariance on non-Euclidean space data, so it needs to transform the non-Euclidean structure data into Euclidean structure by Fourier transform.

The Fourier transform of the graph signal f and the convolution kernel h is used to obtain the Hadamard product of the transformed values, followed by the inverse Fourier transform to obtain the convolution of the graph signal f and the convolution kernel h.

$$
\begin{aligned}
(f * h)_G &= F^{-1}(F(f) \odot F(h)) \\
&= F^{-1}(U^T f \odot U^T h) \\
&= F^{-1}(U^T f \odot \hat{h}) \\
&= U(U^T f \odot \hat{h}) \\
&= U \left(\begin{pmatrix} h_1 & & & \\ \vdots & h_2 & & \vdots \\ & & \ddots & \\ & & & h_n \end{pmatrix} U^T f \right)
\end{aligned} \tag{6}
$$

Since the graph signal f is known, only the convolution kernel h needs to be required, so the learning and training process of the graph convolutional neural network is to find the appropriate value of the convolutional kernel h, which is the value of hi to complete the whole process of GCN.

3.3   The Applications of GCN

Node classification of graphs. Graph, also known as a topology graph, is a network of relationships that is a clear and unambiguous way of representing information. While topological graphs have made the relationships between nodes clear, it is a challenge to classify the nodes in the graph, and the advent of graph convolutional neural networks has made it much easier to classify the nodes in a graph.

For example, to find out which of one's friends like football and which like basketball in a topological graph of one's friends' relationships, one needs to apply a graph convolutional neural network to this graph. First, the label of sports hobby is assigned to each friend node in the graph; then the features of each friend node are listed, including information about school, daily activities, groups to which they belong, etc., which are all features for learning a person's interests; finally, the feature information of the friend nodes and the relationship between the nodes are imported into the graph convolutional neural network, and the relationship between personal information and friends is used to predict each node's The node classification is performed by predicting the sport hobbies of each node through the relationship between personal information and friends.

Social Networks. With the popularity of the Internet, social networks have come to the fore in people's daily lives. In social networks, many social media become an important part of everyday life, and the behaviour of others can be used to influence the user through these media. There are many applications of graph neural networks in social network analysis, for example, the literature proposes a model called DeepInf model, which is based on deep learning techniques and predicts the social influence of nodes in this social network by combining the structure of the social network with information about the characteristics of the user nodes. The DeepInf model can predict the social influence of nodes in this social network based on the action status of neighbor nodes and the user node's The DeepInf model analyses the social group to which a node belongs based on the action status of neighbor nodes and the local structure information of the user node, uses the graph convolutional neural network GCN for feature extraction, and then gives different weights to the nodes by introducing an attention mechanism, and finally classifies the more closely connected nodes into one category.

4 GCN-Based Text Classification Model

4.1 Construct Doc-Word Relationship Graph

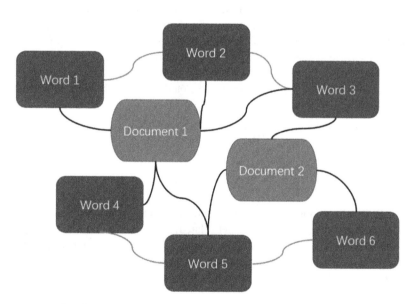

Fig. 3. The Schematic of GCN-based text classification model.

As shown in Fig. 3, the GCN-based text classification technique divides the text into circular article nodes and square word nodes, and then maps these nodes in the text into a topological map through the word co-occurrence technique, where the numbers in the nodes represent the word node and article node numbers, and the different colours represent the different types of article nodes. Edges exist between each associated node, and these are divided into two types, a black article-word edge and a purple word-word edge, with the weight of each edge being calculated based on the node it is connected to.

The article-word edge weights are calculated based on the TF-IDF method, a statistical method used to assess the importance of a word to a text in a text dataset, where a word is considered to be well differentiated if it has a high TF frequency in one article and few occurrences in other articles in the dataset. TF*IDF, where TF represents the frequency of a word or phrase in a document, i.e. the number of occurrences of the word divided by the number of words in the entire document; IDF refers to the Inverse Document Frequency, which is obtained by dividing the total number of documents by the number of documents containing the word, and then taking the logarithm of the result. classification.

$$a_{ij} = \begin{cases} \text{PMI}(i,j), & \text{if i and j are word} \\ \text{TF} - \text{IDF}_{ij}, & \text{if i is doc, and j is word} \\ 1, & \text{if i} = \text{j} \\ 0, & \text{otherwise} \end{cases} \qquad (7)$$

The weight of a word-edge is calculated using a method called PMI, which calculates the weight of a word-edge by counting the frequency of co-occurrences of the two words in a certain range. This is done by using a technique called sliding windows, which simply means defining a window of fixed length (windows) to divide the sentences in the document into segments of equal length, denoting the number of these segments by #W, and then counting the frequency of occurrence of word a in these segments, using #W(a) to denote the frequency with which word a and word b occur together in a count of these word fragments, denoted by #W (a, b). The final PMI value can then be expressed as:

$$\begin{aligned} PMI(a,b) &= \log \frac{p(a,b)}{p(a)p(b)} \\ p(a,b) &= \frac{\#W(a,b)}{\#W(a)} \\ p(a) &= \frac{\#W(a)}{\#W} \end{aligned} \qquad (8)$$

when the PMI value is positive, it means that the relationship between word a and word b is closer and the semantics dare to bet related; when the PMI value is negative, it means that there is little or no semantic relatedness between word a and word b in the corpus, so we only keep the weight values of word-word edges with positive PMI values, so that we can reply to improve the accuracy of text classification.

4.2 TextGCN Model Training

After constructing such a topological map containing word nodes and article nodes, the next step is to put the topological map into the pre-prepared GCN double-layer model for convolution and training. The ReLU function is used as the activation function in the first layer, and the softmax function is used in the second layer for classification optimisation, with the formula defined as:

$$Z = soft \max(\tilde{A} ReLU(\tilde{A} X W_0) W_1) \tag{9}$$

when using the softmax function for classification optimization, the cross-entropy loss function is used:

$$L = -\sum_{d \in y_D} \sum_{f=1}^{F} Y_{df} \ln Z_{df} \tag{10}$$

Documents with labels and F is the dimensionality of the feature vector, i.e. the total number of classes. y is the label indicator matrix. where the weight parameters and can be trained by gradient descent.

The advantage of a two-layer GCN is that it allows interoperability between otherwise unconnected article-article nodes; thus, a two-layer GCN performs better than a single-layer GCN, and continuing to add more layers does not improve performance. This model also has some limitations in that the accuracy of the results depends heavily on the size of the sliding window and the dimensionality of the embedding representation, so constant experimentation is required to select an appropriate sliding window and embedding dimension.

5   Experimental Results and Analysis

5.1   Preparation of the Experiment

In this experiment on the TextGCN model, we have used four widely used text datasets, R8, R52, MR and Ohsumed.

After cleaning the data, splitting the words, removing deactivated words and removing words with a frequency of less than 5, the statistics of the data set resulting from the pre-processing are shown in the table below.

Table 1. Data for the various data sets.

Dataset	Docs	Training	Test	Word	Nodes	Classes	Average Length
R8	18846	11314	7532	42757	61603	20	6572
R52	9100	6532	2568	8892	17992	52	6982
Ohsumed	7400	3357	4043	14157	21557	23	13582
MR	10662	7108	3554	18764	29426	2	2039

5.2   Procedure of the Experiment

The experiment is divided into three parts, namely data cleaning, mapping and model training.

Data Cleaning. First we remove the deactivated words and the low frequency words with a frequency of less than 5 from the document, then we get the target file "dataset_type.clean.txt".

Construct Graph. First, extract the word nodes and article nodes from the datesets, then make a topological graph of the text and the words. A sliding window of size 20 is then defined to divide all the sentences in the dataset into word segments of length 20. The next step is to count the frequency of words in these word fragments and the frequency of two words occurring together. After obtaining the above results, they are brought into the PMI formula to obtain the word-word edge weights. Then the TF-IDF value has to be obtained by calculating the word frequency and the inverse document frequency and assigning it to the article-word edge. In this step, some modifications are made to the original IDF calculation, which is done by dividing the total number of documents by the number of documents containing the word, and then bringing the result into the log formula with base e to obtain the final inverse document frequency.

$$IDF = \frac{n_t}{N} \tag{11}$$

Because there may be many files containing the same word in a dataset, the number of files containing the word is large, which makes the calculated IDF value too small, resulting in a final IDF value that is not significantly different because it is small. This paper therefore attempts to increase the IDF value by decreasing the number of documents containing the word, in order to increase the accuracy of the experiment by increasing the difference between the different IDF values. Through several attempts, it was found that after performing an open operation with a square root of 0.5 for the number of documents containing the word and adjusting the base of the log formula to 2.5, the overall results of the experiment improved somewhat and were more effective than using the original TF-IDF calculation.

$$SquaredIDF = \log_{2.5}\left(\frac{n_t}{\sqrt{N}}\right) \tag{12}$$

5.3   Experimental Results

After the data cleaning process on the R8, R52, Ohsumed and MR datasets and then imported into TextGCN for training, the experimental results are shown in Table 2.

The Text GCN model used in this paper is compared with some commonly used text classification models as shown in Table 6–1 (where the experimental data of TF-IDF + LR, LSTM, fast Text, CNN, and Text GCN models refer to the results in the literature [23]).

Table 2. Comparison of classification results of multiple classification models.

Classification methods	R8	R52	Ohsumed	MR
TF-IDF + LR	0.9374	0.8695	0.5466	0.7459
LSTM	0.9368	0.8554	0.4113	0.7506
Fast Text	0.9613	0.9281	0.5770	0.7514
CNN	0.9571	0.8759	0.5844	0.7775
Text GCN	0.9707	0.9356	0.6836	0.7674
Modified Text GCN	**0.9730**	**0.9408**	-	**0.7799**

From the experimental results, we can conclude that the Text GCN model has the best classification results on all datasets except the MR dataset, and only the improved Text GCN model can reach the level of the CNN model on the MR dataset.

5.4   Experimental Analysis

Based on the experimental results we can conclude that there are two main reasons for the stronger performance of the Text GCN model compared to traditional text classification methods.

1) the topological map constructed by the Text GCN model provides comprehensive access to the article-word relationships as well as the full range of word-word relationships.
2) The GCN model as a special form of Laplace smoothing can compute a weighted average of a node and its second-order neighbours, and use this value as a new feature. As a result, the label information in an article node can then be passed to the word nodes adjacent to it, and then through these word nodes to other word nodes and document nodes adjacent to them.

However, the results also show that the Text GCN model has its shortcomings, and it can be observed that Text GCN performs no better than CNN for classification in the MR dataset, and can only barely reach the level of CNN after a slight improvement. This is because the MR dataset is an emotionally classified dataset, where the order of words is very important, and the Text GCN model just ignores this most important word order, in contrast to the CNN model which explicitly models sequences of consecutive words and therefore does better in the MR dataset.

In summary, the classification accuracy of the GCN-based text classification method proposed in this paper on the R8, R52 and MR corpus has been improved compared with traditional text classification methods such as CNN and LSTM, so it can be concluded that building a topological relationship graph based on the GCN model and then performing convolution operations via Fourier's law has advantages for improving text classification accuracy and can effectively improve text classification efficiency.

References

1. Zhang, X.: Research on the application of improved graph neural network text classification model-an example of NSTL scientific and technical journal literature classification. J. Intelligence **40**(01), 184–188 (2021)
2. Wang, S., Manning, C.D.: Baselines and bigrams: simple, good sentiment and topic classification. In: ACL, pp. 90–94 (2012)
3. Melville, P.C.V., Sindhwani, V., Lawrence, R.D.: Concept labeling: Building text classifiers with minimal supervision. In: IJCAI (2011)
4. Rousseau, F., Kiagias, E., Vazirgiannis, M.: Text categorization as a graph classification problem. ACL **1**, 1702–1712 (2015)
5. Skianis, K., Rousseau, F., Vazirgiannis, M.: Regularizing text categorization with clusters of words. In: EMNLP, pp. 1827–1837 (2016)
6. Mikolov, T., Sutskever, I., Chen, K., Corrado, G.S., Dean, J.: Distributed representations of words and phrases and their compositionality. In: NIPS, pp. 3111–3119 (2013)
7. Pennington, J., Socher, R., Manning, C.: Glove: global vectors for word representation. In EMNLP, 1532–1543 (2014)
8. Le, Q., Mikolov, T.: Distributed representations of sentences and documents. In: ICML, pp. 1188–1196 (2014)
9. Joulin, A., Grave, E., Bojanowski, P., Mikolov, T.: Bag of tricks for efficient text classification. In: EACL, pp. 427–431 (2017)
10. Tang, J., Qu, M., Q, M.: Pte: predictive text embedding through large-scale heterogeneous text networks. In: KDD, pp. 1165–1174. ACM (2015)
11. Wang, G., et al.: Joint embedding of words and labels for text classification. In: ACL, pp. 2321–2331 (2018)
12. Kim, Y.: Convolutional neural networks for sentence classification. In: EMNLP, pp. 1746–1751 (2014)
13. Zhang, X., Zhao, J., Lecun, Y.: Character-level convolutional networks for text classification. In: NIPS, pp. 649–657 (2015)
14. Tai, K.S., Socher, R., Manning, C.D.: Improved semantic representations from tree-structured long short-term memory networks. In: ACL, pp. 1556–1566 (2015)
15. Liu, P., Qiu, X., Huang, X.: Recurrent neural network for text classification with multi-task learning. In: IJCAI, pp. 2873–2879 (2016)
16. Luo, Y.: Recurrent neural networks for classifying relations in clinical notes. J. Biomed. Inform. **72**, 85–95 (2017)
17. Yang, Y.Z., Dyer, D., He, C., Smola, X., Hovy, A., E: Hierarchical attention networks for document classification. In: NAACL, pp. 1480–1489 (2016)
18. Wang, Y., Huang, M., Zhao, L.: Attention-based lstm for aspect-level sentiment classification. In: EMNLP, pp. 606–615 (2016)
19. Schmidhuber, J.: Deep learning in neural networks: An overview. Neural Netw. **61**, 85–117 (2015)
20. Waibel, A.: Phoneme recognition using time-delay neural networks. Meeting of the Institute of Electrical, Information and Communication Engineers (IEICE). Tokyo, Japan (1987)
21. Lecun, Y., et al.: Backpropagation applied to handwritten zip code recognition. Neural Comput. **1**(4), 541–551 (1989)
22. Kipf, T.N., Welling, M.: Semi-supervised classification with graph convolutional networks (2017)
23. Boureau, Y., et al.: Learning mid-level features for recognition (2010)

A Text Multi-label Classification Scheme Based on Resampling and Ensemble Learning

Tianhao Wang[1], Tianrang Weng[1], Jiacheng Ji[1], Mingjun Zhong[4], and Baili Zhang[1,2,3(✉)] (iD)

[1] School of Computer Science and Engineering, Southeast University, Nanjing 211189, China
220191784@seu.edu.cn
[2] Key Laboratory of Computer Network and Information Integration in Southeast University, Ministry of Education, Nanjing 211189, China
[3] Research Center for Judicial Big Data, Supreme Count of China, Nanjing 211189, China
[4] Department of Computing Science, University of Aberdeen, Aberdeen AB24 3UE, UK

Abstract. The medical dispute cases are professional and closely related to medicine. Therefore, the mediation of cases in practice depends heavily on similar historical cases. Multi-label classification of legal documents can efficiently filter irrelevant historical cases, which helps to recommend the similar historical cases faster and better. However, the imbalance and label symbiosis of the data set directly affect multi-label classification of legal documents. Therefore, a multi-label classification scheme based on resampling and ensemble learning is presented in this paper The scheme includes two parts: in the first part, in order to reduce the impact of label symbiosis on resampling, a resampling algorithm based on the average sparsity of the label set is proposed improve the imbalance of the data set; in the second one, a multi-label classification algorithm based on ensemble learning is proposed to train multiple base classifiers and combine each base classifier with a voting strategy of one vote. It can effectively improve the effect of multi-label classification. The experimental results show that the scheme proposed in this paper can improve the effect of multi-label classification and is not only suitable for legal documents but also applicable for other text data sets with imbalanced classes and label symbiosis problems.

Keywords: Class imbalance · Multi-label classification · Ensemble learning · Resampling algorithm · Label symbiosis

1 Introduction

In recent years, the problem of medical disputes has been acute in our country. Because the medical disputes are closely related to the professional field of medicine, the mediation of medical dispute cases is more difficult. In practice, the mediation of cases depend heavily on similar historical cases. Recommendations of legal documents relay on largely on their accurate classification. Among classes, "Department" and

© The Author(s), under exclusive license to Springer Nature Switzerland AG 2022
X. Sun et al. (Eds.): ICAIS 2022, CCIS 1587, pp. 67–80, 2022.
https://doi.org/10.1007/978-3-031-06761-7_6

"Negligence" are most discriminating and important. They reveal what kind of department the patient visited and what kind of possible negligent behavior of the doctor caused the patient's damage. In view of the fact that a medical dispute may correspond to multiple "department" and multiple "negligence", the class labeling of legal documents for medical disputes belongs to the multi-label classification. Since the labeled legal documents will be further filtered by related personnel or algorithms, the multi-label classification of medical dispute legal documents pays more attention to the recall of classification than the accuracy.

At present for multi-label classification issue, there are mainly two solutions based on problem conversion and algorithm adaptation [1]. Among them, BR [2, 3], RAKEL [2], CC [3–5] based on problem conversion methods and Rank-SVM [6], ML-KNN [6] based on algorithm adaptation are widely used in multi-label classification, and have achieved good multi-classification results. Simultaneously, algorithms based on neural networks are gradually being transformed and applied to multi-label classification tasks [7–12].

However, there is a serious imbalance of class distribution in the data set of legal documents, and it is difficult to achieve the ideal classification effect by directly using mainstream multi-label classification algorithms. Existing solutions to the imbalance of classes in text multi-label classification include LP-based resampling schemes and ML-based resampling schemes [13]. The LP-based resampling schemes are represented by LP-RUS [13–15] and LP-ROS [13–15]. The algorithm converts multi-label classification into multi-class classification, under-sampling the majority of classes and over-sampling the minority classes. However, the multi-class classification problem after the conversion will have the problem of a large number of classes and sparse distribution of classes. The ML-based resampling schemes are represented by ML-RUS [13] and ML-ROS [13].The algorithm divides the majority or minority class labels by comparing the frequency difference of each label, and obtains samples containing the corresponding labels, and randomly samples the samples in the sample set, so as to realize the resampling of multi label data sets. However, this algorithm does not take into account the impact of label symbiosis on resampling, and the objective existence of label symbiosis may cause resampled samples. The set still has the problem of imbalance, which makes the selection of samples during resampling more complicated.

Simultaneously, it is difficult for a single multi-label classifier to obtain the ideal classification effect in practical applications. Compared with a single classifier by combining multiple single classifiers with general performance, ensemble learning can often obtain significantly superior classification results [16]. Therefore, solutions based on ensemble learning have also been proposed to solve the problem of class imbalance in multi-label classification. Among them, the Bagging [14] algorithm is a representative of parallel integration, but the bootstrap sampling it adopts cannot avoid the imbalance of the multi-label class distribution, which directly affects the performance of the classifier.

To solve the above problems, firstly, this research proposes the resampling algorithm based on the average sparsity of the label set to resample the training set, and then merges the resampling algorithm based on the algorithm framework of ensemble learning to obtain the final multi-label classifier. Experiments on different data sets show that this solution not only effectively improves the multi-label classification effect of medical dispute legal documents, but also helps to improve the multi-label classification effect of other text data sets with imbalances and label symbiosis problems.

2 The Imbalance of the Types of Legal Documents for Medical Disputes

Through in-depth analysis of medical dispute legal documents, combined with the practice of specific medical dispute contradiction mediation, it is found that among the many labels, "department" and "negligence" belong to the two most basic and most discriminative and important label. However, as shown in Fig. 1 and Fig. 2, both labels of "department" and "negligence" have obvious imbalances in the class distribution [17]. Labels such as "Internal Medicine" and "Surgery" appear frequently, while labels such as "Rheumatology and Immunology" and "Anaesthesia" appear very low. Most classifiers are trained by optimizing the classification accurac, which leads to the classification results being biased to select majority class. Therefore, the data set should be resampled before classification to balance the class distribution to obtain more accurate model. **Sample Heading (Third Level).** Only two levels of headings should be numbered. Lower level headings remain unnumbered; they are formatted as run-in headings.

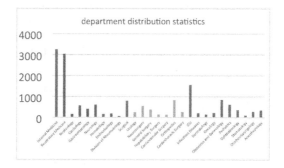

Fig. 1. Department distribution statistics.

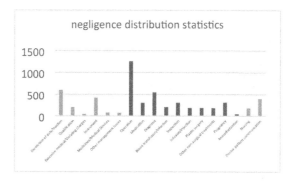

Fig. 2. Negligence distribution statistics.

However, since each instance in the multi-label data set is associated with a certain subset of the label set, and certain labels appear frequently (majority class labels), some labels appear very low (minority class labels), there must be both majority class labels and minority class labels in the label set of some instances, which will increase the number of majority class tags when over-sampling the samples corresponding to the minority class tags, or reduce the number of minority class labels when under-sampling the samples corresponding to majority class labels [18–22]. This phenomenon of label symbiosis makes the selection of samples in multi-label resampling more complicated.

3 Multi-label Classification Based on Resampling and Ensemble Learning

In order to improve the classification effect of multi-label classification for the problem of class imbalance and label symbiosis, this research proposes the evaluation index of label sparsity for the first time, and then uses the resampling algorithm based on the average sparsity of the label set to carry out the self-sampling method in Bagging. Instead, a multi-label classification scheme based on sample resampling and ensemble learning is proposed. This scheme uses a basic algorithm process similar to Bagging. First, the training set is resampled through RCS to obtain multiple different sampling sets. Secondly, a base classifier based on each sampling set is trained. Finally, the base classifier is combined by one vote veto decision voting, so as to improve the effect of multi label classification.

3.1 Resampling Algorithm Based on the Average Sparsity of the Label Set

Before resampling, it is necessary to determine which samples need to be resampled. Existing resampling algorithms, such as ML-based, find minority class labels and majority class labels through the degree of imbalance between the labels, and then over-sample the samples corresponding to the minority class labels, or under-sample the samples corresponding to the majority class labels. Literature [14] proposed that the degree of label imbalance can be measured by IRLbl and MeanIR. IRLbl(y) is the ratio of the most frequent label in the data set to the number of occurrences of label y, which measures the sparseness of label y. The higher the value of IRLbl, the fewer times the corresponding tag appears, and the greater the frequency difference with the tag with the most occurrences; MeanIR is the average of all tag imbalance rates in the tag space, which measures the average imbalance rate of the entire tag set, the greater the

MeanIR, the greater the difference in the number of times the tags appear in the data set as a whole, and the higher the imbalance between the tags.

Based on the calculation of the imbalance rate of a single label, this research proposes the concept MeanIRls of mean sparseness of the label set, that is, the average imbalance rate of the labels contained in a label set. The specific calculation formula is as follows:

$$IRLbl(y) = \frac{argmax_{y=y_1}^{y_q}\left(\sum_{i=1}^{m} h(y', Y_i)\right)}{\sum_{i=1}^{m} h(y', Y_i)} \tag{1}$$

Among them, p is the number of labels contained in the label set.

$$h(y, Y_i) = \begin{cases} 1, y \in Y_i \\ 0, y \notin Y_i \end{cases} \tag{2}$$

Considering that the larger the IRLbl, the smaller the number of occurrences of a single label, and the label is sparser. Therefore, if the average sparseness MeanIRls of a label set is larger, it means that the set contains more minority class labels; if the average sparseness MeanIRls of a label set is smaller, it means that the set contains majority class labels. Sort the average sparsity of the label sets corresponding to all samples in the data set from large to small. Obviously, each over-sampling of samples with larger average sparsity and under-sampling of samples with lower average sparsity will make it is more effective to adjust the unbalanced label distribution of the data set. In view of label imbalance, the traditional resampling method will cause aample to be resampled multiple times due to label symbiosis, and even a sample is under-sampled and over-sampled at the same time. As a result, sampling a sample may not necessarily improve the data. The overall label distribution of the set is unbalanced. In contrast, the resampling algorithm proposed by the text directly samples the samples, avoiding multiple different samplings of a sample, and simultaneously making it possible to effectively adjust the imbalance of the label space for each sample, thereby effectively solving the problem of the impact of label symbiosis on resampling.

On this basis, this research proposes a resampling algorithm based on the average sparsity of the label set. The algorithm calculates the average sparsity of each sample corresponding to the label set, and then obtains the two types of sample sets with higher and lower MeanIRls. Finally, random over-sampling of the samples in the set with higher MeanIRls and under-sampling of the samples in the set with lower MeanIRls to make the resampled data set more balanced in the label distribution. The specific algorithm flow is as follows (Table 1):

Table 1. Algorithm flow.

Input: Unbalanced data set D; up-sampling sample set proportion M, down-sampling sample set proportion N (determine the size of sampling candidate sample set); up-sampling ratio P, down-sampling ratio Q (determine the number of sampled samples)

Output: Approximately balanced data set D'

---

1. $samplesToClone = |D| * P$
2. $samplesToDelete = |D| * Q$
3. $OSNum = |D| * Q$
4. $USNum = |D| * N$
5. / / Get the label space, the sample corresponds to the label collection space
6. / / The same kind of label set corresponds to the sample combination
7. $Lbls, LblSets, lblSetBag \leftarrow$ **labelsInDataset**(D)
8. / / Calculate the imbalance rate of each label
9. **for each** lbl **in** $Lbls$ **do**
10. $IRLbl_{label} \leftarrow$ **calcLIRLbl**(D, lbl)
11. **end**
12. / / Calculate the imbalance rate of the label set corresponding to each sample
13. **for each** $lblSet$ **in** $LblSets$ **do**
14. $MeanIRS_{labelset} \leftarrow$ **caclMeanIRS**($lblSet$)
15. **end**
16. $sortedLblSetBag \leftarrow$ **sorted**($lblSetBag, MeanIRS$)
17. $OSBag, USBag \leftarrow$ **getSamplingBag**($sortedLblSetBag, OSNum, USNum$)
18. / / Oversampling
19. **while** $samplesToClone > 0$ **do**
20. $x \leftarrow$ **random**($1, |OSBag|$)
21.   **cloneSample**(x, D)
22. $samplesToClone \leftarrow samplesToClone - 1$
23. **end**
24. / / Undersampling
25. **while** $samplesToDelete > 0$ **do**
26. $x \leftarrow$ **random**($1, |USBag|$)
27.   **deleteSample**(x, D)
28. $samplesToDelete \leftarrow samplesToDelete - 1$
29. **end**

3.2 Multi-label Classification Algorithm Based on Ensemble Learning

Bagging first uses the self-sampling method to randomly resample the data set n times to obtain n sampling sets of size m, and then trains a classifier based on each sampling set, and finally combines these classifiers. The final effect of ensemble learning is largely affected by the effect of the base classifier. When ensemble learning is used to process data sets that have class imbalance problems and label symbiosis, it is necessary to cooperate with other algorithms to deal with class imbalance. This research replaces the self-sampling method with the resampling algorithm based on the average sparsity of the tag set proposed in the previous article to generate n sample subsets of the original training set. Then, a multi-label classifier is trained based on each sample subset; and the n base classifiers obtained in the previous step are combined by a one-vote veto strategy voting method. The specific process is shown in Fig. 3:

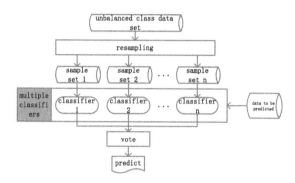

Fig. 3. Multi-label classification model based on ensemble.

For the combination strategy of base classifier ensemble, there are two ways: absolute majority voting and one vote decision. Majority vote means that if more than half of the number of votes cast by multiple base classifiers for a label, it is predicted to be the label. One vote means that if the number of votes of multiple base classifiers for a label is not zero, it is predicted to be the label. Obviously, since the one-vote veto voting combined strategy is that as long as one of the multiple classifiers predicts that the sample has the label y_j, the final sample will be predicted to contain the label. Such a strategy will lead to a decrease in the accuracy of the classifier and an increase in the recall. How to make a choice needs to be determined according to specific application requirements.

Taking into account the research background of this article, the classification of legal documents for medical disputes is for pre-screening documents when recommending similar cases. The high recall can prevent the documents corresponding to the label from being incorrectly filtered. Even if the accuracy rate drops, it can be followed up. The similarity calculation process makes up for it, so it is more appropriate to use the one-vote veto strategy in the integrated learning here.

4   Experimental Results and Analysis

4.1   Data Set

The data set was obtained by downloading medical dispute judgment documents from the Chinese trial documents website and manually marking them. According to the two classes of "department" and "negligence", the medical dispute data set is divided into two multi-label data sets. Among them, the "department" data set has 26 department class labels. Due to the hierarchical relationship between department labels, for example, "respiratory medicine" and "endocrinology" belong to the main "internal medicine", "urology" and "cardiovascular surgery" belong to "major surgery". This research uses a multi-label classification of 24 leaf labels in the hierarchical multi-label. The "Negligence" data set has 18 kinds of Negligence class labels. Figures 1 and 2 show the statistical information of the frequency distribution of each class label in the "Department" and "Negligence" datasets.

In order to verify whether the multi-label classification scheme proposed in this article is also applicable to other multi-label data sets, we chose the cail2018-small data set released by the China Judicial Big Data Research Institute, which is used for the "Fayan Cup" competition. This article uses the cail2018-small validation set as the data set for this article to conduct "crime prediction", and at the same time delete the cost of sample size less than 30. The frequency statistical information of each class label in the data set is shown in Fig. 4, from which it can be found that the class distribution in the data set is also obviously unbalanced.

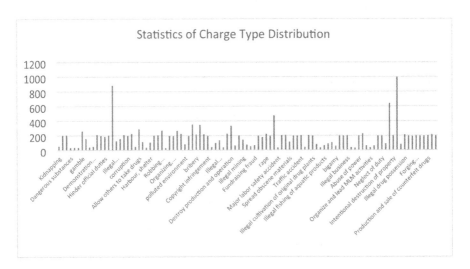

Fig. 4. Statistics of charge type distribution.

4.2 Experimental Results and Analysis

In order to show the effectiveness of the scheme proposed in this research better, this research selects a variety of multi-label classification evaluation indicators, including different forms of accuracy, recall, F1 score and Hamming loss.

In the experiment, the proposed text multi-label classification scheme based on sample resampling and ensemble learning is compared with the ML-ROS, ML-RUS sampling algorithm and the non-resampling algorithm about multi-label classification performance; simultaneously, BR, RAKEL, and CC are used in the experiment. The three multi-label classification algorithms are used as single classifiers to compare the performance improvement effect of the classic multi-label classification algorithm based on the integrated learning algorithm proposed in this research; in addition, two different voting methods are used to integrate the base classifiers, and the different biases of the two methods to the evaluation indicators are compared.

The experimental environment is: CPU Intel i7–6700, 3.40GHz, memory 24G, 64-bit Windows7 operating system. Among them, the specific value settings of related parameters, the up-sampling and down-sampling ratios used by ML-ROS and ML-RUS are 0.1; the up-sampling ratio used by the integrated resampling algorithm based on the unbalanced rate of the tag set is 0.2, and the down-sampling ratio is 0 (The "Department" data set goes up to 0.05), the proportion of up-sampling samples is 0.3, and the proportion of down-sampling samples is 0.1, and a five-fold cross-validation strategy is adopted.

In order to more intuitively analyze the performance of different sampling strategies used in different classification tasks and different base classifier combination strategies on the evaluation indicators described in the previous section, this research uses a line graph to display the experimental results. Figures 5–8 are the performance results on the "Department" data set, Figs. 9–12 are the performance results on the "Negligence" data set, and Figs. 13–16 are on the "Crime Prediction" data set. Performance results. Among them, rcs represents the resampling algorithm proposed in this article, nos represents no resampling, rus represents the ML-RUS resampling algorithm, ros represents the ML-ROS resampling algorithm, BR, rakel, and CC represent three different single multi-labels Classification algorithm, majvote represents an integrated classification algorithm that uses an overwhelming majority of voting strategies, and one vote represents an integrated classification algorithm that uses a one-vote veto strategy:

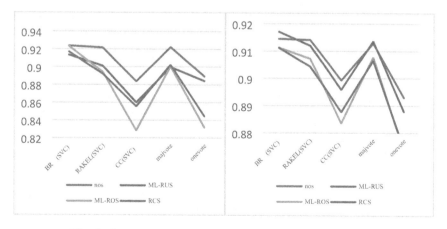

Fig. 5. Department- results-precision. (left: macro, right: micro)

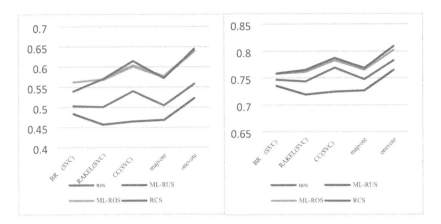

Fig. 6. Department- results-recall. (left: macro, right: micro)

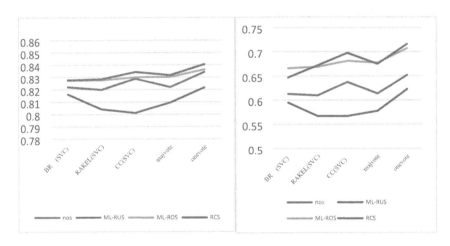

Fig. 7. Department- results-f1. (left: macro, right: micro)

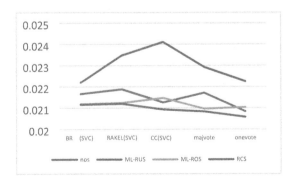

Fig. 8. Department- hamming_loss.

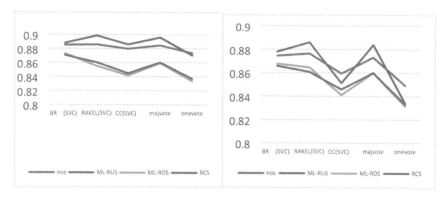

Fig. 9. Negligent behavior- results-precision. (left: macro, right: micro)

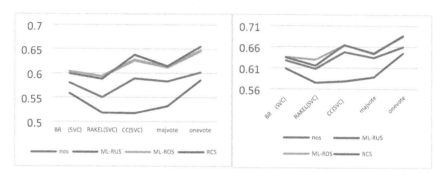

Fig. 10. Negligent behavior- results-recall. (left: macro, right: micro)

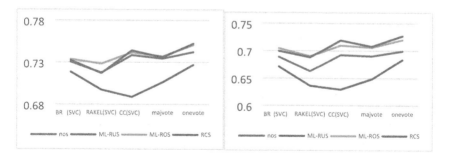

Fig. 11. Negligent behavior- results-f1. (left: macro, right: micro)

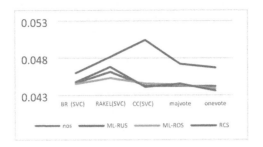

Fig. 12. Negligent behavior- results-hamming_loss.

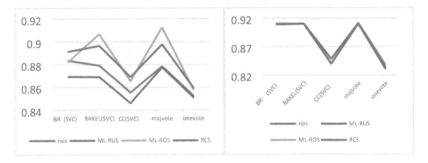

Fig. 13. Charge - results- results-precision. (left: macro, right: micro)

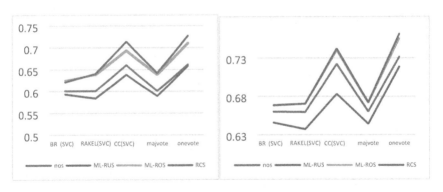

Fig. 14. Charge - results-recall. (left: macro, right: micro)

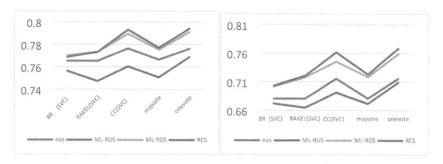

Fig. 15. Charge - results-f1. (left: macro, right: micro)

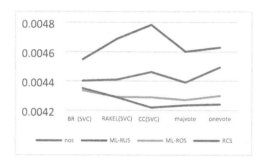

Fig. 16. Charge – hamming-loss.

5 Summary

Aiming at the imbalance of class distribution and label symbiosis in the multi-label classification of medical dispute legal documents, this research proposes a multi-label classification scheme based on sample resampling and ensemble learning. This scheme firstly calculates the average sparsity of the label set corresponding to the sample, and distinguishes the contribution of different samples to the adjustment of the unbalanced label space class distribution. Secondly, it under-samples or over-samples different samples to obtain a new sample subset to reduce the impact of class imbalance on classification. Finally, it trains multiple different base classifiers based on multiple sample sets, and obtains the final multi-label classifier with a one-vote veto integration strategy, which further improves the effect of multi-label classification. The experimental results show that the text multi-label classification scheme based on sample resampling and ensemble learning proposed in this research can effectively improve the multi-label classification effect of text data sets with imbalances and label symbiosis problems.

Acknowledgement. This work was partly supported by the National Key R&D Program of China (2018YFC0830200), the Fundamental Research Funds for the Central Universities (2242018S30021 and 2242017S30023) and Open Research Fund from Key Laboratory of Computer Network and Information Integration in Southeast University, Ministry of Education, China.

References

1. Zhang, M.L., Zhou, Z.: A review on multi-label learning algorithms. IEEE Trans. Knowl. Data Eng. **26**(8), 1819–1837 (2014)
2. Pereira, R.B.: Categorizing feature selection methods for multi-label classification. Artifi. Intel. Rev. Int. Sci. Eng. J. **49**, 57–78 (2018)
3. Wu, Y.P., Lin, H.: Progressive random k-labelsets for cost-sensitive multi-label classification. Mach. Learn. **106**, 671–694 (2017)
4. Read, J., Pfahringer, B., Holmes, G.: Classifier chains for multi-label classification. Mach. Learn. **85**(3), 333–359 (2011)
5. Tsoumakas, G., Katakis, I.: Multi-label claasification: an overview. Int. J. Data Wareh. Mining (IJDWM) **3**(3), 1–13 (2007)
6. Xu, Y., Yang, Y., Wang, Z.: Prediction of acetylation and succinylation in proteins based on multilabel learning ranksvm. Lett. Org. Chem. **8**, 275–282 (2019)
7. Zhang, M.L., Zhou, Z.H.: ML-KNN: a lazy learning approach to multi-label learning. Pattern Recogn. **40**(7), 2038–2048 (2007)
8. Zhang, M.L., Zhou, Z.: Multilabel neural networks with applications to functional genomics and text categorization. IEEE Trans. Knowl. Data Eng. **18**(10), 1338–1351 (2006)
9. Nam, J., Kim, J., Mencía, E., et al.: Large-Scale Multi-label Text Classification-Revisiting Neural Networks, pp. 437–452. Springer, Berlin, Heidelberg (2014)
10. Kurata, G., Bing, X., Zhou, B.: Improved neural network-based multi-label classification with better initialization leveraging label co-occurrence. In: Conference of the North American Chapter of the Association for Computational Linguistics: Human Language Technologies, pp. 521–526 (2016)
11. Hassen, O.A., Abu, N.A., Abidin, Z.Z., Darwish, S.M.: Realistic smile expression recognition approach using ensemble classifier with enhanced bagging. Computers, Materials & Continua **70**(2), 2453–2469 (2022)
12. He, J., Wang, C., Wu, H., Yan, L., Lu, C.: Multi-label Chinese comments categorization: comparison of multi-label learning algorithms. Journal of New Media **1**(2), 51–61 (2019)
13. Charte, F., Rivera, A.J., María, J., Jesus, D.: Addressing imbalance in multilabel classifiction: Measures and random resampling algorithms. Neurocomputing **163**, 3–16 (2015)
14. Emi, N., Abdulhamit, Y.: Comparison of bagging and boosting ensemble machine learning methods for automated emg signal classification. Biomed. Res. Int. **2019**, 9152506 (2019)
15. Charte, F., et al.: A first approach to deal with imbalance in multi-label datasets. In: 8th International Conference on Hybrid Artificial Intelligent Systems-HAIS, pp. 150–160 (2013)
16. Tahir, M.A., Kittler, J., Bouridane, A.: Multilabel classification using heterogeneous ensemble of multi-label classifiers. Pattern Recogn. Lett. **33**(5), 513–523 (2012)
17. Hao, W., Sanhong, D., Xinning, S.: Research on Chinese keyword extraction based on character sequence annotation. Mod. Lib. Info. Technol. **12**, 39–45 (2011)
18. Zhang, J.: Research on opinion extraction of Chinese reviews based on deep learning. Southwest Jiaotong University (2018)
19. Xiao, Y.: Application of multi label learning in the diagnosis of Parkinson's disease in traditional Chinese medicine. Nanjing University (2016)
20. Cao, Y.Q., Tan, C., Ji, G.L.: A multi-label classification method for vehicle video. J. Big Data **2**(1), 19–31 (2020)
21. Vo, M.T., Vo, A.H., Nguyen, T., Sharma, R., Le, T.: Dealing with the class imbalance problem in the detection of fake job descriptions. Computers, Materials & Continua **68**(1), 521–535 (2021)
22. Singla, K., Bashir, A.K., Nam, Y., Hasan, N.U.: Handling class imbalance in online transaction fraud detection. Computers, Materials & Continua **70**(2), 2861–2877 (2022)

Review of Few-Shot Learning in the Text Domain and the Image Domain

Zihang Zhang[1], Yuling Liu[1(✉)], and Junwei Huang[2]

[1] College of Computer Science and Electronic Engineering,
Hunan University, Changsha 410082, China
`yuling_liu@126.com`
[2] HERE North American LLC, Boston, USA

Abstract. Classical machine learning works ineffectively when the data set is small. Recently, few-shot learning is proposed to solve this problem. Few-shot learning models a few samples through the prior knowledge. We could divide few-shot learning into various categories depending on where the prior knowledge is extracted from. There are mainly three classes in this paper: (i) the prior knowledge extracted from the labeled data; (ii) the prior knowledge extracted from a weakly labeled or unlabeled data set; (iii) the prior knowledge extracted from similar data sets. For the convenience of searching corresponding few-shot learning methods in a certain domain, based on the above classification, we further classify few-shot learning models into ones which are applied to the image domain and the other which are applied to the text domain. With this taxonomy, we review the previous works on few-shot learning and discuss them according to these categories. Finally, present challenges and promising directions, in the aspect of few-shot learning, are also proposed.

Keywords: Deep learning · Few-shot learning · Prior knowledge · Data augmentation

1 Introduction

With the advent of the era of big data, AI has also been paid a lot of attention to. More and more excellent AI models have been proposed and have achieved great success in the aspect of the text classification, the image classification and so on. For example, Wang et al. [1] introduce the application of deep learning in object detection field, Deng et al. [2] introduce the application of deep learning in automated question answering field and Liu et al. [3] introduce the application of deep learning in fake faces detection field. However, all of these depend largely on a large-scale data set, which is expensive to get. Hence, in practice, it is impossible for a lot of tasks to select sufficient samples in various classes and not to mention that get a successful result using classical models. To tackle this problem and let machine learning models work efficiently when the data set is small, inspired by the viewpoint of human learning, the concept of few-shot learning(FSL) [4, 5] was proposed, which made machine learning closer to human thinking.

© The Author(s), under exclusive license to Springer Nature Switzerland AG 2022
X. Sun et al. (Eds.): ICAIS 2022, CCIS 1587, pp. 81–92, 2022.
https://doi.org/10.1007/978-3-031-06761-7_7

The concept of FSL first emerged from the field of computer vision [6] and subsequently extensive researches have been carried out in other domains such as natural language processing, intrusion detection systems and so on. For example, model [7] is applied in intrusion detection systems, model [8] is applied in the image domain. In this paper, we mainly introduce FSL in the image domain and the text domain. In contrast to the rapid development of FSL in computer vision, the process of FSL in natural language processing appears to be slower. Because the feature of natural language is hard to be extracted as the data set is small while the one of images is convenient to be extracted. In present, the core problem of FSL is how to improve the accuracy when the number of labeled train samples is few. To tackle this problem, various methods are proposed and all of methods utilize the prior knowledge that we can learn before training model. In this paper, according to where the prior knowledge is extracted from, FSL is divided into three classes including the labeled data D_{label}, a weakly labeled or unlabeled data set $D_{unlabel}$ and similar data sets. We further detail differences among these three classes to help readers to understand them. Firstly, we assume that D_{few} is a few-shot data set which is relevant to our few-shot target tasks and usually contains few labeled samples in each class. Then D_{label} includes all of labeled samples in D_{few}, $D_{unlabel}$ includes all of unlabeled samples in D_{few} and similar data sets include all of samples that don't belong to D_{few}. Note that D_{few} may not be the train set for training the model. Then the test data set is denoted as D_{test}. Meanwhile, according to [9], we divide each category into more detailed sub categories.

This paper firstly introduces several approaches of FSL in three classes and then we present some data sets which are usually used in FSL. Finally, we summarize this paper and give some present challenges and promising directions.

2 The Prior Knowledge from D_{label}

In this section, the prior knowledge from D_{label} is used to improve its accuracy. Let $p = f(D_{label})$, where p is the prior knowledge and $f(\cdot)$ is a function that transforms D_{label} to the prior knowledge p. Thus, according to what $f(\cdot)$ is, we could classify FSL methods as follows.

2.1 Data Augmentation

This strategy augments D_{label} by transforming each $(x_i, y_i) \in D_{label}$ into other variations and the function $f(\cdot)$ aims to generate more samples which are not included in D_{label} through D_{label}.

Firstly, we introduce some FSL models that use this method in the image domain. An early FSL model [10] aligns each sample from D_{label} with other samples from D_{label} and then learns a set of geometric transformations. The FSL model can transform every (x_i, y_i) into other variations which augment the original data set through this set of geometric transformations. In [11], author assumes that there exists some transformable variability among samples from various classes and thus a single transformation function can be learned to apply the variability in other classes to samples from remaining classes. Schwartz et al. [12] propose a network comprising of an encoder and a decoder. There exist a train data set D_{train} and D_{label} in this network and author selects a set of sample pairs $\{(x_i, y_s), (x_j, y_s)\}_1^n$ from the same class in D_{train}, which are fed into the encoder to learn extra information that is required to reconstruct x_i from x_j. Meanwhile, the decoder constructs $\widehat{x}_i$ according to the extra information and x_j. The aim of training this network is to reduce the difference between $\widehat{x}_i$ and x_i. Finally, a trained network is used to reconstruct $\widehat{u}_j$ from u_i in D_{label} through making u_i and the extra information be inputs of the decoder.

Secondly, we introduce some FSL models in the text domain. EDA [13] is proposed to classify text and contains four operations including synonym replacement, random insertion, random swap and random deletion. N sentences are generated to augment the original data using these four operations randomly and author also proves that sentences augmented by EDA conserve their original labels. Ateret Anaby-Tavor et al. [14] propose a LAMBADA approach to solve the text classification task. In this approach, more train data are generated through pre-trained text generator. The detailed process is shown below. Let $D_{label} = \{(x_i, y_i)\}_{i=1}^n$ as train data set, where x_i is i-th sentence and y_i is a corresponding label. Firstly, train a baseline classifier using D_{label}. Then, build the $U^* = y_1 SEPx_1 EOSy_2 SEPx_2 EOS...y_n SEPx_n EOS$ using D_{label}, where tag *SEP* separates y_i from x_i and tag *EOS* terminates a sentence, and fine-tune a pre-trained language model using U^* to obtain a fine-tuned language model. Thirdly, synthesize a set of labeled sentences D_{label}^* using the fine-tuned language model, where the number of samples synthesized far exceeds the one needed. Finally, use the baseline classifier to filter D_{label}^* to retain high-quality sentences.

2.2 Refining Existing Parameters

This strategy gets and refines the parameters of a model using D_{label}.

In the image domain, a method [15] that updates related parts of parameters θ is proposed. This method introduces the struct of the filter and the strength of the filter, corresponding to parameters of the filter and weights of the filter respectively. After learning the struct of the filter through dictionary learning, this method converts the update of parameters of the filter to the update of weights of the filter by freezing the struct of the filter. Thus, the number of parameters that need to be refined is reduced greatly. Then we introduce the algorithm in detail.

Step 1: the method uses hierarchical dictionary filter learning to generate a great struct of the filter. Given the input X, the algorithm gets the struct of the filter D^l through minimize $\frac{1}{2}||X - D^l\alpha||^2 + \lambda||\alpha||_1$. Then the input X is convolved in the filter D^l and the output is denoted as Y. Subsequently the output Y is treated as the input to calculate the struct of next filter until all of structs of filters are calculated.

Step 2: after all of structs of filters are calculated, they are frozen and then strengths of filters are updated by using SGD. When the process of SGD finishes, the trained model can be used to classify images.

3   The Prior Knowledge from $D_{unlabel}$

This section mainly introduces some methods that use the prior knowledge from $D_{unlabel}$ to improve its accuracy. Let $p = f(D_{unlabel})$, where p is the prior knowledge and $f(\cdot)$ is a function that transforms $D_{unlabel}$ to the prior knowledge p. Then we introduce a data augmentation strategy.

This strategy augments D_{label} through selecting a lot of samples from $D_{unlabel}$ and adds these samples to corresponding classes. Thus, how to select samples from $D_{unlabel}$ and how to add these samples to corresponding classes are two main problems in this strategy.

In the image domain, each class in D_{label} learns SVMs [16], which are used to classify samples from $D_{unlabel}$. Thus, every sample from $D_{unlabel}$ gets a class label, either a certain class in D_{label} or not in D_{label}. Then this method adds samples which get a certain class label through SVMs to corresponding classes. In [17], label propagation is used to label samples from $D_{unlabel}$.

In the text domain, a method [18] called Unsupervised Data Augmentation(UDA) is proposed. This method trains a model using labeled samples as well as unlabeled samples. In contrast to conventional strategies, this method uses augmented data as the perturbation. To get a great model $p_\theta(y|x)$, author minimizes the sum of the cross entropy loss on labeled examples and the KL divergence between the predicted distributions on an unlabeled sample set and an augmented unlabeled sample set, i.e., $D_{KL}(p_\theta(y|x)||p_\theta(y|\hat{x}))$, where x is unlabeled samples and $\hat{x}$ is augmented unlabeled samples. Through the method above, the model gets an excellent performance on the IMDb, a text classification dataset. Moreover, author applies this model to the image domain and obtains a comparable performance. An automatic classification method [19] is proposed. Firstly, this method uses pre-trained word embeddings to embed words. Meanwhile, documents are represented by a weighted average of embedded vectors of words from documents. Thus, a few documents are required to be labeled artificially and other unlabeled documents are classified through the distance between them and those labeled documents. Then, those documents are used to train a classification model.

4   The Prior Knowledge from Similar Data Sets

This section presents models using samples from similar data sets D_{extra} as the extra data. Let $p = f(D_{extra})$, where p is the prior knowledge and $f(\cdot)$ is a function that transforms D_{extra} to the prior knowledge p. Thus, according to what $f(\cdot)$ is, we could classify FSL methods as follows.

4.1   Data Augmentation

This strategy augments D_{label} through selecting a lot of samples from similar data sets.

In the image domain, YHH Tsai et al. [20] propose a method that enforces the statistical dependency between data representations and multiple types of side information and then an attention mechanism is proposed to add samples from similar data sets to D_{label}. In [21], a generative adversarial network (GAN) is used to generate indistinguishable synthetic samples. There exist two generators and one maps samples from a small data set to samples from a large-scale data set while the other maps samples from a large-scale data set to samples from a small data set. Wentao Chen et al. [22] propose a method that leverages a sea of unlabeled images from a similar data set to augment the original data. This model contains two parts, one is the part discovery network and the other is the augmentation network. The specific algorithm is shown as following.

Step 1: let $D_{base} = \{x_i\}_{i=1}^N$ from a similar data set and D_{label} of the target task.

Step 2: crop an image x_i from D_{base} into n small patches $\{x_i^j\}_{j=1}^n$ and a larger patch x_i^g. Then random transformations are applied to $\{x_i^j\}_{j=1}^n$.

Step 3: a convolution neural network f transforms $\{x_i^j\}_{j=1}^n$ and x_i^g into embedded representations $\{s_i^j\}_{j=1}^n$ and s_i^g respectively. Then $\{s_i^j\}_{j=1}^n$ and s_i^g are transformed into $\{h_i^j\}_{j=1}^n$ and h_i^g by global average pooling and an MLP.

Step 4: given negative samples $D^- = \{h_i^{g-}\}_{i=1}^{N-}$ that arenot in x_i, the mean distance between h_i^j and D^- is calculated and then h_i^p which has the maximum distance is selected as the discriminative one. Subsequently, the similarity between h_i^p and h_i^g is calculated as the loss to train the MLP and the convolution neural network.

Step 5: f with global average pooling is treated as an embedding function and D_{label} is transformed into vectors through it. Then these vectors are used to train a classifier d.

Step 6: some parts are obtained by d and a Class-Competitive Attention Map from D_{base} and then augments D_{label}. Then the model leverages the augmented D_{label} to refine the parameters of the classifier d.

In the text domain, AugNlg [23] is proposed to solve the FSL problem about natural language generation(NLG). Author pre-trains the model using augmented data. The detail of the model is introduced as following.

Step 1: a number of data from OpenWebText are used to train a GPT-2 model which is treated as the base model.

Step 2: all the n-gram keywords from D_{label} are selected and then TF-IDF scores are used to filter out those keywords that are too general to be effective.

Step 3: in similar data set, all phrases that contain at least one keyword are retrieved and a self-trained neural network is used to filter out selected phrases that are irrelevant to D_{label}.

Step 4: author builds a few-shot NLU model through fine-tuning a BERT model using samples from D_{label}. Then selected phrases are transformed to the format of MR-to-Text.

Step 5: the base model then is fine-tuned using MR-to-Text pairs in D_{label}.

4.2 Multitask Learning

With some related tasks, multitask learning could extract general information and special information from these tasks. This method reduces the portion of model which needs to be trained for FSL. Thus, even with few samples in each class, FSL model still gets a satisfied accuracy. We assume that there exist m tasks and each task has its own data set $\{D_{train}^m, D_{test}^m\}$, and then this method learns general parameters α and special parameters β by joint training.

Firstly, we detail methods in the image domain. In [24], given two data sets, where one has substantial data called the source domain and the other has scarce data called the target domain, i.e. D_{label}, an inference network g and a classifier h are pre-trained using samples from the source domain. For data augmentation, author creates 4 groups of pairs as train data. Then, the train data are leveraged to adversarially train the g, h and a discriminator D. At last, g is able to embed source samples and target samples to a domain invariant space and h is able to classify them correctly. In [25], author proposes two CNN, one is used for the source domain and the other is used for the target domain, i.e. D_{label}. Then, a multi-layer domain transfer network is used to align source representations and target representations and a semantic transfer network is used to transfer information from a labeled set of data to an unlabeled set of data. Yabin Zhang et al. [26] propose a model sharing the information in the front base network and learning different information in last two classifiers. Suppose that the base network shares the same parameters θ_b and two classifiers behind the base network have different parameters θ_t and θ_s. To meta-train the whole network and leverage the public information from other tasks, author modifies the loss function to $Loss = \frac{1}{|D|}L\left(D; (\theta_t, \theta_b) - \eta \frac{1}{|D|}\nabla_{\theta_t, \theta_b}L(D; \theta_t, \theta_b)\right) + \frac{1}{|S|}R(S; \theta_s, \theta_b)$ and then the gradients of $Loss$ with respect to θ_t, θ_s and θ_b are calculated to update the whole network until the network converges.

Meanwhile, there exist some FSL models in the text domain. In [27], two language processing tasks on legal texts are tackled together: charge prediction and legal attribution prediction. In [28], author proposes an adaptive metric learning approach that obtains a set of metrics from meta-training tasks. This approach can determine the best weighted combination for a new few-shot task. ChengCheng Han et al. [29] propose a meta-learning adversarial domain adaptation network which contains a pre-trained word representation layer, a meta-knowledge generator, a domain discriminator, a interaction layer and a classifier. The detailed train process is shown below.

Step 1: D_{label} is divided into $D_{support}$ and D_{query}.

Step 2: words in each sentence of $D_{support}$, $P : [p_1, p_2, \ldots, p_m]$, are embedded into d-dimension vector space through the pre-trained word representation layer.

Step 3: a meta-knowledge generator, consisting of bi-directional LSTM and a fully connected layer, extracts meta-knowledge k^p of each sentence.

Step 4: the k^p and the specific feature of sentences are combined using the interaction layer as the inputs of the classifier to obtain the final outputs and train the classifier using the final outputs.

Step 5: words in each sentence of D_{query} and D_{source}, Q: $[q_1, q_2, \ldots, q_m]$, are embedded into d-dimension vector space through the pre-trained word representation layer and the d-dimension vectors are processed in the same way as step 3 and step 4. But the final outputs are used to train the meta-learning generator and the extracted meta-knowledge is as the input of the domain discriminator to train the domain discriminator.

4.3 Embedding Learning

This strategy uses embedding functions to embed each sample $x_i \in D_{label} \subseteq \mathbb{R}^d$ to a lower-dimensional vector $z_i \in \mathbb{R}^n$. The hypothesis space of tasks becomes smaller through this way and thus it is easier to construct an excellent model with a few of samples. In this section, we focus on specific related models. Models in this section learn general embedding function f from samples in similar data sets to embed $x_i \in D_{label} \subseteq \mathbb{R}^d$ to a lower-dimensional vector $z_i \subseteq \mathbb{R}^n$. In order to make general embedding function more suitable for few-shot scenarios, in [30–32], methods simulate few-shot scenarios when models are pre-trained. For example, there is a data set D_{task}^i in task i, and then this data set D_{task}^i is divided into two parts. One part called the support dataset has P classes while the other called the query dataset has Q classes. We refer samples from support set as $x_{support}$ and samples from query set as x_{query}.

In the image domain, matching network [32] introduces an attention mechanism and a memory mechanism and meta-learns different embedding function f and g to embed $x_{support}$ and x_{query} respectively. In [30], prototypical network is introduced. In this method, $g(x_{query})$ is not compared with every $f(x_{support})$ to find the most similar sample and in contrast $g(x_{query})$ is compared with the mean of $f(x_{support})$ to find the most similar class. This strategy not only improves the accuracy of the model but also reduces the cost of computation. In [31], author proposes a new distance metric approach and uses the feature extractor adaptation methodology in CNAPS [33] as the embedding function. $x_{support}$ and x_{query} are embedded using the feature extractor adaption methodology and then the Mahalanobis distance between embedded $x_{support}$ and x_{query} is calculated to classify samples. All of methods mentioned above learn a fixed prior knowledge from similar data set. For example, once the prior knowledge is learnt from similar data sets and then is directly used in few-shot tasks without any changes. In this situation, the prior knowledge doesn't have any specific information about the few-shot task, which may result in reduced accuracy. To solve this problem, Luca Bertinetto [34] constructs a triplets (x_i, z_i, l_i) as train data and then trains a learnet using the train data whose outputs are the parameters of a discriminative network. So, for various few-shot samples the parameters of a discriminative network are different accordingly. In [35, 36], methods output parameters θ with the input as a whole.

Then we introduce some methods in the text domain. In [37], author proposes a lightweight word embedding model. Firstly, this model pre-trains the word embedding strategy and leverages the knowledge from the source domains to classify the samples from the target task. A multi-label FSL model [38] is proposed to solve a multi-label detection task. The details of this model are introduced as following:

Step 1: the input sentences are embedded using an embedding function and a convolutional neural network.

Step 2: to alleviate the effect about the noise of irrelevant aspects, author designs an attention mechanism called SA. Then the model averages all of the denoised vectors as a prototype.

Step 3: a query sentence is calculated the Euclidean distance from each prototype after processed by a module called QA that aims to reduce the noise of irrelevant aspects in the query sentence.

Step 4: the model uses a softmax function to calculate a ranking of the prototypes and the mean square error(MSE) to train the prototype network.

Step 5: the positive aspects are selected through a dynamic threshold that is obtained using a policy network. This policy network changes the threshold according to various query sentences and input sentences.

Step 6: the model can predict labels of few-shot samples directly without any parameters modifications.

4.4   Refining Existing Parameters

This strategy learns a set of parameters θ as the prior knowledge from similar data sets. Then D_{label} is used to update parameters θ. But if parameters θ are updated only through back propagation, there exists probability that model is over-fitting. Thus, in contrast to models mentioned above, this strategy is about how to update parameters θ to prevent from over-fitting. In contrast to the embedding learning, although refining existing parameters sometimes updates parameters of the embedding functions, it has classifiers that transform the embedded vectors to a certain class while the embedding learning usually uses a similarity function that determines the class.

Firstly, we introduce the methods in the image domain. In [39], author proposes an algorithm whose key strategy is to cluster the model parameters while ensuring intra-cluster similarity and inter-cluster diversity of the parameters. A single gradient is shared among parameters from the same group during back-propagation. Zhiqiang Shen et al. [40] propose a novel fine-tuning strategy for FSL. In contrast to previous fine-tuning strategies, this method learns an optimal transfer strategy that contains optimal learning rates of each layer through the evolutionary search and achieves the state-of-the-art performance on both meta-learning and non-meta based frameworks. In [41], author trains a base leaner f_θ that projects the image x into embedded vector z and a classifier g_θ that projects the embedded vector z into the label y. Meanwhile, author introduces a set of transformations and equivariance as well as invariance to improve the generalization of the model. The detailed process is as followed.

Step 1: a set of transformations T are obtained from a family of geometric transformations D_T and then applied to the input image x to get a set of transformed images $\{x_1, \ldots, x_i, \ldots, x_M\}$ (x_i is transformed through the i-th transformation).

Step 2: these transformed images are combined into a single tensor $x_{all} = \{x_1, \ldots, x_i, \ldots, x_M\}$ and then fed into the base learner to obtain the embedding vector z.

Step 3: to enforce the equivariance and invariance, two extra heads are designed besides the classifier. One of two heads which is a MLP is used to enforce the equivariance and the other which is also a MLP is used to enforce the invariance.
Step 4: a multi-head distillation is introduced to further improve precision.
Step 5: three loss function are designed for three heads respectively to train the model and after the base learner is trained, the classifier is simply trained by using samples from few-shot dataset. Then the model could classify the samples.

Furthermore, we introduce models in the text domain. Universal Language Model Fine-tuning [42] is proposed and contains mainly three steps. Firstly, it pretrains the state-of-art language model using Wikitext-103 dataset and then the pretrained model is fine-tuned through discriminative fine-tuning and slanted triangular learning rates. Finally, it fine-tunes the classifier using concat pooling and gradual unfreezing. In [43], author proposes a model called SC-GPT. This model contains mainly three steps as follows.

Step 1: GPT-2 which is pre-trained on massive training corpus is used as backbone.
Step 2: To enable the guidance of dialog act in response generation, the model is pre-trained on a number of labeled pairs continuously. Meanwhile, the dialog acts and output sequences are pre-processed simultaneously.
Step 3: author leverages the same way as described in step 2 to fine-tune the model by using samples from a new domain, i.e., D_{label}.

5   Data Sets

In this section, we introduce some data sets that are usually used in FSL. Compared to the text domain, datasets in the image domain are more unified. This is due to the property of the text and thus different text tasks have various datasets. Thus, we firstly introduce some datasets in the image domain and then present some datasets in certain text tasks. In the image domain, Omniglot [44], miniImageNet [45], CUB [46] and so on are usually used in FSL. In the NLG task, E2E NLG [47], RNNLG [48] and BAGEL [49] are usually used to train models. Meanwhile FEWSHOTWOZ [43] is a new dataset for the NLG. Then, we introduce some of them simply as follow:

Omniglot. Omniglot contains 1623 handwritten characters with 50 letters and every character is drawn online by different person.

miniImageNet. miniImageNet is selected from the imageNet dataset. Because it is hard to train a model by using samples from imageNet, google DeepMind constructed the miniImageNet dataset. MiniImageNet contains 60000 color pictures in 100 categories, including 600 samples in each category, and the resolution of each picture is 84*84.

CIFAR-100 [50]. CIFAR-100 dataset consists of 60000 32*32 color images in 10 classes, with 6000 images in each class. There are 50000 training images and 10000 test images.

tieredImageNet [32]. tieredImageNet is a smaller but more widely used benchmarks. It is consist of subsets of ILSVRC-2012 and has 608 classes as well as 779165 images.

E2E NLG. E2E NLG contains 1 domain with 42056 training instances and 630 testing instances. Every instance contains 1 intent and 8 slots in average.

BAGEL. BAGEL also contains 1 domain with 363 instances and 41 testing instances. Every instance has 8 intents and 10 slots in average.

RNNLG. there exist 4 domains as well as 4625.5 training instances and 1792.5 testing instances in each domain in average. Every instance contains 11.25 intents and 21 slots averagely.

FEWSHOTWOZ. FEWSHOTWOZ has 7 domains and each domain has 50 training instances and 472.86 testing instances in average. Each instance contains 8.14 intents and 16.15 slots in average.

6 Conclusion

Due to sparse samples in many tasks, classical deep learning models cannot work well. Thus, the concept of FSL is proposed and then various models about FSL begin to emerge. To improve the accuracy, all of models utilize the prior knowledge that is extracted either from D_{label} or from $D_{unlabel}$ or from similar data sets. These few-show learning models can be applied to various tasks via the prior knowledge. In this paper, we firstly introduce various models from above three categories respectively. To help reader to learn about application of FSL in various domains, we further introduce models in the text domain and the image domain respectively. Lastly, we introduce some datasets in the FSL simply. Although FSL is made great progress in, there exist some challenges. Firstly, many methods are required to pre-train by using samples from a large data set, which goes against the concept of FSL. Thus, how to design a model that gets a great accuracy without the help of the prior knowledge extracted from large-scale data sets in FSL is a promising direction. Secondly, there is not a united pre-training data set in the field of text classification. Therefore, constructing a few-shot data set suitable for text classification task is a problem to be considered.

References

1. Wang, J., Zhang, T., Cheng, Y., Al-Nabhan, N.: Deep learning for object detection: a survey. Comput. Syst. Sci. Eng. **38**(2), 165–182 (2021)
2. Deng, C., Zeng, G., Cai, Z., Xiao, X.: A survey of kowledge based question answering with deep learning. J. Artif. Intel. **2**(4), 157–166 (2020)
3. Liu, X., Chen, X.: A survey of gan-generated fake faces detection method based on deep learning. J. Info. Hid. Priva. Protec. **2**(2), 87–94 (2020)
4. Jankowski, N., Duch, W., Grąbczewski, K.: Meta-learning in computational intelligence. Springer Science and Business Media. 97−115 (2011)
5. Lake, B., Salakhutdinov, R.: One-shot learning by inverting a compositional causal process. In: Advances in Neural Information Processing Systems, pp. 2526−2534 (2013)

6. Yang, J., Liu, Y.L.: The latest advances in face recognition with single training sample. J. Xihua Univ. (Natural Science Edition) **33**(4), 1−5 (2014). (in Chinese)

7. Gamal, M., Abbas, H.M., Moustafa, N., Sitnikova, E., Sadek, R.A.: Few-shot learning for discovering anomalous behaviors in edge networks. Computers, Materials & Continua **69**(2), 1823–1837 (2021)

8. Zhang, B., Ling, H., Li, P.: Multi-head attention graph network for few shot learning. Computers, Materials & Continua **68**(2), 1505–1517 (2021)

9. Wang, Y., Yao, Q., Kwok, J.: Generalizing from a few examples: a survey on few-shot. Learning **53**(3), 1–34 (2020)

10. Miller, E., Matsakis, N., Viola P.: Learning from one example through shared densities on transforms. In: CVPR 2000, pp. 464–471. IEEE (2000)

11. Hariharan, B., Girshick, R.: Low-shot visual recognition by shrinking and hallucinating features. In: Proceedings of the IEEE International Conference on Computer Vision, pp. 3018–3027 (2017)

12. Schwartz, E., et al.: Delta-encoder: an effective sample synthesis method for few-shot object recognition. arXiv:1806.04734 (2018)

13. Jason, W., Zou, K.: EDA: Easy data augmentation techniques for boosting performance on text classification tasks. arXiv:1901.11196 (2019)

14. Anaby-Tavor, A., et al.: Do not have enough data? deep learning to the rescue! arXiv: 1911.03118v2 (2019)

15. Keshari, R., et al.: Learning structure and strength of CNN filters for small sample size training. In: Proceedings of the IEEE Conference on Computer Vision and Pattern Recognition, pp. 9349–9358 (2018)

16. Pfister, T., Charles, J., Zisserman, A.: Domain-adaptive discriminative one-shot learning of gestures. In: European Conference on Computer Vision, pp. 814–829 (2014)

17. Douze, M., et al.: Low-shot learning with large-scale diffusion. In: Conference on Computer Vision and Pattern Recognition, pp. 3349–3358 (2018)

18. Xie, Q., et al.: Unsupervised Data Augmentation for Consistency Training. arXiv:1904. 12848 (2019)

19. Bailey, K., Chopra, S.: Few-shot text classification with pre-trained word embeddings and a human in the loop. arXiv: 1804.02063 (2018)

20. Tsai, Y., Salakhutdinov, R.: Improving one-shot learning through fusing side information. arXiv:1710.08347 (2017)

21. Gao, H., et al.: Low-shot learning via covariance-preserving adversarial augmentation networks. In: Advances in Neural Information Processing Systems, pp. 983–993 (2018)

22. Chen, W., et al.: Few-shot learning with part discovery and augmentation from unlabeled images. arXiv:2105.11874 (2021)

23. Xu, X., et al.: AUGNLG: few-shot natural language generation using self-trained data augmentation. arXiv: 2106.05589 (2021)

24. Motiian, S., et al.: Few-shot adversarial domain adaptation. In: Advances in Neural Information Processing Systems, pp. 6670–6680 (2017)

25. Luo, Z., et al.: Label efficient learning of transferable representations across domains and tasks. In: Advances in Neural Information Processing Systems, pp. 165–177 (2017)

26. Zhang, Y., Tang, H., Jia, K.: Fine-grained visual categorization using meta-learning optimization with sample selection of auxiliary data. In: European Conference on Computer Vision, pp. 233–248 (2018)

27. Hu, Z., et al.: Few-shot charge prediction with discriminative legal attributes. In: International Conference on Computational Linguistics, pp. 487–498 (2018)

28. Yu, M., et al.: Diverse few-shot text classification with multiple metrics. arXiv: 1805.07513 (2018)

29. Han, C., et al.: Meta-learning adversarial domain adaptation network for few-shot text classification. arXiv: 2107.12262 (2021)
30. Snell, J., Swersky, K., Zemel, R.: Prototypical networks for few-shot learning. In: Advances in Neural Information Processing Systems, pp. 4077–4087 (2017)
31. Bateni, P., et al.: Improved few-shot visual classification. arXiv: 1912.03432 (2020)
32. Vinyals, O., et al.: Matching networks for one shot learning. In: Advances in Neural Information Processing Systems, pp. 3630–3638 (2016)
33. Requeima, J., et al.: Fast and flexible multi-task classification using conditional neural adaptive processes. arXiv:1906.07697 (2019)
34. Bertinetto, L., et al.: Learning feed-forward one-shot learners. In: Advances in Neural Information Processing Systems, pp. 523–531 (2016)
35. Oreshkin, B., López, P. R., and Lacoste, A.: TADAM: Task dependent adaptive metric for improved few-shot learning. In: Advances in Neural Information Processing Systems, pp. 719–729 (2018)
36. Zhao, F., et al.: Dynamic conditional networks for few-shot learning. In: Proceedings of the European Conference on Computer Vision (ECCV), pp. 19–35 (2018)
37. Pan, C., Huang, J., Gong, J., Yuan, X.: Few-shot transfer learning for text classification with lightweight word embedding based models. IEEE Access 7, 53296–53304 (2019)
38. Hu, M., et al.: Multi-label few-shot learning for aspect category detection. arXiv:2105.14174 (2021)
39. Yoo, D., Fan, H., Boddeti, V.N., Kitani, K.M.: Efficient k-shot learning with regularized deep networks. In: Thirty-Second AAAI Conference on Artificial Intelligence (2018)
40. Shen, Z., et al.: Partial is better than all: revisiting fine-tuning strategy for few-shot learning. In: Proceedings of the AAAI Conference on Artificial Intelligence, vol. 35, no. 11, pp. 9594–9602 (2021)
41. Rizve, M.N., et al.: Exploring complementary strengths of invariant and equivariant representations for few-shot learning. In: Proceedings of the IEEE/CVF Conference on Computer Vision and Pattern Recognition, pp. 10836–10846 (2021)
42. Howard, J., Ruder, S.: Universal language model fine-tuning for text classification. In: Proceedings of the 56th Annual Meeting of the Association for Computational Linguistics (2018)
43. Peng, B., et al.: Few-shot natural language generation for task-oriented dialog. arXiv:2002.1232 (2020)
44. Fort, S.: Gaussian prototypical networks for few-shot learning on Omniglot. arXiv:1708.02735 (2017)
45. Malalur, P., Jaakkola, T.: Alignment based matching networks for one-shot classification and open-set recognition. arXiv:1903.06538 (2019)
46. Cui, Y., et al.: Fine-grained categorization and dataset bootstrapping using deep metric learning with humans in the loop. In: Proc. of the IEEE conference on computer vision and pattern recognition, pp. 1153–1162 (2016)
47. Novikova, J., Dusek, O., Rieser, V.: The e2e dataset: New challenges for end-to-end generation. arXiv:1706.09254 (2017)
48. Wen, T. H., et al.: Multidomain neural network language generation for spoken dialogue systems. arXiv:1603.01232 (2016)
49. Mairesse, F., et al.: Phrase-based statistical language generation using graphical models and active learning. In: Proceedings of the 48th Annual Meeting of the Association for Computational Linguistics, pp. 1552–1561 (2010)
50. Krizhevsky, A., Nair, V., Hinton, G.: Cifar-100 (canadian institute for advanced research) (2009)

A Fire Detection System Based on YOLOv4

Chenhe Fei and Hanwei Qian[✉]

Department of Computer Information and Cyber Security, Jiangsu Police Institute,
Nanjing 210031, China
qianhanwei@jspi.edu.cn

Abstract. Fire is a common disaster which frequently causes serious losses. If it can be found in time in the early stage, the loss can be greatly reduced. Traditional computer vision algorithm segments fire areas via binary processing whose disadvantage lies in its the slow speed and low accuracy, failing to meet the requirement of real-time detection of fire areas. With the development of neural networks, deep learning has been applied in the field of computer vision widely. In this paper, we investigate the recognition algorithm for fire images in YOLOv4 environment based on CSPDarknet-53 framework. Firstly, collected images are preprocessed to get the dataset conforming to the specification image production. Then the server is used to train the model to realize recognition, detection and early warnings of fires. At the same time, the system will be further completed to change the current situation of fire image recognition and real-time detection, and improve working efficiency.

Keywords: Convolutional neural networks · Object detection · YOLO

1 Introduction

Fires are easy to break out, especially in residential houses, warehouses, factory workshops, forests and other places. Once a fire occurs, it will cause serious damage to human life and nature. In some unattended places, the consequence will be more severe. Therefore, it is necessary to design an image recognition system which can be applied to fire detection. If a fire can be detected and extinguished at an early stage, it will significantly reduce its losses [7].

In recent years, convolutional neural networks and deep learning algorithms have made a great breakthrough in the field of computer vision. In this paper, we design an image recognition system based on YOLOv4 and apply it to real-time fire recognition. In a gesture to train the model, image data would be necessary. However, it is difficult to collect fire image data in industry for lack of open access to relevant databases, so it brings a lot of trouble to the process of training models. In this case, we construct the fire image database, making it convenient to change the database content by ourselves according to the demand [5].

With the number of network layers and algorithm complexity increasing, the success rate of fire detection improves as well. Thanks to transfer learning

X. Sun et al. (Eds.): ICAIS 2022, CCIS 1587, pp. 93–104, 2022.
https://doi.org/10.1007/978-3-031-06761-7_8

theory, the number of data sets can be greatly reduced. Firstly, labelImg in the conda environment is used to label the cropped fire images. Secondly, the server environment set up and environment variables imported, the YOLOv4 model will run. Finally, after results get imported to the local virtual machine, fire images can be detected and localized. In a nutshell, we can conclude from the experiment that the image recognition model based on YOLOv4 can effectively improve the accuracy of localization and reduce the false detection rate [10].

2   Object Detection and Deep Learning

2.1   Introduction to Object Detection

Object detection is a computer vision technique for locating instances of objects in images or videos. It has applications in many areas of computer vision, including image retrieval and video surveillance [1]. Since early methods of expressing image features were very limited, various different detection algorithms have been investigated, such as the early Viola-Jone, SIFT, HOG +SVM detection algorithms, and DPM models, which all belong to the traditional detection algorithms under machine vision (Fig. 1).

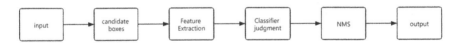

Fig. 1. Traditional object detection algorithm

Traditional object detection methods generally use sliding window detection. A window is used to traverse the image and sequentially determine whether the desired target is in the current window [6]. As the desired candidate region is framed followed by a neural network to extract relevant features, the extracted features are recognized and classified.

Later, with the emergence of deep learning, people started to apply neural networks and deep learning to object detection as well. Gradually, traditional image detection algorithms were replaced by new algorithms related to deep learning. The representative object detection algorithms are mainly divided into two categories: one-stage algorithm and two-stage algorithm. The former has shorter training time but lower accuracy, while the latter is just the opposite. Moreover, object detection algorithms be divided into end-to-end algorithms and candidate region-based algorithms as well. In terms of detection accuracy and localization precision, candidate area-based methods have better performance, while end-to-end algorithms are faster.

In 2014, RBG proposed an algorithm that combines CNN with candidate regions [12]. Compared with traditional sliding window algorithms, R-CNN adopts a new method of extracting candidate frames by using selective search frames. Although the algorithm is much improved than before, it is undeniable that defects remain. While extracting features from all regions, it has a lot of redundant calculations which prevents it from generating positive and negative sample candidates [14]. Therefore, Fast R-CNN was proposed, whose improvement mainly lies in the speed of detection and training and reduction of memory usage [8]. Then comes the Faster R-CNN algorithm, which can be run on the GPU, making it much faster to train and test the neural network. But it is still slower than YOLO.

2.2 Convolutional Neural Networks

Convolutional Layer. The convolutional layer is a complex functional and extraction layer, which completes the convolution process by multiplying each pixel point of the input image with the weights to output a convolutional feature map [3]. The convolution kernel slides sequentially over the input image for feature extraction (Fig. 2).

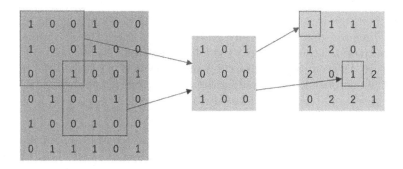

Fig. 2. The process of convolution

Pooling Layer. After the convolution operation, the number of pixel points on the image is significantly reduced and objects we need to detect on the image become more distinguishable. However, there are still too many pixel points on the image for us to detect [11]. At this point, it is necessary to pool the image at the input layer, in order to further reduce the image pixel data.

Maximum pooling is a process that divides an 8×8 region into eight 2×2 regions and takes the maximum value of each of the eight regions. Average pooling, on the other hand, is a pooling operation that calculates the average value for patches of a feature map. This operation of the pooling layer is very effective because the pooling layer can reduce the number of parameters and overfitting to some extent.

The pooling layer, which is modeled after the human visual system has the following features: (1) Dimensionality reduction. As is described above, the amount of input data is reduced, which allows the model to capture a wider range of features; (2) Non-deforming characteristics. The pooling process focuses more on the presence or absence of certain features in the image; (3) Prevention of overfitting.

The pooling layer is calculated as shown in the following equation.

$$X_j^l = f\left(\beta_j^l down\left(X_j^{l-1}\right) + b_j^l\right) \tag{1}$$

Fully Connected Layers. Fully Connected layers in neural networks are those layers where all the inputs from one layer are connected to every activation unit of the next layer, which have been proved to be very effective for both recognition and prediction.

However, its drawbacks are obvious [4]. As the number of hidden layers increases, the network size becomes so large that the high-dimensional matrix multiplication operation becomes more and more complicated. Too much information about the weights needs to be updated in the back-propagation process, which is time-consuming and easily leads to model overfitting. So we need the feature extraction layer to prevent the fully connected network from collapsing. Just in case, Dropout regularization is even introduced to discard the randomness of the neurons in the neural network. When the neural network is needed again, it reverts to the fully connected state.

Activation Functions. The most commonly used activation functions are hyperbolic tangent function, sigmoid function, and so on. Nowadays, the most popular activation function is the Rectified Linear Unit (ReLU). Not only does it speed up the learning speed of deep neural networks, but it also requires no pre-training, effectively avoiding the local optimum problem. Except for the input and output layers, the hidden layers can be regarded as a series of nonlinear transformations [2]. For data points that are relatively obvious to be separated by a straight line, the regression equation can be rectified to characterize the data.

However, some data are not easily separated directly by straight lines. In this case, there are two options. One is to do a linear transformation like transforming the data into a linear regression, the other is to add a suitable activation function to the convolutional pooling layer. Common activation functions are as follows.

Sigmoid Function. A Sigmoid function is a mathematical function which has a characteristic S-shaped curve. It restricts the input value from a large scale to within the range 0–1. Its drawback mainly lies in large computational load and long iteration time.

$$f\left(x\right) = \frac{1}{1 + e^{-x}} \tag{2}$$

Hyperbolic-Tangent Function. While sigmoid functions have been popular, the hyperbolic tangent function is sometimes preferred, partly because it has a steady state at 0.

$$f(x) = \frac{e^x - e^{-x}}{e^x + e^{-x}} \tag{3}$$

ReLu Function. ReLu is a non-linear activation function that is used in multi-layer neural networks or deep neural networks. It is much faster compared to traditional activation functions because it only needs a threshold to get the activation value rather than a large number of complex operations.

$$f(x) = \max(0, x) \tag{4}$$

Leaky ReLu Function. Leaky ReLU is a type of activation function based on a ReLU, but it has a small slope for negative values instead of a flat slope so as to prevent the 'death' of neurons.

$$f(x) = \max(ax, x) \tag{5}$$

3   YOLO Object Detection Algorithm

Since the emergence of R-CNN, YOLO is one of the most effective object detection algorithms in real applications. As a one-stage training approach, the biggest advantage of YOLO is its fast detection speed. Even the basic version of YOLO can achieve a real-time detection speed at 45 FPS, which is much faster than SSD [9].

YOLO can make fuller use of graphical information compared to other algorithms. For example, some algorithms may treat some background regions as detection targets, while YOLO won't be stuck in similar situations. Compared with other object detection algorithms, YOLO uses CNN more directly and thoroughly. By training the model with whole images, YOLO can better distinguish target areas from background areas.

YOLOv4 improves the darknet-53 module on the basis of YOLOv3 [13]. It adds modules such as SPP, PAN combined with Mosaic data enhancement and Mish function to improve the performance of the network. The network structure of YOLOv4 is shown in Fig. 3.

3.1   CSPdarknet-53

Compared with YOLOv3, the feature extraction network of YOLOv4 has added the CSPNet module. CSPResNet adopts a two-block structure–the right side has the same structure as the original module while the left side is a simple residual structure that can be processed with 1 * 1 or a small amount of The left side is a simple residual structure, which can be processed by 1 * 1 or a small amount,

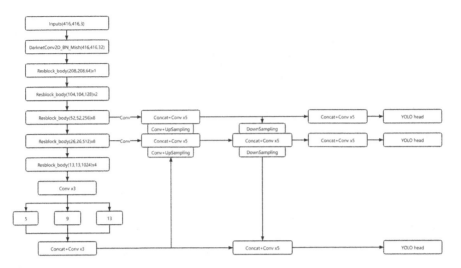

Fig. 3. YOLOv4 network structure

and then connected with the right side to get the final feature layer, so it can be seen that CSP is based on the original YOLOv3 structure with the addition of a residual edge. Therefore, the CSP can be regarded as adding a residual edge to the original YOLO3 structure, which reduces the computational effort and speeds up the computation on the basis of downsampling.

3.2 Spatial Pyramid Pooling (SPP)

SPP is a spatial pyramid pooling, which divides images from fine to coarse levels and aggregates the local features in them. SPP-net enables training of images at multiple scales on the basis of the feature maps of images of different sizes that can be tested. The purpose of increasing the scale invariance and reducing overfitting is achieved by using variable size images for training. In YOLO4, the SPP structure is used to pool the last output feature map at multiple scales, where the size of the last output feature map is 13 * 13, and then the resized images are processed by 5 * 5, 9 * 9, 13 * 13 and maximum pooling to process the images by using the maximum pooling at four different scales respectively, thus greatly increasing the training process the perceptual field and separates the most significant contextual image features. The following figure shows the structure of SPPNet (Figs. 4 and 5).

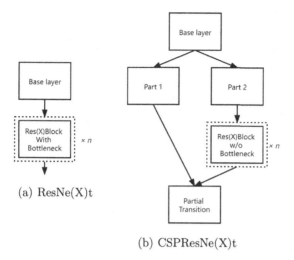

(a) ResNe(X)t

(b) CSPResNe(X)t

Fig. 4. CSPNet

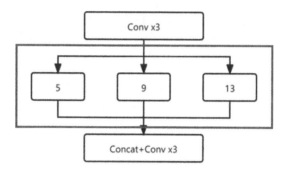

Fig. 5. SPPNet

3.3   PANet

PANet is an instance segmentation algorithm in 2018, which is initially used in the field of instance segmentation to better extract the features of each pixel point, and its specific structure has the meaning of iterative feature enhancement. The high level feature image contains rich semantic information and rich information about the belonging of each region, while the low level features contain rich detail information and more specific description of the details of individual regions. As the feature map gets higher and the perceptual field gets larger, then that neuron is responsible for responding to features in larger regions. Comparing with the structure of FPN, which assigns which feature layer a candidate frame is extracted from based on the size of that candidate frame, this form of feature selection is not an optimal choice; because each layer has a certain importance in target recognition, whether it is large proposals or small proposals, different levels of image feature regions are required. Therefore, after completing the feature extraction of the feature pyramid in the left region, it is also necessary to implement the feature extraction in the right region. The YOLOv4object detection algorithm then draws on PANet's model and takes three effective feature layers with a combination of up and down sampling.

3.4   Loss Function

Compared with YOLOv3, the loss function of YOLOv4 mainly contains three parts: CIoU loss, confidence loss and prediction type loss.

IoU is the degree of overlap between the detection frame and the real frame, which is defined as the ratio of the intersection of the detection frame and the real frame to the concatenation of the detection frame and the real frame, so IoU is also called "intersection and concatenation ratio". Since IoU is a ratio concept, it does not reflect the size of the target object very well. Therefore, CIoU is used in YOLO4 to take into account the distance between target and anchor, overlap rate, scale and penalty term to make the regression and loss calculation of the candidate frame more stable, so that the loss will not be scattered and disappear during the training process, like IoU and GIoU.

$$CIoU = IoU - \frac{\rho^2\left(b, b^{gt}\right)}{c^2} - \alpha\nu \tag{6}$$

$\rho^2\left(b, b^{gt}\right)$ denotes the Euclidean distance of the centroid between the prediction frame and the true frame. c represents the diagonal distance of the smallest closed region that can contain both the prediction frame and the true frame. Equations of α and ν are as follows.

$$\alpha = \frac{1}{1 - IoU + \nu} \tag{7}$$

$$\nu = \frac{4}{\pi^2}\left(\arctan\frac{\omega^{gt}}{h^{gt}} - \arctan\frac{\omega}{h}\right)^2 \tag{8}$$

In all, after subtracting CIoU from one, the corresponding loss will come out.

$$LOSS_{CIoU} = 1 - IoU - \frac{\rho^2\left(b, b^{gt}\right)}{c^2} + \alpha\nu \tag{9}$$

4   Analysis of Experiment Results

4.1   Datasets and Experimental Platforms

In order to test the performance of the object detection algorithm, we applied YOLOv4 to the field of fire monitoring. Since there is no comprehensive fire image dataset available on the Internet, basic data collection is performed by manual photography as well as Internet retrieval for simulated fire data. After that, we use labelImg to label the image. To improve the generalization of the model, we added artificial light sources to the data. Thanks to convolutional neural networks, data information in the deeper layer can be learned by extracting multiple features. Finally, we obtain a dataset of 2000 images, including a training set of 1600 images, a validation set of 200 images, and a test set of 200 images. What's more, we use the open source deep learning framework Pytorch and the experimental platform equipped with a CPU of R5 5900HX, a GPU of NVIDIA RTX 3060, and 16G of memory.

4.2   Training Parameter Setting

In the training, we adopted Mosaic data augmentation, in which four images are randomly selected in the training set and fused on a single image by scaling, flipping, and color gamut changes. To optimize the learning rate, we choose cosine annealing as our optimization strategy where the initial learning rate is set to 0.001. The pre-training weights on the VOC dataset are used to perform transfer learning on the fire detection model. In the first 50 rounds of training, in order to protect the pre-training weights from being destroyed so as to make the model have better detection results, part of the neural network layers are frozen to be out of the training with the Batch-size set to 8. In the second 50 rounds, the frozen layers of the network are unfrozen so that they all participate in the training. The Batch-size is set to 4.

4.3   System Structure

The structure of YOLOv4-based image recognition system consists of three parts: picture detection, video detection, and real-time detection.

As is shown in Fig. 6, the image detection module is designed by PyQt5 to read, detect and save images. By reading a local image with OpenCV, the detection model is called to detect the image and analyze whether there is a fire or not.

Fig. 6. Image detection module

The role of the camera detection module is to detect real-time surveillance videos coming from the local camera or webcam through the detection module, analyzing whether there is a fire situation and giving feedbacks to the computer. It has the speed of real-time detection (30FPS). The video and camera detection module is shown in Fig. 7.

Fig. 7. Video and camera detection module

5   Conclusion

The image recognition system is mainly developed using Python language, deep learning framework PyTorch and object detection algorithm YOLOv4 based on CSPDarkNet-53. To use the image recognition system, the user can directly open the browser to access the website for fire monitoring, fire picture recognition and fire video detection. Through the camera detection system, some specific working areas can be detected in real time to achieve the role of stopping the spread of fire timely.

References

1. Chang, H., Gou, J., Li, X.: Application of faster R-CNN in image defect detection of industrial CT. J. Image Graph. **23**, 1061–1071 (2018)
2. Eker, A.: Evaluation of fabric defect detection based on transfer learning with pre-trained AlexNet. In: 2018 International Conference on Artificial Intelligence and Data Processing (IDAP) (2019)
3. Guo, T., Dong, J., Li, H., Gao, Y.: Simple convolutional neural network on image classification. In: 2017 IEEE 2nd International Conference on Big Data Analysis (ICBDA) (2017)
4. Jia, X.: Fabric defect detection based on open source computer vision library OpenCV. IEEE (2010)
5. Khatoon, S., Hasan, M.M., Asif, A., Alshmari, M., Yap, Y.K.: Image-based automatic diagnostic system for tomato plants using deep learning. Comput. Mater. Contin. **67**(1), 595–612 (2021)
6. Kim, K.J., Kim, P.K., Chung, Y.S., Choi, D.H.: Performance enhancement of YOLOv3 by adding prediction layers with spatial pyramid pooling for vehicle detection. In: 2018 15th IEEE International Conference on Advanced Video and Signal Based Surveillance (AVSS) (2018)
7. Kolar, Z., Chen, H., Luo, X.: Transfer learning and deep convolutional neural networks for safety guardrail detection in 2D images. Autom. Constr. **89**(MAY), 58–70 (2018)
8. Li, Y., Zhang, S., Zhao, J., Tan, W.: Aircraft detection in remote sensing images based on deep convolutional neural network. In: 2017 International Conference on Computer Technology, Electronics and Communication (ICCTEC) (2017)
9. Redmon, J., Farhadi, A.: YOLOv3: an incremental improvement. arXiv e-prints (2018)
10. Wang, Y., Jia, K., Liu, P.: Impolite pedestrian detection by using enhanced YOLOv3-tiny. J. Artif. Intell. **2**(3), 113–124 (2020)
11. Xiao, Y., Keung, J.: Improving bug localization with character-level convolutional neural network and recurrent neural network. In: 2018 25th Asia-Pacific Software Engineering Conference (APSEC) (2018)
12. Yz, A., Kh, A., Hh, B., Xt, A., Bing, W.A.: A visual long-short-term memory based integrated CNN model for fabric defect image classification. Neurocomputing **380**, 259–270 (2020)

13. Zhang, H.W., Zhang, L.J., Li, P.F., Gu, D.: Yarn-dyed fabric defect detection with YOLOV2 based on deep convolution neural networks. In: 2018 IEEE 7th Data Driven Control and Learning Systems Conference (DDCLS) (2018)

14. Zoev, I.V., Beresnev, A.P., Markov, N.G.: Convolutional neural networks of the YOLO class in computer vision systems for mobile robotic complexes. In: 2019 International Siberian Conference on Control and Communications (SIBCON) (2019)

Research on Application of Artificial Intelligence Technology in Education

Shuwen Jia[1]([⊠]), Tingting Yang[2], and Zhiyong Sui[3]

[1] Saxo Fintech Business School, University of Sanya, Hainan, China
jsw2006@163.com
[2] Institute of Information and Intelligence Engineering, University of Sanya, Hainan, China
[3] Erik Jonsson School of Computer Science and Engineering, The University of Texas at Dallas, Dallas, TX, United States

Abstract. With the rapid development of science and technology in China, the continuous progress of artificial intelligence technology has driven the development of all walks of life. The effective application of artificial intelligence system in the field of education and teaching presents a very significant application advantage, and has a profound impact on the whole field of education and teaching. The deep integration of artificial intelligence technology and education has expanded the function of education, improved teaching efficiency and education management services, and promoted the reform of education and teaching. This paper discusses the application of artificial intelligence technology in education and teaching by introducing the meaning of artificial intelligence, its development status in China, and the relationship between artificial intelligence and education and teaching.

Keywords: Education · Wisdom education · Artificial intelligence · Intelligence education

1 Introduction

"Intelligent education" is the application of artificial intelligence technology in education. The application of artificial intelligence technology in education can liberate teachers from the traditional education mode, so that teachers have more time and energy to improve the education content and teaching methods, and achieve better education results. Specifically, the extensive and in-depth application of artificial intelligence technology in education can realize information sharing and data sharing, and promote the change of the overall operation process of education. It is a personalized education under the premise of scale. From beginning to end, "teaching students in accordance with their aptitude" is an effective teaching method in teaching. Confucius, the great educator in ancient China, is the forerunner of "teaching students in accordance with their aptitude". Nowadays, China's education development is unbalanced and high-quality education resources are relatively lacking. Most colleges and universities implement the teaching system of large classes with dozens of students, which makes it difficult for teachers to comprehensively understand and master the

X. Sun et al. (Eds.): ICAIS 2022, CCIS 1587, pp. 105–115, 2022.
https://doi.org/10.1007/978-3-031-06761-7_9

learning situation of all students. This kind of general indoctrination teaching method can not get the effect of "teaching students according to their aptitude". The popularization and application of intelligent education will subversively reform the current "one size fits all" mode of education and teaching in Our country, and promote college teachers to transform from knowledge imitator to designer and instructor of students' learning activities, so as to truly implement personalized education and achieve the goal of "teaching students according to their aptitude" [1].

2   Meaning of Artificial Intelligence

Artificial intelligence is a new technical science that researches and develops theories, methods, technologies and application systems for simulating, extending and expanding human intelligence. Research in this field includes intelligent robots, pattern recognition and intelligent systems, virtual reality technology and applications, System simulation technology and application, industrial process modeling and intelligent control, intelligent computing, artificial intelligence and machine game theory, speech recognition and synthesis, machine translation, image processing and computer vision, computer, computer perception neural network, knowledge discovery and machine learning, intelligent building technology and application, artificial intelligence of other disciplines [2].

Artificial intelligence (AI) is a comprehensive discipline, is a blend of computer science, cybernetics, information theory, psychology, linguistics, and other disciplines and specialties, fusion and mutual infiltration effective development and artificial intelligence to explore the problem is how to more effective use of computer in view of the human brain thinking activities engaged in by simulated and the corresponding behavior, In this way, complex problems that only human experts can deal with can be fundamentally and effectively solved. In other words, artificial intelligence is divided into two parts: artificial intelligence and intelligence, that is, artificial intelligence. Artificial intelligence is a science that studies how to create intelligent machines or intelligent systems and simulates various intelligent activities and thinking patterns of human beings so that people's intelligence can be further extended and expanded through this method [3].

3   The Relationship Between Artificial Intelligence and Education and Teaching

Artificial intelligence and artificial intelligence system was born in 1956. Its initial design, research and application fields are closely related to education and teaching. Artificial intelligence system itself is to fundamentally and effectively study how to fully ensure that computers more effectively integrate education, enhance the science and technology of intelligence. The research results of artificial intelligence technology have played a crucial role in promoting education and teaching, acting on all aspects of education and having the most direct impact on the improvement of teaching quality. For example, the effective application of artificial intelligence system in the process of education and teaching can significantly improve the work efficiency of education and teaching, effectively shorten the amount of work and time of teachers, and also have a very significant role in improving the degree of knowledge mastered by the educated. Thus, the full and effective use of artificial intelligence system can better create a new teaching mode [4].

4 Status Quo of the Application of Artificial Intelligence Technology in Education

The application of artificial intelligence technology in China's education is still in its infancy, and there are many outstanding problems. Although artificial intelligence technology as a new round of technological revolution into the field of education, has made a certain contribution to the reform of China's education system, the development of educational technology and the improvement of teaching methods, but China's artificial intelligence education is still in the initial stage, there are still many problems.

4.1 Artificial Intelligence Education Professional Technical Personnel Training Ability is Weak

At present, Chinese colleges and universities are weak in the cultivation ability of artificial intelligence talents, with weak orientation, lack of deep integration with relevant disciplines, and lack of scientific and reasonable cultivation mechanism, resulting in the lack of talent reserve for intelligent education. According to the global AI Industry Distribution report released in 2018, China's AI talent pool accounted for about 5% of the global AI talent pool in 2017, with a shortfall of more than 5 million. In 2019, Han Min, executive vice president of China Education Development Strategy Association, pointed out that the number of AI enterprises in China occupied the second place in the world, but the number of ai professionals was only the seventh in the world. To address these problems, the Higher Education Law of the People's Republic of China, published by the Ministry of Education in 2019, requires colleges and universities, including higher vocational education, to accelerate the cultivation of AI talents in order to fill the gap of 5 million AI talents in China [5].

4.2 Artificial Intelligence Education is Difficult to Break Through the Technical Bottleneck

As China is still in the primary stage of artificial intelligence – "weak artificial intelligence", artificial intelligence education equipment can only conduct voice recognition evaluation, intelligent marking, photo search and online question answering, far behind the scene education with virtual reality and augmented reality. It is far from the "strong artificial intelligence" stage, which has independent self-awareness, emotional cognition and reasoning ability. Therefore, in the long run, intelligent education also requires to strengthen the ability to distinguish and analyze human emotions and emotions, and closely combine with brain science, cognitive science, psychology and other related disciplines, emphasizing the development of emotion, cognition and intelligent perception technology [6].

4.3   Artificial Intelligence Education Products Are not Perfect and It is Urgent to Innovate and Expand

Market research shows that the intelligent education robot on the market at present is more through audio-visual information output, but does not pay attention to attract users' attention. At present, the intelligent education equipment widely used, has left teachers out of simple repetition and multifarious teaching work, and greatly improve the efficiency of knowledge transfer, but the current numerous products and application of the artificial intelligence education focus too much on the artificial intelligence technology itself, and ignore the education content, education method and education mode of advancing with The Times, As a result, products in the market have serious homogenization phenomenon, and have no significant effect on the cultivation and improvement of learners' ability, which cannot effectively meet the social demand for individualized education of "teaching students in accordance with their aptitude". Therefore, innovation and expansion are needed [7].

4.4   Artificial Intelligence Education Big Data Platform Has Not Yet Been Built

The development of intelligent education needs to be built on big data. On the one hand, there needs to be a series of inherent structural data of education itself, such as grades, attendance, lesson plans, assignments and comments. On the other hand, teaching-related pictures, videos, audio and other unstructured data that reflect teacher-student interaction and belong to the external environment of education are needed. At present, schools in China basically do not have the ability to obtain these data, and China's educational data has been in the process of change, there is no supporting facilities for dynamic data collection and update production, and there is no nationwide construction of a consistent caliber data platform. These deficiencies lead to the failure of effective integration between teaching and learning, teaching and management of intelligent education in China, and the inability to complete immediate information feedback, which makes all data isolated and unable to form large-scale applications, thus seriously affecting the application and promotion of big data technology in the education industry. Therefore, it is an urgent work to actively build a big data platform for intelligent education [8].

4.5   Artificial Intelligence Education May Cause Ethical Risks

With the rapid development of artificial intelligence, many educational institutions have laid out the layout of "AI+ education", hoping to use artificial intelligence to improve the efficiency of education and other purposes, but the excessive reliance on electronic equipment, education apps are intermingled, face recognition monitoring classroom and other problems are gradually exposed. Education itself contains the process of interaction between emotion, psychology and knowledge. Excessive emphasis on the control of technical means on students and teachers will inevitably lead to the lack of education temperature. For example, artificial intelligence monitoring students' learning status through facial recognition may improve students' attention and academic performance, while damaging their personal dignity and healthy growth [9].

5 Application of Artificial Intelligence Technology in Education and Teaching

5.1 Artificial Intelligence Technology Can Be Used for Intelligent Teaching

Artificial intelligence can realize the transition from "teaching before learning" to "learning before teaching", which is helpful to solve the teaching defects. The network has reduced the influence of distance on the equalization of education. The best teachers are selected from the video resources to give the best explanation to a certain knowledge point, which has gradually reduced the necessity for a large number of elementary teachers to teach basic knowledge in ordinary primary and secondary schools. The use of artificial intelligence technology will greatly challenge the traditional teaching concept of teaching and clarifying puzzles, and the function of teachers will be more and more inclined to play the role of "life mentor": Teaching learning methods rather than knowledge points, guiding students to study independently, teaching students the truth of being a person and doing things, cultivating students' emotional intelligence, character and teamwork spirit, and paying more and more attention to the individual development of each student [10].

5.2 Artificial Intelligence Technology Can Be Used for Intelligent Semantic Recognition

Manual marking is usually affected by subjective factors and results of marking deviation machine marking arises at the historic moment. The promotion of domestic applications such as Ali intelligent marking system and IFLYTEK intelligent marking system has opened a new way of marking mainly by machine and supplemented by manual review. Ai can also interact at any time, avoiding a lot of repetitive work [11].

5.3 Artificial Intelligence Technology Can Be Used for Intelligent Evaluation

Intelligent evaluation refers to large-scale autonomous intelligent evaluation of learners' learning process and learning behavior data, and personalized instant feedback. At present, intelligent evaluation applications based on artificial intelligence technology mainly include speaking examiner and examination paper marking. With the increasing accuracy of speech recognition, it has become a reality to use artificial intelligence (AI) speaking examiners to score English listening and speaking tests. By training themselves on sample data, AI speaking examiners can learn to evaluate students' answers in the same way as human examiners [12].

5.4　Artificial Intelligence Technology Can Be Used for Intelligent Learning Guidance

In the past, "sea of questions tactics" is the most commonly used way for our learners to learn, but blind learning often results in a waste of time and half the result with twice the effort. With the help of ai big data analysis, teachers and administrators can comprehensively scan and evaluate our learning behavior and knowledge quantity, find out our weaknesses, and design adaptive learning paths so that they can carry out targeted learning, reduce the time of repeated learning and improve efficiency [13]. The weak link tests itself. In learning, we can self-test the weak link knowledge points. For those who have not mastered the content, we can study for many times and compare with the previous learning situation. In this process, the artificial intelligence learning system can help us query the relevant content of knowledge base in this field and strengthen the weak links. It can also effectively control our learning progress [14].

6　The Significance of Application of Artificial Intelligence Technology in Education and Teaching

6.1　Artificial Intelligence Can Optimize Teaching Tools and Resources for School Education

In this information age, artificial intelligence not only innovates teachers' teaching tools, but also brings students a brand new learning experience. In recent years, the Ministry of Education has issued a series of planning policies for information construction. These policies show that, with the rapid development of artificial intelligence, big data and other technologies, talent demand and education form in the current society have undergone profound changes. The innovation of artificial intelligence on school education and teaching tools will run through every link, and every subject can't do without artificial intelligence. If schools can take artificial intelligence as a teaching tool and make full use of it, the teaching situation will be more real [15].

6.2　Artificial Intelligence Creates an Intelligent Teaching Environment for School Education

With the advent of the information age, artificial intelligence products are gradually entering all departments of schools, bringing a more intelligent interactive environment for teaching and management. With the introduction of artificial intelligence, teachers' educational achievements can be objectively evaluated. How to guide students to study and think should be the direction of future educators or educational system reform. The integration of artificial intelligence into school education and teaching can not only reduce the teaching tasks of teachers, but also improve their information literacy and enhance their ability to use artificial intelligence in teaching. Before learning any subject, students should first learn logical thinking, and then enter into specific subject learning, so as to achieve the "cultivation of the whole person" [16].

6.3 Artificial Intelligence Promotes the Innovative Development of School Teaching Evaluation and Teaching Management

Applying artificial intelligence to school education and teaching can not only innovate teachers' teaching methods and teaching tools, but also provide data support for school teaching evaluation and teaching management. Traditional classroom teaching observation and evaluation are mostly subjective education evaluation based on on-site observation and discussion by educational evaluators, or sharing resources such as video and voice. Due to the limitation of time, space and technology, classroom evaluation lacks objective and comprehensive teaching data aggregation and analysis, and it is difficult to form a standardized evaluation system and objective evaluation data basis. Classroom teaching observation and evaluation face difficulties in methods and subjectivity of evaluation basis. With the technology of artificial intelligence, using artificial intelligence technology to monitor the teaching class in real time, using data to analyze, providing more objective data support for teaching evaluation and teaching management, can better promote teaching evaluation [17].

7 Practical Dilemma of Artificial Intelligence Application in School Education and Teaching

7.1 The Immaturity of Technology Limits the Promotion of Artificial Intelligence in School Education and Teaching

As a product of the information age, artificial intelligence is still in the development stage, so there are still some defects and areas to be improved. Generally speaking, China's artificial intelligence is not mature enough, some technical defects are easy to lead to abnormal work, may also bring security risks. It is the immaturity of artificial intelligence technology itself that limits its application and promotion in school education and teaching. Due to the particularity of education, the business types and scope involved are complicated. Every school has its own school framework and school orientation. The popularization of artificial intelligence technology in the field of school education is not universal and universal, thus limiting its application in school education and teaching [18].

7.2 Lack of Big Data Limits the Application of Artificial Intelligence in School Education and Teaching

With the development of The Times, the era of artificial intelligence is inexorably coming to us, and the penetration and application of artificial intelligence in education will also continue to highlight. However, as far as the current development is concerned, the application of ARTIFICIAL intelligence in the field of education is still in the initial stage. One of the important reasons lies in the lack of educational big data, which limits its application in the field of education. For example, the school roll data of each school has not been shared at the present stage, and there is not much basic student roll information available, which hinders the generation of big data of the school roll information database. Big data is a typical representative of the latest development achievements of information technology. It is the main driver of the new round of major changes in industries such as industry 4.0, and also has a significant impact on the education industry. If we can combine big data, artificial intelligence and school education, it will help solve the problems in traditional teaching [19].

7.3 The Shortage of Talents Restricts the Development of Artificial Intelligence in School Education and Teaching

The application of artificial intelligence in the new era needs professional talents to realize, and the shortage of talents has become a prominent problem at present. The application of artificial intelligence due to its professional requirements, the gap of talent shortage is getting bigger and bigger. Statistics show that in the past five years, the world's investment in ARTIFICIAL intelligence research has grown at a rapid rate of nearly 13% per year. International Data Corporation (IDC) also predicted that China's AI market will reach $9.84 billion by 2022. Some experts predict that in the coming year, various AI technologies will be upgraded at a faster pace and the range of applications will continue to expand. It can be said that artificial intelligence is the hottest sunrise industry in the current era of intelligence. In the new era, to promote the development of artificial intelligence in school education and teaching, the problem of talent gap can not be ignored. At the same time, facing this outstanding talent dilemma, schools should also focus on opening relevant courses to cultivate talents with both RESEARCH and development capabilities and practical experience, so as to accurately meet the needs of industrial upgrading, so as to cope with the current plight of artificial intelligence application in school education and teaching [20].

8 Breakthrough Path of Artificial Intelligence Application in School Education and Teaching

8.1 Optimize Curriculum Design and Reconstruct Artificial Intelligence Education Curriculum System

At present, with the continuous development of science and technology, human beings have made many significant breakthroughs in the algorithm of artificial intelligence. The continuous expansion of educational data can better provide resources for building intelligent schools. Artificial intelligence achieves the marking of artificial intelligence machine through image recognition technology, which greatly saves teachers' time in traditional marking. Artificial intelligence based on speech recognition, face recognition, smart union, natural language processing, image recognition, and other advanced technology, in-depth teaching process of classroom teaching, through the analysis of the students in the classroom activity, the focus of the whole process, multi-dimensional, automation of classroom observation, data gathering and analysis of the teachers and students in the process of teaching behavior, For accurate learning situation analysis, efficient teaching quality, objective teaching evaluation, scientific teaching behavior observation, etc.

8.2 Change the Role of Teachers and Cultivate Service-Oriented Intelligent Teachers

In the new socialist era, information technology is developing rapidly, and education should keep pace with The Times and catch up. Facing the new challenges brought by the development of artificial intelligence, schools should take the initiative to learn new information technology to cope with this challenge, give full play to people's subjective initiative, learn from each other to make up for the deficiency of artificial intelligence. Meanwhile, teachers should keep up with the pace of the information age through their own efforts to learn. Keep up with The Times through constant learning. If artificial intelligence is applied to school education and teaching, the role of teachers will change. Artificial intelligence can better replace the daily teaching work of teachers, which can greatly reduce the daily tedious work for teachers. However, artificial intelligence alone cannot achieve the mission of teaching and educating people. Only when teachers and artificial intelligence education are combined and coordinated with each other can students benefit from the intelligent learning brought by artificial intelligence to a greater extent [21].

8.3 Expand Education Data and Use Artificial Intelligence to Assist School Teaching Management

The application of artificial intelligence in school education and teaching has realized the shift from "teaching before learning" to "learning after teaching", which is helpful to solve some defects existing in traditional teaching. Based on large data support, artificial intelligence technology can be through the behavior of students and the teacher's face, voice, data, multi-dimensional, whole process automation and dynamic quantitative collection and analysis, identify the students in different teaching environment, teaching mode of focus, active state, on the basis of school teaching evaluation standard to custom index modeling, The formation of classroom teaching evaluation and analysis report of each class and school can effectively realize classroom observation, simplify and scientifically evaluate education, so as to truly help teachers, students and education managers of schools to optimize teaching methods and improve the quality of education.

8.4 To Return to the Essence of Education, the Construction of Smart Campus Should Be People-Oriented

When artificial intelligence has an impact on the status of traditional school education, the most basic question we should think about is the nature of education. The essence of education is to cultivate people, so the education of values is becoming more and more important. On the premise of cultivating students with critical thinking, we should teach them how to be a valuable person. Everything has two sides. Seeing the positive aspects brought by artificial intelligence, we should also reflect on the essence of education and re-examine the functions of school education. Therefore, we should follow the basic principle of people-oriented when using artificial intelligence technology to construct smart campus.

9 Conclusion

In recent years, with the rapid development of the Internet, artificial intelligence technology has played an important role in more and more fields. In the field of education, ARTIFICIAL intelligence has gone from pure algorithm to application, from participant to participant, from scattered implementation of functions to close integration with education. In the field of initial education, artificial intelligence only exists as a function due to the strangeness of teachers and students and the imperfect technical support of the whole environment. With the gradual spread of applications, people began to get familiar with and find the convenience brought by artificial intelligence technology, and artificial intelligence began to be rapidly deployed in the field of education. The demand of teachers and students for artificial intelligence also penetrated into all aspects of school affairs. In the future, artificial intelligence technology is bound to become an important technology to change people's way of life. Artificial intelligence technology will become more and more mature, so as to enter thousands of households and bring greater impetus to social progress.

References

1. Quan, H.: Application and exploration of artificial intelligence in computer network technology. South. Agric. Mach. **49**(17), 43–47 (2008)
2. Abu-Alhaija, M., Turab, N.M.: Automated learning of ECG streaming data through machine learning internet of things. Intell. Autom. Soft Comput. **32**(1), 45–53 (2022)
3. Zhang, H.: Practical analysis of the artificial intelligence in computer network technology. Comput. Fan **2018**(10), 16–17 (2018)
4. Liu, C., Wang, H.: Artificial intelligence technology and its application in computer network. Sci. Technol. Innov. **2018**(25), 74–75 (2018)
5. Al-Adhaileh, M.H., Alsaade, F.W.: Detecting and analysing fake opinions using artificial intelligence algorithms. Intell. Autom. Soft Comput. **32**(1), 643–655 (2022)
6. Hinton, G.E., Srivastava, N., Krizhevsky, A.: Improving neural networks by preventing co-adaptation of feature detectors. Comput. Sci. **3**(4), 212–223 (2012)
7. LeCun, Y, Huang, F.J., Bottou, L.: Learning methods for generic object recognition with invariance to pose and lighting. In: Proceedings of the 2004 IEEE Computer Society Conference on Computer Vision and Pattern Recognition (2004)
8. Girshick, R., Donahue, J., Darrell, T.: Rich feature hierarchies for accurate object detection and semantic segmentation. In: Proceedings of the IEEE Conference on Computer Vision and Pattern Recognition, pp. 580–587(2014)
9. Simonyan, K., Zisserman, A.: Very deep convolutional networks for large-scale image recognition. In: Proceedings of ICLR 2015 (2015)

10. Mensink, T., Verbeek, J., Perronnin, F., Csurka, G.: Metric learning for large scale image classification: generalizing to new classes at near-zero cost. In: European Conference on Computer Vision (2012)

11. Russell, B.C., Torralba, A., Murphy, K.P., Freeman, W.T.: Labelme: a database and web-based tool for image annotation. Int. J. Comput. Vision **77**(1), 157–173 (2008)

12. Nair, V., Hinton, G.E.: Rectified linear units improve restricted boltzmann machines. In: Proc. 27th International Conference on Machine Learning (2010)

13. Lecun, Y., Huang, F.J., Bottou, L.: Learning methods for generic object recognition with invariance to pose and lighting. In: Computer Vision and Pattern Recognition (2004)

14. Endres, I., Hoiem, D.: Category independent object proposals. In: Daniilidis, K., Maragos, P., Paragios, N. (eds.) ECCV 2010. LNCS, vol. 6315, pp. 575–588. Springer, Heidelberg (2010). https://doi.org/10.1007/978-3-642-15555-0_42

15. Wang, X., Yang, M., Zhu, S., Lin, Y.: Region lets for generic object detection. IEEE Trans. Pattern Anal. Mach. Intell. **37**(10), 2071–2084 (2015)

16. Zeiler, M., Taylor, G., Fergus, R.: Adaptived econvolutional networks for mid and high level feature learning. In: Computer Vision and Pattern Recognition (CVPR 2011) (2011)

17. Howard, A. G.: Some improvements on deep convolutional neural network based image classification. In: Proc. ICLR 2014 (2014)

18. Sood, I., Sharma, V.: Computational Intelligent techniques to detect DDOS attacks: a survey. J. Cybersecur. **3**(2), 89–106 (2021)

19. Perronnin, F., Sánchez, J., Mensink, T.: Improving the fisher kernel for large-scale image classification. In: Daniilidis, K., Maragos, P., Paragios, N. (eds.) ECCV 2010. LNCS, vol. 6314, pp. 143–156. Springer, Heidelberg (2010). https://doi.org/10.1007/978-3-642-15561-1_11

20. Fei, L., Fergus, R., Perona, P.: Learning generative visual models from few training examples: an incremental bayesian approach tested on 101 object categories. Comput. Vis. Image Underst. **106**(1), 178–187 (2007)

21. Simonyan, K., Zisserman, A.: Very deep convolutional networks for large-scale image recognition. In: ICLR 2015 (2015)

A Data-Driven Machine Learning Spectrum Sharing Mechanism

Fabin Zhu[1(✉)], Feng Li[1], Wentao Song[2], and Yuhang Gu[3]

[1] Zhenjiang Ecological Environment Protection Dispatching Center,
Zhenjiang, China
6331949@qq.com
[2] CETC LES Information System Co., Ltd., Nanjing, China
[3] Nanjing University of Aeronautics and Astronautics, Nanjing, China

Abstract. Spectrum sensing is the most important part of cognitive radio technology, and it is a necessary condition for spectrum sharing. As the radio environment is constantly changing, it is critical to study how to improve the learning ability of cognitive users through machine learning. Based on learning the historical spectrum sensing data collected by the cognitive users, outputting the spectrum resources available in the current spectrum environment is of great significance for improving the accuracy of spectrum sensing, the efficiency of spectrum sharing, and reducing the impact on authorized users. In this paper, a spectrum sensing model based on Autoregressive Integrated Moving Average model (ARIMA) and Long Short-term Memory (LSTM) is proposed. Moreover, the attention mechanism was added to the LSTM, and the retraining process of the model was optimized through feedback records. Experimental results show that the improved LSTM model has better performance in spectrum prediction than traditional machine learning algorithms.

Keywords: Cognitive radio · Spectrum sensing · Machine learning · Deep learning

1 Introduction

In recent years, the rapid development of wireless communication technology has greatly facilitated people's lives, and people's living standards have also been continuously improved. However, the continuous occupation of spectrum by various communication technologies makes the available spectrum resources less and less, and how to improve the utilization rate of limited spectrum resources has become a current problem. In 2003, the Federal Communications Commission (FCC) clearly stated that Cognitive Radio (CR) technology is an effective means to improve spectrum utilization [1]. Therefore, many academic institutions have joined the research of CR.

The most important thing about CR [2, 3] technology is to have cognitive ability. When the CR device is in use, it can autonomously select an idle frequency band through spectrum sensing according to the current wireless environment, and when an authorized user accesses the frequency band, the CR can switch to other idle frequency bands in time or adjust its own frequency band reasonably. parameters to achieve the

X. Sun et al. (Eds.): ICAIS 2022, CCIS 1587, pp. 116–130, 2022.
https://doi.org/10.1007/978-3-031-06761-7_10

purpose of not affecting the normal communication of authorized users. Therefore, spectrum sensing technology is the most core technology in CR, and it is also the basis and premise of spectrum sharing.

Generally speaking, spectrum sensing technology can be divided into two categories, one is single-node sensing and the other is cooperative sensing. The traditional single-node sensing technology can be roughly divided into matched filter, energy detection and cyclisation characteristic detection [4]. The matched filter [5] is a linear filter with the maximum signal-to-noise ratio, it can quickly match the known authorized user spectrum, and then avoid them accurately, the main disadvantage is that it requires sufficient prior knowledge; the energy detection method [6] No prior knowledge is required. It judges whether there is a signal by detecting the amount of channel energy, but the energy threshold is difficult to set, and confusion is easy to occur when the signal is weak; the cyclisation characteristic detection [7] mainly uses large Most signals are artificially modulated and have the characteristic of unavoidable periodic autocorrelation. It can accurately detect and distinguish various signals and performs well in unknown noise and strong interference environments. Its disadvantage is that the computational complexity is too high, resulting in too long detection time. In addition, in terms of collaborative perception, the method of collaborative perception of multiple nodes is mainly used to reduce the workload of a single node. This model structure can be centralized or distributed. Compared with the traditional single-node perception model, which can effectively improve the speed and accuracy of perception. In addition, many literatures [8–11] have integrated and improved these technologies in practical applications, and achieved good results.

In practice, the radio environment is changing all the time, which makes it more difficult to achieve fast and accurate spectrum sharing without affecting the normal use of the spectrum by authorized users; spectrum sensing, then it may lose part of the transmission opportunity. Traditional spectrum sensing methods cannot solve these problems [12], so improving the efficiency of spectrum sensing becomes particularly critical.

Machine learning is a popular artificial intelligence technology, which can effectively improve the learning ability of CR. By learning the historical spectrum sensing data collected by CR, spectrum sensing based on machine learning can predict the available spectrum resources in the current or even future spectrum environment in advance, which can improve the utilization rate of spectrum resources, the efficiency of spectrum sharing, and reduce the need for authorization. User influence is significant.

2 Theoretical Basis

2.1 Spectrum Sharing Mechanism Based on Q-learning

Q-learning is one of the most classic reinforcement learning algorithms. The next Action taken by the Agent is determined by an evaluation function Q. The basic expression is:

$$Q(s,a) = r(s,a) + \gamma max_b Q(s_{next}, b) \qquad (1)$$

In formula (1), The r function represents the reward given by the environment after acting a in the current state s; S_{next} represents the next state the system is about to transition to; γ is the discount factor, representing the impact of future rewards on the current decision; b is the next action to be taken by a state. The Q function is usually stored in the form of a table. When the Agent is in the state S, the most appropriate action in the current state is obtained by querying the form of the Q table. Therefore, the essence of Q-learning is to continuously update and maintain a Q table.

In the spectrum access strategy, the state space S represents the specific occupancy of the current n channels, and each different occupancy represents a different state; the reward function is determined by whether a conflict will be encountered, and when no conflict will occur When r is a positive number, when a conflict occurs, $r = 0$. The experimental results show that when the authorized user frequency is fixed, the spectrum access strategy of Q-learning significantly reduces the probability of collision. However, in practice, the activity rules of authorized users are not completely fixed, and it is difficult for traditional reinforcement learning algorithms to dig out the hidden rules, and the training results are only slightly better than random access strategies.

2.2   Spectrum Sharing Mechanism Based on ARIMA

Many current supervised learning algorithms are still committed to improving the speed and accuracy of signal detection. Although good simulation results have been achieved, the effect of these models is not as good as imagined once they are put into the actual scene due to the addition of many unknown signals. Although reinforcement learning based violation detection strategy is claimed to be able to automatically detect violation behaviors, it is difficult to learn the "habit" of violation behaviors in general reinforcement learning, and the final experimental result is only slightly better than the random detection strategy.

The traditional time series fitting model ARIMA is applied to the detection of violations. The model can detect the occurrence of current and even future violations by fully utilizing the historical violation data and output the available violations. Through detection, violations can be known, and then take appropriate measures. The model is simple in structure, rapid in prediction, and can well capture the "habit" of illegal behavior. Finally, the feasibility of the model will be verified by actual data. There are no longer only 0 and 1 cases for violations.

This rule-breaking behavior model, which is always in a changing state, changes with time. It is a time-series model based on the rule-breaking behavior. Difference ARIMA model is a classic machine learning model, this model has simple structure, to predict quickly, and is a good way to capture the current law of the emergence of irregularities, by predicting the occurrence of irregularities in the future to make response in advance, increase the efficiency of the violation detection.

2.3   Autoregression Model

Autoregressive (AR) model is a traditional statistical model, which is often used in time series prediction and widely used in various fields. Let's say that the value of time series at time T is at the basic principle of AR is to use A_0 to A_{t-1} to predict the current data At, the use of data prior to the sequence itself to predict the current data, also known as autoregression. The specific formula of the model is as follows:

$$y_t = \mu + \sum_{i=1}^{p} \gamma_i y_{t-i} + \epsilon_t \tag{2}$$

In formula (2), y_t represents the current value to be predicted; ε represents the white noise error, which is required to have a mean of 0 and a standard deviation of σ, and σ will not change at any time; the intermediate summation part represents It is that the current y_t is related to the previous p data and is linearly related; the autocorrelation coefficient of y_{t-p} cannot be 0; μ is a constant term.

The principle of this model is very simple, but if you want to achieve a better prediction effect, the sequence itself must have a strong autocorrelation, that is, the autocorrelation coefficient of y is relatively large. If the sequence itself is not strongly autocorrelated, the prediction will be very poor.

2.4   Moving Average Model

The MOVING average (MA) model is like the AR model and is also a basic statistical model. Unlike AR model, MA model has nothing to do with the specific data of the sequence itself. It mainly considers the relationship between noises, and its derivation formula is as follows:

$$y_t = \mu + \epsilon_t + \sum_{i=1}^{q} \theta_i \epsilon_{t-i} \tag{3}$$

In formula (3), y_t represents the current value to be predicted; ε represents the white noise at different time points; θ is a coefficient, and θ_q must not be 0. The essence of the MA model is to use the previous random interference or prediction error to linearly express the current predicted value, which can be used simultaneously with the AR model to eliminate random fluctuations in data prediction.

2.5   Differential Integration Moving Average Autoregressive Model

Autoregressive moving average (ARMA) model is the combination of AR model and MA model. The specific formula is as follows:

$$y_t = \mu + \sum_{i=1}^{p} \gamma_i y_{t-i} + \epsilon_t + \sum_{i=1}^{q} \theta_i \epsilon_{t-i} \tag{4}$$

Here, the noise term in the AR model is expanded into the expression of the MA model, that is, the previous formula (2) and formula (3) are combined. Using MA can effectively eliminate the random fluctuation characteristics of data prediction and improve the accuracy of prediction. ARMA model prediction is mainly through the analysis of time series to determine the appropriate *(p, q)* value.

However, the ARMA model has strict requirements on the time series, that is, the series must satisfy the stationarity condition. Stationarity of a time series requires that the mean and variance of the series do not change significantly over time. Therefore, for those sequences that are inherently unstable, the ARMA model cannot be used directly. The ARIMA model introduces a difference mechanism. Usually, a simple difference operation can make the sequence more stable. Therefore, the ARIMA model has 3 parameters: *(p, d, q)*, where d represents the number of differences.

3   Data-Driven Machine Learning Spectrum Sharing Mechanism

On the theoretical basis, the problem of spectrum sharing is transformed into a time series prediction problem, and the classical time series model ARIMA is adopted. Finally, its feasibility is verified through experiments. Although the prediction effect of ARIMA model is better than that of traditional machine learning algorithm, the result is still unsatisfactory, with 35% misjudgment rate making it unable to be applied in the actual situation. Although ARIMA model is a good way to capture the current irregularities "habit", but, the same place tend to have multiple resources of the irregularities exist, for the same spectrum, he doesn't have to only in the current irregularity's "activity", the relationship between the various irregularities let down by the model. On the other hand, although THE ARIMA model can predict the time series, it essentially requires the series to be a stationary series. In other words, it can only capture the "habits" it wants to capture. In practice, this "habit" of offending behavior tends to be more complex and difficult to capture fully with conventional statistical models. Therefore, we propose a substation three-dimensional space spectrum sharing method based on LSTM. Based on substation three-dimensional security intelligent control platform, LSTM is improved according to the actual situation of spectrum sharing, and attention mechanism and a unique feedback and retraining mechanism are introduced.

3.1   LSTM Model

As a unique branch of machine learning, deep learning has been developing rapidly in recent years. LSTM is a model for dealing with time series problems. It can well control the information it wants to remember or forget through the input gate, forgetting gate and output gate, to improve the accuracy of prediction. As an artificial neural network model, LSTM can capture many laws in time series that cannot be expressed by specific mathematical formulas. However, these laws are often difficult to be learned by traditional machine learning models. Moreover, the structure of deep learning model is very flexible and can be improved according to actual requirements. Therefore, LSTM has natural advantages for long time series prediction.

LSTM evolves from a Recurrent Neural Network (RNN), another artificial Neural Network, which considers not only the impact of current inputs on output, but also the impact of previous inputs, and is therefore mainly applied to deal with a variety of sequential problems. RNN introduces a memory function that allows the network model to determine the current input based on experience, and its basic structure is shown in Fig. 1.

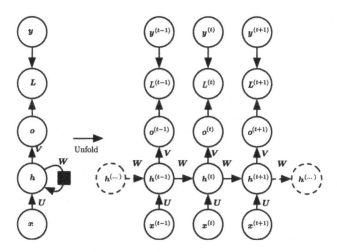

Fig. 1. Basic structure of RNN.

where h represents the hidden information of the current moment, that is, the memory information. In the expanded form of the figure above, we can find that the value of H will propagate forward all the time. O represents the output at the current moment; y is the true value; L stands for error; W, U, and V represent the weight matrix. By observing the expansion diagram, it can be found that the weight matrix is always detected for the input of the same sequence at different times. The specific derivation formula of RNN is as follows:

Although RNN introduces the implicit state of H, it can remember the experience well, but this kind of memory cannot last too long. For longer sequence problems, IT is easy for RNN to occur gradient disappearance. This is because the weight W in the final gradient formula will be multiplied by the derivative of the activation function, such as the activation function tanh commonly used by RNN:

$$h^{(t)} = tanh\left(Wh^{(t-1)} + Ux^{(t)} + b_h\right) \tag{5}$$

$$o^{(t)} = softmax\left(Vh^{(t)} + b_o\right) \tag{6}$$

The loss function is generally the cross entropy:

$$L^{(t)} = -\frac{1}{m}\sum_{i=1}^{m} y_i^{(t)} \log\left(o_i^{(t)}\right) \tag{7}$$

$$L = \sum_{t=1}^{T} L^{(t)} \tag{8}$$

Although RNN introduces the implicit state of H, it can remember the experience well, but this kind of memory cannot last too long. For longer sequence problems, IT is easy for RNN to occur gradient disappearance. This is because the weight W in the final gradient formula will be multiplied by the derivative of the activation function, such as the activation function tanh commonly used by RNN:

$$\prod_{j=k+1}^{t} tanh' W_s \tag{9}$$

The derivative of tanh is mostly going to be a positive number of one less, so if you multiply it all the time, the gradient is going to go to zero, and you're going to lose the gradient. This phenomenon of gradient disappearance will cause the learning efficiency of the front hidden layer to be slower than that of the back layer, thus the final prediction result will become very inaccurate.

Long- and short-term memory network (LSTM) can well solve the phenomenon of RNN gradient disappearance, and greatly improve the memory ability of RNN, which can deal with long sequence problems. LSTM is improved on the original RNN network model, and the specific structure is shown in Fig. 2.

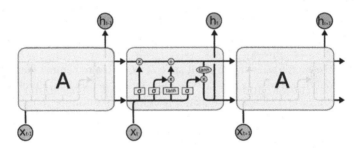

Fig. 2. Specific structure of LSTM.

The LSTM is capable of long-term memory storage due to the introduction of the concept of cellular state. In Fig. 2, in addition to the transfer of h value, there is a line running through the whole structure, which represents the cell state C, and the C value only participates in simple linear operations during the transfer, so that C can be well preserved. The LSTM also introduces a Gate structure that allows it to autonomously remove useless memories or add information that is useful to it. LSTM has three gates, namely forgetting Gate, input Gate and output Gate. The specific calculation formula is shown in (10), (11), (12), (13), (14) and (15). Where x_t Represents the current input, h_{t-1} Represents the output at the previous moment, formula (10) represents the forgetting gate, formula (11) and (12) represent the input gate, and Formula (13) represents the output gate.

$$f_t = \sigma\left(W_f x_t + U_f h_{t-1} + b_f\right) \tag{10}$$

$$i_t = \sigma(W_i x_t + U_i h_{t-1} + b_i) \tag{11}$$

$$\tilde{c}_t = \tanh(W_c x_t + U_c h_{t-1} + b_c) \tag{12}$$

$$o_t = \sigma(W_o x_t + U_o h_{t-1} + b_o) \tag{13}$$

Then update C:

$$c_t = f_t \odot c_{t-1} + i_t \odot \tilde{c}_t \tag{14}$$

Finally, part of C's information is added to H:

$$h_t = o_t \odot \tanh(c_t) \tag{15}$$

Therefore, LSTM is a good model to deal with time series. By introducing the concept of Gate, it compensates for the problem of RNN gradient disappearing to some extent. And through cellular state, it has the capacity for long-term memory. Compared with the previous ARIMA model, The LSTM can further explore the "habit" of spectrums, and make specific improvements based on the actual spectrum sharing model, to improve the accuracy of spectrum sharing.

3.2   Merge Input Sequences

Given that at a given location, there is correlation between spectrums of the same category. These spectrums are often switched from time to time for a variety of reasons. Therefore, simply considering the change of the number of spectrums in the same spectrum, the prediction effect of the model will become very poor. Therefore, when constructing the spectrum sharing model based on LSTM, we combine the historical occurrence of each spectrum in the time dimension.

Suppose there are 4 spectrums, and the time series length of each spectrum is 24, then the combined time series is a 24*4 matrix. This approach not only reduces the complexity of modeling, but also allows for good consideration of the correlation between the occurrence of individual spectrums at each point in time.

3.3   Attention Mechanism

The inspiration of the Attention mechanism comes from the research on the human visual nerve. Usually, when observing an object, people always focus their Attention on a certain part of the object, while playing down their perception of the object's surroundings. This mechanism can help people better understand an object. For example, when we are trying to read a sentence, we often focus on a few words in the sentence to understand the meaning of the sentence, while the words that have little impact on the understanding of the sentence will be ignored by our brain. The essential reason for this phenomenon is the lack of information processing capacity, and for artificial neural network, this kind of information processing shortcomings will be more prominent. Therefore, the introduction of the Attention mechanism enables the model to pay more Attention to the activity rules of important time points, which to some extent improves the model's ability to strengthen memory of key information.

At present, the Attention mechanism has been applied to various fields. Machine translation can improve the accuracy of translation by enabling models to better focus on the important parts of sentences. The original Attention mechanism was proposed by Bahdanau and applied to Encoder-Decoder. The structure used in machine translation is another variant of cyclic neural network – Seq2Seq. This network model does not simply use one RNN but combines two RNN into an Encoder-decoder structure. This allows more freedom in the length of the output sequence, which is more suitable for machine translation. The traditional Attention mechanism is shown in Fig. 3. C stands for semantic vector, which is related to the hidden state H in Encoder. Each C is weighted by H and summed up.

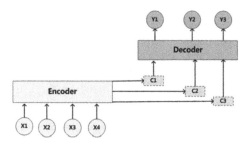

Fig. 3. Attention mechanism in Seq2Seq.

Unlike machine translation, we only need one LSTM for time series prediction. Since Seq2Seq can weight previously hidden states, the LSTM can also introduce this mechanism. In TensorFlow, the Attention mechanism of LSTM is shown in Fig. 4. When calculating the input at the current moment, the output of the first N steps is considered, and the hidden state and other information of the first N steps are weighted and summed up to participate in the input calculation at the current moment. Moreover, the Attention mechanism considers whether the output of the current moment or cell can be added to the current calculation, and whether the output of the current step can be applied to the input of the next moment.

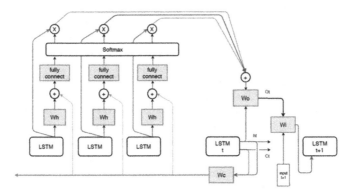

Fig. 4. Attention mechanism in TensorFlow.

The addition of this attention mechanism enables the LSTM to better focus on the more important parts of the input sequence, thus further improving the accuracy of prediction. For the detection of irregularities, the attention mechanism can make predictive models more adaptable. The model can pay more attention to the activity patterns of the spectrums at important points, to predict the occurrence of future spectrums more accurately.

3.4 Feedback Recording and Retraining

In the actual environment of spectrums, even if we grasp the law of spectrums, due to the intervention of some unknown factors, in order to solve this problem, if we only consider the number of spectrums like ARIMA model, the actual effect will not be very ideal. Although LSTM does not require continuous spectrum sharing to predict the occurrence of spectrums, if the model itself is to be applied to practice for a long time, it is obviously not feasible to only carry out the initial training. In general, occasionally, the prediction model of time series based on LSTM needs further training based on the original model, and such training will not take too long, which is also the reason why LSTM has better generalization ability in prediction than the traditional model.

In the example, the ability of the model itself to detect the spectrum is limited to the current spectrum, that is, the model can only record the actual situation of the current spectrum. Based on this premise, we propose a new retraining mechanism based on the idea that reinforcement learning can autonomously optimize itself according to the feedback information from the environment. In practical application, the model needs to obtain the specific occurrence of the current spectrum and record it in a table. This kind of perception of occurrence has no specific speed requirement, but only facilitates the optimization of the subsequent retraining. When the model is further trained, the loss function is calculated using not only the new training data, but also the information recorded by the previous model.

By recording the feedback of actual spectrums and optimizing the retraining process according to the feedback, the adaptability of the model can be effectively improved. In the face of various unknown situations, this continuous feedback recording, and retraining process can enable the model to capture the potential law of unknown factors, to detect spectrums in advance and ensure the safety of personnel.

Due to the nature of the ARIMA model itself, many hidden "habits" of spectrums are not found, and the predictive effects are not satisfactory. As a deep learning model suitable for time series prediction, LSTM can capture many laws that cannot be fitted by traditional statistical models, and it has natural advantages in time series prediction. LSTM has a flexibility that ARIMA cannot match. Based on this, LSTM is optimized in combination with the actual situation of spectrum sharing, and three improvements are proposed: considering the correlation between spectrums themselves, the input sequence of each spectrum is merged, and the overall modeling of all spectrums is carried out; The Attention mechanism commonly used in machine translation is introduced, which enables the model to focus Attention on more important time points. The feedback recording mechanism was added, and the retraining process of the model was optimized through the recorded information, to improve the adaptability of the model to environmental unknown factors.

4   Experiment and Result Analysis

In this experiment, GPU-based TensorFlow framework and python 3.6 were used to compile in Spyder.

4.1   Specific Structure and Parameter Selection

The overall structure of the model is output by Tensorboard. LSTM uses BasicLSTMCell, Attention mechanism USES AttentionCellWrapper, and the length of Attention is 24. The TIME_STEPS of the input sequence is 24. In addition to the input and output layers, there are altogether 3 hidden layers, with 50 neurons in each hidden layer. The LEARNING_RATE is set to 0.001. The loss function is calculated using mean-square error, and the optimizer in the model chooses AdamOptimizer.

4.2   Detection Effect of Spectrum Behavior

The statistical method here is similar to the previous one, but it needs to be divided into two situations: one is that there are only Spectrums and the hypothetical Spectrums in this experiment, in which case the proposed feedback recording mechanism will not affect the experimental results; The other is the interference of other unknown factors in the Spectrum behavior, which is set as the actual occurrence of the Spectrum behavior in this experiment, and limits the model to only observe the actual occurrence of the detected Spectrum behavior. Figure 5 shows the change of loss function during training and lists the effect diagram of one of the predictions (the thick line is the actual data, and the thin line is the predicted data). Finally, the experimental results of the two cases are compared as shown in Fig. 6 and Fig. 7.

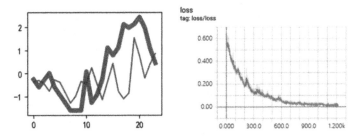

Fig. 5. Prediction results and loss function change curve during training.

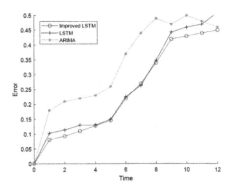

Fig. 6. Comparison of errors in the first case.

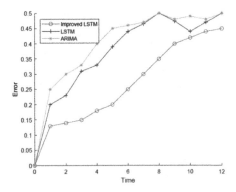

Fig. 7. Comparison of errors in the second case.

Here, we also analyze the misjudgment rate of each algorithm in two cases. See Figs. 8 and 9.

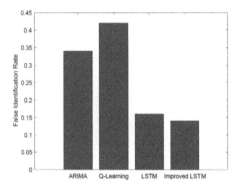

Fig. 8. Comparison of misjudgment rates among algorithms in the first case.

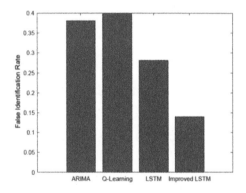

Fig. 9. Comparison of misjudgment rates among algorithms in the second case.

According to the above experiments, in the first case, the improved LSTM is significantly better than the ARIMA model, and the error can be reduced to about 0.1 in the prediction of the first 3 h, slightly better than the model before the improvement. And the error can be kept lower after more than 3 h. Judging from the misjudgment rate, the improved LSTM model reduces the misjudgment rate to about 14%, fully 20% lower than the ARIMA model. In the second case, the improved LSTM can better reflect its adaptability to unknown environment. In the case that the misjudgment rate and error of other methods are significantly increased, the misjudgment rate of the improved LSTM can still be maintained at about 15%.

5 Conclusion

This work first expounds the importance of the Spectrum behavior detection, and then compares and analyzes the advantages and disadvantages of various methods in detail. On this basis, a spectrum sharing model based on ARIMA is proposed to predict the change of Spectrums in the future by fitting the historical occurrence sequence of Spectrums, which improves the efficiency of spectrum sharing in a disguised way. Compared with reinforcement learning model, this model can better grasp the law of Spectrum behavior and improve the accuracy of prediction. Then the feasibility of the model is verified by experiments. However, the misjudgment rate of the model is still high and difficult to be applied to practice. Based on the above Spectrum prediction model and by analyzing the factors ignored by ARIMA model, a spectrum sharing model based on LSTM is proposed. Based on the actual situation, we have made the following three improvements to the LSTM model: First, since the ARIMA model ignores the relationship between each Spectrum itself, the input sequence of each Spectrum is merged in the time dimension. Secondly, in order to further explore the law of illegal activities, attention mechanism is introduced. Finally, considering that in the actual situation, the specific degree of Spectrums will be affected by many unknown factors, a feedback recording mechanism is proposed, and the retraining process is optimized to improve the adaptability of the model to unfamiliar environments. The final experimental results show that the improved LSTM can still maintain a mis-judgment rate of less than 15% under the influence of various unknown factors, which is a good improvement over the traditional prediction model.

References

1. Yucek, T., Arslan, H.: A survey of spectrum sensing algorithms for cognitive radio applications. IEEE Commun. Surv. Tutor. **11**(1), 116–130 (2009)
2. Karimi, M., Sadough, S.M.S., Torabi, M.: Improved joint spectrum sensing and power allocation for cognitive radio networks using probabilistic spectrum access. IEEE Syst. J. **13**(4), 3716–3723 (2019)
3. Arivudainambi, D., Mangairkarasi, S., Varun Kumar, K.A.: Spectrum prediction in cognitive radio network using machine learning techniques. Intell. Autom. Soft Comput. **32**(3), 1525–1540 (2022)
4. Ansere, J.A., Han, G., Wang, H., Choi, C., Wu, C.: A reliable energy efficient dynamic spectrum sensing for cognitive radio iot networks. IEEE Internet Things J. **6**(4), 6748–6759 (2019)
5. Yin, W., Chen, H.: Decision-driven time-adaptive spectrum sensing in cognitive radio networks. IEEE Trans. Wireless Commun. **19**(4), 2756–2769 (2020)
6. Zheng, K., Liu, X., Liu, X., Zhu, Y.: Hybrid overlay-underlay cognitive radio networks with energy harvesting. IEEE Trans. Commun. **67**(7), 4669–4682 (2019)
7. Li, L., Ghasemi, A.: IoT-enabled machine learning for an algorithmic spectrum decision process. IEEE Internet Things J. **6**(2), 1911–1919 (2019)
8. Garg, A., Parashar, A., Barman, D., Jain, S., Singhal, D.: Autism spectrum disorder prediction by an explainable deep learning approach. Comput. Mater. Contin. **71**(1), 1459–1471 (2022)

9. Arunkumar, A., Surendran, D.: Autism spectrum disorder diagnosis using ensemble ml and max voting techniques. Comput. Syst. Sci. Eng. **41**(1), 389–404 (2022)
10. Adarsh, A., Kumar, B., Gupta, M., Kumar, A., Singh, A.: Design of an efficient cooperative spectrum for intra-hospital cognitive radio network. Comput. Mater. Contin. **69**(1), 35–49 (2021)
11. Jacob, S.: A novel spectrum sharing scheme using dynamic long short-term memory with cp-ofdma in 5g networks. IEEE Trans. Cogn. Commun. Netw. **6**(3), 926–934 (2020)
12. Li, B., Li, S., Nallanathan, A., Nan, Y., Zhao, C., Zhou, Z.: Deep sensing for next-generation dynamic spectrum sharing: more than detecting the occupancy state of primary spectrum. IEEE Trans. Commun. **63**(7), 2442–2457 (2015)

Tri-modal Quadruple Constraint Network for Visible-Infrared Person Re-identification

Wanru Song[1(✉)], Xinyi Wang[1], Sijiang Liu[1], Feng Liu[1],
and Hengji Li[2,3]

[1] Nanjing University of Posts and Telecommunications, Nanjing, China
songwanru@njupt.edu.cn
[2] Beijing University of Posts and Telecommunications, Beijing, China
[3] Quantum Technology Lab and Applied Mechanics,
University of Milan, Milan, Italy

Abstract. The visible-infrared person re-identification task remains a challenging issue due to large intra-modality and cross-modality variations. In order to reduce these differences, we propose a novel network model for the visible-infrared task, namely, the tri-modal quadruple constraint network (TQC-Net). First, the TQC-Net converts RGB images to grayscale images through grayscale transformation. The grayscale image loses color information, but is visually more similar to the infrared image. Therefore, it can be used as a bridge between infrared and RGB images. By introducing the grayscale modality, the three-modal image group of the pedestrian is then input to the proposed network, which presents a three-stream framework. In addition, to further reduce the difference between the modalities, we design a hetero-center loss based on a quadruple group and the center loss to train the re-identification model. Extensive experiments are conducted on two datasets, including the SYSU-MM01 and RegDB datasets. The experimental results demonstrate the superiority and effectiveness of the proposed TQC-Net over the state-of-the-art approaches.

Keywords: Person re-identification · Cross-modality · Center loss

1 Introduction

Person re-identification (Person re-id) and vehicle re-identification is an important part of the system of intelligent video analysis and processing [1–5]. The goal of person re-id is to achieve the recognition and retrieval of the same pedestrian under different cameras. The traditional person re-id is performed in the visible light domain. However, in real life, crimes often occur at night with low light. In this case, the visible image shooting cannot capture plenty of effective pedestrian information. Therefore, it is necessary to study the cross-modal retrieval between RGB and infrared images, namely, visible-infrared person re-identification (VI-reid).

In recent years, many studies of VI-reid have emerged one after another. However, most of them obtain poor performance on accuracy. Therefore, the cross-modality task remains a challenging issue. VI-reid faces the same challenges as the traditional task,

X. Sun et al. (Eds.): ICAIS 2022, CCIS 1587, pp. 131–141, 2022.
https://doi.org/10.1007/978-3-031-06761-7_11

such as changes in pose, illumination, and viewpoint. More importantly, VI-reid also needs to consider the differences between different modalities. In other words, in the cross-modality tasks. There are not only intra-modal variations but also huge inter-modal differences (see in Fig. 1). Therefore, it is crucial to explore more discriminative modality-invariant information for the VT-reid task.

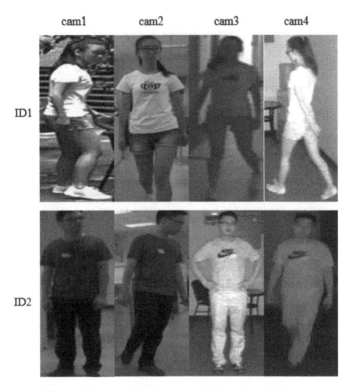

Fig. 1. Some samples from the visible-infrared dataset.

At the beginning of the development of VI-reid, the study on it was basically based on the research of RGB-RGB person re-id. The methods of the RGB-RGB task can be divided into two classes: feature representation learning and metric learning. For the former, its goal is to extract discriminative features that are robust to variations in the external environment. The hand-crafted features are extracted based on color and texture, such as the Local Maximal Occurrence (LOMO) descriptor [6]. In the deep-learned system, the ID-discriminative embedding (IDE) CNN is the most common network. The IDE network regards re-id as the ID classification task and learns the feature of the pedestrian [7]. The metric learning algorithms aim to learn effective similarity measurement. Traditional metric learning methods are almost based on Mahalanobis distance, such as top-push distance learning (TDL) [8]. The metric learning algorithm based on deep learning always trains the model by designing the metric loss function [9].

The studies of VI-reid can be classified into three types, namely learning the modality-invariant feature, designing the metric learning loss function, and heterogeneous image synthesis and conversion. A brief introduction of them is given as follows.

Learning the Modality-Invariant Feature. It is crucial to obtain more modality-shared information. The dual-stream network is the most frequent framework in this research area [10–14]. The visible and infrared images are input to the dual-stream network, respectively. The specific information of them is then mapped to the shared space. Finally, the modality-invariant feature can be extracted. Literature [10] compares the single- and dual-stream structures for VI-reid, and proposes a practical dataset called SYSU-MM01. In [13], the authors propose an improved two-stream CNN to learn the deep cross-modal feature. Additionally, literature [14] designs a shared CNN and fuses the features that came from different levels, and obtains good performance in the cross-modality task.

Designing the Metric Learning Loss Function. The goal of designing the metric loss function is to reduce the intra- and cross-modal distances of the same ID, and to increase the difference between different IDs [12, 15–18]. Ye et al. [12] propose the bi-directional ranking, cross-modality top-ranking constraint and intra-modality top-ranking constraint losses. Combined with cross-entropy loss, the overall embedding loss can simultaneously handle the intra-modality and cross-modality variations. Literature [19] proposes the hetero-center loss, which can improve the accuracy of the VI-reid task by shortening the distance between the center of cross-modal features that came from the same class. In [17], the authors propose the hetero-center triplet loss for visible-infrared person re-id, which refers to triplet loss and center loss.

Heterogeneous Image Synthesis and Conversion. Most of these methods rely on Generative Adversarial Network (GAN). This is because GAN can be used for data augmentation through adversarial training. Therefore, GAN-based methods are commonly used to achieve the mutual conversion between the RGB image and the IR image [20–22]. For example, in [21], the authors propose AlignGAN, which can realize the alignment of pixels and features. First, AlignGAN can generate fake images, and then is used to constrain the real and the fake images into a unified feature space. Different from GAN-based research, some methods also consider utilizing other ways to achieve heterogeneous image synthesis. Li et al. [23] utilize a light network instead of GAN to build the X modality generation network. The paper introduces an auxiliary intermediate modality X to VI-reid, which is reformulated from the RGB channels to a format that can easily perform cross-modal learning.

Obviously, it is important to explore modality-invariant features for the VI-reid task. Generally speaking, various types of improved metric loss functions based on center loss can further improve the accuracy of cross-modal person re-id. However, the effectiveness of GAN-based methods is limited. This is because that we cannot find one-to-one corresponding image pairs in the re-id task. According to the above standpoints, we propose a novel network model for the VI-reid task named the tri-modal quadruple constraint network (TQC-Net). In TQC-Net, the RGB image of pedestrian is first converted to the grayscale images through grayscale transformation instead of GAN. And then, the input of the proposed network is set to the tri-modal image group. TQC-Net utilizes grayscale images as a bridge to reduce the gap between infrared and RGB images. Additionally, a new hetero-center loss based on the quadruple constraint and the center loss is proposed to the training model. It is used to further reduce the variation between the different modalities. In a nutshell, the contributions of this paper are summarized as follows:

(1) We propose a deep feature learning network (TQC-Net) for the VI-reid task, which utilizes the grayscale transformation of visible images to build a tri-modality input. Thus, a three-stream framework is presented and employed to reduce intra- and cross-modality differences of the same person without increasing much calculation cost.
(2) The paper proposes Hetero-center Quadruple Constraint Loss (HCQC loss) for the cross-modal task. The proposed loss just considers the distance between the center points of features in a quadruple group of each modality.
(3) Extensive experiments are conducted on the public VI-reid datasets, and experimental results demonstrate the superiority of the proposed method over the state-of-the-art approaches.

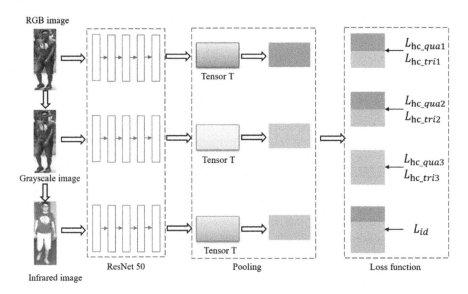

Fig. 2. The framework of the propose TQC-Net.

2 Proposed Method

2.1 Framework

In this paper, we adopt the ResNet50 as a backbone and propose TQC-Net for the VI-reid task. From Fig. 2, it can be seen tat TQC-Net is a three-stream network. First, a simple grayscale transformation is used to achieve the conversion from RGB images to grayscale images. Then, we utilize the framework proposed in [17] as the baseline. The shared layer is set to 0 and local feature learning is ignored in our work. In other words, TQC-Net does not use the shared CNN layer, and just considers the effect of global features. Finally, HCQC loss is proposed for the task. The VI-reid model is trained supervise by the ID classification (L_{id}), hetero-center triplet (L_{hc_tri}) [15] and hetero-center quadruplet (L_{hc_qua}) losses.

2.2 Tri-modal Input

It can be clearly seen that there is a huge difference between the visible image and the infrared image. For the RGB-RGB person re-id task, the color feature of a pedestrian is the crucial appearance information, and plays an important role in the process of re-id. However, we cannot extract color information from the infrared image. Therefore, it is difficult to achieve mutual retrieval between infrared and visible pedestrian images. Considering that there is no color information in the grayscale image, which is visually more similar to the infrared image. We believe that the grayscale modality can be used as an auxiliary mode to reduce the gap between the visible and IR images. Therefore, we convert RGB images to grayscale images in the stage of data processing.

After grayscale transformation, three-modal pedestrian images can be obtained, namely RGB, infrared and grayscale modalities. In the training stage, the input of the network is the tri-modal image group that came from the above modalities.

2.3 Loss Function

In person re-id tasks, the problem of re-id can be regarded as a classification issue. Therefore, the ID classification loss is the most commonly used loss in the task. We first adopt this loss in the training phase:

$$L_{id} = -\sum_{i=1}^{K} \log \frac{e^{W_{y_i}^T x_i + b_{y_i}}}{\sum_{j=1}^{n} e^{W_j^T x_i + b_j}} \tag{1}$$

where K is the batch size and x_i represents the i-th feature. W is the weight matrix, and b is the bias matrix.

In the meantime, by introducing the metric measurement loss function such as triplet loss, the end-to-end network can be built. And meanwhile, the similarity of different features can be calculated. In addition, the center loss sets a center of each class in the feature space, and then drives the features in this class as close as possible to the center. Therefore, center loss is often used in classification tasks.

In the existing research, center loss is widely used in VI-reid. Literature [14, 17] proposes a metric learning loss named the hetero-center triplet loss (L_{hc_tri}). The core of triplet loss is: for each training batch, randomly select P IDs of pedestrians, and each pedestrian randomly selects K different images; thus, a batch contains P × K images; and then, for each image Anchor1 in the batch, we can select a hardest positive sample and a hardest negative sample to form a triple with Anchor1. Literature [14, 17] relax the strict constraints by replacing the comparison of the anchor point with all other samples with the comparison of the anchor point center with all other centers. Experimental results demonstrate that the hetero-center triplet loss obtains good performance in the VI-reid task.

Referring to the hetero-center triplet loss, we propose a new metric loss function, which is also based on center loss. It's worth noting that we introduce a negative sample to form a quadruple. Similar to the hetero-center triplet loss, we also use the center of features as an identity agent and propose the hetero-center quadruplet constraint loss (HCQC loss):

$$
\begin{aligned}
L_{hc\_qua1} = \sum_{i=1}^{P} & \left[\alpha_1 + \left\| c_v^i - c_t^i \right\|_2 - \min_{\substack{n_1 \in \{v,t\} \\ j \neq i}} \left\| c_v^i - c_n^j \right\|_2 \right]_+ \\
+ \sum_{i=1}^{P} & \left[\alpha_3 + \left\| c_v^i - c_t^i \right\|_2 - \min_{\substack{n \in \{v,t\} \\ j \neq i, k \neq i}} \left\| c_n^j - c_n^k \right\|_2 \right]_+
\end{aligned}
\tag{2}
$$

where c_v and c_t represents the centers of feature in the visible and infrared modalities, respectively. c_n denotes the center of features came from negative samples.

In TQC-Net, we calculate the L_{hc_tri1} and L_{hc_qua1} between RGB and grayscale modalities, the L_{hc_tri2} and L_{hc_qua2} between RGB and infrared modalities, and the L_{hc_tri3} and L_{hc_qua3} between infrared and grayscale modalities. Therefore,

$$
L_{hc\_tri} = \frac{\left(L_{hc_{tri1}} + L_{hc_{tri2}} + L_{hc_{tri3}} \right)}{3}
\tag{3}
$$

The final loss function L_{total} is formulated below:

$$
L_{total} = L_{id} + \lambda \left(L_{hc\_tri} + L_{hc\_qua} \right)
\tag{4}
$$

where λ is used to assign a weight to L_{id} and the metric learning function. We set it equals to 0.5 in our work.

3   Experiment

In this section, several experiments are conducted on the two VI-reid datasets, i.e. SYSU-MM01 [10] and RegDB [24]. We first give a brief introduction to the datasets used in the paper. And then, we explain the experimental settings. Next, we conduct a group of ablation experiments on SYSU-MM01 and analyze the experimental results. Finally, the proposed method is compared with the state-of-the-art algorithms.

3.1   Datasets

SYSU-MM01. SYSU-MM01 is the most commonly used large-scale dataset in the VI-reid field. It contains 491 pedestrians. The images of pedestrians are captured by six cameras, of which four cameras are visible light cameras (Cam1, Cam2, Cam5 and Cam6) and the other 2 are infrared cameras (Cam1and Cam6). In addition, each pedestrian is captured by at least two different cameras.

RegDB. RegDB is a small dataset for the VI-reid task. It is captured by two cameras and has 412 pedestrians. Among them, each pedestrian has 10 pairs of visible light and infrared images.

3.2   Experimental Settings

SYSU-MM01 consists of a training set and a testing set. In the training set, there are 395 pedestrians with 22,258 visible images and 11,909 infrared images. The testing set contains 96 pedestrians, with 3,803 infrared images for the query, and 301 randomly selected visible images as the gallery. For RegDB, we randomly divide the dataset into two halves for training and testing according to the evaluation protocol in [12]. Therefore, both the training and testing set consists of 2,060 visible images and 2,060 infrared images. The cumulative matching characteristics (CMC) curve and mean average precision (mAP) are used to evaluate the performance of VI-reid.

All experiments are conducted on the PyTorch architecture and the NVIDIA RTX 2080Ti card. The start learning rate is 0.01 and the batch size is set to 32. Additionally, the momentum is set to 0.9. In the training phase, all images are resized to 288×144. The total number of training epochs is 60. For the loss function, the value of λ is set to 0.5

3.3   Ablation Experiment

In order to evaluate the effect of grayscale transformation and the proposed HCQC loss, we conducted a group of ablation experiments on the SYSU-MM01 dataset, and the results can be seen in Table 1. In Table 1, '$\sqrt{}$' represents adopting the operation or module and '$\times$' means ignoring the above operation.

It can be seen from Table 1 that the performance of using grayscale transformation can achieve 49.92% of CMC matching rate at Rank1 accuracy and 46.73% of mAP in 'All search' mode. In this mode, the performance outperforms baseline by 2.17% at Rank-1 accuracy and 0.75% at mAP. The same is true in 'Indoor search' mode. If adopting HCQC loss to train the network, the performance of the well-trained model is also improved. In 'Indoor search' mode, the use of HCQC loss can bring improvements of 4.63% and 2.94% at Rank1 and mAP accuracy, respectively.

When the proposed method is used, Rank1 can reach 57.42%, and mAP can reach 54.98% in 'All search' mode. In other words, there are 9.67% and 9% improvements compared to baseline. Additionally, TQC-Net outperforms baseline by 11.54% at Rank1 accuracy and 13.44% at mAP in 'Indoor search' mode. The results can illustrate that the grayscale transformation and HCQC loss proposed in this paper are effective in improving VI-reid accuracy.

Table 1. Evaluation of different network setting on SYSU-MM01.

Baseline	Grayscale	HCQC loss	All search		Indoor search	
			Rank1	mAP	Rank1	mAP
√	×	×	47.75	45.98	51.88	55.85
√	√	×	49.92	46.73	53.46	57.76
√	×	√	52.30	48.96	56.51	58.79
√	√	√	57.42	54.98	63.42	69.29

Table 2. Comparison of Rank-k accuracy and mAP (%) with the state-of-the-art methods on SYSU-MM01. **Bold** numbers are the best results.

Method	All search			Indoor search		
	Rank 1	Rank 10	mAP	Rank 1	Rank 10	mAP
Zero-padding [10]	19.13	61.40	10.89	24.43	75.86	18.64
cmGAN [25]	26.97	67.51	31.49	31.63	77.23	42.19
D^{2}RL [26]	28.90	70.60	39.56	28.12	70.23	29.01
AlignGAN [21]	42.40	85.00	40.70	45.90	87.60	54.30
Hi-CMD [20]	34.94	77.58	35.94	-	-	-
XIV [23]	49.92	89.79	50.73	-	-	-
GECNet [27]	53.37	89.86	51.83	60.60	94.29	62.89
HC (baseline) [19]	46.01	88.17	33.99	53.36	94.18	44.90
DGTL [14]	57.34	-	**55.13**	63.11	-	69.20
TQC-Net	**57.42**	**93.60**	54.98	**63.42**	**95.82**	**69.29**

3.4 Comparison with State-of-the-art Methods

In this subsection, we conduct the comparsion experiments on two VI-reid datasets to compare the proposed approach with several state of-the art methods, i.e., Zero-padding [10], cmGAN [25], D^{2}RL [26], AlignGAN [21], Hi-CMD [20], XIV [23], GECNet [27], HC (baseline) [19] and DGTL [14]. Table 2 and Fig. 3 summarized the final results.

From Table 2, it can be found that the proposed TQC-Net obtains the best performance at Rank1 and Rank10 accuracy in 'All search' and 'Indoor search' modes. AlignGAN utilizes GAN to generate fake images, but compared to this method, TQC-Net obtains 15.02% and 14.28% improvements of Rank1 and mAP in 'All search' mode. XIV designs a light network to introduce a new modality–X modality. Similar to it, TQC-Net introduces the grayscale modality for VI-reid. The proposed TQC-Net still significantly outperforms XIV in the two modes. HC (baseline) proposes a heterogeneous center loss and obtains good performance. Compared with it, our method has

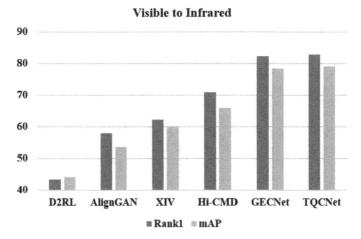

Fig. 3. Comparison of Rank-k accuracy and mAP (%) with the state-of-the-art methods on RegDB.

improvements of Rank1 by 11.41% and 10.06% in the two modes, respectively. Obviously, the mAP of TQC-Net is also improved. DGTL utilizes the hetero-center triplet loss, which is also used in our work. However, the proposed TQC-Net is more effective due to the introduction of grayscale modality and the design of the hetero-center quadruplet constraint loss.

Additionally, as illustrated in Fig. 3, the proposed TQC-Net obtains the best performance of Rank1 and mAP on the RegDB dataset. More specifically, the proposed method can achieve 81.98% Rank1 accuracy and 78.72% mAP accuracy. TQC-Net far exceeds D^2RL, AlignGAN and XIV and Hi-CMD. GECNet utilizes the grayscale enhancement and GAN to the modality extension. However, our method still gains a little advantage over it due to the HCQC loss proposed in the paper.

4 Conclusion

In this paper, in order to further reduce the difference between cross-modal images that came from the pedestrian, a three-stream network TQC-Net is proposed for the VI-reid task. First, our work utilizes grayscale transformation to obtain gray images of pedestrians. And then, a three-stream framework is presented with the tri-modal input. Finally, to further reduce the difference between the modalities, a novel loss based on the quadruple constraint and the center loss is proposed to train the re-id model. Extensive experiments are conducted on the SYSU-MM01 and RegDB datasets, and the results indicate that the proposed TQC-Net outperforms state-of-the-art algorithms.

Acknowledgement. This work was supported in part by the National Natural Science Foundation of China under Grant 62177029 and Grant 61807020, and in part by the Scientific Starting Fund from Nanjing University of Posts and Telecommunications (NUPTSF) under Grant NY221041.

References

1. Wang, T., Gong, S., Zhu, X., Wang, S.: Person re-identification by video ranking. In: Fleet, D., Pajdla, T., Schiele, B., Tuytelaars, T. (eds.) ECCV 2014. LNCS, vol. 8692, pp. 688–703. Springer, Cham (2014). https://doi.org/10.1007/978-3-319-10593-2_45
2. Jiang, T.: A review of person re-identification. J. New Media 2(2), 45–60 (2020)
3. Dai, Y., Luo, Z.: Review of unsupervised person re-identification. J. New Media 3(4), 129–136 (2021)
4. Zhang, X., Chen, X., Sun, W., He, X.: Vehicle re-identification model based on optimized densenet121 with joint loss. Comput. Mater. Continua 67(3), 3933–3948 (2021)
5. Sun, W., Dai, G., Zhang, X., He, X., Chen, X.: TBE-Net: a three-branch embedding network with part-aware ability and feature complementary learning for vehicle re-identification. IEEE Trans. Intell. Transp. Syst. (2021). https://doi.org/10.1109/TITS.2021.3130403
6. Liao, S., Hu, Y., Zhu, X., Li, S.Z.: Person re-identification by local maximal occurrence representation and metric learning. In: Proceedings of the IEEE International Conference Computer Vision Pattern Recognition, Boston, USA, pp. 2197–2206 (2015)
7. Dai, J., Zhang, P., Wang, D., Lu, H., Wang, H.: Video person re-identification by temporal residual learning. IEEE Trans. Image Process. 28(3), 1366–1377 (2019)
8. You, J., Wu, A., Li, X., Zheng, W.S.: Top-push video-based person reidentification. In: Proceedings of the IEEE International Conference Computer Vision Pattern Recognition, Las Vegas, USA, pp. 1345–1353 (2016)
9. Chen, W., et al.: Beyond triplet loss: a deep quadruplet network for person re-identification. In: Proceedings of the IEEE International Conference Computer Vision Pattern Recognition, Hawaii, USA (2017)
10. Wu, A., Zheng, W., Yu, H., Gong, S., Lai, J.: Rgb-infrared crossmodality person re-identification. In: Proceedings of the IEEE/CVF International Conference Computer Vision, Hawaii, USA, pp. 5390–5399 (2017)
11. Liu, H., Cheng, J., Wang, W., Su, Y., Bai, H.: Enhancing the discriminative feature learning for visible-thermal cross-modality person re-identification. Neurocomputing 398, 11–19 (2020)
12. Ye, M., Wang, Z., Lan, X., Yuen, P.C.: Visible thermal person reidentification via dual-constrained top-ranking. In: Proceedings of the International Joint Conference Artificial Intelligence, Stockholm, Sweden, pp. 1092–1099 (2018)
13. Ye, M., Lan, X., Li, J., Yuen, P.C.: Hierarchical discriminative learning for visible thermal person re-identification. In: Proceedings of the AAAI Conference Artificial Intelligence, pp. 7501–7508. New Orleans, Louisiana, USA (2018)
14. Liu, H., Chai, Y., Tan, X., Li, D., Zhou, X.: Strong but simple baseline with dual-granularity triplet loss for visible-thermal person re-identification. IEEE Signal Process. Lett. 28, 653–657 (2021)
15. Ye, M., Lan, X., Wang, Z., Yuen, P.C.: Bi-directional centerconstrained top-ranking for visible thermal person re-identification. IEEE Trans. Inf. Forensics Secur. 15, 407–419 (2020)
16. Ye, H., et al.: Bi-directional exponential angular triplet loss for rgb-infrared person re-identification. IEEE Trans. Image Process. 30, 1583–1595 (2021)
17. Liu, H., Tan, X., Zhou, X.: Parameter sharing exploration and hetero-center triplet loss for visible-thermal person re-identification. IEEE Trans. Multimedia 23, 4414–4425 (2020)
18. Li, Y., Wang, X.: Person re-identification based on joint loss and multiple attention mechanism. Intell. Autom. Soft Comput. 30(2), 563–573 (2021)

19. Zhu, Y., et al.: Hetero-center loss for cross-modality person re-identification. Neurocomputing **38**, 97–109 (2020)
20. Choi, S., Lee, S., Kim, Y., Kim, T., Kim, C.: Hi-CMD: hierarchical cross-modality disentanglement for visible-infrared person reidentification. In: Proceedings of the IEEE/CVF Conference Computing Vision Pattern Recognition, Seattle, USA, pp. 10254–10263 (2020)
21. Wang, G., Zhang, T., Cheng, J., Liu, S., Yang, Y., Hou, Z.: Rgb infrared cross-modality person re-identification via joint pixel and feature alignment. In: Proceedings of the IEEE/CVF International Conference Computing Vision, Long Beach, USA, pp. 3622–3631 (2019)
22. Wang, G.A., et al.: Cross-modality paired-images generation for rgb-infrared person re-identification. In: Proceedings of the AAAI Conference on Artificial Intelligence, New York, USA (2020)
23. Li, D., et al.: Infrared-visible cross-modal person re-identification with an x modality. In: The Thirty-Fourth AAAI Conference on Artificial Intelligence (AAAI-20), New York, USA (2020)
24. Dat, N., et al.: Person recognition system based on a combination of body images from visible light and thermal cameras. Sensors **17**(3), 605 (2017)
25. Dai, P., Ji, R., Wang, H., Wu, Q., Huang, Y.: Cross-modality person re-identification with generative adversarial training. In: Proceedings of the International Joint Conference Artificial Intelligence, Macao, China, pp. 677–683 (2018)
26. Wang, Z., Wang, Z., Zheng, Y., Chuang, Y.Y., Satoh, S.I.: Learning to reduce dual-level discrepancy for infrared-visible person re-identification. In: Proceedings of the IEEE/CVF Conference on Computer Vision and Pattern Recognition, pp. 618–626 (2019)
27. Zhong, X., et al.: Grayscale enhancement colorization network for visible-infrared person re-identification. IEEE Trans. Circuits Syst. Video Technol. (2021). https://doi.org/10.1109/TCSVT.2021.3072171

Continuous Weighted Neural Cognitive Diagnosis Method for Online Education

Shunfeng Wang[1], Peng Fu[1(✉)], Muhui Fu[1], Bingke Li[1],
Bingyu Zhang[2], Zian Chen[2], Zhuonan Liang[2], and Yunlong Chen[2]

[1] School of Computer Science and Engineering, Nanjing University of Science
and Technology, Nanjing 210094, Jiangsu, China
fupeng@njust.edu.cn
[2] School of Science, Nanjing University of Science and Technology,
Nanjing 210094, Jiangsu, China

Abstract. With the rapid development of online education, extensive data records from online education are accumulated in large quantities, therefore the educational evaluation industry is of great potential. Cognitive diagnosis based on machine learning has drawn considerable attention from both the research community and industry, and a lot of works have been proposed. However, many models ignored the point that different knowledge concepts have different important degrees on each exercise. In this paper, we propose the Continuous Weighted Neural Cognitive Diagnosis (CWNCD) model, which is extended from the Neural Cognitive Diagnosis (NCD) framework, a cognitive diagnosis framework based on neural network, to get a more accurate diagnosis result and ensure its interpretability. Specifically, we added information about the importance degree of different knowledge concepts in each exercise for modeling their interactions, in which case we can more comprehensively model the cognitive level of a student. Extensive experiments conducted on real-world datasets show that the CWNCD model is feasible and obtain excellent performance. Finally, the possible future research directions are discussed.

Keywords: Cognitive diagnosis · Learning process · Online education

1 Introduction

Nowadays online education is in the rapid process of scaling up. And the educational diagnosis is in the high demand for AI technology as the manual diagnosis can hardly handle the massive data gathered from learners. In such case, much attention has been drawn to this field. In recent years, there are many studies about student modeling using deep learning methods [1–8], but most of them does not strictly distinguish exercises and knowledge concepts contained in exercises. Therefore, their model lack interpretability, which is required for cognitive diagnosis. To overcome the difficulty, some researchers believe that exercises are related to a set of explicit knowledge concepts, which means a single exercise is related to a certain set of knowledge concepts, which are represented by a Q matrix [9]. Each row of the matrix represents an exercise, and each column represents a knowledge concept. And they think that the score of a certain student on a certain exercise is affected by the student's mastery of the knowledge concepts related to the exercise. The process of modeling students' skills is called the cognitive diagnosis models. Cognitive diagnosis models need to ensure good interpretability while modeling students. Common cognitive diagnosis models include Item response Theory (IRT) [10] model and Deterministic Inputs, Noisy And-gate (DINA). For IRT, students are modeled as a one-dimension ability vectors and the prediction also considers the exercises' information (difficulty, discrimination, etc.). While the DINA employ the Q matrix to model the student as a mastery vector on multi-dimensional knowledge concepts.

However, these works rely on handcrafted interaction functions that just combine the multiplication of student's and exercise's trait features linearly, which usually requires professional expertise and may not be sufficient for capturing the complex relationship between students and exercises. Therefore, the Neural Cognitive Diagnosis (NCD) framework [11] was proposed. By incorporating neural networks to model complex non-linear interactions, it solved the problem.

NCD uses multi-dimensional parameters to describe the cognitive level of student and exercise characteristics (such as difficulty), and combines neural networks instead of manual design function to learn the complex relationship between student factors and exercise factors from heterogeneous data.

However, NCD uses a discrete value of {0, 1} to simply indicate whether the exercises and the knowledge concepts are related. Compared with the method of using continuous values, the discrete values lacks the correlation information between exercises and knowledge concepts. So, we proposed CWNCD that introduces continuous values to describe the relationship between the exercises and the knowledge concepts more concretely and reflect the different importance degree of different knowledge concepts when multiple knowledge concepts are involved in one exercise, thereby improving the effect and interpretability of the entire model.

Our main contributions are summarized as follows:

1. A weight matrix is employed to model the importance degree between different knowledge concepts for each exercise, which provide richer information for the cognitive diagnosis process.
2. CWNCD which we proposed has high scalability with the existing cognitive diagnosis method, which can easily improve the previous cognitive diagnosis research that only simulates student-practice interaction in a natural way.
3. We conducted a lot of experiments on real-world data sets to verify the validity and scalability of CWNCD, including quantitative comparison, qualitative analysis and interpretable visualization.

2   Related Work

2.1   Cognitive Diagnosis

Students are the main target of online education. Accurate analysis of students' knowledge states is of great help to understand students' status and construct appropriate teaching plans [12]. For this reason, researchers in educational psychology proposed cognitive diagnosis to conduct a comprehensive analysis of students' knowledge state. Cognitive diagnosis models and analyzes students' interactions, introduces the correlation between exercises and knowledge concepts, and diagnoses the knowledge state of students [13]. Cognitive diagnosis theory originated in the 1950s. After years of development, education Psychologists have proposed several different cognitive diagnosis models. Common cognitive diagnosis models can be divided into single-dimensional continuous model and multi-dimensional discrete model [14]. Here, "dimension" refers to the number of students' abilities (knowledge concepts and skills related to the exercises), and "discrete" "continuous" corresponds to whether the student's skills obtained by the model diagnosis is discrete (0 or 1) or continuous.

IRT is one of the most commonly used one-dimensional continuous cognitive diagnosis models. It assumes that the results of students' responses to exercises obeyed the independently identically distribution, and modeled the knowledge states of each student as a one-dimensional continuous skill. Finally, the characteristics of exercises (discrimination, difficulty, etc.) are combined to model the student's performance.

Among all the multi-dimensional discrete cognitive diagnosis models, the DINA model is one of the most widely used models. For DINA, each exercise can be represented by explicit knowledge concepts, and Q matrix is used to represent the association relationship. As the Q matrix is usually labeled by experts in education field, it has good interpretability.

2.2 Neural Cognitive Diagnosis Framework

NCD employs neural networks to learn complex interactions to obtain accurate and interpretable diagnostic results. Specifically, students and exercises are projected to factor vectors, and their interaction is modeled using multiple neural layers, where the monotonicity assumption is applied to ensure the interpretability of the two factors.

3   Continuous Weighted Neural Cognitive Diagnosis Model

3.1   Task Overview

In this study, there are N Students, M Exercises and K Knowledge concepts in our focused educational scenarios, which can be represented as $S = \{s_1, s_2, \ldots, s_N\}$ $E = \{e_1, e_2, \ldots, e_M\}$ and $K = \{k_1, k_2, \ldots, k_K\}$ respectively. Each student will do some exercises and each exercise is related to some knowledge concepts. Specifically, we define the response logs R as sets of triplet (s, e, r) where $s \in S, e \in E$ and r is the normalized score that student s got in exercise e. In addition, we have Q-matrix (usually labeled by experts) $Q = \{Q_{ij}\}_{M \times K}$ where $Q_{ij} = 1$ if exercise e_i relates to knowledge concept k_j; otherwise, $Q_{ij} = 0$. And in this article, the Q-matrix is additionally influenced by a parametric adjacency matrix $P \in (0, 1)^{M \times K}$, which define the importance degree between different knowledge concepts for each exercise. Now, our cognitive diagnosis task aims to evaluate students' knowledge level on knowledge concepts through the student performance prediction process.

3.2   Neural Cognitive Diagnosis Model

To solve the problem mentioned, we propose CWNCD model, which is illustrated in Fig. 1. Generally, we considered student factors, exercise, factors and the interaction function and use multi-layer neural network to model students' cognitive level. Specifically, corresponding student and exercise are represented as one-hot vectors for each input response log. Then we obtain the diagnostic factors of the student and exercise including knowledge relevancy, cognitive level, knowledge difficulty and exercise discrimination. And as the previous methods (such as NCD) didn't take the importance degree of different knowledge concepts for each exercise into consideration, we specially designed a novel knowledge relevancy matrix to reveal it. Finally, the interactive layers learn the interaction function among the factors and output the student performance prediction. After training, we get students' cognitive vectors as diagnostic results. Details are introduced as follow.

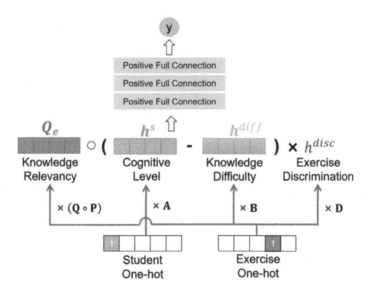

Fig. 1. Neural cognitive diagnosis + model. The color of orange, blue and yellow indicate student factors, exercise factors and interaction function respectively (Color figure online).

Student Factors. Student factors reflect the students' cognitive level of knowledge concepts, which would affect the students' response to exercises. In CWNCD, each student is represented with a continuous knowledge cognition vector h^s, each entry of which is continuous ($[0, 1]$) indicating the student's cognitive level. And h^s is obtained by multiplying the corresponding student's one-hot vector x^s with a trainable matrix A:

$$h^s = \text{sigmoid}(x^s \times A) \tag{1}$$

in which $h^s \in (0, 1)^{1 \times K}$, $x^s \in \{0, 1\}^{1 \times N}$, $A \in \mathbb{R}^{N \times K}$.

Exercise Factors. Exercise factors are divided into three categories.

The first indicates the relationship between exercises and knowledge concepts, which is represented as knowledge relevancy vector Q_e. Q_e has the same dimension as h^s, with the i th entry indicating the relevancy between the exercise and the knowledge concept k_i. In addition, each entry of Q_e is continuous ($[0, 1]$) resulted from the element-wise product between the aforementioned Q-matrix Q and the corresponding trainable parameter matrix P. Specifically, the i th entry of P indicating the importance degree between different knowledge concepts for the i th exercise. For example, $x^e \times P = [0.7, 0.3, 0]$ indicates the first knowledge concept is more significant than the second one, while the third one is not implicit in the corresponding exercise. And x^e is the corresponding student's one-hot vector like x^s. That is,

$$Q_e = x^e \times (Q \circ P) \tag{2}$$

where $Q_e \in (0, 1)^{1 \times K}$, $x^e \in \{0, 1\}^{1 \times M}$, $P \in (0, 1)^{M \times K}$, $\circ$ is element-wise product.

The second indicates knowledge difficulty examined by the exercise, which is represented as knowledge difficulty vector $h^{diff} \in (0, 1)^{1 \times K}$. It can be obtained by:

$$h^{diff} = \text{sigmoid}(x^e \times B), B \in \mathbb{R}^{M \times K} \tag{3}$$

where B is a trainable matrix.

The third indicates the capabilities of the exercise to differentiate multiple cognitive levels, which is represented as exercise discrimination scalar $h^{disc} \in (0, 1)$. It can be obtained by:

$$h^{disc} = \text{sigmoid}(x^e \times D), D \in \mathbb{R}^{M \times 1} \tag{4}$$

where D is a trainable matrix.

Interaction Function. In this part, we use artificial neural network to obtain the interaction function. And we employ the monotonicity assumption to our neural network inspired by some IRT and MIRT models to ensure the interpretation between student and exercise factors, which means the optimization algorithm should increase the student's cognitive level if the model output a wrong prediction during training. So here we restrict each element of W_1, W_2, W_3 to be positive. It can be easily proved that $\frac{\partial y}{\partial h_i^s}$ is positive for each entry h_i^s in h^s. Thus, monotonicity assumption is always satisfied during training. In such case, the first layer of the interaction layers can be intuitively formulated as:

$$x = Q_e \circ \left(h^s - h^{diff} \right) \times h^{disc} \tag{5}$$

where $\circ$ is element-wise product.

Following are two full connection layers and an output layer:

$$f_1 = \text{sigmoid}\left(W_1 \times x^T + b_1\right) \tag{6}$$

$$f_2 = \text{sigmoid}(W_2 \times f_1 + b_2) \tag{7}$$

$$y = \text{sigmoid}(W_3 \times f_2 + b_3) \tag{8}$$

The loss function of CWNCD is cross entropy between output y and true label r:

$$loss_{CDM} = -\sum_i \left(r_i \log y_i + (1 - r_i) \log(1 - y_i)\right) \tag{9}$$

After training, the value of h^s is what we get as diagnosis result, which denotes the student's cognitive level on each knowledge concepts.

4 Experiments

We compare our CWNCD models with some baselines on the student performance prediction task.

4.1 Dataset Description

In the experiments, we used the real-world dataset ASSISTment2009 which contain learners' exercising performance records and exercise-concept correlations. This dataset was collected from ASSISTments system in 2009, which has been widely used in students' performance prediction tasks. ASSISTments is a free public service operated jointly by Worcester Polytechnic Institute and the ASSISTments Foundation which is a non-profit organization sponsored by Worcester Polytechnic Institute created in 2019.

We choose the public corrected version that eliminates the duplicated data issue proposed by previous work [15], and perform a 70%/20%/10% train/test/val split of each student's response log.

4.2 Experimental Setup

We use three full connection layers in CWNCD and the activation function of all layers is Sigmoid. The dimensions of the fully connected layer are (k,512), (512,256) and (256,1), where k is the number of knowledge concept. The dropout function is used between the first full connection layer and the third, we set p = 0.3.

By comparing them with previous approaches, i.e. IRT, MIRT and PMF [16], we have evaluated the performance of our CWNCD models.

4.3   Experimental Results

Table 1. Experimental results on student performance prediction.

ASSISTment2009			
Model	Accuracy	RMSE	AUC
IRT	0.674	0.464	0.685
MIRT	0.701	0.461	0.719
PMF	0.661	0.476	0.732
NCD	0.719	0.439	0.749
CWNCD	**0.889**	**0.302**	**0.762**

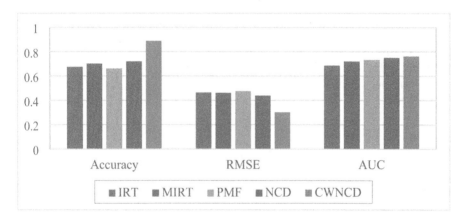

Fig. 2. Histogram of student performance prediction experimental results.

The performance of cognitive diagnostic models is difficult to evaluate because we cannot obtain the true knowledge proficiency of students. Since the diagnosis results are usually obtained by predicting the performance of students in most works, the performance of these prediction tasks can indirectly evaluate the model from one aspect [17]. Considering that all the exercises we use in the data are objective exercises, we use evaluation indicators from the classification and regression aspects, including accuracy, root mean square error (RMSE) [18] and area under the curve (AUC) [19].

Table 1 shows the experimental results of all models on the task of predicting student performance. In addition to the CWNCD, the models involved in the task also include IRT, MIRT, PMF and NCD. From the table, we can observe that the performance of the CWNCD is better than NCD, and it is also better than almost all other baselines. This proves the effectiveness of the Q-matrix method, and also illustrates the importance of the finely estimated knowledge relevance vector for cognitive diagnosis. Figure 2 uses a bar graph to more intuitively show the superiority of the CWNCD model compared to other models.

4.4 Discussion

Through the above experiments, we can observe that the improved NCD model provides more accurate and interpretable results for cognitive diagnosis than the NCD model, but there is still room for further exploration. There is still a long way to study and design a more effective knowledge concept prediction model. Since the knowledge status of students will change in many online self-learning environments, we hope to extend NCD to dynamic cognitive diagnosis. In addition, you can consider using multi-head attention in the model to infer the weight of the relationship between the knowledge concepts, which helps to further reveal the implicit correlation between the knowledge concepts. From the results, we can see that, owing to the ability of modeling the reliance on exercises and knowledge concepts, CWNCD can focus on the relationship between exercises and knowledge concepts, which can contribute to the improvement of the accuracy of student evaluation in the online teaching process.

5 Conclusion

In this paper, we propose a specific CWNCD framework. Generally, we considered student factors, exercise, factors and the interaction function and use multilayer neural network to model students' cognitive level. Specifically, corresponding student and exercise are represented as one-hot vectors for each input response log. Then we obtain the diagnostic factors of the student and exercise. Finally, the interactive layers learn the interaction function among the factors and output the student performance prediction. After training, we get students' cognitive vectors as diagnostic results. The results of extended experiments on real-world data sets show the accuracy and interpretability of our model.

References

1. Piech, C., et al.: Deep knowledge tracing. Adv. Neural Inf. Process. Syst. 505–513 (2015)
2. Zhang, J., Shi, X., King, I., Yeung, D.Y.: Dynamic key-value memory networks for knowledge tracing. In: WWW (2017)
3. Huang, Z., Yin, Y., Chen, E., Xiong, H., Su, Y., Hu, G.: Ekt: exercise-aware knowledge tracing for student performance prediction. IEEE Trans. Knowl. Data Eng. (2019)
4. Dubey, R., Agrawal, J.: An improved genetic algorithm for automated convolutional neural network design. Intell. Autom. Soft Comput. 32, 747–763 (2022)
5. Haq, M.A., Abdul, M.: Dnnbot: deep neural network-based botnet detection and classification. Comput. Mater. Continua 71, 1729–1750 (2022)
6. Ketu, S., Mishra, P.K.: A hybrid deep learning model for covid-19 prediction and current status of clinical trials worldwide. Comput. Mater. Continua 66, 1896–1919 (2021)
7. Deng, C., Zeng, G., Cai, Z., Xiao, X.: A survey of knowledge based question answering with deep learning. J. Artif. Intell. 2, 157–166 (2020)
8. Hussain, S.I., Ruza, N.: Automated deep learning of covid-19 and pneumonia detection using google automl. Intell. Autom. Soft Comput. 31, 1143–1156 (2022)
9. Torre, J.D.L.: Dina model and parameter estimation: a didactic. J. Educ. Behav. Stat. 34(1), 115–130 (2009)

10. Embretson, S.E., Reise, S.P.: Item Response Theory. Psychology Press (2013). https://doi.org/10.4324/9781410605269
11. Wang, F., et al.: Neural cognitive diagnosis for intelligent education systems. AAAI **34**, 6153–6161 (2020)
12. Anderson, T.: The Theory and Practice of Online Learning. Athabasca University Press, Athabasca, Canada (2008)
13. Leighton, J.P., Gierl, M.J.: Cognitive Diagnostic Assessment for Education: Theory and Applications. Cambridge, UK, Cambridge (2008)
14. Dibello, L.V., Roussos, L.A., Stout, W.: A review of cognitively diagnostic assessment and a summary of psychometric models. Handb. Statist. **26**(6), 979–1030 (2006)
15. Xiong, X., Zhao, S., Inwegen, E.V., Beck, J.E.: Going deeper with deep knowledge tracing. Int. Educ. Data Min. Soc. (2018)
16. Salakhutdinov, R., Mnih, A.: Probabilistic matrix factorization. In: Proceedings of the 21st Neural Information Processing Systems, pp. 1257–1264 (2007)
17. Bradley, A.P.: The use of the area under the roc curve in the evaluation of machine learning algorithms. Pattern Recogn. **30**(7), 1145–1159 (1997)
18. Liu, Q., et al.: Fuzzy cognitive diagnosis for modelling examinee performance. ACM Trans. Intell. Syst. Technol. **9**(4), 1–26 (2018)
19. Pei, H., Yang, B., Liu, J., Dong, L.: Group sparse bayesian learning for active surveillance on epidemic dynamics. In: Thirty-Second AAAI Conference on Artificial Intelligence (2018)

User-Oriented Data and Model Privacy Protection Technology

Gengtian Niu[1(✉)], Feng Zhu[1], Zhong Chen[1], Zilu Yang[2], Jiale Chen[2], and Feng Hu[2]

[1] The 28th Research Institute of China Electronics Technology Group Corporation, Nanjing 210007, Jiangsu, China
jsshngtt@163.com

[2] Nanjing University of Aeronautics and Astronautics, Nanjing 211106, Jiangsu, China

Abstract. Machine learning algorithms based on deep neural networks have achieved remarkable results and have been widely used in different fields. Currently, it is necessary to fully solve privacy issues in machine learning systems, and be able to efficiently encrypt and decrypt data involved in calculations. This article aims to provide the intersection of these two fields, and highlight the technologies used to protect data and models. It introduces the privacy protection capabilities of homomorphic encryption for smart algorithms and efficient data encryption and decryption algorithms, and the benefits of user-oriented privacy protection technologies. The research has certain reference significance.

Keywords: Privacy preserving deep learning · Secure multi-party computing · Blowfish algorithm

1 Introduction

Machine learning has proven to be a very effective tool for generating predictive models for a wide range of applications such as medical care, image classification, and finance. As the amount of training data increases, the accuracy of these models becomes better. Machine learning models can obtain large amounts of training data by aggregating data from multiple contributors, but the data involved in machine learning calculations are usually highly confidential and valuable, so it is essential to encrypt the entire process of data storage, data training and data inference. The aim of this paper is to provide the intersection of the two fields of cryptography and machine learning and to highlight the techniques used to protect data and models for intelligent algorithms, the privacy-preserving features of homomorphic encryption for efficient data encryption and decryption algorithms, and the advantages of user-oriented privacy-preserving techniques. The research has some applicability in the military domain.

© The Author(s), under exclusive license to Springer Nature Switzerland AG 2022
X. Sun et al. (Eds.): ICAIS 2022, CCIS 1587, pp. 151–161, 2022.
https://doi.org/10.1007/978-3-031-06761-7_13

2 Intelligent Algorithm-Oriented Homomorphic Encryption for Data Privacy Protection

2.1 Background

Homomorphic encryption is a cryptographic technique based on the computational complexity theory of mathematical puzzles. Homomorphic encrypted data is processed to produce an output that is decrypted in the same way as the original, unencrypted data. Homomorphic encryption is now beginning to be combined with novel computing architectures such as federation learning to secure data in communication transmissions and computational processes. Homomorphic encryption, which processes directly on ciphertext data, frees ciphertext computation from the traditional cumbersome steps of decrypting, then computing, then encrypting large ciphertext data, ensuring both security and computational cost savings.

Secure multi-party computation (MPC) techniques enable mutually untrusted parties to correctly compute any function, while also guaranteeing the privacy of the parties' input and output information. Partial homomorphic encryption (PHE) can be used to assist secure multi-party computation by generating multiplicative triples for auxiliary computation in the SPDZ [1] or ABY [2] protocols without an independent third party, i.e. under the premise of "no independent third party" Under the premise of "no independent third party", partially homomorphic cryptographic algorithms are an indispensable basis for secure multi-party computation and can be used together with secure multi-party computation to accomplish secure intelligent reasoning.

While secure multi-party computing is primarily designed to ensure security at the protocol level and is a common data security technique in collaborative computing, homomorphic encryption uses the qualities of the algorithm itself to ensure the effectiveness of the encryption method. The two are in fact not exact parallel opposites, but rather two concepts in different directions. Homomorphic encryption is more of a cryptographic primitive than secure multi-party computation, and the contrasting secure computation is an advanced protocol, i.e. a protocol constructed from cryptographic primitives.

When designing specific computational tasks, special secure computation protocols may exist with good computational results. However, in the computation of generic functions, homomorphic encryption has a huge efficiency advantage over secure computation. Even though the efficiency of full homomorphic encryption is still not sufficient for daily use, for the computation of arbitrary functions, such as in cloud computing scenarios, the computational efficiency, the complexity of the interaction logic, the communication bandwidth and the communication latency are all far less than for secure multi-party computation.

Secure multi-party computing provides a solution to the privacy protection problem in the N-server model. Model the problem as follows: a set of M data owners wish to use N servers to perform training on their federated data. First, these M participants encrypt their input data and send it to the N servers. Together, these servers run an interactive protocol to generate training models that can be used for inference.

The security requirement is that neither party nor any server can get any information about any other party's training data through analysis. The model is called the

N-server model. The scheme currently focuses on a setting of N = 3, while M can be arbitrary, the scheme is currently set to M = 1.

The trained model can be hidden in any single server party and kept as a secret shared share between servers (or rebuilt to obtain an explicit model). Even if the model is kept secret and shared across N servers, and inference predictions can still be performed on any new input using the trained model, keeping the model, new input and prediction output private to third party servers. The architecture is shown in Fig. 1.

Fig. 1. Homomorphic encryption intelligent reasoning architecture diagram.

2.2 Homomorphic Cryptographic Privacy Protection System for Intelligent Algorithms

Secure, privacy-preserving machine learning inference is constructed by using homomorphic addition and homomorphic multiplication algorithms to construct convolutions, pooling and approximating various activation functions such as Sigmoid, ReLU, Matmul, etc., combined with secure data interaction using secure multi-party computing. The technology is adapted to six machine learning algorithms (including Convolutional Neural Network (CNN), Back Propagation (BP), Logistic Regression, Support Vector Machine (SVM), Linear Regression, and Multilayer Perceptron (MLP)). Under this architecture, the inference side consists of three servers. The user data is automatically encrypted locally and the server side does not need to decrypt it, it is directly calculated on the cipher text and the settlement result is returned to the user, who decrypts it to get the inference result. The user is indifferent to the whole reasoning process. Only the user will decrypt the key during the whole calculation process, which guarantees the security of the whole process.

2.3 Implementation Principles

Paillier homomorphic encryption utilizes the classical Paillier encryption algorithm, which can be oriented to take ciphertext calculations for addition and multiplication. the Paillier homomorphic encryption algorithm is shown in Eq. (1)

$$c = Enc(x, r) = g^x * r^n mod\ n\text{^}2 \tag{1}$$

where (g, n) is used as the encryption public key, r is a random number greater than 0 and less than n, and r is mutually prime with n. g is a random number less than n^2, and n is usually more than 4000 bits, so the overhead of the computation is very large.

Paillier homomorphic addition is calculated as in (2).
Paillier homomorphic addition calculation formula is as (2):

$$Enc(x,r) * Enc(y,s) = \left(g^{x}* r^{n}\bmod n^2\right)*\left(g^{y}* s^{n}\bmod n^2\right)$$
$$= g^{x+y} * (r*s)^{n}\bmod n^2 \tag{2}$$
$$= Enc(x+y, r*s)$$

Paillier homomorphic multiplication calculation formula is as (3):

$$Enc(x,r) \quad w$$
$$= (g^{x} * r^{n}\bmod n^2) \quad w$$
$$= g^{x*w} * (r^{w})^{n}\bmod n^2 \tag{3}$$
$$= Enc(x*w, r{\wedge}w)$$

Once the data has been encrypted, the data is transmitted and interacted with using the well-known SPDZ protocol for secret sharing. The secure multi-party computation (MPC) on which we are based is a cryptographic computation technique that allows multiple parties to work together to securely hide the value of the data itself without affecting the computational functionality.

Specifically, MPC splits a piece of data into multiple encoded parts (secret sharing), without any of the original data being displayed in the sharing itself. Two computational participants perform the same operation on a set of secret shares and then recombine them as if the operation had been performed on the original data.

Secret sharing involves dividing the data into two parts, which are used by both participants, and then recombining these shares to obtain the result. During the computation, the two computational participants usually need to interact, and also with third parties.

The private tensor <x> is split on the user side into two shares (shares), x_0 and x_1, with x = x_0 + x_1, and the two tensors x_0 and x_1 are sent to two servers, S_0 and S_1, to hold them respectively. Having x_0 or x_1 alone is not a threat to the privacy of data x.

The formula for disassembling x = x_0 + x_1 is as follows [10]:

$$x_0 = share1x, r = r\bmod m \tag{4}$$

$$x_1 = share2(x,r) = x - r\bmod m \tag{5}$$

Both r and m are random numbers.

For the specific implementation, we will set up with two party servers (P0, P1) and one auxiliary server (P2), all three of which form the computing cluster. When creating the shared shares specifically, and before performing any operations on the shares, we need to know how the shares will be allocated. To generate a secret share, simply separate the numbers that are to be converted into two values. For example, 5 could be divided into 3 and 2, or 8 and −3. This is done by P2 generating a cryptographically secure random number and then subtracting what is to be shared. Both P0 and P1 will exchange half of their shares with each other, they will then operate with their shares and exchange the results, and then recombine their shares into the final answer. p0 will send a_1 to P1, and P1 will send b_0 to P0. Since P0 does not have access to b_1, it cannot determine the value of b.

Addition is the simplest operation we can perform using secret sharing. Each party adds its share and then exchanges the result. Addition can be described as follows.

$$a + b = (a_0 + a_1) + (b_0 + b_1)$$

We can rearrange this formula using the commutative law of addition and the associative law of addition

$$a + b = (a\_0 + b\_0) + (a\_1 + b\_1)$$

where P0 will solve a_0 + b_0, and P1 will solve a_1 + b_1. This ensures that P0 only obtains part of b, and P1 only obtains part of a.

The parties performing the multiplication need to communicate during the calculation process. We can use the same notation as above to define multiplication using secret sharing.

$$a * b = (a\_0 + a\_1) * (b\_0 + b\_1)$$

This can be expanded to:

$$= (a\_0 * b\_0) + (a\_0 * b\_1) + (a\_1 * b\_0) + (a\_1 * b\_1)$$

We can see that P0 can be responsible for a_0 * b_0, and P1 can be responsible for a_1 * b_1.

However, the middle ((a_0 * b_1) + (a_1 * b_0)) has a problem, because neither party can execute it safely and will expose a and b, which will require each party to have another share. For example, if P0 wants to solve a_0 * b_1, they will need b_1, but they already have b_0, which will allow them to access the value of b. We want to keep P0 secret b.

The solution to this problem is the so-called mask hiding. When the shares need to be covered, we will introduce a new unknown number to all parties. When the shares are finally merged, the mask number will disappear. In order to maintain privacy, we need a third party (P2) to generate these unknown numbers, which will be used to cover up data they do not want to share with the other party. This means that we will block b_1 in P0 and a_0 in P1. We refer to these masks as s and t, and alpha and beta as mask values.

The multiplication of a * b performed by P0 becomes:

$$z\_0 = s * t\_0 + (s\_0 * beta) + (alpha * t\_0) + (alpha * beta)$$

The multiplication performed by P1 becomes:

$$z\_1 = s * t\_1 + (s\_1 * beta) + (alpha * t\_1)$$

We will start with a third party (P2) to create some masking values. P2 generates three new values and then divides them into multiple shares. The first two numbers are random, and the third is the product of these two numbers.

The way to use these values is to subtract them from the original data

$$alpha = (a\_0 - s\_0) + (a\_1 - s\_1)$$

$$beta = (b\_0 - t\_0) + (b\_1 - t\_1)$$

P2 sends the values of s_0 and t_0 to P0, and sends the values of s_1 and t_1 to P1. The values of s_0 and t_0 can take any integer, and the values of s_1 and t_1 can be directly used to subtract s_0 and t_0 from s and t. Then, P0 creates the (a_0 − s_0) part of alpha and the (b_0 − t_0) part of beta respectively, and P1 creates the (a_1 − s_1) part of alpha and the (b_1 − t_1) part of beta respectively. Next, P0 and P1 can exchange their alpha and beta shares without revealing any information about a or b. This is because the true values of a and b are hidden by the value given by P2. Now we are ready to insert these values into the above formula.

Calculation of P0:

$$z\_0 = s * t\_0 + (s\_0 * beta) + (alpha * t_0) + (alpha * beta)$$

Calculation of P1:

$$z\_1 = s * t\_1 + (s\_1 * beta) + (alpha * t\_1)$$

Then we merge the results:

$$z\_0 + z\_1 = a * b$$

In summary, we have demonstrated in a case study that secure interaction of data is achieved by secret sharing. All expressions can be modelled using homomorphic addition and homomorphic multiplication (subtraction is achieved by adding negative numbers instead, and division by multiplying by the inverse). Many machine learning models [11–13] can be further supported by the construction of homomorphic addition and multiplication as well. These two primitives can implement layers such as convolution, pooling and approximate activation functions. This is sufficient for many computer vision algorithms, linear or logistic regression, etc. Specifically in the implementation, the algorithm functions need to be adapted accordingly. CNN, BP, MLP, logistic regression, etc. are mainly rewrites of the activation functions, approximating the differentiable functions in the algorithm by Taylor expansions, keeping them only in a form that can be computed additively and multiplicatively in homomorphic encryption. Linear layers and convolution (essentially matrix multiplication), rectified linear units (ReLU), Maxpool, normalisation, etc. These protocols are compatible with each other and, for a given inference algorithm, can be effectively combined to provide the required secure computational protocol.

2.4   Experimental Evaluation

In verifying the cryptographic inference function of several machine learning algorithms, namely Convolutional Neural Network (CNN), Back Propagation Algorithm (BP), Logistic Regression Algorithm, Support Vector Machine (SVM) and Multilayer Perceptron (MLP), the data used in this scheme is the test set of the MNIST handwritten dataset; in verifying the cryptographic inference function of Linear Regression Algorithm, this scheme uses the test set of the Boston House Price dataset. It is important to emphasise that this scheme transfers the encrypted data to a model that has been transformed and trained for efficient and secure intelligent inference, and therefore does not involve the initial training of the model. The intelligent model is still trained and tuned using plaintext data after its activation function has been transformed, and this stage is beyond the scope of this paper. Lightweight security for the model will be described in detail in a later section. The test set evaluation data is chosen for the experiments to facilitate verification of the correctness of the inference of these algorithms with the addition of homomorphic encryption mechanisms.

In evaluating the performance of five algorithms, including convolutional neural network (CNN), back propagation algorithm (BP), logistic regression algorithm, support vector machine (SVM) and multilayer perceptron (MLP), 200 and 500 MNIST data were predicted and the correct prediction rate was calculated, as shown in Fig. 2; the linear regression algorithm was evaluated by calculating the predicted value and the true value, as shown in Table 1. In terms of inference elapsed time, as shown in Table 2, the batch inference times for the 200 and 500 samples remained at the second level, and the average inference elapsed time for a single sample was approximately 0.67 s. It can be concluded that this homomorphic cryptographic inference mechanism for intelligent algorithms not only provides good performance, but also ensures the security of inference. The accuracy of the predictions and the accuracy of the model are in approximate agreement, and the sample average error rate is within an acceptable range. In military application scenarios, the fast and secure intelligent inference technology will efficiently help combat units to make judgments on battlefield situations without the risk of data theft and tampering.

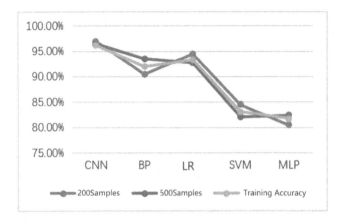

Fig. 2. Encrypted inference performance for intelligent algorithms.

Table 1. Encrypted inference performance for linear regression.

	200 samples	500 samples	Accuracy
Average error rate (%)	3.16%	6.21%	81.5%

Table 2. Performance evaluation of homomorphic encryption computing.

	200 samples	500 samples
Prediction duration (s)	135.4	328.7

3 Efficient Model Privacy Protection Function Based on Blowfish Cryptographic Algorithm

3.1 Lightweight Encryption and Decryption of User Model Data Based on Blowfish

Due to the military application scenario, massive model files not only need to guarantee extremely high security, but also have high requirements for the encryption and decryption performance of massive data. This is one of the bottlenecks that hinder the implementation of cryptographic algorithms.

The user-oriented model data encryption and decryption algorithm design in this project designs a lightweight Blowfish method, which not only guarantees the security of model data encryption through symmetric encryption mechanism, but also meets the platform's efficiency requirements for data encryption storage and decryption reading through multi-threaded computation, segmentation encryption, secret key splitting and S-box bit conversion mechanism. After several tests, the encryption and decryption time of the cryptographic algorithm proposed in this project is less than 999 ms for 100 MB of model data under 1024 bit secret key length, and the encryption and decryption performance reaches millisecond level, which achieves excellent performance in model privacy protection.

3.2   Principle of Optimized Lightweight Blowfish Algorithm

Blowfish algorithm is a 64 bit grouping symmetric encryption algorithm, which uses variable length key for grouping encryption. The main advantages of this algorithm are fast and compact encryption, variable key length, and not easy to crack, etc. Its encryption process is mainly divided into two parts: key processing and data encryption, and due to the nature of its symmetric algorithm, the decryption process is the inverse process of the encryption process.

Key Pre-processing Process. The Blowfish algorithm uses the p-box and s-box of the original key to preprocess the input key. In the encryption process, unlike traditional encryption algorithms, the algorithm does not use the original key for encryption, but uses the two arrays of key_p[18] and key_s[4][256] generated after key preprocessing. The initialization data of the p-box and s-box of the original key is fixed using the fractional part of π assigned to p[18] and s[4][256] every 4 bytes. The advantage of this is that the algorithm does not need to deal directly with very long plaintext segments, but uses a splitting approach to encrypt the spaced plaintext segments and thus obtain the overall ciphertext.

Key Encryption Process. Blowfish algorithm is based on Feistel cryptographic structure, both are symmetric encryption algorithms used for group encryption, because of their symmetric characteristics, the encryption and decryption process of both are almost the same. In the encryption process, the algorithm first groups the plaintext data to be encrypted, and the length of each group is m bit (m = 2n), and for each grouping of plaintext data, it is divided into two equal parts L(m/2) and R(m/2) from the middle; the advantage of multi-threaded computation is that it can encrypt many equal-length plaintext segments in parallel. Assuming that the round function is F and K_i is the subkey of round i, the encryption process of this algorithm is as follows: (1) the plaintext data is divided into two blocks L_0 and R_0 on the left and right; (2) the encryption process of round i depends on the encryption result of round $i - 1$: $L\_i = R\_i - 1$; $R\_i = L\_i - 1$ xor $F(R\_i - 1, K\_i - 1)$.

Key Decryption Process. Due to the symmetric characteristic of Blowfish algorithm, its decryption process is the inverse process of encryption process, so the decryption process should use the same key as the encryption process, and it also needs to preprocess the key before decryption, which can directly use the preprocessing result of the key before encryption to use, and the decryption process only needs to use the value in key_p[] in reverse order to perform the dissimilarity process.

3.3   Performance Comparison Between Blowfish Algorithm and Other Algorithms

DES Algorithm Performance Analysis. DES algorithm is the first encryption technology based on Lucifer algorithm, which is applied to the security protection in various fields as soon as it appears, and it has certain security problems in itself as the first encryption standard. Firstly, the key of traditional DES algorithm is 64 bit, among which there are 8 bit check bits that need to be parity checked, so the actual key length of DES algorithm is only 56 bit, which leads to the short key length of the algorithm, thus leading to low security performance; secondly, DES algorithm will divide the subkeys in the process of generating subkeys, if the two parts after division are all 0 or all This makes the DES algorithm have the problem of weak keys, which greatly reduces the security of the algorithm, and in the existing computer environment, the performance of DES algorithm can no longer meet the needs of data security.

AES Algorithm Performance Analysis. Due to the insecurity of DES algorithm, AES algorithm is proposed as a new generation of encryption standard, as a replacement of DES algorithm, in comparison, AES algorithm has better security, higher algorithm execution efficiency, faster execution speed, whether using software encryption or hardware encryption than DES algorithm, and requires less memory in the process of algorithm execution, which can better save CPU computing resources, so AES algorithm is widely used in the security encryption of data at present.

Blowfish Algorithm Performance Analysis. Blowfish algorithm is a symmetric group encryption algorithm with variable key length, which was first invented in 1994 and has the characteristics of symmetry and variable key length, so the algorithm has high security. Compared with DES and AES algorithms, Blowfish algorithm takes up very little CPU resources and memory, and the comprehensive performance is also optimal. Some scholars have used 3DES algorithm to encrypt a 6 MB file, after finishing the encryption of the 6 MB file, nearly 45% of the remaining power of the encryption device was used up, which shows that the 3DES algorithm consumes great computing resources. This makes the key of Blowfish algorithm almost unanalyzable. Meanwhile, Blowfish algorithm uses variable length key in the range of 32–448 bits, which also makes it almost impossible to crack Blowfish algorithm by exhaustive cracking, so Blowfish algorithm has high security.

A more authoritative result on the performance comparison of the above cryptographic algorithms is published by Professor Nathan Bell of Google and Professor Michael Garland, Senior Research Director of NIVIDA, in the paper [9], which has been cited by Google nearly 900 times and is currently used as the main reference in major cryptographic research organizations and has a high influence in the cryptographic field.

The two professors in this literature used the single-threaded CPU versions of DES, 3DES, AES, and Blowfish algorithms to encrypt and decrypt 256M of data respectively, and the statistical encryption and decryption times are shown in Table 2. It can be seen that Blowfish algorithm has the fastest encryption speed and higher security performance. Therefore, Blowfish algorithm is used in this project to achieve fast encryption and decryption of user model data, which has high utilization efficiency while ensuring privacy.

4 Conclusion

Machine learning algorithms based on homomorphic encryption as a breakthrough in artificial intelligence effectively combine intelligent computing and privacy protection, and have very important uses in military battlefield, medical and financial. The efficient BlowFish algorithm has good performance for encryption and decryption of large-scale user data and model data. The development and application of user-oriented data and model privacy protection technology is of strategic importance for China to promote scientific and technological progress and implement the integration of industrialization and informatization.

References

1. Sharma, S., Xing, C., Liu, Y., Kang, Y.: Secure and efficient federated transfer learning. In: 2019 IEEE International Conference on Big Data (Big Data), pp. 2569–2576 (2019)
2. Wu, Y., et al.: Efficient server-aided secure two-party computation in heterogeneous mobile cloud computing. IEEE Trans. Dependable Secure Comput. **18**, 2820–2834 (2021)
3. Nam, M., Kim, J., Nam, B.: Parallel tree traversal for nearest neighbor query on the GPU. In: 45th International Conference on Parallel Processing (ICPP), pp. 113–122 (2016)
4. Anish, D.J.: Usage of botnets for high speed MD5 hash cracking. In: Third International Conference on Innovative Computing Technology (INTECH 2013), pp. 314–320 (2013)
5. Houshmand, S., Aggarwal, S., Flood, R.: Next gen PCFG password cracking. IEEE Trans. Inf. Forensics Secur. **10**, 1776–1791 (2015)
6. Karale, S.N., Pendke, K., Dahiwale, P.: The survey of various techniques & algorithms for SMS security. In: 2015 International Conference on Innovations in Information, Embedded and Communication Systems (ICIIECS), pp. 1–6 (2015)
7. Dang, T.N., Vo, H.M.: Advanced AES algorithm using dynamic key in the internet of things system. In: 2019 IEEE 4th International Conference on Computer and Communication Systems (ICCCS), pp. 682–686 (2019)
8. Barbosa, F.M., Vidal, A.R.S.F., Almeida, H.L.S., Mello, F.L.D.: Machine learning applied to the recognition of cryptographic algorithms used for multimedia encryption. IEEE Lat. Am. Trans. **15**(7), 1301–1305 (2017)
9. Maggioni, M., Berger-Wolf, T.: AdELL: an adaptive warp-balancing ELL format for efficient sparse matrix-vector multiplication on GPUs. In: 2013 42nd International Conference on Parallel Processing, pp. 11–20 (2013)
10. Kapadiya, V.J., Desai, L.S., Meghrajani, Y.K.: Boolean-based multi secret sharing scheme using meaningful shares. In: 2018 Second International Conference on Inventive Communication and Computational Technologies (ICICCT), pp. 840–844 (2018)
11. Nithyanantham, S., Singaravel, G.: Hybrid deep learning framework for privacy preservation in geo-distributed data centre. Intell. Autom. Soft Comput. **32**(3), 1905–1919 (2022)
12. Wazirali, R.: A review on privacy preservation of location-based services in internet of things. Intell. Autom. Soft Comput. **31**(2), 767–779 (2022)
13. Alotaibi, L.S., Alshamrani, S.S.: Smart contract: security and privacy. Comput. Syst. Sci. Eng. **38**(1), 93–101 (2021)

DICDP: Deep Incomplete Clustering with Distribution Preserving

Mingjie Luo[1], Siwei Wang[1], Chengyu Wang[1], Wei Chen[2], En Zhu[1(✉)], and Xinwang Liu[1]

[1] National University of Defense Technology, Changsha, China
{luomingjie13,wangsiwei13,chengyu,enzhu,xinwangliu}@nudt.edu.cn
[2] School of Computer Science, University of Birmingham, Birmingham, UK
wxc795@cs.bham.ac.uk

Abstract. Clustering is a fundamental task in the computer vision and machine learning community. Although various methods have been proposed, the performance of existing approaches drops dramatically when handling incomplete high-dimensional data (which is common in real world applications). To solve the problem, we propose a novel deep incomplete clustering method, named <u>D</u>eep <u>I</u>ncomplete <u>C</u>lustering with <u>D</u>istribution <u>P</u>reserving (DICDP). To avoid insufficient sample utilization in existing methods limited by few fully-observed samples, we propose to measure distribution distance with the optimal transport for reconstruction evaluation instead of traditional pixel-wise loss function. Moreover, the clustering loss of the latent feature is introduced to regularize the embedding with more discrimination capability. As a consequence, the network becomes more robust against missing features and the unified framework which combines clustering and sample imputation enables the two procedures to negotiate to better serve for each other. Extensive experiments demonstrate that the proposed network achieves superior and stable clustering performance improvement against existing state-of-the-art incomplete clustering methods over different missing ratios.

Keywords: Incomplete clustering · Optimal transport

1 Introduction

Clustering is one of the fundamental and important unsupervised learning tasks in data science, image analysis and machine learning community [1,10,14–16, 21,27,29,33,34]. A wide variety of data clustering methods have been proposed to organise similar items into same groups and achieve promising performance, e.g., k-means clustering, Gaussian Mixture Model (GMM), spectral clustering

Supplementary Information The online version contains supplementary material available at https://doi.org/10.1007/978-3-031-06761-7_14.

X. Sun et al. (Eds.): ICAIS 2022, CCIS 1587, pp. 162–175, 2022.
https://doi.org/10.1007/978-3-031-06761-7_14

and deep clustering recently. However, existing clustering approaches all hold one premise that the data themselves are complete while data with missing features are quite common in reality. Data incompleteness occurs due to many factors, e.g. sensor failure, unfinished collection and data storage corruption [6]. When facing with various types of missing features, incomplete data clustering has drawn increasing attention in recent years [13–15,24,25,30]

Existing incomplete clustering can be roughly categorized into two mechanisms, **heuristic-based** and **learning-based** respectively. Both of them firstly impute the missing features and then the full data matrix can be applied with traditional clustering algorithms. The heuristic imputation methods often rely on statistic property, e.g., zero-filling (ZF) and mean-filling (MF) after normalizing. But when facing with complex high-dimensional data, heuristic-based methods perform poorly since the simple imputations cannot obtain enough information to precisely recover data.

Recently, learning-based imputation methods receive enormous attention and become to be the mainstream. Existing work can be categorized into shallow and deep learning framework. The shallow representatives normally assume that the data are low-rank and therefore apply iterative methods to recover missing values [4,9,17,20,26]. With the improvements of deep learning architectures, various deep networks have been proposed to handle incompleteness. Variants of generation-style networks are introduced including Generative Adversarial Networks (GAN) and Variational Auto-Encoder (VAE). Followed this line, enormous GAN and VAE-based approaches are put forward to minimizing the distances between real values and imputed matrices [18,31,32].

Although these aforementioned methods offer solutions for incomplete data clustering, several drawbacks in existing mechanism cannot be neglected: i) Existing incomplete clustering methods follow a two-step manner, where the imputation stage and the clustering stage are separated from each other. In other words, the imputed features are not designed for clustering task, which may heavily degrade the clustering performance in return. ii) When facing with high-dimensional data (e.g., images, text), both of the shallow and deep methods perform poorly due to the insufficient observed information with inaccurate imputation. These results in sharp degradation in clustering task performance.

In this paper, we propose a novel deep incomplete clustering method, which we refer as Deep Incomplete Clustering with Distribution Preserving (DICDP), that generalizes the well-known Deep Embedding Clustering network (DEC) to handle missing features. Different from existing pixel-by-pixel reconstruction in traditional autoencoder, we propose to minimize the Wasserstein distance between observed data and the reconstructed data with optimal transport. By optimizing the novel network, the distribution of original data can be well-preserved and in return the missing features can be more accurately imputed by guidance of latent clustering structures. Thus, the proposed DICDP simultaneously utilizes the imputation and the embedded clustering procedures so that they can be jointly negotiated with each other. Finally, the proposed DICDP is showcased in extensive experiments on a wide variety of benchmarks with different missing ratios, to evaluate its effectiveness. As demonstrated, the proposed network enjoys superior clustering performance in comparison with existing state-of-the-art imputation methods by large margins.

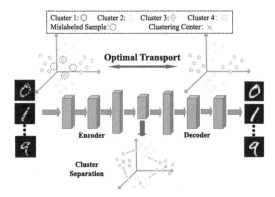

Fig. 1. The framework of the proposed DICDP. Instead of pixel-to-pixel reconstruction, we impute features by minimizing the distribution distance with optimal transport. Moreover, the latent embedding representations are regularized with clustering loss to ensure intra-cluster discrimination. The joint loss functions seamlessly negotiate incomplete imputation and clustering tasks as a unified framework to improve the performance of each other.

The contributions of our DICDP are summarized as follows,

1. We mathematically analyze the failures of existing incomplete clustering methods in theory when facing with high-dimensional data. To avoid insufficient training brought by the spareness of full-observed data, a novel end-to-end deep clustering network is proposed to minimize the wasserstein distances between original and reconstructed distribution.
2. We regularize the latent distribution with more discriminate separation to further enhance task performance. By the guidance of the unified loss function, the network decodes the informative latent representations contributing to better recovery and clustering. To the best of our knowledge, this could be the first work of end-to-end deep incomplete clustering network.
3. Comprehensive experiments are conducted on six high-dimensional benchmarks datasets with various incomplete ratios. As the experimental results show, the proposed network significantly outperforms state-of-the-art incomplete clustering methods by large margins.

2   Related Work

2.1   Statistical Imputation

Basic statistical methods try to utilize information from the missing data by the means of numerical property. Most of them use statistical attributes to estimate the missing feature values, rather than directly discard incomplete feature information. Incomplete entries are filled with constants to obtain complete data so that they can be directly applied to machine learning tasks, e.g., zero, mean and median. Additionally, KNN imputation method has been considered as an alternative estimating the missing features with the mean of k nearest reliable neighbors [2]. The Bayesian framework considers the joint and conditional distribution for dealing with incomplete features. These frames are generally expressed in terms of a maximum-likelihood method, which estimate missing values with the most probable numbers. The most popular method of Bayesian framework is the Expectation Maximization (EM) algorithm [3,5].

2.2 Deep Incomplete Clustering

Although deep clustering mechanism has received much attention in recent years, none of existing methods has considered to cluster with incomplete features in an end-to-end manner yet. They propose to fill missing values through neural networks and then apply clustering algorithms on the estimated dataset. GAIN [31] firstly proposes to impute incomplete features with GAN. Different from the traditional GAN networks, the goal of the discriminator in GAIN is to accurately distinguish whether the data are imputed or real. Unfortunately, the same problems as common GANs, these models are generally difficult to train since the optimization processes are hardly stable. Apart from GAN-like networks, VAEAC [8] proposes a neural probabilistic model based on variational autoencoder, which can estimate the observed features using stochastic gradient variational inference [11]. However these VAE-based method may lead to poor results when the posterior approximation of variational inference is far from the actual posterior approximation. In addition, based on fitting the conditional distribution of the missing data, a Markov chain Monte Carlo (MCMC) scheme has been developed in [23].

2.3 Deep Incomplete Clustering

Let $\alpha = \sum_{i=1}^{n} a_i \delta_{\mathbf{X}_i}$, $\beta = \sum_{i=1}^{n} b_i \delta_{\mathbf{Y}_i}$ be two discrete distributions formed by empirical given data samples $\mathbf{X}, \mathbf{Y}$, and their supports $\mathbf{X} \in \mathbb{R}^{n \times d}, \mathbf{Y} \in \mathbb{R}^{n' \times d}$ and frequency vectors $\mathbf{a}, \mathbf{b}$. It can be easily obtained that $\mathbf{a}^\top \mathbf{1} = 1, \mathbf{a} \geq 0, \mathbf{b}^\top \mathbf{1} = 1, \mathbf{b} \geq 0$. The q-th Wasserstein distance corresponds to these two distributions α and β is denoted as follows,

$$W_q(\alpha, \beta) \stackrel{\text{def}}{=} \min_{\mathbf{P} \in U(\mathbf{a},\mathbf{b})} \langle \mathbf{F}, \mathbf{C} \rangle, \tag{1}$$

where $U(\mathbf{a}, \mathbf{b}) \stackrel{\text{def}}{=} \left\{ \mathbf{F} \in \mathbb{R}_+^{n \times n'} : \mathbf{F1} = \mathbf{a}, \mathbf{F}^\top \mathbf{1}_n = \mathbf{b} \right\}$ and $\mathbf{C} = (\|x_i - y_j\|^q)_{ij} \in \mathbb{R}^{n \times n'}$ denotes as the cost matrix of pairwise squared distances between the support sets. In our paper, we set $q = 2$. The Wasserstein distance denoted in Eq. (1) is often jointly introduced with an entropy regularization,

$$W_q^\epsilon(\alpha, \beta) \stackrel{\text{def}}{=} \min_{\mathbf{F} \in U(\mathbf{a},\mathbf{b})} \langle \mathbf{F}, \mathbf{C} \rangle - \epsilon h(\mathbf{F}), \tag{2}$$

where $h(\mathbf{F}) \stackrel{\text{def}}{=} -\sum_{ij} f_{ij} \log f_{ij}$ denotes the entropy regularization. Equation (2) can be efficiently optimized using Sinkhorn algorithm [22]. Based on Eq. (2), a symmetric divergence can be represented as

$$S_\epsilon(\alpha, \beta) \stackrel{\text{def}}{=} \text{OT}_\epsilon(\alpha, \beta) - \frac{1}{2} \left(\text{OT}_\epsilon(\alpha, \alpha) + \text{OT}_\epsilon(\beta, \beta) \right). \tag{3}$$

The Sinkhorn divergence in Eq. (3) offers a tractable alternative for Wasserstein distance calculations, and easily be accelerated by GPU. In our paper, we use the sinkhorn divergence to measure the optimal transport distance of two distributions.

3   DICDP

3.1   Motivation

Problem Analysis. Although the aforementioned methods have been proposed to solve incomplete data clustering to some extent, most of them are evaluated with very small-dimensional data and make them unpractical in real scenarios. When facing with high-dimensional data (e.g., images, text), both of the existing shallow and deep methods perform poorly due to the insufficient observed information with inaccurate imputation. We theoretically analyze this phenomenon with the following Theorem 1.

Theorem 1. *Suppose the data are i.i.d (independently and identically distributed), a fully-observed high-dimensional data sample exists with low probability when facing incompleteness.*

Proof. Suppose the missing ratio is $p(0 \le p \le 1)$. Given a matrix $\mathbf{X} \in \mathbb{R}^{n \times d}$. For each sample x_i, we can obtain the following equation.

$$P(\mathbf{X}_{i1}, \ldots, \mathbf{X}_{id}) = P(\mathbf{X}_{i1}) \cdots P(\mathbf{X}_{id}) = (1 - p)^d, \tag{4}$$

where $P(\mathbf{X}_{i1})$ denotes the probability $\mathbf{X}_{i1}$ can be observed.

Taking $p = 0.1, d = 300$ as an example, with 10^{-14} probability the sample x_i can be fully-observed. With the increasing dimension d, the probability becomes smaller and approximates 0. This completes the proof.

Theorem 1 illustrates that very few samples are fully complete when the dimensions are relatively high. Therefore, the traditional statistical and deep generative methods fail to impute proper values lacking of sufficient information, e.g., knn-filling and GAN-style solutions. In [19], the Wasserstein distance is firstly applied to impute missing features where the assumption is to minimize the discrepancy of missing data distribution and the complete data distribution. In the low-dimensional incomplete setting (less than 50), the experiments results are promising and proven to show more stable along with change of the incomplete ratios. However, as confronting with much higher dimension data types (e.g., images, videos and text), very few fully-complete data can be obtained making the empirical estimation of target distribution (complete data distribution) difficult and inaccurate. Therefore these methods perform poorly in downstream clustering tasks (see results in Table 1).

Different from existing assumptions, we propose to jointly solve the two processes in a unified framework: reconstruction and clustering. The natural way of reconstruction is to apply autoencoder models. The observed values can be regraded as 'supervised' signals for the reconstruction. However, with few informative information, it is not reasonable to only reconstruct the missing counterparts since the reconstruction may destroy the geometry distribution features for the data and the clustering performance is heavily affected. In this paper, we decide to recover the latent distribution instead of pixel-level approximation. Specially, we adopt the latent variable models defined by an encoder-decoder manner, where we firstly encode original data x_i into the latent code z_i in the latent space $\mathcal{Z}$ and then z_i is decoded to the reconstructed image $\hat{x}_i$. This process can be expressed as,

$$p_{\hat{X}}(\hat{x}) := \int_{\mathcal{Z}} p_{p_{\hat{X}}(\hat{x}|z)}(\hat{x}|z)p_z(z)dz, \quad \forall x \in \mathcal{X} \tag{5}$$

where $p_x(z|x), p_{\hat{X}}(\hat{x}|z)$ are parameterized with the encoder f_e and decoder f_d network. Then the distribution-preserving loss can be measured with Eq. (3) respecting to p_X and $p_{\hat{X}}$,

$$L_s(\mathbf{X}, \hat{\mathbf{X}}) = S_\epsilon(\mathbf{X}, f_d(f_e(\mathbf{X}))). \tag{6}$$

3.2 Overall Network Architecture

In this section, we leverage the one-stage deep incomplete clustering introduced in the previous section as a basis to demonstrate the process of the proposed learning algorithm, the overall flowchart is illustrated in Fig. 1. The proposed clustering model consists of three parts, an encoder, a decoder, and a soft clustering layer, specifically, the method relies on a linear combination based on two objective functions, representing the optimal transport distance and clustering loss respectively. The joint optimization process can be described as follows:

$$L = L_s + \gamma L_c, \tag{7}$$

where L_s is the sinkhorn divergence shown in Eq. (3) and L_c is the clustering loss. γ is a hyper-parameter, which is used to balance the two costs. Consider a dataset $\mathbf{X}$ with n samples, and each $x_i \in \mathbb{R}^d$ where d is the dimension. The number of clusters k is known, for each input data x_i we denote the nonlinear mapping $f_e : x_i \rightarrow z_i$ and $f_d : z_i \rightarrow \hat{x}_i$ where z_i is the low dimensional feature space, $\hat{x}_i$ is the complete data learned through the network.

The clustering loss is defined as KL divergence between distributions $\mathbf{P}$ and $\mathbf{Q}$ proposed in [28], where $\mathbf{P}$ is the soft assignment of the distribution $\mathcal{Z}$:

$$p_{ij} = \frac{\left(1 + \|z_i - \mu_j\|^2\right)^{-1}}{\sum_j \left(1 + \|z_i - \mu_j\|^2\right)^{-1}}, \tag{8}$$

and then the cluster assignment can be obtained $s_i = \arg\max_j p_{ij}$. Then $\mathbf{Q}$ is the target distribution derived from $\mathbf{P}$,

$$q_{ij} = \frac{p_{ij}^2 / \sum_i p_{ij}}{\sum_j \left(p_{ij}^2 / \sum_i p_{ij}\right)}. \tag{9}$$

Therefore, the clustering loss is defined as

$$L_c = KL(\mathbf{Q}\|\mathbf{P}) = \sum_i \sum_j q_{ij} \log \frac{q_{ij}}{p_{ij}}. \tag{10}$$

We summarize the merits of our proposed framework with the following factors: i) more naturally handle with incomplete clustering in high-dimensional space. The L_s loss accomplishes the reconstruction samples with preserving geometry characteristics. ii) more flexible that does not require the prior distribution of $\mathbf{X}$ or $\mathbf{Z}$. Instead of explicit distribution formulation, our encoder and decoder network implicitly estimate the latent distribution with more flexibility; iii) regularizing the latent distribution q with more discriminate separation to further enhance task performance. As the empirical experimental results show, the guidance of the joint loss function updates the network leading to the improvement of clustering performance. The full training procedure is summarized in Algorithm 1.

4   Experiments

4.1   Experiments Setup

Datasets. In this paper, we conduct extensive experiments on the six widely-used large-scale benchmark datasets. (1) **MNIST-full** and **Fashion-MNIST** [12]: 70000 images including the training and testing split are combined into a unified dataset. (2) **USPS** [7]: This dataset contains a total of 9298 grayscale samples with 16 × 16 pixels. (3) **COIL-20**: COIL-20 consists of 1440 images of 20 objects taken by cameras from varying angles. (4) **Reuters-10K**: We used 4 root categories: corporate/industrial, government/social, markets and economics as labels and excluded all documents with multiple labels. We randomly sampled a subset of 10000 examples and computed features on the 2000 most frequent words. We term this dataset as Reuters-10K. (5) **Letter**: The Letter dataset merges a balanced set of the 26 letters with 800 images each class.

Followed by existing incomplete clustering task setting, we set seven groups of incomplete ratios as $\{0.1, 0.2, 0.3, \cdots 0.6, 0.7\}$ for each dataset in our experiments. Incomplete ration means the percentage of missing features in all samples.

Algorithm 1. DICDP

Input: Missing data $\mathbf{X}_m$; Cluster number k; Hyper-parameter λ; Batchsize N; Maximum iterations $MaxIter$; Stopping threshold δ; Learning rate η.

Output: Clustering Assignment $\mathbf{S}$.

1: Initialize $\mathbf{X}_m$ with mean filling.
2: Initialize clustering centroids u.
3: **for** $iter = 0$ to $Maxiter$ **do**
4:      **for** $i = 0$ to $\lfloor n/N \rfloor$ **do**
5:          Sample a minibatch $\{x_i\}_{i=1}^m$ from $\mathbf{X}$.
6:          Compute related variables by $z_i = f_e(x_i)$, $\hat{x}_i =$
7:          $f_d(z_i)$.
8:          Compute P_i, Q_i using Eq. (8) and Eq. (9)
9:          Compute clustering assignment for $\{x_i\}_{i=1}^m$.
10:         Compute overall loss L by Eq. (7).
11:         Back-propagation and update model weights.
12:      **end for**
13:      Compute $Z = f_e(\mathbf{X})$.
14:      Compute $\mathbf{P}$ and $\mathbf{Q}$.
15:      Compute clustering assignment $\mathbf{S}$.
16:      **if** $sum(\mathbf{S}_{iter+1} \neq \mathbf{S}_{iter})/n < \delta$ **then**
17:          Stop training.
18:      **end if**
19: **end for**

Evaluation Metrics. In our experiments, we used three standard clustering performance metrics for evaluation: (1) **Accuracy (ACC)** is computed by assigning each cluster with the dominating class label and taking the average correct classification rate as the final score, (2) **Normalised Mutual Information (NMI)** quantifies the normalised mutual dependence between the predicted labels and the ground-truth, and (3) **Purity** measures the proportion of the number of samples correctly clustered to the total number of samples.

4.2 Compared SOTA Methods

(1) **Mean-Filling (MF)**: The missing features are imputed with the mean of the observed values in the corresponding dimensions. (2) **Mean-Filling (MF)**: The missing features are imputed with zeros in the normalized data matrix. (3) **Low-rank Completion (LRC)** [20]: The method attempts to recover data matrix with low-rank assumption. (4) **Max Norm Completion (MNC)** [4]: MNC adopts the max-norm to complete missing features. (5) **Factor Group-Sparse Regularization for Efficient Low-Rank Matrix Recovery (FSGR)** [4] The author proposes factor group-sparse regularizers to accomplish low-rank matrix completion task. (6) **GAIN** [31]: **Missing data imputing using Generative Adversarial Nets**. It proposes a method that uses GAN to estimate and complete the work of filling missing values. (7) **VAEAC:** [8] **Variational Autoencoder with Arbitrary Conditioning**. It is a latent variable model

trained using stochastic gradient variational Bayes. (8) **MIVAE** [18]: MIWAE is based on the importance-weighted autoencoder, and maximises a potentially tight lower bound of the log-likelihood of the observed data. (9) **MDIOT** [19]: **Missing Data Imputing using Optimal Transport.** This paper leverages OT to define a loss function for missing data distribution and complete data distribution. The hyper-parameters used in all our comparative experiments follow their corresponding papers.

For all the compared methods above, we have downloaded their public implementations with Matlab and Pytorch. All our experiments are conducted on desktop computer with Intel i7-9700K CPU @ 3.60 GHz × 12, 64 GB RAM and GeForce RTX 3090 25GB.

4.3   Results Comparisons to Alternative Methods

In this section, we deeply analyze the clustering performance regarding to various ratios and the evolution of the learned representation. Table 1 shows the aggregated clustering comparison of the above algorithms on the benchmark datasets. The best results are highlighted with boldface and '–' means the out of GPU memory failure. Based on the results, we have the following observations:

1. Our proposed method outperforms all the SOTA imputation competitors in clustering performance by large margins. For example, our algorithm surpasses the second best by **53.9%, 15.7%, 14.8%, 23.6%, 10%** and **28.1%**, in terms of ACC on all benchmark datasets. In particular, the margins for the four datasets (Mnist, Usps, Reuters and Letter) are very impressive. These results clearly verify the effectiveness of the proposed network.
2. Comparing with the generative-style methods, the proposed DICDP consistently further improves the clustering performance and achieves better results among the benchmark datasets. GAIN, VAEAC and MIWAE are the chosen representative methods. As can be seen, they concentrate on the generation or imputation task while ignoring the impacts of downstream clustering procedure. The joint optimization framework further contributes to improving performance.
3. MDIOT has been considered as a strong baseline for incomplete data imputation. It outperforms other competitors among most of the datasets. Our proposed algorithm surpasses MDIOT by **54.9%, 15.7%,17.5%, 42.7%,12.4%** and **33.7%** in terms of ACC on all benchmark datasets. The phenomenon demonstrates the effectiveness of the proposed architecture. Regardless of directly computing distribution distances in original space, the bottleneck of our embedding layer serves for clustering task and make distributions more discriminate.

In order to show the comparison between different methods more clearly, we draw the ACC of compared methods under different missing rates as line graphs as shown in Fig. 2 and illustrates different imputation performance of the competing method in Fig. 3.

From the Fig. 2, we can obtain the following observations: **(1)** As can be seen, with the incomplete ratios increasing, all the methods suffers the degradation of clustering performance due to more unavailable information. Especially for the generative-based methods (VAEAC and MDIOT), their performance drops sharply due to inaccurate imputations. **(2)** The results of our proposed method in terms of ACC are higher than all the competing algorithms for different incomplete ratios. Moreover, our method achieves stable performance against the increasing incomplete ratios. These results clearly demonstrates the effectiveness of DICDP. In addition, **(3)** The relative NMI and Purity performance of the compared methods are omitted due to space limit and provided in supplementary materials. As can be seen, the clustering performance results are consistent with the ACC observations.

Table 1. The aggregated ACC, NMI and Purity comparison (mean ± std) of different algorithms on benchmark datasets. '–' means out of the GPU memory. The detailed results are omitted due to space limit and provided in supplementary materials.

Method	Shallow					Deep				
Dataset	MF	ZF	LRC	MNC	FSGR	GAIN	VAEAC	MIWAE	MDIOT	Ours
ACC (%)										
Mnist	54.66 ± 3.13	52.48 ± 3.33	51.82 ± 3.46	53.28 ± 3.08	53.22 ± 2.97	52.05 ± 3.06	53.73 ± 3.63	–	54.31 ± 3.46	$\mathbf{84.16 \pm 0.35}$
Usps	61.63 ± 3.92	60.72 ± 3.24	61.78 ± 3.63	61.80 ± 3.61	60.22 ± 3.38	60.20 ± 3.11	61.90 ± 3.51	48.75 ± 4.73	63.63 ± 4.07	$\mathbf{73.61 \pm 0.23}$
Fmnist	51.14 ± 3.87	49.56 ± 3.84	51.70 ± 3.75	51.56 ± 3.44	52.12 ± 4.16	50.75 ± 4.39	52.04 ± 4.05	–	50.91 ± 3.54	$\mathbf{59.85 \pm 0.38}$
Reuters	56.26 ± 11.67	50.96 ± 9.15	53.79 ± 5.48	54.17 ± 5.27	53.72 ± 5.47	51.25 ± 9.49	60.22 ± 8.62	54.51 ± 10.00	52.18 ± 8.21	$\mathbf{74.45 \pm 0.20}$
COIL20	54.33 ± 4.95	42.77 ± 5.86	58.73 ± 4.56	59.10 ± 4.47	55.00 ± 4.74	55.10 ± 4.42	60.21 ± 4.22	57.87 ± 5.13	58.95 ± 4.67	$\mathbf{66.25 \pm 0.17}$
Letter	35.77 ± 1.22	33.40 ± 1.47	36.95 ± 1.36	33.68 ± 1.53	37.34 ± 1.05	35.54 ± 1.23	36.11 ± 1.32	27.42 ± 0.91	35.40 ± 1.39	$\mathbf{47.33 \pm 0.33}$
NMI (%)										
Mnist	47.82 ± 1.42	45.48 ± 1.53	46.07 ± 1.59	46.55 ± 1.36	46.57 ± 1.27	46.06 ± 1.31	47.62 ± 1.19	–	49.62 ± 1.07	$\mathbf{76.74 \pm 0.19}$
Usps	58.51 ± 3.92	55.89 ± 3.24	57.56 ± 3.63	58.02 ± 3.61	56.21 ± 3.38	57.54 ± 1.51	58.32 ± 1.25	44.60 ± 4.38	62.33 ± 1.37	$\mathbf{70.14 \pm 0.13}$
Fmnist	49.83 ± 3.87	47.03 ± 3.84	49.98 ± 3.75	50.07 ± 3.44	50.19 ± 4.16	50.55 ± 1.16	49.93 ± 1.08	–	49.49 ± 1.03	$\mathbf{61.21 \pm 0.17}$
Reuters	26.37 ± 11.67	21.41 ± 9.15	26.43 ± 5.48	27.37 ± 5.27	25.82 ± 5.47	21.26 ± 9.94	31.99 ± 8.04	23.71 ± 9.67	22.28 ± 11.42	$\mathbf{44.37 \pm 0.19}$
COIL20	68.89 ± 4.95	55.75 ± 5.86	73.38 ± 4.56	74.05 ± 4.47	70.22 ± 4.74	69.14 ± 2.67	74.36 ± 2.38	71.72 ± 2.64	73.43 ± 2.10	$\mathbf{76.68 \pm 0.19}$
Letter	37.58 ± 1.22	34.79 ± 1.47	39.18 ± 1.36	35.06 ± 1.53	39.43 ± 1.05	37.98 ± 0.57	$38.56 \pm 0,57$	30.045 ± 0.63	37.45 ± 0.72	$\mathbf{51.82 \pm 0.18}$
Purity (%)										
Mnist	58.37 ± 1.62	56.64 ± 2.21	57.35 ± 1.79	57.96 ± 1.83	58.09 ± 1.81	56.78 ± 1.89	57.91 ± 1.57	–	59.28 ± 1.47	$\mathbf{84.03 \pm 0.35}$
Usps	69.40 ± 2.47	67.74 ± 2.74	69.11 ± 2.47	69.55 ± 2.00	67.70 ± 2.29	67.72 ± 2.34	69.36 ± 2.45	55.40 ± 5.35	71.35 ± 2.77	$\mathbf{80.04 \pm 0.13}$
Fmnist	56.09 ± 2.20	53.03 ± 2.84	56.71 ± 2.22	56.61 ± 2.42	57.15 ± 1.52	55.98 ± 2.16	56.62 ± 1.87	–	56.27 ± 1.88	$\mathbf{64.34 \pm 0.52}$
Reuters	74.71 ± 5.10	74.21 ± 4.97	78.41 ± 4.08	$\mathbf{78.97 \pm 3.59}$	77.79 ± 3.91	73.78 ± 5.12	78.18 ± 3.94	74.43 ± 4.99	73.67 ± 4.76	75.49 ± 0.15
COIL20	58.03 ± 5.49	45.63 ± 4.97	63.25 ± 3.93	63.96 ± 4.09	59.38 ± 3.83	58.77 ± 4.19	64.63 ± 4.16	61.30 ± 4.04	63.48 ± 3.67	$\mathbf{69.85 \pm 0.19}$
Letter	37.90 ± 1.01	35.23 ± 1.89	39.30 ± 1.02	35.49 ± 1.67	39.76 ± 0.99	38.12 ± 0.99	38.68 ± 0.88	29.04 ± 0.83	37.66 ± 1.14	$\mathbf{50.06 \pm 0.34}$

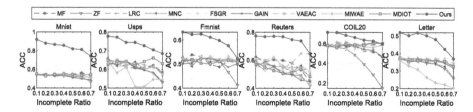

Fig. 2. The clustering results of ACC metric on the benchmark datasets with different incomplete ratios. The results of NMI and Purity are provided in supplementary materials due to space limit.

In addition, Fig. 3 illustrates the complete data and the imputation performance of the competing method with 30% missing rate on the Mnist. Images
along rows (a) and (b) contains the complete data images and initialized data
images which represents mean-imputed data at 30% missing rate, respectively.
The compared imputation methods take the observed images (b) for input, and
the complete images are shown for reference. Images along rows (c), (d) include
the imputed results after using GAIN, MDIOT respectively. Compared with
GAIN and MDIOT, it can be seen from row (e) that our method is visually
impressive. More importantly, our work is better at preserving the structure of
the intended image which is benefit for clustering task. Specifically, the embedding layer has learned the structural information and removed the noise from
our network, and this is why our method can obtain leading clustering effects
in the face of missing data. The experimental results in Table 1 also verified our
statement.

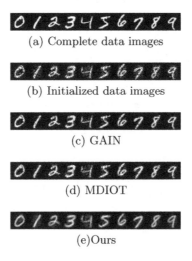

(a) Complete data images

(b) Initialized data images

(c) GAIN

(d) MDIOT

(e)Ours

Fig. 3. Sample imputation results for Mnist at 0.3 missing rate: (a) Complete data
images, (b) Initialized data images, (c) GAIN-imputed data images, (d) MDIOT-
imputed data images, (e) The reconstruction data of proposed network.

4.4   Ablation Study

Loss Ablation Study

We first investigate how the clustering loss and the distribution-preserving loss
affect the clustering performance on Mnist/Usps/Reuters, and the results are
shown in Table 2. In this experiment, we uniformly adopt datasets with 10%
missing ratio. It seems that the L_c has more contributions than L_s on Mnist/Usps
for clustering, and inversely on Reuters. We also conclude that the joint of two
counterpart losses further contributes to better performance.

Table 2. Loss ablation study with 10% missing ratio.

Dataset	Mnist		Usps		Reuters	
Loss	ACC	NMI	ACC	NMI	ACC	NMI
L_s	72.24	62.36	55.59	53.29	76.47	44.58
L_c	86.84	77.7	74.81	73.88	72.42	43.09
$L_s + L_c$	**92.16**	**85.77**	**77.5**	**77.35**	**77.7**	**47.93**

Sensitivity to Initialization Imputed Values

The initialization of imputed values has been demonstrated to be an essential part of incomplete clustering. We tested its sensitivity in our DICDP, w.r.t. model performance on Mnist/Usps/Reuters. We evaluated two commonly-used initialization values: zero-filling (ZF) and mean-filling (MF). Table 3 shows that DICDP can work stably without clear variation in the overall performance when using different initialization. This verifies that our method is insensitive to network initialization.

Table 3. Model sensitivity to different initialization of imputed values of three different missing ratios (10%/30%50%) on three benchmarks. Metric: ACC.

Dataset	Mnist		Usps		Reuters	
Initialization	ZF	MF	ZF	MF	ZF	MF
10%	90.75	92.16	74.19	77.5	74.03	77.7
30%	83.36	86.74	72.46	75.65	72.47	77.23
50%	78.61	82.15	71.77	73.77	72.03	75.53

5 Conclusion

In this paper, we propose a novel incomplete clustering methods termed DICDP, which jointly performs clustering and missing data imputation into a unified framework. Extensive experiments are conducted to demonstrate the effectiveness of optimal transport for clustering tasks. In the future, we will consider to construct more advanced network to further improve incomplete clustering performance and extend our proposed framework for other applications.

References

1. Chowdhury, S., Needham, T.: Generalized spectral clustering via Gromov-Wasserstein learning. In: International Conference on Artificial Intelligence and Statistics, pp. 712–720. PMLR (2021)

2. Crookston, N.L., Finley, A.O.: yaimpute: an R package for KNN imputation. J. Stat. Softw. **23**(10), 1–16 (2008)
3. Dempster, A.P., Laird, N.M., Rubin, D.B.: Maximum likelihood from incomplete data via the EM algorithm. J. Roy. Stat. Soc.: Ser. B (Methodol.) **39**(1), 1–22 (1977)
4. Fan, J., Ding, L., Chen, Y., Udell, M.: Factor group-sparse regularization for efficient low-rank matrix recovery. In: 33rd Conference on Neural Information Processing Systems (NeurIPS 2019) (2019)
5. Ghahramani, Z., Jordan, M.I.: Supervised learning from incomplete data via an EM approach. In: Advances in Neural Information Processing Systems, pp. 120–127 (1994)
6. Greenhalgh, T., Schmid, M.B., Czypionka, T., Bassler, D., Gruer, L.: Face masks for the public during the covid-19 crisis. BMJ **369**, m1435 (2020)
7. Hull, J.J.: A database for handwritten text recognition research. IEEE Trans. Pattern Anal. Mach. Intell. **16**(5), 550–554 (1994)
8. Ivanov, O., Figurnov, M., Vetrov, D.: Variational autoencoder with arbitrary conditioning. In: 7th International Conference on Learning Representations, ICLR 2019 (2019)
9. Jain, P., Netrapalli, P., Sanghavi, S.: Low-rank matrix completion using alternating minimization. In: Proceedings of the Forty-Fifth Annual ACM Symposium on Theory of Computing, pp. 665–674 (2013)
10. Kang, Z., et al.: Partition level multiview subspace clustering. Neural Netw. **122**, 279–288 (2020)
11. Kingma, D.P., Welling, M.: Stochastic gradient VB and the variational autoencoder. In: Second International Conference on Learning Representations, ICLR, vol. 19 (2014)
12. LeCun, Y., Bottou, L., Bengio, Y., Haffner, P.: Gradient-based learning applied to document recognition. Proc. IEEE **86**(11), 2278–2324 (1998)
13. Li, S.Y., Jiang, Y., Zhou, Z.H.: Partial multi-view clustering. In: Proceedings of the AAAI Conference on Artificial Intelligence, vol. 28 (2014)
14. Liu, X., et al.: Efficient and effective regularized incomplete multi-view clustering. IEEE Trans. Pattern Anal. Mach. Intell. **43**, 2634–2646 (2020)
15. Liu, X., et al.: Late fusion incomplete multi-view clustering. IEEE Trans. Pattern Anal. Mach. Intell. **41**(10), 2410–2423 (2018)
16. Liu, X., et al.: Multiple kernel k k-means with incomplete kernels. IEEE Trans. Pattern Anal. Mach. Intell. **42**(5), 1191–1204 (2019)
17. Lu, S., Ren, X., Liu, F.: Depth enhancement via low-rank matrix completion. In: Proceedings of the IEEE Conference on Computer Vision and Pattern Recognition, pp. 3390–3397 (2014)
18. Mattei, P.A., Frellsen, J.: MIWAE: deep generative modelling and imputation of incomplete data sets. In: International Conference on Machine Learning, pp. 4413–4423. PMLR (2019)
19. Muzellec, B., Josse, J., Boyer, C., Cuturi, M.: Missing data imputation using optimal transport. In: International Conference on Machine Learning, pp. 7130–7140. PMLR (2020)
20. Nie, F., Huang, H., Ding, C.: Low-rank matrix recovery via efficient schatten p-Norm minimization. In: Proceedings of the AAAI Conference on Artificial Intelligence, vol. 26 (2012)
21. Peng, X., Feng, J., Xiao, S., Yau, W.Y., Zhou, J.T., Yang, S.: Structured autoencoders for subspace clustering. IEEE Trans. Image Process. **27**(10), 5076–5086 (2018)

22. Peyré, G., Cuturi, M., et al.: Computational optimal transport: With applications to data science. Found. Trends® Mach. Learn. **11**(5–6), 355–607 (2019)
23. Richardson, T.W., Wu, W., Lin, L., Xu, B., Bernal, E.A.: MCFlow: Monte Carlo flow models for data imputation. In: Proceedings of the IEEE/CVF Conference on Computer Vision and Pattern Recognition (CVPR), June 2020
24. Tian, Y., Liu, W., Xiao, R., Wen, F., Tang, X.: A face annotation framework with partial clustering and interactive labeling. In: 2007 IEEE Conference on Computer Vision and Pattern Recognition, pp. 1–8. IEEE (2007)
25. Wang, Q., Ding, Z., Tao, Z., Gao, Q., Fu, Y.: Partial multi-view clustering via consistent GAN. In: 2018 IEEE International Conference on Data Mining (ICDM), pp. 1290–1295. IEEE (2018)
26. Wen, Z., Yin, W., Zhang, Y.: Solving a low-rank factorization model for matrix completion by a nonlinear successive over-relaxation algorithm. Math. Program. Comput. **4**(4), 333–361 (2012)
27. Wu, J., et al.: Deep comprehensive correlation mining for image clustering. In: Proceedings of the IEEE/CVF International Conference on Computer Vision, pp. 8150–8159 (2019)
28. Xie, J., Girshick, R., Farhadi, A.: Unsupervised deep embedding for clustering analysis. In: International Conference on Machine Learning, pp. 478–487. PMLR (2016)
29. Yang, C., Robinson, D., Vidal, R.: Sparse subspace clustering with missing entries. In: International Conference on Machine Learning, pp. 2463–2472. PMLR (2015)
30. Yang, L., Shen, C., Hu, Q., Jing, L., Li, Y.: Adaptive sample-level graph combination for partial multiview clustering. IEEE Trans. Image Process. **29**, 2780–2794 (2019)
31. Yoon, J., Jordon, J., Schaar, M.: GAIN: missing data imputation using generative adversarial nets. In: International Conference on Machine Learning, pp. 5689–5698. PMLR (2018)
32. Yoon, S., Sull, S.: GAMIN: generative adversarial multiple imputation network for highly missing data. In: Proceedings of the IEEE/CVF Conference on Computer Vision and Pattern Recognition, pp. 8456–8464 (2020)
33. Zhang, C., Cui, Y., Han, Z., Zhou, J.T., Fu, H., Hu, Q.: Deep partial multi-view learning. IEEE Trans. Pattern Anal. Mach. Intell. (2020)
34. Zhang, C., Fu, H., Liu, S., Liu, G., Cao, X.: Low-rank tensor constrained multi-view subspace clustering. In: Proceedings of the IEEE International Conference on Computer Vision, pp. 1582–1590 (2015)

A Review of Client Scheduling Strategies in Federated Learning

Zhikai Yang[1], Yaping Liu[1,2(✉)], Shuo Zhang[1,2], Xingyu Lv[1],
and Fangyu Shen[1]

[1] Cyberspace Institute of Advanced Technology, Guangzhou University,
Guangzhou 510000, China
ypliu@gzhu.edu.cn
[2] Peng Cheng Laboratory Shenzhen, Shenzhen 518000, China

Abstract. Federated learning is a distributed machine learning method to solve the problems of 'data islands' and privacy protection. Now it has become one of the research hotspots in the field of learning. Like many learning methods, Federated Learning is a data-driven learning framework. When facing the challenges of devices heterogeneity, non identically and independently distributed (Non-IID) data and data's security, it could not be processed simply and abstractly like other learning paradigms. This paper briefly introduces the definition of Federated Learning and the challenges faced by all parties, and mainly summarizes the client scheduling strategies in Federated Learning in recent years. Client scheduling is an important part of the aggregation strategy of Federated Learning. At present, it is very difficult to reduce resource consumption and make the joint model more excellent and personalized. Client scheduling strategy needs to balance the relationship between optimization objectives and task objectives. The summary will help us understand the development situation of the current field and provide a clear direction for future research.

Keywords: Federated Learning · Aggregation · Client scheduling strategy

1 Introduction

The EU issued the general data protection regulation (GDPR) in 2018, which is a privacy protection regulation, which aims to specify the regulations that enterprises should abide by when collecting, processing and using users' data. The implementation of GDPR makes people living in the digital age re-examine the necessity of data privacy protection. Machine learning has long become a hot topic in the field of computer science. Most of the models need a considerable amount of data to support their training and application. The data from open channels probably not meet the growing data needs of enterprise production, scientific research and public services. We do not want the data with privacy attributes held by users to be publicly used for corporate profits or scientific research. Enterprises with reasoning model requirements also do not want to share their private data. We call those individuals, research groups or enterprises who are unwilling or even unable to share private data in violation of the rules as data islands. These data islands may have similar data environment and the need to establish efficient models. How to break the shackles of data islands and carry out joint learning has become a challenge in front of people. Google provides us with an effective joint learning paradigm. In 2016, Google [1] proposed the concept of Federated Learning (FL) and successfully applied it to Google Keyboard [2], providing a powerful tool to break the barrier of data islands. FL can share the internal distribution of data on the premise of protecting users' privacy, and jointly establish a more accurate and efficient federated model than the model established by single user machine learning through the communication and interaction of multiple participants. FL will play an irreplaceable role in finance, health care, Internet of things and intergovernmental cooperation, and will significantly improve the service quality without violating privacy regulations and data security ethics.

This paper will focus on one of the core problems of FL, the client scheduling strategy in the aggregation process. Aggregation occurs in the process that each participant merges the models generated by their potential distribution of data into a global model. It affects the speed of federated model establishment, model quality and data security. This paper is organized according to the following structure. In the second part, we will introduce the concept, basic framework and factors affecting the aggregation effect of FL; In the third part, we will briefly analyze and summarize the client scheduling strategies in the recent FL aggregation strategies; Finally, we will give a summary and some personal prospects for the future of this field.

2   A Brief Introduction of Federated Learning

In this part, we will summarize the definition, infrastructure and challenges of FL. The elaboration of these aspects will help us understand the aggregation strategy of FL.

2.1   Definition and Characteristics of FL

FL involves many computer science fields, including machine learning, distributed systems, privacy protection technology and communication. FL is a joint learning model, which allows multiple participants to conduct joint machine learning and establish appropriate models without exchanging their own data or under the condition of more strict privacy protection, such as preventing gradient attacks. FL is generally defined as follows:

Assume that there are N different parties, and each party is denoted by T_i, where $i \in [1, N]$. We use D_i to denote the data of T_i. For the non-federated setting, each party T_i uses only its local data D_i to train a machine learning model M_i. The predictive accuracy of M_i is denoted as P_i. For the federated setting, all the parties jointly train a model M_f while each party T_i protects its data D_i according to its specific privacy restrictions. The predictive accuracy of M_f is denoted as P_f. Then, for a valid FL system, there exists $i \in [1, N]$ such that $P_f \geq P_i$. The general FL process is shown in Fig. 1.

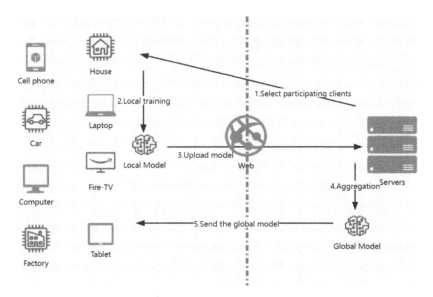

Fig. 1. FL's procession.

Unlike distributed machine learning (DML), FL has different purposes and characteristics. Due to the heterogeneity of devices and the personalized behavior of different users, the self-owned data located in the FL computing node is often non independent and identically distributed (Non-IID), which is different from DML. In DML, the data owned by different computing nodes are generally independent and identically distributed (IID), which will weaken the differences of different computing nodes in joint modeling.

2.2 FL's Infrastructure and Classification

There are two types of FL infrastructure communication architecture, including distributed configuration of central server and peer-to-peer network configuration (P2P). Both architectures have their own application scenarios and advantages.

The central communication architecture consists of a central server or server group and clients participating in learning. The central server is responsible for coordinating the training process of the overall system and managing the communication process between the clients and the server. The client is a FL participant, holds private data and is willing to participate in joint learning.

In order to avoid the negative impact of untrusted central server on the FL system, Abhijit Guha Roy et al. [3] proposed the P2P network architecture Brain Torrent. In this architecture, there is no central server. Instead, a client is randomly selected as a temporary server after each round of training to perform aggregation operation. The p2p network architecture Biscotti [4] based on blockchain technology has made considerable progress in security.

According to the difference of feature space and sample space of data held by different clients, FL system can be divided into three categories: horizontal federated learning, vertical federated learning and federated transfer learning [5].

2.3 Challenges of FL

FL system faces many challenges due to the growth of participants, the increase of system complexity and the increase of attack means. These problems should be considered when designing relevant architectures and algorithms [6].

In FL, the nature of Non-IID datasets is inevitable. Due to the differences of users' personal habits, task objectives and even geographical location, the generated local datasets are not always IID. There may be differences in hardware resources and effective learning time between different client devices. These differences may have a negative impact on the data set generation process and subsequent training and aggregation processes, which may drag down the learning efficiency of the whole system. Heterogeneous devices and Non-IID datasets are two of the important features that distinguish FL from DML.

Communication efficiency is also one of the important factors restricting the development of FL. Deep learning models widely used in modern industry and academia often contain dozens or even hundreds of layers of neural network structure, with millions of parameters. On the other hand, FL participants are mostly mobile edge devices. The network connection quality between these devices and the central server depends on many factors. Some privacy protection technologies also need efficient compression technology and stable transmission technology.

Even though the goal of FL is joint learning without divulging privacy, in fact, FL system is facing severe security challenges. The more complex the system, the more vulnerabilities there are, and so is the FL system.

Personalization is aimed at the experience of the participants. The global aggregation model may not have an outstanding local effect on the participants because of the Non-IID problem mentioned above. Adjusting the training and model according to the characteristics of the participants is helpful to the application effect of the local model. In order to maintain the long-term and active participation of all participants in FL, the incentive mechanism of FL sponsors is necessary.

3 FL Clients Scheduling Strategies

In this section, we will focus on the scheduling management of the clients in the FL aggregation policy. We divide the aggregation strategy into three parts: overall architecture design and optimization, clients scheduling and management, parameter processing and optimization algorithm.

Due to the heterogeneity and large number of client devices in the actual environment, which often reaches the order of millions, the scheduling and management of the clients has become one of the challenges we encounter. To manage such a large user group, the design of scheduling architecture is very important. At the same time, for the central FL system, according to the load capacity of the server, we can only select some clients for aggregation after each round of training. The clients' sampling strategy and the processing and sampling of client data derived therefrom have an important impact on the aggregation efficiency and model quality.

Let's first introduce the FedAvg [1] algorithm, pseudocode in Fig. 2. The clients sampling method adopted by FedAvg is to randomly sample of all clients with probability after each round of training for the next step of model aggregation. In an ideal state, such as when the computing resources of all clients are similar, the network communication state is stable, and the generated data comes from the same distribution, the effect is good. But the actual performance is bad, because we are facing more complex scenarios: heterogeneous clients and Non-IID data. The update delay caused by the network fluctuation of some clients will affect the convergence speed of the global model.

Algorithm 1 FedAvg

Input: The K clients are indexed by k; B is the local minibatch size, E is the number of local epochs, and η is the learning rate.
Server:
initialize w_0
for each round $t = 1, 2, \ldots$ **do**
    $m \leftarrow \max(C \cdot K, 1)$
    $S_t \leftarrow$ (random set of m clients)
    for each client $k \in S_t$ **in parallel do**
        $w_{t+1}^k \leftarrow$ ClientUpdate (k, w_t)
    end for
    $w_{t+1} \leftarrow \sum_{k=1}^{K} \frac{n_k}{n} w_{t+1}^k$
end for

Client Update(k, w): //*Run on client k*
$\mathcal{B} \leftarrow$(split $\mathcal{P}_k$ into batches of size B)
for each local epoch i from 1 to E **do**
    for batch $b \in \mathcal{B}$ **do**
        $w \leftarrow w - \eta \nabla \ell(w; b)$
    end for
end for
return w to server

Fig. 2. FedAvg algorithm.

3.1   Client Management Architecture Design

Although the design of scheduling management system architecture for large-scale equipment has been studied for many years in the field of traditional communication and edge computing, and the technology is becoming more and more perfect, it is still difficult and challenging to expand it to FL. Keith Bonawitz et al. [7] systematically described the components that should be considered in an FL system from the macro and micro perspectives, including network protocol, software architecture of client equipment, server infrastructure, analysis and monitoring, security aggregation and other modules, and described in detail the specific functions contained in each component. It provides an architecture design reference for us to build an operational FL system from scratch.

SmartPC [8] is a FL framework that can effectively balance training progress, model accuracy and energy consumption in real time. SmartPC contains two control layers: global control layer and local control layer. The global control layer collects information such as hardware configuration and runtime performance from the training clients, intelligently determines the global deadline for each round of learning, and prevents the server from falling into a long wait due to the disconnection of individual clients. The local controller intelligently adjusts the computing resources of the training clients according to the global deadline, and minimizes the energy consumption. Wang et al. [9] established a scheduling framework from the perspective of dynamic task load allocation, and configured different workloads for IID and Non-IID tasks. Intelligent scheduling is one of the important directions of client architecture design, which improves the robustness of the whole system to complex situations.

For the architecture that a few servers correspond to large-scale clients, many researchers put forward the idea of layering, adding proxy servers or edge servers between servers and clients as a new hierarchical structure to undertake some scheduling and aggregation functions. HFL [10] is a hierarchical aggregation architecture based on the geographical distribution of clients. Considering the clients under the jurisdiction of a base station, the architecture clusters the clients into clusters located in different geographical locations according to the geographical distribution of clients, sets up small base stations in the cluster to manage the clients in the cluster. Small base stations will regularly send local models to base stations for averaging and updating to establish global consistency. When the client is stable and joins the edge server, HFEL [11] is an efficient scheduling algorithm. HFEL decomposes the cost minimization problem into two sub problems: the resource allocation of each edge server and the edge association of all clients are given. By optimizing the client resource allocation under each edge server, finally the resource cost of the whole FL system is minimized.

Considering the introduction of P2P idea, if the server is completely cancelled and a P2P architecture is formed between clients for FL, the time required for a round of learning is unacceptable due to the huge number of clients, but canceling the central server and retaining the edge server on the basis of hierarchical architecture is an acceptable compromise. P-FedAvg [12] is a parallel FL algorithm. Multiple edge servers are set in the FL system, which are respectively responsible for the scheduling and aggregation of some clients. After the edge server obtains the aggregation model, it will communicate with its neighbor servers and mix the model parameters. When the client scale is large, the effect is better than FedAvg, and the robustness against risk is high.

Table 1 gives a summary of this section. Efficient and intelligent scheduling architecture helps to overcome the communication resource bottleneck in FL and build a good foundation for the operation of FL system.

Table 1. Client management architecture design.

Studies	Communication architecture	Targets
FedAvg [1]	Centralized	Basic algorithm
Keith Bonawitz et al. [7]		Theoretical analysis, design guidance
SmartPC [8]		Balance model accuracy and energy consumption
Wang et al. [9]		Dynamic load adjustment
HFL [10]		Geographical distribution, hierarchical structure
HFEL [11]		Resource allocation
P-FedAvg [12]	P2P	P2P structure

3.2   Client Sampling

In this section, we mainly focus on the sampling strategies for the clients of the organization responsible for aggregation in FL. There are two levels of clients sampling. One is that the server samples the client itself. The client distributes Q_i, from which the server samples $C \sim Q_i$; The other is that the client samples private data. For customer C_i, the data distribution of C_i meets $C_i \sim Q_{c_i}$. In the FedAvg algorithm, the sampling method of the server to the client is to randomly sample a fixed M. The algorithms summarized below are improvements to this random sampling idea, and FedAvg has been the benchmark of most FL aggregation algorithms. Table 2 summarizes various client-side sampling algorithms.

Sampling Based on Mathematical Method. The FedAvg algorithm based on static sampling can not adapt to the changes of dynamic environment. Ji et al. [13] proposed a dynamic sampling algorithm. The idea of dynamic sampling algorithm is that the server tries to accommodate more clients to participate in the training at the beginning to ensure the rapid convergence of the global model. In the later stage of training, because the convergence speed of the model decreases, a large number of clients can not ensure the rapid convergence of the global model, so the number of clients participating in aggregation can be appropriately reduced after several rounds of training. Compared with static sampling, after selecting the appropriate down sampling rate, although the cost of dynamic sampling increases in the previous rounds of training, the total amount of parameter transmission of dynamic sampling is less than that of static sampling, which can reduce the communication consumption of FL system. At the same time, the author proposes a masking parameter algorithm, which only transmits the parameters that are too different from the model after the last round of training to the server, so as to reduce the amount of communication data.

Lokesh Nagalapatti et al. [14] proposed a novel client sampling algorithm S-FedAvg based on game theory. The problem solved by this algorithm is how to select relevant clients. Relevant clients refer to those clients whose data can accelerate the global training speed, while irrelevant clients refer to those clients whose data has nothing to do with the goal of FL system or may even have a reaction. The researcher establishes a cooperative game model to calculate the client shapley value and client correlation coefficient, and then establishes the client sampling strategy.

The sampling based on mathematical method has good interpretability and fast sampling speed. It has unique requirements in scenes that are relatively stable and do not need too high model accuracy.

Sampling Under Resource Constraints. We consider the heterogeneity of devices in FL system. Some clients cannot upload model updates in time due to insufficient computing resources, low network bandwidth and high network delay, which makes the server fall into a long waiting process, slows down the convergence process of FL model, and finally reduces the aggregation efficiency.

FedCS [15] is a representative algorithm for sampling client clusters according to client resources in FL, it solves the problem of client selection with resource constraints. FedCS first requests the resource information of the client before selecting the client that really participates in aggregation, and limits the time for the client to download, update and upload the model, select those clients that can participate in the aggregation in time to construct a selected client set, maximize the number of clients that can participate in the aggregation, and dynamically update the set according to the resource information obtained from each round of communication.

FL is an unstable distributed system most of the time. The client may drop due to its own or network problems. When it goes online again, the client's too old model may have a negative impact on the global model aggregation. FedLaAvg [16] algorithm considers the client sampling strategy in this case, some clients' long-term absence from training will lead to other clients being frequently selected for training, which introduces some deviations. In order to alleviate this deviation, the main idea of the algorithm is to keep the latest gradient information of each client in the server. During client sampling, select those clients who have been absent from training for a long time from the available clients for model aggregation, so as to reduce the error. SAFA [17] is a semi asynchronous client sampling protocol. It divides the clients into three types according to the network conditions that the clients depend on: up to date clients, deprecated clients and tolerable clients, only up to date and deprecated clients is selected for each sampling, and cache some of the updates uploaded by clients, which will be adopted in the next round of aggregation. The adoption of semi asynchronous protocol makes the sampling efficiency higher. Astw_FedAvg [18] considers the asynchronous update mode of the model as deep neural network. In FL, shallow neural network updating has a greater impact on the performance of the global model than deep network updating, so the author uses this feature to design an asynchronous protocol. The parameters of the shallow network will be updated in each communication, while the parameters of the deep network will be updated every few rounds of communication, so as to reduce the consumption of communication resources.

Still considering resource constraints, we discuss client selection from the perspective of reducing resource consumption. Due to unnecessary over training and frequent parameter uploading and downloading, mobile devices will aggravate resource consumption (such as power consumption), which may not be acceptable in some cases. For example, in wireless networks, the communication consumption accounts for the largest proportion of the total consumption of mobile devices. Bing Luo et al. [19] theoretically gave the relationship between the total cost, control variables (client sampling number K and local iteration number E) and the upper limit of convergence, and gave the optimization algorithm. The theory shows that a large K value is conducive to the reduction of learning time, while a small K value is conducive to cost saving, and shows that a relatively low sampling rate will not seriously affect the convergence of the global model, while the selection of E value depends on the relationship between calculation cost and communication cost. This study helps to determine the design principles of different optimization objectives. In the paper [20], the author proposes a control algorithm using time-varying nonlinear integer programming. Under the condition of making the model converge, the client that minimizes the cumulative resource usage can be selected online.

Next, we focus on a specific scenario, the client sampling method in wireless network. Yang et al. [21] studied the effectiveness of three different client sampling methods in wireless networks. The three sampling methods are: random scheduling (RS), which randomly selects clients to participate in aggregation in each round of communication; round robin (RR) divides the client into arrays, and selects a group to update in turn during each round of communication; proportional fair scheduling (PF) selects high-quality clients weighted by signal-to-noise ratio (SNR). The results show that PF is better than RS and RR at high signal to interference noise ratio (SNIR), while RR is better at low SNIR. The OCEAN [22] algorithm considers the relationship between client sampling, bandwidth allocation and final model quality in each round of aggregation under long-term training, and gives the wireless bandwidth allocation strategy. Yang et al. [23] proposed an iterative algorithm based on the energy efficient transmission and computing resource allocation of FL in wireless networks, derived the closed solutions of time allocation, bandwidth allocation, power control, computing frequency and learning accuracy, and gave the feasible solution of the energy minimization problem. Experiments show that the algorithm can reduce the energy consumption by 59.5% compared with the traditional FL algorithm. The optimization problem FEDL [24] is considered from the balance between the amount of calculation and communication delay determined by the learning accuracy, and the balance between the learning time and energy consumption. It is transformed into three convex subproblems to solve, which provides a theoretical analysis for different objective optimization algorithms.

Client scheduling under resource constraints is a multi-objective balancing problem. Different algorithms have tendencies for different optimization objectives.

Sampling Based on Machine Learning Method. Traditional machine learning methods and deep learning methods, which have sprung up in recent years, have been applied in various fields and achieved very good results.

Clustering is a machine learning algorithm that divides individuals similar in mathematical or physical sense into the same cluster. Yann Fraboni et al. [25] cluster the client and local models from the two aspects of client similarity and model similarity, and sample and aggregate from each cluster. Experiments show that the clustering sampling method in heterogeneous datasets has faster convergence speed and smoother convergence curve than the general method. IFCA [26] framework is a multitask FL framework based on clustering. The server clusters the clients according to different tasks of the client, and performs FL aggregation operation for each cluster respectively, so as to realize multitask parallelism. Unlike the above-mentioned thorough clustering of all clients from beginning to end to perform the same task or multi task parallel from the beginning, FL+HC [27] algorithm balances these two situations. After the first few rounds of joint training, the clients are clustered, and the clustered client clusters are trained independently, this not only takes advantage of the rapid convergence of the global model due to the joint learning of a large number of clients at the beginning of FL, but also ensures the personalization of the internal models of each cluster in the later stage. CFL and DCFL [28] search the client cluster structure from the perspective of optimizing resource consumption to obtain the cluster structure that minimizes resource consumption. Clustering and sampling clients have been proved to alleviate the negative impact of heterogeneous devices and data on FL system.

Reinforcement learning is one of the paradigms and methodologies of machine learning. It is used to describe and solve the problem that agents maximize returns or achieve specific goals through learning strategies in the process of interaction with the environment. FAVOR [29] is a client-side sampling mechanism based on deep Q-learning in reinforcement learning. This strategy learns to sample a set of clients in each round of communication to maximize reward, so as to encourage FL system to improve accuracy and punish the use of more communication rounds. P. Tam et al. [30] propose a scheme combines deep Q-networks and mainly considers the criticality of FL model service and congestion state to optimize the long-term strategy. Wang et al. [31] proposed a scheduling algorithm based on graph convolution neural network (GCN). The algorithm determines the sampling strategy by learning the relationship between network attributes, unloading topology, client cluster and learning accuracy.

It is a good research direction to migrate the existing scheduling strategy based on machine learning to the new FL system.

Other Sampling Methods. In essence, sampling the client is to sample all the data of the client that meets the sampling conditions. We call resampling the data as fine-grained sampling. Fine-grained sampling can avoid the impact of task independent data held by the client on the overall FL process. Through the sampling and analysis of private datasets, we can provide reference for the sampling at the client level. Anran Li et al. [32] first select those clients with high coincidence between the sample category and the data category required by the target task, and then conduct further screening: dynamically select the clients and samples that are more important for global model update. Tiffany Tuor et al. [33] proposed that the task related sub datasets can be obtained by correlation sampling of the client's datasets. In each round of training, the client only uses the sub datasets for learning.

In the SGD algorithms, the large loss means that the current convergence speed is fast. The Power-Of-Choice [34] sampling strategy selects those clients with large local loss to participate in the aggregation to accelerate the global convergence speed. FOLB [35] deals with communication and heterogeneous problems by estimating the contribution of local updates to global updates and adjusting the aggregation process.

FREPD [36] and Fed-DFE [37] contribute to the safety of FL system.

Table 2. Client sampling methods.

Studies	Main area	Targets
FedAvg [1]	Mathematical method	Basic algorithm
Ji et al. [13]		Dynamic sampling rate
S-FedAvg [14]		Game theory
FedCS [15]	Resource constraints	Resource constraints, accommodates more clients to participate
FedLaAvg [16]		Relieve long-term absence from training
SAFA [17]		Semi asynchronous, client classification
Astw_FedAvg [18]		Asynchronous update, hierarchical updating of deep neural network
Bing Luo et al. [19]		Theoretical analysis,
Y. Jin [20]		Minimizes the cumulative resource usage
Yang et al. [21]		Wireless network, different SNIR
OCEAN [22]		Wireless bandwidth allocation, long-term training
Yang et al. [23]		Energy efficient transmission, computing resource allocation, wireless networks
FEDL [24]		Amount of calculation, communication delay
Yann Fraboni et al. [25]	Machine learning	Clustering, client similarity and model similarity
IFCA [26]		Clustering, multitask
FL+HC [27]		Clustering
CFL and DCFL [28]		Clustering, search cluster structure
FAVOR [29]		Reinforcement learning
P. Tam et al. [30]		Deep Q-networks
Wang et al. [31]		GCN
Anran Li et al. [32]	Others	Fine-grained sampling
Tiffany Tuor et al. [33]		Fine-grained sampling, task related sub datasets
Power-Of-Choice [34]		Clients with large local loss
FOLB [35]		Estimating the contribution of local updates

4 Conclusions and Prospects

This paper summarizes the client scheduling strategies in FL system, and briefly explains it from two aspects: architecture design and sampling strategies. When designing the scheduling strategy, we should focus on the heterogeneity of devices and the Non-IID data, which seriously affect the joint learning process of FL system. At the same time, a trade-off needs to be made between learning rate, model accuracy, resource consumption and security. The proposed method is to optimize different objectives through intelligent strategies, which is also one of the development directions of FL scheduling strategies in the future.

Acknowledgement. We thank anonymous reviewers for their helpful comments in improving the paper. This work is supported in part by Key-Area Research and Development Program of Guangdong Province (No. 2019B010137005).

Funding Statement. Key-Area Research and Development Program of Guangdong Province No. 2019B010137005.

Conflicts of Interest. The authors declare there is no conflicts of interest regarding the publication of this paper.

References

1. McMahan, B., Moore, E., Ramage, D., Hampson, S., Arcas, B.A.: Communication-efficient learning of deep networks from decentralized data. In: Artificial Intelligence and Statistics, pp. 1273–1282. PMLR (2017)
2. Hard, A., et al.: Federated learning for mobile keyboard prediction. arXiv:1811.03604 (2018)
3. Roy, A.G., Siddiqui, S., Pölsterl, S., Navab, N., Wachinger, C.: BrainTorrent: a peer-to-peer environment for decentralized federated learning. arXiv:1905.06731 (2019)
4. Shayan, M., Fung, C., Yoon, C.J., Beschastnikh, I.: Biscotti: a ledger for private and secure peer-to-peer machine learning. arXiv:1811.09904. (2018)
5. Yang, Q., Liu, Y., Chen, T., Tong, Y.: Federated machine learning: concept and applications. ACM Trans. Intell. Syst. Technol **10**(2), 1–19 (2019)
6. Kairouz, P., et al.: Advances and open problems in federated learning. Found. Trends Mach. Learn. **14**(1–2), 1–210 (2021)
7. Bonawitz, K.: Towards federated learning at scale: system design. In: Proceedings of Machine Learning and Systems, vol. 1, pp. 374–88 (2019)
8. Li, L., Xiong, H., Guo, Z., Wang, J., Xu, C.Z.: SmartPC: hierarchical pace control in real-time federated learning system. In: 2019 IEEE Real-Time Systems Symposium (RTSS), pp. 406–418 (2019)
9. Wang, C., Yang, Y., Zhou, P.: Towards efficient scheduling of federated mobile devices under computational and statistical heterogeneity. IEEE Trans. Parallel Distrib. Syst. **32**(2), 394–410 (2021)
10. Abad, M.S.H., Ozfatura, E., Gunduz, D., Ercetin, O.: Hierarchical federated learning across heterogeneous cellular networks. In: ICASSP 2020–2020 IEEE International Conference on Acoustics, Speech and Signal Processing (ICASSP), pp. 8866–8870 (2020)
11. Luo, S., Chen, X., Wu, Q., Zhou, Z., Yu, S.: HFEL: joint edge association and resource allocation for cost-efficient hierarchical federated edge learning. IEEE Trans. Wirel. Commun. **19**(10), 6535–6548 (2020)
12. Zhong, Z.: P-FedAvg: parallelizing federated learning with theoretical guarantees. In: IEEE INFOCOM 2021-IEEE Conference on Computer Communications, pp. 1–10 (2021)
13. Ji, S., Jiang, W., Walid, A., Li, X.: Dynamic sampling and selective masking for communication-efficient federated learning. arXiv:2003.09603 (2020)

14. Nagalapatti, L., Narayanam, R.: Game of gradients: mitigating irrelevant clients in federated learning. arXiv:2110.12257 (2021)
15. Nishio, T., Yonetani, R.: Client selection for federated learning with heterogeneous resources in mobile edge. In: ICC 2019–2019 IEEE International Conference on Communications (ICC), pp. 1–7 (2019)
16. Yan, Y., et al.: Distributed non-convex optimization with sublinear speedup under intermittent client availability. arXiv:2002.07399 (2020)
17. Wu, W., He, L., Lin, W., Mao, R., Maple, C., Jarvis, S.: SAFA: a semi-asynchronous protocol for fast federated learning with low overhead. IEEE Trans. Comput. **70**(5), 655–668 (2021)
18. Chen, Y., Sun, X., Jin, Y.: Communication-efficient federated deep learning with layerwise asynchronous model update and temporally weighted aggregation. IEEE Trans. Neural Netw. Learn. Syst. **31**(10), 4229–4238 (2020)
19. Luo, B., Li, X., Wang, S., Huang, J., Tassiulas, L.: Cost-effective federated learning design. In: IEEE INFOCOM 2021-IEEE Conference on Computer Communications, pp. 1–10 (2021)
20. Jin, Y., Jiao, L., Qian, Z., Zhang, S., Lu, S., Wang, X.: Resource-efficient and convergence-preserving online participant selection in federated learning. In: 2020 IEEE 40th International Conference on Distributed Computing Systems (ICDCS), pp. 606–616 (2020)
21. Yang, H.H., Liu, Z., Quek, T.Q.S., Poor, H.V.: Scheduling policies for federated learning in wireless networks. IEEE Trans. Commun. **68**(1), 317–333 (2020)
22. Xu, J., Wang, H.: Client selection and bandwidth allocation in wireless federated learning networks: a long-term perspective. IEEE Trans. Wirel. Commun. **20**(2), 1188–1200 (2021)
23. Yang, Z., Chen, M., Saad, W., Hong, C.S., Shikh-Bahaei, M.: Energy efficient federated learning over wireless communication networks. IEEE Trans. Wirel. Commun. **20**(3), 1935–1949 (2021)
24. Tran, N.H., Bao, W., Zomaya, A., Nguyen, M.N.H., Hong, C.S.: Federated learning over wireless networks: optimization model design and analysis. In: IEEE INFOCOM 2019-IEEE Conference on Computer Communications, pp. 1387–1395 (2019)
25. Fraboni, Y., Vidal, R., Kameni, L., Lorenzi, M.: Clustered sampling: low-variance and improved representativity for clients selection in federated learning. In: International Conference on Machine Learning, pp. 3407–3416. PMLR (2021)
26. Ghosh, A., Chung, J., Yin, D., Ramchandran, K.: An efficient framework for clustered federated learning. In: Advances in Neural Information Processing Systems, vol. 33, pp. 19586–19597 (2020)
27. Briggs, C., Fan, Z., Andras, P.: Federated learning with hierarchical clustering of local updates to improve training on non IID data. In: 2020 International Joint Conference on Neural Networks (IJCNN), pp. 1–9 (2020)
28. Wang, Z., Xu, H., Liu, J., Huang, H., Qiao, C., Zhao, Y.: Resource-efficient federated learning with hierarchical aggregation in edge computing. In: IEEE INFOCOM 2021-IEEE Conference on Computer Communications, pp. 1–10 (2021)
29. Wang, H., Kaplan, Z., Niu, D., Li, B.: Optimizing federated learning on non IID data with reinforcement learning. In: IEEE INFOCOM 2020-IEEE Conference on Computer Communications, pp. 1698–1707 (2020)
30. Tam, P., Math, S., Lee, A., Kim, S.: Multi-agent deep Q-networks for efficient edge federated learning communications in software-defined IoT. Comput. Mater. Contin. **71**(2), 3319–3335 (2022)
31. Wang, S., Lee, M., Hosseinalipour, S., Morabito, R., Chiang, M., Brinton, C.G.: Device sampling for heterogeneous federated learning: theory, algorithms, and implementation. In: IEEE INFOCOM 2021-IEEE Conference on Computer Communications, pp. 1–10 (2021)

32. Li, A., Zhang, L., Tan, J., Qin, Y., Wang, J., Li, X.Y.: Sample-level data selection for federated learning. In: IEEE INFOCOM 2021-IEEE Conference on Computer Communications, pp. 1–10 (2021)
33. Tuor, T., Wang, S., Ko, B.J., Liu, C., Leung, K.K.: Overcoming noisy and irrelevant data in federated learning. arXiv:2001.08300 (2020)
34. Cho, Y.J., Wang, J., Joshi, G.: Client selection in federated learning: convergence analysis and power-of-choice selection strategies. arXiv:2010.01243 (2020)
35. Nguyen, H.T., Sehwag, V., Hosseinalipour, S., Brinton, C.G., Chiang, M., Poor, H.V.: Fast-convergent federated learning. IEEE J. Select. Areas Commun. **39**(1), 201–218 (2021)
36. Gu, Z., He, L., Li, P., Sun, P., Shi, J.: FREPD: a robust federated learning framework on variational autoencoder. Comput. Syst. Sci. Eng. **39**(3), 307–320 (2021)
37. Sun, Z., Feng, J., Yin, L., Zhang, Z., Li, R.: Fed-DFE: a decentralized function encryption-based privacy-preserving scheme for federated learning. Comput. Mater. Contin. **71**(1), 1867–1886 (2022)

Error Sensitivity Based Redundancy Analysis for Kinematic Calibration of Industrial Robot

Guifang Qiao[1,2(✉)], Lei Tian[1], Ying Zhang[1], Di Liu[1],
and Guangming Song[2]

[1] School of Automation, Nanjing Institute of Technology,
Nanjing 211167, China
qiaoguifang@126.com
[2] School of Instrument Science and Engineering, Southeast University,
Nanjing 210096, China

Abstract. Kinematic parameter error is the main factor that affects the accuracy of industrial robots. The accuracy of robots can be effectively improved through calibration technology. The error model based method is one of main calibration methods for calibrating robots. This paper presents the error sensitivity based redundancy analysis for kinematic calibration of industrial robot. The pose error model is firstly established based on the M-DH model. By introducing the concept of error sensitivity, the effects of kinematic parameter error on the end pose error of industrial robot is analyzed. The redundant parameters of pose error model are analyzed based on the error sensitivity. Secondly, the effectiveness of the non-redundant pose error model is verified through experiments. The average comprehensive position error of Staubli TX60 robot is reduced by 88.7%. The average comprehensive attitude error of Staubli TX60 robot is reduced by 75.4%.

Keywords: Serial robot · Error sensitivity · M-DH model · Pose error · Pose measurement

1 Introduction

With the rapid development of robotic technology, industrial robots are gradually being used in high-end manufacturing fields, such as intelligent grinding and polishing operations for aerospace engines, drilling and riveting in the aerospace industry, and online measurement systems in the industrial fields [1, 2]. In 2017–2019, the national key research and development project 'Intelligent robot' of China pointed out that the position and attitude accuracy should be better than 0.1 mm and 0.1° respectively in the high-end manufacturing fields. At present, the repeat position accuracy of the most industrial robots can meet the accuracy requirement. While the absolute position and attitude accuracy of the robot are still poor.

A number of studies have shown that robot calibration technology can effectively improve the absolute accuracy of industrial robots [3, 4]. The robot calibration technology is mainly divided into on-line calibration and off-line calibration. Qu X. et al. proposed an on-line pose compensation method for the KUKA KR-5 robot [5]. The on-line compensation system is restricted by field environments. And the real-time

© The Author(s), under exclusive license to Springer Nature Switzerland AG 2022
X. Sun et al. (Eds.): ICAIS 2022, CCIS 1587, pp. 190–201, 2022.
https://doi.org/10.1007/978-3-031-06761-7_16

performance of the compensation algorithm cannot meet the requirements of high-end manufacturing field. The off-line robot calibration process generally contains the joint error calibration, the kinematic errors calibration and the non-kinematic errors calibration [6]. The kinematic errors are the main errors which affect the absolute accuracy of the industrial robots. Kinematic calibration can be mainly divided into two methods, i.e. error model based calibration [7] and screw axis measurement based calibration [8]. Compared with the error model based calibration, the accuracy of the screw axis measurement based calibration is lower. The process of the error model based calibration includes four critical steps, i.e. error modeling, pose/position measurement, parameters identification, and error compensation. To overcome the problems of completeness and continuity of the kinematic models, the zero reference model, exponential product model, M-DH model have been proposed [9–11]. The established error models are divided into the position error model, the pose error model, and the distance error model [12]. Compared with the other two models, the pose error model comprehensively describes the position and attitude errors of the industrial robot. The error model used for calibration is mainly determined by the measurement equipment. The laser tracker is the most widely used measuring equipment for robot calibration [13]. The identification of the kinematic parameters is a problem of solving nonlinear functions. Wen X. et al. applied the improved crow (ICSA) algorithm to increase the pose accuracy by 70% [14]. The minimization of error model can improve the identification performance, such as convergence rate and calculation accuracy. This can be obtained based on the model redundancy analysis. Two mathematical analysis methods are applied to solve the problem of redundancy analysis, i.e. singular value decomposition (SVD) and QR decomposition [7, 15]. In this paper, a new redundancy analysis method based on the error sensitivity is proposed for kinematic calibration of industrial robot.

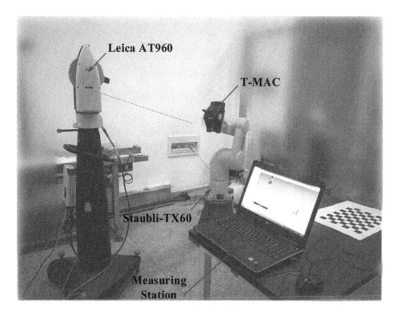

Fig. 1. The calibration system of industrial robot.

2 Overview of Industrial Robot Calibration System

The calibration system of industrial robot built in this paper is shown in Fig. 1. The laser tracker used in this system is Leica AT960. The measurement uncertainty of the laser tracker is ±(15 μm + 6 μm/m). The industrial robot to be calibrated is Staubli TX60. The repositioning accuracy of the robot is ±0.02 mm. The measurement tools of the laser tracker can be a 1.5-in target ball and a T-MAC tool. The 1.5-in target ball can only obtain the position of robot. The T-MAC tool can obtain the pose of robot. The weight of T-MAC tool is nearly 1.5 kg. It is not suitable for measuring the pose of robot with a small load. The rated load of Staubli TX60 is only 3 kg. The measurement processes involved in this paper are in compliance with standards GB/T-12642-2013 and ISO-9283.

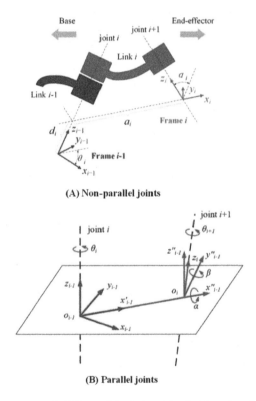

(A) Non-parallel joints

(B) Parallel joints

Fig. 2. The parameter definition of the industrial robot based on M-DH model.

3   Pose Error Model Based on M-DH Model

Four parameters, i.e., the link length a, the link distance d, the link torsion angle α, and the joint angle θ, are used to describe the pose relation between the neighboring links in the DH model. When the two neighboring axes are parallel or nearly parallel, the DH model has the singularity problem. It is not conducive to the kinematic calibration. To solve the singularity problems, Hayati proposed the M-DH model which uses an angle parameter β to describe the position relation between neighboring parallel axes [9]. The parameter definition of the industrial robot based on M-DH model is shown in Fig. 2.

The end pose of robot in the base coordinate system can be expressed as

$$T = A_0A_1A_2A_3A_4A_5A_6A_7$$
$$= \begin{bmatrix} R & P \\ 0 & 1 \end{bmatrix}$$
$$= \begin{bmatrix} n & o & a & P \\ 0 & 0 & 0 & 1 \end{bmatrix} \tag{1}$$

where $P \in R^{3\times1}$ is the position translation vector and $n, o, a \in R^{3\times1}$ is the column vector of the attitude rotation matrix R.

Due to the errors of kinematic parameters, the nominal and actual end pose can be calculated by the matrix T_N and T_R. The joint frames are defined and shown in Fig. 3. The nominal M-DH parameters of Staubli TX60 are shown in Table 1.

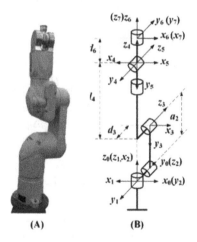

Fig. 3. The industrial robot Staubli TX60 (A) and its M-DH model (B).

Table 1. The nominal parameters of robot based on M-DH model.

i	θ_i/rad	d_i/mm	a_i/mm	α_i/rad	β_i/rad	–
1	π	0	0	$\pi/2$	–	–
2	$\pi/2$	0	290	0	0	–
3	$\pi/2$	20	0	$\pi/2$	–	–
4	π	310	0	$\pi/2$	–	–
5	π	0	0	$\pi/2$	–	–
6	0	70	0	0	0	–

i	a_i/mm	b_i/mm	c_i/mm	α_i/rad	β_i/rad	γ_i/rad
0	0	0	0	0	0	0
7	0	0	0	0	0	0

The end pose error of industrial robot is defined as

$$\Delta T = T_R - T_N$$
$$= \begin{bmatrix} \Delta n & \Delta o & \Delta a & \Delta p \\ 0 & 0 & 0 & 0 \end{bmatrix} \tag{2}$$

where ΔT is the difference between the actual end pose T_R and nominal end pose T_N.

The column vectors of transformation T are partially differentiated with respect to the kinematic parameters, and the high-order terms are ignored.

$$\begin{cases} \Delta n = \sum_{i=1}^{n} \frac{\partial n}{\partial \eta_i} \Delta \eta_i = H_n \Delta \eta, \\ \Delta o = \sum_{i=1}^{n} \frac{\partial o}{\partial \eta_i} \Delta \eta_i = H_o \Delta \eta \\ \Delta a = \sum_{i=1}^{n} \frac{\partial a}{\partial \eta_i} \Delta \eta_i = H_a \Delta \eta, \\ \Delta p = \sum_{i=1}^{n} \frac{\partial p}{\partial \eta_i} \Delta \eta_i = H_p \Delta \eta \end{cases} \tag{3}$$

where $\Delta \eta = [..., \Delta \theta_i \ \Delta d_i \ \Delta a_i \ \Delta \alpha_i \ \Delta \beta_i \ ...]$ are the kinematic parameter errors to be identified, and n is the number of robot joints. The Jacobian matrix of the M-DH kinematic model is given as

$$\begin{cases} H_p = \left[\cdots \frac{\partial p_j}{\partial \theta_i} \ \frac{\partial p_j}{\partial d_i} \ \frac{\partial p_j}{\partial a_i} \ \frac{\partial p_j}{\partial \alpha_i} \ \frac{\partial p_j}{\partial \beta_i} \cdots \right]^T \\ H_n = \left[\cdots \frac{\partial n_j}{\partial \theta_i} \ \frac{\partial n_j}{\partial d_i} \ \frac{\partial n_j}{\partial a_i} \ \frac{\partial n_j}{\partial \alpha_i} \ \frac{\partial n_j}{\partial \beta_i} \cdots \right]^T \\ H_o = \left[\cdots \frac{\partial o_j}{\partial \theta_i} \ \frac{\partial o_j}{\partial d_i} \ \frac{\partial o_j}{\partial a_i} \ \frac{\partial o_j}{\partial \alpha_i} \ \frac{\partial o_j}{\partial \beta_i} \cdots \right]^T \\ H_a = \left[\cdots \frac{\partial a_j}{\partial \theta_i} \ \frac{\partial a_j}{\partial d_i} \ \frac{\partial a_j}{\partial a_i} \ \frac{\partial a_j}{\partial \alpha_i} \ \frac{\partial a_j}{\partial \beta_i} \cdots \right]^T \end{cases} \tag{4}$$

where j is the pose sequence index.

4   Redundancy Analysis of Pose Error Model

The Eq. (1) shows that the end pose of industrial robot is a function of kinematic parameters. Therefore, the Eq. (1) is rewritten as

$$T = F(\boldsymbol{\theta}, \boldsymbol{a}, \boldsymbol{d}, \boldsymbol{\alpha}, \boldsymbol{\beta}) \tag{5}$$

where $\boldsymbol{\theta} = [\theta_1\ \theta_2\ \theta_3\ \theta_4\ \theta_5\ \theta_6]$, $\boldsymbol{a} = [a_1\ a_2\ a_3\ a_4\ a_5\ a_6]$, $\boldsymbol{d} = [d_1\ d_2\ d_3\ d_4\ d_5\ d_6]$, $\boldsymbol{\alpha} = [\alpha_1\ \alpha_2\ \alpha_3\ \alpha_4\ \alpha_5\ \alpha_6]$, $\boldsymbol{\beta} = [\beta_1\ \beta_2\ \beta_3\ \beta_4\ \beta_5\ \beta_6]$.

The errors of kinematic parameters synthetically result in the end pose error of robot. Each kinematic parameter error has different effects on the end pose error. In this paper, the error sensitivity is used to analyze the effects of each parameter error. The error sensitivity of kinematic parameters is donated as

$$\begin{cases} S_{Pi} = \frac{\partial P}{\partial q_i} \\ S_{oi} = \frac{\partial o}{\partial q_i} \\ S_{ni} = \frac{\partial n}{\partial q_i} \\ S_{ai} = \frac{\partial a}{\partial q_i} \end{cases} \tag{6}$$

where S_{Pi} is the position error sensitive vector of each kinematic parameter. (S_{ni}, S_{oi}, S_{ai}) is the attitude error sensitive vector of each kinematic parameter. The error sensitive vectors are all 3×1 column vectors. The sign of each vector component determines the effect direction of each kinematic parameter. q_i represents the kinematic parameter and i is the sequence number of the kinematic parameter in the vector $\boldsymbol{\eta}$.

However, the three-dimensional vectors cannot quantitatively express the effects on the end pose error. This paper defines a quantitative significance index as follows

$$\begin{cases} e_{pi} = \dfrac{dP_i \cdot dP}{\|dP\|} \\ e_{oi} = \dfrac{do_i \cdot do}{\|do\|} \\ e_{ni} = \dfrac{dn_i \cdot dn}{\|dn\|} \\ e_{ai} = \dfrac{da_i \cdot da}{\|da\|} \end{cases} \tag{7}$$

where dP_i, dn_i, do_i, da_i are the error vectors generated by the i-th kinematic parameter. dP, dn, do, da are the total error vectors generated by all kinematic parameter errors. The physical meanings of the quantitative significance index $e_{pi}, e_{ni}, e_{oi}, e_{ai}$ are the projection of the error sensitive vectors generated by the i-th kinematic parameter in the direction of the total error vector.

When the number of sampling points is N, the average quantitative significance indexes are statistically given as

$$\begin{cases} \bar{e}_{pi} = \dfrac{1}{N}\sum_{k=1}^{N} e_{pik} \\[2mm] \bar{e}_{ni} = \dfrac{1}{N}\sum_{k=1}^{N} e_{nik} \\[2mm] \bar{e}_{oi} = \dfrac{1}{N}\sum_{k=1}^{N} e_{oik} \\[2mm] \bar{e}_{ai} = \dfrac{1}{N}\sum_{k=1}^{N} e_{aik} \end{cases} \qquad (8)$$

A test set, which contains 50 points, is applied to calculate the average quantitative significance index of each kinematic parameter. The 50 points are randomly selected in

Table 2. The average quantitative significance index of M-DH kinematic parameters of TX60 robot.

i	DH	Position	Attitude		
		P	N	o	a
1	a_0	0.00021	0	0	0
2	b_0	0.00029	0	0	0
3	c_0	−0.00038	0	0	0
4	α_0	−0.12856	0.142873	0.081936	−0.012826
5	β_0	0.20552	0.069272	−0.021684	0.021104
6	γ_0	0.08811	0.037192	0.100129	0.208291
7	a_1	−0.00027	0	0	0
8	d_1	−0.00038	0	0	0
9	α_1	0.10183	−0.152964	−0.067887	−0.002170
10	θ_1	0.08811	0.037192	0.100129	0.208291
11	a_2	−0.00041	0	0	0
12	d_2	0.00028	0	0	0
13	α_2	0.09434	0.026996	0.092958	0.199853
14	θ_2	0.23327	0.043069	−0.024088	0.019536
15	β_2	−0.01919	0.147924	0.068812	0.011732
16	a_3	0.00046	0	0	0
17	d_3	0.00028	0	0	0
18	α_3	−0.10253	0.005488	−0.079901	−0.193921
19	θ_3	0.16631	0.043069	−0.024088	0.019536
20	a_4	4.7505E−05	0	0	0

(continued)

Table 2. (*continued*)

i	DH	Position	Attitude		
		P	N	o	a
21	d_4	0.00015	0	0	0
22	α_4	−0.00604	0.033534	0.043628	−0.037822
23	θ_4	0.005419	0.147217	0.085209	0.038111
24	a_5	4.1887E−05	0	0	0
25	d_5	−0.000118	0	0	0
26	α_5	0.008268	0.053628	0.008669	0.053310
27	θ_5	0.00293	0.007553	0.045184	−0.014814
28	a_6	−0.000453	0	0	0
29	d_6	0.000144	0	0	0
30	α_6	0	0	0.091710	0.195888
31	θ_6	0	0.137126	0.100569	0
32	β_6	0	−0.075663	0	−0.080554
33	a_7	−0.000453	0	0	0
34	b_7	−0.000154	0	0	0
35	c_7	0.000144	0	0	0
36	α_7	0	0	0.091710	0.195888
37	β_7	0	−0.075663	0	−0.080554
38	γ_7	0	0.137126	0.100569	0

the workspace of the robot. In the simulation analysis, the errors of kinematic parameters a_i and d_i are set as 0.1 mm. The errors of kinematic parameters α_i, β_i, θ_i are set as 0.1 rad. The nominal pose $\boldsymbol{T}_N$ without kinematic parameter errors and the actual pose $\boldsymbol{T}_R$ with kinematic parameter errors are both calculated respectively. The average quantitative significance index of each kinematic parameter is calculated according to (8). The calculation results are shown in Table 2. It can be seen that the kinematic parameters α_0, β_0, α_1, θ_2, α_3, θ_3 have great impacts on the position error, while the kinematic parameters α_0, γ_0, α_1, θ_1, α_2, β_2, α_3, θ_4, α_6, θ_6, α_7, γ_7 have great impacts on the attitude error. When the average quantitative significance index is zero, the corresponding kinematic parameter does not have effect on the pose errors. The kinematic parameters with equal average quantitative significance index have same effects on the end pose error. It can be seen that a_6 and a_7, c_0 and d_1, γ_0 and θ_1, d_2 and d_3, d_6 and c_7, θ_6 and γ_7, α_6 and α_7, β_6 and β_7 are equal. The redundant kinematic parameters obtained by QR decomposition method are all contained. Therefore, the average quantitative significance index can be used for redundancy analysis.

5 Robot Calibration Experiment Based on Non-redundant Error Model

The non-redundant pose error model is constructed after removing the parameters c_0, γ_0, d_2, a_6, d_6, α_6, γ_7 and β_6 from the M-DH pose error model. The optimization objective function is defined as

$$f = \min \left(\sum_{j=1}^{N} \sqrt{\left\| \Delta n_j \right\|^2 + \left\| \Delta o_j \right\|^2 + \left\| \Delta a_j \right\|^2 + \left\| \Delta p_j \right\|^2} \right) \tag{9}$$

where j represents the j-th measurement data, and N represents the total number of calibration measurement data. In this paper, the number N is equal to 200.

The M-DH parameter error is identified based on the LM optimization algorithm. In order to comprehensively evaluate the calibration effect of the robot, the average comprehensive position error e_p and the average comprehensive attitude error e_δ are defined as

$$\begin{cases} e_p = \frac{1}{N} \sum_{i=1}^{N} \sqrt{\Delta p_{ix}^2 + \Delta p_{iy}^2 + \Delta p_{iz}^2} \\ e_\delta = \frac{1}{N} \sum_{i=1}^{N} \sqrt{\delta_{ix}^2 + \delta_{iy}^2 + \delta_{iz}^2} \end{cases} \tag{10}$$

where $\Delta p_{ix}, \Delta p_{iy}, \Delta p_{iz}$ indicate the position error in x-axis, y-axis, and z-axis respectively. And $\delta_{ix}, \delta_{iy}, \delta_{iz}$ indicate the attitude error in x-axis, y-axis, and z-axis respectively.Fig. 5.The attitude errors of TX60 robot before and after calibration.

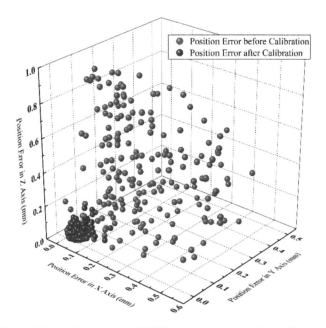

Fig. 4. The position errors of TX60 robot before and after calibration.

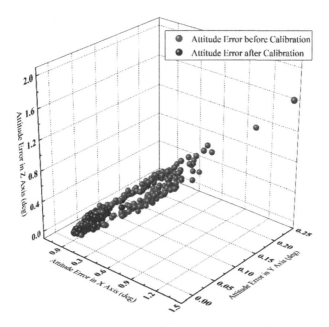

Fig. 5. The attitude errors of TX60 robot before and after calibration.

The pose accuracy of Staubli TX60 robot before and after kinematic calibration are shown in Fig. 4 and Fig. 5 respectively. The average position errors on the x-, y-, and z-axes of Staubli TX60 robot before calibration are (0.214 mm, 0.179 mm, 0.399 mm). The average position error on the x-, y-, z-axes after calibration are (0.028 mm, 0.027 mm, 0.038 mm). The position accuracy of Staubli TX60 robot after calibration in the three axes has been greatly improved. The average comprehensive position error is reduced from 0.547 mm to 0.062 mm, and the maximum comprehensive position error of the robot is reduced from 1.049 mm to 0.170 mm. The attitude errors of Staubli TX60 robot have also been improved obviously. The average attitude errors on the x-, y-, and z-axes of Staubli TX60 robot before calibration are (0.309°, 0.112°, 0.320°). The average attitude errors on the x-, y-, and z-axes of Staubli TX60 robot after calibration are (0.068°, 0.022°, 0.087°). The average comprehensive attitude error is reduced from 0.484° to 0.119°, and the maximum comprehensive attitude error is reduced from 3.232° to 0.412°.

6 Conclusion

This paper presents the error sensitivity based redundancy analysis for kinematic calibration of industrial robot. Firstly, the pose error model is established based on the M-DH model. By introducing the concept of error sensitivity in error theory, the effects of kinematic parameter error on the end pose error is analyzed. The redundant parameters of the pose error model are analyzed based on the error sensitivity. The analysis result is same as the QR decomposition method. Secondly, the effectiveness of the non-redundant pose error model is verified through experiments. The average comprehensive position error of the Staubli TX60 robot is reduced from 0.547 mm to 0.062 mm, and the maximum comprehensive position error of the robot is reduced from 1.049 mm to 0.170 mm. The average comprehensive attitude error of the robot is reduced from 0.484° to 0.119°, and the maximum comprehensive attitude error of the robot is reduced from 3.232° to 0.412°. The accuracy of the industrial robot is improved remarkably. Future work will focus on the quantitative analysis of the associated effect of the kinematic parameters.

Acknowledgement. The research reported in this paper was carried out at School of Automation, Nanjing Institute of Technology, Nanjing, China, and School of Instrument Science and Engineering, Southeast University, Nanjing, China.

Funding Statement. This work was supported in part by Natural Science Foundation of China under Grant 51905258, Natural Science Foundation of Jiangsu Province under Grant BK20170763, China Postdoctoral Science Foundation 2019M650095.

Conflicts of Interest. The authors declare that they have no conflicts of interest to report regarding the present study.

References

1. Mejri, S., Gagnol, V., Le, T.-P., Sabourin, L., Ray, P., Paultre, P.: Dynamic characterization of machining robot and stability analysis. Int. J. Adv. Manuf. Technol. **82**(1–4), 351–359 (2015)
2. Lin, Y., Zhao, H., Ding, H.: Posture optimization methodology of 6R industrial robots for machining using performance evaluation indexes. Robot. Comput. Integ. Manuf. **48**, 59–72 (2017)
3. Sun, T., Lian, B., Yang, S., Song, Y.: Kinematic calibration of serial and parallel robots based on finite and instantaneous screw theory. IEEE Trans. Rob. **36**(3), 816–834 (2020)
4. Du, G., Liang, Y., Li, C., Liu, P., Li, D.: Online robot kinematic calibration using hybrid filter with multiple sensors. IEEE Trans. Instrum. Meas. **69**(9), 7092–7107 (2020)
5. Shi, X., Zhang, F., Qu, X., Liu, B., Wang, J.: Position and attitude measurement and online errors compensation for KUKA industrial robots. J. Mech. Eng. **53**(8), 1–7 (2017)
6. Guo, Y., Yin, S., Ren, Y., Zhu, J., Yang, S., Ye, S.: A multilevel calibration technique for an industrial robot with parallelogram mechanism. Precis. Eng. **40**, 261–272 (2015)
7. Gao, G., Sun, G., Na, J., Guo, Y., Xu, X.: Structural parameter identification for 6 DOF industrial robots. Mech. Syst. Sig. Process. **113**, 145–155 (2018)
8. Cho, Y., Do, H., Cheong, J.: Screw based kinematic calibration method for robot manipulators with joint compliance using circular point analysis. Robot. Comput. Integr. Manuf. **60**, 63–76 (2019)
9. Hayati, S., Mirmirani, M.: Improving the absolute positioning accuracy of robot manipulators. J. Robot. Syst. **2**(4), 397–413 (1985)
10. Gupta, K.: Kinematic analysis of manipulators using the zero reference position description. Int. J. Robot. Res. **5**(2), 5–13 (1986)

11. Rocha, C., Tonetto, C., Dias, A.: A comparison between the Denavit-Hartenberg and the screw-based methods used in kinematic modeling of robot manipulators. Robot. Comput. Integr. Manuf. **27**(4), 723–728 (2011)
12. Xuan, J., Xu, S.: Review on kinematics calibration technology of serial robots. Int. J. Precis. Eng. Manuf. **15**(8), 1759–1774 (2014)
13. Nubiola, A., Bonev, I.: Absolute calibration of an ABB IRB 1600 robot using a laser tracker. Robot. Comput. Integr. Manuf. **29**(1), 236–245 (2013)
14. Wen, X., Kang, C., Qiao, G., Wang, D., Han, Y., Song, A.: Study on robot accuracy based on full pose measurement and optimization. Yi Qi Yi Biao Xue Bao **40**(7), 81–89 (2019)
15. Judd, R.P., Knasinski, A.B.: A technique to calibrate industrial robots with experimental verification. IEEE Trans. Robot. Autom. **6**(1), 20–30 (1990)

Re-introduction to Tibetan Case Structure and Its Grammatical Functions

Hua Cai[1(✉)], Bai Guan[2], and Kai Li[3]

[1] Key Laboratory of Artificial Intelligence Application Technology State Ethnic Affairs Commission, Qinghai Minzu University, Xining 810007, China
tshe_dpal@163.com
[2] Computer College of Qinghai Normal University, Xining 810007, China
[3] Graduate School of Advanced Science and Technology, Japan Advanced Institute of Science and Technology, 1-1 Asahidai, Nomi 923-1292, Ishikawa, Japan

Abstract. Tibetan linguistics has a long history and has formed a relatively complete traditional grammar system, but there is no recognized and relatively complete modern formal grammar framework of Tibetan. In order to inherit, expand, extend and deepen the traditional Tibetan grammar and its formal requirements, this paper makes comparative study on Fillmore case grammar with traditional Tibetan grammar, and introduces a new Tibetan grammatical unit called case structure, and demonstrates that the case structure plays an important role in Tibetan syntactic and semantic analysis. Different case structures of the same verb form Tibetan sentences, and one Tibetan sentence can be uniquely decomposed into one or more case structures. Case structure not only carries the syntactic structure of the sentence, but also reflects the semantic components of the sentence. Therefore, under this grammatical framework, Tibetan syntactic and semantic analysis can be studied in an integrated way. This opinion has some certain theoretical significance for Tibetan grammar research and Tibetan natural language processing.

Keywords: Tibetan grammar · Syntactic analysis · Semantic analysis · Case structure

1 Introduction

The syntactic and semantic analysis of Tibetan natural language is not only the premise and foundation for the intelligent development of Tibetan information processing technology, but also provides theoretical support and technical solutions for the problems encountered in the field of Tibetan morphology, such as inconsistent word segmentation units, inconsistent part of speech markers and related technical bottlenecks, and plays a connecting role in Tibetan natural language processing.

Tibetan linguistics has a long history and has formed a relatively complete grammar system. However, traditional Tibetan grammar pays attention to the phonetic [1] form and grammatical function of function words and does not pay much attention to the semantic relationship between concepts and the structure between sentence

X. Sun et al. (Eds.): ICAIS 2022, CCIS 1587, pp. 202–213, 2022.
https://doi.org/10.1007/978-3-031-06761-7_17

components [2]. Therefore, from the perspective of information processing, traditional Tibetan grammar is difficult to achieve formalization. The research on Tibetan syntax and semantic analysis for natural language processing is in its infancy. Because the traditional Tibetan grammar lacks the description of grammatical structure, some research institutions, experts and scholars use Chinese or English syntactic theory and semantic analysis methods [3–5] to analyze Tibetan. But this research method has the following problems worth thinking about:

Structural differences exist between individual languages [6]. Such kind of differences is superficial and individual and is embodied in the syntactic rules of different languages. However, the semantic relations among sentences are deep and common and are general phenomena in all languages [7].

For languages under standard grammatical patterns, such as English and Chinese, there is no direct mapping relation between the underlying semantics and superficial forms of sentences, so their syntactic and semantic analyses are regarded as two different linguistic research levels. Therefore, the tripartite research framework of syntax, semantics and pragmatics forms [8]. In English or Chinese, the correspondence between syntactic function and semantic structure varies from word to word [9]. Therefore, case grammar has some limitations in description of Chinese or English [10]. Based on these, Fillmore further developed case grammar into frame semantics.

Different from Chinese or English, Tibetan sentences include a large number of functional words which are natural syntactic and semantic analysis symbols of Tibetan. The underlying semantic relations and superficial syntactic structures of Tibetan sentences stay on the same level of research. Therefore, Tibetan syntactic and semantic analyses should be synchronous and parallel.

2   Structural Features of Tibetan Sentences

English or Chinese sentences are formed by word sequences. The arrangement of constituents of a sentence is exactly the basic content of its syntax.

Example 1:

Jhon bought the sandwich from Tom for three dollars.

The nine words can form a grammatical English sentence only when they're arranged in the above sequence. If not, they can't constitute a sentence. However, Tibetan is different. The sentence showed in Example 1 in Tibetan is:

jon   gyis bga zas de   thom   las   a sgor gsum   gyis   nyos .
tɕhon[13] chi?[132] ka[13]sɛ?[132] the[13] thom[55] lɛ?[132] a[55]kor[13] sum[55] chi?[132] ŋø?[132] .

Jhon   K3   sandwich K1 Tom   K5   three dollars   K3   bought.

In a Tibetan sentence, the predicate shall be put at the end of the sentence while the substantive shall be proposed. Kn in Tibetan is a set of grammatical markers that are added between the substantive and the predicate, called case markers (rnam dbyevi phrad) to show "the transitivity between substantives, nouns, pronouns, etc. and predicate verbs, adjectives, etc., such as the relationship between an action and its implementer, the relationship between an action and its receiver, the relationship between an action and the privies, etc. [11]" For example, K3 which is set between Jhon and bought is called the third case marker (rnam dbye gsum pa byed sgra), showing the semantic relation between the action and its implementer.

It's because different case markers are used to bind the semantic relation between each substantive and predicate in Tibetan that the syntactic function and semantic relation of the substantive are no longer affected by change of its position in the sentence. Therefore,

1 Jhon K3 sandwich K1 Tom K5 three dollars K3 bought.
2 sandwich K1 Jhon K3 Tom K5 three dollars K3 bought.
3 Tom K5 sandwich K1 Jhon K3 three dollars K3 bought.
4 Tom K5 three dollars K3 sandwich K1 Jhon K3 bought.
5 Jhon K3 sandwich K1 Tom K5 three dollars K3 bought.
6 sandwich K1 Jhon K3 Tom K5 three dollars K3 bought.
7 Tom K5 Jhon K3 sandwich K1 three dollars K3 bought.
8 Tom K5 Jhon K3 three dollars K3 sandwich K1 bought.
9 Tom K5 Jhon K3 sandwich K1 three dollars K3 bought.
8 Jhon K3 Tom K5 three dollars K3 sandwich K1 bought.
9 Jhon K3 Tom K5 sandwich K1 three dollars K3 bought.
10 sandwich K1 Jhon K3 three dollars K3 Tom K5 bought.
…

For example1, Theoretically, there are 24 different constructions of sentences that correspond to it in Tibetan, and these sentences are all right sentences that conform to the Tibetan grammar. But each sentence is representing a different perspective of the same scene. Therefore, we are think that the Tibetan language is much more capable of describing scenes than Chinese or English.

3 Case Structure in Tibetan

By comparison, we can see that there is a very similar cognitive framework between the case structure mentioned in Tibetan traditional grammar and the case in Fillmore's grammatical theory. Tibetan traditional grammar has always paid great attention to the study of the semantic relations between concepts, but never formed a syntactic analysis method that regards verbs as the core. Therefore, Tibetan has never formed an advanced and self-contained grammar theory. If we re-understand and organize the Tibetan traditional grammar theory with the Fillmore grammatical perspective, we can find that the case grammar could better reflect the grammatical features of Tibetan language than the standard grammar.

3.1 Form of Case Structure

After making some necessary changes to the first case and sixth case of the Tibetan traditional grammar, we can see that the Tibetan case structure has a fixed organizational form, which is NP + K + VP and indicating the semantic relation between NP and VP. NP is known as the case with K as the case marker and VP as the core and predicate of a sentence. The semantic relation between NP and VP varies with K as a case marker. In other words, the first seven cases are used to describe the outside world, and the seventh case to express the speaker's psychological activity.

Case structure in Tibetan is divided into eight categories by semantics, the so-called eight cases. Each category is further detailed into multiple kinds of semantic relations. Eight cases of Tibetan language can be distributed into three groups, as shown in Fig. 1. The first case, the second case, the third case and the fourth case are listed as the first group with a topic describing an action, respectively expressing such main semantic relations as *"what to do"*, *"where to do it"*, *"who to do it"*, *"how to do it"*; the second group includes the first case, the fifth case, the sixth case and the seventh case respectively expressing such semantic relations as *"how do you find it"*, *"where to get it"*, *"who does it belong to"* and *"where is it"* to describing an object. The eighth case can be classified as the third group, mainly describing the way a speaker expresses his/her feelings. The eight cases are named after these main semantic relations in Tibetan in which it is considered that subordinate semantic relations are included in the above-mentioned eight cases.

The eight cases of Tibetan are respectively named according to the partial semantic relations mentioned above, and each case can be subdivided into a case relation related to many semantic meanings. For example, the second case is generally called the dative case, but it can not only represent the semantic relationship between the action and the object, but also represent action as well as the semantic relationship between the place, time and result of the action. The third case is generally called implementation case, which not only represents the semantic relationship between actions and implementers, but also semantic relations such as actions and tools, causes and methods.

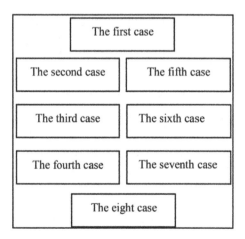

Fig. 1. The Tibetan case structure.

3.2   The Classification of Tibetan Verbs and Semantic Case Priority

Case is a basic tool of case grammar to interpret semantic and syntax relations. But it is quite difficult to define a case list. Fillmore never makes an entire and clear case list. In different articles, number of cases varies with their names changed frequently [12]. What has caused the difficulty? In our opinion, first, there is a lack of research on the classification of verbs; second, the issue of preference for multiple semantic cases.

Tibetan traditional grammar attaches great importance to the classification of verbs, and has produced a variety of classification methods. Among them, what has an important influence on grammar is the classification of Tibetan verbs based on subjects and objects. According to the differentiation between subject and object, the method divides the verb into subject-object separable verbs (bya byed tha dad pavi bya tshig) and subject-object inseparable verbs (bya byed tha mi dad pavi bya tshig). The subject-object separable verbs means that the subject of the action can be separated from the object on which the action exerts an "influence". If they can't be separated, it is called the subject-object inseparable verb. For example, "plant" (vdebs) is a subject-object separable verb, because the subject of this action (or actor. E.g., students) and the object (or patient. E.g. trees) are two different things; "go" (vgro) is a subject-object inseparable verb, because the subject and object of this action has to be the same animal indistinguishably. In many literatures, this classification is equal to that of transitivity. However, the classification of Tibetan verbs is based on the semantic level while the classification of transitivity focuses on the morphological differences, which lies a big difference between these two.

In addition, according to two different angles, Tibetan divides verbs into subject verbs (byed las), object verbs (bya las) as well as natural verbs (ngang gis byung ba) [13], tense verbs (dus gsum gyi dbye bas khyab pa) and normal verb (dus gsum gyi dbye bas ma khyab pa) and so on. For example: cut (bcad), is an subject verb, having subject-object reparability and variations in tense; break (chad), is an object verb, which could be separated from the subject and is a normal verb; go (འགྲོ), is an automatic verb, subject-object inseparable verb and tense verb.

It is believed that in the natural language processing and comprehension of Tibetan, a comprehensive utilization of verbal classification will extract more grammatical information about Tibetan verbs.

Example 2: "I climb trees." and "I cut trees." are corresponding to the following ones in Tibetan:

$$
\begin{aligned}
&\text{nga} \quad \text{sdong bo} \quad \text{la} \quad \text{vdzegs}. \\
&\text{ŋa}^{13} \quad \text{toŋ}^{13}\ \text{pho}^{13} \quad \text{la}^{13} \quad \text{tseʔ}^{132}. \\
&\text{I} \quad \text{trees} \qquad \text{K2} \quad \text{climb.} \\
&\text{nga s} \quad \text{sdong bo} \qquad \text{bcad}. \\
&\text{I} \quad \text{K3}\ \text{tree} \qquad \text{cut.} \\
&\text{ŋɛʔ}^{132} \quad \text{toŋ}^{13} \quad \text{pho}^{13} \quad \text{tɕɛʔ}^{51}.
\end{aligned}
$$

Obviously, we cannot differentiate the syntactic and semantic differences between the two Chinese sentences through part-of-speech, transitivity, or sentence structure. However, there are obvious differences in the syntactic structure of the two corresponding Tibetan sentences. This is because Tibetan constructs the sentence structure according to the semantic relations of core verbs. Before the construction of sentences, the semantic relations between predicates and argument are definite.

In Tibetan, the object of action must respond to the action, in other words, the action of the subject must affect the state of the object. Tibetans believe that "climbing" and "walking" have the same effect, which both belong to subject-object inseparable verbs. The subject and the object of "climbing" is both "I", so there is a dual semantic relationship between me and climbing. In this regard, the semantic case priority should be used in Tibetan language choice. The first case takes precedence over the third grid, that is, I K1 climb. Because climbing this action will not cause the "tree" state to change, which is only the place where the action occurs, so the semantic relationship between the tree and climbing is the location-action relationship, that is, tree K2 climb.

"Cut" is a subject-object separable verb. In terms of this action, the subject is "I" and the object affected by the action is "tree". Therefore, different markers Kn are used between each nominal and predicate, that is, I K3 cut and tree K1 cut, which reflects the deep semantic differences (Table 1).

Table 1. Tibetan verb classification and semantic case.

	Example	Font size and style
I	K_1	K_3
Trees	K_2	K_1

As shown in Fig. 2, the second case structure is formed between "climb" and "tree" while the first case structure is formed between "cut" and "tree"; there is a first case formed between "climb" and "me", however, a third case construction is formed between "cut" and "me". This subtle grammatical difference results from the classification of Tibetan verbs and the semantic case prioritization.

When a substantive matches with the predicate constituted by multiple verbs, its form of semantic case depends on the first verb.

Example 3: "He sings song and goes away" is corresponding to the following sentence in Tibetan:

kho s   glu   len   nas   bud   song .
khø?^{51} lu^{55} len^{13} nɛ?^{132} phy?^{132} soŋ^{55} .
He K3 songs K1 sing F   goes   away."

The serial verb in Tibetan is generally the verb phase in the form of V1 + F + V2, where F is a function word. When a substantive matches with a verb phase, the semantic case follows the former verb. In Example 3, the third case is between "He" and "sings" and the first case is between "sings" and "goes away". But after "sings" and "goes" form a verb phase by the function word F, only K3 is used for the semantic case between "He" and "sings F goes". Different function words, often occurring between two verbs of a Tibetan serial-verb sentence to mark their semantic relations, are organized through semantic relations as done in Chinese pivotal sentences.

Therefore, the "limitation" in Chinese won't be encountered with when case grammar is adopted for description in Tibetan [14].

3.3   Nested Structure in Sentence

There is a widespread phenomenon of nominalization of forms in Tibetan language [15]. As a kind of independent grammatical unit, the part-of-speech of case structure is the same as that of verb phrase. When a verb, a verb phrase or a case structure acts as a case character of another verb or nests in another sentence, nominalization must be achieved through certain grammatical means.

Example 4: "He was right!" or "He is right!" corresponds to the Tibetan sentence:

khong	gis	gsungs	pa	bden .
khoŋ^{55}	khiʔ^{132}	sup^{51}	pa^{55}	ten^{13} .
He	K3	said	ba	right.

Among which, ba is an nominalization maker. Formally, the maker is added after the verb, but whether to analysis from the perspective of grammar or the semantic relation, this maker should be added after the case structure "He K3 said". In this way, the nominal component of nominalization is different from the original predicative component, but it is related to a certain lattice that is governed by the predicate. The nominalized case structure and the central predicate of the whole sentence "right" constitute a new case structure.

In Example 4, "He K3 said" firstly constitutes the third case structure CP3 with the verb "said" as its core, expressing the semantic relation between the action and the subject of the action. Secondly, nominalization the case structure by adding nominalization markers and transferred designation [15] to "what he said". The noun phrase acts as the described object of the core word "right", and thus forms the first case structure finally. In Example 4, if the marker "ba" was not used, the corresponding Tibetan sentence "He K3 said right" would be a grammatically wrong sentence. The syntax structure of Example 4 can be described as show in Fig. 2.

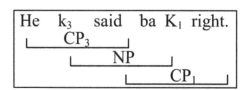

Fig. 2. Nesting of the Tibetan case structure.

A general grammar rule in Tibetan is that, only after nominalization the Tibetan non-nominal grammar unit can act as the case role of another verb.

Example 5: "He is writing characters." It corresponds to the following complete sentence:

khong	gis	yi ge	vbri bzhin vdug
khoŋ⁵⁵	khi?¹³² ji¹³khe¹³	tṣi¹³ ɕin¹³ tu?¹³²
He.	K3 characters K1	is writing.

khong gis yi ge vbri bzhin vdug
khoŋ⁵⁵ khi?¹³² ji¹³khe¹³ tṣi¹³ ɕin¹³ tu?¹³²
He.   K3 characters K1 is writing.

If this sentence acts as the case role of another verb, it needs to be nominalized first.

Example 6: "I saw him writing characters." It is a pivotal sentence and it corresponds to the Tibetan sentence:

nga yis khong gis yi ge vbri ba mthong song .
ŋa¹³ ji?¹³² khoŋ⁵⁵ khi?¹³² ji¹³khe¹³ tṣi¹³ pha¹³ thoŋ⁵⁵ soŋ⁵⁵ .
I   K3 him   k3 characters writing ba saw.

Among which, "*He k3 characters k1 writing*" is a complete sentence, which is postposition by the character ba and becomes the object clause of "*saw*", hence forms a certain case relation with the core verb "*saw*". If no postposition like "*ba*" is makers, "*I K3 he k3 characters k1 writing K1 saw.*" will be a character string that does not conform to Tibetan grammar.

3.4   Case Structure Serving as the Most Direct Unit of Tibetan Sentences

In order to reflect the grammatical features of Tibetan, this paper expands its grammatical units into six units: phonemes, characters, words, phrases, case structures and sentences. A case structure is a special grammatical unit between a phrase and a sentence. A phrase is a component of a case structure, and a case structure is the very direct constituent of a sentence.

In example 2, the "*I K3 cut*" and "*tree K1 cut*" are both standard Tibetan case structures. The first seven case structures in Tibetan have a unified structural construction, which is V + Kn + P. The combination with different case structures of the same verb will result in Tibetan sentences with the verb as the core. For example, "*I K3 cut*" and "*tree K1 cut*" can form two Tibetan sentences with "*cut*" as the core, i.e.

1. *I K3 tree K1 cut.*
2. *tree K1 I K3 cut.*

These two sentences are equivalent to "I cut the tree." and "The tree is cut by me." in Chinese, equally English.

Similarly, there are four case structures in Example 1:

1. *Jhon K3 bought,*
2. *sandwich K1 bought,*
3. *Tom K5 bough,*
4. *three dollars K3 bought.*

In theory, these case structures can be combined into 24 different Tibetan sentences with "bought" as the core.

4 Terms Tree Diagram of Tibetan Case Grammar

4.1 Fillmore Case Grammar

In Fillmore case grammar, a sentence consists of modality and proposition. If we represent a sentence with S, modality with M and proposition with P respectively, they can be written as: $S \rightarrow M + P$. P can be extended to a scope of one verb and one or more cases. If V stands for a verb, the scope of case can be represented with , , ..., , and they can be written as: $C \rightarrow K + NP$.

In this way, a sentence expressed by case grammar can be drawn into a tree diagram as Fig. 3.

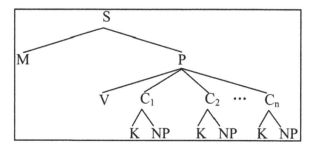

Fig. 3. Fillmore case grammar tree.

4.2 Tibetan Tree Diagram Based on Case Grammar

In order to embody the grammar characteristics of Tibetan itself, this paper has adjusted the original tree diagram of Fillmore case grammar as follow:

1. location interchange between modality and proposition;
2. location interchange between case and verb;
3. location interchange between case and case mark, and synchronization of the subscript of C and K. Of course, such adjustment is only change in form, without influencing the main idea of the case grammar.

Example 7: For building a house, Tashi will cut trees in the forest from tomorrow.

> khang ba bzo par bkra shis kyis sang nyin nas nags tshal du sdong bo gcod rgyu red .
> khaŋ⁵⁵pha¹³ so¹³ par⁵⁵ tʂa⁵⁵ɕiʔ⁵¹ciʔ⁵¹ saŋ⁵⁵ɲin¹³ nɛʔ¹³² naʔ¹³²tshɛː⁵⁵ thu¹³ toŋ¹³pho¹³ tɕøʔ⁵¹ cu¹³ ɹeʔ¹³² .

> building a house K4 Tashi K3 tomorrow K5 forest K2 tree K1 will cut.
> The corresponding Tibetan syntax of the sentence can be expressed as the following tree diagram (Fig. 4):

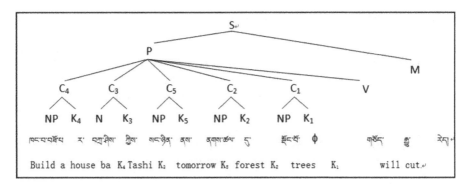

Fig. 4. The Tibetan case grammar tree.

As shown in the diagram, the core verb "cut" divides the sentence into two parts, with every case role at the left, and the modality part at the right. Each C and V form a Tibetan case structure, in which V is the core verb: the first case CP1 in Tibetan grammar is composed of C1 and V, K1 is the empty mark, and NP denotes the object affected by V; the second case of Tibetan is composed of C2 and V, the case mark is K2, and NP denotes the place where V occurs [16]; the fifth case of Tibetan is composed of C5 and V, the case mark is K5, and NP denotes the start time of V [17]; the fourth case of Tibetan is composed of C4 and V, the case mark is K4, and NP denotes the purpose of the implementation of V [18]; the third case of Tibetan is composed of C3 and V, the case mark is K3, and NP denotes the implementer of V [19]. Among them, C4 has a nested case structure. Taking verb "*build*" as the core verb of "*house*",

"*house k1 build*" forms a first case structure. The postposition of the word case "*ba*" changes into the self-reference nominal component, serving as the destinative of the core verb "*cut*".

The modality in the case grammar mainly refers to the tense, aspect and voice of a verb and positive, negative, imperative, interrogative, exclamation and statement and so on. In Tibetan, these modalities of verb will be present on the right of a verb: the "tense" of a verb reflects in the verb itself [20] or the add-on component; the modality components of positive, imperative, interrogative, exclamation and statement etc. will be also present after the verb; the negative component of the Tibetan verb will appear ahead of the verb. As shown in the diagram, "will" represents the tense and "can" indicates the positive.

The syntax structure of Example 7 may also be expressed as

$$(C4\ (C3\ (C5\ (C2\ (C1\ (V,\ M)))))),$$

from which the hierarchical relationship of the case structures can be seen clearly.

5   Conclusion

In view of the grammatical features of Tibetan itself, it is necessary to introduce a new grammatical unit into Tibetan grammar, which is the case structure. Lying between phrases and sentences, it plays a connecting role in the study of Tibetan grammar. Case structure not only inherits the characteristics of Tibetan traditional grammar, but also facilitates the uncovering of the correspondence between the surface structure and deep meaning of Tibetan sentences. This paper holds the point that case grammar is more suitable to describe the language characteristics of Tibetan than standard grammar. Therefore, the case structure can be applied not only to the teaching and research of Tibetan language, but also to the technology oriented to natural language processing in Tibetan language. Moreover, case grammar can also be used to in the parallel study of syntax and semantics of Tibetan language and to construct a Tibetan language model.

Acknowledgement. We would like to thank the anonymous reviewers for their valuable comments. This work was partially funded by the planning projects foundation of Department of Education of China (21YJA740001); Qinghai Province Natural Science Foundation of China (2021-ZJ-727); National Natural Science Foundation of China (62007019/62166034); Young and middle-aged scientific research fund project of Qinghai Normal University (2019zr013); Scientific research projects of the State Key Laboratory of Tibetan intelligent information processing and application and Qinghai Key Laboratory of Tibetan information processing and machine translation (2020-ZJ-Y05).

References

1. Zhao, Y., et al.: Tibetan multi-dialect speech recognition using latent regression Bayesian network and end-to-end mode. J. Internet of Things **1**(1), 17–23 (2019)
2. Kumar, S., Sastry, H.G., Marriboyina, V., Alshazly, H., Idris, S.A.: Semantic information extraction from multi-corpora using deep learning. Comput. Mater. Continua **70**(3), 5021–5038 (2022)
3. Rana, T.A., et al.: Extraction of opinion target using syntactic rules in Urdu text. Intell. Autom. Soft Comput. **29**(3), 839–853 (2021)
4. Ji, H., Oh, S., Kim, J., Choi, S., Park, E.: Integrating deep learning and machine translation for understanding unrefined languages. Comput. Mater. Continua **70**(1), 669–678 (2022)
5. Kolhar, M., Alameen, A.: Artificial intelligence based language translation platform. Intell. Autom. Soft Comput. **28**(1), 1–9 (2021)
6. Humboldt, W.V.: The Diversity of Human Language-Structure and its Influence on the Mental Development of Mankind. The Commercial Press (1998)
7. Liu, Y.: Computational Linguistics, p. 204. Tsinghua University Press, Beijing (2014)
8. Cai, S., Zou, C.: Formal Theoretical Research on Natural Language, p. 5. People's Publishing House, Beijing (2010)
9. Feng, Z.: Formal Model of Natural Language Processing, p. 306. University of Science and Technology of China Press, Beijing (2010)
10. Liu, Y.: Computational linguistics, p. 198. Tsinghua University Press, Beijing (2014)
11. Feng, Z.: Formal Model of Natural Language Processing, p. 295. University of Science and Technology of China Press, Beijing (2010)

12. Ma, J.: Clarification of the Four Structures of Tibetan Grammar: Tibtan, p. 62. Ethnic Publishing House, Beijing (2008)
13. Yuan, Y.: Research on the Valence Grammar in Chinese, vol. 3, pp. 73–74. Commerce and Trade Press, Beijing (2010)
14. Feng, Z.: Formal Model of Natural Language Processing, p. 294. Beijing: University of Science and Technology of China Press (2010)
15. Ma, J.: Tibetan Grammar: Tibetan, p. 281. Qinghai Ethnic Publishing House, Xining (1998)
16. Gesangjumei, G.: Practical Tutorial Tibetan Grammar, p. 112. Sichuan Ethnic Publishing House, Sichuan (2004)
17. Ji, T.: Research on Syntax of Tibetan Language, p. 294. China Tibetology Press (2013)
18. Nog, D., Jia, Z.: The Computational Linguistics of Tibetan. Southwest Jiaotong University Press, Sichuan, p. 127 (2014)
19. Zu, G.: Tibetan Verb List: Tibetan, p. 2. Tibetan people's Publishing House, Lhasa (1999)
20. Rao, D., McMahan, B.: Natural Language Processing with PyTorch. China Electric Power Press (2021)

Modelling the Precipitation Nowcasting ZR Relationship Based on Deep Learning

Jianbing Ma[1](✉), Xianghao Cui[1], and Nan Jiang[2]

[1] Chengdu University of Information Technology, Chengdu 610225, China
mjb@cuit.edu.cn
[2] Bournemouth University, Bournemouth BH12 5BB, UK

Abstract. Sudden precipitations, especially heavy ones, usually bring troubles or even huge harm to people's daily lives. Hence a timely and accurate precipitation nowcasting is expected to be an indispensable part of our modern life. Given that the current precipitation nowcasting methods are based on radar echo maps, the ZR relation that transforms radar echoes into precipitation amounts is crucial. However, traditionally the ZR relation was typically estimated by location-dependent experiential formula which is not satisfactory in both accuracy and universality. Therefore, in this paper, we propose a deep learning based method to model the ZR relation. To evaluate, we conducted our experiment with the Shenzhen precipitation data as the dataset. We introduced and compared several deep learning models, such as CNN, LSTM, and Transformer. The experimental results show that Transformer + CNN has a higher prediction accuracy. Furthermore, to deal with the unbalanced datasets and emphasize on heavy precipitation, we tried to use the SMOTE algorithm to expand heavy precipitation samples, and it shows that it can effectively improve the prediction accuracy of heavy precipitation. Similarly, we also tried to use a customized loss function to enhance the weight of heavy precipitation samples during model training, and it also demonstrate that it can achieve a better accuracy of heavy precipitations. Both approaches can improve the prediction of heavy Precipitation samples by more than 30% on average.

Keywords: Precipitation nowcasting · Radar reflectivity · Transformer · SMOTE · CNN

1 Introduction

Nowcast is a type of weather forecast which makes predictions in the very short term, typically less than two hours - a period in which traditional numerical weather prediction can be limited [1]. Since precipitation nowcasting has a wide range of applications such as agriculture, aviation control, and transportation, intensive research efforts have been proposed in this area [1–4, 7]. The traditional Numerical Weather Prediction (NWP) has been proved to be infeasible in dealing with this problem. Due to the dynamic and non-linear nature of nowcasting, linear extrapolation techniques cannot capture the underlying patterns of aberrations and trends based on the historical data. Given that precipitation nowcasting involves a big amount of data, researchers have started to exploit the processing capabilities of sequence-based deep neural networks [2].

© The Author(s), under exclusive license to Springer Nature Switzerland AG 2022
X. Sun et al. (Eds.): ICAIS 2022, CCIS 1587, pp. 214–224, 2022.
https://doi.org/10.1007/978-3-031-06761-7_18

In precipitation nowcasting, there are typically a series of radar data in chronological order. Clearly, we can resort to methods that can process time series data, namely, deep learning methods such as LSTM [2], 3D-CNN [2] and the recently proposed Transformer based on the attention mechanism [6].

In [3], Shi et al. proposed the ConvLSTM network to solve the image data with timing characteristics. They used it to build an end-to-end trainable model of precipitation nowcasting. Experiments showed that the ConvLSTM network can better capture the temporal and spatial correlation, and the result outperformed FC-LSTM and an advanced business ROVER algorithm used for precipitation nowcasting [3]. However, in the ConvLSTM-based model, the convolutional recursive structure is position-invariant, while natural movement and transformation (rotation) are usually positional changes. So later Shi. et al. proposed the Trajectory GRU (TrajGRU) model [4], which can actively learn the structure of recursively connected position variables and showed that training with balanced loss functions is essential for good nowcasting performance of heavier rainfall. And among the deep learning models, TrajGRU performs the best and 3D CNN outperforms 2D CNN, which shows that an appropriate network structure is crucial to achieving good performance.

In the prediction of precipitation, the radar reflection echo diagram is the most widely used. The relationship between radar reflectivity (Z) and precipitation (R) is also the key to predicting precipitation in the past. In previous precipitation predictions, many experiments directly used the ZR formula (Z = aRb) derived from the data by the predecessors. For instance, the Marshall–Palmer formula [5] ($Z = 200 \, R^{1.6}$ where Z is in mm^6/m^3 and R is in mm/h) converts radar reflectivity into precipitation rate. This method may have some shortcomings. Firstly, the values of the parameters are different for different regions; Secondly, the formula is quite simple, and some important factors or functions may be ignored, and the fit for precipitation is low; Lastly, for some special terrains, it may lead to larger prediction loss. To remedy these weaknesses, in this paper we propose deep learning-based methods to model the ZR relation.

The main contributions of this paper are:

1. The effectiveness of multiple deep learning models for simulating ZR relations is compared. It is concluded that Transformer + CNN works best.
2. A comparison was made between the model emphasizing the strong precipitation sample and the untreated model. It is concluded that the above method can lead to an average improvement of more than 30% in the accuracy of heavy rainfall samples.

The rest of the paper is organized as follows. In Sect. 2, We present some background knowledge that needs to be understood for this paper. Section 3 describes the details of the deep evidence dataset, including dimensions, data significance, etc. In Sect. 4, we describe in detail the principles of each deep learning model and how they are combined. In Sect. 5, we analyzed and discussed the experimental results. And finally we conclude our paper in Sect. 6.

2 Related Work

2.1 Traditional Methods

In traditional weather forecasting systems, Numerical Weather Prediction (NWP) is a widely used method in the past. It relies on the mathematical and physical equations of atmospheric motion to infer the future weather. However, it involve solving highly complex mathematical models which are computationally expensive and require enormous computing power and thus usually are performed on expensive supercomputers [7]. Due to their high computational and time requirements, NWP models are less suitable for short-term forecasts ranging from minutes to up to 6 h, also referred to as now-casting [2]. Nowcasting models are able to use the latest available observational weather data to create their predictions, making them more responsive compared to the NWP models [3]. This responsiveness is critical to increase the accuracy of predictions for dynamic and rapidly changing environments such as the atmosphere. Nowcasts have therefore become important tools to complement NWP approaches, especially in the context of meteorologically unstable conditions typical for severe weather hazards such as thunderstorms and heavy rainfall [8].

The conventional approaches to precipitation nowcasting used by existing operational systems rely on optical flow [14]. Recently, progress has been made by utilizing supervised deep learning [15] techniques for precipitation nowcasting. Shi et al. [16] formulated precipitation nowcasting as a spatiotemporal sequence forecasting problem and proposed the Convolutional Long Short-Term Memory (ConvLSTM) model, which extends the LSTM [17] by having convolutional structures in both the input-to-state and state-to-state transitions, to solve the problem. Using the radar echo sequences for model training, the authors showed that ConvLSTM is better at capturing the spatiotemporal correlations than the fully-connected LSTM and gives more accurate predictions than the Real-time Optical flow by Variational methods for Echoes of Radar (ROVER) algorithm [14] currently used by the Hong Kong Observatory (HKO).

2.2 SMOTE for Data Processing

In daily weather, precipitation samples are not available every day, and heavy precipitation samples are even rarer, and heavy Precipitation is the most influential part of people's daily life, so how to deal with the imbalance of Precipitation samples and improve heavy precipitation. The accuracy of prediction is an urgent task to be solved. SMOTE (Synthetic Minority Oversampling Technique), synthetic minority oversampling technique. It is an improved scheme based on the random oversampling algorithm. Because random oversampling adopts a simple copy sample strategy to increase the minority samples, it is easy to cause the problem of model overfitting, making the information learned by the model too special and not general enough. The basic idea of the SMOTE algorithm is to analyze the minority samples and artificially synthesize new samples based on the minority samples and add them to the data set. The algorithm is shown in the figure below, and the algorithm flow is as follows:

A. For each sample x in the minority class, use the Euclidean distance as the standard to calculate the distance from all samples in the minority class sample set to obtain its k nearest neighbors.
B. Set a sampling ratio according to the sample imbalance ratio to determine the sampling magnification N. For each minority sample x, randomly select several.
C. Samples from its k nearest neighbors, assuming that the selected nearest neighbor is xn.
D. For each randomly selected neighbor xn, construct a new sample with the original sample according to the following formula (Fig. 1).

$$x_{new} = x + rand(0, 1) * (\underset{x}{\sim} - x)$$

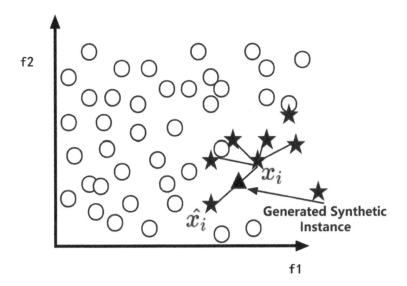

Fig. 1. SMOTE randomly generated data.

3   ShengZheng Dataset

The dataset contains real radar images and precipitation at the target site collected by the Meteorological Observation Center. The data covers the following dimensions:

1. Each radar chart contains a target site (located in the center of the map);
2. Each radar chart contains the total amount of precipitation at the target site in the next 1 h and 2 h. Please note that we do not consider the amount of precipitation in the next hour;
3. Radar images under different time spans, with an interval of 6 min, a total of 15 time spans; radar images at different heights, with an interval of 1 km, ranging from a distance of 0.5 km to 3.5 km, a total of 4 heights;

4. According to the latitude and longitude of the target location, each radar map covers an area of 101×101 km^2. The area is marked as 101×101 grids, and the target position is in the center, that is, (50, 50). Each precipitation sample contains radar echo maps of 4 heights at 15 time points, forming a dataset of dimension (batch, 15, 4, 101, 101).

The following is an example of a visualization of radar echo data for a given sample at a given height. From left to right and top to bottom are arranged in chronological order. Above each graph is the average pixel value (average of reflected echo intensity) for that graph. From left to right and top to bottom are arranged in chronological order. The average pixel value (average of reflected echo intensity) for that plot is shown above each plot. Row is the sample ordinate, high is the height ordinate, and rain is the precipitation amount (Fig. 2).

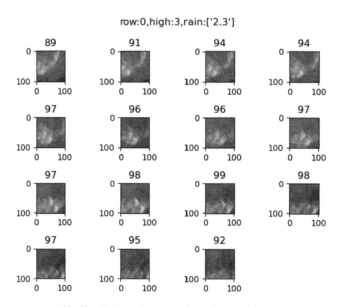

Fig. 2. Radar echo map of the fourth altitude.

Table 1. The precipitation proportion of the dataset.

	Size	Precipitation (mm/h)	Proportion (%)
Training	5000	$0 \leq x < 30$	81.46
		$30 \leq x$	18.54
Test	3000	$0 \leq x < 30$	82.77
		$30 \leq x$	17.23

Among them, there are 5000 training samples and 3000 testing samples, and the percentage of heavy precipitation samples (>30 mm/h) in each sample is shown in the Table 1.

4   Case Design and Algorithms

In our experiments, we selected the fourth altitude (3.5 km) of radar echo data for training because of the high accuracy at this altitude. Several different combinations of deep learning models were chosen for the model. The general idea is to use CNN to extract the graph as feature values, and then use FC networks or RNN networks to process the feature values. The specific model combinations are described in detail below. Among them, the effects of using only the last radar plot (case1 & case2) and the time-series data using 15 plots (case3 & case4) are compared in the use of data. Case 1 & Case 2 use the last radar map from the time-series radar data as input, so the data dimension is (b, 101, 101). In addition, Case3 & Case4 use the data dimension of (b, 15, 101, 101).

4.1   CNN + FC + ZR Formula

In Case 1, the model construction is based on the traditional Z-R formula ($Z = aR_b$), and the radar map is processed into a feature vector h using CNN, and then h is put into two FC networks to obtain parameters a and b. The precipitation R is inverse according to the ZR formula. Theoretically, the model generalizes better and works better with a smaller amount of data.

4.2   CNN + FC

In Case 2, the model directly uses the combination of CNN + FC for prediction, forming a control group with Case 1.

4.3   CNN + LSTM + FC

In Case 3, we use CNN to extract the feature vectors, and then feed the temporal feature vectors of length 15 into the LSTM. Finally, the output of the LSTM is used as the input of the FC layer to output the predicted precipitation.

4.4   CNN + LSTM + ZR Formula + FC

In Case 4, based on Case 1 and Case 3, the radar map in each time series is operated as Case 1 to obtain the time series feature vector h, and then h is used as the input to the LSTM.

4.5   CNN + Transformer + FC

In Case 5, the Transformer is used instead of LSTM to process temporal type data. The model is based entirely on the attention mechanism and completely dispenses with recursion and convolution. Experiments on two machine translation tasks show that these models are qualitatively superior, while being more parallelizable and requiring less training time [6]. Some modifications were made to the original Transformer model and only the encode layer was used in the experiments, removing the original decode layer.

The network structure of the model is shown in the Fig. 3 below (Figs. 4, 5 and 6):

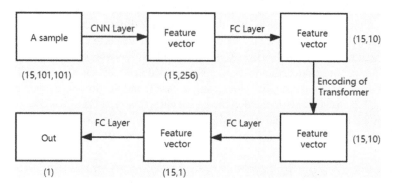

Fig. 3. The overall model structure diagram.

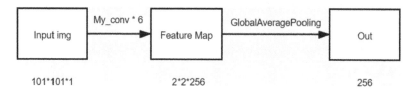

Fig. 4. CNN layer.

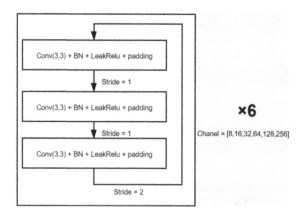

Fig. 5. The conv layer used in CNN layer.

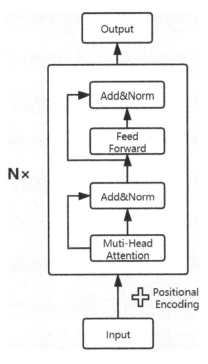

Fig. 6. Encoder of transformer.

Transformer works best in this experiment when processing timing data. The Transformer model in this experiment uses only the Encoder part of the native model with some modifications.

4.6   CNN + Transformer + FC + SMOTE

In Case 6, since the precipitation data have a clear imbalance, i.e., the proportion of heavy precipitation weather is much smaller than that of non-heavy precipitation weather. Therefore, in order to improve the prediction accuracy of strong precipitation days, we need to SMOTE the data and randomly supplement some strong precipitation samples to make the sample proportion balanced.

4.7   CNN + Transformer + FC + Customized Loss Function

In Case 7, a custom loss function is used to improve the prediction accuracy of the strong precipitation samples. This is done by multiplying the loss of the strong precipitation samples by a factor A (factor A = 2 in this paper), which makes the gradient of the model in the strong precipitation samples increase, and thus biases the model to predict the strong precipitation data. Recently, it was shown that attention in CNNs can be a very useful tool to enhance performance for an underlying task [9–13]. Attention is a mechanism that amplifies wanted signals and suppresses unwanted ones. This directs the network to pay more attention to features important for the task at hand.

5   Evaluation and Discussion

This section evaluates different combinations of deep learning methods. Table 2 gives the MSE loss for each combination on the val dataset under training and it is found that the combination of Transformer + CNN + FC performs the best. Table 3 gives the MSE loss on the test set using the Transformer + CNN + FC combination comparing the MSE loss on the test set using the SMOTE extended dataset and the original dataset, and it is found that although the overall loss has increased instead of decreased, the loss on the strong precipitation sample data has decreased a lot.

Table 2. Comparison of MSE loss for each model combination.

Model	MSE
CNN + FC + ZR formula	*130*
CNN + FC	*240*
CNN + LSTM + FC	*100*
CNN + LSTM + ZR formula + FC	*130*
CNN + Transformer + FC	**85**

Table 3. Impact of dataset pre-processing on heavy precipitation.

Dataset	MSE	
	All samples	Heavy precipitation
Unprocessed	**315**	*835*
SMOTE data extensions	*357*	**107**
Modify the loss function	*335*	*347*

Through the experiment results above, it can be concluded that when using one radar map to infer precipitation, a combination of mathematical formulas and BP networks can be used to achieve optimal results. The reason for this may be the fact that using the deep learning approach alone may lead to severe overfitting when the amount of data is not sufficient. And adding mathematical formulas as constraints can improve the generalization of the model. When multiple radar maps are used to form a temporal data, the results are better than when only one radar map is used. The reason for this is the increased amount of data and the fact that the radar plots at different times may have some correlation. In the comparison of the time-series models, Transformer works better, thanks to its attention mechanism. It can both make the training faster and compute the gradients of each time series in parallel, which solves the problem of gradient disappearance. Finally, both the customized loss function and the SMOTE supplemental data approaches can improve the prediction accuracy of heavy precipitation samples. However, it should be noted that due to the black box nature of the deep learning model and the randomness of the initialization, the effect of different experimental models may have some deviation.

6 Evaluation and Discussion

In this paper, we presented a deep learning-based methods to model the ZR relation which was traditionally estimated by experiential formula. We used a meteorological dataset from Shenzhen, which consists of radar reflectivity maps, precipitation and precipitation times recorded by ground monitoring stations, and height/ of each station. A variety of deep learning methods were experimentally compared in simulating the ZR relationship. Among them, the combination of Transformer + CNN has the best result with an MSE loss of 85 on the Val dataset, compared with MSE loss of 100 of the LSTM method. Furthermore, to deal with the unbalanced datasets and emphasize on heavy precipitation, we tried to use the SMOTE algorithm to expand heavy precipitation samples, and it shows that it can effectively improve the prediction accuracy of heavy precipitation. Similarly, we also tried to use a customized loss function to enhance the weight of heavy precipitation samples during model training, and it also demonstrate that it can achieve a better accuracy of heavy precipitations. The MSE loss for heavy precipitation on the unpreprocessed dataset is 800. After SMOTE processing, the MSE loss can be reduced to 100, which is an 8-fold improvement. Using the custom loss function, the MSE loss of strong Precipitation can be reduced to 347 even without multiple parameter adjustments, which is an 50% improvement.

As a future work, we will perform more detailed tuning to improve model accuracy. The GAN model will also be used to expand the low percentage data for unbalanced data samples. The idea of fighting against loss in GAN models is also the focus of our future research. GAN can be used not only for generative models, but also for predictive models.

References

1. Prudden, R., et al.: A review of radar-based nowcasting of precipitation and applicable machine learning techniques (2020)
2. Patel, M., Patel, A., Ghosh, R.: Precipitation nowcasting: leveraging bidirectional LSTM and 1D CNN (2018)
3. Shi, X., et al.: Convolutional LSTM Network: A Machine Learning Approach for Precipitation Nowcasting. MIT Press (2015)
4. Shi, X., et al.: Deep learning for precipitation nowcasting: a benchmark and a new model (2017)
5. Marshall, J.S., Palmer, W.: The distribution of raindrops with size. Meteor 5(4), 165–166 (1948)
6. Vaswani, A., et al.: Attention is all you need. In: Advances in Neural Information Processing Systems (2017)

7. Soman, S.S., et al.: A review of wind power and wind speed forecasting methods with different time horizons. In: North American Power Symposium (NAPS) (2010)
8. Hering, A.M., et al.: Nowcasting thunderstorms in the Alpine region using a radar based adaptive thresholding scheme (2004)
9. Hu, J., Shen, L., Sun, G.: Squeeze-and-excitation networks. In: Proceedings of the IEEE Conference on Computer Vision and Pattern Recognition, pp. 7132–7141 (2018)
10. Jaderberg, M., Simonyan, K., Zisserman, A.: Spatial transformer networks. In: Advances in Neural Information Processing Systems (2015)
11. Bello, I., et al.: Attention augmented convolutional networks. In: 2019 IEEE/CVF International Conference on Computer Vision (ICCV) (2020)
12. Oktay, O., et al.: Attention u-net: learning where to look for the pancreas. arXiv arXiv:1804. 03999 (2018)
13. Zhang, X., Zhou, X., Lin, M., Sun, J.: ShuffleNet: an extremely efficient convolutional neural network for mobile devices. In: Proceedings of the IEEE Conference on Computer Vision and Pattern Recognition, pp. 6848–6856 (2017)
14. Woo, W., Wong, W.: Operational application of optical flow techniques to radar-based rainfall nowcasting. Atmosphere 8(3), 48 (2017)
15. LeCun, Y., Bengio, Y., Hinton, G.: Deep learning. Nature 521(7553), 436–444 (2015)
16. Shi, X., Chen, Z., Wang, H., Yeung, D.Y., Wong, W.K., Woo, W.C.: Convolutional LSTM network: a machine learning approach for precipitation nowcasting. In: Advances in Neural Information Processing Systems (2015)
17. Sepp, H., Jürgen, S.: Long short-term memory. Neural Comput. 9(8), 1735–1780 (1997)

Multi-task Parallel: A Tumor Segmentation Approach of Specific Task Attention

Yanfen Guo[✉], Xiaojie Li, Tao Wu, Jinrong Hu, and Jing Peng

Department of Computer Science, Chengdu University of Information
Technology, Chengdu 610225, China
gyf@cuit.edu.cn

Abstract. It is of great significance to make full use of the complementary advantages of different modality imaging information for improving the accuracy of tumor segmentation and formulating precise radiotherapy plans. This paper proposed a multi-tasking parallel training method, which combined the attention mechanism of specific tasks to mine the effective information of different modals. It has three parallel learning networks based on parameter sharing, including CT segmentation network, MRI segmentation network, and the joint learning network of similarity measurement between CT and MRI images. CT and MRI segmentation networks learned their specific task features, and used the attention module of specific tasks to enhance the utilization of effective features while learning shared features. The similarity measurement learning network jointly learned the similarity between CT and MRI images, and combined the specific task features shared by CT and MRI segmentation networks to segment multimodal tumor images. Comparing the results of single-modal and multi-modal tumor image segmentation, it is proved that multi-modal segmentation can provide more abundant features and effectively locate the tumor location, especially in the fuzzy adhesion region of the tumor boundary. In addition, other multi-modal image segmentation methods were compared, and the results also prove that the multi-task learning method is suitable for multi-modal image segmentation and has achieved better segmentation results.

Keywords: Multi-modal · Tumor segmentation · Multi-task learning · Specific task attention · Similarity measurement

1 Introduction

CT or MRI images are usually used in the clinical diagnosis of tumors. CT images are usually used as the localization, and MRI images are used for auxiliary diagnosis. The segmentation of multimodal medical images needs to consider the features of different modal images. Because CT locates accurately and determines the location of the lesion, MRI has a higher soft tissue resolution. It is necessary to combine CT and MRI images for tumor image segmentation, which can provide more information to reflect the tumor and its infiltrating tissues for diagnosis and treatment.

X. Sun et al. (Eds.): ICAIS 2022, CCIS 1587, pp. 225–238, 2022.
https://doi.org/10.1007/978-3-031-06761-7_19

How to mine the useful information of different modals and fuse the information for the segmentation network is an important problem. Multi-task learning [1] is a joint learning model, which learns multiple tasks in parallel and makes the results affect each other. This learning mode is very suitable for multimodal images [2]. Multi-modal image learning cannot be separated from similarity measurement. Inspired by multi-task learning, we proposed a multi-modal image segmentation method for nasopharyngeal carcinoma (NPC) based on multi-task similarity measurement learning. It has three parallel learning networks based on parameter sharing, including CT segmentation network, MRI segmentation network, and the joint learning network of similarity measurement between CT and MRI images. In this method, the multimodal information utilization ability of the network was improved by the joint training of different modal similarity learning task and segmentation task. The attention modules of specific tasks were used to avoid overfitting. While learning shared features, the utilization of effective features was enhanced, and the guiding significance of features in the segmentation process was strengthened, so as to promote the improvement of network segmentation performance.

Authors are required to adhere to this Microsoft Word template in preparing their manuscripts for submission. It will speed up the review and typesetting process.

2   Related Work

2.1   Multi-task Learning

Multi-task learning is an inductive transfer mechanism that trains multiple related tasks in parallel through the use of shared representations. In the process of learning, a shared representation is used to share and supplement the information related to the learned field, so as to improve the effect of generalization [3–5]. For medical images with scarce training data, multi-task learning jointly learns the similarity between different modal images by means of sharing models, so that image features learned by different tasks can be shared, and useful information can be obtained from other associated tasks.

The shared representation methods of multi-task learning include parameter-based sharing and constraint-based sharing. The former is to share the same parameters between different tasks; the latter is to mine the common data features hidden between different tasks. Parameter-based sharing is the most common way in neural networks to reduce the risk of overfitting, such as Gaussian processing; Constraint-based sharing is that each task has its own model and parameters, and parameter similarity is stimulated by regularization distance [6, 7]. The shared representation of multi-tasking learning is shown in Fig. 1.

In medical image segmentation, multi-task learning is mainly used for segmentation tasks of multiple categories, labeling of different tissues and organs, such as cell image segmentation, rib segmentation in chest X-ray images, detection and segmentation of pulmonary nodules and so on [8–12].

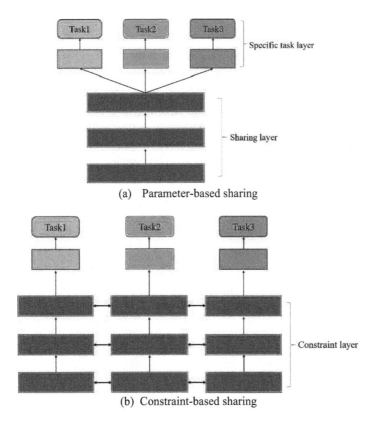

(a)   Parameter-based sharing

(b)   Constraint-based sharing

Fig. 1. Shared representations in multi-tasking learning.

2.2   Attention of Specifical Task

There are both sharing-task features and specific-task features in multi-task learning. In the case of limited sample data, the task model may be difficult to distinguish the correlation and non-correlation of image features. How to balance the task is an issue that must be considered in network learning. Attention of Specifical Task [13] is also called Dynamic Weight Generation Network. The relative contribution of each task is weighted by the network, and different weights are given to different features according to the importance of feature extraction, so as to achieve feature-level attention. Attention of specific task has two functions. One is to avoid overfitting and let the network learn the general feature representation of the image. On the other hand, it is helpful to enhance the feature expression ability of the model by learning the specific tasks' features, generating attention weights and enhancing the role of useful features [14].

Since there are few samples of medical images, it is necessary to fully extract the information contained in the samples, so that the network can learn more useful features of different modal images and retain specific tasks at the output layer.

3 Methodology

3.1 Multi-task Similarity Measurement Learning

Influenced by the imaging principle of medical image, the feature difference of tissue and the registration accuracy, the appearance and location of tumor may not be completely consistent in different modal images [15]. In order to extract the features of multimodal images, we proposed a multimodal image segmentation method for nasopharyngeal carcinoma based on Multi-task Similarity Learning Network (MSLN). MSLN consists of three tasks, two segmentation tasks for CT and MRI single modes, and a joint learning task for similarity measurement of CT and MRI images. The segmentation network uses U-Net as the backbone and uses image block sampling for data enhancement, so the segmentation network is named Block U-Net (BUNet). The segmentation networks for CT and MRI are named BUNet-CT and BUNet-MRI respectively. The joint learning network is named JUNet. In addition, we used the DenseNet [16] injected with Atrous Convolution [17] to fine-divide the features extracted from the multi-task network, which was named ACDNet. The network framework for extracting CT and MRI multi-timodal image features of NPC is shown in Fig. 2.

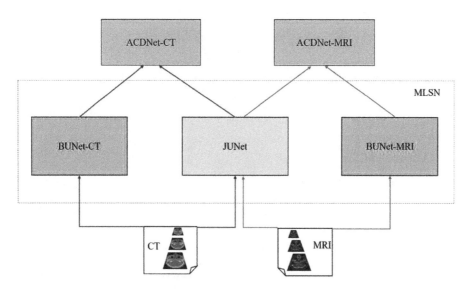

Fig. 2. Multi-task Similarity Learning Network (MSLN).

JUNet is an improved network based on the Siamese Network [18], which is used to calculate the similarity [19] of CT and MRI. The principle is to map a pair of input to the target feature space through a weight-sharing twin convolutional neural network, and measure the similarity with the distance function on the feature. In the training stage, the loss function value of the same class of sample pairs is minimized, and the loss function value of different class of sample pairs is maximized. The Siamese network has great advantages in image similarity matching, but it maps the images in two branches respectively and connects the related neurons of the two images until the last layer. Therefore, JUNet improved the Siamese network. When the images were input, they were merged into a two-channel image, and the weighted mapping was used to learn the similarity measure of the neurons of the two images. Figure 3 shows the network framework of JUNet.

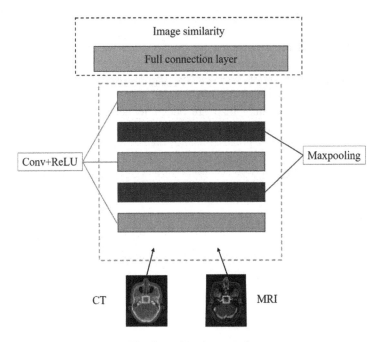

Fig. 3. JUNet framework.

ACDNet uses DenseNet as backboneand adds Atrous Spatial Pyramid Pooling (ASPP) [20] into the Dense Block. The purpose is to increase the receptive field, extract multi-scale features and improve the segmentation accuracy.

MSLN is multi-task learning based on parameter sharing. BUNet-CT and BUNet-MRI are the main tasks that use image block sampling to extract contextual information, which is used to extract hierarchical abstract features, complete single-modal image segmentation, and generate pixel-level tumor probability response maps. JUNet is an auxiliary task, which directly learns the similarity evaluation function of CT and MRI images, and constrains the network to learn the optimal shared weight w, so as to accurately judge the similarity of two images in the same feature map. The main task segmentation network and the auxiliary task similarity measurement learning network were used to share the convolutional layer for feature extraction, and the three tasks were mutually constrained and jointly learned.

3.2   Task-Specific Attention Mechanism

By using task-specific attention mechanisms, the network can filter out a large amount of information irrelevant to the task. BUNet-CT and BUNet-MRI have their own specific task features respectively. According to the discriminative characteristics of NPC tumors, the network will generate an attention weight matrix, and assign a higher attention weight distribution to the effective features of the segmentation task. CT and MRI images have obvious features and differences in NPC images. We proposed task-specific attention to enhance the expressive ability of single-modal image features. By using high-level features to guide low-level feature weighting, the pixel-level attention of low-level feature maps is generated, so that the network can pay attention to the feature with more information and improve the effectiveness of feature representation. When the high-level features are encoded, the attention weight matrix W of the corresponding low-level feature map can be obtained. Then, the weighted low-level feature map and high-level feature map are added to achieve more accurate spatial information selection. The structure of task-specific attention is shown in Fig. 4.

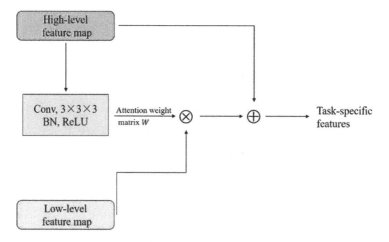

Fig. 4. Attention of specifical task.

Task-specific attention takes the useful features from the main task and weights them so that the JUNET auxiliary task can automatically determine the importance of shared features to the network. This method can not only generalize between different tasks, but also allows specific tasks to be customized for each task to learn more useful features.

3.3   Loss Metrics

The loss function uses dynamic weighting to assign a weighting factor gamma to each task. The loss function of MSLN is the weighted loss of the three subtasks. Focal loss was used for the loss functions of BUNet-CT and BUNet-MRI, which were denoted as

L_{CT} and L_{MRI}, respectively. The loss function L_J of JUNet used contrast loss, which was defined as follows:

$$L_J = \frac{1}{2n} \sum_{i=1}^{n} yD^2 + (1-y)\max(margin - D, 0)^2 \tag{1}$$

where, n is the number of training samples, $margin$ is the set threshold, and y is the binary label of whether the CT and MRI sample pairs match. $y = 1$ means the two samples are similar or match, $y = 0$ means they don't match. D represents the Euclidean distance between samples and features, which is defined as,

$$D = \|G_w(x_{CT}) - G_w(x_{MRI})\| \tag{2}$$

wherein, x_{CT} and x_{MRI} are image blocks extracted from CT and MRI images respectively, and G_w is the mapping function corresponding to image blocks. The loss function of MSLN is shown in Eq. (3).

$$L = \gamma_1 L_{CT} + \gamma_2 L_{MRI} + \gamma_3 L_J \tag{3}$$

The weight factor γ is used to maintain the balance between the three sub-networks during the training process, and the total is 1. It adjusts the weight of the task by considering the loss change rate of each task. During training, CT and MRI images were segmented and predicted independently by Bunet-CT and Bunet-MRI, and three tasks were jointly learned and optimized.

4 Experiments and Results

4.1 Dataset and Pre-processing

The experimental data set consists of CT and MRI images of 120 NPC patients, and all imaging data are encoded in DICOM format. The dataset includes 63 male patients and 57 female patients. The voxel size of CT data ranges from $0.88 \times 0.88 \times 3.0$ mm^3 to $0.97 \times 0.97 \times 3.0$ mm^3, and that of MRI data was $0.6 \times 0.6 \times 3.0$ mm^3. First, the original images were cropped to retain only the head images of the nasopharyngeal tumor at the neck and above, and the CT and MRI images were resampled to isotropic resolution. Secondly, CT and MRI images were registered to solve the image differences caused by different imaging devices. Thirdly, the images were normalized, sampled as $24 \times 24 \times 8$ image block, and rotated and flipped to increase the data. CT and MRI images were used as input to the main task. The registered image was used as the input for the auxiliary task. Tumor labeled images were manually delineated by two experienced clinicians. The determined segmentation label was used as the actual segmentation result image of this experiment.

4.2   Training Details

During network training, BUNet-CT and BUNet-MRI used CT and MRI image blocks respectively as input, and the similarity measurement learning network JUNet used CT and MRI sample pairs as input. The similarity label of JUNet was calculated by the Euclidean distance of the sample to the center point of the image block. The label was set to binary, and the value in 16 individual pixels was 1, otherwise it was 0. The network weight parameters were initialized by random Gaussian distribution, and the Adam optimizer was used for network optimization. The initial learning rate was set as 0.001, the attenuation rate was 0.9, and the weight attenuation item was 0.0005. The training iteration was 45000 times. The network training loss curve is shown in Fig. 5.

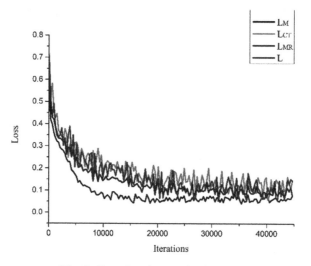

Fig. 5. Loss function graph of MSLN.

It can be seen from Fig. 5 that the training loss gradually decreases as the number of iterations increases. In 50,000 training iterations, the training loss gradually stabilizes when the network is around 20,000 iterations.

4.3   Evaluation Metrics

In order to quantitatively evaluate the performance of the network model, Dice Similarity Coefficient (DSC), Average Symmetric Surface Distance (ASSD) Sensitivity (SE) and Positive Predictive Value (PPV) were used in this paper.

DSC is used to measure the similarity between the segmentation results and the ground-truth [21]. For the given manually labeled tumor segmentation result X and predicted result Y of network segmentation, DSC is defined as:

$$DSC = \frac{2 \times |X \cap Y|}{|X| + |Y|} \tag{4}$$

The value range of DSC is [0, 1]. If the value of DSC is larger, the similarity between the network segmentation result and the real result is higher.

The ASSD index represents the average surface distance between the predicted results of network segmentation and the results of manual labeling segmentation. Its formula is shown in Eq. (5).

$$ASSD = \frac{1}{2} \left(\frac{\sum_{g \in G} min_{p \in P} d(g, p)}{|G|} + \frac{\sum_{p \in P} min_{g \in G} d(p, g)}{|P|} \right) \tag{5}$$

where G and P represent the surface voxels of ground-truth and network prediction segmentation results respectively, and $d(p, g)$ represents the Euclides distance between g and p.

The Sensitivity (SE), known as recall rate or true positive rate, was used to evaluate the proportion of tumor regions with correct segmentation to tumor regions in the truth map. It can be shown in Eq. (6).

$$R = \frac{TP}{TP + FN} \tag{6}$$

The positive predictive value (PPV) was used to estimate the proportion of correctly segmented tumor regions to total segmented outcomes. The definition formula is shown in Eq. (7).

$$P = \frac{TP}{TP + FP} \tag{7}$$

where, TP is the true positive sample set, indicating the number of samples whose actual and predicted values are positive, that is, the predicted answer is correct. FP is the false positive sample set, representing the number of samples that are actually negative but predicted to be positive. FN is also the false negative sample set, which represents the number of samples that are actually positive but predicted to be negative.

The combination of higher SE and lower PPV indicates that there may be over-segmentation in the segmentation results of network prediction. Otherwise, it indicates that there may be under-segmentation. Both of them are commonly used in evaluation of multimodal image segmentation.

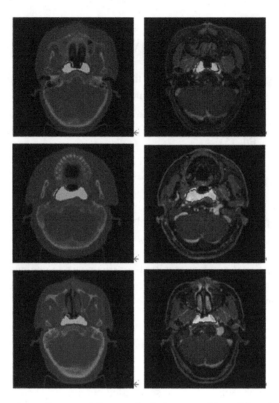

Fig. 6. Comparison of segmentation results between multi-modal and single-modal.

4.4 Results

In order to verify the segmentation effect of multimodal nasopharyngeal carcinoma images, we compared the multi-modal segmentation algorithm based on MLSN with the single-modal segmentation networks BUNET CT and BUNET MRI. Figure 6 shows the comparison of segmentation results. The red region is the real segmentation result manually labeled by clinicians, the blue line is the segmentation result of single-mode BUNet, and the green line is the segmentation result of multi-modal MLSN.

It can be seen from the Fig. 6 that the single-mode segmentation effect is unstable, and there are over-segmentation or under-segmentation. The segmentation effect of multi-modal is more stable than that of single-modal, especially in the tumor boundary region. The segmentation boundary of multi-modal is accurate and close to the real result, while the single-modal has the fuzzy region of adhesion.

Table 1 shows the comparison of the quantitative evaluation of multi-modal and single-modal segmentation effects. The segmentation effect of BUNet in MRI image is better than CT image, which shows that MRI image has more advantages in the segmentation of nasopharyngeal carcinoma and has better resolution ability for soft tissues. The DSC and ASSD values of MSLN are better than those of BUNet, indicating that the multi-modal network segmentation results are more similar to the real results, and its accuracy is higher than that of single-modal segmentation.

In order to verify the effectiveness of the proposed method in this chapter, there are two comparison networks as the comparison, including network stack method [22] (denoted as NetA) and feature fusion method [23] (denoted as NetB). The comparison of segmentation results is shown in Fig. 7.

Table 1. Comparison of segmentation results between multi-modal and single-modal.

Network	DSC	ASSD	PPV	SE
BUNet-CT	0.712	1.298 mm	0.701	0.743
BUNet-MRI	0.741	1.212 mm	0.731	0.756
MSLN	0.768	1.101 mm	0.779	0.812

In order to verify the effectiveness of the proposed method in this chapter, there are two comparison networks as the comparison, including network stack method [22] (denoted as NetA) and feature fusion method [23] (denoted as NetB). The comparison of segmentation results is shown in Fig. 7.

In Fig. 7, the red area is the real segmentation results manually labeled by physicians, the green line is the segmentation results of MLSN network, the blue line is the segmentation results of NetA, and the yellow line is the segmentation results of NetB. On the whole, the segmentation effect of MLSN network was closer to the labeling segmentation result given by physicians. The quantitative evaluation results of the method in this chapter and the comparison method are shown in Table 2.

The DSC and SE values of the three methods are close, but the ASSD and PPV values of MSLN are obviously better than those of the other two methods, which further shows the effectiveness of the method from the basis of quantitative evaluation.

On one hand, multi-modal image can provide pathological information from many aspects due to different imaging mechanisms, and the accuracy of segmentation results is higher than that of single-mode image segmentation. On the other hand, the results of multimodal image segmentation based on multi-task learning are better than the two methods.

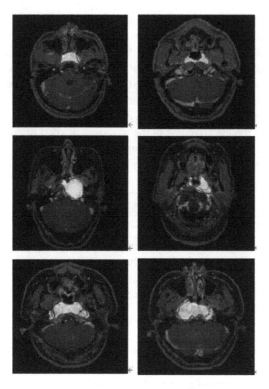

Fig. 7. Comparison of segmentation results between MSLN and other networks.

Table 2. Quantitative evaluation results of three segmentation networks.

Network	DSC	ASSD	PPV	SE
NetA	0.725	1.347 mm	0.675	0.743
NetB	0.723	1.365 mm	0.668	0.738
MSLN	0.768	1.101 mm	0.779	0.812

5 Discussion and Conclusion

The segmentation of multi-modal medical images needs to consider the features of different modal images. It is an important issue to extract important information from different modals and effectively fuse them for segmentation, which is different from single-modal medical image segmentation. Multi-task learning makes the image features learned by different tasks share, and obtains useful information from other related tasks, which is very suitable for multimodal medical image segmentation. In this paper, multi-task learning networks based on parameter sharing were used for joint training of different modal similarity learning tasks and segmentation tasks. It is helpful to promote the utilization of multimodal information in the network. Task-specific attention can help the network avoid overfitting, enhance the use of important features, and improve the segmentation accuracy of images. Experiments show that multi-modal segmentation can provide more abundant features and effectively locate the tumor location, especially in dealing with the fuzzy adhesion area of the tumor boundary. The advantages of multi-modal segmentation are obvious.

Acknowledgement. This work was supported by the Sichuan Science and Technology program (Grant No. 2019JDJQ0002), Key R& D projects in Sichuan Province (Grant No. 2020YFG0189) and the Education Department Foundation of Chongqing (Grant No. 19ZB0257).

References

1. Ruder, S.: An overview of multi-task learning in deep neural networks. Computer Science Machine Learning (2017)
2. Wang, J., Wang, J.L.: Multi-task diagnosis for autism spectrum disorders using multi-modality features: a multi-center study. Hum. Brain Mapp. **38**(6), 3081–3097 (2017)
3. Zhang, Y., Yang: A survey on multi-task learning. Computer Science Machine Learning (2018)
4. Alrajhi, H.: A generalized state space average model for parallel DC-to-DC converters. Comput. Syst. Sci. Eng. **41**(2), 717–734 (2022)
5. Zheng, H., Shi, D.: A multi-agent system for environmental monitoring using Boolean networks and reinforcement learning. J. Cyber Secur. **2**(2), 85–96 (2020)
6. Lee, S.: A study on classification and detection of small moths using CNN model. Comput. Mater. Continua **71**(1), 1987–1998 (1987)
7. Duong, L., Cohn, Bird, S.: Low resource dependency parsing: cross-lingual parameter sharing in a neural network parser. In: Proceedings of the ACL-IJCNLP, pp. 2115–2139 (2015)
8. Wang, X., Wang, Q.: Application of dynamic programming algorithm based on model predictive control in hybrid electric vehicle control strategy. J. IoT **2**(2), 81–87 (2020)
9. Al-Adhaileh, M.H., Alsaade, F.W.: Detecting and analysing fake opinions using artificial intelligence algorithms. Intell. Autom. Soft Comput. **32**(1), 643–655 (2022)
10. Li, C.S.L., Zhang, X.M.: Shape-aware semi-supervised 3D semantic segmentation for medical images. Comput. Sci. Comput. Vis. Pattern Recogn. (2019)
11. Chaichulee, S., Villarroel, J.: Multi-task convolutional neural network for patient detection and skin segmentation in continuous non-contact vital sign monitoring. In: Proceedings of the ICAFGR (2017)
12. Moeskops, P., et al.: Deep learning for multi-task medical image segmentation in multiple modalities. In: Ourselin, S., Joskowicz, L., Sabuncu, M.R., Unal, G., Wells, W. (eds.) MICCAI 2016. LNCS, vol. 9901, pp. 478–486. Springer, Cham (2016). https://doi.org/10.1007/978-3-319-46723-8_55
13. Lee, J.B., Rossi, K.: Attention models in graphs: a survey. ACM Trans. Knowl. Discov. Data **13**(6), 62–63 (2019)
14. Feng, L.X.J., Zhang, Y.Z., Zeng, Y.: Question similarity calculation model based on multi-attention CNN. Comput. Eng. **45**(9), 284–290 (2019)
15. Chen, H., Qi, Y.X., Yin, Y.: MMFNet: a multi-modality MRI fusion network for segmentation of nasopharyngeal carcinoma. Neurocomputing **394**(21), 27–40 (2020)
16. Huang, G., Liu, L., Maaten, V.D.: Densely connected convolutional networks. Proc. CVPR, 4700–4708 (2017)

17. Yu, F., Koltun, V.: Multi-scale context aggregation by dilated convolutions. Computer Science Computer Vision and Pattern Recognition (2016)
18. Bromley, J., Bentz, B.: Signature verification using a Siamese time delay neural network. Int. J. Pattern Recogn. Artif. Intell. 7(4), 669–688 (1993)
19. Zagoruyko, S., Komodakis, N.: Learning to compare image patches via convolutional neural networks. Computer Science Computer Vision and Pattern Recognition (2015)
20. Chen, G.L.C., Papandreou, S.: Rethinking atrous convolution for semantic image segmentation. Computer Science Computer Vision and Pattern Recognition (2017)
21. Zou, S.K.K.H., Warfield, A.: Statistical validation of image segmentation quality based on a spatial overlap index. Acad. Radiol. 11(2), 178–189 (2004). Scientific reports
22. Pereira, S., Pinto, A.: Brain tumor segmentation using convolutional neural networks in MRI images. IEEE Trans. Med. Imaging 35(5), 1240–1251 (2016)
23. Nie, D., Wang, L., Gao, Y.: Fully convolutional networks for multi-modality isointense infant brain image segmentation. In: Proceedings of the ISBI, pp. 1342–1345 (2016)

The Optimization Method of the Layout of Integrated Passenger Transport Terminals in Beijing-Tianjin- Hebei Urban Agglomeration

Chen Sun[1], Xuting Duan[1(✉)], Daxin Tian[1], Shudong Xia[2],
Xuejun Ran[2], Xu Han[1,3], and Yafu Sun[2]

[1] School of Transportation Science and Engineering, Beihang University,
Beiijng 102206, China
duanxuting@buaa.edu.cn
[2] China TransInfo Co. Ltd., Beijing 100085, China
[3] Department of Engineering and Design, University of Sussex, Brighton BN1
9RH, UK

Abstract. In order to meet the demand for passenger transport and improve the overall operation efficiency of the integrated passenger transport system in the region within the urban agglomeration, the optimization method of the layout of integrated passenger transport terminals in the urban agglomeration are researched in this paper, and the Beijing-Tianjin-Hebei urban agglomeration is considered as our research object. Firstly, the influential factors of the location and layout of the integrated passenger transport terminal are qualitatively analyzed. Secondly the degree of charm indexes are defined, and next the selection model of alternative points based on the degree of charm of the terminal is built, and then the degree of charm value is calculated comprehensively by the analytic hierarchy process (AHP) and multi-level fuzzy evaluation method. Then, on the basis of determined the alternative points of the terminal, the layout of the terminals is optimized based on the P-median location model, and Microcity software is used to solve the model. Finally, an instance is given to prove that the model method has a certain guiding effect on the layout optimization of urban agglomeration comprehensive passenger terminals.

Keywords: Comprehensive passenger terminal · Attractiveness index · Multi-level fuzzy evaluation · Microcity

1 Introduction

With the rapid development of society and economy, Urbanization process is increasingly advanced in China, which leads to the change of the regional spatial form and layout structure, and urban agglomerations gradually form and obtain development continuously. With the growth of urban population and the rise of motorization level, the travel demand between different urban agglomerations and between different cities within a urban agglomeration has increased significantly, the integrated passenger terminals have played a more and more important role as key nodes which are vital places for passengers to arrive, distribute and transfer within the regional passenger transport network. In addition, the continuous innovation of scientific technology and transportation modes has constantly promoted the network construction of various transportation modes and the integration construction of regional comprehensive transportation systems.

To meet the travel demand of urban agglomeration passenger, the Outline of the National Integrated Three-dimensional Network Plan has clearly pointed out that the focus area of China is divided into "four poles, 8 groups, 9 clusters", and the construction of "six main spindles, seven corridors, eight channels", which consist of the main frame of national comprehensive three-dimensional traffic network. Besides, it is aimed at the optimization transport layout of national integrated three-dimensional traffic layout, promoting the development of the integrated transportation as a whole fusion and with high quality. Therefore, it is extremely essential to study the coordinated optimization layout of urban agglomeration hubs. Scientific and reasonable coordinated layout planning for the integrated passenger transport hubs in urban agglomerations is conducive to improving the overall efficiency of the integrated passenger transport system within the urban agglomeration and providing passengers with efficient, convenient, comfortable and safe travel services.

At present, a lot of studies on the layout optimization of integrated passenger transport hubs have been carried out from domestic and foreign scholars. In terms of the research on the layout of hubs, Marianov, V., et al. [1] considers the relationship between the selection of hub location and time cost, and a 0-1 programming model is constructed and solved by the Tabu heuristic algorithm. Costa, M.D.G., et al. [2] takes the cost minimization as the first goal function, and on this premise, total service time and maximum service time minimization is taken as the second goal, and a double-standard method for the selection and allocation of hub location is proposed. Khasnabis, S., et al. [3] elaborates the influence and function of the interactive relationship between urban land use and the layout of integrated passenger terminal while analyzing economic growth. Alumur, S., et al. [4] establishes an integer programming model for the selection of hub location based on fixed cost after classifying and sorting out currently existing hub models. Li, T.T. [5] builds a hierarchical layout optimization model for integrated passenger transport hubs in urban agglomerations based on the multi-flow nested hierarchical facility location model, and the CPLEX software is applied to accurately solve the model. Lv, S., et al. [6] applies the TOD planning concept to determine the best hub position combined with macro layout and micro layout. Wu, D. [7] constructs a mixed integer programming model, and the minimum of sum of total passenger travel costs including the investment cost of the construction, the operating cost, the cost of occupancy on passing capacity and the total cost of passenger travel is taken as the objective function. In terms of algorithm research on the optimization layout of comprehensive passenger transport hubs, common intelligent algorithms such as genetic algorithm and clone algorithm are widely used. The latest research progress of optimization algorithms provides new thinking for solving the optimization problem of the layout of hubs. Xu, B., et al. [8] proposes a multi-strategy differential evolutionary greedy algorithm, which is effective to solve NP-hard problem. Al-Khateeb, B., et al. [9] presents a new algorithm called Rock Hyraxes Swarm

Optimization (RHSO), which belongs to a novel metaheuristic algorithm. It is very effective to solve the problems with constraints. Devi, R.M., et al. [10] proposes a new improved Runge-Kutta Optimization algorithm to solve optimization problems, and it has an advantage in discovering the optimal results for all selected optimization problems compared to other algorithm. Zeidabadi, F.A., et al. [11] proposes a new optimization algorithm called All Members-Based Optimizer (AMBO) to various optimization problems, and verifies it is more superior and more competitive in providing suitable solution than other mentioned algorithm. Jan, A.M., et al. [12] presents an improved Particle Swarm Optimization (PSO) which is combined with the superiority of feasibility and the violation constraint-handling to make PSO is more suitable for the problems with constraints. The existing research on hub site selection and layout is rarely carried out at the level of urban agglomeration, and there is a lack of systematic theoretical system for the layout of integrated passenger hubs in urban agglomeration. A method of the location selection and layout of integrated passenger transport hubs from the level of urban agglomeration is proposed in this paper, which aims at providing a reference method for the site selection and service scope determination of regional integrated passenger hubs in the urban agglomeration.

The region of the Beijing-Tianjin-Hebei urban agglomeration is taken as the research object in this paper. and the process of layout optimization of integrated passenger terminals is divided into two steps, including the selection of the alternative points site and the selection of the final points site of the integrated passenger terminal. For the first step, a selection model of alternative points based on attractiveness is proposed to determine the alternative points set combined with the method of qualitative and quantitative analysis about the key influential factors of integrated passenger terminal location layout. For the second step, when the set of alternative points is established, the final layout scheme of the integrated passenger terminals can be determined based on the P-median location and layout optimization model, which provides an idea and method for the layout optimization of the integrated passenger transport terminals in the Beijing-Tianjin-Hebei urban agglomeration.

The main technical route of this paper is shown in Fig. 1:

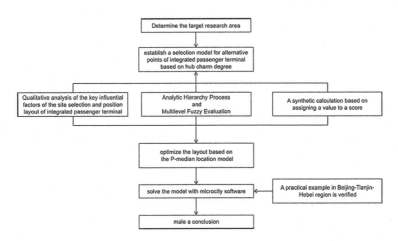

Fig. 1. Technology roadmap.

2 Establish a Selection Model of Alternative Points Based on the Degree of Charm of Hubs

The layout of integrated passenger transport terminals in Beijing-Tianjin-Hebei urban agglomeration is a complex engineering problem, which involves various and complicated key factors. What's more, if there are a large number of alternative hubs, it is difficult to find a reasonable layout scheme within a limited time. Consider establishing a screening model for alternative hubs to screen out non-feasible nodes to construct alternative hubs target set.

Table 1. The charm index system of the set of alternative points of comprehensive passenger terminals.

Criterion layer			
Index layer	The coordination and matching index w_1	The demand adaptability index w_2	The social impact index w_3
	The degree of coordination with the city master plan w_{11}	The service radiation range of the transport terminal w_{21}	The degree of influence on the loading degree of the road network around the transport terminal w_{31}
	The degree of coordination with various modes of transportation w_{12}	The adaptability of construction scale of the transport terminal w_{22}	The degree of influence on urban population and industrial layout w_{32}
	The degree of coordination with the layout of urban road route network w_{13}	The reserved space for future development of the transport terminal w_{23}	The degree of influence on the urban environment w_{33}

2.1 Select and Define the Degree of Charm Index

Factors such as passenger flow scale, aggregation and connection degree of various transportation modes in the transport hub, coordination and matching degree with the surrounding road network capacity, and coordination and adaptation degree with the overall planning and spatial layout of cities in the Beijing-Tianjin-Hebei urban agglomeration have an important influence on the site selection and layout of the integrated passenger transport terminal. The degree of charm index system is established based on the analysis of key influential factors, as shown in Table 1. The charm value is used to reflect the degree of charm and possibility of each alternative point to become an integrated passenger transport terminal. And the most likely alternative point set to become an integrated passenger transport hub is selected by calculating the degree of charm of each alternative point.

2.2   Calculate the Degree of Charm

Determine the Weight Coefficients by Analytic Hierarchy Process. The process of applying AHP (Analytic Hierarchy Process) is as follows:

1. Select a set of factors

According to the evaluation criteria, it can be divided into the following factor sets: $w_1 = \{w_{11}, w_{12}, w_{13}\}$, $w_2 = \{w_{21}, w_{22}, w_{23}\}$, $w_3 = \{w_{31}, w_{32}, w_{33}\}$.

2. Determine the evaluation set

The following evaluation sets are determined according to the four grades of excellent, good, average and poor: {excellent V_1, good V_2, average V_3, poor V_4}.

3. Calculate the factor importance degree coefficient

AHP is applied to assign the weight A_i by using the maximum characteristic root. Taking factor set $W = \{w_1, w_2, w_3\}$ as an example, and the 1–9 scale method is used to determine the importance of w_i relative to w_j (i, j = 1, 2, 3).

4. Construct the judgment matrix U

The judgment matrix U is as shown in Eq. (1):

$$U = \begin{bmatrix} u_{11} & u_{12} & u_{13} \\ u_{21} & u_{22} & u_{23} \\ u_{31} & u_{31} & u_{33} \end{bmatrix} \tag{1}$$

5. Hierarchical single sorting

Each column vector of the judgment matrix U is normalized, as shown in Eq. (2):

$$M_{ij} = \frac{u_{ij}}{\sum_{i=1}^{3} u_{ij}}, i = 1, 2, 3, j = 1, 2, 3 \tag{2}$$

Sum each row of M_{ij} obtained above, as shown in Eq. (3):

$$M_i = \sum_{j=1}^{3} M_{ij}, i = 1, 2, 3 \tag{3}$$

Normalization of M_i is carried out to obtain the calculated feature vector $A = (A_1, A_2, A_3)^T$ of the factor set $W = \{w_1, w_2, w_3\}$, as shown in Eq. (4):

$$a_i = \frac{M_i}{\sum_{i=1}^{3} M_i}, \quad i = 1, 2, 3 \tag{4}$$

Calculate the maximum characteristic root of the judgment matrix U, as shown in Eq. (5):

$$\lambda \sum_{i=1}^{3} \frac{(Ua)i}{3ai_{max}} \tag{5}$$

Consistency checking, as shown in Eq. (6) and Eq. (7):

$$CI = \frac{\lambda_{max}}{f - 1} \tag{6}$$

$$CR = \frac{CI}{RI} \tag{7}$$

RI is the average random consistency index of the judgment matrix, corresponding to order f, which can be queried in Table 2.

Table 2. Corresponding table of average random consistency index of judgment matrix.

Order	1	2	3	4	5	6	7	8	9
RI	0	0	0.58	0.9	1.12	1.24	1.32	1.41	1.45

If CR is less than 0.1, it is considered that the judgment matrix meets the consistency test. Otherwise, the judgment matrix U should be reconstructed according to the above five steps. Similarly, the weight distribution vectors A_1, A_2 and A_3 corresponding to the factor set $w_1 = \{w_{11}, w_{12}, w_{13}\}$, $w_2 = \{w_{21}, w_{22}, w_{23}\}$ and $w3 = \{w_{31}, w_{32}, w_{33}\}$ can be obtained respectively.

Determine the Value of Charm Degree by Multi-level Fuzzy Comprehensive Evaluation. The process of applying multi-level fuzzy comprehensive evaluation is as follows:

1. The first layer of fuzzy comprehensive evaluation

The expert scoring method is applied to evaluate each factor in the index layer. The evaluation grades V_1, V_2, V_3 and V_4 obtained by each factor are voted and counted. The evaluation matrices R_1, R_2 and R_3 corresponding to the factor sets w_1, w_2 and w_3 in each criterion layer are obtained. The corresponding first-level comprehensive evaluation results of the single factor set w_1, w_2 and w_3 in this study are as follows:

$$B_1 = A_1 R_1 = \begin{pmatrix} a_1 & a_2 & a_3 \end{pmatrix} \begin{pmatrix} r_{11} & r_{12} & r_{13} & r_{14} \\ r_{21} & r_{22} & r_{23} & r_{24} \\ r_{31} & r_{32} & r_{33} & r_{34} \end{pmatrix} = \begin{pmatrix} b_{11}, & b_{12}, & b_{13}, & b_{14} \end{pmatrix} \tag{8}$$

$$B_2 = A_2R_2 = \begin{pmatrix} a_1 & a_2 & a_3 \end{pmatrix} \begin{pmatrix} r_{11} & r_{12} & r_{13} & r_{14} \\ r_{21} & r_{22} & r_{23} & r_{24} \\ r_{31} & r_{32} & r_{33} & r_{34} \end{pmatrix} = \begin{pmatrix} b_{21}, & b_{22}, & b_{23}, & b_{24} \end{pmatrix} \quad (9)$$

$$B_3 = A_3R_3 = \begin{pmatrix} a_1 & a_2 & a_3 \end{pmatrix} \begin{pmatrix} r_{11} & r_{12} & r_{13} & r_{14} \\ r_{21} & r_{22} & r_{23} & r_{24} \\ r_{31} & r_{32} & r_{33} & r_{34} \end{pmatrix} = \begin{pmatrix} b_{31}, & b_{32}, & b_{33}, & b_{34} \end{pmatrix}$$

$$(10)$$

2. The second layer of fuzzy comprehensive evaluation

For the factor set $W = \{w_1, w_2, w_3\}$, the important factor distribution vector is A, so the second-level fuzzy evaluation results are as follows:

$$B = (b_1, b_2, b_3, b_4) = A(B_1, B_2, B_3)^T = (a_1, a_2, a_3) \begin{bmatrix} b_{11} & b_{12} & b_{13} & b_{14} \\ b_{21} & b_{22} & b_{23} & b_{24} \\ b_{31} & b_{32} & b_{33} & b_{34} \end{bmatrix} \quad (11)$$

Assign scores to the evaluation levels in the evaluation set, making excellent = 95, good = 80, average = 65 and poor = 50. A comprehensive evaluation method is adopted, that is, fuzzy evaluation results and evaluation grades are used to calculate the score of this point.

The score G is taken as the charm value of this point.

$$G = 95 \times b_1 + 80 \times b_2 + 65 \times b_3 + 50 \times b_4 \quad (12)$$

G is considered as the degree of charm of the alternative point. After calculating the charm degree of all the alternative points, the charm degree is sorted from large to small, and a certain number of alternative points are screened from high to low according to the charm degree, so as to determine the final size of alternative hub point set.

Random Examples. Taking an alternative point in the alternative points set of the original integrated passenger transport terminal as an example, through summarizing the literature, it is considered that the factor set $W = \{w_1, w_2, w_3\}$, and the judgment matrix is constructed according to the 1–9 scale method as shown in Table 3:

Table 3. The judgment matrix of factor set W.

Factor collection W	w_1	w_2	w_3
w_1	1	3	5
w_2	1/3	1	3
w_3	1/5	1/3	1

The feature vectors A and the maximum characteristic root λmax of the factor set can be calculated according to the above methods and steps. The results are shown in Table 4:

Table 4. The weight calculation process of factor set W and the results of each step.

Symbol	Value		
U	1	3	5
	1/3	1	3
	1/5	1/3	1
U_i	1.5333	4.3333	9
Mij	0.6522	0.6923	0.5556
	0.2174	0.2308	0.3333
	0.1304	0.0769	0.1111
Mi	1.9000	0.7815	0.3185
A	0.6333	0.2605	0.1062
U·A	1.9456	0.7901	0.3197
λ_{max}	3.0387		
F	3		
RI	0.58		
CI	0.0194		
CR	0.0334		

From the Table 4, it can be seen that CR < 0.1, so the judgment matrix meets the consistency test, and the weight distribution corresponding to the factor set W is A = (0.6333, 0.2605, 0.1062). Similarly, corresponding judgment matrices can be constructed respectively for the above factor sets w_1, w_2, and w_3. $w_1 = \{w_{11}, w_{12}, w_{13}\}$, $w_2 = \{w_{21}, w_{22}, w_{23}\}$, $w_3 = \{w_{31}, w_{32}, w_{33}\}$ and corresponding weights A_1, A_2, and A_3 can be calculated respectively.

After the corresponding weight distribution coefficients A, A_1, A_2 and A_3 are worked out, 10 experts are selected to vote on the importance degree. The attractiveness index evaluation system of an alternative point and the relevant weight distribution obtained by summarizing the votes according to relevant literature are shown in Table 5:

Table 5. Evaluation system and weight distribution of each factor.

Index layer	Excellence of evaluation sets	Good of evaluation sets	Average of evaluation sets	Poor of evaluation sets	Weight
w_{11}	6	2	1	1	0.5247
w_{12}	5	2	2	1	0.3338
w_{13}	8	1	1	0	0.1416
w_{21}	4	3	2	1	0.6080
w_{22}	3	6	1	0	0.2721
w_{23}	3	4	2	1	0.1199
w_{31}	2	2	2	4	0.5390
w_{32}	2	3	1	4	0.2973
w_{33}	1	2	2	5	0.1638

The first-level evaluation results calculated by the multi-level fuzzy evaluation method are shown in Table 6:

Table 6. Results of the first layer evaluation.

Symbol	Value			
A_1	0.5247	0.3338	0.1416	
R_1	0.6	0.2	0.1	0.1
	0.5	0.2	0.2	0.1
	0.8	0.1	0.1	0
$B_1 = A_1R_1$	0.5950	0.1859	0.1334	0.0859
A_2	0.6080	0.2721	0.1199	
R_2	0.4	0.3	0.2	0.1
	0.3	0.6	0.1	0
	0.3	0.4	0.2	0.1
$B_2 = A_2R_2$	0.3608	0.3936	0.1728	0.0728
A_3	0.5390	0.2973	0.1638	
R_3	0.2	0.2	0.2	0.4
	0.2	0.3	0.1	0.4
	0.1	0.2	0.2	0.5
$B_3 = A_3R_3$	0.1836	0.2298	0.1703	0.4164

Thus, the comprehensive evaluation results of factor sets w_1, w_2 and w_3 are as follows: $B_1 = A_1 \cdot R_1 = (0.5950\ 0.1859\ 0.1334\ 0.0859)$. $B_2 = A_2 \cdot R_2 = (0.3608\ 0.3936\ 0.1728\ 0.0728)$. $B_3 = R_3 \cdot A_3 = (0.1836\ 0.2298\ 0.1703\ 0.4164)$.

The second-level evaluation results are shown in Table 7:

Table 7. Results of the second level evaluation.

Symbol	Value			
A	0.6333	0.2605	0.1062	
$(B_1, B_2, B_3)^T$	0.5950	0.1859	0.1334	0.0859
	0.3608	0.3936	0.1728	0.0728
	0.1836	0.2298	0.1703	0.4164
B	0.4903	0.2446	0.1476	0.1175

From this instance, for the importance of the alternative point, the proportion of excellence is 49.03%, the proportion of good is 24.46%, the proportion of average is 14.76%, the proportion of poor is 11.75% consider it poor.

Then, a comprehensive evaluation method proposed above is applied to calculate the final charm value of this alternative point:

$$G = 95 \times 0.4903 + 80 \times 0.2446 + 65 \times 0.1476 + 50 \times 0.1175 = 81.62 \qquad (13)$$

Thus, the value of the degree of charm of the alternative point is 81.62, in the same way, we can obtain the actual judgment matrix and real expert scoring data of corresponding factor sets of alternative points of integrated passenger transport terminals within Beijing-Tianjin-Hebei urban agglomeration. And then all the value of the degree of charm can be calculated. In the end, the final alternative sets K can be screened according to the sorting of the degree of charm from large to small.

3   Layout of Optimization Based on P-Median Location Model

3.1   Description of Problem

In this paper, the target study area is selected from Beijing-Tianjin-Hebei urban agglomeration. And then the amount of passenger demand points divided in the planned area is Q. The amount of the alternative points screened by the model based on the degree of charm is K. The passenger volume of each transportation district as demand points and the distance between each alternative integrated passenger terminal and the center of the transportation district are all known quantities. The P-median model is applied to determine the position and the service scope of integrated passenger terminals which amount is E.

3.2   Model Assumptions

To simplify the problem, this paper puts forward the following assumptions:

1. Transshipment of passenger flow between integrated passenger terminals is temporarily not considered.
2. There is a line connection between the alternative stations of the integrated passenger terminal and the demand points, that is, each demand point is accessible to each integrated passenger terminal.
3. E is known as the amount of integrated passenger transport terminals to be established.

3.3   Symbol Description

The symbolic meanings involved in the model are shown in Table 8:

Table 8. Corresponding table of symbol meaning of model.

Model symbol	Meaning of the symbol
x_i	0-1 variable, indicating whether to establish an integrated passenger terminal at the alternative point i
y_{ij}	0-1 variable, indicating whether the integrate passenger terminal i serves the urban traffic district j
q_j	Represents the demand for passenger transport in the urban traffic district
E	Represents the number of integrated passenger terminal construction
d_{ij}	Represents the distance between the integrated passenger terminal i and the urban traffic district j
K	Represents a set of alternative integrated passenger terminals
Q	Represents a set of demand points in urban traffic districts

3.4   Model Construction

The minimization of the sum of the product of the distance between alternative points and demand points and the passenger flow volume at demand points as the objective function. The specific model is as follows:

$$\min Z = \sum_{i \in K} \sum_{j \in Q} q_j d_{ij} y_{ij} \tag{14}$$

$$s.t. \ \sum_{i \in K} y_{ij} = 1, \ \forall j \in Q \tag{15}$$

$$\sum_{i \in K} x_i = E \tag{16}$$

$$x_i \geq y_{ij}, \ \forall i \in K, \ j \in Q \tag{17}$$

$$x_i = 0, 1, \ \forall i \in K \tag{18}$$

$$y_{ij} = 0, 1, \ \forall i \in K, \ j \in Q \tag{19}$$

1. Target function:

Equation (14) represents the minimization of the sum of the product of the distance between each alternative point and each the demand point and the passenger volume at the demand point, namely, the total weighted travel distance and the minimization.

2. Constraint conditions:

Equation (15) indicates that each demand point can only be served by one comprehensive passenger terminal, that is, each traffic district can only be assigned to one integrated passenger terminal.

Equation (16) represents the number limit of integrated passenger terminals.

Equation (17) represents that only when the alternative point i is determined as the integrated passenger terminal, can it serve the demand point.

Equation (18) represents the constraint of decision variable. If it is 1, it means that the alternative point i is selected as the construction site of the integrated passenger terminal. If it is 0, it means that the alternative point i is not selected as the site for the construction of the comprehensive passenger terminal.

Equation (19) represents the constraint of the decision variable. If it is 1, it means that the integrated passenger terminal i provides services to the traffic district j. If it is 0, it means that the he integrated passenger terminal i does not serve the traffic district j.

3.5 Model Solution

Microcity is a software for spatial analysis, which is fast, extensible, visual and user-friendly. It can be used in GIS, operating geographic information system and spatial data processing, and can be widely used in network fractal, 3D simulation and modeling solution, etc. Microcity software is used in this paper to establish spatial data and process the data, then uses its own programming language and built-in functions to solve the P-median site selection model, and returns the calculation results to determine the final layout scheme.

4 Example Verification

4.1 Select the Target Research Area

The railway integrated passenger terminals within the Beijing-Tianjin-Hebei urban agglomeration are taken as the actual example, and the cities of the Beijing, Tianjin and Hebei Zhangjiakou, Chengde, Qinhuangdao, Tangshan, Langfang, Baoding,

Shijiazhuang, Xingtai, Handan, Hengshui, Cangzhou are taken as traffic districts, generating 13 passenger demand point, namely the $Q = 13$. 11 integrated passenger terminals are selected as the alternative points with the screening model based on the degree of charm, including Beijing Railway Station, Beijingxi Railway Station, Beijingbei Railway Station, Beijingnan Railway Station, Shijiazhuang Railway Station, Tianjinxi Railway Station, Tianjin Railway Station, Qinhuangdao Railway Station, Tangshan Railway Station, Baoding Railway Station, Handandong Railway Station, namely $K = 11$.

Among them, Zhangjiakou City, Cheng de City, Qinhuangdao City, Tangshan City, Tianjin City, Langfang City, Beijing City, Bao ding City, Shijiazhuang City, Xing tai City, Han dan City, Heng shui City, Cangzhou City are respectively marked as No. 1, No. 2, No. 3, No. 4, No. 5, No. 6, No. 7, No. 8, No. 9, No. 10, No. 11, No. 12, No. 13 passenger transport demand points. Beijingnan Railway Station, Beijing Railway Station, Beijingxi Railway Station, Beijingbei Railway Station, Shijiazhuang Railway Station, Tianjinxi Railway Station, Tianjin Railway Station, Tangshan Railway Station, Qinhuangdao Railway Station, Baoding Railway Station, Handandong Railway Station are respectively labeled alternative point 1, 2, 3, 4, 5, 6, 7, 8, 9, 10, 11.

4.2   Model Solving

The distance between each target demand point and each alternative point is measured by Baidu Map. The passenger flow of the target demand points of passenger transport is obtained by searching a lot of literatures and relevant passenger transport data, as shown in Table 9:

Table 9. Passenger demand at each demand point of passenger transport in the target planning area.

Demand points of passenger transport	Annual passenger volume (ten thousand)
1 Zhangjiakou	914
2 Chengde	544
3 Qinhuangdao	1264
4 Tangshan	1076
5 Tianjin	5372
6 Langfang	611
7 Beijing	17051
8 Baoding	1824
9 Shijiazhuang	3648
10 Xingtai	587
11 Handan	1063
12 Hengshui	1011
13 Cangzhou	967

In this study, Microcity software is used to solve the model. According to the relative positions of the demand points and alternative points in the selected target area, the spatial relative positions are shown in Microcity, and the passenger flow data at the demand points and the OD distance between alternative points and demand points are input into the corresponding spatial data tables on the corresponding points and links map layer. Spatial representation is shown in Fig. 2 and Fig. 3:

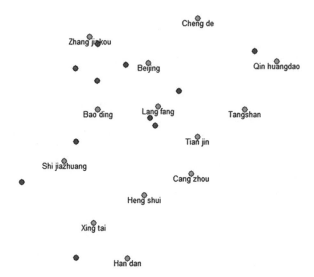

Fig. 2. The relative location map of demand points and alternative points of integrated passenger terminals drawn in microcity.

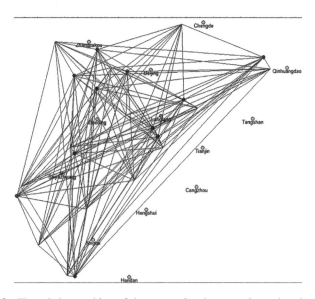

Fig. 3. The relative position of the target planning area drawn in microcity.

Microcity software is used to solve the P-median location selection model, the results of solution can be obtained by running the program, as shown in Fig. 4:

```
[2021-05-11/15:09:49] Executing module: main
[2021-05-11/15:09:49] choose 9 stations from 11 alternative sites to build integrated passenger terminal to provide 13 demandpoints
[2021-05-11/15:09:49] The minimum of the sum of the product of the passenger flow among the demandpoints
                     and the distance between the demandpoints and the alternativepoints is 640655.90000018
[2021-05-11/15:09:49] The construction plan is as follows:
[2021-05-11/15:09:49] Integrated passenger terminal numbered 1
                     provides service to the demandpoint numbered6
[2021-05-11/15:09:49] Integrated passenger terminal numbered 2
                     provides service to the demandpoint numbered7
[2021-05-11/15:09:49] Integrated passenger terminal numbered 4
                     provides service to the demandpoint numbered1
[2021-05-11/15:09:49] Integrated passenger terminal numbered 5
                     provides service to the demandpoint numbered9
[2021-05-11/15:09:49] Integrated passenger terminal numbered 5
                     provides service to the demandpoint numbered12
[2021-05-11/15:09:49] Integrated passenger terminal numbered 7
                     provides service to the demandpoint numbered5
[2021-05-11/15:09:49] Integrated passenger terminal numbered 7
                     provides service to the demandpoint numbered13
[2021-05-11/15:09:49] Integrated passenger terminal numbered 8
                     provides service to the demandpoint numbered2
[2021-05-11/15:09:49] Integrated passenger terminal numbered 8
                     provides service to the demandpoint numbered4
[2021-05-11/15:09:49] Integrated passenger terminal numbered 9
                     provides service to the demandpoint numbered3
[2021-05-11/15:09:49] Integrated passenger terminal numbered 10
                     provides service to the demandpoint numbered8
[2021-05-11/15:09:49] Integrated passenger terminal numbered 11
                     provides service to the demandpoint numbered10
[2021-05-11/15:09:49] Integrated passenger terminal numbered 11
                     provides service to the demandpoint numbered11
[2021-05-11/15:09:49] Module execution succeeded
```

Fig. 4. The optimization scheme of location selection and layout of the integrated passenger terminals.

4.3   Result Analysis

After solving the model by Microcity, It is seen that the minimum total weighted travel distance is 6406.559 ten thousand people · kilometer. Through the P-median location model, 9 out of 11 alternative points of integrated passenger transport terminals are selected as the optimal P-median integrated passenger transport terminals in the Beijing-Tianjin-Hebei urban agglomeration. The selected integrated passenger terminals and their service scope are shown in Table 10:

Table 10. Optimal sites of the integrated passengertransport terminals and their corresponding radiation ranges of passengerservices.

The integrated passenger transport terminals	Demand points of passenger transport
No. 1 (Beijingnan Railway Station)	No. 6 (Langfang)
No. 2 (Beijing Railway Station)	No. 7 (Beijing)
No. 4 (Beijingbei Railway Station)	No. 1 (Zhangjiakou)
No. 5 (Shijiazhuang Railway Station)	No. 9 (Shi jiazhuang)
No.7 (Tianjin Railway Station)	No. 5 (Tianjin), No. 13 (Cangzhou)
No. 8 (Tangshan Railway Station)	No. 2 (Chengde) No. 4 (Tangshan)
No. 9 (Qinhuangdao Railway Station)	No. 3 (Qin huangdao)
No. 10 (Baoding Railway Station)	No. 8 (Baoding)
No. 11 (Handandong Railway Station)	No. 10 (Xingtai), No.11 (Handan)

The results of the instance show that the P-median site selection model for the layout of integrated passenger transport terminal has a certain guiding role, namely it can determine P-median optimal integrated passenger transport terminals from a known set of alternative points. From the Table 10, Beijingnan Railway Station provides traffic service for Lang fang. Beijingbei Railway Station serves the passenger of Zhangjiakou. The radiation scope of Tianjin Railway Station includes Cangzhou. Tangshan Railway Station can provide traffic service service for Cheng de. The radiation range of Handan Railway Station includes Xingtai. Based on the results, from the view of the integrated passenger terminal capacity adjustment, we can consider to enlarge the scale of Beijingnan Railway Station, Beijingbei Railway Station, Tianjin Railway Station, Tangshan Railway Station, Handandong Railway Station. From the perspective of feeder lines, we can increase Dedicated lines from Langfang to Beijingnan Railway Station, from Zhangjiakou to Beijingbei Railway Station, from Chengde to Tianjin Railway Station, from Xing tai to Handan Railway Station. As a result, the layout optimization of the integrated passenger terminals within Beijing-Tianjin-Hebei urban agglomeration practice can provide a certain reference function.

5   Conclusion

In this paper, Firstly, the key factors affecting the layout of integrated passenger transport terminals are selected for qualitative analysis. Secondly, the degree of charm index is defined, and next a screening model of alternative points of passenger transport based on the degree of charm is proposed, and then a comprehensive evaluation method is applied to quantitatively calculate the charm value of each alternative points in combination with the multi-level fuzzy evaluation model. It provides a way to get the alternative points set of integrated passenger terminal in the planned area. On the basis of the determined alternative points set, P-medium site selection model is applied to optimize the layout of integrated passenger terminals. The minimization of the sum of product of the distance between each alternative point and each the demand point and the passenger volume at the demand point is considered as the objective function. In addition, Microcity soft is used to process the spatial data and solve P-medium site selection model. In the end, the P-middle optimal layout scheme can be obtained. The proposed method provides a design idea for the optimization of the layout of integrated passenger transport terminals in Beijing-Tianjin-Hebei urban agglomeration.

Acknowledgement. This research was supported by the National Key Research and Development Program of China (2018YFB1601300).

References

1. Marianov, V., Figuera, D., Revelle, C.: Location of hubs in a competitive environment. Eur. J. Oper. Res. **14**(2), 363–371 (1999)
2. Costa, M.D.G., Captive, M.E., Climaco, J.: Capacitated single allocation hub location problem-a bi-criteria approach. Comput. Oper. Res. **35**(11), 3671–3695 (2008)
3. Khasnabis, S.: Land use and transit integration and transit use incentives. Transp. Res. Rec. J. Transp. Res. Board **1618**(1), 39–47 (1998)
4. Alumur, S., Kara, B.Y.: Network hub location problems: the state of the art. Eur. J. Oper. Res. **190**(1), 19–121 (2008)
5. Li, T.T.: Hierarchical location problem of comprehensive passenger transport hub in city cluster under urbanization background. M.S. Dissertation, Jiaotong University, Beijing (2017)
6. Lv, S., Tian, F.: Location model of urban passenger intermodal transfer terminals. J. Shenzhen Univ. Sci. Eng. **24**(2), 194–199 (2007)
7. Wu, D.: Study on problems of passenger site layout in railway terminal. M.S. Dissertation. Southwest Jiaotong University (2010)
8. Xu, B., Zhu, J., Wen, J., Lin, S., Zhao, Y., et al.: Optimization for variable height wind farm layout model. Intell. Autom. Soft Comput. **29**(2), 525–537 (2021)
9. Al-Khateeb, B., Ahmed, K., Mahmood, M., Le, D.: Rock hyraxes swarm optimization: a new nature-inspired metaheuristic optimization algorithm. Comput. Mater. Continua **68**(1), 643–654 (2021)
10. Devi, R.M., Premkumar, M., Jangir, P., Elkotb, M.A., Elavarasan, R.M., et al.: IRKO: an improved Runge-Kutta optimization algorithm for global optimization problems. Comput. Mater. Continua **70**(3), 4803–4827 (2022)
11. Zeidabadi, F.A., Doumari, S.A., Dehghani, M., Montazeri, Z., Trojovský, P., et al.: Ambo: all members-based optimizer for solving optimization problems. Comput. Mater. Continua **70**(2), 2905–2921 (2022)
12. Jan, A.M., Mahmood, Y., Khan, H.U., Mashwani, W.K., Uddin, M.I., et al.: Feasibility-guided constraint-handling techniques for engineering optimization problems. Comput. Mater. Continua **67**(3), 2845–2862 (2021)

Review of Research on Named Entity Recognition

Xiaole Li[1], Tianyu Wang[2], Yadan Pang[2], Jin Han[2(✉)], and Jin Shi[1]

[1] Nanjing University, Nanjing, China
[2] Nanjing University of Information Science and Technology, Nanjing, China
hjhaohj@126.com

Abstract. With the development of Web2.0, huge amount of text information is produced. It's important to extract useful information from data. This paper systematically analyzes the main research progress and methods of named entity recognition (NER), and grasps the development context to help researchers quickly understand NER. [Method/process] We select representative literature for review, summarize and comb the mainstream methods by bibliometrics and literature research, and count the keywords of relevant papers in Web of Science to support this view, and finally summarize the applications and the development trends of NER. [Result/conclusion] Research shows that common recognition methods include rule-based, statistics-based, hybrid methods, and more and more tend to integrate multiple methods; in recent 5 years, hybrid and joint models based on deep learning are currently dominating the latest technology.

Keywords: Named entity recognition · Information extraction · Machine learning

1 Introduction

1.1 The Current Research Framework

The rapid development of the Internet and the diversification of information carriers have made the information that people contact with become complex and diverse, the way to find key information in the massive data has become an urgent problem to be solved, so information extraction has emerged. As the important semantic knowledge in text, named entity is the basic information unit in natural language, which must be the prerequisite and foundation for researchers to conduct research on natural language understanding and text mining. Therefore, one of the core tasks of information extraction is: NER. The goal of NER is to identify and classify meaningful time, date or other quantitative phrases and proper nouns such as person or place names in the text [1]. Therefore, it is also called named entity recognition and classification (NERC). Among various natural language processing (NLP) technologies such as knowledge question answering systems, machine translation, and knowledge ontology construction, NER is indispensable.

X. Sun et al. (Eds.): ICAIS 2022, CCIS 1587, pp. 256–267, 2022.
https://doi.org/10.1007/978-3-031-06761-7_21

Through extensive literature research and text analysis, this paper sorts out the development history of NER at home and abroad, summarizes the research status of this field and forms a full-process research framework as shown in Fig. 1. For the task of NER, the main process is to publish different types of entities to be recognized by the relevant evaluation conference. Scholars will use and improve algorithms, and measure the recognition result by evaluation indicators; at the same time, scholars can also collect data for labeling and research on their specific problems. Then final model can be applied to different fields.

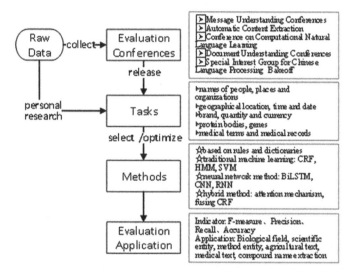

Fig. 1. Research framework of NER task.

In 1991, Rau proposed an algorithm to automatically extract company names from financial news combined with a large amount of corpus. This research is regarded as the beginning of NER [2]. Before reviewing the development history of NER, we must first clarify what are named entities.

1.2 What Are Named Entities

In 1995, the sixth in a series of Message Understanding Conferences, named entity (NE) was proposed as a clear concept. In MUC-6 and MUC-7, three categories and seven subcategories of entities that need to be identified for NER evaluation were stipulated. The three categories of entities include NEs, time expressions and quantitative expressions, and the seven subcategories include people names, place names, organizations names, time expressions, and certain types of numerical expressions [3]. The meeting also stipulated that entities to be marked were "unique identifiers of entities".

In addition to some mainstream evaluation conferences, many scholars have researched on the meaning and types of named entities. Sekine et al. [4] extended the original 7 subcategories of named entities to include 150 entity categories in order to better meet the needs of information retrieval. Cucchiarelli et al. [5] stipulated that NE is a proper noun that can be used as the name of someone or something. Borrega et al. [6] considered the characteristics of NEs to be "unique and unambiguous" and defined NEs from a linguistic point of view. Researchers in different research directions often determine named entities based on specific applications.

At present, the academic circle has not unified the definition of NE, and the extension and connotation of NE are constantly enriched, and the discussion about it is far from over. We believe that researchers need to focus their research on how to design models and use appropriate methods to identify NEs, without paying too much attention to what are NEs.

1.3   Research History

In 1999, Bikel et al. [7] proposed a hidden markov model (HMM), which can identify and classify English NEs. In the test set provided by MUC-6, the recall and precision of institution names, person names and place names of the model exceeded 90%. After that, in CoNLL-2002 and CoNLL-2003 conferences. The participating groups all used machine learning methods, like Maximum Entropy, Support Vector Machine, Conditional Random Field, AdaBoost, etc.

The development of Chinese NER started a little later, and the reason is obvious: Chinese NER includes word segmentation, which is very different from English entity recognition relying on spaces, and it is more difficult to implement. In 863 Information Retrieval Evaluation held in 2004, the highest F1 of the names of person, places and organizations reach 85.51%, 82.51%, and 60.81%, respectively. Particularly, Chinese organization names often use abbreviations, which makes it more difficult to identify. With the improvement of technology, the development of machine learning has been gaining momentum in recent years. Zhang Min [8] used SVM and CRF to extract disease entities; Wang Dongbo et al. [9] compared the results of extracting data science recruitment entities through a variety of deep learning models, and constructed a corresponding entity network.

1.4   Evaluation Conferences

There are many evaluation conferences for NER at home and abroad, and the conferences have greatly promoted the development of entity extraction technology. See Table 1 for details.

Table 1. Different evaluation conferences and detail information.

Evaluation conference	Data	Meaning
MUC	English military report and news report	Muc-6 makes NER a meeting evaluation task
ACE	English, Chinese, Spanish news, blogs, etc.	Three stages of development, the development of NER to a new perspective
CoNLL	News columns in English and German	Machine learning has become the mainstream in this conference
DUC	Associated Press, New York Times and Xinhua news	From entity recognition to deep text analysis
SIGHAN Bakeoff	Chinese Corpus	For Chinese automatic word segmentation and entity extraction

2   NER Methods

According to the development history of NER, the methods widely used by scholars generally include three categories, namely: rules and dictionaries-based methods, machine learning-based methods, and hybrid methods.

2.1   Rules and Dictionaries-Based Methods

In the early development of NER, the method based on rules and dictionaries was the first choice of researchers because of its simple principle. For example, the system in MUC-7 conference was all based on handwritten rules. Linguists manually construct templates based on commonly features (such as punctuation, keywords, demonstrative words, position words, etc.), and then establish a system based on the dictionary and knowledge given by domain experts.

Generally speaking, the more rules are formulated, the better the recognition result. But it is obviously unreasonable to recognize infinite entities by limited rules. Especially when the domains are different, the manually rules are often difficult to transplant, which means that different domains require different experts to write the rules, and it is an extremely time-consuming job. On the other hand, the rule-based method is too costly, the compilation process is time-consuming and cannot cover all language phenomena. Therefore, researchers have also tried to use computer to automatically discover and generate rules. For example, Collins and Singer [10] trained a pre-defined seed-set based on unsupervised iterative training, and then used the iterative rules to recognize NEs. The final result was that the recognition precision of three types of entities exceeded 90%. Cucerzan [11] used Bootstrapping algorithm to automatically generate rules. Before 2000, researchers mostly used rule-based methods. With the rise of machine learning, more researchers made new attempts in NER. The research work of rule-based NER is summarized in Table 2.

Table 2. NER research based on rules and dictionaries.

Authors and publish year	NEs	Methods	Results
Singh et al. 2012	Name of people, place, organization, quantity, date, brand, etc.	Place name dictionary and manual rules	F-score: 74.09%
Gupta et al. 2011	Proper noun entity	Catalogue of place names	Precision: 89.22% Recall: 83.4%
Shaalan et al. 2009	Name of people, place, organization, date, company, time	Dictionary and grammar rules	F-score: People 87.7% Date 91.6% Company 83.15% Place 85.9% Time 95.4%

From the research work summarized above, it is not difficult to see that the rule-based research method has good results in extracting the traditional three types of NEs (person names, place names, organization names), and often needs to cooperate with dictionaries and knowledge vocabulary to assist the rule to complete the extraction. With the expansion of the extraction scope, the enrichment of content and fields, the high dependence, heavy task, and non-transferability of the rule-based extraction method have become obstacles to its continued development.

2.2 Machine Learning-Based Methods

Compared with rule-based methods, machine learning-based methods can be completed in a shorter time because researchers no longer need to understand linguistics. In the CoNLL-2003 conference mentioned in Sect. 1.3, all participating systems used machine learning methods. The advantage of the method is that when transplanted to other fields, you can use the new corpus to retrain, basically without major changes.

Early neural networks are rarely used in the field of NLP, because artificial neural networks have certain limitations. In 2006, Hinton [12] proposed to complete model training and prediction tasks through layer-by-layer pre-training and back propagation to make up for the learning difficulties of multi-layer neural network models. At the same time, with the improvement of computing power, the method based on neural network has attracted the attention of scholars. Deep learning is a technology to realize machine learning, and neural network is the core of deep learning. Therefore, this section divides machine learning methods into two categories: non-neural network and neural network.

In actual research, traditional machine learning methods mainly include: hidden markov model [13] (HMM), maximum entropy [14] (ME), conditional random fields [15] (CRF) and support vector machine [16] (SVM) and so on. The comparison of these four classic methods is shown in Table 3.

Table 3. Comparison of advantages and disadvantages of different algorithms.

Algorithm	Advantages	Disadvantages
HMM	High speed and efficiency	Accuracy is not high
ME	Compact structure and versatility	Time-consuming
CRF	Flexible and globally optimal	Slow convergence and time-consuming
SVM	High accuracy	Time-consuming

The above four methods are all based on supervised learning methods. Firstly the implementation of these methods is to select the appropriate training corpus, then analyze the text information in the corpus to form an appropriate training set, and finally use data mining to select appropriate features for algorithm improvement. Among the above algorithms, HMM is more suitable for small dataset and is a generative model; ME adapts to the data by setting constraints, but it is time-consuming; CRF can use the context information provided in the text to be recognized to get better results, and it is the most widely used; SVM treats recognition as a classification problem to solve. The non-neural network method named entity recognition research situation is summarized as shown in Table 4.

Table 4. NER research based on non-neural network.

Authors and publish year	NEs	Methods	Results
Chen et al. 2015	Clinical diagnosis, problems and testing	CRF	F-score: 80%
Wang et al. 2014	name of people, place, organization	HMM, MEMM, CRF	Highest-F is 95.12% based on CRF
Jung et al. 2012	Name of people, place, organization	CRF	F-score: 90.3%
Borthwick et al. 1999	Name of people, place, organization, date, time	ME	F-score: 85.9%
Bikel et al. 1997	Non recursive entity	HMM	F-score: English-entity is 93% Spain-entity is 90%

Gallo et al. [17] regarded NER as a word classification problem. They managed the context information of the input information through the sliding window of the multi-layer perceptron, and evaluated the performance in commercial quotation dataset and seminar announcement dataset. This method provides solutions for the field of informal documents. Peters et al. [18] proposed a semi-supervised method based on a neural language model, which can encode words and their semantic roles in the context, and used RNN for sequence modeling, and embed the trained context for NER. The F1 of the method on CoNLL reached 91.93%.

Chiu and Nichols [19] proposed a BiLSTM-CNNs model that can automatically detect word and character-level features. Ma and Hovy [20] further extended it to the BiLSTM-CNNs-CRF architecture, which added a CRF module to optimize the output tag sequence. Traditional RNN can't handle long-term dependence well. The method based on LSTM can better capture the long-distance dependence in the text, which is suitable for modeling text data. Later, the BiLSTM method is improved on the basis of the LSTM model, which can better capture the two-way semantic dependence, so it has become one of the most widely used methods for NER in recent years. Zhang et al. [21] were based on the LSTM framework and combined with the CRF to consider the dependency between context words. This method has an F1 of 89.94% in medical text BioCreative II GM. Table 5 summarizes the research status of NER based on neural network.

Table 5. NER research based on neural network.

Authors and publish year	NEs	Methods	Results
Zhang et al. 2021	Diseases, drugs, genes and proteins	LSTM-CRF	F1-score: 89.94%
Peters et al. 2017	Name of people, place, organization (CoNLL)	Language model	F-score: 91.93%
Chiu et al. 2016	Name of people, place, organization	BiLSTM-CNNs	Highest F-score: 91.55%
Ma et al. 2016	Name of people, place, organization	BiLSTM-CNNs-CRF	F-score: 92.21%

NER can use the non-linear characteristics of deep learning to establish a non-linear mapping from input to output. Compared with linear models (such as linear chain CRF), deep learning models can use massive amounts of data to learn more complex and refined features through nonlinear activation function learning. Deep learning does not require complex feature engineering, it can automatically discover information from the input and learn the representation of the information, and usually the results of such automatic learning are not bad. At present, the biggest challenge of deep learning is data annotation, informal text and invisible entities.

2.3   Hybrid Method

Natural language processing is not entirely a random process. If you do not rely on the knowledge of rules to filter in advance, only rely on machine learning methods will make the state search space very large, and take a long time. Judging from the current research, it is better to mix the two methods. The combination of these two methods can be either a hierarchical relationship or a sequential relationship. From the earliest method of internal integration to the use of external dictionaries, it has developed to the current popular deep learning methods.

(1) The machine learning methods are overlapped and integrated.

Etkinson and Bull [22] combined support vector machine and hidden markov model to identify biological entities (like genes, proteins, cells, etc.), and obtained an F of 85.14% by preprocessing and adding feature representation.

(2) The technical integration of rules, dictionaries and machine learning. In order to reduce the limitation of the corpus, some rules can be introduced in the method based on machine learning.

Moradi and Ahmadi [23] used two HMM and Viterbi methods, a set of vocabulary and pattern library construction rules were used to identify named entities, and fused the two to identify entities in Persian texts, and obtained 89.73% precision. Liu et al. [24] added the Gazetteers geographical name dictionary based on the architecture of hybrid semi-markov conditional random fields (HSCRFs), and used the matching of entities in the geographical name dictionary to increase recognition features.

(3) Combination of various models or algorithms: the training data of the next level is derived from the results of the previous level, and then repeat the training to get the next level model. How to efficiently combine the two methods and what kind of fusion technology to use is the focus for researchers.

Lin et al. [25] combined the rule-based post-processing with ME to construct a "MENE" system, used machine learning to identify biological entities, and the entity boundary is corrected through post-matching processing based on rule patterns to reduce identification and classification errors. Strubell et al. [26] proposed the method of using an expanded CNN with CRF in the output layer. He used iterative expansion to capture sentence context and this method obtained F-measure of 86.84% and 90.65% in OntoNotes and CONLL datasets, respectively. The research work status of NER based on hybrid method is summarized in Table 6.

Table 6. NER research based on hybrid method.

Authors and publish year	NEs	Methods	Results
Ali et al. 2019	ANERCorpus	LSTM + self attention mechanism	F-score: 91%
Zhu et al. 2019	Chinese RESUME + MSRA	CNN + local attention mechanism	F-score of RESUME: 94.94% F-score of MSRA: 92.97%
Munkhjargal et al. 2015	NEs in Mongolian	CRF + SVM + ME	F-score: CRF:87.36% SVM:87.43% ME:82.72%
Guanming et al. 2009	Name of people, place, organization	CRF + tagsets + TL	F-score: 93.49%

3 New Stage of NER

3.1 Specific Application

With the development of the times and technological progress, the effect of NER has been continuously improved. Nowadays, the focus of NER research is no longer on the improvement of the model but on practical applications. Although the high accuracy and recall rate cannot be achieved for large-scale text-based named entity recognition tasks, the effects of most machine learning methods are also satisfactory. Subsequently, researchers began to try named entity recognition in the text corpus of various disciplines and fields. Such as scientific entity extraction, compound name extraction, medical entity extraction, etc. Oliveira et al. [27] identify the names of people, places, and organizations mentioned in Twitter based on five filters: nouns, affixes, terms, dictionaries, and contextual information. The research does not rely on grammatical rules and is more efficient. In recent years, entity recognition in the field of NER biomedicine has been the most successful. Zhao et al. [28] proposed a CNN-based model that uses character embedding, word embedding, and dictionary feature embedding as input for disease named entity recognition. In recent years, the hot social media has developed rapidly, attracting a large number of researchers to conduct network analysis and emotional evaluation on it. This research has also become an important subfield of natural language processing (NLP). There is reason to believe that with the advent of the era of big data and the improvement of computer performance, people have obtained enough corpus, and the previous restrictions on certain algorithms will no longer exist. In the future, named entity recognition will play an active role in many other fields.

3.2 NER Method Research

In order to understand the usage of the method of NER task from a more extensive research process. Based on the idea of bibliographic data analysis, this article uses advanced search in WoS. The search formula is "TS = (Named entity recognition OR Named entity recognition and classification OR NER OR NERC)". The search date was January 10, 2021 and 7228 papers were retrieved. Manually export the bibliographic information of the document, and extract the research methods involved in keywords.

After statistics, 4848 papers contain keywords, and then select the method keywords whose word frequency is more than 30, as shown in Table 7.

Table 7. Results of methodological keywords.

Rank	Keyword	Frequency	Rank	Keyword	Frequency
1	CRFs	231	8	RNN	41
2	Machine learning	176	9	CNN	39
3	Deep learning	126	10	BiLSTM	38
4	Neural networks	94	11	HMM	38
5	SVM	72	12	Semi-supervised learning	34
6	Word embedding	69	13	Active learning	32
7	LSTM	45	14	ME	31

It is found from Table 7 that the CRF has been used the most times, and this method is also a very classic algorithm. The sequence labeling and recognition performance of this algorithm has been affirmed by most researchers. In the past three years, deep learning is also ranked third, which is widely used by scholars. There are reasons to believe that deep learning will have greater development in the future. The three types of classic machine learning algorithms, HMM, ME, and SVM, are widely used, indicating that the three types of methods have a strong fusion degree, and the use of other models or rule methods can improve the performance of the model. The research hotspots in this field also include active learning and transfer learning. In view of historical development, more and more articles in the field of NER have been published, and scholars have conducted more in-depth research on it, and the sub-categories extended from it are also richer. We believe that with the in-depth study of syntactic knowledge and semantics in the field of NLP, the application of NER in other disciplines will become an important research direction in the future.

4   Conclusion

Starting from the current research status, this article leads to the subject of NER. This topic has been developed for more than 20 years. This paper reviews the academic papers related to NEs and NER at home and abroad in recent 20 years. Obviously, since NER was proposed as a subtask of information extraction, researchers have been expanding the scope of application and applicable methods of the task, and the current mainstream methods have also achieved good results. Many evaluation conferences at home and abroad have limited the scope of NER, and spawned a series of important machine learning or deep learning algorithms. After combing through its mainstream algorithms, it is easy to conclude that NER is promising in many fields such as machine translation, information retrieval, data mining, and NLP.

Judging from the existing research results, NER is still challenging. On the one hand, in big data era, the development of deep learning has increased infinite possibilities for the emergence of new algorithms, and the effect and importance of NER will gradually become prominent. On the other hand, how to choose different feature enhancement algorithms and how to expand the corpus both are researchers need to consider. We believe that the most important value of NER is to help other disciplines obtain NEs that need attention, build entity libraries in various fields, help researchers better standardize the research process, and promote cross-learning and development in different fields.

For citations of references, we prefer the use of square brackets and consecutive numbers. Citations using labels or the author/year convention are also acceptable. The following bibliography provides a sample reference list with entries for journal articles [1], an LNCS chapter [2], a book [3], proceedings without editors [4], as well as a URL [5].

Acknowledgement. This work is supported by Engineering Research Center of Digital Forensics, Ministry of Education, Nanjing University of Information Science and Technology.

References

1. Chinchor, N.: MUC7 named entity task definition. In: Proceedings of the 7th Message Understanding Conference (1997)
2. Rau, L.F.: Extracting company names from text. In: Proceedings of the 7th IEEE Conference on Artificial Intelligence Applications, pp. 29–32. IEEE (1991)
3. Sundheim, B.M.: Named entity task definition, version 2.1. In: Proceedings of the 6th Conference on Message Understanding (MUC-6) (1995)
4. Sekine, S., Sudo, K., Nobata, C.: Extended named entity hierarchy. In: Proceedings of the 3rd International Conference on Language Resources and Evaluation, pp. 1818–1824 (2002)
5. Petasis, G., Cucchiarelli, A., Velardi, P., et al.: Automatic adaptation of proper noun dictionaries through cooperation of machine learning and probabilistic methods. In: International ACM SIGIR Conference on Research & Development in Information Retrieval, pp. 128–135. ACM (2000)
6. Borrega, O., Taulé, M., Martí, M.A.: What do we mean when we speak about Named Entities. In: Proceedings of Corpus Linguistics (2007)
7. Bikel, D.M., Schwartz, R., Weischedel, R.M.: An algorithm that learns what's in a name. Mach. Learn. **34**(1), 211–231 (1999)
8. Zhang, M.: Research on medical entity extraction based on SVM and CRF. Chengdu University of Technology (2018)
9. Wang, D., Hu, H., Zhou, X., et al.: Research of automatic extraction of entities of data science recruitment and analysis based on deep learning. Libr. Inf. Serv. **62**(13), 64–73 (2018)
10. Collins, M., Singer, Y.: Unsupervised models for named entity classification. In: Proceedings of the Joint SIGDAT Conference on Empirical Methods in Natural Language Processing and Very Large Corpora, pp. 10–20 (1999)
11. Cucerzan, S., Yarowsky, D.: Language independent named entity recognition combining morphological and contextual evidence. In: Proceedings of the 1999 Joint SIGDAT Conference on EMNLP and VLC, pp. 90–99 (1999)
12. Hinton, G.E., Salakhutdinov, R.R.: Reducing the dimensionality of data with neural networks. Science **313**, 504–507 (2006)
13. Bikel, D.M., Miller, S., Schwartz, R., et al.: Nymble: a high-performance learning name-finder. In: Proceedings of the 5th Conference on Applied Natural Language Processing, pp. 194–201. Association for Computational Linguistics, Stroudsburg (1997)

14. Borthwick, A.E.: A maximum entropy approach to named entity recognition. New York University, New York (1999)
15. McCallum, A., Li, W.: Early results for named entity recognition with conditional random fields, feature induction and web-enhanced lexicons. In: Proceedings of the 7th Conference on Natural Language Learning at HLT-NAACL, vol. 4, pp. 188–191. Association for Computational Linguistics, Stroudsburg (2003)
16. Isozaki, H., Kazawa, H.: Efficient support vector classifiers for named entity recognition. In: Proceedings of the 19th International Conference on Computational Linguistics, vol. 1, pp. 1–7. Association for Computational Linguistics, Stroudsburg (2002)
17. Gallo, I., Binaghi, E., Carullo, M., et al.: Named entity recognition by neural sliding window. In: 8th IAPR International Workshop on Document Analysis Systems. IEEE Computer Society (2008)
18. Peters, M.E., Ammar, W., Bhagavatula, C., et al.: Semi-supervised sequence tagging with bidirectional language models. In: Proceedings of the 55th Annual Meeting of the Association for Computational Linguistics, pp. 1756–1765 (2017)
19. Chiu, J., Nichols, E.: Named entity recognition with bidirectional LSTM-CNNS. Trans. Assoc. Comput. Linguist. **4**, 357–370 (2016)
20. Ma, X., Hovy, E.: End-to-end sequence labeling via bi-directional LSTM-CNNs-CRF. In: Proceedings of the 54th Annual Meeting of the Association for Computational Linguistics (Volume 1: Long Papers) (2016)
21. Zhang, L., Wu, H.: Medical text entity recognition based on deep learning. J. Phys: Conf. Ser. **1744**(4), 042209 (2021)
22. Atkinson, J., Bull, V.: A multi-strategy approach to biological named entity recognition. Exp. Syst. Appl. **39**, 12968–12974 (2012)
23. Moradi, H., Ahmadi, F., Feizi-Derakhshi, M.R.: A hybrid approach for Persian named entity recognition. Iran. J. Sci. Technol. Trans. A Sci. **41**(1), 215–222 (2017)
24. Liu, T., Yao, J.G., Lin, C.Y.: Towards improving neural named entity recognition with gazetteers. In: Proceedings of the 57th Annual Meeting of the Association for Computational Linguistics, pp. 5301–5307 (2019)
25. Lin, Y., Tsai, T., Chou, W., et al.: A maximum entropy approach to biomedical named entity recognition. In: Proceedings of the 4th ACM SIGKDD Workshop on Data Mining in Bioinformatics (2004)
26. Strubell, E., Verga, P., Belanger, D., et al.: Fast and accurate sequence labeling with iterated dilated convolutions (2017)
27. de Oliveira, D.M., Laender, A.H., Veloso, A., da Silva, A.S.: FS-NER: a lightweight filter-stream approach to named entity recognition on twitter data. In: Proceedings of the 22nd International Conference on World Wide Web, pp. 597–604 (2013)
28. Zhao, Z., Yang, Z., Ling, L., et al.: ML-CNN: a novel deep learning based disease named entity recognition architecture. In: 2016 IEEE International Conference on Bioinformatics and Biomedicine (BIBM). IEEE (2016)

Big Data

Large-Scale Mobile Edge Computing with Joint Offloading Decision and Resource Allocation

Yongnan Lu[1], Ming-Xing Luo[1(✉)], and Xiaojun Wang[2]

[1] The School of Information Science and Technology, Southwest Jiaotong University, Chengdu 610031, China
mxluo@home.swjtu.edu.cn
[2] School of Electronic Engineering, Dubin City University, Dublin 9, Ireland

Abstract. Mobile Edge Computing (MEC) marginalizes the computing resources of the core network. So far, most of results have only focused on small number of users or servers. In this paper, a large-scale MEC wireless network is considered with multi-user multi-MEC servers. The random task calculation with normal distribution is proposed. The joint task offloading and resource allocation is investigated by maximizing the average user offloading utility. The delay and energy consumption offloading benefits is formalized as a mixed integer nonlinear program (MINLP) which is general difficult. Our method is to decompose the original problem into resource allocations (RA) under the fixed offloading decision, and the offloading decision (OD) under the optimal resource allocation. RA is further consisting of one convex optimization and quasi-convex optimization. OD is then solved by using a heuristic search algorithm based on simulated annealing principle. The total simulation time complexity is polynomial in the numbers of users and servers. Simulations show that the proposed algorithms performs closely to the optimal solution and achieve higher system utility than traditional methods in small-size networks. Interestingly, it is also applicable for large-scale networks consisting of more than one thousand users. This provides an efficient way for MEC in practical applications.

Keywords: MEC · Task offloading · Resource allocation · Mixed integer nonlinear program

1 Introduction

With the rapid development of the Internet of Things, the computation-intensive nature of many emerging applications leads to high latency and high energy consumption [1–3]. This brings main contradiction between the limited computing power and the battery capacity of smart mobile devices and the ultra-intensive computing tasks. In wireless networks, MEC servers can provide unload services for mobile devices, thus offloading computation-intensive tasks that cannot be handled locally due to limited resources [4]. In the process of offloading tasks

X. Sun et al. (Eds.): ICAIS 2022, CCIS 1587, pp. 271–286, 2022.
https://doi.org/10.1007/978-3-031-06761-7_22

to edge servers, both transmission tasks and processing tasks have delay and energy consumption, which may generate higher delay and power consumption than local execution in ultra-dense networks [5]. Therefore, it is very important to design reasonable strategies to make effective unload decisions, allocate wireless resources and computing resources, and fundamentally improve QoE.

In recent years, the task offloading problem of moving edge computing has attracted a great deal of attention. Some studies focus on reducing delay [6–8], some on reducing power consumption [4,9–11]. Due to the limited resources of a single edge node, some tasks are relatively intensive and still lead to high delay. Therefore, the delay can be reduced by dividing tasks into multiple sub-tasks [6]. In order to reduce system energy consumption, in reference [4], the author studied the energy-saving calculation and unloading mechanism of MEC in 5G heterogeneous network, and designed an EECO scheme to jointly optimize the energy consumption and radio resource allocation of the unloading system. There are also a large number of studies focus on combining the two [12–14]. Meanwhile, the problem of competition between wireless and computing resources caused by a large number of users uploading computing tasks is a hot topic [15–17]. Among them, reference [15] studies the offloading optimization of joint communication, computing resource allocation and energy perception to minimize the tradeoff between energy consumption and delay.

The above studies were conducted mainly when the computational requirements of the task were known, but in most cases, the computational requirements of the task were unknown. In reference [18], a task offloading and resource allocation algorithm for uncertain computing was proposed based on the study of unknown computing requirements. However, the network model based on cloud center and remote server in this study is not necessarily applicable to large-scale multi-user multi-server network model. The actual application scenarios of the system in this paper are mainly applicable to small scale scenarios with concentrated user distribution (such as schools, large sports fields, shopping malls, etc.). In this scenario, users' task types are similar, and it is easy to obtain the statistical value of task computing requirements through certain statistical methods. Therefore, this paper studies the joint task offloading and resource allocation of multi-user and multi-server MEC systems with normally distributed task computing requirements. The offloading utility of each user is modeled as a weighted sum of the benefits of offloading execution relative to local execution latency and energy consumption. Based on the normal distribution of task computing requirements, to maximize the total utility of the system for user unloading, joint task unloading and resource allocation are studied. The problem is formulated as mixed integer nonlinear programming (MINLP). In order to reduce the difficulty of solving MINLP problem, the joint task assignment problem is decomposed into two sub-problems: the task offloading (OD) problem under optimal resource allocation condition and the resource allocation (RA) problem with fixed task unloading decision. The KKT condition of binary search method and Lagrange multiplier method is used to solve the computational resource allocation problem. In the offloading decision part, a heuristic search algorithm based on the principle of simulated annealing (HS-AP) is proposed to approximate the optimal solution and obtain the suboptimal solution.

2   System Model

We consider a large-scale multi-user multi-base MEC network, as shown in Fig. 1. Assume that the actual application scenario of the network model is a large commercial and financial center. There are N users and K base stations (BS). Each BS is deplored as a MEC server. Denote $\mathcal{N} = (1, 2, \cdots, N)$ and $\mathcal{K} = (1, 2, \cdots, K)$ be respective user and server set. The mobile device communicates with BS through wireless channel. MEC servers provide computing offloading services for the mobile device. Each user can perform one computation-intensive non-separable task, which may be completed locally or uploaded to the MEC server. These offloading decisions are respectively represented by a binary variable $a_{n,k} = 0$ or $a_{n,k} = 1$. Denote $U_k = \{n \in \mathcal{N} | a_{n,k} = 1, k \in \mathcal{K}\}$ as the set of users who offload tasks to the server k. Let $\mathcal{A} = \{a_{n,k} | n \in \mathcal{N}, k \in \mathcal{K}\}$ be the offloading decision set of all users.

The computation task of user n is represented by Tk_n, which is defined as a tuple of two parameters, (D_n, C_n). D_n is the data size of the task that may include programs and input parameters. C_n is the number of CPU cycles required for the task D_n. Given specific applications, C_n may be evaluated by statistics. In what follows, assume that the task Tk_n obeys the normal distribution with the mean μ_{cn} and variance σ_{cn}^2, that is, $C_n \sim N(\mu_{cn}, \sigma_{cn}^2)$.

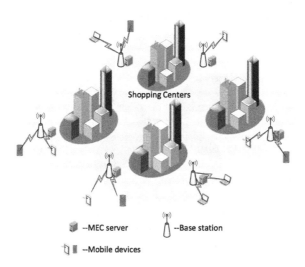

Fig. 1. System model.

2.1   Local Execution

Let $f_{n,l}$ be the local processing rate of the user n. The delay and the energy consumption for the user n with local computation can be calculated as

$$T_{n,l} = \frac{C_n}{f_{n,l}}, E_{n,l} = k_l f_{n,l}^2 C_n \tag{1}$$

where k_l is the energy consumed per CPU cycle, which depends on the chip structure of the mobile device. As in Ref. [19], we take use of $k_l = 5 \times 10^{-27}$.

2.2   Remote Execution

Due to the limitation of its own limited computing resources, users can choose to upload the task to the edge server for calculation, so as to reduce the calculation delay and system energy consumption. When the user chooses to perform the unloading task remotely, we only consider the delay and energy consumption generated by the two processes of upstream data and remote execution, and ignore the feedback process with much less data [20].

Uplink Transmission. The total bandwidth of the base station is W, and we assume that the bandwidth is equally divided by the users offloading in this base station, then the uplink transmission bandwidth of each user offloading is calculated as $B = W/\sum_{n=1}^{N} a_{n,k}$. In this paper, we use orthogonal frequency division multiplexing (OFDM) multiple access technology to make the communication between users in the same cell orthogonal, so the interference in the system mainly comes from different cells. Let $\mathcal{P} = \{p_1, p_2, \cdots, p_N\}$ represent the uplink transmission power set of users, and p_n satisfies $0 \le p_n \le P_{max}$. P_{max} is the maximum transmitted power. By Shannon's theorem [21], the uplink transmission rate of user n is calculated as

$$r_{n,k} = B \log_2(1 + \frac{p_n h_{n,k}}{\omega_0 + I_{in}}) \tag{2}$$

where $h_{n,k}$ is the channel gain from the user n to BS k, and ω_0 is the background noise power. $I_{in} = \sum_{s \ne k}^{K} \sum_{m}^{N} p_m h_{m,s}$ is interference from other cells. In the process of uplink transmission, the time delay and energy consumption of user n are respectively represented by $T_{n,k}^t$ and $E_{n,k}^t$. Then, we have

$$T_{n,k}^t = \frac{D_n}{r_{n,k}}, E_{n,k}^t = T_{n,k}^t p_n = \frac{D_n p_n}{r_{n,k}} \tag{3}$$

Task Execution. The total computing resources of each MEC server is defined f_k, The computing resources allocated by server k to user n is represented as $f_{n,k}$. $\mathcal{F} = \{f_{n,k}|n \in \mathcal{N}, k \in \mathcal{K}\}$ is computing resource allocation decisions. It is obvious that $\sum_{n \in N} f_{n,k} \le f_k, \forall k \in \mathcal{K}$.

When user n offloads the task, the delay of user n during the processing of the task by the server k is defined as $T_{n,k}^c$ which is given by $T_{n,k}^c = \frac{C_n}{f_{n,k}}$. For user n, the total energy consumption generated by the task offloading and execution is only related to the task data uploading, that is, the energy consumption generated by the server-side processing tasks is not considered. Therefore, the total energy consumption $E_{n,s}$ and the total delay $T_{n,s}$ generated by the task offloading by user n are calculated as

$$T_{n,s} = T_{n,k}^t + T_{n,k}^c, E_{n,s} = E_{n,k}^t \qquad (4)$$

User Offloading Utility. In mobile edge network, time delay and energy consumption are the main indicators of QoE. Therefore, we define the utility of the system as the tradeoff between the time delay and energy consumption generated by the offload task and the gain from local execution [22]. When user n executes the task locally, the system utility is 0. If user n offloads the task to the server, the system utility will be positive only if the process produces low energy consumption and low time delay. Otherwise the system utility will be negative. Therefore, the system utility of user offloading can well reflect the rationality of offloading decision. $J_n^T = (T_{n,l} - T_{n,s})/(T_{n,l})$ and $J_n^E = (E_{n,l} - E_{n,s})/(E_{n,l})$ represent the utility of time delay and energy consumption of user n, respectively.

Set β_n as the weighting factor between the delay and energy consumption, and $\beta_n \in [0,1]$. Users can set β_n according to specific requirements (such as battery percentage) to save more energy or reduce delay. Meanwhile, the battery residual energy rate γ_n is introduced into the weighting factor, which is defined as the ratio of the current remaining energy of the mobile device battery to the total battery capacity [15]. Here, the weighting factor is expressed as $\beta_n\gamma_n$. So, the offloading utility of the user n is defined as $J_n = (\beta_n\gamma_n J_n^T + (1 - \beta_n\gamma_n)J_n^E)a_{n,k}$, where $n \in \mathcal{N}, k \in \mathcal{K}$. So the total offloading utility of the system is calculated as

$$J = \sum_{n=1}^{N} \lambda_n J_n \qquad (5)$$

where $\lambda_n \in (0,1)$ means the operator's preference for user n. The operator can set the λ_n of the app paying user n to a higher level to obtain a higher profit.

3 Problem Formulation

3.1 Optimization Problem

The goal of this paper is to combine task offload scheduling with resource allocation to maximize system utility, so we have

$$\max_{\mathcal{A},\mathcal{P},\mathcal{F}} \quad J(\mathcal{A},\mathcal{P},\mathcal{F}) \qquad (6)$$

Since C_n is a random variable subject to normal distribution, after averaging the objective function in Eq. (6), the objective function is defined as

$$\max_{\mathcal{A},\mathcal{P},\mathcal{F}} \quad \mathbb{E}(J(\mathcal{A},\mathcal{P},\mathcal{F})) \tag{7}$$

$$\text{s.t.} \quad a_{nk} \in \{0,1\}, \forall n \in \mathcal{N}, k \in \mathcal{K} \tag{7a}$$

$$\sum_{k=1}^{K}\sum_{n=1}^{N} a_{nk} \leq N \tag{7b}$$

$$0 \leq p_n \leq P^{max}, \forall n \in \mathcal{N} \tag{7c}$$

$$f_n^k > 0,, \forall n \in U_n, k \in \mathcal{K} \tag{7d}$$

$$\sum_{n\in\mathcal{N}} f_n^k \leq f^k, \forall k \in \mathcal{K} \tag{7e}$$

where Eqs. (7a) and (7b) represent that each user's task is an indivisible task, and each task can only be handled one way at a time; Eq. (7c) means that the transmitted power of each user is constrained by the maximum transmitted power; Eqs. (7d) and (7e) indicate that each user to be offloaded must be allocated positive computing resources and that the total computing resources allocated to all users for each server must not exceed the maximum computing capacity of the server.

Due to the integer constraint, the problem becomes a mixed integer nonlinear programming problem, which is difficult to solve directly. Therefore, it is necessary to find a solution with low complexity that is easy to implement.

3.2 Equivalent Problem

In order to reduce the difficulty of solving the problem in Eq. (7), the problem is decomposed into sub-problems. By fixing the binary variable $a_{n,k}$, the problem in Eq. (7) can be rewritten as

$$\max_{\mathcal{A}} \max_{\mathcal{P},\mathcal{F}} \mathbb{E}(J(\mathcal{A},\mathcal{P},\mathcal{F}) \tag{8}$$

It can be seen from the constraints of Eqs. (7a)-(7e) that the offloading decision and the constraints of resources are decoupled. Firstly, in the case of specific offloading decision $\mathcal{A}$, we can find $\mathcal{P}^*$ and $\mathcal{F}^*$; then, based on the optimal resource allocation, the optimal offloading decision problem can be solved. So that the offloading decision problem turns into

$$\max_{\mathcal{A}} \quad \mathbb{E}(J(\mathcal{A},\mathcal{P}^*,\mathcal{F}^*)) \tag{9}$$

$$\text{s.t.} \quad (7a) - (7b)$$

where $\mathbb{E}(J(\mathcal{A},\mathcal{P}^*,\mathcal{F}^*))$ is the optimal solution of RA problem, which is expressed as

$$\mathbb{E}(J(\mathcal{A},\mathcal{P}^*,\mathcal{F}^*)) = \arg\max_{\mathcal{P},\mathcal{F}} \mathbb{E}(J(\mathcal{A},\mathcal{P},\mathcal{F})) \tag{10}$$

$$\text{s.t.} \quad (7c) - (7e)$$

In the RA problem stated above, by substituting Eqs. (5 into 10) we obtain for the fixed offloading decision set $\mathcal{A}$ as

$$\mathbb{E}(J(\mathcal{A}, \mathcal{P}, \mathcal{F})) = \sum_{n \in U_k} \lambda_n (\beta_n \gamma_n \hat{J^T} + (1 - \beta_n \gamma_n) \hat{J^E}) a_{n,k}$$

$$= \sum_{k \in \mathcal{K}} \sum_{n \in U_k} \lambda_n - C(\mathcal{A}, \mathcal{P}, \mathcal{F}) \tag{11}$$

in which

$$C(\mathcal{A}, \mathcal{P}, \mathcal{F}) = \sum_{k \in \mathcal{K}} \sum_{n \in U_k} \lambda_n \beta_n \gamma_n \frac{\hat{T_n^s}}{\hat{T_n^l}}$$

$$+ \sum_{k \in \mathcal{K}} \sum_{n \in U_k} \lambda_n (1 - \beta_n \gamma_n) \frac{E_n^s}{\hat{E_n^l}} \tag{12}$$

Obviously, when the offloading decision is fixed, $\sum_{k \in \mathcal{K}} \sum_{n \in U_k} \lambda_n$ is a constant. The problem in Eq. (10) is equivalent to

$$\min_{\mathcal{P}, \mathcal{F}} \quad C(\mathcal{A}, \mathcal{P}, \mathcal{F}) \tag{13}$$

$$\text{s.t.} \quad (7c) - (7e)$$

By sorting out the formula, Eq. (12) can be calculated as

$$C(\mathcal{A}, \mathcal{P}, \mathcal{F}) = \sum_{k \in \mathcal{K}} \sum_{n \in U_k} \frac{v_n + \eta_n p_n}{\log_2(1 + \frac{h_{n,k}}{\omega_0 + I_{in}} p_n)}$$

$$+ \sum_{k \in \mathcal{K}} \sum_{n \in U_k} \frac{\delta_n}{f_{n,k}} \tag{14}$$

where $v_n = (\lambda_n \beta_n \gamma_n D_n)/(B\hat{T_{n,l}})$, $\eta_n = (\lambda_n (1 - \beta_n \gamma_n) D_n)/(B\hat{E_{n,l}})$, $\delta_n = \lambda_n \beta_n \gamma_n f_n^l$. As can be seen from the constraint conditions in Eqs. (13) and (14), the problem in Eq. (13) can be further decomposed into two sub-problems: uplink power allocation problem which is defined at the first term of Eq. (14) and server computing resource allocation problem which is defined at the second term of Eq. (14). By the decomposition of the problem, it can be easily solved.

4   Joint Resource Allocation and Offloading Decision Algorithm

4.1   Uplink Power Allocation Algorithm

According to Eqs. (13) and (14), the objective function of uplink power allocation problem can be expressed as

$$\min_{P} \sum_{k \in \mathcal{K}} \sum_{n \in U_k} g(p_n) = \sum_{k \in \mathcal{K}} \sum_{n \in U_k} \frac{v_n + \eta_n p_n}{\log_2(1 + \frac{h_{n,k}}{\omega_0 + I_{in}} p_n)} \tag{15}$$

$$\text{s.t.} \quad (7c)$$

We assume that the base stations of the system in this paper distribute power independently to the users who communicate with them, so the power between users of different base stations is independent of each other, that is, when studying the power p_n for the user n communicating with the base station k. $I_{in} = \sum_{s \neq k}^{K} \sum_{m}^{N} p_m h_{m,s}$ can be regarded as a constant. Through calculation, it can be proved that in the domain of constraints, the second derivative of the point where the first derivative of $g(p_n)$ is equal to 0 is greater than 0, so the problem is quasi-convex. At the same time, it can be seen that the first derivative is a monotone increasing function with negative starting point in the constraint region. So the binary search algorithm is used to solve the problem. The algorithm is described in Algorithm 1.

Algorithm 1. Power Allocation Algorithm

Input: Input: P_{max}, β_n, γ_n, h_n, ω_0, B
Output: Output: p_n^*
1: Initialize ε
2: Calculate $g'(P_{max})$
3: **if** $g'(P_{max}) \leq 0$ **then**
4:     $p_n^* = P_{max}$
5: **else**
6:     Initialize $p_L = 0$, $p_H = P_{max}$
7:     **while** $p_H - p_L > \varepsilon$ **do**
8:         Set $p_n^* = (p_L + p_H)/2$
9:         **if** $g'(p_n^*) \leq 0$ **then**
10:             Set $p_L = p_n^*$
11:         **else**
12:             Set $p_H = p_n^*$
13:         **end if**
14:     **end while**
15:     Set $p_n^* = (p_L + p_H)/2$
16: **end if**

4.2   Computing Resource Allocation Algorithm

According to Eq. (14), the computational resource allocation problem can be modeled as

$$\min_{\mathcal{F}} \quad S(\mathcal{A}, \mathcal{F}) = \sum_{k \in \mathcal{K}} \sum_{n \in U_k} \frac{\delta_n}{f_{n,k}} \tag{16}$$

$$\text{s.t.} \quad (7d) - (7e)$$

It's easy to know that the second derivative of Eq. (16) with respect to $f_{n,k}$ is greater than 0, and the second partial is equal to 0. Therefore, its second partial derivative matrix is positive qualitative, so the problem is convex and can be solved by KKT condition. Thus, the optimal resource allocation strategy and the optimal object function to the problem defined in Eq. (16) can be respectively calculated as

$$f_{n,k}^* = \frac{f_k \sqrt{\delta_n}}{\sum_{n \in U_k} \sqrt{\delta_n}}, \forall k \in \mathcal{K}, n \in U_k \tag{17}$$

$$S(\mathcal{A}, \mathcal{F}^*) = \sum_{k \in \mathcal{K}} \frac{1}{f_k} \left(\sum_{n \in U_k} \sqrt{\delta_n} \right)^2 \tag{18}$$

4.3   Offloading Decision Algorithm

In the above section, the optimal value of resource allocation has been obtained for a given offload decision. The optimal uplink power allocation can be obtained by Algorithm 1. The optimal computing resource allocation can be obtained by Eq. (18). So, Eq. (11) can be rewrite as

$$\mathbb{E}(J^*(\mathcal{A})) = \sum_{k \in \mathcal{K}} \sum_{n \in U_k} \lambda_n - \sum_{k \in \mathcal{K}} \sum_{n \in U_k} g(p_n^*) - S(\mathcal{A}, \mathcal{F}^*)$$

$$\tag{19}$$

According to Eqs. (11), (14), (15) and (18), the offload decision problem under the optimal resource allocation which was defined in Eq. (19) can be transformed into

$$\max_{\mathcal{A}} \sum_{k \in \mathcal{K}} \sum_{n \in U_k} \lambda_n - \sum_{k \in \mathcal{K}} \sum_{n \in U_k} g(p_n^*) - S(\mathcal{A}, \mathcal{F}^*) \tag{20}$$

$$\text{s.t.} \quad (7a) - (7b)$$

In order to solve the combinatorial problem in Eq. (20), a low-complexity heuristic search algorithm (HS-AP) is proposed, by combining with the idea that the simulated annealing algorithm accepts the difference solution with a certain probability. This is avoid falling into the local optimal solution and seek the global optimal solution. The offloading decision algorithm (HS-AP) is described as Algorithm 2.

Algorithm 2. Offloading Decision Algorithm(HS-AP)

Input: $T, T_{min}, num, \alpha, \mathcal{A}$
Output: $\mathcal{A}^*, J^*$
1: Initialize $J^* = 0$
2: Calculate $old_{\mathcal{A}}$.
3: **while** $T > T_{min}$ **do**
4:     **for** each $i \in num$ **do**
5:         Calculate $new_{\mathcal{A}}$.
6:         Calculate $\mathbb{E}(J^*(old_{\mathcal{A}}))$ according to Eq.(20)
7:         Calculate $\mathbb{E}(J^*(new_{\mathcal{A}}))$ according to Eq.(20)
8:         **if** $\mathbb{E}(J^*(old_{\mathcal{A}})) < \mathbb{E}(J^*(new_{\mathcal{A}}))$ **then**
9:             Set $\mathbb{E}(J^*(old_{\mathcal{A}})) = \mathbb{E}(J^*(new_{\mathcal{A}}))$
10:            Set $old_{\mathcal{A}} = new_{\mathcal{A}}$
11:            **if** $\mathbb{E}(J^*(new_{\mathcal{A}})) > J^*$ **then**
12:                Set $J^* = \mathbb{E}(J^*(new_{\mathcal{A}}))$
13:                Set $A^* = new_{\mathcal{A}}$
14:            **end if**
15:        **else**
16:            Generates a random number $\theta \in (0,1)$
17:            **if** $\exp(\mathbb{E}(J^*(new_{\mathcal{A}})) - \mathbb{E}(J^*(old_{\mathcal{A}})) > \theta$ **then**
18:                Set $\mathbb{E}(J^*(old_{\mathcal{A}})) = \mathbb{E}(J^*(new_{\mathcal{A}}))$
19:                Set $old_{\mathcal{A}} = new_{\mathcal{A}}$
20:            **end if**
21:        **end if**
22:    **end for**
23:    Set $T = T\alpha$
24: **end while**

In Algorithm 2, the task of calculating $old_{\mathcal{A}}$ is completed as follows : the user offloads specific task to the server according to the channel gain from large to small. The system benefit is calculated once for each iteration. If positive benefits can be generated, it will continue until the current decision fails to generate higher system benefits. And then the current solution is the initial solution of the offload decision. The channel gain matrix of the user is $\mathbf{H}$. Moreover, the task of calculating $new_{\mathcal{A}}$ is completed as follows : three schemes that interfere with the initial offloading decision are defined : (a). Exchange servers between users who want to offloading tasks; (b). Change offloading server of users who need to offloading tasks; (c). Change the offloading decision $(a_{n,k} = 1 - a_{n,k})$. A random variable uniformly distributed between (0,1) is defined to represent the probability of selecting the perturbation scheme.

5   Simulation and Analysis

In this section, the performance of the proposed heuristic joint task offloading scheduling and resource allocation strategy are verified through simulations. We consider a square area with 16 base stations evenly arranged, and each base station will deploy a MEC server. Mobile users are randomly distributed within the region. Adjacent base stations are 300 m away from each other. The path loss model between the user and base station is $L[dB] = 140.7 + 36.7 \log_{10} d_{[km]}$ [23].

In the following experiments, the main setting ups are shown in Table 1. The system utility performance of the algorithm in this paper is compared with the following basic algorithm:

Table 1. Simulation parameters.

Notation	Description	Value
N	Number of users	1600
K	Number of servers	16
D_n	Data size of users' task\ KB	$U(320, 520)$
C_n	User task loading	$N(3000, 45)$
$f_{n,l}$	Local processing rate\ GHz	1
W	Bandwidth of server\ MHz	20
P_{max}	Maximum transmission power\ dBm	20
ω_0	Background noise power\ dBm	−100
β_n	The weighting factor	0.5
γ_n	The battery residual energy rate	0.8
λ_n	The operator's preference for user n	1

(1) Greedy Algorithm: Only make the best choice in the current view.
(2) Local Search Algorithm: Starting from the local execution of all users, the iterative search is conducted directly through Algorithm 3 to obtain the optimal solution within the maximum number of iterations setted in advanced.
(3) User Independent Decision (UID) Algorithm: Each user, in the case of exclusive resources, makes its own offloading decision only by comparing the utility of local and offload. And finally, the system distributes resources equally to each user who decides to offload.
(4) Game Algorithm: Offloading users in turn and calculate the offloading utility of users until one user changes his decision and the utility of the whole system cannot be higher and the optimal solution can be obtained.

Cause local execution will bring 0 utility, it does not participate in the comparison.

In Fig. 2(a,b), we compare the performance of the HS-AP algorithm in this paper with other three basic algorithms. Experiments perform with $\mu_{cn} = 1000, 2000$, and 3000 Megacycles, where $\sigma_{cn}^2 = 5, 20, 45$ are carried out, respectively. At the same time, we carry out simulation experiments for each algorithm in the small-scale network (a) and the large-scale network (b) respectively. As its shown in Figs. 2, the HS-AP algorithm in this paper is better than other

three algorithms in both Fig. 2(a) and 2(b). And, with the increase of computing load, the performance of several algorithms are increasing. Its performance
is improved by 26%, 26%, 25% and 36% respectively in small-scale network.
Interestingly, the average system utility is greatly enhanced in the large-scale
scenario, to 118.4%, 118.4%, 45% and 50%, respectively. Greedy algorithm and
UID algorithm show poor performance in the large scale network. So, they are
only suitable for small-scale networks. As shown in Figs. 2, the proposed HS-
AP algorithm is better than the other four algorithms in both small-scale and
large-scale networks. Hence, the HS-AP algorithm scales well with network size.

The effect of users on each algorithm is shown in Fig. 3. The number of users
take (100, 400, 700, 1000, 1300, 1600) respectively. As its shown in Fig. 3, the
algorithm in this paper is better than other algorithms. It can also be observed in
Fig. 4 that when the number of users is small, the growth rate of user offloading
utility with the increase of users is relatively high. However, when the number of
users reaches a certain level, the growth rate of system utility starts to decrease
or even turn negative. This is due to the increasing number of users competing

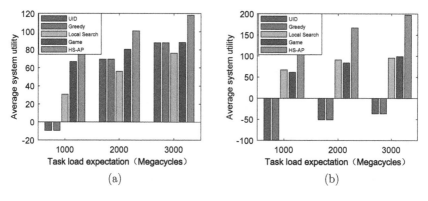

Fig. 2. Average system utility vs Task workload. (a) $N = 300$ and $K = 9$; (b) $N = 1600$
and $K = 16$

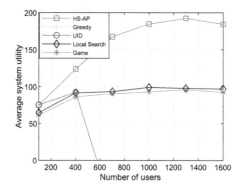

Fig. 3. Average system utility vs User number

for radio and computing resources, and the higher cost of sending tasks and performing tasks on the MEC server, thus reducing the offload utility. With the rapid increase in the number of users, the competition for resources becomes more and more intense, and the offload efficiency of users becomes lower.

To evaluate the performance of Algorithm 4 when more base stations cooperate with each other, we compared the average system utility and algorithm running time for different network deployment scales. Network deployment size is defined as a triad with three elements, the number of base stations, the distance between base stations, and the number of users. Figure 4 shows the average system utility for different network deployments. And the algorithm running time under different network deployments is shown in Table 2. As can be seen from the figure and the table, the more intensive the network deployment is, the higher the system benefits will be achieved, and the running time also shows an increasing trend. This is because the denser the network deployment, the more intensive the computation and the longer the computation time will be. Thus, it can be seen that the algorithm proposed in this paper has the best performance in ultra-dense network, but its running time is longer. Therefore, it is better to divide the network and reduce the density appropriately.

In Figs. 5(a,b) show the impact of average user task load and task data size on algorithm performance respectively. As its shown in the figures, the average system utility of all algorithms increase with the increase of the average task workload and decrease with the increase of the task data volume. This is because tasks with high user task load and low data volumes can be more profitable when executed remotely than locally, so such users are better suited to offload execution tasks.

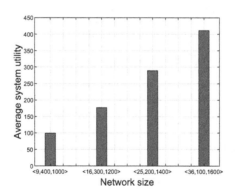

Fig. 4. Average system utility for different network sizes

Table 2. The running time of algorithm 4 under different network scales.

No. BSs	BS spacing	No. users	Runtime
9	$400m$	1000	$1405.9s$
16	$300m$	1200	$4366.7s$
25	$200m$	1400	$10189.3s$
36	$100m$	1600	$21132.6s$

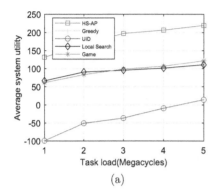
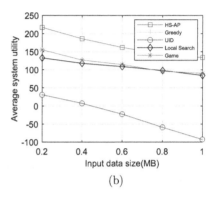

(a)   (b)

Fig. 5. Task load and input data size vs Average system utility

6   Conclusion

In this paper, we study the overall strategy of joint task offloading and resource allocation in a large scale mobile edge computing network with multi-user and multi-server task computing requirements subject to normal distribution. The optimization problem in this paper is formulated as a mixed integer nonlinear programming problem (MINLP). To solve this problem, the original problem is decomposed into uplink power allocation and computing resource allocation problems under specific offloading decisions and the offloading decision problem under optimal resource allocation. The resource allocation problem is solved by the binary search algorithm and the Lagrange multiplier algorithm, and the offloading decision problem is solved by heuristic search algorithm based on the principle of simulated annealing (HS-AP). Simulation results show that the proposed algorithm can achieve high system utility in both small-scale and large-scale edge computing networks. In the future, we will study the direction of further optimization algorithm.

References

1. Sreekanth, G.R., Ahmed, S., Sarac, M., Strumberger, I., Bacanin, N.: Mobile fog computing by using sdn/nfv on 5g edge nodes. Comput. Syst. Sci. Eng. **41**(2), 751–765 (2022)

2. Fan, B., Leng, S., Yang, K.: A dynamic bandwidth allocation algorithm in mobile networks with big data of users and networks. IEEE Network **30**(1), 6–10 (2016)
3. Yang, Y., Li, X., Zhu, D., Hu, H., Du, H.: A resource-constrained edge IoT device data-deduplication method with dynamic asymmetric maximum. Intell. Autom. Soft Comput. **30**(2), 481–494 (2021)
4. Zhang, K., et al.: Energy-efficient offloading for mobile edge computing in 5g heterogeneous networks. IEEE Access **4**, 5896–5907 (2016)
5. Deng, M., Tian, H., Lyu, X.: Adaptive sequential offloading game for multi-cell mobile edge computing. In: 2016 23rd International Conference on Telecommunications, ICT, pp. 1–5. IEEE (2016)
6. Nan, Z., Wen, L., Zhu, L., Zhi, L., Yu, L.: A new task scheduling scheme based on genetic algorithm for edge computing. Comput. Mater. Continua **71**(1), 843–854 (2022)
7. Almutairi, J., Aldossary, M.: Investigating and modelling of task offloading latency in edge-cloud environment. Comput. Mater. Continua **68**(3), 4143–4160 (2021)
8. Sun, Y., Gou, X., Song, J.: Adaptive learning-based task offloading for vehicular edge computing systems. IEEE Trans. Veh. Technol. **68**(4), 3061–3074 (2019)
9. Zhang, J., et al.: Joint resource allocation for latency-sensitive services over mobile edge computing networks with caching. IEEE Internet Things J. **6**(3), 4283–4294 (2018)
10. Chang, Y., Yong, Z., Rui, Z., Kai, H.: Asynchronous mobile-edge computation offloading: energy-efficient resource management. IEEE Trans. Wireless Commun. **17**(11), 7590–7605 (2018)
11. Xiong, A., Chen, M., Guo, S., Li, Y., Zhao, Y.: An energy aware algorithm for edge task offloading. Intell. Autom/ Soft Comput. **31**(5), 1641–1654 (2022)
12. Wu, H., Wolter, K.: Stochastic analysis of delayed mobile offloading in heterogeneous networks. IEEE Trans. Mob. Comput. **17**(2), 461–477 (2018)
13. Dinh, T., Tang, J., La, Q., Quek, T.: Offloading in mobile edge computing: task allocation and computational frequency scaling. IEEE Trans. Commun. **65**(8), 3571–3584 (2017)
14. Gu, B., Zhou, Z.: Task offloading in vehicular mobile edge computing: a matching-theoretic framework. IEEE Trans. Veh. Technol. Mag. **14**(3), 100–106 (2019)
15. Zhang, J., et al.: Energy-latency tradeoff for energy-aware offloading in mobile edge computing networks. IEEE Internet Things J. **5**(4), 2633–2645 (2017)
16. Tran, T., Pompili, D.: Joint task offloading and resource allocation for multi-server mobile-edge computing networks. IEEE Trans. Veh. Technol. **68**(1), 856–868 (2019)
17. Zhan, W., Luo, C., Min, G., Wang, C., Zhu, Q., Duan, H.: Mobility-aware multi-user offloading optimization for mobile edge computing. IEEE Trans. Veh. Technol. **69**(3), 3341–3356 (2020)
18. Eshraghi, N., Liang, B.: Joint offloading decision and resource allocation with uncertain task computing requirement. In: IEEE INFOCOM 2019-IEEE Conference on Computer Communications, pp. 1414–1422. IEEE (2019)
19. Miettinen, A., Nurminen, J.: Energy efficiency of mobile clients in cloud computing. HotCloud **10**(4), 19 (2010)
20. Cheng, K., Teng, Y., Sun, W., Liu, A., Wang, X.: Energy-efficient joint offloading and wireless resource allocation strategy in multi-mec server systems. In: 2018 IEEE international conference on communications, ICC, pp. 1–6. IEEE (2018)
21. Shannon, C.E.: A mathematical theory of communication. The Bell Syst Tech. J. **27**(3), 379–423 (1948)

22. Hong, S., Kim, H.: QoE-aware computation offloading to capture energy-latency-pricing tradeoff in mobile clouds. IEEE Trans. on Mobile Computing **18**(9), 2174–2189 (2018)
23. Chu, X., Lopez-Perez, D., Yang, Y., Gunnarsson, F.: Heterogeneous cellular networks: theory, simulation and deployment. Cambridge University Press (2013)

Tibetan Literature Recommendation Based on Vague Similarity of Cited Number and Downloads

Yongzhi Liu[1,3,4(✉)], Gang Wu[2], and Zangtai Cai[3,4]

[1] College of Alibaba Big Data, Fuzhou Polytechnic, Fuzhou 350108, China
y_zliu@163.com
[2] College of Information Engineering, Tarim University, Alar 843300, China
[3] Tibetan Information Processing and Machine Translation Key Laboratory of Qinghai Province, Xining 810008, China
[4] Key Laboratory of Tibetan Information Processing, Ministry of Education, Xining 810008, China

Abstract. In scientific research, it is very important to quickly and accurately retrieve relevant important documents. This paper sorts the keywords according to their importance and calculates the fuzzy membership degree of keywords; The literatures with the same keywords enter the recommendation set, and two kinds of experiments are carried out on the literatures entering the recommendation set: one is to use vague similarity technology to recommend documents according to keywords; Second, on the basis of the first experiment, vague similarity technology is used to fuse the cited numbers and downloads for literature recommendation. Experiments show that the recommendation algorithm proposed in this paper is reasonable and effective, and can give a reasonable ranking, which meets the needs of researchers to retrieve literatures.

Keywords: Tibetan · Academic resources · Recommend · Vague technology

1 Introduction

1.1 A Subsection Sample

With the development of storage technology and emerging technology, more and more academic resources are accumulated, including academic journals, dissertations, conference papers and newspapers, which provide researchers with a rich scientific research library and literature foundation. As a written communication medium for Tibetans, Tibetan has been widely used in five Tibetan areas, including Tibet, Qinghai, Sichuan, Gansu and Yunnan. With the development of the new generation of information technology, more and more attention has been paid to the research of Tibetan, and there are more and more Tibetan documents. By searching the CNKI website in Tibetan with theme, we can find 4988 articles (as of May 22, 2021), including 3200 academic journals and 687 dissertations. Facing so many academic resources, relying on retrieval, sorting and other technologies can not meet the needs of searchers. How to

© The Author(s), under exclusive license to Springer Nature Switzerland AG 2022
X. Sun et al. (Eds.): ICAIS 2022, CCIS 1587, pp. 287–294, 2022.
https://doi.org/10.1007/978-3-031-06761-7_23

make efficient use of literature resources and provide high-quality literature recommendation has become a hot issue that researchers must face.

Common recommendation technologies include content-based recommendations, collaborative filtering recommendations and hybrid recommendations [1, 2]. The content-based recommendation algorithm is more suitable for the recommendation of academic resources. Because the user information is insufficient and the resources are rich, the user only needs to interact with the resources, extract the features from the interactive resources, compare them with the features of the resources to be recommended, and find out the resources with high acquaintance. Feature extraction and acquaintance measurement are the key technologies for content recommendation.

For content recommendation, the key lies in feature extraction, such as product color, appearance, brand qualitative indicators, specific to the characteristics of academic resources, such as title, summary and keywords. Unlike qualitative indicators, quantitative indicators have measurable values and generally have fuzzy attributes. Fuzzy set theory and vague set theory are generally used to measure fuzzy attributes. Vague inherits the fuzziness of fuzzy, describes the degree of membership from true support and false support, and can also represent the degree of neutrality. Vague has done a lot of research on scoring function, similarity measurement and unknown degree allocation, and produced a lot of theoretical and application results [3, 4], which lays a foundation for the application of vague set in the field of recommendation.

This paper uses the vague similarity algorithm [5, 6] proposed by Liu Yongzhi and others to extract the keywords of Tibetan documents; Then, the keywords are sorted according to the importance, the fuzzy membership degree is calculated by using the relevant theory, and then the true membership degree and false membership degree are extracted to provide the basis for similarity measurement. The experimental results show that the proposed algorithm is effective for Tibetan literature recommendation.

2 Keyword Sorting

Let K be the set of keywords, expressed as $K = \{k_1, k_2, \cdots k_m\}$, and determine its importance according to the number of times it appears in the summary and title. The more times it appears, the higher the importance.

$$w_i = Count(k_i)_{abstract} + 2 * Count(k_i)_{title} \tag{1}$$

If several keywords appear the same times, the one appearing in the title takes precedence. Otherwise, the original position can be defaulted. If $K = \{k_1, k_2, k_3, k_4\}$, $w_1 = 2 + 2 * 0 = 2$, $w_2 = 2 + 1 * 2 = 4$, $w_3 = 3 + 2 * 0 = 3$, $w_4 = 1 + 2 * 1 = 3$ the keywords will be reordered as $K = \{k_2, k_4, k_3, k_1\}$ according to importance.

3   Turn to Fuzzy Membership

Only by numerically converting the keyword features of the literature can we carry out mathematical processing research. This paper selects the theory of literature [7] to convert the keyword features. Literature [7] believes that the fuzzy membership basically conforms to the characteristics of Gaussian function. The Gaussian function is used to obtain the eigenvalues of each literature I, |L| represents the number of keywords, and R represents the ordered position ordinal number.

$$V_{I_i} = \frac{r}{2\sqrt{\alpha|L|(r-1)}} \tag{2}$$

α is a constant greater than 1, which affects the value of each keyword. In the actual operation process, the selected keyword features are important, and some minor features are not selected as keywords. In this paper, a Kx representative is added after each keyword feature set, so that the number of features becomes |L|+1.

4   The Fuzzy Membership Degree is Transformed into Vague Function Value

The fuzzy membership degree of keyword features is obtained by Gaussian function. In order to make use of vague similarity, it needs to be transformed into vague function value. Suppose that the fuzzy membership value of the keyword feature attribute value processed by Gaussian function is $V = \{v_1, v_2, v_3, v_4, v_x\}$, and its value is sorted according to the importance. v_1 is the most important value, v_2 is the second important value, and the value of v_2 can also be regarded as an objection to the value of v_1. The value of v_1-v_2 is the true support value, v_1 is the support with unknown information, and is the maximum support. Therefore, use $(v_1 - v_2, v_1)$ to represent the vague function value of the characteristic attribute. According to this idea, it is converted into the vague function set as follows:

$$V = \{(v_1 - v_2, v_1), (v_2 - v_3, v_2), (v_3 - v_4, v_3), (v_4 - v_x, v_4))\} \tag{3}$$

5   Recommended Ranking

This paper defines I as the set of documents to be recommended, expressed as $I = \{I_1, I_2, I_3 \cdots I_m\}$. The n keyword attributes of each document $I_i(i = 1,2,...m)$ in the document set I constitute a vector set $K_{I_i} = \{K_{i1}, K_{i2}, K_{i3} \cdots K_{in}\}$, which can uniquely represent the characteristics of document I_i The vague function set of document characteristics is:

$$X_{kp}(I_i) = \{\langle t_{k_1}(I_i), 1 - f_{k_1}(I_i)\rangle, \langle t_{k_2}(I_i), 1 - f_{k_2}(I_i)\rangle \cdots \langle t_{k_n}(I_i), 1 - f_{k_n}(I_i)\rangle\} \quad (4)$$

where, $t_{k_n}(I_i)$ represents the true support of product features, $f_{k_n}(I_i)$ represents the false support of product features, and $u_{k_n}(I_i)$ represents the hesitation of product features. The relationship between the three is $u_{k_n}(I_i) = 1 - t_{k_n}(I_i) - f_{k_n}(I_i)$.

In this paper, $S_j(I_k, I_i)$ is defined as the similarity between documents I_k and I_i about feature attribute K_j. The similarity is calculated according to documents [9, 10], and then the similarity between documents I_k and I_i is:

$$S(I_k, I_i) = \sum_{j=1}^{n} S_j(I_k, I_i), \ 0 \le S(I_k, I_i) \le 1 \quad (5)$$

The score value of literature is determined by the number of downloads and citations, and the degree of importance is different. Due to the different publication time of literature, the number of downloads and citations need to be processed. This paper is processed according to the annual average, and the score value of literature I_i is defined as $r(I_i)$:

$$r(I_i) = \varepsilon * \frac{C_d(I_i) - min_d}{max_d - min_d} + \phi * \frac{C_y(I_i) - min_y}{max_y - min_y} \quad (6)$$

where, $0 < \varepsilon < 1, 0 < \varphi < 1$, and $\varphi > \varepsilon$, $C_d(I_i)$ is the average annual download volume of Literature I_i, min_d is the minimum value of the average annual download volume of literature, and max_d is the maximum value of the average annual download volume of literature; $C_y(I_i)$ is the average annual citation of Literature I_i, min_y is the minimum value of the average annual citation of literature, and max_y is the maximum value of the average annual citation of literature. The weighted sum is used to recommend the literature. The formula is $R(I_k) = r(I_i)S(I_k, I_i)$, and the literature is sorted and recommended according to the size of $R(I_k)$.

6   Experiment

6.1   Data Sources

Taking the title as the condition and inputting Tibetan keywords, you can query 1741 Tibetan research literatures (as of May 22, 2021, www.cnki.net). 373 literatures are collected for recommendation research, and the collected literature collection is expressed as $F = \{f_1, f_2 \cdots f_{373}\}$.

6.2   Experimental Process

Firstly, the researcher randomly selects a document to download in F, such as f_9 [8], extracts the keywords in document F and sorts them according to the importance, finds the documents with the same keywords as f_9 in the collected document set F, and those with the same keywords enter the recommendation set as $R = \{f_{108}^{[9]}, f_{111}^{[10]}, f_{116}^{[11]},$

$f_{127}^{[12]}, f_{150}^{[13]}, f_{335}^{[14]}, f_{347}^{[15]}$}. Then, each document in the recommendation set R is sorted by keywords, the fuzzy membership degree of keywords is calculated and transformed into vague function. Finally, the similarity of vague is calculated by using the similarity of vague proposed by Liu Yongzhi and others, and the recommendation order is given. The specific process is shown in Fig. 1.

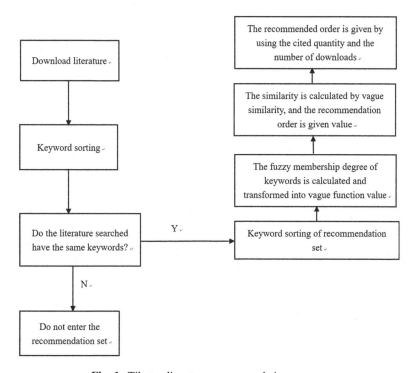

Fig. 1 Tibetan literature recommendation process

6.3 Keyword Sorting of Recommendation Set

There are generally 3 to 8 keywords in the literature. The author is very cautious in selecting keywords. Generally, he can choose the key words that reflect the content of this study, but he doesn't pay much attention to the ranking of keywords. Therefore, we need to rank keywords to reflect the importance of keywords. For example, the keyword with serial number f_9 is "KNN algorithm; Tibetan text; Feature selection; Text classification". According to the theory in Sect. 2 above, the keywords are reordered according to their importance as follows: Tibetan text; KNN algorithm; Text classification; Feature selection. This order can better reflect the core content of the article and lay a foundation for similarity measurement. We rank the documents entering the recommendation set according to the importance of keywords, as shown in Table 1.

6.4   Keywords Fuzzy Membership Degree and Vague Function Value

Let $\alpha = 1.25$, use the theories in Sects. 3 and 4 to obtain the value of characteristic fuzzy membership degree of each literature keyword in the recommendation set, and put it in the same column as the value of fuzzy membership degree of f_9 keyword. And perform vague conversion, as shown in Table 1.

Table 1. Keyword fuzzy membership and vague value.

f_9	1	0.354	0.259	0.199	0	0	0
f_{108}	0	0	0.199	0	1	0.354	0.259
f_{111}	0	0	0	0.425	1	0.335	0
f_{116}	0	0	0	0.199	1	0.354	0.259
f_{127}	0.335	0	0	0	1	0.425	0
f_{150}	0	0	0.165	0	1	0.257	0.115
f_{335}	1	0	0	0	0.425	0.335	0
f_{347}	0	0	0	0.354	1	0.259	0.199
f_9Vague	0.646,1	0.095,0.354	0.06,0.259	0.043,0.199	0,0	0,0	0,0
f_{108}Vague	0,0	0,0	0.043,0.199	0,0	0.646,1	0.095,0.354	0.06,0.259
f_{111}Vague	0,0	0,0	0,0	0.09,0.425	0.575,1	0.062,0.335	0,0
f_{116}Vague	0,0	0,0	0,0	0.043,0.199	0.646,1	0.095,0.354	0.06,0.259
f_{127}Vague	0.062,0.335	0,0	0,0	0,0	0.575,1	0.09,0.425	0,0
f_{150}Vague	0,0	0,0	0.05,0.165	0,0	0.743,1	0.03,0.115	0.02,0.061
F_{335}Vague	0.575,1	0,0	0,0	0,0	0.09,0.425	0.062,0.335	0.0
F_{347}Vague	0,0	0,0	0,0	0.095,0.354	0.646,1	0.06,0.259	0.043,0.199

6.5   Using Vague Similarity Recommendation

Using the vague similarity proposed in references [5, 6], calculate the similarity between the recommendation set and f_9, as shown in Table 2.

Table 2. Similarity between recommendation set and f_9.

	f_9	f_{108}	f_{111}	f_{116}	f_{127}	f_{150}	f_{335}	f_{347}
f_9	1	0.656	0.661	0.656	0.671	0.678	0.932	0.656

This table shows that the recommended order is:

$R(f_{335}) > R(f_{150}) > R(f_{127}) > R(f_{111}) > R(f_{108}) = R(f_{116}) = R(f_{347})$.

This result can well find out the most relevant literature, but f_{111}, which has the highest number of downloads and citations in Tibetan research, is ranked lower, and the recommended values of f_{108}, f_{116} and f_{347} are the same, which can not be distinguished. There are some defects in using vague similarity for recommendation.

6.6 Fuse the Vague Similarity of the Number of Arguments and the Number of Downloads

The weight is determined by the downloaded and cited quantity. Let $\phi = 0.6$, $\varepsilon = 0.4$, $min_d = 9$, $max_d = 50$, $min_y = 0.2$, $max_y = 3$. The minimum and maximum values are slightly larger than the maximum value of the recommendation set and slightly smaller than the minimum value, so as to avoid the situation that the score value is 0. The results are calculated by using the formula in Sect. 5, as shown in Table 3.

Table 3. Literature score

f_{108}	f_{111}	f_{116}	f_{127}	f_{150}	f_{335}	f_{347}
0.007	0.764	0.176	0.069	0.537	0.337	0.35

Using $R(I_k) = r(I_i)S(I_k, I_i)$, calculate the recommended value (with three decimal places) as follows:

$R(f_{108}) = 0.007*0.656 = 0.005$
$R(f_{111}) = 0.764*0.661 = 0.505$
$R(f_{116}) = 0.176*0.656 = 0.116$
$R(f_{127}) = 0.069*0.671 = 0.046$
$R(f_{150}) = 0.0537*0.678 = 0.364$
$R(f_{335}) = 0.337*0.932 = 0.314$
$R(f_{347}) = 0.35*0.656 = 0.229$

According to the recommended values, the recommended order is:

$R(f_{111}) > R(f_{150}) > R(f_{335}) > R(f_{347}) > R(f_{116}) > R(f_{127}) > R(f_{108})$.

This recommendation not only reflects the ranking of the literature f_{111} with the highest number of downloads and citations in Tibetan research, and presents the heat of the current research, but also distinguishes the literature f_{108}, f_{116} and f_{347}, which shows the effectiveness of the algorithm proposed in this paper.

7 Conclusion

Taking Tibetan research literature as an example, this paper sorts the keyword feature attributes of Tibetan literature according to their importance, and describes the fuzzy membership of keyword features of Tibetan literature by using the fuzzy membership formula proposed in the literature; Then, the eigenvalues are transformed into vague values, and the vague similarity [16, 17] is used to measure the correlation of Tibetan documents; Combined with the average annual downloads and average annual citations, the documents entering the recommendation set are sorted, which solves the defects of difficult representation of content recommendation feature attributes and relying only on vague recommendation to a certain extent. New ideas are also put forward on the conversion of vague value, which provides a new method for literature content recommendation.

Acknowledgements. Supported by the State Key Laboratory of Tibetan intelligent information processing and Application/Tibetan Information Processing and Machine Translation Key Laboratory of Qinghai Province (2020Z003) and scientific research of Fuzhou Polytechnic (FZYRCQD201901).

References

1. Lin, L., Shoulian, T.: Metric ranking learning recommendation model based on content representation. Acta Electron. Sin. **48**(08), 1615–1622 (2020)
2. Sun, Y., Zhu, J., Li, Y.: Research development of information recommendation based on big data in China: core content. J. Mod. Inf. **40**(08), 156–165 (2020)
3. Zang, Z., Hui, X., Cui, C.: Model and application of e-commerce shopping decision-making based on vague set. J. Syst. Sci. Math. Sci. **37**(12), 2375–2388 (2017)
4. Zang, Z., Cui, C.: Research on knowledge-based recommendation by one-dimensional of properties and requirement matching based on vague sets. Oper. Res. Manage. Sci. **29**(08), 112–119 (2020)
5. Liu, Y., Pi, D., Rao, X.: A new method for measuring vague similarity. Math. Pract. Theory **50**(05), 263–267 (2020)
6. Liu, Y., Pi, D.: A new method for measuring the similarity of vague sets and its application in fault diagnosis. In: 6th International Conference, vol. 2020, pp. 539–548 (1920)
7. Zenebe, A., Anthony, F.: Norcio: representation, similarity measures and aggregation methods using fuzzy sets for content-based recommender systems. Fuzzy Sets Syst. **160**, 76–94 (2009)
8. Jia, H.: Research on key technologies of Tibetan text classification based on KNN algorithm. J. Northwest Univ. Nationalities (Nat. Sci.) **32**(03), 24–29 (2011)
9. Jiang, T., Yu, H., Xu, T.: Research on Internet Tibetan content security detection and filtering system. Netinfo Secur. **10**, 47–48 (2009)
10. Zhu, J., Li, T., Liu, S.: Research on Tibetan name recognition technology under CRF. J. Nanjing Univ. (Nat. Sci.) **52**(02), 289–299 (2016)
11. Wang, W., Ding, X., Qi, K.: Study on similitude characters in Tibetan character recognition. J. Chin. Inf. Process. **04**, 60–65 (2002)
12. Ransanzhi, C.: Research on algorithm of word segmentation in Tibetan search engine. J. Tibet Univ. (Nat. Sci.) **28**(02), 53–57 (2013)
13. An, J., La, M., Sun, Q.: Design of internet public opinion analysis system of Tibetan information. Microprocessors **38**(02), 56–58 (2017)
14. Ai, J.: Research on normalization method of Tibetan text for information processing. J. Northwest Normal Univ. (Nat. Sci.) **53**(02), 52–56 (2017)
15. Wang, W., Ding, X., Chen, L., et al.: Study on printed Tibetn character recognition. Comput. Eng. **03**, 37–38 (2003)
16. Hidayat, R., Tri, I., Ramli, A.A., Farhan, M., Ahmar, A.S.: Generalized normalized Euclidean distance based fuzzy soft set similarity for data classification. Comput. Syst. Sci. Eng. **38**(1), 119–130 (2021)
17. Irshad, K., Afzal, M.T., Rizvi, S.S., Shahid, A., Riaz, R.: SWCS: section-wise content similarity approach to exploit scientific big data. Comput. Mater. Continua **67**(1), 877–894 (2021)

Design of Provincial Comprehensive Energy Service Platform Based on SCADA

Xudong Wang[2]([✉]), Xueqin Zhang[1], Jing Duan[3], Wei Chen[2], Xiaojun Sun[2], and Jinyue Xia[4]

[1] State Grid of Shanxi Branch, Taiyuan 030021, China
[2] Shanxi Yi Tong Gird Protection Co. Ltd., Taiyuan 030021, China
1928879373@qq.com
[3] State Grid Shanxi Electric Power Company Information and Communication Branch, Taiyuan 030021, China
[4] International Business Machines Corporation (IBM), New York 10041NY212, USA

Abstract. Under the trend of the new national energy security strategy, my country's comprehensive energy development and market competition have become increasingly fierce. This has also led grid companies to continue to innovate comprehensive energy coordination, utilization, and service models. In order to meet the needs of the times, this article focuses on comprehensive The background of energy research puts forward a plan for a provincial integrated energy service platform based on SCADA. The platform is based on CPS and takes the construction of smart energy interactive applications and business management applications as the main line to connect with power customers, energy service providers, government departments and other parties. The platform provides comprehensive energy services externally, and internally relies on professional customer services and diversified service content to promote extensive interconnection and in-depth perception of various energy facilities on the customer side with the power grid. Based on source-network-load-storage collaborative services, it aggregates user resources Implement demand response to support the sustainable development of traditional power supply services and the high-quality development of emerging integrated energy businesses.

Keywords: Energy internet · SCADA · Integrated energy · Management and dispatch

1 Introduction

1.1 Background

Today, energy has become an indispensable basic element of human society. On this planet, with increasing energy shortages and environmental degradation, access to economically convenient and environmentally friendly energy has become an urgent problem related to human survival and sustainable development. Finding a solution to improve energy efficiency has become a common responsibility of the whole society, ranging from social families to large enterprises and governments. Various types of water, electricity, gas equipment and classified energy consumption are one of the main components of industrial facilities, social infrastructure, and various building construction investment and daily operating costs. A reasonable layout of energy facility configuration and management and control functions can significantly improve facilities and energy Use efficiency and reduce costs.

1.2   Research Purpose and Significance

Improve the collection, storage, management and utilization of energy information. The complete SCADA system is convenient for obtaining first-hand operational industrial data, real-time understanding of system operation, and timely dispatching measures, so that the system can operate in the best possible state, and the accident. The impact is minimized. Under the guidance of the energy management department of the enterprise, decentralized control and centralized management of the energy system are adopted. In view of the decentralization of the energy industry system and the centralized energy management requirements, the establishment of an energy management system can meet the decentralized control and centralized management of the energy industry system characteristics, so that the enterprise's energy management level can adapt to the company's strategic development needs. The construction of energy management system can realize energy monitoring and energy management process optimization reengineering based on information analysis, realize energy equipment management and operation management, and effectively implement an objective data-based energy consumption evaluation system, and efficiency assessment. Reduce the cost of energy management, improve the efficiency of energy management, understand the real energy consumption in a timely manner, and propose energy-saving and consumption-reducing technologies and management measures, and ask for benefits from energy management. The traditional on-site management, operation on-duty, overhaul and management are heavy and costly. The construction of the energy center will play an important role in the energy reform.

1.3   Research Content

Energy control SCADA (hereinafter referred to as SCADA) is the basic application of the smart energy service platform. It is responsible for accessing multiple types of CPS data to achieve complete, high-performance monitoring and security of the steady-state information of the client-side energy equipment and pipeline network in real time. Reliable equipment control provides comprehensive and highly reliable data services for other applications.

According to the connected customer-side CPS energy monitoring and integrated display data of graphs, numbers, and models, the flexible control framework uses standardized communication protocols to realize demand transmission and policy release, and realize the real-time regulation of flexible interruptible loads. SCADA access uses data and CPS data. There are differences in data types and data formats. Data interaction center, data synchronization, data cleaning, data sampling and other functions are required to ensure data quality, mine data value, realize data exchange, and support advanced Application; this service platform should be based on the data processed by SCADA, and connect to a large number of client-side CPSs, through panoramic monitoring, power quality monitoring, multi-energy monitoring, and auxiliary monitoring to perform energy monitoring throughout the entire process [1]. in the process of energy monitoring It needs to achieve remote control under necessary conditions through single-point control, control assistance, batch control, control inversion, and emergency control; only through display and monitoring, business alarms cannot be ensured, and over-limit alarms, working condition alarms, etc. Alarm monitoring is realized through functions such as fault alarm, alarm shunting, alarm query, alarm definition, alarm operation, and alarm push [2]. In order to support demand response adjustment needs, it is necessary to implement strategy reception and strategy decomposition through strategy management; through pre-communication and pre-collection, Collection management, equipment management and other methods to realize the management of the Internet of Things; according to the users associated with the system, display the user's CPS homepage, early warning system, and energy dispatch system [3].

The main content of this article is as follows:

Section 1 mainly describes the purpose and significance of the research of this service platform, and comprehensively elaborates the research content of this article.

Section 2 focuses on the analysis of the two major requirements of the service platform: functional requirements and non-functional requirements, and then summarizes some requirements in actual scenarios, and completes all related work of the service platform's needs analysis.

Section 3 first describes the overall functions of the service platform and the overall system architecture. In order to be able to express clearly, more popular diagrams are used, including architecture diagrams.

2 Demand Analysis

2.1 Feasibility Analysis

The traditional energy management method adopts manual management. The information is chaotic, inefficient, and wasteful, which affects the operation and control management of the entire energy management and distribution process. In contrast, it promotes the revolution of energy production and consumption, and builds a clean, low-carbon, safe and efficient The national advocacy of the energy system has also brought about the continuous expansion of the Internet+energy system, a set of reasonable, effective, efficient, and practical integrated energy service strategies to realize the systematization, standardization and automation of energy industry management, and to achieve comprehensive energy Centralized and unified management of information. However, the feasibility of an idea needs to be analyzed. Therefore, the feasibility of this service platform needs to be analyzed in detail, which will be carried out from the following aspects [4].

In terms of technology, it is mainly to examine whether the existing mature technology in the current environment can realize the functions that need to be realized.

In terms of operation, first of all, it depends on whether this service platform can allow multiple users to easily operate, meet the needs of multiple users, and achieve a win-win effect.

In terms of economy, it is necessary to evaluate the platform's architecture hardware, software development costs, and maintenance costs. The main goal is to control the costs in an acceptable range.

Technically Feasible. In terms of technology, collection control applications, business management applications, and external user interaction applications can adopt different technical routes.

Collection and Control Applications. Collection and control applications should adopt a service-oriented software architecture (SOA), which has good openness and can better meet the needs of system integration and the continuous development of applications; hierarchical functional design can effectively control hardware resources, data and The software function modules are well organized to provide an ideal environment for application development and operation; public application support and management functions developed for system and application operation and maintenance requirements can provide comprehensive support for the operation and management of application systems [5].

Business Management Applications. It should be based on the State Grid cloud architecture and design a layered architecture in accordance with the three levels of infrastructure layer (IaaS layer), application platform layer (PaaS layer), and software service layer (SaaS layer) [6].

External User Interaction Applications. The interface display layer should provide the display, layout, rendering, operation response, data verification, etc. of system page elements; the service access layer should provide unified access to service requests, protocol conversion, interface resources, load balancing and other services [7]. Service processing layer Provide user interaction services, process and respond to user requests. The management information data should be accessed through the isolation interaction layer, and capabilities such as service governance, distributed message queues, and real-time service monitoring should be provided; the isolation interaction layer realizes the isolation of internal and external network interactions. The data drive corresponding to the isolation device is used to complete the internal network storage of external network data and ensure a good user experience; the platform support layer includes two parts: a development platform and a security management. The development platform includes development kits, frameworks, functional components, etc. Security management includes security controls, security certificates, DDOS protection, etc. [8, 9].

Operation is Feasible. For operation, the interface of this service platform should use a way that conforms to human operating habits, which is easy to understand and easy to use for ordinary users. This service platform can provide users with WEB services based on the B/S architecture, as long as users can Access to the Internet, you can operate this service platform.

Economically Feasible. In terms of economy, this service platform builds a business system based on SCADA basic components. The economic expenditure is mainly on some high-performance servers and software developers, and there is no huge expenditure. In the previous process of traditional energy information management, a lot of financial resources, material resources, and manpower were spent. This was invisible and cost a lot of costs. However, after applying this service platform, all energy-related information is stored. In the cloud database, the data is updated in real time and is visible to all Internet users, saving a lot of publicity costs and manual maintenance of information costs.

2.2 Functional Requirements Analysis

As an integrated platform for energy production, supply and marketing, the integrated energy service platform can organically coordinate and optimize various links including energy production, transmission, storage, distribution and consumption in the process of energy construction, planning and operation. In the regional integrated energy system, the organic integration of multiple energy sources will result in the use of a large number of distributed power generation technology and energy coupling equipment, which puts forward higher requirements for the operation of integrated energy, and the system must meet a certain degree of economy [10]. The various needs of users, comprehensively consider the impact of external factors such as price and environment, and realize the operation optimization and efficient utilization of the energy system through reasonable dispatch. At the same time, from a service perspective, with the widespread application of distributed energy technology and the promotion of energy service concepts, there will be diversified users such as energy suppliers, energy service providers, consumers, producers and consumers in the regional integrated energy system. Roles exist. Participants are no longer the traditional pure relationship between energy supply and consumption [11]. The interaction of energy flow, information flow, and business flow is the basis for the continuous and stable operation of integrated energy services. Therefore, under the new business form of integrated energy service, the design of an integrated energy service platform should focus on the following issues from the application layer [12].

Collection control applications, business management applications, and external user interaction applications should adopt different technical routes.

Collection and Control Applications. Collection and control applications should adopt a service-oriented software architecture (SOA), which has good openness and can better meet the needs of system integration and the continuous development of applications; hierarchical functional design can effectively control hardware resources, data and The software function modules are well organized to provide an ideal environment for application development and operation; public application support and management functions developed for system and application operation and maintenance requirements can provide comprehensive support for the operation and management of application systems [13] (Fig. 1).

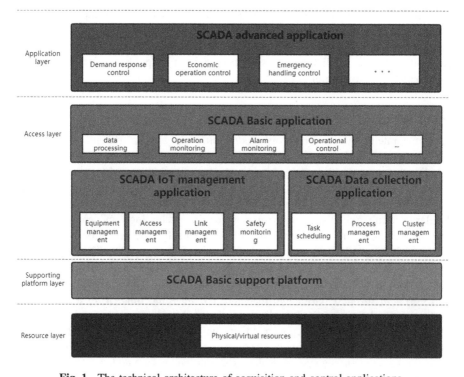

Fig. 1. The technical architecture of acquisition and control applications.

Business Management Applications. It should be based on the State Grid Cloud, in accordance with the three levels of infrastructure layer (IaaS layer), application platform layer (PaaS layer), and software service layer (SaaS layer) for layered architecture design (Fig. 2).

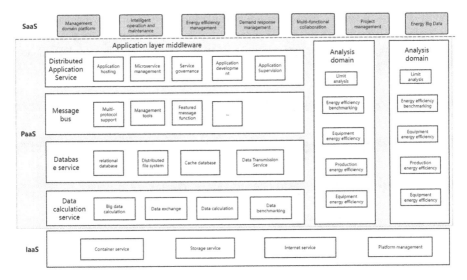

Fig. 2. Business management application technology architecture.

The cloud platform IaaS and PaaS capabilities should be used to build the SaaS layer application of the provincial integrated energy service platform.

The SaaS layer should at least include energy efficiency management, intelligent operation and maintenance, demand response, multi-energy collaboration, spot trading services, energy big data, energy finance and project management.

The SaaS layer platform should make full use of the distributed service capabilities, distributed data storage capabilities, distributed message transmission capabilities, distributed transaction consistency capabilities, and real-time monitoring capabilities provided by the PaaS layer.

The SaaS layer should be based on the elastic scaling of the resources of the IaaS layer to achieve dynamic scaling of service capabilities.

The SaaS layer should provide a multi-tenant model to implement hierarchical account management and function management of tenants.

External User Interaction Applications. The interface display layer should provide the display, layout, rendering, operation response, data verification, etc. of the system page elements. The service access layer should provide services such as unified access for service requests, protocol conversion, interface resources, and load balancing. The service processing layer provides user interaction services, processes and responds to user requests. The management information data should be accessed through the isolation and interaction layer, and capabilities such as service governance, distributed message queues, and real-time service monitoring should be provided. The isolation interaction layer realizes the isolation of internal and external network interactions. Use the data driver corresponding to the isolation device to complete the internal network storage of external network data and ensure a good user experience [14]. The platform support layer includes two parts: development platform and security management. The development platform includes development kits, frameworks, functional components, etc. Security management includes security controls, security certificates, DDOS protection, etc. (Fig. 3).

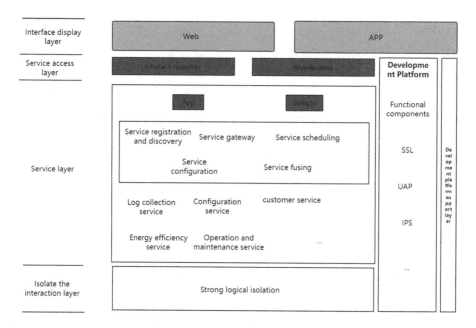

Fig. 3. External user interaction application technology architecture.

3   Platform Design and Implementation

3.1   The Overall Design of the System

The SCADA-based provincial integrated energy service platform is based on CPS, with the construction of smart energy interactive applications and business management applications as the main line, connecting power customers, energy service providers, government departments and other parties. The platform relies on the green national grid to provide comprehensive energy services externally, reduce user energy costs, increase user benefits, and increase customer stickiness; internally, relying on professional customer services and diversified service content, it promotes the development of various energy facilities and power grids on the customer side [15]. Extensive interconnection and in-depth perception, based on source-network-load-storage collaborative services, implement demand response by aggregating user resources, improve grid asset utilization, new energy consumption levels and risk prevention capabilities, and support the sustainable development and sustainable development of the company's traditional business of power supply services High-quality development of integrated energy emerging business [16]. The provincial integrated energy service platform system structure based on SCADA is divided into equipment physical layer, business management layer and interactive application layer. Each layer depends on each other and cooperates with each other. The system structure of the provincial integrated energy service platform based on SCADA should include the equipment physical layer, the business management layer and the interactive application layer, and each layer depends on and cooperates with each other [17] (Fig. 4).

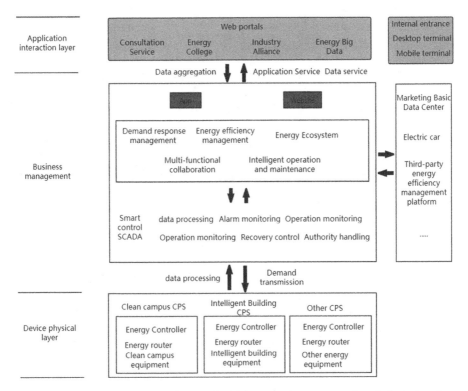

Fig. 4. The overall framework of a provincial integrated energy service platform based on SCADA.

3.2   Application Architecture Design

The SCADA-based provincial integrated energy service platform includes three categories: integrated energy monitoring applications, integrated energy service applications, and integrated energy business management applications, with a total of 19 application functions [18] (Fig. 5).

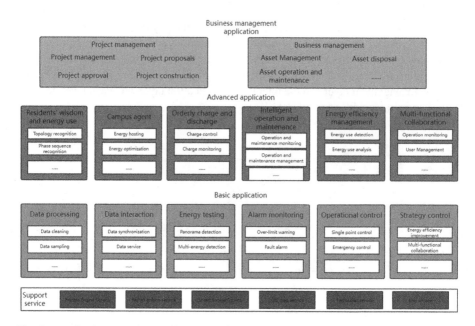

Fig. 5. Application architecture diagram of provincial integrated energy service platform based on SCADA.

3.3 Data Architecture Design

The provincial integrated energy service platform based on SCADA follows the SG-CIM data model of State Grid Corporation of China and belongs to the category of customer domain. The current sorting involves: support domain, shared domain, user domain, equipment domain, measurement domain, organization domain, and analysis domain. Operation domain, settlement domain, project domain 10 s-level subject areas, combined with external systems and emerging business applications, learn from IEC-CIM, synchronously expand and supplement related equipment models, if necessary, will expand the second-level subject areas [19] (Figs. 6 and 7).

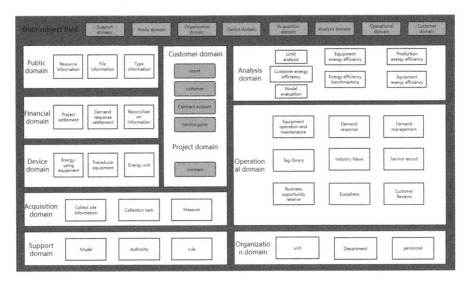

Fig. 6. Data architecture diagram of the provincial integrated energy service platform based on SCADA.

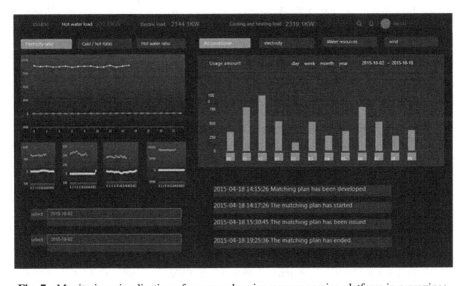

Fig. 7. Monitoring visualization of a comprehensive energy service platform in a province.

4   Conclusion

In this paper, the design of a provincial integrated energy service platform based on SCADA is based on CPS, with the construction of smart energy interactive applications and business management applications as the main line. Based on energy control, SCADA should achieve panoramic monitoring, alarm monitoring, alarm management, and adjustable resources. Core functions such as visualization, CPS station-level monitoring, and authority management. The differences between natural gas, cold (heat), power and other energy subsystems in the integrated energy system pose huge challenges to the integrated energy management and control system for multi-energy data optimization and regulation, energy operation, and collection. Data is collected through real-time monitoring technology. And make full use of the complementation of multiple energy sources and meet the diverse requirements of multiple users for comprehensive energy management and services under the new energy situation. This article comprehensively elaborates on the analysis of system energy demand, rationalized architecture design of integrated energy service system, and service system business function design. Compared with the traditional single control form of energy management and control system, the provincial integrated energy service platform based on SCADA presents new value space in terms of economy, energy efficiency improvement, peak reduction and valley filling, and renewable energy utilization. Carbon energy provides technical support for sustainable development, making the advantages of an integrated energy system more prominent.

References

1. Jia, J.H., Wang, D., Xu, X.D.: Research on several issues of regional integrated energy system. Autom. Electr. Power Syst. **39**(7), 198–207 (2015)
2. Wu, P., Guo, W., Jin, C.J.: Talking about the current situation and solutions of my country's electric power and energy. Electr. Technol. **5**(5), 1–4 (2018)
3. Geng, H., Zhang, H., Zhang, Y.: Efficient routing protection algorithm in large-scale networks. Comput. Mater. Continua **66**(2), 1733–1744 (2021)
4. Wu, J.Z.: The driving force and status quo of the development of European integrated energy system. Autom. Electr. Power Syst. **40**(5), 1–7 (2016)
5. Cheng, L.: Energy Internet concept and practice. Power Supply **34**(2), 1–13 (2017)
6. Ma, K.Q., Wu, D., Zheng, H.: Discussion on hybrid simulation technology route of integrated energy system. Power Supply **7**, 28–33 (2018)
7. Sun, H.B., Pan, Z.G., Guo, Q.L.: Research on multi-energy flow energy management: challenges and prospects. Autom. Electr. Power Syst. **40**(15), 1–8 (2016)
8. Khan, M., Ali, I., Nisar, W., Saleem, M.Q., Ahmed, A.S.: Modernization framework to enhance the security of legacy information systems. Intell. Autom. Soft Comput. **32**(1), 543–555 (2022)
9. Zheng, G.T., Li, H., Tang, Y.H.: Comprehensive optimization configuration of electric/thermal energy storage equipment of user-side integrated energy system based on energy balance of supply and demand. Power Syst. Protect. Control **46**(16), 8–18 (2018)
10. Cheng, C., Lin, D.: Based on compressed sensing of orthogonal matching pursuit algorithm image recovery. J. Internet Things **2**(1), 37–45 (2020)
11. Dong, S., Whang, F.C., Liang, J.: Multi-objective day-ahead optimal dispatch of an integrated energy system taking into account the operating cost of electricity-to-gas conversion. Autom. Electr. Power Syst. **42**(11), 8–15 (2018)
12. Zheng, H., Shi, D.: A multi-agent system for environmental monitoring using boolean networks and reinforcement learning. J. Cyber Secur. **2**(2), 85–96 (2020)
13. Wang, X.D., Zhuang, J., Ge, L.J.: Comprehensive user energy benefit evaluation based on BSC. J. Electr. Power Syst. Autom. **27**(S1), 114–119 (2015)

14. Yu, X., Wang, D., Zhang, D., et al.: Construction of Tianjin eco-city smart grid innovation demonstration zone for multi-energy interconnection. Electr. Power Construct. **36**(11), 58–63 (2015)
15. Asiri, Y.: Short text mining for classifying educational objectives and outcomes. Comput. Syst. Sci. Eng. **41**(1), 35–50 (2022)
16. Huang, R.L., Pu, T.J., Liu, K.W.: Urban energy internet function system and application scheme design. Autom. Electr. Power Syst. **39**(9), 26–33 (2015)
17. Liu, F., Bie, C.H., Liu, S.Y.: Energy Internet market system design, transaction mechanism and key issues. Autom. Electr. Power Syst. **42**(13), 108–117 (2018)
18. Zhang, J.H.: Research on optimal operation of integrated energy system and its decision-making algorithm, Guangzhou (2017)
19. Tian, J.Y.: Preliminary exploration of regional energy planning model from the perspective of distributed integrated energy system, Shanghai (2013)

Research on Process Oriented Emergency Management and Control Model Under the Background of Big Data

Shiqi Zhang[1] , Junren Ming[1(✉)], Huan Liu[1], Yujie Ma[1], Jie Luo[1], and Yu Zhou[2]

[1] School of Management, Wuhan Institute of Technology, Wuhan 430205, China
82464119@qq.com
[2] Hungarian University of Agriculture and Life SciencesBusiness Administration and Management, Gödöllő, Hungary

Abstract. At the time of the rapid development of the national economy, various types of emergencies occur frequently, and it is urgent to design a reasonable and effective control model to evaluate and control the scope and extent of the incident. Based on a comprehensive analysis of the characteristics of emergencies, this paper proposes a process oriented management and control model consisting of three sub-modules of data support, intelligence control and event management, and proposes a guarantee strategy for the realization of key aspects of the model. The control activities of the event provide a reference for practical work.

Keywords: Emergency control · Emergencies · Big data · Process oriented

1 Introduction

Emergencies refer to natural disasters, accident disasters, public health events and social security events that occur suddenly, cause or may cause serious social harm and require emergency response measures [1]. It can be seen from the concept that emergencies are unpredictable in time, wide in space and serious in harm [2]. With the rapid development of market economy, the society gathers wealth as well as risks. The frequency of emergencies is becoming more and more frequent, the degree of damage is becoming more and more serious, and the coupling relationship between events is becoming more and more complex, which brings difficulties to the corresponding control work [3]. Based on the existing research, it can be found that emergencies have certain social attributes, complex connotation and extensive extension. How to effectively control emergencies and avoid secondary disasters has gradually become a hot research topic of common concern in emergency management, information science, sociology and other disciplines [4]. As a new era background in the world today, 'big data' brings new opportunities for emergency management and control in terms of thinking, technology and management methods. The research on emergency management and control model in the context of big data is not only the integration of big data theory, platform construction theory and crisis management theory, but also the practical exploration of improving the rapid response to emergencies and the ability to resist risks and enhance the emergency management ability of emergencies.

As an important part of social governance, emergency management is particularly important to change by using the unique characteristics of the big data era. Research shows that information asymmetry is the root cause of the difficulty of emergency control [5, 6]. The relationship between the influencing factors of the event in the latent stage, the evolution law after the event, the direction of public opinion in the process of event control, and the possibility of triggering other events are all priori information that is difficult to fully grasp [7]. Due to the obvious social attributes and information characteristics of emergencies, the current academic research mainly focuses on the development of 'emergency decision support system [8], the construction of event case base [9] and the key nodes of public opinion control [10]. However, most of the relevant studies look at events from an isolated and static perspective, and seldom consider the complex relationship between different stages of event development. At the same time, they do not fully consider the change of information demand in the process of event development. In fact, due to many related factors that lead to emergencies, the development of events has the characteristics of unpredictable and difficult to control, and even backtracking to a certain extent.

In view of this problem, the Sect. 1 of this paper introduces the research background and expounds related concepts. The Sect. 2 analyzes the process characteristics of the four periods of initiation, expansion, change, and fading of emergencies, and constructs emergency management and control models based on the characteristics of the entire process of emergencies. Section 3 proposes practical solutions from three aspects: multi-source data fusion, multi-subject co-governance and case base intelligence. The Sect. 4 is the concluding part, which explains the research significance of constructing emergency management and control models for emergencies under the background of big data. Based on the characteristics of emergencies, this article examines the entire process of emergencies in the context of big data, and puts forward a process oriented emergency management and control model, and uses big data technology to design and discuss the key problems of model construction from data support, intelligence control and state control, in order to provide reference for solving related problems.

2 Construction of Process Oriented Emergency Management and Control Model

To build a process oriented emergency management and control model, we need to analyze the process characteristics of emergencies, find out the activities of various subjects and the evolution law of events in the process of events, and analyze the different needs of emergency information in each stage and link, so as to build a complete process oriented multi module management and control model.

2.1   Analysis of Process Characteristics of Emergencies

Building a process oriented emergency management model based on the perspective of information flow requires analysis of the evolution process of events and the information characteristics displayed in the evolution process, to clarify the characteristics of each stage and link of the emergency, as well as the requirements for emergency intelligence. Overall, emergencies have distinct event boundaries. The evolution process includes initiation period, expansion period, change period and fading period. After the early warning system takes effect or fails, it enters the emergency initiation period; enter the expansion period of the situation according to the different conditions of the initiation period; with the change of the subject, object and environment of the event, it enters a period of change. Finally, after the event subsides, the relevant information is summarized and integrated to form a case base. In the whole process, there is a positive information prediction flow and a reverse information feedback flow. The information prediction flow mainly predicts the evolution of the next stage according to the current stage of the emergency and the management strategies to be adopted. The information feedback flow mainly evaluates the rationality and validity of the previous stage management behavior based on the current stage performance characteristics of the emergency. The overall evolution process is shown in Fig. 1.

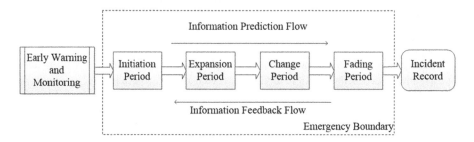

Fig. 1.   Evolution of emergency process from the perspective of intelligence control.

Emergencies Initiation Period. Due to the long-term accumulation of social contradictions, or the existing emergencies have not been effectively handled, the accumulation of many factors or problems has changed from quantitative change to qualitative change, and the problems have changed from latent state to triggering state. If the emergency in the initiation period is well controlled, the damage intensity of the event can be weakened or spread range can be reduced; if the content of events is complex and cannot grasp comprehensive information and is forced to allow the situation to enter the deployment period, the impact of the deployment period needs to be predicted and corresponding control measures need to be formulated.

Emergencies Expansion Period. The emergencies in the expansion period show more characteristics and involve more social subjects. The stakeholders began to increase, and the internal logic of events and the correlation between events gradually reflected. The scope of influence of events itself continued to spread, and the influence continued to strengthen. The attraction and linkage between events continued to be complicated. In addition to the relevant government departments and the media, the masses, as an important part of the social structure, continue to cross the system boundaries, and become an important part of the evolution of emergencies in a way of forced participation or active attention. At this time, the amount of information increases sharply and the density of information value is low. It is necessary to use information analysis and prediction technology to sort out the situation, predict the characteristics of the next period of events and propose control strategies. And the effectiveness of the response strategy in the initiation period is evaluated according to the current situation.

Emergency Change Period. The change period is the most complex period for the emergencies. Firstly, according to the plan of event control in the expand period, there may be a large difference in the satisfaction level of each stakeholder to the progress and status of the event. The evolution and impact of the emergency are at the peak of complex conditions. At the same time, due to the diversity and complexity of the participants, the difficulty of event control further increases. For the same event, the division of powers and responsibilities between different government departments and the definition of management scope, the confirmation of intensive information exchange and communication, the views and attitudes of different influential media in the event, and the spontaneous behavior of the masses, all burst out centrally during the changing period of the emergency.

Emergency Fading Period. With the intervention and control of administrative departments, the life cycle of an emergency gradually enters a fading period, at which time the attention of social media and users gradually decreases to exit the event boundary. From the perspective of control subjects, it is necessary to analyze the process of events, enrich the case base of events, and provide reference for the follow-up control of similar events. In addition, it is necessary to analyze whether the evolution of events in the fading period is expected, so as to prevent the re-complication of events caused by improper handling of events in the fading period, preventing a backtracking of the emergency cycle or triggering new related events.

2.2 Emergency Management Model Construction

Through the analysis of the whole process characteristics of emergencies, it can be seen that with the evolution of events, the stakeholders involved are more diversified, the relationship between problems is more complex, and the entropy increase of information is increasing. In this case, the static control of a single link is easy to remain on the surface of the event, and it is difficult to penetrate into the essence and core of the problem. Therefore, it is necessary to build a cross departmental collaborative emergency management and control model combined with the process characteristics of emergencies. At the same time, based on the obvious process characteristics and close relationship of emergencies, event handling and control need to focus on the whole process of events. In addition, the emergency response and management of emergencies in the era of big data has changed from emphasizing data collection to data processing [11]. Therefore, it is necessary to design the information control module, which is used to connect the basic data with the actual work, so as to prevent event backtracking, triggering and the occurrence of secondary events [12]. According to the process characteristics of emergencies, a process oriented emergency management and control model is designed, as shown in Fig. 2.

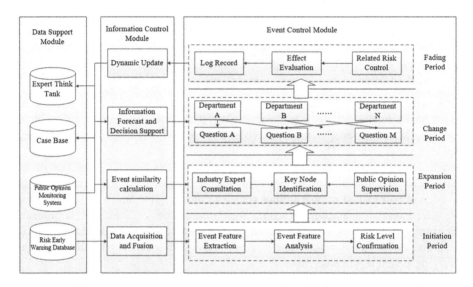

Fig. 2. Emergency management and control model for emergencies.

The process oriented emergency management and control model is mainly composed of three modules: data support module, information control module and event control module. The data support module and event control module obtain the support of effect evaluation and decision-making information through the information control module. This paper analyzes the model according to the evolution process of emergencies.

During the initiation period of emergencies, the risk early warning database in the data support module automatically integrates the monitoring results, and the data support module sends them to the event control module. According to the push results of the early warning system, the event control module preliminarily analyzes the risk characteristics of the event, including dividing the event type, determining the risk level, evaluating the involved personnel and regions, analyzing the information needs, etc., then matches the event characteristics with the blacklist and whitelist in the system through anomaly detection and misuse detection, provide reference for various control activities in the risk expansion period. The key to control initiation period is obtaining and integrating risk early warning data to reduce the uncertainty of events.

During the expansion period of emergencies, the model calls data from the case base in the data support module and the public opinion monitoring system respectively. On the one hand, it measures the situation of the emergency itself, and on the other hand, it investigates the public opinion dynamics of the public and the media on the incident, and grasps and correctly guides it in time to avoid panic and large-scale mass incidents. At this time, the event control module automatically conducts industry expert consultation according to the event type, identifies the key points in the event, and calculates the similarity between the characteristic information of this event and the previous events in the case base through the intelligence support module. Finally, the subjective judgment of experts and the characteristics of objective events are integrated, and targeted control strategies are adopted to optimize the allocation of limited control resources. And public opinion is supervised to control the development of the situation within an acceptable range.

When emergencies enter a period of change, from the perspective of information science, the information entropy value of the event is maximized, the development and change of the event itself are complex, and the event is closely related to other events. At this stage, the case base and expert think tank information in the data support module need to be called through the intelligence control module to predict the trend and make auxiliary decisions. On the basis that the key nodes of the problems have been identified at the upper level, the corresponding relationship between the problems and departments in the nodes is divided, different problems are implemented to specific departments, the information processing problems of case base and expert think tanks are integrated, and the advantages of cross departmental coordination are used to deal with emergencies in the changing period.

After the event enters the fading period, it mainly evaluates the effect of this control, including whether to use reasonable resources to suppress the spread of events as much as possible; whether to effectively prevent the damage within acceptable limits. In this stage, on the one hand, the event control module needs to be called to control the associated risk, so as to avoid retroactive problems after extinction or linkage with other events. On the other hand, it is necessary to complete the effect evaluation work, record the whole process of event control, and dynamically update the expert think tank and case base in the data support module by using the intelligence control module to optimize the next event processing activity.

To sum up, the process oriented emergency management and control model mainly controls the problem from the perspectives of data, information and event itself. (1) From the perspective of data. The risk early warning data, public opinion data, case base and expert think tank provided by the data module jointly deal with different stages of emergencies, ensuring that the events have relevant data support at different stages. (2) From the perspective of information. Contrary to the evolution trend of events, intelligence information can verify whether the activities of the previous stage are effective and reasonable, and predict the information accordingly, which has the ability of regression analysis. Therefore, the intelligence control module is designed according to the occurrence process of the event. While continuously updating the content of the data support module, the information flow transmitted to the event control module is preprocessed, fused and assisted in decision-making, thereby controlling the situation. (3) From the perspective of the event itself. The event control module plays a cross-sectoral collaborative advantage in the process of event management and control. By integrating the event content and the experience of industry experts, formulate targeted strategies for all links of the event evolution, control the situation from both the scope of influence and the degree of injury, then simultaneously supervise the public opinion information.

3 Key Issues and Implementation Strategies of Emergency Management and Control Model

In order to ensure the effectiveness of the process oriented emergency management and control model, it is necessary to design practical solutions to the key links and key issues of the model. This paper designs the model from the perspectives of data provision, intelligence management and control. Overall, it is necessary to solve three aspects: multi-source data fusion, multi-subject co-governance and case base intelligence.

3.1 Multi-source Data Fusion

Emergencies involve a large amount of data and have a wide range of sources, including the problem sensing data before the event and the public opinion data generated with the evolution of events. Due to the different types of emergencies, data types, representation and storage methods are different and the depth and angle of data expression are also significantly different. Data is the basis of the control model. The effective integration of multi-source heterogeneous data according to the characteristics of event process and data itself is the key to improving the level of emergency crisis management and control, and can promote the targeted control strategy [13]. In this paper, according to the needs of emergency crisis management and control, hierarchical fusion is carried out from the perspective of scenario, case and public opinion. The fusion scheme is shown in Fig. 3.

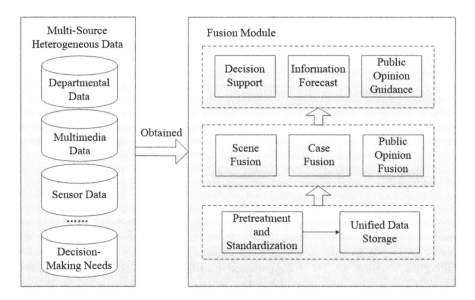

Fig. 3. Multi- source data fusion scheme for emergencies.

According to the requirements of emergency for information fusion types and the phased information needs of emergency management and control, multi-sectoral and multi-source data are collected intelligently, and media data are collected in the process of event development to grasp the trend of public opinion. At the same time, the performance of the same event in different environments is recorded, and emergency management and control strategies are formulated in accordance with specific scenarios to achieve the integration of event scenario information [14]. After collecting all kinds of data comprehensively, preprocess the data, and use the cloud storage technology to store the data uniformly. The functional integration of data from the perspectives of scenarios, cases and public opinion provides a data basis for the management and control model to play the role of decision support, information prediction and public opinion guidance [15]. Through multi-source data fusion and multi-level analysis, big data technology processes different events in different periods and different locations, and finds the uniqueness of different events, which can enhance the pertinence of emergency management and make emergency management more flexible.

3.2   The Co-governance of Multiple Subjects

The various problems caused by emergencies during the evolution are the most critical and prominent. Not only the damage degree and evolution direction of the risk itself are unpredictable, but also the linkage relationship with other risks is very complex and easy to cause a series of chain reactions. Because of the large difference in the follow-up work caused by emergencies, it needs to be solved by multiple departments, including the prevention of potential problems, evacuation or appeasing stakeholders [16]. The subject involved in emergency management and control is no longer a single government subject, but multiple cooperation and collaborative governance of the government, citizens, enterprises, experts, social organizations and the media. Based on this, this paper puts forward a guarantee scheme of cross departmental collaboration, as shown in Fig. 4.

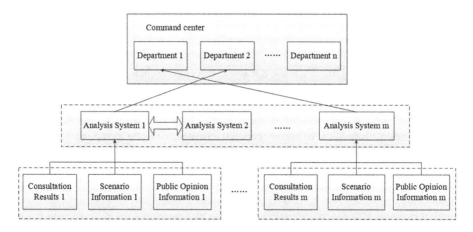

Fig. 4. Cross-departmental collaboration scheme of emergency.

According to the needs of collaborative work, the expert consultation information provided in the third layer of the management and control model, the public opinion information in the data support module and the fused scenario information are fully integrated. From the perspective of event type, different decision-making auxiliary information is empowered, and the results are fed back to the command center. The command center distributes the results of the analysis system to each department to realize the division of labor and cooperation among departments [17]. Each subsystem in the system layer can not only complete the analysis of the current problems, but also realize the interaction of the information of the adjacent system. Besides, the subsystem can calculate the optimal solution of the work allocation and the management and control resource allocation. It can also effectively solve the department collaboration and division of labor, optimize the matching results between the management and control departments and the problems, reduce the cost of information transmission, reduce the confusion of responsibility and power, and form a situation of multi-governance and win-win cooperation.

3.3   Construction of Intelligent Case Base

Case base is the core part of data support module. The comprehensiveness, reliability and timeliness of its content information directly affect the emergency management and control effect of emergencies [18]. A complete process oriented emergency management and control model needs to build a smart case base to provide prior knowledge for the whole management and control system. On the basis of comprehensive and complete cases and real-time updating of content, this paper fully integrates case reasoning results with expert think tanks in emergency management and control activities through case base intelligent reasoning mechanism to provide comprehensive and reliable decision support information [19]. The smart case base build process is shown in Fig. 5.

The construction of smart case base mainly includes: case acquisition, case key factor expression, case knowledge organization based on key factors, case reasoning mechanism design, and case writing. First, obtain the original data of various cases and extract the key fields in the cases. And structurally extract and represent the cases, such as stakeholders, high-risk areas, frequent occurrence time, background characteristics, risk correlation and other information, so as to complete the construction of the basic data table of the cases [20]. Then use the above information fields to associate multiple cases, and establish the network relationship of cases from the aspects of time, place, audience, triggering factors and so on. Finally, the case-based reasoning mechanism is designed to provide a logical basis for the similarity of cases, the universality of methods and the formation of recommended schemes. And the complete case-based reasoning engine and case knowledge organization content are written into the case base.

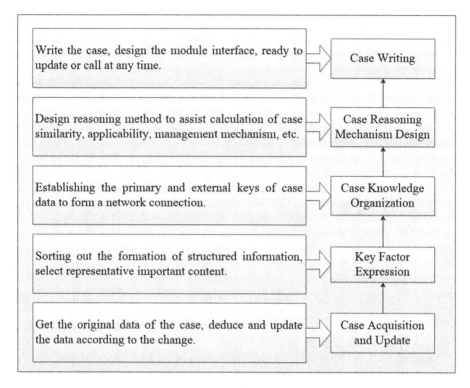

Fig. 5. Construction process of intelligent case base.

4 Conclusion

While the economy is developing at a high speed, various emergencies occur frequently, which poses a serious threat to the people's personal and property safety. Improper handling will lead to the linkage of events, which further increases the scope of influence and damage of risks. Therefore, emergency management and control has become a hot research issue of interdisciplinary and multi-industry common concern. However, at present, emergency management and control is mainly based on specific work details, and few models are designed from the perspective of process and combined with the information characteristics of each stage of emergency management and control. Based on the analysis of the stage characteristics of emergencies, this paper integrates big data technology with the emergency management process, construct a process oriented emergency crisis management model, and structure the model from the perspectives of data support, information control, and event management, emphasizes the importance of information flow at different stages of emergencies. At the same time, the key links involved in the model were discussed to optimize emergency management procedures and provide references for related theoretical research and practice.

References

1. Overall national emergency plan for public emergencies. http://www.gov.cn/yjgl/2006-01/08/content_21048.html
2. Song, H.Y., Liu, C., Zhang, X.Y.: Study on the factors influencing government response effect of major public health emergencies: an empirical analysis based on 36 major public health emergencies in China from. Inf. Stud. Theory Appl. 1–11 (2021)
3. Carter, H., Weston, D., Symon, C.: Public perceptions of pre-incident information campaign materials for the initial response to a chemical incident. Disaster Prev. Manag. **28**(5), 565–584 (2019)
4. Wang, L., Wang, K., Wu, J.: Public opinion propagation and evolution of public health emergencies in social media era: a case study of 2018 vaccine event. Data Anal. Knowl. Discov. **3**(04), 42–52 (2019)
5. Youngblood, S.A., Youngblood, N.E.: Usability, content, and connections: how county-level Alabama emergency management agencies communicate with their online public. Govern. Inf. Q. **35**(1), 20–60 (2018)
6. Zhang, X.R., Zhang, H.T., Li, Y.L., Zhang, L.F.: Research on the identification of key elements of information collaboration for emergent public health events. Inf. Stud. Theory Appl. **2018**, 1–13 (2018)
7. Li, Y.: Consideration on the construction of intelligence capability oriented to urban emergency management. Mod. Inf. **39**, 17–23 (2019)
8. Sene, B., Kamsu-Foguem, P., Rumeau, P.: Decision support system for in-flight emergency events. Technol. Work **20**(2), 245–266 (2018)
9. Jiang, X., Su, X.N., Chen, Z.Q.: Exploratory research on the knowledge base structure of a fast response informatics management system on multi-dimensional integration. J. China Soc. Sci. Tech. Inf. **36**(10), 1008–1022 (2017)
10. Jiang, J., Shen, Q., Ma, N., Liu, Y.J.: A study on microblog public opinion ecological niche based on the ecology of network public opinions. J. Inf. **35**(05), 52–57 (2016)
11. Palfy, A.: Bridging the gap between collection and analysis: intelligence information processing and data governance. Int. J. Intell. Counter Intell. **28**(2), 365–376 (2015)
12. Fan, B., Liu, R., Huang, K.: Embeddedness in cross-agency collaboration and emergency management capability: evidence from Shanghai's urban contingency plans. Gov. Inf. Q. **36**(4), 1–12 (2019)
13. Liu, Y.S., Zhang, H.T., Xu, H.L., Wei, P.: Research on evolutionary topic map of internet public opinion with multi-dimensional feature fusion. J. China Soc. Sci. Tech. Inf. **38**(08), 798–806 (2019)
14. Gao, S., Wang, Y.H.: Deductive scenario of public health emergencies based on dynamic Bayesian network. J. Catastrophol. **36**(03), 28–34 (2021)
15. Alotaibi, Y.: A new database intrusion detection approach based on hybrid meta-heuristics. Comput. Mater. Continua **66**(2), 1879–1895 (2021)
16. Qi, J., Ren, Y.J., Wang, Q.R.: Network electronic record management based on linked data. J. Big Data **1**(1), 9–15 (2019)
17. Fan, B., Liu, R.X.: Collaborative management theory on emergency information exchanging systems. J. Inf. Resour. Manage. **9**(04), 10–17 (2019)

18. Rudniy, A.: Data warehouse design for big data in academia. Comput. Mater. Continua **71** (1), 979–992 (2022)
19. Dhaya, R., Kanthavel, R.: Dynamic automated infrastructure for efficient cloud data centre. Comput. Mater. Continua **71**(1), 1625–1639 (2022)
20. Ramakrishnan, U., Nachimuthu, N.: An enhanced memetic algorithm for feature selection in big data analytics with mapreduce. Intell. Autom. Soft Comput. **31**(3), 1547–1559 (2022)

Analysis of Factors Influencing Carbon Emissions from Civil Aviation Transportation Based on LMDI and STIRPAT Models

Hang He[1(✉)], Biao Wang[1], Shanshan Li[1], and Jinghui Zhang[2]

[1] School of Airport Engineering and Transport Management, Civil Aviation
Flight University of China, Guanghan 618307, China
43162164@qq.com
[2] WebChain Pty Ltd., Sydney, NSW 2118, Australia

Abstract. The analysis of factors influencing the carbon emissions of civil aviation transport is of great significance to the low-carbon development of civil aviation transport. In order to quantify the relationship between the change of carbon emission of civil aviation transportation and each influencing factor, this paper decomposes the total carbon emission of civil aviation transportation into four influencing factors through LMDI model. Among them, population size, GDP per capita and turnover per unit of GDP contribute to the growth of carbon emissions, with contribution rates of 5.04%, 81.73% and 21.03%. Respectively, while energy consumption per unit of turnover inhibits the growth of carbon emissions, with a contribution rate of −7.81%. In order to deeply study the change response relationship among the influencing factors of civil aviation transportation carbon emission, the regression equation between civil aviation transportation carbon emission and each influencing factor was obtained by constructing STIRPAT model and ridge regression analysis. Finally, based on the analysis of each influencing factor, targeted suggestions and measures are proposed for energy saving and emission reduction in civil aviation transportation industry.

Keywords: LMDI · STIRPAT · Civil aviation transport · Carbon emissions

1 Introduction

In the face of the growing prominence of global climate problems, a wave of carbon peaking and carbon neutrality has been set in motion worldwide. At the national level, China has pledged that China will reach peak CO2 emissions around 2030 and strive to achieve the goal of carbon neutrality by 2060 [1], and the construction of the national ecological civilization system will take a new height. China's civil aviation industry as a key industry sector of energy saving and emission reduction, the low carbon development of civil aviation industry not only has the necessity and urgency, but also responds to the development needs of China's carbon peak and carbon neutral [14–16], and the carbon emission of civil aviation transportation has become a popular issue in the industry and research field.

X. Sun et al. (Eds.): ICAIS 2022, CCIS 1587, pp. 320–330, 2022.
https://doi.org/10.1007/978-3-031-06761-7_26

At present, domestic and foreign research on the factors influencing carbon emissions has been extensive, but mainly focused on agriculture, construction and the entire transport sector, and less research on the influencing factors for the civil aviation transport sector [2]. From foreign studies, Sgouridis et al. (2011) used econometric method regression to analyze five influencing factors on CO2 emissions in civil aviation sector [3]. Arjomandi et al. (2014) used a sample of 48 low-cost airlines, they empirically measured the environmental and technical efficiency impacts between 2007 and 2010 [4]. Brueckner (2017) regressed fuel consumption on variables such as average number of seats and range, and conducted an empirical analysis based on data from 16 U.S. airlines to obtain the relationship between the variation of influencing factors and carbon emissions [5]. From domestic studies, Chen et al. (2014) used LMDI model to decompose and analyze the influencing factors of civil aviation transportation industry [6]. Yao (2014) empirically analyzed the influencing factors of carbon emissions of Chinese airlines [7]. Shi et al. (2019) used LMDI method to empirically analyze the driving factors of carbon emissions of Chinese aviation industry [2]. Guo (2020) used STIRPAT model to analyze the influencing factors of carbon emissions of civil aviation passenger transport and its carbon emission forecast [8].

The quantitative study of the influencing factors affecting the carbon emissions of civil aviation transportation can help the civil aviation industry to formulate targeted emission reduction strategies and thus promote the low-carbon development of the civil aviation industry [12, 13]. From the research on the influencing factors of carbon emissions in domestic civil aviation industry, although some scholars have used decomposition analysis method to study the main influencing factors affecting carbon emissions of civil aviation transportation, there is still great room for expansion and deepening of the research degree. Therefore, this paper adopts the LMDI model to decompose the influencing factors of carbon emissions of civil aviation transportation, and then adopts the STIRPAT model to explore the change response relationship among the influencing factors, so as to provide energy-saving and emission reduction suggestions for the low-carbon development of civil aviation transportation industry.

2   Introduction

2.1   A Subsection Sample

According to the IPCC National Greenhouse Gas Emission Guidelines, carbon emission measurement mainly includes "top-down" and "bottom-up" methods [2]. In this paper, a "top-down" approach is used to measure the carbon emissions of the civil aviation transport sector, whereby the product of aviation paraffin consumption and carbon emission factors is calculated to obtain the total estimated CO_2 emissions of the civil aviation transport sector. In particular, the carbon emission factor of aviation kerosene is 3.15 [7].

$$C = E \times I \tag{1}$$

E: Aviation paraffin consumption in the civil aviation transport sector.
I: Aviation paraffin carbon emission factor.

2.2   The Kaya Constant and the LMDI Model

The Kaya constant equation links energy carbon emissions to influencing factors such as population, economy and energy, and is a common decomposition model in the field of carbon emission influencing factors 7. Its expression is:

$$C = P \times \frac{GDP}{P} \times \frac{E}{GDP} \times \frac{C}{E} \tag{2}$$

C: Carbon emissions.
P: Population size.
GDP: Gross Domestic Product.
E: Energy consumption.
In this paper, for each influencing factor of the civil aviation transportation industry, it is expanded on the basis of the above Kaya's constant equation, and the carbon emissions are interlinked with the influencing factors of population size, gross domestic product, civil aviation transportation turnover and aviation paraffin consumption to obtain the following equation:

$$C = P \times \frac{GDP}{P} \times \frac{S}{GDP} \times \frac{E}{S} \times \frac{C}{E} \tag{3}$$

S: Transport turnover in the civil aviation transport sector.
GDP/P: GDP per capita.
S/GDP: Civil aviation transport intensity (i.e. civil aviation transport turnover per unit of GDP).
E/S: Aviation paraffin consumption per unit of turnover.
C/E: Aviation paraffin carbon emission factor.
Based on the Kaya constant equation, the LMDI model decomposes civil aviation transportation carbon emissions into multiple influencing factors and quantifies the contribution value of individual influencing factors. Based on the LMDI summation decomposition method, the factors in the expanded Kaya constant equation are decomposed without residuals, and the contribution values are solved as follows:

$$\Delta C = \Delta C_P + \Delta C_{\frac{GDP}{P}} + \Delta C_{\frac{S}{GDP}} + \Delta C_{\frac{E}{S}} + \Delta C_{\frac{C}{E}} \tag{4}$$

$$\Delta C_P = \frac{C_T^t - C_T^0}{\ln C_T^t - \ln C_T^0} \left(\ln P^t - \ln P^0 \right) \tag{5}$$

$$\Delta C_{\frac{GDP}{P}} = \frac{C_T^t - C_T^0}{\ln C_T^t - \ln C_T^0} \left[\ln \left(\frac{GDP}{P} \right)^t - \ln \left(\frac{GDP}{P} \right)^0 \right] \tag{6}$$

$$\Delta C_{\frac{S}{GDP}} = \frac{C_T^t - C_T^0}{\ln C_T^t - \ln C_T^0} \left[\ln \left(\frac{S}{GDP} \right)^t - \ln \left(\frac{S}{GDP} \right)^0 \right] \tag{7}$$

$$\Delta C_{\frac{E}{S}} = \frac{C_T^t - C_T^0}{\ln C_T^t - \ln C_T^0} \left[\ln \left(\frac{E}{S} \right)^t - \ln \left(\frac{E}{S} \right)^0 \right] \tag{8}$$

where ΔC_P, $\Delta C_{\frac{GDP}{P}}$, $\Delta C_{\frac{S}{GDP}}$, $\Delta C_{\frac{E}{S}}$ denote the contribution value of each influencing factor to the change of carbon emission of civil aviation transportation, respectively. Since the aviation kerosene carbon emission factor is considered as a constant in this paper, disregarded the $\Delta C_{\frac{C}{E}}$ impact on the carbon emissions of civil transport. In the calculation results of LMDI sum decomposition method, when the contribution value is greater than 0, it indicates that the influence factor has a contributing effect on the carbon emission of civil aviation transportation; when the contribution value is less than 0, it indicates that the influence factor has a suppressing effect on the carbon emission of civil aviation transportation.

2.3 STIRPAT Model

The STIRPAT model is based on the IPAT model [9], which considers three main human influences on the environment: population size, economic level and technological level [10], and has the standard form of

$$I = aP^b A^c T^d e \tag{9}$$

where a are the model coefficients, the b, c, d is the variable index, and e is the random error term. The STIRPAT model can be obtained by taking the logarithm of the IPAT model.

$$\ln I = \ln a + b\ln P + c\ln A + d\ln T + \ln e \tag{10}$$

For the influence factors of carbon emission of civil aviation transportation industry, STIRPAT model can be improved for three influence factors of population size, economic level and technology level. Since the influence of population size on the carbon emission of civil aviation transportation industry is mainly in the turnover of passengers and cargo, and considering that the great impact of the Newcastle pneumonia epidemic on civil aviation industry in 2020 is mainly in the reduction of civil aviation transportation turnover, the passenger and cargo turnover of civil aviation transportation is introduced into the STIRPAT model instead of population size; economic development plays an important role in the carbon emission of civil aviation transportation, so the GDP per capita is introduced into the STIRPAT model; energy consumption per unit of turnover represents the technical level of civil aviation transportation industry, so energy consumption per unit of turnover is introduced into STIRPAT model.

To sum up, this paper improves the population size as civil aviation transport turnover, the economic level as GDP per capita, and the technology level as energy consumption per unit of turnover, so as to analyze the carbon emission influencing factors of civil aviation transport industry. The expressions are as follows:

$$\ln C = \ln a + b\ln S + c\ln GDP + d\ln SE + \ln e \tag{11}$$

C: Carbon emissions from civil aviation transport.
S: Civil aviation traffic turnover.
GDP: Gross Domestic Product.
SE: Energy consumption per unit of turnover.

b, c, d the regression coefficients of each influencing factor are denoted separately, and under the condition that other influencing factors are kept constant, each 1% change in civil aviation transport turnover, GDP per capita and energy consumption per unit of turnover will affect the occurrence of carbon emissions from civil aviation transport respectively b%, c%, d% which the change in.

2.4 Data Sources

The aviation kerosene consumption data for 2013–2018 is sourced from 《From Statistics to Civil Aviation》 for 2014–2019, and the aviation kerosene consumption for 2019 and 2020 is sourced from Luo [11], the population, GDP and GDP per capita data for 2013–2020 are sourced from the official website of the National Bureau of Statistics, the data on civil aviation transportation turnover from 2013 to 2020 are from the official website of the Civil Aviation Administration of China.

3   Decomposition of Carbon Emission Influencing Factors Based on LMDI Model

According to the "top-down" method, the carbon emissions of the civil aviation transportation industry from 2013 to 2020 are shown in "Fig. 1", in which the calculated carbon emissions in 2020 will decrease due to the reduction of aviation kerosene consumption as a result of the impact of the Newcastle pneumonia epidemic. In order to explore the contribution value of each influencing factor of carbon emission in civil aviation transportation industry, the LMDI model was used to decompose each factor; due to the huge impact of Newcastle pneumonia epidemic on civil aviation industry in 2020, which led to large deviation of data, the decomposition of influencing factors of carbon emission in civil aviation transportation was done up to 2019, and the decomposition results are shown in "Table 1".

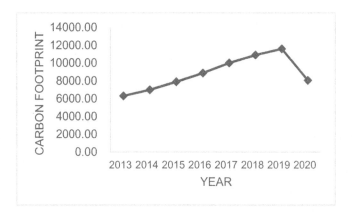

Fig. 1. Carbon emissions from civil aviation transport, 2013–2020.

According to the results of the decomposition of the contribution value of the influencing factors of carbon emissions of civil aviation transportation industry in "Table 1", taking 2013 as the base period, the cumulative increase of carbon emissions of civil aviation transportation industry in China will be 52,606,400 tons by 2019. According to the results of the cumulative effect can be divided into promoting and inhibiting effects of the impact factors.

Table 1. Results of the decomposition of carbon emission changes.

Year	ΔC	ΔC_P	$\Delta C_{\frac{GDP}{P}}$	$\Delta C_{\frac{S}{GDP}}$	$\Delta C_{\frac{E}{S}}$
2013–2014	626.34	44.47	501.20	108.68	−28.01
2014–2015	948.16	36.60	461.81	502.42	−52.66
2015–2016	985.00	54.64	623.46	354.31	−47.41
2016–2017	1090.18	52.56	966.18	54.02	17.42
2017–2018	933.77	39.46	992.76	118.20	−216.65
2018–2019	677.19	37.33	754.34	-31.15	−83.33
Accumulate	5260.64	265.05	4299.75	1106.48	−410.64
Percentage	100%	5.04%	81.73%	21.03%	−7.81%

Population size, GDP per capita and unit GDP turnover contribute to the carbon emissions of civil aviation transportation. The change in population size leads to a cumulative increase of 2.650 million tons of carbon emissions in the civil aviation transportation industry, which shows that the contribution of population size to carbon emissions in the civil aviation transportation industry is not significant; the change in GDP per capita leads to a cumulative increase of 42.997 million tons of carbon emissions in the civil aviation transportation industry, which has the most significant impact on carbon emissions in the civil aviation transportation industry; the unit GDP turnover leads to a cumulative increase of carbon emissions in the civil aviation transportation industry 110.648 million tons, which has a more significant contribution to the carbon emissions of the civil aviation transportation industry. Energy consumption per unit of turnover plays a suppressing role in carbon emissions of civil aviation transportation industry, leading to a cumulative reduction of 410.64; energy consumption per unit of turnover represents the technological level of civil aviation transportation industry, indicating that technological progress can suppress the rapid growth of carbon emissions of civil aviation transportation industry to a certain extent.

4 Analysis of the Factors Influencing Carbon Emissions Based on the STIRPAT Model

LMDI model can quantitatively analyze the contribution degree of each influencing factor of civil aviation transportation carbon emission, but it lacks elasticity analysis for the influencing factors of civil aviation transportation carbon emission, so STIRPAT model is introduced at this time to explore the change response relationship of each influencing factor of civil aviation transportation carbon emission. In this paper, the STIRPAT model is constructed by selecting civil aviation transportation turnover, GDP per capita and energy consumption per unit of turnover as the explanatory variables of civil aviation transportation carbon emissions, and then using SPSS software to conduct multiple linear regression analysis on each variable. The results are shown in "Table 2". The ADF unit root test for carbon emissions, civil aviation turnover and energy consumption per unit of turnover passed the 5% significant level, and the ADF unit root test for GDP per capita passed the 10% significant level, indicating that the original series of each variable is smooth.

Table 2. ADF unit root test results.

Variable	ADF value	Threshold value			P-value	Conclude
		1%	5%	10%		
$\ln C$	−3.400162	−3.007406	−2.021193	−1.597291	0.0056	Smoothly
$\ln S$	−5.094239	−3.007406	−2.021193	−1.597291	0.0006	Smoothly
$\ln GDP$	−4.612708	−7.006336	−4.773194	−3.877714	0.0589	Smoothly
$\ln SE$	−22.23316	−7.006336	−4.773194	−3.877714	0.0001	Smoothly

After the variables passed the ADF unit root test, ordinary least squares regression analysis was performed on each variable using SPSS software, and the regression results are shown in "Table 3", where the VIF values of civil aviation transport turnover, GDP per capita and energy consumption per unit of turnover are all greater than 10, indicating that there is a multicollinearity problem between the factors and the results obtained are not desirable.

Table 3. Results of ordinary least squares regression analysis

Variable	t	Saliency	Tolerances	VIF
Constant	−12390952.7	0.000		
S	16595205.69	0.000	0.026	37.891
GDP	0.033	0.975	0.042	23.967
SE	3468518.46	0.000	0.050	19.921

In order to avoid the problem of multicollinearity among the factors, the multiple linear regression analysis was performed again for each factor using the ridge regression method. The results of the ridge regression analysis were obtained by plotting the ridge traces and selecting K = 0.3, while the regression coefficients of the variables were also output in the results, as shown in "Table 4" (Fig. 2).

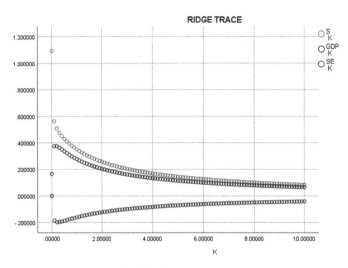

Fig. 2. Ridge trace map.

Table 4. Results of the ridge regression analysis.

Variable	B	SE (B)	Beta	T	Sig
S	0.4354	0.03926	0.4759	11.0909	0.0004
GDP	0.4115	0.0582	0.3628	7.0676	0.0021
SE	−1.15	0.3231	−0.1971	−3.6829	0.0212
Constant	−1.1351	1.1015	0.0000	−1.0305	0.3609

Note: R Square = 0.9728; F value = 47.74; Sig F = 0.00137178

From the results of the ridge regression analysis, it is known that the value of Sig F passed the 5% significance test and The R2 value is equal to 0.9728. The regression equation can be obtained as follows.

$$\ln C = 0.4354\ln S + 0.4115\ln GDP - 1.15\ln SE - 1.1351 \tag{12}$$

The actual values of carbon emissions in the civil aviation transport sector from 2013–2020 were compared with the predicted values in the regression equation to test the error of this regression equation. The results are shown in "Table 5". The errors between the actual values of carbon emissions from the civil aviation transport sector and the predicted values from the regression equation are within manageable limits.

From the regression coefficients obtained, holding other influencing factors constant, civil aviation transport carbon emissions change by 0.4354% for every 1% change in civil aviation transport turnover; holding other influencing factors constant, civil aviation transport carbon emissions change by 0.4115% for every 1% change in GDP per capita; holding other influencing factors constant, civil aviation transport carbon emissions change by −1.15% for every 1% change in energy consumption per unit of turnover.

Table 5. Error between actual and forecasted carbon emissions in the civil aviation transport sector.

Year	Actual carbon emissions (million tonnes)	Projected carbon emissions (million tonnes)	Error (%)
2013	6294.09	6980.24	10.90%
2014	6980.34	7583.24	8.64%
2015	7890.24	8298.90	5.18%
2016	8866.94	9084.51	2.45%
2017	9996.08	9954.57	−0.42%
2018	10906.87	11111.67	1.88%
2019	11604.60	11873.66	2.32%
2020	8051.40	8511.48	5.71%

5   Conclusions and Recommendations

5.1   Analysis of the Results of Factors Influencing Carbon Emissions from Civil Aviation Transport

Based on the LMDI model and STIRPAT model, this paper quantitatively analyzes the relationship between carbon emissions from civil aviation transportation and influencing factors such as the level of economic development, energy-saving and emission reduction technologies, and population size, and obtains the following conclusions.

1) The decomposition analysis of the influencing factors of civil aviation transportation carbon emissions using LMDI model shows that economic development, unit GDP turnover and population size play a role in promoting civil aviation transportation carbon emissions, among which economic development plays the most significant role in promoting civil aviation transportation carbon emissions; energy-saving and emission reduction technologies play a suppressing role in civil aviation transportation carbon emissions, which can effectively slow down the rapid growth of civil aviation transportation carbon emissions.

2) The regression equations between civil aviation transport carbon emissions and civil aviation transport turnover, GDP per capita and energy consumption per unit of turnover were obtained by constructing the STIRPAT model and the ridge regression method. The regression equation can further understand the change response relationship between the carbon emission of civil aviation transportation and each influencing factor.

5.2   Suggestions for Energy Saving and Emission Reduction in the Civil Aviation Transport Industry

1) In terms of economic development: economic development will cause civil aviation transport CO2 emissions, but it does not mean that the low-carbon development of

civil aviation transportation should be at the expense of the overall socio-economic development. Good socio-economic development will promote the business improvement of the civil aviation transportation industry, bring a lot of revenue to the civil aviation transportation industry, make a lot of investment in the green development of the civil aviation transportation industry, promote the progress of energy-saving and emission reduction technology in the civil aviation transportation industry, and improve the operational efficiency of the civil aviation transportation industry, forming a virtuous cycle.

2) In terms of civil aviation turnover: the increase in civil aviation turnover will more directly cause emissions in the civil aviation transport CO2 emissions, so it is necessary to improve the efficiency of civil aviation operation and management, and guide aviation enterprises to strengthen intelligent operation to achieve systematic energy saving and carbon reduction. For example, when planning routes, it should shorten the route distance as much as possible and choose flight routes and flight altitudes that are conducive to energy saving and emission reduction; optimise the take-off and landing procedures when aircraft are at the airport, minimise the frequency of aircraft take-off and landing, and reduce unnecessary ground taxiing and air waiting time, among other measures.

3) In the area of energy conservation and emission reduction: increase investment in the research and development of energy conservation and emission reduction technologies, and promote the application of advanced practical energy conservation technologies in the civil aviation transportation industry; vigorously promote the replacement of traditional fuels by advanced bio-liquid fuels and sustainable aviation fuels, and improve the energy efficiency of terminal fuel products; introduce policies to encourage technological innovation in energy conservation and emission reduction, and provide human resources as well as management support for energy conservation and emission reduction efforts.

References

1. Yu, Z.: Global aviation carbon reduction efforts are steadily advancing. China Aviation News, 2021-09-10 (006)
2. Shi, Y., Wu, W., Li, X.: Research on the development characteristics and influencing factors of China's aviation carbon emissions. J. East China Jiaotong Univ. 36(06), 32–38 (2019)
3. Sgouris, S., Bonnefoy, P.A., Hansman, R.J.: Air transportation in a carbon constrained world: long-term dynamics of policies and strategies for mitigating the carbon footprint of commercial aviation. Transp. Res. Part A Policy Pract. 45(10), 1077–1091 (2011)
4. Arjomandi, A., Seufert, J.H.: An evaluation of the world's major airlines' technical and environmental performance. Econ. Model. 41, 133–144 (2014)
5. Brueckner, J.K., Abreu, C.: Airline fuel usage and carbon emissions: determining factors. J. Air Transp. Manag. 62, 10–17 (2017)
6. Chen, Q., Lu, C., Zhou, D.: Exponential decomposition of carbon emission factors in China's civil aviation industry based on LMDI method. J. Tianjin Univ. (Soc. Sci. Ed.) 16 (05), 397–403 (2014)

7. Yao, S.: An empirical analysis of the factors influencing carbon emissions of Chinese airlines. Civil Aviation University of China (2014)

8. Guo, P.: Study on the spatial and temporal evolution and influencing factors of carbon emissions of civil aviation passenger transportation in China. Northwest Normal University (2020)

9. York, R., Rosa, E.A., Dietz, T.: STIRPAT, IPAT and ImPACT: analytic tools for unpacking the driving forces of environmental impacts. Ecol. Econ. **46**(3), 351–365 (2003)

10. Ehrlich, P.R., Holdren, J.P.: Impact of population growth. Science **171**(3977), 1212–1217 (1971)

11. Luo, Y., Xing, Z., Zhang, Q.: Analysis of the impact of the New Crown epidemic on China's aviation coal consumption and forecast of aviation coal demand in the 14th Five-Year Plan. Oil Gas New Energy **33**(03), 17–21 (2021)

12. He, H., Zhao, Z., Luo, W., Zhang, J.: Community detection in aviation network based on k-means and complex network. Comput. Syst. Sci. Eng. **39**(2), 251–264 (2021)

13. Tang, Y., Liu, W., He, Y., Zhang, Y., Zhang, F.: The development of generalized public bicycles in China and its role in the urban transportation system. J. Internet Things **2**(3), 101–107 (2020)

14. Lu, C., Zhao, M., Khan, I., Uthansakul, P.: Prospect theory based hesitant fuzzy multi-criteria decision making for low sulphur fuel of maritime transportation. Comput. Mater. Contin. **66**(2), 1511–1528 (2021)

15. Zaini, H.G.: Forecasting of appliances house in a low-energy depend on grey wolf optimizer. Comput. Mater. Contin. **71**(2), 2303–2314 (2022)

16. Chen, Y., Chen, Y., Lou, S., Huang, C.: Energy saving control approach for trajectory tracking of autonomous mobile robots. Intell. Autom. Soft Comput. **31**(1), 357–372 (2022)

Design and Implementation of Hadoop-Based Campus Cloud Drive

Lei Xiang[1], Qi He[1(✉)], Zhuo Li[1,2], and Jun Guo[1]

[1] Hunan Automotive Engineering Vocational College, Zhuzhou 412000, China
279487906@qq.com
[2] The University of Lahore, Lahore 54660, Pakistan

Abstract. Campus network users have an increasing demand for file storage and sharing, and the traditional storage and sharing methods cannot adapt to this demand. This study proposes a campus network cloud disk system based on cloud storage, which uses a network asynchronous communication mode to cope with the high load of user concurrency. Besides, the file hashing algorithm is used to solve the problem of multiple copies of files stored on the network, which enables multiple users to share one copy. Symmetric key algorithm is used for file sharing and inexpensive distributed storage is used to facilitate storage space expansion. Finally, Hadoop technology is used for implementation. This campus network cloud disk system adapts to the characteristics of high network bandwidth and low egress bandwidth of campus network, and solves the problem of remote file storage and sharing for teachers and students.

Keywords: Hadoop · Campus cloud · Distributed

Teachers and students in higher education generate a large amount of data information in their study and work, such as courseware, videos, experimental data, etc. A large amount of disk space is needed to store these materials. Due to the limitation of storage space and bandwidth, traditional local storage and remote mailbox storage cannot provide large capacity and high bandwidth storage space. A personal file storage and sharing system applicable to campus network is needed [1].

In recent years, big data technologies have developed rapidly and new technologies have emerged continuously, such as Hadoop, Flink, Beam, Spark, etc. [2]. HDFS distributed file storage system, one of the core components of Hadoop, has strong fault tolerance and can improve its fault tolerance [3] by adding copies of data, capable of storing such as GB, TB level or more massive data, and can also be built on inexpensive machines to achieve features such as secure reading and writing of big data at low cost. Using Hadoop HDFS big data technology to build campus cloud system can better solve the above problems.

1 Analysis of Campus Network Cloud Disk System

Cloud storage is a distributed storage method relying on high-speed network, which provides low-cost, easily scalable and reliable mass storage resources and migrates users' local storage to a remote server cluster. Campus networks of universities are user-dense, with large and frequent data storage, complex network division, and low network utilization. Due to campus network characteristics and egress bandwidth limitations, public network storage methods are not adapted to campus network users [4]. The high-speed bandwidth of campus network with 10-gigabit backbone and 100-gigabit to desktop provides an excellent infrastructure for storing big data, especially with the users' Internet location moves frequently, the cloud disk can access data at any location in the campus network. Therefore, the campus network-based cloud drive is the best solution to meet the storage needs of teachers and students [5].

Requirement analysis:

1) The default LAN privatization deployment is required. The client is based on the windows operating system, and the system is deployed to the server (either Linux or windows) [6].
2) Each user space is freely allocated.
3) Each teacher in the school has an account. Teachers can log in and access it through PC client and web page.
4) Data among teachers can be sent, shared and stored, and permissions can be set [7].
5) Teachers can create their own external chain folder, teachers can distribute materials through the external chain folder, and students can upload and save their homework through their own external chain folder without logging in to their account [8].

1.1 Automatic Data Backup

The campus cloud disk supports the simultaneous access of web and PC clients, establishes shared folders according to the organizational structure of school functional departments, departments or classes, and uniformly archives and stores the documents scattered in the computers of teachers, information classrooms and scientific researchers, so as to realize the safe storage of excellent courseware, scientific research project materials, academic papers, class assignments and other materials. Then, with a complete automatic backup mechanism, prevent virus attacks, recover quickly after data loss, and stick to the post of document protection [9].

1.2 Build a Teaching Resource Bank and Improve the Level of Education

The campus cloud disk creates a cloud virtual teaching resource library to quickly share the cloud teaching and scientific research materials among teachers and students, and supports rapid retrieval and search of relevant literature. Teachers share the latest teaching materials, high-quality courseware and teaching plans in real time in yueku campus cloud disk [10].

1.3 Cloud Electronic Classroom, Orderly Submission of Homework

Teachers can teach in any classroom without taking courseware with them. Whiteboard and courseware modification during class are saved to the cloud in real time. Students' classroom homework is submitted to yueku campus cloud disk in real time. Through permission control, students' homework can be copied and viewed from each other.

Teachers can not only receive the reminder of homework submission in real time, but also review and feed back to students online. There is no need to download one by one by email, and reply by email after approval. Make the classroom homework communication between teachers and students more convenient [11].

2   Design of Overall System

The system uses C/S model. The client side is responsible for user interaction, user login, file upload, synchronization, download, rename, delete, share and other operations. The server side is divided into three layers: the access layer, the service layer and the cloud storage layer. The access layer is responsible for user authentication and monitoring user information, and users connect to the system through the access layer and send operation requests to the service layer. The service layer is the core functional layer of the system, responsible for responding to the requests of the access layer and realizing the requested operations. The storage function of the cloud storage layer is invoked to complete the storage of files. The cloud storage layer provides storage resources to provide distributed mass storage. The system structure is shown in Fig. 1 below [12].

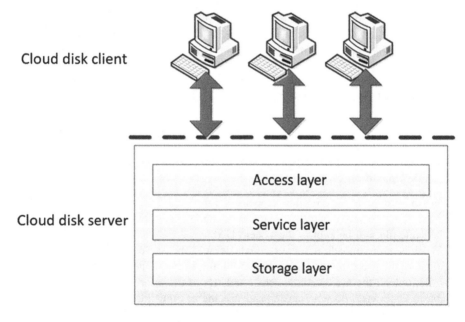

Fig. 1. System architecture.

3   System Design and Implementation

The campus network-based cloud drive system is divided into several parts: user management, file management, data transfer, data multi-copy identification and sharing, and distributed file storage.

3.1   User Authentication Login Process

Users who log in to the cloud disk account and use the campus network are not allowed to register their own account. Each legitimate user in the campus network has a "cloud disk" account. The combination of user management and campus network user management can greatly facilitate the use of teachers and students. At the same time, it ensures the security of the account [13].

The client sends the user's login request through the access layer, the service layer accepts the user request and queries whether the database user name and password are legal. The user logs into the system through authentication and returns to the request state while fails to authenticate [14].

3.2   Data Transmission

The data transmission between client and server uses socket word connection based on TCP. The server side uses the IOCP model to meet the concurrent processing under high load and the concurrent data transmission of multiple users. The IOCP model is an I/O asynchronous operation that can efficiently handle data exchange for multiple clients.

$$clientSocket = socket(AF\_INET, SOCK\_STREAM, IPPRO - TO\_TCP);$$

$$nRet = connect(clientSocket, (sockaddr*)\&SockAddr, sizeof(SockAddr));$$

3.3   File Upload and Management

During the storage of files, it often happens that the same files are stored separately by different users. To save cloud storage resources and network bandwidth, only one copy of the same file will be kept in the system [15].

When a user uploads a file to cloud storage, the server will compare the file information database to determine whether the file is a new file or an old file. If it is a new file, upload the file data completely and record the information of the file in the database. Otherwise, do not transfer and use the existing file copy. The file upload process is shown in Fig. 2 below.

Before uploading a file to the server, the user first calculates the file identification code (file-hash). FileHash is the hash value of the file, using MD5 and SHA-1 methods.

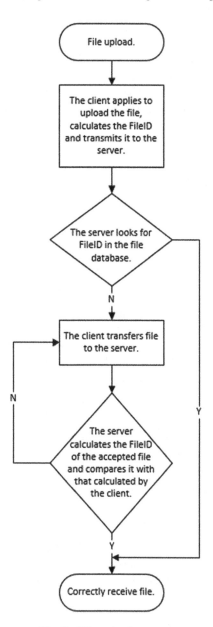

Fig. 2. File upload process.

$$FileHash = MD5(file) + SHA(file) \tag{1}$$

$$FileID = FileHash + FileName + FileLength \tag{2}$$

FileHash, file name and file length are used together as the unique identification information FileID of the file. The client calculates the FileHash of the file locally, synthesizes the FileID and transmits it to the server. The server retrieves the file information database. If there is no match, the server notifies the client to upload the file. Otherwise, if there is a match, it has no need to upload. After receiving the file, the server shall determine the data integrity during transmission. The server recalculates the FileID of the file and compares it with that calculated by the client. If it is the same, it will be accepted. If not, it will be retransmitted. In the file storage process, the server establishes meta information records for the correctly accepted files and stores them into the file database. File meta information records include file name, file length, identification information, storage location and number of references (name, length, FileID, place, quote). The field place records the location information of the file in the cloud storage, and the field quote records the number of times the file is referenced by the user [16].

The server creates for each user a list of the user's files, which records the information (name, length, place) of all the files owned by the user. The add and delete operations of the user's files are the addition and deletion of file information records in the file list. The rename of a file only modifies the name field of the file information in the list.

3.4   File Download

The user selects the file to be downloaded on the client side and requests the server to download it. The server looks up the user's file list, finds the storage location of the selected file, and transfers it to the client [17].

3.5   File Sharing

File sharing among users conveniently enables data sharing. The data sharing process of cloud drive avoids data copying without consuming a lot of computing resources and storage space, and different users share one copy of files in the cloud drive system.

The client selects the file to be shared and applies for sharing to the server; the server randomly selects the sharing code K, uses the encryption algorithm E, encrypts the FileID of this file and calculates the ciphertext M as the sharing link.

$$M = E(FileID, K) \tag{3}$$

The user passes the sharing link and share to other users. Users who get the share link and share code request the server to get the shared file through the client, and the server receives the request and uses the decryption algorithm D to calculate the FileID.

$$FileID = D(M, K) \qquad (4)$$

The server queries the file information database to get the information of the shared file (name, length, place) and adds it to the user's file list.

3.6   Storage of Documents

A distributed cloud storage solution is used for file storage. Cloud storage has the advantages of low cost, flexible scaling and easy deployment for big data storage. The open-source project OpenStack Object Storage (Swift) is used, which is an inexpensive standard hardware as the storage medium, and uses hashing technology and data redundancy in the hardware layer to ensure efficient and reliable data, with high scalability.

4   System Coding and Testing

The user needs to upload the files. The file is stored in the cluster server, and the system classifies the file according to the file size and suffix name, and stores the file information in the database, displaying "File upload successful" or "File upload failed". The user executes the "Download" command, the system matches the file information, downloads the file from the server, and returns the download progress, displaying "Download Successful" or "Download Failed". Enter the "Delete" command and the system will receive the command and delete the file from the server, and updates the current directory, outputting "Delete Success" or "Delete Failure".

The file upload and download function is the main function of this system. For this function, there are tests on file size, file format and other aspects to test the efficiency of uploading and downloading files. There are many factors that affect the efficiency of this part, such as hardware parameters of machine, network speed, etc. The test data of the efficiency of uploading and downloading files are shown in Table 1.

Table 1.   Upload and download file efficiency test.

File size	1 MB	10 MB	100 MB	1 GB	10 GB
Upload	0.1 s	0.3 s	7.2 s	161.8 s	1803.3 s
Download	0.1 s	0.2 s	1.1 s	12.9 s	131.5 s

5   Operating Environment and Installation Deployment

Before development, four virtual machines with Linux distribution CentOS7 (64-bit) are installed to build Hadoop fully distributed cluster nodes as shown in Table 2. After setting fixed IPs on the virtual machines and installing JDK, uploading Hadoop-2.7.2 to build a Hadoop cluster requires modifying seven configuration files, including core-site.xml, hadoop-env.sh, yarn-env.sh, mapred-site.xml, yarn-site.xml, slaves, hdfs-site.xml, as well as cloning virtual machines, configuring SSH login without password, configuring time synchronization service, starting/shutting down the cluster, etc.

Table 2. Hadoop fully distributed cluster hosting plan

Host name (FQDN)	RAM	HDD	IP address	Role
master	8 GB	100 GB	192.168.137.140	Namenode
slave1	4 GB	60 GB	192.168.137.141	Secondary namenode, datanode
slave2	4 GB	60 GB	192.168.137.142	Datanode
slave3	4 GB	60 GB	192.168.137.143	Datanode

To package the project, select Export, War file in Eclipse, and in the pop-up dialog box, select the path to be packaged and other information, and select the webapps directory under the Tomcat installation directory to facilitate compilation when starting Tomcat. Start Tomcat, go to the bin directory under the Tomcat installation directory, double-click startup.bat to start Tomcat, and then you can access https://local-host:8888/CloudDisk in your browser.

6   Summary

The cloud disk system based on Hadoop has the following features. The file storage system adopts Hadoop HDFS distributed file system and the file metadata storage adopts MySQL database. It has visual pages, for example, when operating file upload and download, the page can display the progress information in real time. However, there are still some shortcomings in the system, such as file deletion is only deleted from the server HDFS file system [10], and then the metadata of deleted files is stored in the database. The deleted file data is displayed in the recycle bin page, which does not really realize the recycling function, and the file transmission is not encrypted. In view of the above shortcomings, the next step can be optimized in the following aspects such as designing storage space for files, adding the recycle function, and using encryption algorithms to encrypt files.

Funding Statement. This research is supported by 2019 training object project of young backbone teachers in Colleges and universities in Hunan Province.

References

1. Desai, H.G.: Dr Ratanlal Harichand Kalro (1945–2013). Indian J. Gastroenterol. **33**(2), 101 (2014). https://doi.org/10.1007/s12664-013-0442-y
2. Gankhuyag, U., Han, J.: Automatic BIM indoor modelling from unstructured point clouds using a convolutional neural network. Intell. Autom. Soft Comput. **28**(1), 133–152 (2021)
3. Zhu, X., Jing, Z.: SWOT analysis and strategy research on campus e-commerce. In: 2011 International Conference on E-Business and E-Government (ICEE) (2011)
4. Adillah, I., Arifin, Y., Permai, S.D., Limarja, C.: Nitipyuk: a crowdsourcing marketplace for personal shopper. Procedia Comput. Sci. **157**(4), 514–520 (2019)
5. Jayamala, R., Valarmathi, A.: An enhanced decentralized virtual machine migration approach for energy-aware cloud data centers. Intell. Autom. Soft Comput. **27**(2), 347–358 (2021)
6. Li, T.: Construction of multi-platform for campus e-commerce. Eurasian Bus. Rev. **11**(4), 40–42 (2015)
7. Aldossary, M.: A review of dynamic resource management in cloud computing environments. Comput. Syst. Sci. Eng. **36**(3), 461–476 (2021)
8. Fang, Z., et al.: Abnormal event detection in crowded scenes based on deep learning. Multimedia Tools Appl. **75**(22), 14617–14639 (2016). https://doi.org/10.1007/s11042-016-3316-3
9. Adnan, K., Akbar, R.: An analytical study of information extraction from unstructured and multidimensional big data. J. Big Data **6**(1), 1–38 (2019). https://doi.org/10.1186/s40537-019-0254-8
10. Jiang, L., Fu, Z.: Privacy-preserving genetic algorithm outsourcing in cloud computing. J. Cyber Secur. **2**(1), 49–61 (2020)
11. Mavridis, L., Karatza, H.: Performance evaluation of cloud-based log file analysis with Apache Hadoop and Apache Spark. J. Syst. Softw. **15**(125), 133–151 (2017)
12. Rudniy, A.: Data warehouse design for big data in academia. Comput. Mater. Contin. **71**(1), 979–992 (2021)
13. Rospocher, F.C.M., Cattoni, R., Magnini, B., Serafini, L.: The knowledge store: a storage framework for interlinking unstructured and structured knowledge. Int. J. Semant. Web Inf. Syst. **11**(2), 1–35 (2017)
14. Lee, S.: A study on classification and detection of small moths using CNN model. Comput. Mater. Contin. **71**(1), 1987–1998 (2020)
15. Swain, N.R., et al.: A review of open source software solutions for developing water resources web applications. Environ. Model. Softw. **67**(9), 108–117 (2015)
16. Wickramasinghe, C., Wallace, L., Reinke, K., Jones, S.: Implementation of a new algorithm resulting in improvements in accuracy and resolution of SEVIRI hotspot products. Remote Sens. Lett. **9**(9), 877–885 (2018)
17. Shankar, K., Venkatraman, S.: A secure encrypted classified electronic healthcare data for public cloud environment. Intell. Autom. Soft Comput. **32**(2), 765–779 (2021)

Correlation Analysis of Water Temperature and Dissolved Oxygen Based on Water Quality Monitoring Data

Wenwu Tan[1], Jianjun Zhang[1], Jiang Wu[1], Yifu Sheng[1], Xing Liu[1], Manqin Lei[2], Ziqiu Zhang[2(✉)], Haijun Lin[1], Guang Sun[3], and Peng Guo[4]

[1] College of Engineering and Design, Hunan Normal University, Changsha 410081, China
[2] LIHERO Technology (Hunan) Co. Ltd., Changsha 410205, China
283870277@qq.com
[3] Big Data Institute, Hunan University of Finance and Economics, Changsha 410205, China
[4] University Malaysia Sabah, 88400 Sabah, Malaysia

Abstract. The content of dissolved oxygen in water is an important index to detect and evaluate water quality, and the change of its concentration is greatly affected by algae factors, and water temperature is an important factor to affect algae reproduction. The study of the relationship between water temperature and dissolved oxygen can play a better guiding role in water quality evaluation. In this paper, the web crawler was designed to crawl the water quality monitoring data of the relevant monitoring waters from the Internet, and then the correlation analysis was conducted after the pretreatment. Correlation analysis is mainly divided into three steps: Firstly, analyze the correlation between the obtained water temperature data and dissolved oxygen data in the time domain; Secondly, from the statistical point of view of correlation analysis, perform a regression analysis and get the correlation coefficient; Finally, use the correlation analysis results to predict the future data. The experiment shows that the established correlation analysis model has a good effect on the prediction of dissolved oxygen concentration.

Keywords: Correlation · Regression analysis · Water temperature · Dissolved oxygen · Prediction

1 Introduction

In recent years, a large increase in water pollution load has led to a large increase in plankton and plants in water [1], and water hypoxia has become a serious global problem. However, water hypoxia will have many negative effects, such as hypoxia death of fish and other aquatic organisms, and harmful gases released from sediments will damage water bodies [2] At the same time, as a large number of nitrogen and phosphorus pollutants released by sediments provide nutrients for algae and other plankton, the growth of algae is intensified, thus damaging the stability of the

X. Sun et al. (Eds.): ICAIS 2022, CCIS 1587, pp. 340–352, 2022.
https://doi.org/10.1007/978-3-031-06761-7_28

ecosystem. Dissolved molecular oxygen in air is called dissolved oxygen in water, and the content of dissolved oxygen in water is an important indicator to measure the self-purification capacity of water. When dissolved oxygen in water decreases, the shorter the time required to restore to the initial state means the stronger the self-purification capacity of water. Dissolved oxygen is mainly affected by photosynthesis, respiration and oxidation [3], in which both photosynthesis and respiration are related to the reproduction of algae, while water temperature is a key factor determining whether algae can reproduce. Therefore, analyzing the correlation between dissolved oxygen and water temperature and solving their correlation coefficient in the same watershed has important reference value for future water quality evaluation.

With the continuous development of Internet of Things technology and the Internet, digital economy is developing rapidly, and big data and related technologies are increasingly affecting our daily life. By analyzing the big data produced in production and life, it has become possible to analyze and predict the big data of water quality monitoring [4, 5]. Based on the design of web crawler, climb from water quality monitoring online platform to take the monitoring water quality monitoring data of water using big data related technology analysis of monitoring data of water quality processing, the corresponding water quality index correlation analysis model is established, the correlation analysis of water temperature and dissolved oxygen, and use its correlation analysis results to predict future data [6, 7].

2 Related Technology

2.1 Web Crawler

Web crawler is a kind of software that automatically extracts network information according to a specific setting method, so as to realize the function of local backup of the required information on the network, and is also one of the main components of search engines [8]. The architecture of the web crawler is mainly composed of three parts, which are the scheduling end of the crawler, the core module of the crawler and the storage data [9], as shown in Fig. 1. The scheduling terminal is the entrance of the entire crawler program, which is mainly used to control the start, execution and stop of the entire crawler program and to monitor various running conditions in the crawler. The core module of the whole crawler program is composed of three parts: the URL management part, the web page download part and the web page parsing part. The URL management part downloads the URL data waiting to be crawled through the network downloader and converts it into a string form, and then uses the regular expression, BeautifulSoup and other methods to filter out redundant information on the transmitted string information through the web page parsing part. Therefore, valuable information is extracted, and finally the information is transferred to the storage module for storage. The processing process is shown in Fig. 1. In addition, in the process of crawling, we often encounter URLs pointing to other pages in web pages. The URLs of these web pages will also be parsed by the web page parser and passed to the URL management part for further crawling.

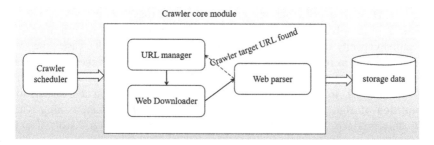

Fig. 1. The working principle of crawler.

2.2 Introduction to Pandas

Pandas is one of the plugins for Python. It is very powerful. It contains advanced data structures and sophisticated tools that make working with data in python very fast and easy. Pandas is built on NumPy. It contains two data structures: list and data frame. The data frame class is commonly used to store values and characters in two dimensions. Pandas provides various powerful functions such as grouping, counting, and merging. It is not only widely used in data input and output, data cleaning and data mining [10], but also can eliminate abnormal data. It can be used in conjunction with other efficient scientific computing methods such as SciPy, NumPy and Matplotlib in data analysis, and can create end-to-end analytical work to solve problems during the modeling process.

3 Data Preprocessing

3.1 Construction of Big Data for Water Quality Monitoring

First, enter the water resources platform through a browser, and the distribution of some water resources will be displayed on its page, and then click the link to enter the water quality testing platform, and obtain the URL of the link, as shown in Fig. 2. After entering the page, you can find that the data of the page is dynamically loaded. Therefore, if a crawler is used to directly request the URL of the interface, the returned HTML is only the source code of the current interface, and the complete source code of all interfaces cannot be obtained.

For webpages with dynamically loaded data, there are usually two ways to crawl the data. The first way is to analyze the data interface of the dynamically loaded data, and the second way is to use selenium and browsers to simulate the habits of natural people to load the webpage and parse the rendered source code. Since the second method consumes CPU and memory and has low performance and slow speed, this paper uses the first method to read JSON format strings from files and convert them into Python objects for data processing. By entering the developer mode, the source code of web pages and related files are viewed to analyze the data interface for dynamically loading data. After extracting the required form through the POST request method, all information is crawled by changing the page number Pageindex and page display number PageSize.

After analyzing the data, the obtained water quality monitoring data sets in the past three years are summarized, and the sorted data are shown in Table 1.

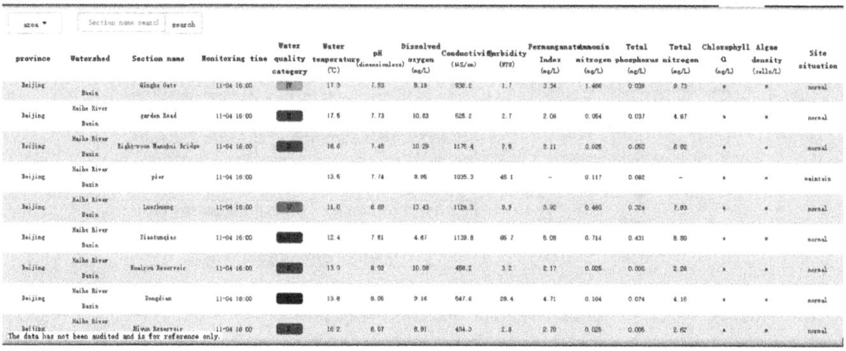

Fig. 2. Water platform

Table 1. Standard item standard limits for surface water environmental quality standards.

Indicator	Number of data	Value
Dissolved oxygen	4792	1.04–19.55
Water temperature	4792	2.48–33.5
PH	4787	4.06–9.23
Conductivity	4791	197.80–732.10
Turbidity	4791	3.39–2571.46
Permanganate index	1550	1.67–12.33
Ammonia nitrogen	1554	−0.02–1.62
Total phosphorus	1681	0.02–0.36
Total nitrogen	1613	1.45–9.93

3.2 Data Preprocessing

With the advent of the era of big data, the clutter, complexity and fuzziness of the original data make the data face huge challenges in many aspects such as perception and calculation [11]. Data preprocessing is a very important preparatory work before data analysis and mining. On the one hand, it can ensure the accuracy and validity of the data, and on the other hand, by adjusting the data format, it is more in line with the needs of data mining [12].

Data preprocessing technology mainly consists of data cleaning, data transformation, data integration and so on. Data cleaning mainly includes processing missing data, filtering outliers and eliminating duplicate values. The data transformation part includes converting index into time series type and processing data according to different time and frequency. The data integration part mainly includes merging DataFrame tables with key parameters, etc. The data preprocessing flow chart is shown in Fig. 3.

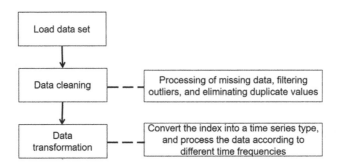

Fig. 3. Data preprocessing process.

Data Cleaning. Data cleaning analyzes the causes and existing ways of "dirty data", fully uses emerging technologies and methods to clean it, and converts "dirty data" into data that meets data quality requirements, thereby improving the quality of data sets. Therefore, different cleaning methods and the intensity of cleaning determine the quality of the cleaned data. The method of data cleaning mainly consists of two parts: the processing of missing values and the processing of outliers.

Missing Value Handling. The reasons for missing values are mainly divided into natural factors and human factors. The reason for natural factors is that in the process of data collection, some of the data collection failed due to machine reasons or the collected data could not be saved, resulting in some of them. Part of the data is missing; human factors are due to human errors in the collection process, resulting in the omission of some data. For the processing of missing values in the data, the following two methods are commonly used:

Delete Missing Values. When the number of samples in the data set is large enough, and the proportion of missing values is relatively small, the most simple and effective method can be used to deal with the missing values in the case where such a small amount of missing has a small impact on the whole, that is, the missing value samples Direct removal is also one of the commonly used strategies.

Interpolation Filling Method. Interpolation filling is to find the law through the distribution of the known sequence, and then estimate the missing values according to the found law. Linear interpolation is one of the commonly used methods for interpolating one-dimensional data. It is allocated by calculating the proportion of the distance between the two data on the left and right of the interpolation point to the point.

Outliers and Noisy Data Cleaning. In the process of data collection, due to the different types of data sources, there will be abnormal objects in data measurement and collection errors, and abnormal objects are often called outliers. Outlier detection, also known as deviation detection and exception mining, is often used as an important part of data mining. Its task is to find objects that are significantly different from most data, so most data mining methods regard this difference information as an important part of data mining noise to deal with [13]. There are two commonly used outlier processing methods:

Box Plot Method. The library provides a standard for detecting outliers by calling box graphs. Data between QL-1.5*IQR and QU-1.5*IQR are considered normal. Anything outside this range is considered an outlier. Quartile in QL, indicating that one quarter of the total data is smaller than it. QU is the upper quartile, indicating that a quarter of all numbers are greater than it. IQR is the difference between the upper quartile and the lower quartile and contains general data. The box plot is judged by the spacing between quartiles, and 25% of the data does not interfere with the quartiles, so outliers do not affect this criterion.

Normal Distribution Method. The 3σ principle is the most commonly used method for dealing with outliers when the data follows a normal distribution. The 3σ principle is also known as the Laida principle. Its function is to determine the appropriate interval according to a certain probability according to the standard deviation method of the random error and gross error appearing in the data. Since the values outside the interval are also called gross errors, they can be eliminated, and the probability density of normal distribution is shown in Fig. 4.

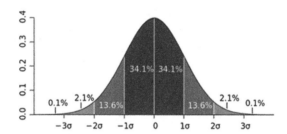

Fig. 4. Normal distribution probability density plot.

In the 3σ principle, σ represents the standard deviation and X represents the mean. From the probability density of the normal distribution shown in Fig. 4, the probability of a data point falling within one plus or minus standard deviation is 68.2%; the probability of a data point falling within twice plus or minus standard deviation is 95.4%; The probability of falling within three plus or minus standard deviations is 99.6%. Therefore, when the data is outside the probability of two standard deviations, such data points are considered as outliers; When the data is more than three times the standard deviation, such data points are considered as extreme outliers.

Water Quality Data Cleaning. In data cleaning, the Pandas library is called first to import and convert the data into a Dataframe type, and then the data of water temperature and dissolved oxygen are selected from the water resources data for analysis.

Because the data interval of the study is not long and there is no large missing value, this paper uses the linear interpolation method to fill the missing data in the text. Finally, the overall analysis is carried out, so as to selectively process the outliers in the process of data collection. The analysis process usually uses the maximum, minimum, mean and standard deviation commonly used in statistics to describe the data. By calling pandas, the data is converted into Dataframe type, and then the library function is called to obtain the corresponding value, which will make the data display more intuitive, as shown in Table 2.

Table 2. Data integrity analysis.

Statistic	Water temperature	Dissolved oxygen
Mean	16.70	9.83
Std	8.76	2.41
Min	2.48	1.04
Max	33.5	19.55

It can be seen from the above table that there are exaggerated data for the maximum and minimum values of dissolved oxygen, which may be due to the long working time of the instrument and the problem of aging of the instrument causing errors in the data at some time points. When performing data analysis, these data can be identified as outliers. The effect of removing outliers from the box plot is shown in Fig. 5.

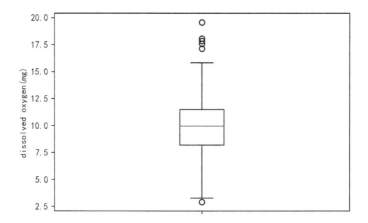

Fig. 5. Dissolved oxygen outlier box plot.

3.3   Data Transformation

Time series is a sequence of factors that are analyzed in chronological order. It is one of the commonly used methods for statistical analysis [14], so it is also called dynamic sequence, which can usually use existing data to predict future conditions. A time series consists of S, T, C, I, where S represents seasonal fluctuations, T represents long-term trends, C represents cyclic changes, and I represents irregular changes. There are two main analysis methods for time series, one is the index analysis method, and the other is the component analysis method [15].

From the obtained water quality data, it can be found that the relevant variables are closely related to the changes of time, and have the characteristics of seasonality and periodicity. Therefore, in the process of analysis, the data is also compared through different time frequencies. In this paper, the data is first converted into a time-series format through pandas, and then by calling the library function, the data is resampled in the form of daily mean and monthly mean, respectively, to analyze the impact of water temperature on dissolved oxygen from different time perspectives.

4 Correlation Analysis

4.1 Principles of Correlation Analysis

Correlation analysis is used to measure the degree of linear correlation between two things, or between two variables, and express it with specific indicators. It is a correlation method for studying the closeness between variables. Commonly used correlation coefficient calculation methods are Pearson, Spearman, Kendall [16], the method we calculated in the experiment is the pearson correlation coefficient, so we only introduce the pearson correlation coefficient below, and its formula is:

$$p = \frac{\sum(X - \overline{X})(Y - \overline{\overline{Y}})}{\sqrt{\sum(X - \overline{X})^2 \sum(Y - \overline{Y})^2}} \tag{1}$$

The corresponding size of its correlation coefficient P can be represented by a correlation degree table, as shown in Table 3.

Table 3. Correlation table.

$|p|$	Relevance
$0.8 < |p| \leq 1$	Very strong correlation
$0.6 < |p| \leq 0.8$	Strong correlation
$0.4 < |p| \leq 0.6$	Moderately relevant
$0.2 < |p| \leq 0.4$	Weak correlation
$0 < |p| \leq 0.2$	Irrelevant

Due to the existence of sampling error, the correlation coefficient between two variables in the sample is not 0, and the correlation coefficient between two variables that cannot represent the total amount is not 0, so it must pass the test. The T test is used in this paper. When the correlation coefficient tests the significance probability of the t statistic P < 0.05, it can indicate that the correlation between the two variables is significant; when the correlation coefficient tests the significance probability of the t statistic P < 0.01, it can indicate that the significance between the two variables is very significant; when the significance probability of the correlation coefficient test t statistic is P > 0.05, it indicates that there is no correlation between the two variables.

4.2   Visual Analysis

In order to reflect the water temperature and dissolved oxygen in the same coordinate system, we set up a double Y-axis coordinate system, so that the two can be reflected in the same time series as the coordinate axis. The daily and monthly average data of water temperature and dissolved oxygen after processing outliers were visually analyzed.

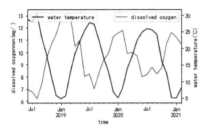

Fig. 6. Monthly mean visual analysis.

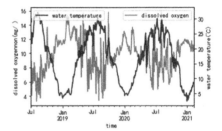

Fig. 7. Visual analysis of daily averages.

The changes of water temperature and dissolved oxygen are shown in Figs. 6 and 7. From the monthly average visual analysis, it can be seen that from July 2018 to February 21, the water temperature and dissolved oxygen showed opposite periodic changes. The water temperature will reach the lowest point in January each year and the highest point in July each year, forming a similar inverted 'W' curve; while the dissolved oxygen will reach the highest point in January and reach the highest point in July each year. The lowest, forming a 'W' curve, just the opposite of the change curve of water temperature. From the daily average curve, it can be seen that the dissolved oxygen concentration fluctuated in a small range compared with the slow change of water temperature, because the eutrophication of the water body caused its change to be relatively unstable. This situation will be more obvious in summer, because the water temperature in summer is the highest in the whole year, which promotes the repro-duction of algae and plankton, which makes the photosynthesis of algae stronger, causing the change of dissolved oxygen to exceed the change of water temperature condition. It can be seen that there is a negative correlation between water temperature and dissolved oxygen.

4.3 Regression Analysis

From the above visualization based on monthly and daily averages, we can see that the above graphs of changes in water temperature and dissolved oxygen tend to be almost opposite. The following linear regression analysis will be performed on these data to obtain the changing relationship between them and the influencing factors. By directly calling the sklearn library for machine learning commonly used in python, the following variables can be analyzed.

We selected the monthly average data of water temperature and dissolved oxygen in a basin from 2018 to 2020 for linear fitting, and the obtained effect is shown in Fig. 8. It can be seen from Fig. 8 that the univariate linear regression line of the monthly mean value of water temperature and dissolved oxygen is $y = 0.189x + 13.06$, and the correlation coefficient between them is $R = -0.87$, and the significance probability is $P < 0.01$.

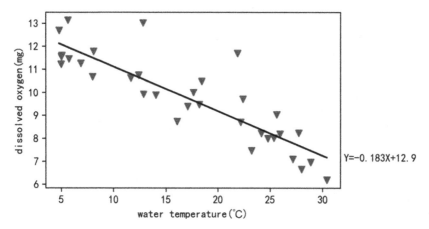

Fig. 8. Linear regression line of monthly mean value of water temperature and dissolved oxygen.

Next, linear fitting was performed on the daily average data of water temperature and dissolved oxygen in a certain watershed from 2018 to 2020. The obtained effect is shown in Fig. 9. The univariate linear regression line of water temperature and dissolved oxygen is $y = -0.183x + 12.9$, and the correlation coefficient between them is $R = -0.79$, and the significance probability is $P < 0.01$.

To sum up, it can be proved that water temperature and dissolved oxygen have a strong negative correlation, and the two variables are very significant.

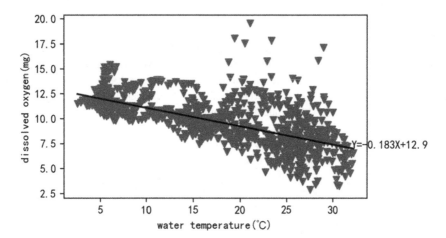

Fig. 9. Linear regression line of daily mean value of water temperature and dissolved oxygen.

4.4   Correlation Prediction

In order to verify the practicability of the model, the data of the next 5 days is analyzed through the water temperature variable, the predicted curve and the actual curve are visualized through matplotlib, and the error rate between the actual value and the predicted value is compared, and the visualized image is shown in the Fig. 10.

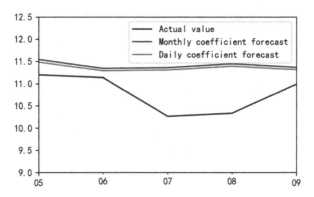

Fig.10.   Predicted curve vs. actual value.

The comparison between the predicted value and the actual value is shown in Table 4.

Table 4. Comparison of predicted and actual values.

Item	Value
Daily coefficient forecast	11.36
Monthly coefficient forecast	11.41
Actual value	10.78
Daily coefficient error rate	5%
Monthly coefficient error rate	6%

From the above-mentioned Fig. 10 and Table 4, the following conclusions can be drawn through the analysis of the forecast of the data in the next five days:

(1) The error rate of dissolved oxygen prediction by water temperature is very low, and the obtained prediction value has high accuracy. Therefore, this experiment has practical significance in the early warning of water quality in the actual process.

(2) The error between the daily average coefficient of each data and the predicted value of the monthly average coefficient is not large, basically about 1%, but the predicted value of the correlation coefficient of the monthly average is slightly higher than the predicted value of the correlation coefficient of the daily average, indicating that the daily In the process of measuring the mean value, there may be instrument measurement problems and the influence of natural factors, which may cause errors in the measured dissolved oxygen concentration on some days, while the monthly mean value reduces the impact of these errors.

(3) The change range of the curve of the predicted variable and the curve of the actual variable is basically the same, so the change trend of water quality in the next few days can be analyzed through the correlation line.

5 Summary

In this paper, the correlation analysis of dissolved oxygen is carried out by taking the water temperature in the water quality as a variable, and the correlation between them is verified after visual display and significant T test, and the daily average linear regression line and monthly average linear regression line are obtained respectively straight line. Finally, the dissolved oxygen in the water quality in the next five days is predicted through the correlation line, and the predicted value is compared with the actual value. From the perspective of forecasting, this prediction of data in the next few days through the correlation between variables can provide early warning of potential risks to water quality in the future, and provide a basis for the study of the safety management of regional waters. In addition, due to its limited level, we only add univariate factors as a correlation analysis in this paper. In the next process, we will use multivariate and more advanced elastic network for prediction.

Acknowledgement. This research was funded by the National Natural Science Foundation of China (No. 61304208), Scientific Research Fund of Hunan Province Education Department (18C0003), Research project on teaching reform in colleges and universities of Hunan Province Education Department (20190147), Changsha City Science and Technology Plan Program (K1501013-11), Hunan Normal University University-Industry Cooperation. This work is implemented at the 2011 Collaborative Innovation Center for Development and Utilization of Finance and Economics Big Data Property, Universities of Hunan Province, Open project, grant number 20181901CRP04.

References

1. Xiao, Y., Yisi, Z.G., Xiaobo, L., Qiang, D., Hong, T.: Evolution mechanism of dissolved oxygen stratification structure in large deep-water reservoirs. Lake Sci. **30**(05), 1496–1507 (2020)
2. Jia, J., Hua, Z., Xiao, T.: Status and progress of surface water monitoring in environmental monitoring. Low Carbon World **9**(03), 22–23 (2019)
3. Xiao, Y.: Variation of dissolved oxygen in Manju reservoir and analysis of influencing factors. Environ. Sci. Guide **40**(01), 56–58 (2021)
4. Zhang, J., Sheng, Y., Chen, W., Lin, H., Sun, G., et al.: Design and analysis of a water quality monitoring data service platform. Comput. Mater. Continua **66**(1), 389–405 (2021)
5. Sun, G., Li, F.H., Jiang, W.D.: Brief talk about big data graph analysis and visualization. J. Big Data **1**(1), 25–38 (2019)
6. Yang, B., Xiang, L., Chen, X., Jia, W.: An online chronic disease prediction system based on incremental deep neural network. Comput. Mater. Continua **67**(1), 951–964 (2021)
7. Sheng, Y., Zhang, J., Tan, W., Wu, J., Lin, H., et al.: Application of grey model and neural network in financial revenue forecast. Comput. Mater. Continua **69**(3), 4043–4059 (2021)
8. Chun, L.: Design of big data acquisition system based on web crawler technology. Mod. Electron. Tech. **44**(16), 115–119 (2021)
9. Yan, Z., Yuquan, W.: Design of network data crawler program based on python. Comput. Program. Skills Maintenance **04**, 26–27 (2020)
10. Cheng, T., Hang, C., Hai, T., Ze, W.: Research and application of data preprocessing methods in the context of big data. Inf. Record. Mater. **22**(09), 199–200 (2021)
11. Shi, Y., Xiao, C., Lin, S.: Python-based data desensitization and visual analysis. Comput. Knowl. Technol. **15**(06), 14–17 (2019)
12. Qin, S., Chang, Y.: Research on data preprocessing methods for big data. Comput. Technol. Dev. **28**(05), 1–4 (2018)
13. Ying, Y.: Big data cleaning method for transmission and transformation equipment status based on time series analysis. Autom. Power Syst. **39**(07), 138–144 (2015)
14. Li, X.: Algorithms and applications of cluster analysis. Jilin University, pp. 13–20 (2010)
15. Jian, L., Huan, X., Yi, X., Yi, S.: Tea price forecast in Guizhou based on time series and logistic regression. Inf. Technol. Inform. **07**, 70–75 (2021)
16. Jin, Q., Chun, Z.: Analysis of correlation between land use pattern and water quality in Hanfeng lake watershed of Kaizhou. Sichuan Environ. **36**(01), 58–63 (2017)

A Database File Storage Optimization Strategy Based on High-Relevance Mode Access Data Compression

Rui Gao[1], Yixuan Lu[2], Jian Liu[3], Jun Yu[1], Weiguo Tian[2], Haiwen Du[4],
Chuanmeng Kang[2], Weiqi Yin[2], and Dongjie Zhu[2(✉)]

[1] Shanghai J.Y-JZ Network Technology Service Co., Ltd., Shanghai 200233, China
[2] School of Computer Science and Technology, Harbin Institute of Technology,
Weihai 264209, China
`zhudongjie@hit.edu.cn`
[3] Shanghai J.Y Ba-Shi Passenger Transport (Group) Co., Ltd.,
Shanghai 200065, China
[4] School of Astronautics, Harbin Institute of Technology, Harbin 150001, China

Abstract. With the improvement of social informatization and the popularization of Internet of Things devices, the scale, complexity and diversity of data are currently growing rapidly, and traditional storage solutions have been unable to meet the complex and diverse applications and large-scale new storage requirements. Existing storage solutions still have deficiencies in data compression and adapting to the diversity of system architectures, resulting in a large waste of storage space resources, which in turn increases the total cost of ownership of platform data. Therefore, this paper will study the data compression strategy of database file storage, and propose a high-relevance mode access data compression method. The data request of the write-only instance of the database hosted on the cloud platform is aggregated with the system workload. The data stored in the write-only instance is compressed, which improves data storage efficiency and storage space utilization. The method was validated using data in real enterprise scenarios. The experimental results show that the proposed method has a certain degree of improvement in storage space utilization compared with the original method.

Keywords: Storage space optimization · Data compression

1 Introduction

In recent years, with the popularization of 5G technology and the derivation of new concepts of the iot such as smart city [4], smart transportation [1], smart wellness service [2], and smart home [6], the scale of network data has expanded rapidly, and the complexity and diversity have also increased[7]. In comparison to 2009, the data production will be 44 times greater with rapid increase in volume, velocity and variety of the data [8].

© The Author(s), under exclusive license to Springer Nature Switzerland AG 2022
X. Sun et al. (Eds.): ICAIS 2022, CCIS 1587, pp. 353–363, 2022.
https://doi.org/10.1007/978-3-031-06761-7_29

As the scale of big data applications continues to expand, traditional single-node services can no longer meet the current explosive business requests. At the same time, currently cloud computing plays an important role in the provision of services such as storage, resource access, and resource pooling [10]. Therefore, users and enterprises are gradually using rapidly evolving cloud platforms to host databases to support real-time addition, deletion, modification, and checking of high-throughput data [3]. At present, the database hosted on the cloud platform is mainly oriented to scenarios with a large amount of visits and many read requests, so a "read-write separation" infrastructure is adopted [11]. The read-only instance is only used as data storage, and it performs real-time data synchronization with the bound write-only instance to ensure data consistency. In addition, the size of a single data request of many systems is much less than 1 KB, which will cause CPU performance to become a bottleneck for system throughput [13]. Frequent data I/O operations will also result in huge waste of resources and reduce the disk space life of cloud service providers [12]. In order to ensure the use of scenarios such as expansion and disaster recovery, the database will regularly back up the data files stored in the cloud platform [9].

However, the current method does not compress the data files, resulting in a large waste of network bandwidth for data transmission, and unable to effectively utilize storage space. At the same time, due to the diversity of data access, data requests generate additional processing overhead on critical I/O paths. Mao et al. proposed an elastic data compression scheme called EDC, which uses the compression characteristics of different compression algorithms to compress access data and write it to the storage system, which significantly improves I/O performance [5], but may increase the burden of resources such as cpu. In response to the above problems, we analyze the current data access mode, include the CPU and memory usage of the system load into the research scope, and combine the characteristics of SSD storage media to propose a high-relevance mode access data compression strategy, which improves the overall utilization of the media storage space in the cloud platform, thereby reducing the total cost of data ownership of the cloud platform, and ensuring the speed and efficiency of data processing.

2   Data Compression

In the era of big data, as the amount of data stored by users continues to grow, it is necessary to improve the overall utilization of system resources on the premise of ensuring the total cost of data ownership. In the database system, its architecture is divided into application layer, logical layer and physical layer (storage layer). The application layer is responsible for information interaction with the client, and the logic layer is responsible for additional functions such as data query processing and storage management. The physical layer is the storage layer, which stores database files, such as various user data and log files. The database infrastructure widely used by cloud service providers is shown in Fig. 1.

It can be seen from Fig. 1 that the database infrastructure of cloud service providers nowadays adopts a read-write separation architecture model. Proxy

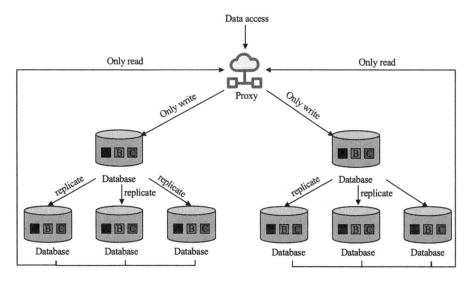

Fig. 1. database infrastructure

divides which read-only or write-only instance each data request should be allocated to for processing. The requests can be allocated based on hashing, the remainder of the number of requests, etc. The write-only instance handles frequent data write requests. In real scenarios, the data write size is mostly less than 1 KB. Such frequent data write requests of less than 1 KB will deplete the life of the new NVMe SSD hard drive. The subject's research on the data storage method in the database found that the requested data is not written directly into the data file, but written into the log file. When the log is saved successfully, the client can consider that the data has been successfully stored, and does not need to save the data to the data file immediately. This method can effectively reduce the overall data request delay and make the user unaware of the specific operation of the data. Therefore, the subject proposes a high-relevance mode access data compression strategy design. Set a time window to accumulate access requests for data requests in the write-only instance, and then sample the data in the time window to detect the data content to determine whether it is suitable for data compressing, then select the data compression algorithm according to the current system workload to compress and store the data in the time window, as shown in Fig. 2.

We set the time window threshold $Time_{th}$ and the expected data length threshold $Size_{th}$ in the time window. Within the threshold time range and when the expected data length threshold is not met, the data requests within the time window will not be stored persistently, but will be accumulated Called a data file. Only when the data accumulation time is greater than the time window threshold $Time_{th}$ or the data length in the time window is greater than the expected data length threshold, the sampler will detect the data in the time window and determine which compression algorithm it uses is more suitable for

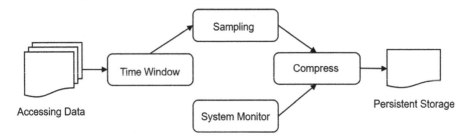

Fig. 2. High-relevance mode access data compression strategy design schematic

the current workload. Then obtain the CPU and memory of the current system workload through the system monitor, construct a dynamic compression strategy based on the workload, and select a data compression algorithm to compress and store the data files accumulated in the time window. The dynamic compression strategy formula based on workload is shown in (1).

$$Level(D) = D \times \bar{R}_x + \widehat{T_{cx}}(D) + \alpha \cdot \widehat{C_{cx}}(D) + \beta \cdot \widehat{M_{cx}}(D) \tag{1}$$

Among them, D represents the data size, $\bar{R}_x$ represents the average compression rate of the selected x compression algorithm, $\widehat{T_{cx}}$ is the predicted compression time of the selected x compression algorithm, $\widehat{C_{cx}}(D)$ and $\widehat{M_{cx}}(D)$ are the impact values of the CPU and memory changes caused by the selected x compression algorithm. α and β are the weight coefficients of CPU and memory respectively.

This paper uses a multi-threaded approach to process data in a time window. However, if threads are frequently created and destroyed or threads are frequently switched to process data, it will cause higher thread processing costs and reduce data processing efficiency. Therefore, this paper proposes a data processing thread model, as shown in Fig. 3.

As shown in the data processing thread model in Fig. 3, when the number of currently active worker threads exceeds the threshold, idle threads will be put into the thread waiting queue for waiting. If the thread in the waiting queue waits for a timeout, it will be destroyed. The thread waiting queue adopts the head insertion method, which can ensure that the thread used must be the thread that finishes the work last, which improves the efficiency of thread usage. For the listener, when the data request receiver receives a data processing request, it will get data from the request queue. Then try to wake up the thread from the thread waiting queue. If the wake-up is successful, use the awakened thread to process the data in the data request queue. If the wake-up fails, a new thread is created as the data request processing thread. The pseudo code of the data processing thread model is shown in Table 1.

As the database infrastructure in the cloud platform is shown in Fig. 1, data is only written to write-only nodes, not read-only nodes. Data synchronization

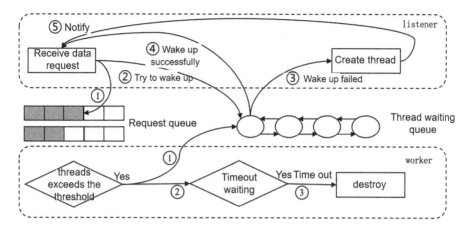

Fig. 3. Data processing thread model

between write-only nodes and read-only nodes can only be done through write-only nodes. We use parallel replication to replicate the binlog, as shown in Fig. 4.

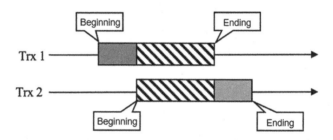

Fig. 4. Data parallel replication

When the storage engine of the read-only node submits the data, the first lock held is released, and the time interval for the transaction to hold the lock ends. When the last holding lock is acquired, the lock holding interval of the transaction starts to count.

In the Trx 1 transaction in Fig. 4, the *Beginning* and *Ending* represent the time interval for a transaction to hold the lock, and the *Beginning* represents the binlog_prepare phase of the transaction. The transaction holding lock of Trx 1 started earlier than Trx 2, but the time interval of the transaction holding the lock between Trx 1 and Trx 2 overlaps, and then the binlog log can be copied in parallel. At the end of the lock-holding interval of each transaction, each transaction will be assigned a logical timestamp. If the minimum logical timestamp of the transaction being executed is greater than the timestamp of the last transaction commit of a transaction, the write-only node can execute the transaction and continue processing the data.

Table 1. Data processing thread model pseudo code.

Algorithm model name: data processing thread model
Algorithm model input: data request
Algorithm model output: processed data

```
Begin
1   if threadpool_max_threads ¿ active_thread:
2       wait_header_insert(thread_id):
3       if check_timeout:
4           destroy_thread(thread_id)
5       end if
6   end if
8   while monitor_data_queue:
9       if wait_begin:
10          // Data processing
11      else
12          create_thread()
13  end while
14  return // Processed data
End
```

3 Experiment

The subject conducts experiments of the access compression strategy algorithm for the high-relevance mode, compares with the existing methods, and analyzes from the storage space.

3.1 Experimental Configuration

The experimental operating environment of this paper is shown in Table 2.

Table 2. Experimental environment configuration.

Property	Type
CPU	Intel (R) Xeon (R) Gold 6240 @2.60 GHz
DRAM	378 GB 2400 MHz
SSD	Intel DC P4510 2TB
OS	CentOS release 6.1, 64bit
Linux kernal version	3.10.0

The workload of the high-relevance mode access compression strategy comes from the real enterprise scenario, and the access data set is randomly generated.

3.2   Experimental Results and Analysis

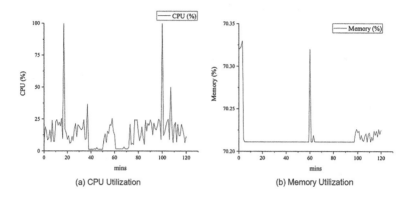

(a) CPU Utilization   (b) Memory Utilization

Fig. 5. Burst task workload

Figure 5 shows the 2 h workload of an enterprise server we collected. From Fig. 5, it can be seen that the system workload CPU and memory may increase sharply in a certain period of time, and in Most of the time memory utilization has not changed much.

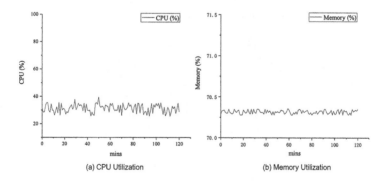

(a) CPU Utilization   (b) Memory Utilization

Fig. 6. Smooth task workload 1

Figure 6 is a diagram of a stable task workload. The CPU and memory usage within 2 h is relatively stable, the CPU utilization rate is low, and the memory usage rate is close to the memory usage rate of the burst task workload. The workload in Fig. 7 comes from application services deployed on cloud servers. It is found that the memory usage rate may change with the changes in the CPU usage rate, but the overall change is not large, while the CPU usage rate changes bigger.

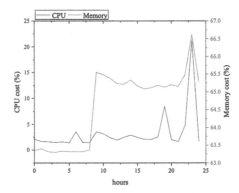

Fig. 7. Smooth task workload 2

Our research on workloads in real scenarios found that the smallest TPS in a day is 209, so the window time in the high-relevancy mode access compression strategy is set to 1 s, and the expected data length in the time window is 128 KB. In real scenes, the CPU usage is often less than half, while the memory usage is usually above 60%. Therefore, set α in formula (1) to 0.3 and β to 0.7.

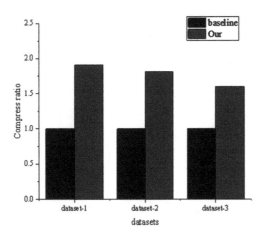

Fig. 8. Data compression for write-only node storage space

From Fig. 8, it can be found that the data storage space of the write-only node is better optimized when the high-relevancy mode access compression strategy algorithm is used compared with the baseline that does not use the compression algorithm for data processing. Moreover, due to the particularity of database data persistence, the system delay will not change. Accumulation and processing of data in the access request can reduce I/O jitter and frequent write overhead.

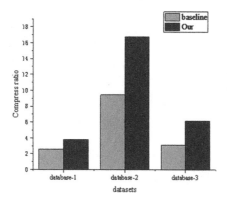

Fig. 9. Database backup file compression ratio

The compression algorithm used by the baseline in Fig. 9 is the quicklz algorithm, which is compared with the algorithm proposed in this article. The comparison between different database backups can show the effectiveness of the algorithm proposed in this paper. When testing the database file backup, 4 threads are used to (de)compress the data file, and the result is shown in Fig. 10. It can be seen from the figure that the algorithm proposed in this paper has a greater improvement in decompression time compared with the baseline, and the performance of the compression speed on the data set is the same as that of the baseline.

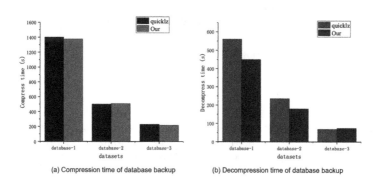

Fig. 10. Time of (de)compressing database backup files

4   Conclusion

This article addresses the problem of low storage efficiency of database files currently hosted on cloud platforms. Aiming at the waste of storage space for read-only instance data in the database infrastructure, a high-relevance mode access data compression strategy is proposed, which combines system resources to compress data storage and reduces the total cost of data ownership. Experiments show that the database storage optimization strategy proposed in this paper has improved the data storage utilization rate, and the space utilization rate of the write-only instance in the database has been improved.

There are still some shortcomings and room for improvement in this article. In the future, improvements will be made in the following aspects:

(1) The current data compression technology needs to be compatible with the diversity of data access, and the data request generates additional processing overhead on the key I/O path, and it will occupy the original system resources when processing the data online. Therefore, for requests with a small data scale, the compression category can be added as a window cumulative dimension to split data with different characteristics. Perform aggregate compression on data requests applicable to the same compression algorithm to improve compression efficiency.
(2) With the development of memory computing technology in recent years, data can be placed in the storage layer for calculation, reducing data I/O overhead.

Acknowledgement. The authors would like to thank the associate editor and the reviewers for their time and effort provided to review the manuscript.

Funding Information. This work is supported by the Fundamental Research Funds for the Central Universities (Grant No. HIT. NSRIF. 201714), Weihai Science and Technology Development Program (2016DX GJMS15), Future Network Scientific Research Fund Project (SN: FNSRFP-2021-YB-56) and Key Research and Development Program in Shandong Provincial (2017GGX90103).

Conflicts of Interest. The authors declare that they have no conflicts of interest to report regarding the present study.

References

1. Babar, M., Arif, F.: Real-time data processing scheme using big data analytics in internet of things based smart transportation environment. J. Ambient. Intell. Humaniz. Comput. **10**(10), 4167–4177 (2018). https://doi.org/10.1007/s12652-018-0820-5
2. Farooq, U., Ryoo, I., Khang, G.: A smart wellness service platform and its practical implementation. Comput. Mater. Continua **66**(1), 45–57 (2021)
3. Khan, A., et al.: Intelligent cloud based load balancing system empowered with fuzzy logic. Comput. Mater. Continua **67**, 519–528 (2021)
4. Hoon Kim, T., Ramos, C., Mohammed, S.: Smart city and IOT. Futur. Gener. Comput. Syst. **76**, 159–162 (2017)
5. Mao, B., Wu, S., Jiang, H., Yang, Y., Xi, Z.: Edc: Improving the performance and space efficiency of flash-based storage systems with elastic data compression. IEEE Trans. Parallel Distrib. Syst. **29**(6), 1261–1274 (2018)

6. Marikyan, D., Papagiannidis, S., Alamanos, E.: A systematic review of the smart home literature: a user perspective. Technol. Forecast. Soc. Chang. **138**, 139–154 (2019)
7. Mehmood, F., Ahmad, S., Ullah, I., Jamil, F., Kim, D.: Towards a dynamic virtual IOT network based on user requirements. Comput. Mater. Continua **69**, 2231–2244 (2021)
8. Sahu, P., Singh, D., Singh, A.: Blockchain based secure solution for cloud storage: a model for synchronizing industry 4.0 and IOT. J. Cyber Security **3**, 107–115 (2021)
9. Son, Y., et al.: Ssd-assisted backup and recovery for database systems. In: 2017 IEEE 33rd International Conference on Data Engineering, ICDE, pp. 285–296 (2017)
10. Sridharan, M., Murugaiyan, C.: Virtualized load balancer for hybrid cloud using genetic algorithm. Intell. Autom. Soft Comput. **32**, 1459–1466 (2021)
11. Takruri, H., Kettaneh, I., Alquraan, A., Al-Kiswany, S.: FLAIR: accelerating reads with consistency-aware network routing. In: 17th USENIX Symposium on Networked Systems Design and Implementation, NSDI 20, pp. 723–737. USENIX Association, Santa Clara, Febuary 2020
12. Wu, S., Yi, Y., Xiao, J., Jin, H., Ye, M.: A large-scale study of i/o workload's impact on disk failure. IEEE Access **6**, 47385–47396 (2018)
13. Yang, J., Yue, Y., Rashmi, K.V.: A large scale analysis of hundreds of in-memory cache clusters at twitter. In: 14th USENIX Symposium on Operating Systems Design and Implementation, OSDI 2020, pp. 191–208. USENIX Association, November 2020

Efficient Designated-Server Proxy Re-encryption with Keyword Search for Big Data

Miaolei Deng[1(✉)], Wenshuai Song[1], Mimi Ma[1], Haochen Li[1],
and Muhammad Israr[2]

[1] College of Information Science and Engineering, Henan University of Technology,
Zhengzhou 450001, China
`dengmiaolei@163.com`
[2] Department of Information Technology, Hazara University,
Mansehra 21300, Pakistan

Abstract. Against the background of the era of big data and cloud computing, cloud platforms have become the first choice for data storage. While cloud platforms also face serious threats to data security and user privacy. At the same time, users will be faced with the problem of how to efficiently retrieve ciphertext on the cloud. Searchable encryption allows users to directly retrieve ciphertext data on the cloud through keywords, which provides an effective method for solving efficient retrieval of ciphertext on the cloud. As an important branch of searchable encryption technology, proxy re-encryption can realize the sharing of ciphertext among multiple users. However, most of the existing schemes have security shortcomings or functional defects, such as inability to resist keyword guessing attack, and do not support search authority authorization. A new designated-server proxy re-encryption with keyword search scheme was proposed, which not only can resist keyword guessing attack, but also realizes the function of sharing search authority. Finally, we give the performance and security analysis. The experimental results show that our scheme is superior compared with other related schemes.

Keywords: Cloud security · Big data · Keyword guessing attack · Proxy re-encryption · Searchable encryption

1 Introduction

With the rapid development of 5G and Internet of Things (IoT) technology [25], the amount of data is growing explosively. The technology of processing big data through artificial intelligence and security are constantly being proposed [1,2,22]. However, traditional storage systems have been unable to satisfy the needs of big data storage. Cloud storage has attracted wide attention due to its advantages of high flexibility, on-demand purchase and convenient access. At present, it has been involved in several areas [16]. To solve how to efficiently retrieve ciphertext on the cloud, searchable encryption (SE) was proposed. The

X. Sun et al. (Eds.): ICAIS 2022, CCIS 1587, pp. 364–377, 2022.
https://doi.org/10.1007/978-3-031-06761-7_30

first public key encryption with keyword search (PEKS) scheme for mail routing was proposed by Boneh et al. [5]. In the PEKS scheme, the ciphertext is encrypted with the public key of the e-mail receiver and uploaded to the cloud server by e-mail encryption user. The receiver uses the private key to generate keyword trapdoors for matching ciphertext retrieval. So as to improve the efficiency of ciphertext retrieval. Later, a lot of PEKS schemes have been proposed to improve security and extend functions [9,12,13]. Proxy re-encryption with keyword search (PREKS) as a new cryptographic primitive was first proposed by Shao et al. [17]. However, traditional PREKS scheme cannot resist inside keyword guessing attack. In order to solve these issues, we construct a new designated-server proxy re-encryption with keyword search scheme.

2   Related Works

2.1   Keyword Guessing Attack

keyword guessing attack (KGA) called an adversary can guess all possible keywords and verify the speculation in the form of offline or online. Byun et al. [6] found that in real life users usually choose keywords that have special meaning to them. As a result, the information entropy in the keyword space is relatively small. Attackers can carry out offline keyword guessing attack by exhaustively enumerating common keywords when obtaining an effective trapdoors. Jeong et al. [11] pointed that there is no PEKS scheme can satisfy both algorithm consistency and security under KGA. In order to resist KGA, Baek et al. [3], Rhee et al. [14,15] and others have successively made research and Rhee proposed the concept of indistinguishability of trapdoors. Rhee proved that the indistinguishability of trapdoors is a sufficient condition to resist KGA. When a malicious server attacks trapdoor, it is called inside keyword guessing attack (IKGA). Wang et al. [20] introduced a dual-server model. However, this scheme is computationally expensive and can defend IKGA only when the servers are not complicit. The literature [19] generates ciphertext by means of signcryption algorithm, and uses an additional message authentication code to verify the return result to the data receiver. But this scheme has a higher communication cost. Huang et al. [10] designed a public key authenticated encryption with keyword search (PAEKS). With this method, the cloud server cannot generate search trapdoors to guess keywords, but it cannot completely resist KGA. The search trapdoor generation algorithm in this scheme is a deterministic algorithm, keyword statistics cannot be hidden, so there is still the problem of inside guessing attacks. The current solution to defend inside keyword guessing attacks does not have a limited calculation and a good balance of efficiency.

2.2   Proxy Re-encryption with Keyword Search

When it was necessary to share plaintext information in the past, User A downloads the ciphertext to the local for decryption, and sends the plaintext to user B. However, this method consumes a lot of resources and is inefficient. Therefore, the proxy spontaneously arises. The concept of proxy was proposed by Blaze et al. [4]. The proposal of proxy provides a new idea for data sharing. In proxy re-encryption concept, a semi-trusted proxy server implements the conversion of user A's ciphertext into a ciphertext that can be decrypted by user B's private key. During the entire encryption and decryption process, the proxy server cannot derive any relevant information in the plaintext, thus ensuring the privacy and security of information. The existence of an agent makes information sharing safer and more convenient. Subsequently, many PRES schemes [7,8,24] have been constructed. Chen et al. [7] designed a PREKS model with restricted keyword search. Xu et al. [23] also designed a scheme for proxy authorization designation in electronic health record.

2.3 Our Contribution

In order to resist keyword guessing attack, we propose a new designated-server PREKS scheme. Specific contributions are where:

1. We designed a new proxy re-encryption algorithm to resist IKGA.
2. This scheme designs a new proxy key generation method to re-encrypt ciphertext.
3. Based on the assumption of the decision liner problem (DLIN) problem, the keyword ciphertext and trapdoor are both generated by non-deterministic algorithms to meet the indistinguishability of search trapdoor and keyword ciphertext, and security has been proved in the random oracle model.

3   Preliminaries

3.1   Bilinear Pairing

Definition 1: G_1 and G_T are two cyclic groups with prime order p, g is a generator of the group G_1 . We say $\hat{e} : G_1 \times G_1 \rightarrow G_T$ is a bilinear pairing if it satisfies the following properties:

(1) Bilinear: $\forall a, b \in Z_q^*$, $\hat{e}(g^a, g^b) = \hat{e}(g, g)^{ab}$.
(2) Non-degenerate: $\exists g \in G_1$, s.t. $\hat{e}(g, g) \neq 1$.
(3) Computablity: $\forall u, v \in G_1$, there are effective algorithms to compute $\hat{e}(u, v)$.

3.2   Difficult Problem Assumptions

Definition 2 (DLIN): Given $g, g^x, g^y, g^{xr}, g^{sy}, g^u \in G_1$, where $x, y, r, s, u \in Z_p^*$ are random numbers, g is a generator of G_1. For any probabilistic polynomial time algorithm A, if A correctly distinguishing g^{r+s} from g^u is negligible, then the DLIN problem is difficult.

Definition 3 (mDLIN): Given $g, g^x, g^y, g^{r/x}, g^{sy}, g^u \in G_1$, where $x, y, r, s, u \in Z_p^*$ are random numbers, g is a generator of G_1. For any probabilistic polynomial time algorithm A, if A correctly distinguishing g^{r+s} from g^u is negligible, then the DLIN problem is difficult.

Definition 4 (mDLIN*) [21]: Given $g, g^x, g^{r/x}, g^{sx}, g^u \in G_1$, where $x, y, r, s, u \in Z_p^*$ are random numbers, g is a generator of G_1. For any probabilistic polynomial time algorithm A, if A correctly distinguishing $g^{r+s^{-1}}$ from g^u is negligible, then the DLIN problem is difficult.

3.3   System Model

Figure 1 shows the four participants of our scheme and the interaction between them.

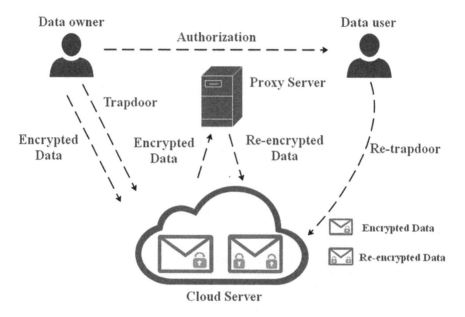

Fig. 1. Framework of scheme model

Data owner (DO): DO encrypts the data and uploads to the cloud server. Moreover, DO authorizes data user search permission.

Data user (DU): DU can perform keyword matching on the re-encrypted ciphertext after obtaining the authorization qualification.

Cloud server (CS): CS stores ciphertext and re-encrypted ciphertext.

Proxy server (PS): PS uses relevant information to generate a proxy key and re-encrypts the ciphertext to send the CS.

9 polynomial-time algorithms of the scheme are where:

1) $Setup(\lambda)$: Input the given security parameters and the system generates public parameters $params$ through algorithms.
2) $KeyGen(params)$: Input system parameter $params$. Then output key pair (PK_{do}, SK_{do}), (PK_{du}, SK_{du}), (PK_{cs}, SK_{cs}).

3) $Encrypt(params, w, SK_{do}, PK_{cs})$: DO inputs the keyword w, SK_{do} and PK_{cs}, outputs the ciphertext C.

4) $Trapdoor(params, w, SK_{do}, PK_{cs})$: DO inputs keyword w, SK_{do} and PK_{cs}. Outputs the trapdoor T_w.

5) $Test(params, PK_{do}, SK_{cs}, C, T_w)$: Input ciphertext C, trapdoor T_w, DO's public key PK_{do} and CS's private key SK_{cs}. If the match is successful, output 1 and return the ciphertext to DO, otherwise return 0.

6) $Proxy(params, SK_{do}, SK_{du})$: DO authorizes to DU, The algorithms outputs the proxy key rk.

7) $Re-encrypt(params, C, rk)$: Input the ciphertext C and the proxy key rk. Output the re-encrypted ciphertext $\hat{C}$.

8) $Re-trapdoor(params, SK_{du}, w)$: Input SK_{du} and w. Output re-trapdoor $\hat{T}_w$.

9) $Re-test(params, \hat{C}, \hat{T}_w, PK_{du}, SK_{cs})$: Input re-encryption ciphertext $\hat{C}$, trapdoor $\hat{T}_w$, when the match is successful, output 1 and return the ciphertext to DU, otherwise output 0.

3.4 Security Model

In the literature [15], Rhee pointed that sufficient condition is the indistinguishability of ciphertext and trapdoor of KGA. Therefore, in order to resistance KGA by an inside adversary, the solution needs to ensure that the adversary meets the following requirements under the premise of the known server private key: Game I the indistinguishability of the trapdoor. Game II the indistinguishability of the keyword ciphertext. The definition is given below through two games.

Game I (Indistinguishability of trapdoor): Challenger $\mathcal{C}$ generates the global parameter P, the key pair of (PK_{do}, SK_{do}), (PK_{du}, SK_{du}), (PK_{cs}, SK_{cs}). $\mathcal{C}$ send P, PK_{do}, PK_{du} and the CS key pair (PK_{cs}, SK_{cs}) to the adversary $\mathcal{A}$.

Adversary $\mathcal{A}$ adaptively queries oracles. Given CS public key PK_{cs} and keyword w, the keyword ciphertext oracle O_C returns the keyword ciphertext C to $\mathcal{A}$. Given PK_{cs} and w, the search trapdoor oracle O_T returns T_w and $\hat{T}_w$ to $\mathcal{A}$. The oracle O_{rk} obtains the re-encryption key rk, and sends rk to $\mathcal{A}$. The O_C runs the $Re-proxy$ algorithm to obtain the re-encryption ciphertext $\hat{C}$, and gives $\hat{C}$ to $\mathcal{A}$.

$\mathcal{A}$ chooses two keywords w_0^*, w_1^* that has not been asked about the oracle O_C, and sends them to $\mathcal{C}$, and the $\mathcal{C}$ randomly selects $b \in \{0, 1\}$ to send $T_{w_b^*}$ and $\hat{T}_{w_b^*}$ to $\mathcal{A}$. Adversary $\mathcal{A}$ can continue to access the oracle machine but cannot access oracle machine O_C on the keywords w_0^*, w_1^*. Adversary $\mathcal{A}$ outputs $b' \in \{0, 1\}$ to guess the keyword w_b^*. If $b' = b$, then adversary $\mathcal{A}$ wins.

Define the advantage of $\mathcal{A}$ to successfully distinguish the keyword search trapdoor as:

$$Adv_A^T(\lambda) = |Pr[b' = b] - \frac{1}{2}| \tag{1}$$

Game II (Indistinguishability of ciphertext): Same as above Game I, challenger $\mathcal{C}$ generates the global parameter p, the key pair of DO (PK_{do}, SK_{do}), DU (PK_{du}, SK_{du}), and CS (PK_{cs}, SK_{cs}) according to the given security parameter

λ. $\mathcal{C}$ send p, PK_{do}, PK_{du} and the CS key pair (PK_{cs}, SK_{cs}) to the adversary $\mathcal{A}$. Same as above Game I, $\mathcal{A}$ can adaptively challenge the oracles O_C, O_T and 0_{rk}, and the number of queries is limited by polynomial time. Two keywords w_0^*, w_1^* are selected by $\mathcal{A}$ that has not been asked about the oracle O_T, and sends them to challenger $\mathcal{C}$, and the challenger $\mathcal{C}$ randomly selects $b \in \{0, 1\}$. And calculate the ciphertext C_b^* and $\hat{C}_b^*$ of the keyword w_b^* and send to $\mathcal{A}$. $\mathcal{A}$ outputs $b' \in \{0, 1\}$ to guess the keyword w_b^*. If $b' = b$, then $\mathcal{A}$ wins.

Define the advantage of $\mathcal{A}$ to successfully distinguish the ciphertext as:

$$Adv_A^C(\lambda) = |Pr[b' = b] - \frac{1}{2}| \tag{2}$$

4   Concrete Structure of the Proposed Scheme

This section presents the concrete structure and correctness verification of the scheme algorithm.

4.1   The Algorithm Structure

1) *Setup(λ)*: Input the security parameter λ to generate the public parameter $params = \{p, g, h, G_1, G_T, \hat{e}, H\}$ where G_1 and G_T are cyclic group of with order p, g and h are generators of group G_1, $\hat{e}: G_1 \times G_1 \to G_T$ is a bilinear mapping. $H : \{0, 1\}^* \to G_1$ is a hash function.

2) *KeyGen(params)*: DO randomly selects $x \leftarrow Z_p^*$ as the private key SK_{do}, and $PK_{do} = g^x$ as the public key; DU randomly selects $y \leftarrow Z_p^*$ to generate SK_{du} and $PK_{du} = g^y$; CS selects the random number $z \leftarrow Z_p^*$ to generate SK_{cs} and $PK_{cs} = g^z$.

3) *Encrypt(params, w, SK_{do}, PK_{cs})* $\to$ C: Given CS public key PK_{cs}, DO selects a random number $r \leftarrow Z_p$ and calculates the key word ciphertext $C = (C_1, C_2)$, where:

$$C_1 = H(w)^{SK_{do}} \cdot (PK_{cs})^{SK_{do} \cdot r}, C_2 = h^r \tag{3}$$

4) *Trapdoor(params, w, SK_{do}, PK_{cs})* $\to$ T_w: DO selects the random number $s \leftarrow Z_p^*$, and uses private key SK_{do} to calculate the search trapdoor $T_w = (T_1, T_2)$ corresponding to the query keyword w, where:

$$T_1 = H(w)^{SK_{do}} \cdot (PK_{cs})^{SK_{do} \cdot s}, T_2 = h^s \tag{4}$$

5) *Test(parmas, PK_{do}, SK_{cs}, C, T_w)* $\to$ *0/1*: After CS receives the DO's query trapdoor T_w, if the matching relationship satisfies $\hat{e}(\frac{C_1}{T_1}, h) = \hat{e}(PK_{do}, \frac{C_2}{T_2})^{SK_{cs}}$, then output 1; Otherwise output 0.

6) *Proxy(parmas, SK_{do}, SK_{du})* $\to$ *rk*: The ps generates a DO to DU re-encrypt key $rk = y/x$ for the first time by interacting with DO and DU. The interaction method is as follows:

    1. DO randomly selects $m \leftarrow Z_p^*$, sends $(x \cdot m)^{-1}$ to DU, and sends m to PS.

2. DU sends $(x \cdot m)^{-1} \cdot y$ to PS.
3. Combining the information sent by DO and DU, the PS calculates $rk = y/x$.

7) *Re-encrypt(params, C, rk)$\rightarrow \hat{C}$*: For ciphertext C, the PS uses rk generates re-encrypted ciphertext $\hat{C} = (\hat{C}_1, \hat{C}_2)$, and uploads to the CS, where:

$$\hat{C}_1 = C_1^{rk} = (H(w)^{SK_{do}} \cdot (PK_{cs})^{SK_{do} \cdot r})^{rk}, \hat{C}_2 = h^r \tag{5}$$

8) *Re-trapdoor(params, SK_{du}, Pk_{cs}, w)$\rightarrow \hat{T}_w$*: DU randomly selects $s \rightarrow Z_p^*$ and calculates the re-trapdoor corresponding to the query keyword w $\hat{T}_w = (\hat{T}_1, \hat{T}_2)$, where:

$$\hat{T}_1 = H(w)^{Sk_{du}} \cdot (PK_{cs})^{SK_{du} \cdot s}, \hat{T}_2 = h^s \tag{6}$$

9) *Test(params, $\hat{C}$, $\hat{T}_w$, PK_{du}, SK_{cs})$\rightarrow$ 0/1*: The CS receives DU's re-trapdoor $\hat{T}_w$, if the matching relationship satisfies $\hat{e}(\frac{\hat{C}_1}{\hat{T}_1}, h) = \hat{e}(PK_{du}, \frac{\hat{C}_2}{\hat{T}_2})^{SK_{cs}}$, then output 1; Otherwise output 0.

4.2   Correctness of the Scheme

The description of correctness in the proposed efficient designated-server PREKS scheme is divided into two parts: 1. The correctness of the Encrypt. 2. The correctness of the Re-encrypt.

1. The Correctness of the Encrypt

Given the query keywords w, DO's key pair $(PK_{do}, SK_{do}) = (g^x, x)$, CS key pair $(PK_{cs}, SK_{cs}) = (g^z, z)$, if the keyword ciphertext matches the search trapdoor, there are:

$$\begin{aligned} \hat{e}(C_1/T_1, h) &= \hat{e}(H(w)^x g^{zxr}/H(w)^x g^{zxs}, h) \\ &= \hat{e}(g^{zx(r-s)}, h) = \hat{e}(g^x, h^{r-s})^z \\ &= \hat{e}(g^x, h^r/h^s)^z = \hat{e}(PK_{do}, C_2/T_2)^{SK_{cs}} \end{aligned} \tag{7}$$

2. The Correctness of the Re-encrypted

Given the query keywords w, DU's key pair $(PK_{du}, SK_{du}) = (g^y, y)$, CS key pair $(PK_{cs}, SK_{cs}) = (g^z, z)$, proxy key rk, if the re-encrypted keyword ciphertext matches the search proxy trapdoor, there are:

$$\begin{aligned} \hat{e}(\hat{C}_1/\hat{T}_1, h) &= \hat{e}((C_1)^{rk}/\hat{T}_1, h) \\ &= \hat{e}((H(w)^x g^{zxr})^{rk}/H(w)^y g^{zys}, h) \\ &= \hat{e}(g^{zy(r-s)}, h) = \hat{e}(g^y, h^{r-s})^z \\ &= \hat{e}(g^y, h^r/h^s)^z = \hat{e}(PK_{du}, C_2/T_2)^{SK_{cs}} \end{aligned} \tag{8}$$

5   Security and Performance Analysis

5.1   Security Proof

Based on the mDLIN* difficult problem hypothesis, the following two lemmas can prove that the new scheme satisfies keyword indistinguishability and trapdoor indistinguishability under the random oracle model, then come to the Theorem 1.

Lemma 1. Adversary $\mathcal{A}$'s probabilistic advantage $Adv_{\mathcal{A}}^C(\lambda)$ of being able to distinguish keyword ciphertext under any probability polynomial time algorithm can be ignored.

Proof. Assume that non-negligible probability advantage ϵ_A of adversary $\mathcal{A}$ to correctly distinguish the keyword ciphertext, we construct a new probability polynomial time algorithm $\mathcal{B}$ to solve the mDLIN* problem. Given $\{g, g^x, g^{r/x}, g^{sx}, g^u\} \in G_1$, algorithm $\mathcal{B}$ determines whether $Z = g^u$ is the same as $Z = g^{r+s^{-1}}$ are equal. Challenger $\mathcal{C}$ randomly selects a random number b to determine the value of Z. When $b = 0$, $u = r + s^{-1}$; when $b = 1$, u is any element in the cyclic group G_T.

The public parameters are $\{p, g, h, G_1, G_T, \hat{e}, H\}$, $\mathcal{B}$ randomly select $t \in Z_p^*$, let $h = (g^{sx})^t$. $\mathcal{B}$ selects a random value $z \in Z_p^*$, define the CS key pair $(SK_{cs}, PK_{cs}) = (z, g^z)$ and send to the adversary $\mathcal{A}$. In other words the cloud server knows own private key z. The DO's public key is set to $PK_{do} = g^x$, and the private key is set to $SK_{do} = x$ to save to list. In the same way, DU's key pair is $PK_{du} = g^y, SK_{du} = y$ to save to list. The adversary $\mathcal{A}$ asks the following oracle machine, and the algorithm $\mathcal{B}$ answers the question of $\mathcal{A}$.

The Hash Oracle O_H: Algorithm $\mathcal{B}$ maintains a list L_H, the initial value of the list L_H is empty, which is used to store a four-tuple $\langle w_i, h_i, a_i, c_i \rangle$, w_i is keyword. The adversary $\mathcal{A}$ requests the hash of the keyword w_i, $\mathcal{B}$ does the following to reply to $\mathcal{A}$'s inquiry.

1) If the keyword w_i exists in L_H, algorithm $\mathcal{B}$ will return $H(w_i) = h_i \in G_1$.
2) If the keyword w_i not exists in L_H, algorithm $\mathcal{B}$ selects $c_i \in \{0, 1\}$ with the probability of $Pr[c_i = 0] = \theta$. If $c_i = 0$, algorithm $\mathcal{B}$ randomly selects $a_i \in Z_p^*$ and sets $h_i = g^{r/x}g^{a_i} \in G_1$; otherwise, let $h_i = g^{a_i} \in G_1$.
3) Algorithm $\mathcal{B}$ stores the value of the four-tuple $\langle w_i, h_i, a_i, c_i \rangle$ into L_H, and returns h_i to adversary $\mathcal{A}$.

Proxy Oracle O_{rk}: The adversary $\mathcal{A}$ makes an adaptive query to the oracle O_{rk}, algorithm $\mathcal{B}$ first queries the list. If SK_{do} and SK_{du} are not in the list, $\mathcal{B}$ terminates the operation. Otherwise, algorithm $\mathcal{B}$ returns $rk = y/x$ to $\mathcal{A}$.

Keyword Ciphertext Oracle O_C: When $\mathcal{A}$ performs ciphertext C_{w_i} and re-encrypted ciphertext $\hat{C}_{w_i}$ on the keyword w_i on the oracle O_C, $\mathcal{B}$ first queries the quadruple $\langle w_i, h_i, a_i, c_i \rangle$.

1) Keyword ciphertext queries for the DO: If $c_i = 0$, algorithm $\mathcal{B}$ terminates the operation and randomly outputs b's guess $b' \in \{0, 1\}$; otherwise, $\mathcal{B}$ randomly selects $r_i \in Z_p^*$, calculates and returns to $\mathcal{A}$ DO's keyword ciphertext C_{w_i}:

$$C_{w_i} = (C_{w_i,1}, C_{w_i,2}) = PK_{do}^{a_i} \cdot (PK_{do})^{z \cdot r_i}, h^{r_i} \qquad (9)$$

2) Keyword ciphertext queries for the DU: If $c_i = 0$, algorithm $\mathcal{B}$ terminates the operation and randomly outputs b's guess $b' \in \{0, 1\}$; otherwise, $\mathcal{B}$ randomly selects $r_i \in Z_p$, calculates and returns to $\mathcal{A}$ DU's keyword ciphertext $\hat{C}_{w_i}$:

$$\hat{C}_{w_i} = (\hat{C}_{w_i,1}, \hat{C}_{w_i,2}) = PK_{do}^{a_i \cdot rk} \cdot (PK_{do})^{z \cdot r_i \cdot rk}, h^{r_i} \tag{10}$$

Trapdoor Oracle O_T: Adversary $\mathcal{A}$ uses the keyword w_i to perform ciphertext query trapdoor and re-encryption ciphertext query trapdoor on the oracle O_T for adaptive query. Algorithm $\mathcal{B}$ first queries the quadruple $\langle w_i, h_i, a_i, c_i \rangle$.If $c_i = 0$, algorithm $\mathcal{B}$ terminates the operation and randomly outputs b's guess $b' \in \{0, 1\}$; otherwise, $\mathcal{B}$ randomly selects $\mu_i \in Z_p^*$, calculates and returns to the opponent Keyword ciphertext search trapdoor T_{w_i} and keyword re-encryption ciphertext search trapdoor $\hat{T}_{w_i}$:

$$T_{w_i} = (T_{w_i,1}, T_{w_i,2}) = PK_{do}^{a_i} \cdot (PK_{do})^{z \cdot \mu_i}, h^{\mu_i}$$
$$\hat{T}_{w_i} = (\hat{T}_{w_i,1}, \hat{T}_{w_i,2}) = PK_{du}^{a_i} \cdot (PK_{du})^{z \cdot \mu_i}, h^{\mu_i} \tag{11}$$

After inquiring through the above steps, $\mathcal{A}$ selects two challenge keywords w_0^* and w_1^* that have not been asked about the O_T oracle and send them to algorithm $\mathcal{B}$. Algorithm $\mathcal{B}$ first queries the list L_H to obtain the four-tuples $\langle w_0^*, h_0^*, a_0^*, c_0^* \rangle, \langle w_1^*, h_1^*, a_1^*, c_1^* \rangle$ corresponding to the keywords w_0^* and w_1^*. If $c_0^* = c_1^*$, algorithm $\mathcal{B}$ terminates the operation and randomly outputs the guess value $b' \in \{0, 1\}$ of b; If c_0^* or c_1^* has a value of 0, set $c_{b'}^* = 0$, $\mathcal{B}$ randomly selects $r' \in Z_p^*$, calculates and returns the keyword ciphertext and keyword re-encrypted ciphertext:

$$C^* = (C_1^*, C_2^*) = (Z \cdot (g^x)^{a_{b'}^*} \cdot (g^x)^{z \cdot r'}, g^{t/z} \cdot (h)^{r'})$$
$$\hat{C}^* = (\hat{C}_1^*, \hat{C}_2^*) = (Z \cdot (g^x)^{a_{b'}^* \cdot y \cdot x^{-1}} \cdot (g^x)^{z \cdot r' \cdot y \cdot x^{-1}}, g^{t/z} \cdot (h)^{r'}) \tag{12}$$

When $Z = g^{r+s^{-1}}$:

$$C_1^* = g^{r+s^{-1}} \cdot (g^x)^{a_{b'}^*} \cdot (g^x)^{z \cdot r'} = (g^{r/x} \cdot g^{a_{b'}^*})^x (g^{xz})^{(\frac{1}{sxz}+r')}$$
$$C_2^* = h^{(\frac{1}{sxz}+r')} = (g^{sxt})^{(\frac{1}{sxz}+r')} = g^{t/z} \cdot (h)^{r'} \tag{13}$$

The same can be obtained

$$\hat{C}_1^* = g^{r+s^{-1}} \cdot (g^y)^{a_{b'}^*} \cdot (g^y)^{z \cdot r'} = (g^{r/y} \cdot g^{a_{b'}^*})^y (g^{yz})^{(\frac{1}{syz}+r')}$$
$$\hat{C}_2^* = h^{(\frac{1}{syz}+r')} = (g^{syt})^{(\frac{1}{syz}+r')} = g^{t/z} \cdot (h)^{r'} \tag{14}$$

Among them, $\frac{1}{sxz}+r'$ meets the random distribution of $\mathcal{A}$. When Z is a random element, C_2^* is also random to $\mathcal{A}$. Similarly, $\frac{1}{syz}+r'$ meets a random distribution to $\mathcal{A}$. When Z is a random element, $\hat{C}_2^*$ is also random to $\mathcal{A}$.

Adversary $\mathcal{A}$ continues to perform adaptive queries on oracles O_C and O_T until the guessing result b'' is output, but adversary $\mathcal{A}$ cannot perform keywords

w_0^* and on the oracle O_T Adaptive query of w_1^*. If $b'' = b'$, Algorithm $\mathcal{B}$ outputs $b' = 0$, that is $u = r + s^{-1}$; otherwise, it outputs $b' = 1$, that is u is a random number.

Suppose that adversary $\mathcal{A}$ performs q_H times O_H oracle adaptive query, q_T times O_T oracle adaptive query, q_C times O_C oracle adaptive query, refer to the literature [16] set ter represents the situation where Algorithm $\mathcal{B}$ terminates the game.

(1) When algorithm $\mathcal{B}$ simulates O_T or O_C oracle machine, when $c_i = 0$. Because c_i is independent and identically distributed, the probability that $\mathcal{B}$ terminates the game is: $Pr[ter_1] = 1 - (1 - \theta)^{q_T + q_C}$
(2) Among the keywords that adversary $\mathcal{A}$ chooses to challenge, $c_0^* = c_1^* = 1$, the probability that algorithm $\mathcal{B}$ terminates the game is: $Pr[ter_2] = (1 - \theta)^2$

Algorithm $\mathcal{B}$ continues to prove that the probability of the game is:

$$Pr[\overline{ter}] = (1 - Pr[ter_1])(1 - Pr[ter_2])$$
$$= (1 - \theta)^{q_T + q_C}(1 - (1 - \theta)^2) \tag{15}$$

As in literature [18], when $\theta = 1 - \sqrt{\dfrac{q_T + q_C}{q_T + q_C + 2}}$, $\mathcal{B}$ with a non-negligible probability advantage $\epsilon_T = \dfrac{2}{e(q_T + q_C)}$ ends the safe proof game. Assuming that ϵ_{adv} is the advantage of adversary $\mathcal{A}$ to break through the solution, the probability that algorithm $\mathcal{B}$ can defeat mDLIN* through adversary $\mathcal{A}$ at this time is:

$$Pr[b' = b] = Pr[b' = b \wedge ter] + Pr[b' = b \wedge \overline{ter}]$$
$$= Pr[b' = b|ter]Pr[ter] + Pr[b' = b|\overline{ter}]Pr[\overline{ter}] \tag{16}$$
$$= \frac{1}{2}(1 - Pr[\overline{ter}]) + (\epsilon_{adv} + \frac{1}{2}) \cdot Pr[\overline{ter}] = \frac{1}{2} + \epsilon_{adv} \cdot Pr[\overline{ter}]$$

So, $Adv_A^C(\lambda) = |Pr[b' = b] - \dfrac{1}{2}| = \epsilon_{adv} \cdot Pr[\overline{ter}]$. Because both ϵ_{adv} and $Pr[\overline{ter}]$ cannot be ignored, algorithm $\mathcal{B}$ use a non-negligible probability advantage to solve the mDLIN* problem. This contradicts the difficult assumption of the mDLIN* problem, so the solution satisfies the indistinguishability of ciphertext.

It can be seen that the construction of T_w, $\hat{T}_w$ and keyword ciphertext C and keyword re-encryption ciphertext $\hat{C}$ in the scheme of this paper are consistent, so it can be known from Lemma 1. The $\mathcal{A}$'s probabilistic advantage in distinguishing trapdoors is negligible. The following Lemma 2 where:

Lemma 2. If the mDLIN* problem is difficult, then adversary $\mathcal{A}$ of arbitrary probability polynomial time can distinguish the probability advantage of searching trapdoors $Adv_A^T(\lambda)$ can be ignored.

Combining Lemma 1 and Lemma 2, we shows that this scheme is safe under the IKGA in Theorem 1.

Theorem 1. *Assuming that the mDLIN* problem is difficult, the new scheme is proved to be resistant to inside keyword guessing attack under random oracle model.*

5.2   Performance Analysis

The operation execution time of this scheme in the encryption phase, trapdoor generation phase, and test phase is shown in this section. Then discuss the performance of our scheme and other schemes. We use C++ language to test algorithms based on Miracl cryptographic library under Window 10 operating system. It runs on an HP personal notebook with i5-6300HQ, 2.3 GHz, and 16.0 GB of RAM.

Table 1 shows the symbols and calculation time of the basic operations involved in our scheme. Since exponential operation, bilinear pairing operation, and hash operation time are relatively long in the calculation cost, only the calculation time of these three aspects is considered. We will use the data in Table 1 to compare the running time of each stage with other schemes.

Table 1. Basic operation execution time (ms).

Symbol	Description	Time
E	Exponential calculation time	0.012
P	Bilinear pairing operation time	5.127
h	General hash operation time	0.005
H	Hash-to-point computing time	8.445

Table 2 shows the calculation amount of each scheme's keyword encryption phase, search trapdoor generation phase, test phase and whether to resist IKGA. From the perspective of the encryption stage, the performance of our scheme is significantly better than other schemes. In the trapdoor generation stage, the calculation performance of our scheme is equivalent to other schemes. From a security point of view, the literature [10] and the literature [18] can resist inside keyword guessing attacks, but the search trapdoor algorithm is a deterministic algorithm, which can easily cause the leakage of keyword statistics. In our scheme, the search trapdoor generation algorithm uses a non-deterministic algorithm, which makes it difficult to cause keyword information leakage. In summary, the new scheme proposed in our article has greater advantages in terms of security and computing performance compared to other schemes.

Table 2. Performance and safety analysis.

Scheme	Encrypt	Trapdoor	Test	IKGA
[5]	$2E + P + 2H = 13.596$	$E + H = 8.457$	$H + P = 13.572$	No
[18]	$9E + 3P + 3H = 40.824$	$2E = 0.024$	$5E + 4P + H = 29.013$	Yes
[10]	$3E + H = 8.481$	$E + P + H = 13.584$	$2P = 10.254$	Yes
Our scheme	$3E + H = 8.481$	$3E + H = 8.481$	$E + 2P = 10.266$	Yes

6 Conclusion

With the wide application of cloud storage technology and big data, the research on PEKS is becoming more and more mature, but it will still be one of the hot areas of research by scholars for a long time to come. As one of the important technologies for realizing ciphertext sharing, proxy re-encryption saves resource utilization among users. However, most existing PREKS schemes cannot resist IKGA. In order to enhance safety performance, we propose an efficient designated-server PREKS scheme. Our scheme can meet the necessary security requirements, and can defend inside keyword guessing attack. Section 5 shows that our scheme is more efficient than the previous related schemes.

The next step of the scheme, we will consider how to achieve the security verification under the standard model. In addition, the next step is to design an efficient PREKS scheme based with multi-keyword and PEKS scheme combined with blockchain.

Acknowledgements. We thank the anonymous ICAIS 2022 reviewers for their helpful comments. This work was supported by the National Natural Science Foundation of China (No. 61902111), Major Public Welfare Project of Henan Province (No. 201300311200), and the High-level talent Fund Project of Henan University of Technology, China (No. 2018BS052).

References

1. Alameen, A.: Repeated attribute optimization for big data encryption. Comput. Syst. Sci. Eng. **40**(1), 53–64 (2022)
2. Attaallah, A., Alsuhabi, H., Shukla, S., Kumar, R., Gupta, B.K., Khan, R.A.: Analyzing the big data security through a unified decision-making approach. Intell. Autom. Soft Comput. **32**(2), 1071–1088 (2022)
3. Baek, J., Safavi-Naini, R., Susilo, W.: Public key encryption with keyword search revisited. In: Gervasi, O., Murgante, B., Laganà, A., Taniar, D., Mun, Y., Gavrilova, M.L. (eds.) ICCSA 2008. LNCS, vol. 5072, pp. 1249–1259. Springer, Heidelberg (2008). https://doi.org/10.1007/978-3-540-69839-5_96
4. Blaze, M., Bleumer, G., Strauss, M.: Divertible protocols and atomic proxy cryptography. In: Nyberg, K. (ed.) EUROCRYPT 1998. LNCS, vol. 1403, pp. 127–144. Springer, Heidelberg (1998). https://doi.org/10.1007/BFb0054122
5. Boneh, D., Di Crescenzo, G., Ostrovsky, R., Persiano, G.: Public key encryption with keyword search. In: Cachin, C., Camenisch, J.L. (eds.) EUROCRYPT 2004. LNCS, vol. 3027, pp. 506–522. Springer, Heidelberg (2004). https://doi.org/10.1007/978-3-540-24676-3_30
6. Byun, J.W., Rhee, H.S., Park, H.-A., Lee, D.H.: Off-line keyword guessing attacks on recent keyword search schemes over encrypted data. In: Jonker, W., Petković, M. (eds.) SDM 2006. LNCS, vol. 4165, pp. 75–83. Springer, Heidelberg (2006). https://doi.org/10.1007/11844662_6
7. Chen, Z., Li, S., Guo, Y., Wang, Y., Chu, Y.: A limited proxy re-encryption with keyword search for data access control in cloud computing. In: Au, M.H., Carminati, B., Kuo, C.-C.J. (eds.) NSS 2014. LNCS, vol. 8792, pp. 82–95. Springer, Cham (2014). https://doi.org/10.1007/978-3-319-11698-3_7

8. Guo, L., Lu, B.: Efficient proxy re-encryption with keyword search scheme. J. Comput. Res. Dev. **51**(6), 1221 (2014)

9. Hahn, F., Kerschbaum, F.: Searchable encryption with secure and efficient updates. In: Proceedings of the 2014 ACM SIGSAC Conference on Computer and Communications Security, CCS 2014, pp. 310–320. Association for Computing Machinery, New York (2014). https://doi.org/10.1145/2660267.2660297

10. Huang, Q., Li, H.: An efficient public-key searchable encryption scheme secure against inside keyword guessing attacks. Inf. Sci. **403-404**, 1–14 (2017). https://doi.org/10.1016/j.ins.2017.03.038. https://www.sciencedirect.com/science/article/pii/S0020025516321090

11. Jeong, I.R., Kwon, J.O., Hong, D., Lee, D.H.: Constructing PEKS schemes secure against keyword guessing attacks is possible? Comput. Commun. **32**(2), 394–396 (2009). https://doi.org/10.1016/j.comcom.2008.11.018. https://www.sciencedirect.com/science/article/pii/S0140366408005768

12. Kamara, S., Papamanthou, C.: Parallel and dynamic searchable symmetric encryption. In: Sadeghi, A.-R. (ed.) FC 2013. LNCS, vol. 7859, pp. 258–274. Springer, Heidelberg (2013). https://doi.org/10.1007/978-3-642-39884-1_22

13. Kamara, S., Papamanthou, C., Roeder, T.: Dynamic searchable symmetric encryption. In: Proceedings of the 2012 ACM Conference on Computer and Communications Security, CCS 2012, pp. 965–976. Association for Computing Machinery, New York (2012). https://doi.org/10.1145/2382196.2382298

14. Rhee, H.S., Park, J.H., Susilo, W., Lee, D.H.: Trapdoor security in a searchable public-key encryption scheme with a designated tester. J. Syst. Softw. **83**(5), 763–771 (2010). https://doi.org/10.1016/j.jss.2009.11.726. https://www.sciencedirect.com/science/article/pii/S0164121209003100

15. Rhee, H.S., Susilo, W., Kim, H.J.: Secure searchable public key encryption scheme against keyword guessing attacks. IEICE Electron. Exp. **6**(5), 237–243 (2009). https://doi.org/10.1587/elex.6.237

16. Riad, K., Hamza, R., Yan, H.: Sensitive and energetic IoT access control for managing cloud electronic health records. IEEE Access **7**, 86384–86393 (2019). https://doi.org/10.1109/ACCESS.2019.2926354

17. Shao, J., Cao, Z., Liang, X., Lin, H.: Proxy re-encryption with keyword search. Inf. Sci. **180**(13), 2576–2587 (2010). https://doi.org/10.1016/j.ins.2010.03.026. https://www.sciencedirect.com/science/article/pii/S0020025510001386

18. Shao, Z.Y., Yang, B.: On security against the server in designated tester public key encryption with keyword search. Inf. Process. Lett. **115**(12), 957–961 (2015). https://doi.org/10.1016/j.ipl.2015.07.006. https://www.sciencedirect.com/science/article/pii/S0020019015001283

19. Sun, L., Xu, C., Zhang, M., Chen, K., Li, H.: Secure searchable public key encryption against insider keyword guessing attacks from indistinguishability obfuscation. Sci. Chin. Inf. Sci. **61**(3), 1–3 (2017). https://doi.org/10.1007/s11432-017-9124-0

20. Wang, C., Tu, T.: Keyword search encryption scheme resistant against keyword-guessing attack by the untrusted server. J. Shanghai Jiaotong Univ. (Sci.) **19**(4), 440–442 (2014). https://doi.org/10.1007/s12204-014-1522-6

21. Wang, S.H., Zhang, Y.X., Wang, H.Q., Xiao, F., Wang, R.C.: Efficient public-key searchable encryption scheme against inside keyword guessing attack. Comput. Sci. **46**, 91–95 (2019)

22. Xu, C., Xu, J.: Provenance method of electronic archives based on knowledge graph in big data environment. J. Inf. Hiding Priv. Prot. **3**(2), 91 (2021)

23. Xu, L., Sun, Z., Li, W., Yan, H.: Delegatable searchable encryption with specified keywords for EHR systems. Wirel. Netw. (2020). https://doi.org/10.1007/s11276-020-02410-3
24. Liu, Y., Ren, Y., Wang, Q., Wang, Q., Xia, J.: The development of proxy re-encryption. J. Cyber Secur. **2**(1), 1–8 (2020). https://doi.org/10.32604/jcs.2020.05878
25. Zhou, Y., Luo, W.: A QR data hiding method based on redundant region and BCH. J. Big Data **3**(3), 127 (2021)

HotLT: LT Code-Based Secure and Reliable Consortium Blockchain Storage Systems

Yang Liu[1,3], Boai Yang[2], Jiabin Wu[1], Zhiguang Chen[3], Ou Yang[1], Fang Liu[3(✉)], and Nong Xiao[1]

[1] College of Computer, National University of Defense Technology, Changsha 410000, China
[2] School of Design, HuNan University, Changsha 410000, China
[3] School of Computer Science and Engineering, Sun Yat-Sen University, Guangzhou 510000, China
fangl@hnu.edu.cn

Abstract. The consortium blockchain is deployed in many key industries because decentralization is irreversible and traceable. However, the storage system of the alliance chain usually adopts a full copy method, which leads to an explosive increase in storage overhead over time. What is worse, this will become a hidden threshold for companies to join the alliance to a greater extent and then evolve into an industry-centric model again. In this paper, we propose a novel storage solution named HotLT, which adopts a distributed storage system coding scheme to reduce the storage overhead of the alliance chain and enhance scalability. Secondly, to solve the bottleneck of concurrent access to encoded data and improve the average decoding speed, HotLT dynamically adjusts the generating matrix during the encoding process to adopt different encoding strategies for data blocks of different hot. Finally, the data access frequency is further divided, low-complexity coding is performed on data with high access frequency, and high-complexity coding is performed on cold data. Compared with the encoding time of traditional LT encoding, the experimental results show that the encoding time of HotLT is almost the same, and its average access speed gradually approaches the speed of direct reading as the proportion of access hot data increases.

Keywords: Consortium blockchain · Distributed storage system · Concurrent access

1 Introduction

With the development and broad application of the Internet, the Domain Name System (DNS) has become a key infrastructure and must meet security and efficiency requirements. The existing DNS system has problems such as a single point of failure and abuse of power due to its topological tree structure and centralized management of root servers and is extremely vulnerable to network attacks [1]. To solve problems, a new DNS system based on blockchain has been designed. Namecoin [2] is a Bitcoin application that implements a decentralized DNS system. Each DNS server needs to save all blocks since the genesis block can prevent data tampering, ensure data security, and have better access performance. BlockStack [3] introduces the idea of virtual blockchain and off-chain storage. It saves the operation record of the domain name into the blockchain to ensure the data's Non-repudiation and traceability. Meanwhile, it maps and stores the real domain name status information to third-party storage space via the virtual blockchain. Handshake [4] uses an improved flat file Merkel tree structure to reduce data query overhead and integrates a fair bidding mechanism into the blockchain consensus protocol, which is applied to establish a decentralized root domain name service management system. DNSLedger [5] is an advanced DNS system based on Consortium Blockchain proposed by CNNIC. In order to make the transition from the existing DNS system to a new one, the solution follows the DNS hierarchical management mechanism and realizes the root domain name chain and TLD chain, respectively.

The decentralized distributed DNS systems meet new challenges to access and storage performance. Since the blockchain adopts a full-replica storage method, as the scale of data and server nodes increases, the overall storage overhead of the system will explode, which is not conducive to system management and maintenance. Therefore, some mechanisms that combine erasure codes and decentralized consensus protocols have been designed to reduce the redundant storage overhead caused by the full-replica storage mechanism and ensure that distributed nodes can reach a consensus. RS-Paxos [6] and Craft [7] combine erasure code mechanisms with consensus algorithms such as Paxos and Raft to realize a decentralized private system with low storage overhead. BFT-Store [8] is an erasure code storage engine suitable for the Byzantine environment to reduce the storage overhead of decentralized systems.

On the one hand, there are significant differences in the access frequency of different domain names in actual application scenarios, which is likely to cause severe load skew on the DNS server cluster [9]. On the other hand, the DNS system is experiencing a surge in traffic due to emergencies, which will cause the DNS service to degrade or even crash in a short period, causing system bottlenecks [10]. Existing distributed encoding storage solutions with low storage overhead based on erasure codes cannot adapt to heterogeneous and dynamic DNS service scenarios. According to the data heat, the dynamic encoding schema is adjusted, so the access delay of high-heat data is lower. Therefore, it is necessary to design a lightweight distributed DNS system that can dynamically adjust the encoding rate for heterogeneous resource scenarios while reducing storage overhead.

In response to the low performance problems of erasure code storage systems in heterogeneous dynamic environments, we combined the fountain code solution and the heat perception mechanism to implement HotLT. It minimizes the cost of data access and repair transmission to ensure request efficiency. In the encoding stage, by optimizing the generator matrix, different encoding strategies can be used for data blocks of different degrees. Based on the heat perception mechanism, the more frequently accessed data block has a smaller degree level in encoding. Therefore, the degree value in the encoding mode is inversely proportional to the decoding speed. The decoding process uses idle time to calculate different decoding paths, and comprehensively selects the optimal decoding path according to the busyness of the node, the path length and the network quality to improve the decoding speed. In the repair process, the metadata information generates different transmission topology modes and optimizes the generation matrix in advance. HotLT re-adjusts the data block of the repaired node according to the heat of the data block at the time of repair, and ensures the decodability of the entire storage system. In order to achieve the purpose of continuously adjusting the proportion of data blocks in the system as the heat of the data blocks changes. By setting the data popularity matrix, analyzing different decoding strategies, repairing and adding hot data blocks, HotLT can make better balance among the coding or decoding efficiency, hot accessing and node repairing.

Our main contributions are as follows:

(1) During the encoding process, we set the heat information for the data block. By optimizing the generator matrix, original data blocks of different popularity use different coding strategies to accelerate the average read performance.

(2) During the decoding process, we use helpers' computing power to perform partial decoding calculations. The optimal decoding method is selected according to the path length, the busy state of the node and the network quality.

(3) During the repair process, we use functional repair. The repair strategy is dynamically adjusted according to the value of the popularity of the data block at the time of repair. This strategy ensures that the hot data block is always kept at a smaller encoding degree value and provides a more efficient service to the requester.

2 Related Work

Blockchain is a decentralized, highly secure distributed computing technology. The peer nodes in the blockchain network complete decentralized collective decision-making by implementing the consensus protocol [24], and each node will keep a completely consistent ledger (that is, the operation data of the data). Therefore, when there are individual malicious nodes in the blockchain, it itself cannot interfere with the final query result of the blockchain by providing wrong data, so as to ensure that the data cannot be tampered with. Blockchain nodes adopt a full copy data redundancy strategy. As the number of nodes and blocks increase, the storage performance will inevitably decrease. A large amount of data redundancy has caused the problem of excessive storage overhead, which is a bottleneck. The promotion of blockchain technology in general systems is restricted.

BFT-store [8] proposed the use of erasure codes to solve the blockchain storage problem. Erasure coding technology is widely used in distributed storage systems to reduce the overall storage overhead of distributed storage systems. A distributed storage system that encodes data into multiple fixed-size blocks stored in distributed storage nodes. Each node only saves a part of the data. When the data needs to be read, the target data fragments are taken out from the related nodes, and these fragments are spliced to obtain the target data. When these data fragments are lost due to the failure of the node where they are located, they can be restored to the original data through erasure code decoding. Erasure code technology has been widely used in distributed storage systems, for example, LRC [25] coding scheme both can reduce the overall overhead of the distributed system while ensuring the high reliability of the system.

HRepair [26] proposed a large number of code repair schemes across data centers, which has important practical significance in blockchain system. PBS [27] presented a speculative partial write scheme that supports fast small writes in erasure-coded storage systems. The current mainstream erasure coding scheme is a fixed coding stripe scheme, which is a strategy of exchanging calculation time for storage space, and is suitable for cold data storage systems with fixed system nodes and low data popularity.

3   Background and Motivation

3.1   LT Codes

LT codes is a classic fountain code with no bit rate compared to traditional erasure codes, which means that any number of code blocks can be generated [11]. Correspondingly, the code rate $r = k/n$ no longer makes sense. LT codes can generate any number of coded data blocks from k original data blocks that are combined by exclusive-or (XOR) operations to generate n encoded blocks, $\{\{C_i\}, 1 \leq i \leq n\}$. Data reading only needs any m coded data blocks to recover the original data. The LT encoding process is shown in Fig. 1.

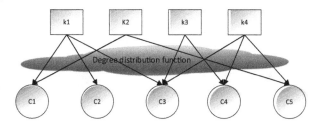

Fig. 1. LT encoding process

In general, m here is slightly larger than k, which introduces a certain decoding overhead ε, which is defined as $\varepsilon = \frac{m}{k} - 1$. Code degree d is the number of original data blocks combined into one coding block. The degree probability distribution function $\rho(d)$ represents the proportion of coded data packets of the degree in all coded data packets (Eq. (1)). n_i is the number of coded blocks with degree i, and n is the number of all coded blocks.

$$\rho(d) = n_i/n \tag{1}$$

In LT codes, degree distribution function usually adopts Ideal Soliton distribution or Robust Soliton distribution. It has a significant influence on the decoding process of rate-less codes [12–15]. The Ideal Soliton distribution is $\rho(1), \ldots, \rho(d)$, which represents the probability of the occurrence of different degree coded data packets, k is the number of original data blocks selected, as Eq. (2).

$$\begin{cases} \rho(1) = \frac{1}{k}, & d = 1 \\ \rho(d) = \frac{1}{d(d-1)}, & d = 2, \ldots, k \end{cases} \tag{2}$$

In order to improve the practicability, Luby made further improvements to Ideal Soliton distribution to obtain Robust Soliton distribution (Eqs. (3) and (4)).

$$\tau(d) = \begin{cases} \frac{s}{k} \cdot \frac{1}{d}, & d = 1, 2, \ldots, \left(\frac{k}{s} - 1\right) \\ \frac{s}{k} ln(s/\sigma), & d = k/s \\ 0, & d > k/s \end{cases} \tag{3}$$

$$s = cln\left(\frac{k}{\sigma}\right)\sqrt{k} \tag{4}$$

In order to ensure the number of data packets with degree 1 in each decoding process, two parameters σ and c are introduced. σ is the probability that the decoding fails when the decoding receives N coded data packets. c is an arbitrary constant. In practical applications, the value of c is generally less than 1, and the value is usually 0.02. The introduction of the two parameters ensures that the degree value in the decoding process can obtain the required decoding performance. The LT decoding process is shown in Fig. 2.

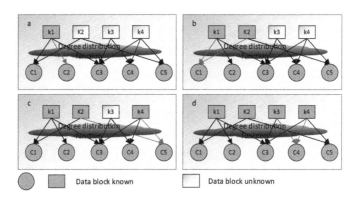

Fig. 2. LT decoding process

3.2 Consortium Blockchains

Consortium blockchains is a semi-open distributed system with a high degree of decentralization. Members need to obtain permission before they can access it. Consortium blockchains can determine the degree of openness to the public according to application scenarios, and its network is jointly maintained by member institutions. Therefore, it is suitable for the storage, management, authorization, monitoring and auditing of dynamic data by multiple member institutions under the domain name system. At present, the HyperLedger project is a relatively mature alliance chain [16].

Consortium blockchains enterprises need to conduct real-name authentication, and organizations joining the consortium chain need authoritative authentication to prove their identity. After the certification is completed, other companies on the alliance chain will allow this institution or node to enter and obtain the rights of communication and voting. Compared with the traditional centralized technology architecture, financial institutions in the alliance chain can better solve cooperation problems such as efficiency and trust among enterprises.

3.3   Motivation

At present, the consortium chain system is mainly based on the way nodes store the entire blockchain, which will eventually lead to insufficient storage resources, which in disguise increases the entry barrier of the consortium chain. Therefore, the scalability issue has become one of the main concerns of the alliance chain, because it is essential for large-scale applications. For the ever-increasing storage problem, there are two commonly used solutions. One solution is to use light nodes [17]. Light nodes only store block headers instead of complete data, resulting in light nodes not being able to work independently. Another method is to reclaim disk space by deleting old transactions [18]. This method affects data integrity. Recently, the use of coding technology has been proposed one after another [6–8, 19–21]. However, the complexity of their encoding and decoding is usually ignored, and the heterogeneity of nodes in the blockchain system is not considered. Therefore, it is vital to dynamically adjust the coding complexity on the basis of reducing storage overhead, considering the heterogeneity of nodes and the popularity of data access, which is also the motivation of this paper.

4   Design of HotLT

HotLT is designed to reduce the storage overhead of the domain naming system and speed up access based on the blockchain. In this section, we describe how HotLT uses the consortium blockchain for system security, and present how it copes with different hot data blocks.

4.1   HotLT System Architecture

In the system architecture, the client sends requests for registration, update, and cancellation. All requests are collectively referred to as transactions, and are first stored in transaction pools, and after transaction verification, they are packaged into a block on the chain. In the data storage stage, we use a encoding data block for every two blocks for data encoding. This is done to be consistent with the size of the SST (sorted string table) in leveldb to facilitate database writing [22]. Figure 3 shows a HotLT system architecture.

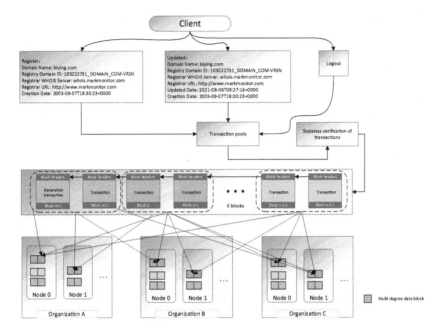

Fig. 3. HotLT system architecture

4.2 Dynamic Decoding Strategy

The coded data block is distributed to multiple nodes for storage, and the data decoding operation is performed during data reconstruction. The traditional solution is to decode after the repair node receives a certain amount of coded data from neighboring nodes. Figure 4 shows the network bottleneck of the disadvantages of this scheme. Therefore, we adopted a local decoding method for data restoration.

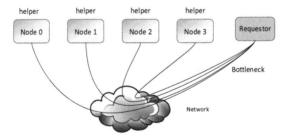

Fig. 4. The network bottleneck

The nodes on the consortium chain in the domain name system may be distributed in every corner of the world. The traditional decoding method will further amplify the data transmission bottleneck. Therefore, this paper proposes a pipelined dynamic decoding strategy to make full use of the computing resources of the storage node to initiate multi-threaded operations, as shown in Fig. 5. This paper give full play to the computing power of each node and delegate the work of computing to storage nodes. LT decoding itself is not complicated, so the storage node can do some simple work. We assume that both the client and the repair end need raw data, and the storage node stores the encoded data. The following is a data analysis within a single organization. The storage node performs a data transmission to the repair end or the client at the same time as the calculation. After a single storage node is decoded, the remaining Tanner graph is used for internal transmission between storage nodes. In order to reduce the overhead of remote transmission, all decoding work is completed between storage nodes.

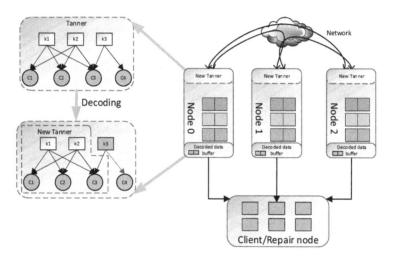

Fig. 5. Schematic diagram of pipeline decoding

4.3 Repair Strategy Based on Data Hot Perception

In Sect. 4.2, we propose a local pipeline repair strategy to reduce the decoding overhead. However, the query performance of the data has a certain impact on the reading speed due to the different coding complexity, and the heat of the data varies with time.

As a result, the system cannot provide fast data retrieval and reasonable load balancing ability in the face of data with hot difference. Therefore, the strategy of negative correlation between data access hot and coding complexity is added on the basis of Sect. 4.2.

The traditional measure to deal with hot data perception and query is to use the data cold and hot separation mechanism. For the domain name system, the highly popular domain name data can be transferred to an additional hot data storage system, which can avoid repeatedly searching for target data in the huge retrieval space of the index and the blockchain. Under the condition of data popularity perception, the access of domain name data includes the process of data conversion between cold and hot. The domain name data in the storage space is heated by the query request, and the data records are transferred to the hot data storage system. After a period of time, the amount of data query is zero for a long time, and this batch of cooled data will be moved out of the hot data storage system. This section proposes a repair and optimization mechanism for data heat perception, and sets up a linked list of hot data storage for data blocks. When a piece of domain name data is queried, the popularity of the data increases, and its related domain name will also be considered to be accessed in a short time. Therefore, the popularity of the entire data block where the domain name data is located will also increase.

The linked list receives the data block file as input for re-coding and marks the heat value of the data block. Cooling blocks for which there are no new query requests for a long time and the data heat life value expires will be removed from the linked list. The coding window is a collection of coding blocks, which is used as a set of encoded data. For each coding window, HotLT coding repair first randomly reads k data blocks that do not participate in the coding, and generates k values for them. Different from the LT fountain code mechanism, HotLT exchanges values to make the hottest data blocks in the coding window have a degree of 1, and low-hot data blocks get higher values, that is, a more complex coding strategy. A degree of 1 ensures that high-heat data can be accessed directly. After the value assignment is completed, the set of data blocks in the coding window are encoded and then distributed to the hot data block storage space of the distributed storage node.

Algorithm1:	HotLT
Input:	Original data block (k_i), Degree distribution (d_i), Data popularity(w_j)
Output:	Decoded data block (c_i)
	Record the number of data accesses (N)
if	N>=1000 **then**
	Mark data blocks as hot data (H_i)
	H_i=1
else if	N>=500 && N <1000 **then**
	Mark data blocks as slight hot data
	H_i=2
else	
	Genral data
end if	
function	HotLT
if	There are hot data blocks in the coding group
	Obtain degree distribution according to Robust Soliton distribution
for	Each data block
if	H_i=1 && degree ≠1
	Exchange between 1 degree data block and heat data block
end if	
	Verify the decoding ability
end for	
end if	
end	

In the process of data restoration, the HotLT dynamic restoration coding scheme considers the hotspot distribution of the data and adjusts the original degree distribution scheme. In the process of data recovery, the data is dynamically adjusted without additional overhead.

5 Evaluation

Consortium blockchain on a virtual machine and allocates different hard disk space and CPU cores when creating the virtual machine. In this way, it simulates blockchain nodes with different resources. Each virtual machine is equipped with a Linux environment, ubuntu 20.04 operating system, and docker is installed. Also, Hyperledger Caliper [23] was used to test the tool for experiments. The server is equipped with Intel (R) Xeon(R) CPU E5-2620 v3 @ 2.40 GHz 2.40 GHz, 40G DRAM.

In order to evaluate the performance of HotLT, the encoding time, storage overhead and access time are studied. In the experiment, we set the percentage of the popularity data in different access data. Define the proportion of random read popularity data as 0 and when the total access popularity is $H_i = 1$, the proportion is defined as 100%.

We analyzed the storage overhead of the full copy state and the storage overhead of HotLT. With the increase of nodes, the storage overhead of HotLT increases slowly, and the full copy grows faster, as shown in Fig. 6.

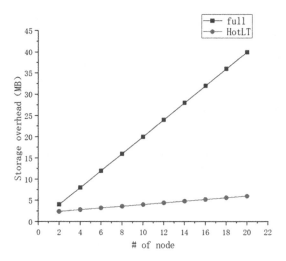

Fig. 6. Storage overhead

From the analysis of the Fig. 7, it can be seen that when the block hot is dynamically added during the encoding process, the encoding time is increased by a small amount of time due to obtaining and searching whether the current heat block data is the data content in the reconstructed node. The overall time is basically the same, and the average time is basically the same. Under the circumstance that the encoding time is basically unchanged, we further conduct experimental analysis on the reading time of the thermal data.

From the analysis of the Fig. 8, it can be seen that the higher the proportion of the read hot data, the more obvious the advantages of the HotLT solution, while the LT code basically remains unchanged. When the hot data reaches 100%, HotLT is basically close to the direct reading time. Therefore, the small amount of time added in the encoding process is acceptable for reading overhead.

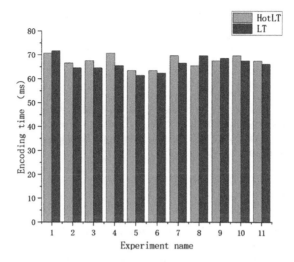

Fig. 7. LT encoding VS HotLT encoding time

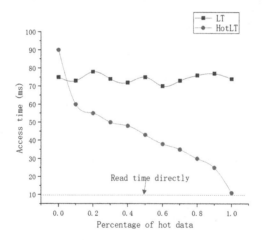

Fig. 8. LT encoding VS HotLT access time

6 Conclusion

This article optimizes the storage cost of the consortium chain of the domain name system. The storage system of the consortium chain usually adopts a full copy method, which leads to explosive growth of storage costs over time. This has increased the hidden barriers for many small and medium-sized enterprises to join the alliance, and then evolve into an industry-centric model again. Therefore, in this article, we propose a new storage solution called HotLT, which uses a distributed storage system coding scheme to reduce the storage overhead of the alliance chain and enhance scalability. Second, we use the method of decoding at the storage node in the decoding process to reduce the total amount of data transmission. Finally, the data access frequency is further divided, and the data with high access frequency is encoded with low complexity. Compared with the encoding time of traditional LT encoding, as the proportion of access to hot data increases, the average access speed gradually approaches the direct reading speed.

Acknowledgements. This work is supported by The National Key Research and Development Program of China (2019YFB1804502), National Natural Science Foundation of China (61872392, 61832020, 61802418), and the Major Program of Guangdong Basic and Applied Research (2019B030302002).

References

1. Almeida, V.A.F., Doneda, D., de Souza Abreu, J.: Cyberwarfare and digital governance. IEEE Internet Comput. **21**(2), 68–71 (2017). https://doi.org/10.1109/MIC.2017.23
2. Loibl, A.: Namecoin (2014) [Online]. https://namecoin.info.
3. Ali, M., Nelson, J.C., Shea, R., et al.: Blockstack: a global naming and storage system secured by blockchains. In: 2016 USENIX Annual Technical Conference, USENIX ATC 2016, Denver, CO, USA, 22–24 June 2016, pp. 181–194. USENIX Association (2016)
4. Community H. Handshake [EB/OL]. (2014). https://hsd-dev.org/files/handshake.txt. Accessed 23 Feb 2021
5. Duan, X., Yan, Z., Geng, G., et al.: Dnsledger: decentralized and distributed name resolution for ubiquitous iot. In: IEEE International Conference on Consumer Electronics, ICCE 2018, Las Vegas, 12–14 January 2018, pp. 1–3. IEEE (2018)
6. Mu, S., Chen, K., Wu, Y., Zheng, W.: When paxos meets erasure code: reduce network and storage cost in state machine replication. In: Proceedings of the 23rd International Symposium on High-Performance Parallel and Distributed Computing (HPDC '14), pp. 61–72. Association for Computing Machinery, New York (2014). https://doi.org/10.1145/2600212.2600218
7. Wang, Z., Li, T., Wang, H., et al.: CRaft: an erasure-coding-supported version of raft for reducing storage cost and network cost (2020)
8. Qi, X., Zhang, Z., Jin, C., et al.: BFT-store: storage partition for permissioned blockchain via erasure coding. In: 2020 IEEE 36th International Conference on Data Engineering (ICDE). IEEE (2020)
9. Zhauniarovich, Y., Khalil, I., Yu, T., et al.: A survey on malicious domains detection through DNS data analysis. ACM Comput. Surv. **1**(1) (2018)
10. Fan, B., Lim, H., Andersen, D.G., et al.: Small cache, big effect: provable load balancing for randomly partitioned cluster services. In: ACM Symposium on Cloud Computing in conjunction with SOSP 2011, SOCC 2011, Cascais, 26–28 October 2011, p. 23. ACM (2011)
11. Luby, M.: LT codes. In: Proceedings of the 43rd Annual IEEE Symposium on Foundations of Computer Science, pp. 271–280 (2002)
12. Yen, K.-K., Liao, Y.-C., Chen, C.-L., Chang, H.-C.: Modified robust soliton distribution (MRSD) with improved ripple size for LT codes. IEEE Commun. Lett. **17**(5), 976–979 (2013)
13. Yao, W., Yi, B., Huang, T., Li, W.: Poisson robust soliton distribution for LT codes. IEEE Commun. Lett. **20**(8), 1499–1502 (2016)

14. Luo, P., Fan, H., Shi, W., Qi, X., Zhao, Y., Zhou, X.: An ECSO-based approach for optimizing degree distribution of short-length LT codes. EURASIP J. Wirel. Commun. Netw. **2019**(1), 76 (2019)
15. Chen, C.-M., Chen, Y.-P., Shen, T.-C., Zao, J.K.: On the optimization of degree distributions in LT code with covariance matrix adaptation evolution strategy. In: Proceedings of the IEEE Congress on Evolutionary Computation, pp. 1–8 (2010)
16. Androulaki, E., Manevich, Y., Muralidharan, S., et al.: Hyperledger fabric: a distributed operating system for permissioned blockchains. In: The Thirteenth EuroSys Conference (2018)
17. Churyumov, A.: ByteBall: A Decentralized System for Storage and Transfer of Value. [Online] (2016). https://byteball.org/Byteball.pdf
18. Nakamoto, S.: Bitcoin: A Peer-to-Peer Electronic Cash System. [Online]. (2008). http://bitcoin.org/bitcoin.pdf
19. Dai, M., Zhang, S., Wang, H., Jin, S.: A low storage room requirement framework for distributed ledger in blockchain. IEEE Access **6**, 22970–22975 (2018)
20. Raman, R.K., Varshney, L.R.: Dynamic distributed storage for blockchains. In: Proceedings of the IEEE International Symposium on Information Theory (ISIT), June 2018, pp. 2619–2623 (2018)
21. Perard, D., Lacan, J., Bachy, Y., Detchart, J.: Erasure code-based low storage blockchain node. In: Proceedings of the IEEE International Conference Internet Things (iThings) IEEE Green Computer Communication (GreenCom) IEEE Cyber-Physical-Social Computing (CPSCom) IEEE Smart Data (SmartData), July 2018, pp. 1622–1627 (2018)
22. Chang, F.: Bigtable: A Distributed Storage System for Structured Data. In: 7th USENIX Symposium on Operating Systems Design and Implementation (OSDI), 2006 (2006)
23. Hyperledger Caliper. https://github.com/hyperledger/caliper. Accessed 10 Nov 2019
24. Lepore, C., Ceria, M., Visconti, A., et al.: A Survey on Blockchain Consensus with a Performance Comparison of PoW, PoS and Pure PoS (2020)
25. Huang, C., Simitci, H., Xu, Y., et al.: Erasure coding in windows azure storage. In: 2012 {USENIX} Annual Technical Conference ({USENIX}{ATC} 12), pp. 15–26 (2012)
26. Bao, H., Wang, Y., Xu, F.: Reducing network cost of data repair in erasure-coded cross-datacenter storage. Future Gen. Comput. Syst. **102**, 494–506 (2020)
27. Zhang, Y., Li, H., Liu, S., et al.: PBS: an efficient erasure-coded block storage system based on speculative partial writes. ACM Trans. Storage **16**(1), 1–25 (2020)

Research on Key Word Information Retrieval Based on Inverted Index

Meihan Qi[1], Wei Fang[1,2(✉)], Yongming Zhao[3], Yu Sha[1],
and Victor S. Sheng[4]

[1] School of Computer and Software Engineering, Research Center of Digital Forensics, Ministry of Education, Nanjing University of Information Science and Technology, Nanjing 210044, China
Fangwei@nuist.edu.cn
[2] State Key Laboratory of Severe Weather, Chinese Academy of Meteorological Sciences, Beijing 100081, China
[3] China Meteorological Administration Training Center, Beijing, China
[4] Department of Computer, Texas Tech University, Lubbock, TX 79409, USA

Abstract. With the advent of the era of big data, data has penetrated into every aspect of social life and become an important production factor in various industries. However, while providing convenience to our life, massive information also brings difficulties to information retrieval, which has problems of low retrieval efficiency and poor retrieval accuracy. Therefore, how to improve the efficiency and accuracy of information retrieval has become a key technical problem to be solved. In this paper, we propose a key word information retrieval scheme based on inverted index, which uses the inverted index segmentation algorithm based on keywords to realize the block retrieval of information, improves the efficiency of information retrieval, and improves the accuracy of retrieval content through reasonable error correction of keywords. The results of evaluation indicate that compared with the mainstream information retrieval methods, the keyword information retrieval scheme based on inverted index can carry out faster and more accurate information retrieval. Experimental results show that the keyword information retrieval scheme with inverted index can further improve the efficiency and accuracy of information retrieval.

Keywords: Inverted index · Keyword retrieval · Chunked retrieval · Retrieval efficiency · Retrieval accuracy

1 Introduction

With the rapid development and wide application of network and information technology, the tide of information has impacted every field of social life. The automation of data generation and the fast speed of data generation make the amount of data increase rapidly. However, as the data structure is complex and changeable, efficient and accurate information retrieval from complex data is faced with great challenges.

At present, the information retrieval method used by the mainstream relational database is SQL fuzzy query, and the data structure used by the underlying storage mechanism of its storage engine is B+ Tree data structure, which can greatly improve the query speed of the data in the database. However, with the increase of data volume, the speed of SQL fuzzy query of relational database will decrease rapidly, which cannot meet the demand of real-time retrieval by users. In order to improve the efficiency and accuracy of information retrieval and bring better retrieval experience to users, we propose a keyword information retrieval scheme based on inverted index. Through the use of keywords based on the inverted index segmentation algorithm [1] to achieve the block retrieval of information, each retrieval operation is performed by extracting and calculating part of the index file, this method greatly improves the efficiency of information retrieval. At the same time, the accuracy of information retrieval is further improved by using the method of word segmentation and error correction.

Specifically, the inverted index is composed of dictionary and inverted file. The dictionary is a set of all keywords, and the inverted file is composed of the inverted list corresponding to the keywords, and each keyword maintains a specific logical relationship with the corresponding inverted list. The keyword based inversion index segmentation algorithm is based on the constructed inverted file. Firstly, the dictionary is divided into several subsets according to the order of the keywords in the dictionary, and then the number of inverted items in the inversion list corresponding to the keywords is calculated statistically to achieve the balanced partition of sub-index files. The inverted index file is divided into multiple sub-index files, which are independent of each other. Each index stores only part of the keywords and the inverted list, reducing the size of the sub-index file. In the process of information retrieval, the server will search the sub-index file corresponding to the keyword, and then load it into the memory for retrieval, which greatly improves the retrieval efficiency. Keyword error correction is mainly used to discover possible keyword errors during information retrieval and recommend possible correct keywords. Firstly, some keywords in the dictionary are extracted for training, and then the storage structure of character tree is trained for the subsequent keyword correction operations. Then the entered keywords are processed by word segmentation, error correction and character tree search, and the recommended entries are given for the keywords that may have errors, which greatly improves the accuracy of information retrieval.

2   Related Work

With the development of information retrieval technology, users have higher and higher requirements for information retrieval. Keywords [2] are highly refined and generalized to the content of the document, which to some extent reflects the theme of the document and the content of research and analysis. Through the statistical analysis of keywords, the core problems of a certain field can be known, and research hotspots can be obtained by analyzing the closeness of connection between nodes, the strength of centrality and the size of frequency. In recent years, many methods have been proposed to solve the problem of keyword information retrieval [3]. Cao et al. [4] proposed that vectors of equal length should be used to represent documents and retrieval traps, and the correlation degree between documents and retrieval words could be obtained by calculating the inner product of documents and retrieval traps.

Documents were sorted according to the correlation degree and the documents with the highest correlation degree were returned, so as to achieve more accurate retrieval. Yang Yang et al. [5] set different weights for keywords in different areas of the document, and expressed the importance of keywords through weighted average score, so as to improve the efficiency of multi-keyword ranking retrieval scheme. References [6, 7] proposed the combination of multi-keyword retrieval with the information retrieval mode of sorting according to the correlation degree between documents and keywords, so as to make the information retrieval scheme more secure and efficient. Reference [8] proposed to combine fuzzy retrieval with the retrieval mode of sorting according to relevance, realize fuzzy retrieval through semantic analysis of keywords, and sort according to the degree of correlation between documents and retrieval words, so as to improve the accuracy of retrieval results [9]. Bosch et al. [10] proposed a keyword retrieval method using wildcard characters. Vigna [11] proposed to use ELISA-Fano index to build a mixed index, so as to obtain better compression effect. Learned index [12, 13] constructed based on machine learning has also gradually received attention due to its characteristics of fast retrieval speed and small space occupation. Nowadays, the development of hardware, especially the development of SIMD parallel instruction set and hierarchical storage architecture, has also spawned a large number of adaptive applications [14, 15].

Index [16–19] is one of the most core technologies in search engines, and the main research direction of index technology is to optimize and improve the index model [20–23], in which it is of great significance to build an efficient inverted index model and optimize and improve it. As a typical and efficient information data retrieval structure, inverted index is the core unit of full-text index [24]. Inverted index [17, 25–29] has great advantages in fuzzy retrieval [30] and information retrieval [31] compared with mainstream relational database [32–34]. However, when the amount of data is large [35], quick retrieval of documents containing or not containing some keywords and accurate positioning of the query will have a great impact on the query results and query efficiency. In order to achieve the ideal effect, it needs special treatment in the process of use.

In order to further improve the efficiency and accuracy of information retrieval, we propose a keyword information retrieval scheme based on inverted retrieval, which realizes the block retrieval of information by using the inverted index segmentation algorithm based on keywords. Each retrieval operation is performed by extracting and calculating a portion of the contents of the index file. This method greatly improves the efficiency of information retrieval. At the same time, through the parallel processing of word segmentation and error correction, the retrieval keywords are reasonably corrected, which further improves the accuracy of information retrieval.

3   Method

Nowadays, the mainstream relational database index adopts B+ Tree structure, which can support the important features of relational database in query, such as range query, prefix matching fuzzy query, sorting and paging. However, with the increase of data volume, the query speed of the relational database based on B+ Tree index will also decline rapidly, which cannot meet the needs of users for real-time retrieval. In order to solve the above problems, we use an information retrieval method based on inverted index to ensure that each time a specific keyword is retrieved, the document scope of the keyword can be quickly located, so as to greatly improve the efficiency of information retrieval. At the same time, in order to improve the accuracy of information retrieval, we propose a keyword error correction method, which is mainly used to find the possible errors of keywords in information retrieval and recommend the possible correct keywords. In this paper, the main optimization methods include inverted index, inverted index segmentation algorithm and Keyword Error Correction.

3.1 Inverted Index

Inverted index, also known as reverse index, is a relative concept to forward index. In search engines, to facilitate internal processing, each document in the document collection is assigned a document number as the unique identification of the document. The content of the document is processed with word segmentation. The document is represented as a set of words, each of which is also given a word number to represent its uniqueness. The data structure of forward index is the linked list structure from document to word, where each document node contains the information of document number, and word node is the information set of word, occurrence times of the word and occurrence position list of the word. The forward index structure is shown in Fig. 1.

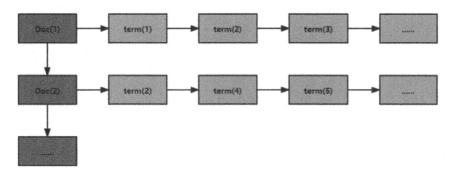

Fig. 1. Forward index structure.

When using the forward index for keyword retrieval, it is necessary to scan all the documents used in the index library, extract the documents containing specific keywords, score and rank them according to the scoring model and present them to users. However, with the rapid increase of data volume, the number of documents is often astronomical, and forward indexes cannot meet the need to return ranking results in real time. Therefore, the search engine introduces the inverted index, which is the reconstruction of the structure of the forward index, that is, the mapping from file number to keyword is transformed into keyword to file mapping, in which each keyword corresponds to a series of files containing the keyword. Inverted index is a linked list structure from keywords to documents. The inverted index structure is shown in Fig. 2.

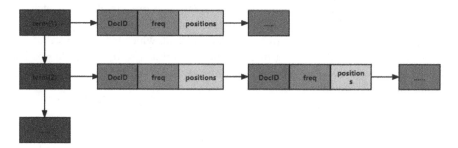

Fig. 2. Inverted index structure.

The retrieval of search engine is actually a concrete data structure that implements "word-document matrix". Word-document matrix is a conceptual model that expresses the inclusion relationship between words and documents. In the keyword document matrix, from the horizontal dimension, each row represents the specific documents containing a keyword. From the vertical dimension, each column represents the keywords contained in the document, and the checkbox position represents the inclusion relationship. The conceptual model of word-document matrix can be implemented in many different ways, but inverted index is the best implementation. The keyword - document matrix is shown in Table 1.

Table 1. Keyword - document matrix.

Term	Doc1	Doc2	Doc3	Doc4	Doc5
Term1	✓		✓		
Term2		✓	✓		
Term3				✓	
Term4	✓	✓		✓	
Term5			✓		✓

Inverted index consists of word dictionary and inverted file. Word is the basic index unit of a search engine, while a dictionary is a collection of strings containing all the words that appear in a collection of documents. Each index item in a dictionary contains information about the word itself and a pointer to an inverted list. The document list of all documents corresponding to the keyword and the location information of the keyword in the document are recorded in the inverted list, and each keyword in the inverted list maintains the corresponding logical relationship with the specific inverted list. An inverted file is a physical file that stores an inverted list of all the words. The structure of the inverted index is shown in Fig. 3.

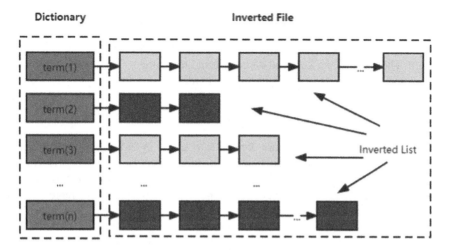

Fig. 3. Inverted index structure.

3.2 Inverted Index Segmentation Algorithm

The inverted index segmentation scheme based on keywords realizes the index segmentation based on the index files that have been built. Firstly, keywords are divided into several dictionary subsets according to the order of keywords in the dictionary, and then the inverted list files are divided into multiple sub-index files according to the corresponding relationship between keywords and inverted list. The sub-index files are independent of each other and do not intersect each other. To ensure the balanced division of index files, it is necessary to calculate the number of inverted items in the inverted list corresponding to keywords, so that the number of inverted items maintained by each sub-index is equal.

The inverted index segmentation algorithm takes the inverted index Ω and the number of sharding index k as input, and the output is the sub-index set $\{\Omega1, \Omega2, \ldots, \Omega k\}$. The segmentation standard of inverted index is to count the total number of inverted items P contained in all inverted lists $P(i \leq i \leq n)$ in the index file. According to the formula

$$\text{SLoad(post)} \cong \frac{\sum_{i=1}^{n} |P_i|}{k}, \tag{1}$$

the number of inverted items contained in each sub index is approximately calculated, so as to determine the segmentation standard of keywords in the dictionary. $L = \{P_1, P_2, P_3, \ldots, P_n\}$ is inverted list file and $P = \{P_{1i}, P_{i2}, P_{i3}, \ldots, P_{ij}\}$ is the inverted list corresponding to the keyword t_i. P_{ij} is the j inverted item in the inversion list P_i, which contains the identification information of the document and other relevant information. K is the number of sub-indexes segmented, $|P_i|$ is the number of inverted items in the i inverted list, $\sum_{i=1}^{n} |P_i|$ is the number of all inverted items in the inverted index.

SLoad(post) is the approximate number of inverted items that a sub-index file contains and maintains.

The keyword segmentation in the dictionary takes SLoad(post) as the segmentation standard. The order of the keyword dictionary and the number of inverted items $|P_i|$ in the corresponding inverted list are known. According to the formula

$$\sum_{i=1}^{m_1} t_i \langle df \rangle \cong \sum_{i=m_1+1}^{m_2} t_i \langle df \rangle \cong \ldots \cong \sum_{i=m_{k-1}+1}^{n} t_i \langle df \rangle, \qquad (2)$$

the key words in the dictionary are divided into k sets in order to form k keyword dictionary. $t_i < df >$ indicates the number of documents related to the keyword t_i, which is equivalent to the number of inverted items $|P_i|$ in the corresponding inverted list. $m_{k-1} + 1$ represents the first keyword in the k keyword set, and m_k represents the last keyword in the k keyword set.

The inverted index segmentation algorithm is to segment the inverted file into multiple sub-index files based on keywords, and each sub-index is independent of each other. Each index saves only a part of the keywords and inverted list, thus reducing the size of the sub index file. In the process of information retrieval, the server will search the sub-index file corresponding to the keyword, and then load it into the memory for retrieval, which greatly improves the retrieval efficiency.

3.3   Keyword Error Correction

We realize the reasonable error correction of retrieval keywords by parallel processing of word segmentation and error correction, so as to improve the accuracy of information retrieval. Keyword error correction is mainly used to find possible errors in keywords during information retrieval and recommend possible correct keywords. Firstly, some keywords in the dictionary are extracted for training and trained into the storage structure of character tree for subsequent keyword error correction operations. Then the input keywords are processed by word segmentation, error correction and character tree search, and the possible error keywords are recommended. Specifically, input the keywords and word processing, for more than two words and words of the key words need to look for in the corresponding character tree and the match of entry, if not found matching entries that input keywords there may be errors, error correction of the keywords to search operation in the corresponding character in the tree. Among them, the word segmentation operation uses a recursive segmentation strategy, if it is a single word of keywords are not for word processing, if is a word of keywords, the length of the first keyword statistics, when keywords length shall not exceed the maximum length, then the entire string as a key word in character tree to find the matching error and try, if find failure, The previous word segmentation operation is performed recursively on the substring in the string. The character tree structure and recursive word segmentation process are shown in Fig. 4 and Fig. 5 respectively.

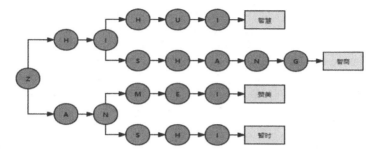

Fig. 4. Character tree structure.

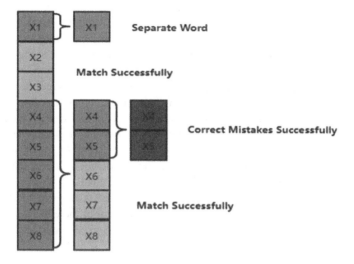

Fig. 5. Recursive word segmentation.

4 Experiments

4.1 Data

The keyword information retrieval experiment based on inverted index uses Wang Xiaobo's books, and puts Wang Xiaobo's books into the data pool of the data retrieval system to provide data support for the keyword information retrieval experiment based on inverted index. The book information in the data pool includes the title, introduction, and original text of the article.

4.2 Evaluation Methods

The evaluation standard used in the experiment is the time of searching for a keyword, that is, searching for a keyword in the data retrieval system, searching the article introduction containing the keyword through the inverted index and the B+ Tree index adopted by the mainstream relational database, and counting the time consumed by two different retrieval methods to search the same keyword. By comparing the time of the two retrieval methods, it is verified whether the keyword information retrieval method based on inverted index is superior to the B+ Tree retrieval method adopted by the mainstream relational database in terms of retrieval efficiency. At the same time, through the wrong input of keywords, it is tested whether the error correction reminder can be given to the input errors of keywords, so as to verify the retrieval accuracy of keyword information retrieval based on inverted index.

4.3   Analysis of Experimental Results

Evaluation of Retrieval Efficiency. The experiment selects several keywords to evaluate the efficiency of keyword information retrieval through self-comparison and comparison with mainstream methods. Self-comparison is achieved by retrieving keywords of different lengths. By setting keywords of different lengths, it verifies whether the keyword retrieval method based on inverted index is effective in different situations. Comparison with the mainstream methods, mainly through the comparison with the information retrieval method of B+ Tree index adopted by the mainstream relational database, it is used to verify the efficiency of the retrieval keywords of the proposed method, which is higher than that of the mainstream relational database. For different keywords, experiments are carried out on the retrieval of specified keywords by two retrieval methods: inverted index and B+ Tree index of relational database. The experimental results are shown in Table 2, in which the evaluation index is the time consumed in keyword retrieval. At the same time, in order to observe the comparison results more intuitively, the corresponding plane histogram of the experimental results is also drawn, which makes the comparison results of the experiment more clear. The experimental results are shown in Fig. 6.

Table 2. Time comparison of different retrieval methods (Tips: Keywords are used in Chinese in practice, and keywords in table case are used in English).

Keyword	Inverted index (second)	B+ Tree index (second)
Impression	0.031	0.594
Two o'clock	0.001	0.031
Wisdom	0.001	0.047
Smile a little	0.017	0.063
More deep	0.001	0.531

As can be seen from Table 1 and Fig. 6, in terms of self-comparison experiments, there is no significant difference in the retrieval time of keywords of different lengths, indicating that the length of keywords does not affect the retrieval efficiency. Compared with the mainstream methods, the keyword information retrieval method based on inverted index has an obvious gap in the retrieval time compared with the B+ Tree index of the mainstream relational database, indicating that the keyword retrieval method proposed in this paper greatly improves the retrieval efficiency.

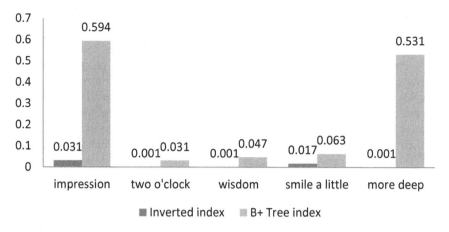

Fig. 6. Time comparison of different retrieval methods.

Evaluation of Retrieval Accuracy. The experiment selects several keywords, and searches the article profile containing the retrieved keywords through the keyword information retrieval method based on inverted index to see whether the article profile containing the retrieved keywords can be accurately output, and then view the full text of the article. Based on the correct retrieval of documents, we test whether the input errors of keywords can be properly corrected, so as to improve the accuracy of information retrieval.

Table 3. Keyword error correction (Tips: Keywords are used in Chinese in practice, and keywords in table case are used in English).

Keyword	Retrieval time (s)	Retrieval results
Motherland	0.001	Search [motherland], find 14 results
自激	0.047	Search [自己], find 35 results, still search [自激]?
Easy	0.001	Search [easy], find 28 results
More deep	0.001	Search [More deep], find 35 results
多年不间	0.047	Search [多年不见], find 8 results, still search [多年不间]?
笔计本	0.063	Search [笔记本], find 13 results, still search [笔计本]?
Author	0.017	Search [author], find 26 results

It can be seen from Table 3 that the keyword information retrieval scheme based on inverted index can correctly output the document content according to the input keywords. In addition, when there is incorrect input of the keyword information, it can make reasonable error correction according to the keywords, and then carry out information retrieval for the correct keywords and output the corresponding document content. This function of keyword error correction makes the accuracy of information retrieval function further improved.

5 Conclusion

The existing information retrieval methods have the problems of low retrieval efficiency and accuracy. In order to solve the above problems, we propose a keyword retrieval method based on inverted index. Firstly, the traditional information retrieval method is improved by inverted index algorithm, and then the inverted index based on keywords is realized by index segmentation algorithm based on the constructed index file, so as to improve the efficiency of information retrieval. Finally, the key words are corrected reasonably to improve the accuracy of retrieval information. In the experiment, taking data retrieval as an example, the retrieval efficiency and accuracy of keyword information retrieval method based on inverted index are tested, and compared with traditional information retrieval. The experimental results show that compared with traditional information retrieval methods, the keyword information retrieval method based on inverted index proposed in this paper can improve the efficiency and accuracy of information retrieval. Experiments verify the effectiveness of the proposed method.

Acknowledgement. This work was supported by the National Natural Science Foundation of China (Grant No. 42075007), the Open Grants of the State Key Laboratory of Severe Weather (No. 2021LASW-B19).

References

1. Ali, U., Mahmood, M.T.: Defocus blur segmentation using local binary patterns with adaptive threshold. Comput. Mater. Continua **71**(1), 1597–1611 (2022)
2. Jo, B., Ahn, J., Jung, S.: Efficient spatial keyword search methods for reflecting multiple keyword domains. J. Inf. Record. **35**(4), 903–921 (2019)
3. Ezhilarasi, K., Kalavathy, G.M.: Enhanced neuro-fuzzy-based crop ontology for effective information retrieval. Comput. Syst. Sci. Eng. **41**(2), 569–582 (2022)
4. Cao, N., Wang, C., Li, M.: Privacy-preserving multi-keyword ranked search over encrypted cloud data. IEEE Trans. Parallel Distrib. Syst. **25**(1), 222–223 (2014)
5. Yang, Y., Yang, S.L., Cai, S.B.: A sort verifiable semantic fuzzy searchable encryption scheme. J. Sichuan Univ. **49**(4), 119–128 (2017)
6. Fu, Z., Sun, X., Linge, N.: Achieving effective cloud search services: multi-keyword ranked search over encrypted cloud data supporting synonym query. IEEE Trans. Consum. Electron. **60**(1), 164–172 (2014)
7. Xia, Z., Wang, X., Sun, X.: A secure and dynamic multi-keyword ranked search scheme over encrypted cloud data. IEEE Trans. Parallel Distrib. Syst. **27**(2), 340–352 (2015)
8. Fu, Z., Shu, J., Sun, X., et al.: Smart cloud search services: verifiable keyword-based semantic search over encrypted cloud data. IEEE Trans. Consum. Electron. **60**(4), 762–770 (2014)
9. Wang, Q.Y., Dong, H.B.: Book retrieval method based on QR code and CBIR technology. J. Artif. Intell. **1**(2), 101–110 (2019)
10. Bösch, C., Brinkman, R., Hartel, P., Jonker, W.: Conjunctive wildcard search over encrypted data. In: Jonker, W., Petković, M. (eds.) SDM 2011. LNCS, vol. 6933, pp. 114–127. Springer, Heidelberg (2011). https://doi.org/10.1007/978-3-642-23556-6_8

11. Vigna, S.: Quasi-succinct indices. In: Proceedings of the Sixth ACM International Conference on Web Search and Data Mining, pp. 83–92. Springer, Heidelberg (2013). https://doi.org/10.1145/2433396.2433409

12. Kraska, T., Beutel, A., Chi, E.H., et al.: The case for learned index structures. In: Proceedings of the 2018 International Conference on Management of Data, pp. 489–504. Springer, Heidelberg (2018). https://doi.org/10.1145/3183713.3196909

13. Ooslerhuis, H., Culpepper, J.S., de Rijke, M.: The potential of learned index structures for index compression. In: Proceedings of the 23rd Australasian Document Computing Symposium, pp. 1–4. Springer, Heidelberg (2018). https://doi.org/10.1145/3291992.3291993

14. Zhang, J., Lu, Y., Sparnpinato, D.G., et al.: FESIA: a fast and SIMD-efficient set intersection approach on modern CPUs. In: 2020 IEEE 36th International Conference on Data Engineering, ICDE, pp. 1465–1476. IEEE (2020)

15. Lemire, D., Boytsov, L., Kurz, N.: SIMD compression and the intersection of sorted integers. Softw. Pract. Exp. **46**(6), 723–749 (2016)

16. Gossard, E.E.: The height distribution of refractive index structure parameter in an atmosphere being modified by spatial transition at its lower boundary. Radio Sci. **13**(3), 489–500 (2016)

17. Li, Y., Wang, J., Pullman, B., et al.: Index-based, high-dimensional, cosine threshold querying with optimality guarantees. Theory Comput. Syst. **65**(4), 1–42 (2021)

18. Zhong, H., Li, Z., Xu, Y., Chen, Z., Cui, J.: Two-stage index-based central keyword-ranked searches over encrypted cloud data. Sci. China Inf. Sci. **63**(3), 1–3 (2020)

19. Lekshmi, K.K., Prem, M.V.: Multi-keyword score threshold and B+ tree indexing based top-K query retrieval in cloud. Peer-to-Peer Netw. Appl. **13**(6), 1990–2000 (2019)

20. Bai, F.J., Gao, J.L., Li, W.R., et al.: An inverted index compression method. Appl. Res. Comput. **36**(1), 106–109 (2019)

21. Zhu, J., Liu, Z., Qiao, D., et al.: Construction and optimization of spatial index model for massive geospatial data based on hbase. Geolog. Sci. Technol. Inf. **35**(4), 1–8 (2019)

22. Yang, M., Ma, K., Yu, X.: An efficient index structure for distributed k-nearest neighbours query processing. Soft. Comput. **24**(8), 5539–5550 (2020)

23. Hao, R.Z., Li, J.W., Guang, J.: A privacy-preserved indexing schema in DaaS model for range queries. High Technol. Newslett. Eng. Vers. **26**(4), 7 (2020)

24. Qiao, Y.C., Yun, X.C., Tuo, Y.P., et al.: Fast traceability method for reuse code based on simhash and inverted index. J. Commun. **37**(11), 10 (2016)

25. Huang, Y., Li, X., Zhang, G.Q.: ELII: a novel inverted index for fast temporal query, with application to a large covid-19 ehr dataset. J. Biomed. Inform. **117**(4), 103744 (2021)

26. Peng, Y., Xu, Y., Zhao, H., Zhou, Z., Han, H.: Most similar maximal clique query on large graphs. Front. Comp. Sci. **14**(3), 1–16 (2019)

27. Du, R.Z., Li, M.Y., Tian, J.F., et al.: Verifiable obfuscated keyword ciphertext retrieval scheme based on inverted index. J. Softw. **30**(8), 2362–2374 (2019)

28. Zheng, Z., Ruan, K., Yu, M., et al.: k-Dominant skyline query algorithm for dynamic datasets. Front. Comp. Sci. **15**(1), 1–9 (2021)

29. Boucenna, F., Nouali, O., Kechid, S., et al.: Secure inverted index based search over encrypted cloud data with user access rights management. J. Comput. Sci. Technol. **34**(1), 133–154 (2019)

30. Hua, J., Liu, Y., Chen, H., Tian, X., Jin, C.: An enhanced wildcard-based fuzzy searching scheme in encrypted databases. World Wide Web **23**(3), 2185–2214 (2020)

31. Lilian, J.F., Sundarakantham, K., Shalinie, S.M.: QeCSO: design of hybrid cuckoo search based query expansion model for efficient information retrieval. Sādhanā **46**(3), 1–11 (2021)

32. Wang, P., Susilo, W.: Data security storage model of the internet of things based on blockchain. Comput. Syst. Sci. Eng. **36**(1), 213–224 (2021)
33. Ntshalintshali, G.M., Clariana, R.B.: Paraphrasing refutation text and knowledge form: examples from repairing relational database design misconceptions. Educ. Tech. Res. Dev. **68**(5), 2165–2183 (2020)
34. Jose, B., Abraham, S.: Performance analysis of NoSQL and relational databases with MongoDB and MySQL. Mater. Today Proc. **24**(7), 2036–2043 (2020)
35. Ragavan, N., Rubavathi, C.Y.: A novel big data storage reduction model for drill down search. Comput. Syst. Sci. Eng. **41**(1), 373–387 (2022)

An Optimization Strategy for Spatial Information Network Topology

Jiaying Zhang⬛, Peng Yang$^{(\boxtimes)}$, and Shuang Hu

University of Electronic Science and Technology of China,
Chengdu 610054, China
yang_peng_26@163.com

Abstract. Aiming at the characteristics of high-speed movement of SIN network nodes, this article studies the invulnerability of SIN network from the perspective of topological structure. According to the periodicity of satellite constellation, a satellite cycle is divided into multiple time slices and optimized respectively. Taking network redundancy as the optimization goal, the main consideration is the full connectivity of network nodes, the number of nodes and links, and the node load, etc., to construct a network topology invulnerability optimization model. Model solving is an NP-hard problem, this paper proposes a neighbor immune algorithm (NIA) based on simulated annealing update. This method applies improved simulated annealing algorithm (ISAA) before neighbor immune algorithm falls into the local optimum, replacing part of the antibody, so that the population continues to evolve to a better solution. This strategy overcomes the shortcomings of neighbor immune algorithm that it is easy to fall into the local optimum at the later stage of the iteration, and at the same time improves the convergence speed. Finally, the simulation is based on the Iridium constellation with 66 low orbit (LEO), experiments show that the improved algorithm effectively optimizes the optimization effect of the original algorithm, and can obtain a topological structure with good invulnerability.

Keywords: Neighbor immune algorithm · Simulated annealing algorithm · Network topology · Invulnerability

1 Introduction

With the advancement of the "air-space-ground integration" process, the spatial information network (SIN) plays an extremely important role in the task of information transmission, acquisition and distribution. The nodes in the SIN network are in high-speed motion at all times. Due to the occlusion of the earth, the communicable links between satellites are sometimes disconnected. At the same time, high-speed movement can easily lead to the failure of nodes and links. For highly dynamic satellite networks, the number of satellite links that can be established is much smaller than the number of satellite links that can be established. Therefore, in the case of limited resources, designing a topological structure with high invulnerability is of great significance to the acquisition and transmission of satellite network information.

© The Author(s), under exclusive license to Springer Nature Switzerland AG 2022
X. Sun et al. (Eds.): ICAIS 2022, CCIS 1587, pp. 405–418, 2022.
https://doi.org/10.1007/978-3-031-06761-7_33

At present, the research on satellite network topology generation has achieved certain results. SHI et al. used a greedy algorithm for link allocation [1] and optimized the number of inter-satellite observations, but the algorithm's convergence was very poor. ZHENG et al. proposed a multi-objective optimization path selection algorithm based on priority queues to optimize the shortest transmission path of the link [9]. PAN et al. innovatively considered the particularity of the satellite multi-state system, and also used simulated annealing algorithm to obtain the optimal topology for the transmission delay. However, the random update method of link exchange adopted by its algorithm is easy to fall into a local optimal solution [3].

In the optimization algorithms used in the above studies, random link switching methods are used when generating neighborhood solutions, which are prone to fall into the optimal solution and slow convergence. This paper takes network redundancy as the optimization goal, optimizes the invulnerability of the topology, and considers the problem of satellite link resource constraints, and proposes NIA based on simulated annealing. When NIA falls into the optimal solution, this method uses simulated annealing algorithm to update the neighborhood solution, which expands the population iteration advantage of NIA and improves the optimization result.

2   Satellite Network Topology

The satellite network studied in this paper is mainly composed of satellites and inter-satellite links. From the perspective of graph theory, every satellite in the network can be regarded as a node $s_i(i = 1, 2, \ldots n)$, which forms the point set of a graph regarded as $S = \{s_1, s_2, \ldots, s_n\}$. After recording the links between any two satellites s_i and s_j as $e(s_i, s_j)$, the edge set $E = \{e_1, e_2, \ldots, e_m\}$ composed of these edges is defined. So a satellite network can be regarded as an undirected graph $G = \{S, E\}$. Then define $A_{n \times n} = a_{ij}$ as the adjacency matrix of a satellite network G. When there is an edge $e(s_i, s_j)$ between s_i and s_j, let the corresponding value in matrix A be 1, that is, $a_{ij} = a_{ji} = 1$, otherwise $a_{ij} = a_{ji} = 0$.

During the movement of the satellites, the visibility between the satellites will change every few seconds. Define the matrix $V_{n \times n} = v_{ij}$ as the visible matrix, That is, when an inter-satellite link can be established between the satellite s_i and the satellite s_j, $v_{ij} = v_{ji} = 1$, otherwise $v_{ij} = v_{ji} = 0$. In order to solve the problem of high-speed movement of satellites, one cycle of the satellite constellation movement is divided into multiple time periods, and the time period from each change of the visible matrix to the last change is called a time slice. The algorithm in this paper divides the entire satellite period into M time slices, within each time slice, the topology of the constellation will not change. In this way, a single time slice can be used to design an optimization algorithm for the object for calculation.

3 Satellite Network Optimization Model

Optimizing the satellite network topology is essentially to find the optimal solution of the satellite network adjacency matrix A with high invulnerability under constraint conditions. It is believed that the more edges in the network, the higher the redundancy. Then for a network with n satellites and at most m edges, the topology to be selected has $C_{\frac{(n-1)n}{2}}^{m}$. It is an NP-hard problem to find the highest invulnerability from all the topological structures. There is currently no algorithm that can be proven to find the optimal solution for this type of problem.

With the deepening of research, adopting some optimization algorithms to find a better solution has become a research hotspot. In this paper, NIA is adopted. Compared with sorting genetic algorithm II (SGA II), the use of cloning operation expands the search range of optimal solutions and suppresses the degradation phenomenon in the optimization process of SGA II to a certain extent. But under the same number of iterations, NIA runs slowly, and the particularity of its population optimization is easy to fall into the local optimal solution. The simulated annealing algorithm can speed up the search speed and accept inferior solutions with a certain probability, which can effectively jump out of the local optimum and make up for the deficiencies of NIA.

3.1 Objective Function

In this paper, redundancy is used as the optimization goal of network invulnerability. After verification, network redundancy can effectively measure the invulnerability of complex networks. The invulnerability of the network topology can be defined as: the ability of the topology to maintain connectivity when a node or edge in the network fails immediately. The essence of network redundancy is to measure the number of all closed loops in the network. Network redundancy is essentially a measure of the number of all closed loops in a network. The more closed loops there are, the more alternative paths there are between nodes, and the higher the damage resistance. According to the knowledge of graph theory, the kth power matrix A^k of the adjacency matrix $A(G)$, the element a_{ii}^k on the main diagonal of the i-th row, is a closed loop with node s_i as the starting point and end point and length k number.

Therefore, the total number of closed loops of various lengths in the network:

$$L' = \sum_{k=0}^{\infty} \sum_{i=1}^{n} a_{ii}^k \tag{1}$$

The adjacency matrix A is a real symmetric matrix, which can be known from matrix theory:

$$L' = \sum_{k=0}^{\infty} \sum_{i=1}^{n} a_{ii}^k = \sum_{k=0}^{\infty} tr\left(A^k\right) = \sum_{k=0}^{\infty} \sum_{i=1}^{n} (\lambda_i)^k \tag{2}$$

Among them, there are n real eigenvalues of matrix A defined as $\lambda_i(i = 1, 2, \ldots n)$. As the above formula has a problem of repeatedly superimposing the number of closed loops with actual contributions. Penalty coefficient A_k^k is used to process it, as a result:

$$L = \frac{1}{A_k^k} \times L = \sum_{i=1}^{n} \sum_{k=0}^{\infty} \frac{(\lambda_i)^k}{k!} = \sum_{i=1}^{n} e^{\lambda_i} \tag{3}$$

At the same time, in order to ensure the convergence of L, define the redundancy of the complex network:

$$R = \ln\left(\sum_{i=1}^{n} e^{\lambda_i}\right) \tag{4}$$

3.2 Model Building

In the actual satellite network, affected by the power of the nodes and the surface area of the satellite itself, the upper limit of the actual number of links for each satellite is less than the number of visible satellites. That is, the sum of elements in each row of the adjacency matrix $\sum_{j=1}^{n} a_{ij}$ has an upper limit D_{max}. At the same time, the connectivity of the network and ensuring the visibility between the chain-building satellites are one of the constraints. For the adjacency matrix A of the graph, its Laplacian matrix:

$$L = D - A \tag{5}$$

Among them, $D = diag(d_i) = diag\left(\sum_{j=1}^{n} a_{ij}\right)$ is the diagonal matrix formed by the degree of nodes. Solve the eigenvalues of the Laplacian matrix, sort from small to large $0 \leq \mu_1 \leq \mu_2 \leq \cdots \leq \mu_n$. Then A is connected when μ_2 is greater than 0. According to the constraints and objective function, the satellite network optimization model is established as follows:

$$max\, R = ln\left(\sum_{i=1}^{N} e^{\lambda_i}\right) \tag{6}$$

$$\begin{cases} \mu_2 > 0 \\ \sum_{j=1}^{N} a_{ij} \leq 4 \\ \forall a_{ij} = 1, v_{ij} = 1 \end{cases} \tag{7}$$

In the formula, the adjacency matrix is $A_{n \times n} = a_{ij}$, and the visible matrix is $V_{n \times n} = v_{ij}$. This paper comprehensively considers the network connectivity, resource constraints, and satellite visibility, and obtains a better topology by solving the adjacency matrix that makes the network redundant.

4 Neighbor Immune Algorithm Based on Simulated Annealing

4.1 Simulated Annealing Algorithm

Simulated annealing algorithm uses the annealing idea, and each new solution is randomly obtained from the current solution neighborhood, which is equivalent to the mutation operation in NIA. The advantage of the temperature in the algorithm is that it adopts the Metropolis criterion, which can accept inferior solutions with a certain probability, and thus has the ability to jump out of the local optimal solution. The detailed flow of ISAA used in this paper is shown in Fig. 1.

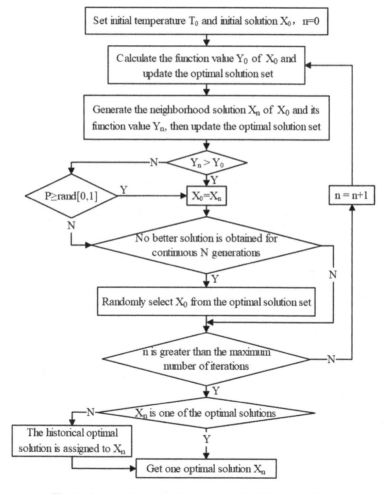

Fig. 1. Improved simulated annealing algorithm flow chart.

The temperature T_i of the i-th iteration is obtained by annealing the temperature T_{i-1} of the previous generation:

$$T_i = q \times T_{i-1} \tag{8}$$

where q is the set cooling rate. The probability P of accepting a new solution is affected by the current temperature, and the higher the temperature, the easier it is to accept the new solution.

$$P = \begin{cases} 1, & f(x_{i+1}) > f(x_i) \\ e^{\frac{f(x_{i+1}) - f(x_i)}{T_i}}, & f(x_{i+1}) > f(x_i) \end{cases} \tag{9}$$

4.2   Neighbor Immune Algorithm

The idea of neighbor immune algorithm is to imitate the principle of antibody formation of human immune viruses, with the objective function to be optimized as the antigen and solution as the antibody. The basic steps are:

① Initialization generates a set of solutions randomly, and calculates its affinity according to the designed solution model.

② According to the affinity of the antibody, the higher n_D dominant individuals are selected to form the first-generation dominant population D.

③ Cloning: Select n_B individuals of the dominant population D species with high adaptability to copy, and obtain the clone population B.

④ Cross mutation: Cross and mutate individuals in the clonal population to obtain a series of new individuals to form the population R.

⑤ Merge the dominant population D and population R, and retain n_D with higher affinity to form the next generation dominant population.

⑥ If the current iteration number is greater than the set value, proceed to step ⑦; otherwise, repeat step ③–step ⑤.

⑦ Output the individual with the highest affinity in the current population as the final solution.

In step ③ of the algorithm, each individual is stratified according to their dominance and non-dominated relationship, and the fitness value reflects the crowdedness distance of the individual in the population. That is, the local density between each point in the target space and two adjacent points of the same level. This operation copies individuals with sparse function values more times, which improves the diversity of the search range. The calculation formula for the number of clones q_i of individual b_i is as follows:

$$q_i = n_C \times \frac{I(b_i, B)}{\sum_{j=1}^{|B|} I(b_j, B)} \tag{10}$$

Among them, n_C is the number of individuals in the cloned population C, and $I(b_i, B)$ is the crowding degree of the individual b_i in the population B, which is determined by the individual's antigen affinity: Sort all individuals in population B according to their affinity to get $b_1, b_2, \ldots, b_{n_B}$, and define the crowding degree of b_i as the ratio of the difference between the affinity before and after it and the difference between the maximum and minimum values of the population, namely:

$$I(b_i, B) = \frac{|R(b_{i-1}) - R(b_{i+1})|}{|R(b_1) - R(b_{n_B})|} \tag{11}$$

The mutation operation in step ④ of the above algorithm is usually the method of random mutation in the neighborhood. However, unlike other function optimization problems, due to the limitation of the visible matrix and the number of established chains in the satellite network, the matrix cannot quickly obtain new individuals that meet the constraints by simply breaking the chain and building a new chain. In order to keep the degree value of each node of the matrix unchanged after the mutation, the link is updated by switching the link. Randomly select two satellites s_1, s_2, according to the adjacency matrix A and the visible matrix V, the s_1, s_2 established chain satellites and the set of visible satellites are obtained respectively: a_1, a_2, v_1, v_2. From the visible satellite set v_1 of s_1, the satellite s_3 that has not been linked but is linked to s_2 is randomly selected, and the satellite s_4 that is not linked but is linked to s_1 is randomly selected from the visual satellite set v_1 of s_2. The links $e(s_1, s_4)$ and $e(s_2, s_3)$ are deleted, and $e(s_2, s_4)$ and $e(s_1, s_3)$ are established to complete the link exchange. This kind of exchange has randomness, does not change the degree of nodes, and can meet the visibility requirements at the same time.

NIA does not require external storage. Step ⑤ adopts an elite retention strategy that merges all the parents and offspring into a unified population, and the algorithm has a higher computational efficiency.

4.3   NIA Based on Simulated Annealing Algorithm

Different from multi-dimensional vector optimization, the search direction of the matrix optimization process is very broad and complicated. Aiming at the problem of finding the approximate optimal solution of the network adjacency matrix, the method of finding the optimal solution by switching links successively has strong randomness. Although the number of selectable topologies is an astronomical number, multiple similar topologies actually have the same degree of redundancy. And due to the limitation of the visibility of the satellite network, not all structures with the same degree of redundancy can obtain a solution with better invulnerability through the exchange of links.

The advantage of NIA to solve this problem is that the characteristics of population optimization can retain the same redundant topological structure, and improve the diversity and optimization speed through cross mutation within the population and large-scale mutation of the population as a whole, thereby improving the performance of the algorithm. This idea is suitable for solving large-scale and high-complexity optimization problems. Its disadvantage is that the elite retention strategy in the selection process still adopts the idea of greedy algorithm, that is, the objective function value is the largest. This makes it easy to obtain populations with identical individuals or identical redundancy in the process of random search from generation to generation. This situation increases the possibility of the algorithm falling into a local optimum in the later stage, and weakens the advantage of NIA population evolution (Fig. 2).

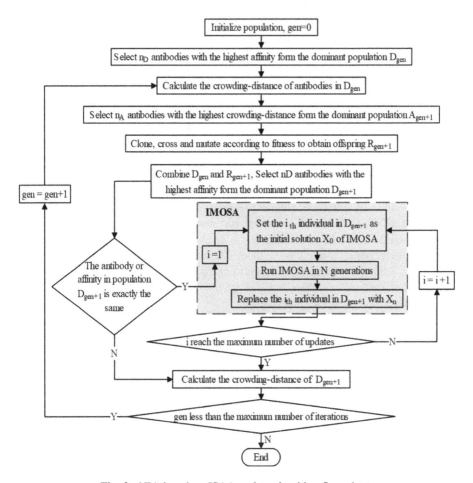

Fig. 2. NIA based on ISAA-update algorithm flow chart.

In order to solve the problem that NIA is easy to fall into the local optimum in the later stage, this paper combines simulated annealing algorithm, and adds a set to store the historical optimal solution in simulated annealing algorithm. When NIA tends to become uniform, improved simulated annealing algorithm is used to update some individuals, which can quickly improve the affinity of individuals and speed up the convergence speed, and at the same time improve the optimization ability of the population.

The flow of neighbor immune optimization algorithm based on simulated annealing is shown in the Fig. 1. In the Fig. 1, P is the probability of simulated annealing accepting bad solutions, and i is the number of antibodies in the updated population.

5 Simulation Experiment and Analysis

5.1 Simulation Environment and Parameter Setting

In this paper, MATLAB and STK software are used for joint simulation. The iridium constellation with 66 Leo is used as the constellation configuration. The specific parameters are shown in Table 1.

Table 1. Parameters of constellation simulation.

Parameters of satellite	Value
Altitude/km	780
Inclination/(°)	86.3
Amount of orbit	6
Satellite amount of one orbit	11
Total number of satellites	66
RAAN/(°)	60
Period/s	6027.1
Connectivity	4

In NIA, the number of initialization population is 50, and the number of dominant population, active population and clone population are respectively set to 20, 5 and 20. When ISAA is used for updating, 8 individuals are updated at a time, the initial temperature is 1000 and the annealing rate is 0.95. Each individual iterates 500 times. The number of external loop iterations is 2000.

5.2 Comparison of the Algorithms

The invulnerability optimization model is a single-object and multi-constraint optimization model. However, considering the complexity of solving the adjacency matrix of the object network, the multi-objective population optimization algorithms, NIA and SGA II are selected to compared with ISAA. The experimental results are shown in the figure below.

For a single time slice, Fig. 3 shows the astringency comparison of three existing algorithms. On the premise that other conditions are consistent, the convergence of the three algorithms under the 18 s running time is intercepted, there was no obvious optimization in the subsequent operation. Firstly, from the optimization results in the Table 2, there is little difference between NIA and SGA II, also they are much better than simulated annealing algorithm; Secondly, from the perspective of optimization speed, ISAA has great advantages followed by NIA. However, when it's focused on the last stage of iteration shown in Fig. 4 and Table 2, it's clearly that NIA converges much earlier than SGA II. That means the optimization ability of NIA is much stronger than that of SGA II. On the other hand, it is also more difficult for NIA to jump out of the local optimal solution, so there is still a large optimization space in the overall topology for NIA.

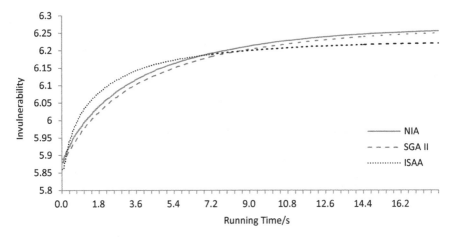

Fig. 3. Comparison of running times among ISAA, NIA, SGA II.

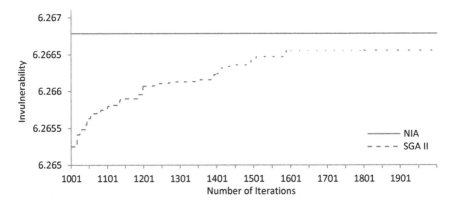

Fig. 4. The last 1000 iterations comparison of NIA and SGA II.

Figure 5 shows the comparison of the improved algorithm with NIA and ISAA. By analyzing the experimental results, the former convergence speed of NIA based on simulated annealing update proposed in this paper is very close to that of ISAA, and the optimization result is significantly improved. In the process of the algorithm, some similar individuals are updated repeatedly because of the need to jump out of the local

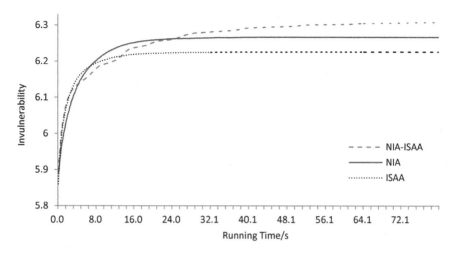

Fig. 5. Comparison of running times among NIA-ISAA, ISAA and NIA.

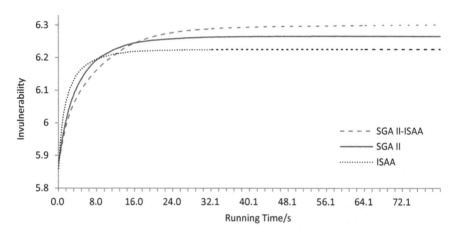

Fig. 6. Comparison of running times among SGA II-ISAA, ISAA and SGA II.

optimal solution, which leads to a certain fluctuation in the mid-term of convergence. But during its optimization process still exceeds ISAA and NIA in their 4340th and 411th iterations respectively. Overall, the improved algorithm does help NIA get a good ability to jump out of the local optimal solution as well as getting faster update speed in the early stage. It can be seen from the Table 2 that the solution result of the algorithm proposed in this paper is significantly higher, which proves the effective improvement of the algorithm.

Similarly, the ISAA-improved method is also used in SGA II for the same experiment a as the result in Fig. 6. This updating method just has a certain ability to jump out from the local optimization without higher convergence speed. That's because compared with NIA, SGA II has no cloning step in its flow which makes it

Table 2. The average optimal value, time to maximum and running time of five algorithms.

Algorithm	Optimal value	Time to its maximum	Running time/s
ISAA	6.2264	108.263	115.666
NIA	6.2668	44.952	134.587
NIA-ISAA	6.312	121.102	121.406
SGA II	6.2666	68.068	85.674
SGA II-ISAA	6.303	104.688	104.898

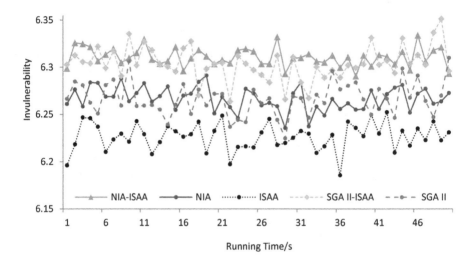

Fig. 7. ISAA, NIA and NIA-ISAA's comparison of topology invulnerability optimization results on 50 time slices

difficult to meet the conditions for accepting updates when looking for a better topology. When compared with NIS-ISAA, NIS-ISAA already get the maximum result of SGA II-ISAA at 64 s. In other words, it's not essential for SGA II to be updated by ISAA whose process would slow down the algorithm without more effective optimization capability. However, the fast search ability of ISAA does have an effect on the search of better solutions, which confirms the effectiveness of the update method proposed in this paper.

Now Fig. 7 compares the optimization results for the overall dynamic topology of five algorithms. Because there are too many time slices, only the first 50 are chosen for comparison.

After the optimization of the algorithm, the value of redundancy in iridium constellation increases. Due to the constraints, the connectivity of satellite nodes is small, and the increase is not obvious (about 6%). However, due to the strict monotonicity of the optimization results in each time slice which SGA II-ISAA does not achieve, it is ensured that the topology obtained by the algorithm has higher invulnerability. In addition, the variance of the overall topology is smaller, and the invulnerability stability of the network is improved in the whole operation cycle, which further proves the effectiveness of the improved algorithm proposed in this paper in dealing with the invulnerability optimization problem of SIN network topology.

6   Conclusion

Considering that the network topology fundamentally affects the network invulnerability, this paper optimizes the topology invulnerability according to the high dynamic and periodic characteristics of spatial information network, mainly considering the constraints such as the full connectivity of network nodes, the number of nodes and links and node load, and proposes a NIA based on simulated annealing update with network redundancy as the objective function. Verified by simulation:

1)   The convergence result of the algorithm in iridium constellation is better than that of ISAA and NIA. For a single time slice, a topology with higher invulnerability can be obtained. At the same time, the overall redundancy of sin network is increased by 6%, that is, the global network topology generated by the algorithm has better invulnerability. The update method proposed in this paper is more effective when combined with NIA.
2)   NIA-ISAA does not converge in 2000 iterations in this experiment, and according to the experimental results in the Fig. 7, it is found that the algorithm still has a certain optimization space for multiple time slices.

Acknowledgement. Research supported by Major Science and Technology Special Project of Sichuan Province, P.R. China (Grant no. 2019ZDZX0007).

References

1. Shi, L.Y., Xiang, W., Tang, X.M.: A link assignment algorithm applicable to crosslink ranging and data exchange for satellite navigation system. J. Astronaut. **32**(9), 1971–1977 (2011)
2. Wang, Z.X., Jiang, D.L., Qi, L.: Complex network invulnerability and node importance evaluation model based on redundancy. Compl. Syst. Complex. Sci. **17**(3), 78–85 (2020)
3. Pan, C.S., Xing, G.X., Qi, Y.W.: Topology generation method in multi-state space information network. Acta Aeronaut. Astronaut. Sin. **41**(4), 323546 (2020)
4. Gong, M.G., Jiao, L.C., Du, H.F.: Multi-objective immune algorithm with nondominated neighbor-based selection. Evol. Comput. **16**(2), 225–255 (2008)
5. Li, S.D., Zhu, J., Li, G.X.: Optimization of LEO regional communication satellite constellation with GA algorithm. J. China Inst. Commun. **26**(8), 122–128 (2005). (in Chinese)
6. Jiang, X.L., Jiang, Q.J., Liu, H.J.: Design optimization of hybrid leo constellation using modified non-dominated neighbor immune algorithm. J. Astronaut. **35**(9), 1007–1014 (2014)
7. Kirkpatrick, S., Gelatt, C.D., Vecchi, M.P.: Optimization by simulated annealing. Science **220**(4598), 606–680 (1983)

8. Yan, C., Ou, Z.C., Liu, W.: Research on UBI auto insurance pricing model based on adaptive SAPSO to optimize the fuzzy controller. Int. J. Fuzzy Syst. **22**(3), 491–503 (2020)

9. Zheng, G.M.: Research on satellite constellation design and routing based on multi-objective optimization. M. S. Dissertation, Chongqing University of Posts and Telecommunications, Chong Qing (2019). (in Chinese)

10. Wei, D.B., Qin, Y.F., Yu, R.: Research on satellite network topologies survivability evaluation method. Comput. Sci. **43**(11A), 301–310 (2016). (in Chinese)

11. Dong, F.H., Lv, J., Gong, X.W.: Optimization design of structure invulnerability in space information network. J. Commun. **35**(10), 50–58 (2014). (in Chinese)

12. Nie, Y.Y., Fang, Z.G., Liu, S.F.: Dynamic invulnerability model of LEO satellite network based on node repair. Contr. Decis. **35**(5), 1247–1252 (2020). (in Chinese)

13. Huang, J., Su, Y., Liu, W.: Optimization design of inter-satellite link (ISL) assignment parameters in GNSS based on genetic algorithm. Adv. Space Res. **60**(12), 2574–2580 (2017). (in Chinese)

14. Dong, M.Z., Lin, B.J., Liu, Y.C.: Topology dynamic optimization for inter-satellite laser links of navigation satellite based on multi-objective simulated annealing method. Chin. J. Lasers **45**(7), 1–12 (2018). (in Chinese)

15. Shi, W.B., Liu, D., Yang, B.W.: Research on network invulnerability optimization based on link reconfiguration. Strategy **30**, 6–9 (2020). (in Chinese)

16. Castet, J.F., Saleh, J.H.: Beyond reliability, multi-state failure analysis of satellite subsystems: a statistical approach. Reliab. Eng. Syst. Saf. **95**(4), 311–322 (2009)

17. Mo, Y., Yan, D.W., You, P.: A survey of constellation optimization design for satellite communications. Telecommun. Eng. **56**(11), 1293–1300 (2016). (in Chinese)

18. Jian, G., Liora, M., Eberhard, G.: Statistical analysis and modelling of small satellite reliability. Acta Astronaut. **98**, 97–110 (2014)

19. Erlank, A.O., Bridges, C.P.: Reliability analysis of multicellular system architectures for low-cost satellites. Acta Astronaut. **147**, 183–194 (2018)

20. Matthew, P.F., David, B.S.: Satellite constellation design tradeoffs using multiple-objective evolutionary computation. J. Spacecr. Rocket. **43**(6), 1404–1411 (2006)

21. Oh, E., Lee, H.: Development of a convolution-based multi-directional and parallel ant colony algorithm considering a network with dynamic topology changes. Appl. Sci. **9**, 3646 (2019)

22. Wang, X., Wang, Q.: Study on optimization of urban rail operation control curve based on improved multi-objective genetic algorithm. J. Internet Things **3**(1), 1–9 (2021)

23. Assiri, A.: Anomaly classification using genetic algorithm-based random forest model for network attack detection. Comput. Mater. Continua **66**(1), 767–778 (2021)

24. Mei, P., Ding, G., Jin, Q.: Reconstruction and optimization of complex network community structure under deep learning and quantum ant colony optimization algorithm. Intell. Autom. Soft Comput. **27**(1), 159–171 (2021)

25. Li, Y., Xie, J., Xia, M.: Dynamic resource pricing and allocation in multilayer satellite network. Comput. Mater. Continua **69**(3), 3619–3628 (2021)

26. Wang, H., Zhu, C., Shen, Z.: A network security risk assessment method based on a b_nag model. Comput. Syst. Sci. Eng. **38**(1), 103–117 (2021)

Research on Driving Factors of Independent Innovation Capability of New Energy Equipment Manufacturing Enterprises

Ruhao Ma[1(✉)], Haiwen Du[2,3], Fansheng Meng[1], and Dongjie Zhu[4]

[1] School of Economics and Management, Harbin Engineering University,
Harbin 150001, China
mrh9506@163.com

[2] School of Astronautics, Harbin Institute of Technology, Harbin 150001, China

[3] School of Computer Science, University College Dublin, Dublin, Ireland

[4] School of Computer Science and Technology, Harbin Institute of Technology,
Weihai 264209, China

Abstract. With the implementation of the "Made in China 2025" plan and the promulgation of the "Renewable Energy Law", China's new energy equipment manufacturing industry has developed rapidly. At the same time, it has also revealed that China's new energy equipment manufacturing enterprises have issues such as a high degree of external dependence on key technologies and low-level international competitiveness. Facing the complex international market environment, Chinese new energy equipment manufacturing enterprises urgently need to improve their independent innovation capabilities. This paper establishes the driving factors of independent innovation by sorting out domestic and international independent innovation-related research and combining the opinions of new energy equipment manufacturing experts. By using the exploratory factor analysis, five dimensions that affect independent innovation capability are extracted: independent innovation input capability, external environmental support, internal environmental support, knowledge management capability, and independent innovation output capability. Finally, it establishes the structural equation model of the driving factors of the independent innovation capability of new energy equipment manufacturing enterprises and proposes the driving path of the independent innovation capability of new energy equipment manufacturing enterprises. The research results show that both independent innovation input ability and knowledge management ability can directly have a positive impact on independent innovation output ability, and the influence of knowledge management ability is more significant; while the external environmental support and internal environmental support influence the enterprise's knowledge management ability Indirectly affect the output capacity of independent innovation.

Keywords: New energy equipment manufacturing industry · Independent innovation capability · Structural equation model · Driving factors

X. Sun et al. (Eds.): ICAIS 2022, CCIS 1587, pp. 419–429, 2022.
https://doi.org/10.1007/978-3-031-06761-7_34

1 Introduction

The implementation of the "Made in China 2025" plan has promoted the transformation of China's manufacturing industry from "manufacturing" to "intelligent manufacturing" [1]. The equipment manufacturing industry is at the high end of a country's value chain and the core link of the industrial chain. It is the engine that promotes industrial transformation and upgrading, and energy is the source of power for the operation of the engine [2, 3]. Due to the non-renewability of traditional fossil energy represented by oil and coal and the environmental problems caused by the extensive use of fossil energy, many countries have turned their attention to the development and utilization of new energy such as hydropower, wind energy, and solar energy, and new energy equipment manufacturing [4]. The development of China is also booming day by day. In the past, China used cheap labor and imported technology to make the equipment manufacturing industry advance by leaps and bounds. However, due to misunderstandings and strategic mistakes, China's equipment manufacturing capability is weak in independent innovation and lacks core technologies, and many strategic equipment manufacturing products are severely constrained by others. As a result, the overall competitiveness of the equipment manufacturing industry is not strong. In particular, the new energy equipment manufacturing industry is promoted by high and new technology. Although the traditional "technology introduction-backward-re-introduction-further backward" model has allowed it to develop for a period of time, the effective international demand for new energy is insufficient, and developed countries have "high-end" under the background of "return" and "mid-to-low-end diversion" in developing countries, when the market share of China's new energy equipment manufacturing industry grows to a certain extent, technology acquisition will become more and more difficult [5]. The traditional "introduction" innovation restricts its further development [6]. For Chinese new energy equipment manufacturing enterprises, it is particularly important to enhance independent innovation capabilities and improve international competitiveness.

At present, "building an innovative country" has become the direction of China's efforts. The independent innovation capability and overall development level of the equipment manufacturing industry determine China's economic strength, scientific and technological strength, national defense strength, and position in global competition [7, 8]. China attaches great importance to the development of the equipment manufacturing industry. It puts forward the goals, principles, tasks, and policies of the equipment manufacturing industry at the national level, and has issued a series of major decisions and policy support, focusing on strengthening the independent innovation capability of China's equipment manufacturing industry [9]. China's equipment manufacturing industry is shouldering the important task of moving from "Made in China" to "Intelligent Manufacturing in China", and the new energy equipment manufacturing industry is the "leader" in the army of "Intelligent Manufacturing" [10]. Therefore, this research aims to explore the driving factors and influence paths of China's new energy equipment manufacturing industry's independent innovation capabilities based on previous research on equipment manufacturing and independent innovation, combined with the actual situation of China's new energy equipment manufacturing enterprises.

2 Determining the Driving Factors of Independent Innovation Capability

This study has compiled the research results of relevant experts and scholars, combined with the actual situation of my country's new energy equipment manufacturing enterprises, referred to the expert opinions of new energy equipment manufacturing, and summarized and extracted 16 new energy equipment manufacturing enterprises' independent innovation capabilities.

2.1 Data Analysis

In this study, Windows SPSS 20.0 software was used to perform exploratory factor analysis on 158 original data. Through calculation, the KMO value is 0.812 (close to 1), the Bartlett sphericity test result is 787.329, and the significance level is 0.000, indicating that the factor analysis method can be used to extract several dimensions of the driving factors of the independent innovation capability of new energy equipment manufacturing enterprises. After that, we used principal component analysis and the maximum variance orthogonal rotation method and used the eigenvalue greater than 1 and the factor load not less than 0.50 to extract five dimensions. The results are shown in Table 1. In the table, the abbreviations are as follows: WZ is the external environment support; NZ is the internal environment support; CC is the independent innovation output capacity; ZS is the knowledge management ability; TR is the Independent innovation investment capacity. We refer to the relevant literature on the influencing factors of independent innovation at home and abroad, and based on the analysis of the data results of the questionnaire, we named the measurement dimensions of the independent innovation capability of five new energy equipment manufacturers, and for the convenience of displaying in the model, And influencing factors are expressed in English letters.

2.2 Reliability Test

In this study, Cronbach's Alpha coefficient was used to test the reliability of the scale. The value of Cronbach's Alpha coefficient between 0.65 and 0.70 is the minimum acceptable value. A value greater than 0.7 indicates that the scale is reliable. Table 2 shows the Cronbach's Alpha coefficient value of each latent variable analyzed by SPSS20.0 software. Except for the external environmental support, the other latent variable coefficient values are all greater than 0.7, and there is no latent variable less than 0.65. The Cronbach's Alpha coefficient value of the scale is 0.841, which indicates that the scale is highly reliable and requires a composite reliability test.

Table 1. Exploratory factor analysis results of independent innovation capabilities of new energy equipment manufacturing enterprises (N = 158).

Indicator	Code	Factor				
		WZ	NZ	CC	ZS	TR
R&D human resource investment intensity	TR1					.667
R&D expenditure input intensity	TR2					.797
Number of R&D institutions and technology centers	TR3					.830
Entrepreneurs' emphasis on independent innovation	NZ1		.784			
Number of enterprise innovation incentive methods	NZ2		.816			
The corporate values of advocating innovation and emphasizing talents	NZ3		.691			
Accumulation of corporate innovation knowledge	ZS1				.822	
Learning ability of enterprise R&D personnel	ZS2				.668	
Knowledge Sharing in Organizational Communication	ZS3				.630	
Absorption and utilization of knowledge or technology	ZS4				.596	
Government policy support	WZ1	.711				
Cooperation between enterprises and external scientific research institutions	WZ2	.772				
The level of enterprises attracting and utilizing foreign capital	WZ3	.708				
Number of achievements of innovative products	CC1			.731		
Market competitiveness of innovative products	CC2			.811		
Number of enterprise invention patents	CC3			.771		
Eigenvalue (rotation value)		2.195	2.155	2.049	2.045	1.988
Explainable amount of variance (%)		13.722	13.467	12.808	12.783	12.423
Cumulative explainable variance (%)		13.722	27.189	39.997	52.780	65.203

Note:

1. The method of extracting factors is Principal Component Analysis.

2. The rotation method is Varimax with Kaiser Normalization

Table 2. Latent variables and Cronbach's alpha coefficient value of scale.

Latent variable	Cronbach's alpha coefficient	Number of measurable variables	Scale Cronbach's alpha coefficient
Independent innovation investment capacity	0.725	3	0.841
Internal environment support	0.747	3	
External environment support	0.657	3	
Knowledge management ability	0.777	4	
Independent innovation output capacity	0.700	3	

3 Construction of Structural Equation Model

3.1 Basic Principles of Structural Equation Modeling

Structural equation model (SEM) is a confirmatory model, mainly used to analyze the complex relationship between observed variables. There are three types of random variables included in the SEM equation: observed variables, latent variables, and error variables. SEM can estimate the measurement indicators and latent variables in the model at the same time. It can not only estimate the measurement error of the indicator variables in the measurement process but also evaluate the reliability and validity of the measurement. The latent variable itself cannot be measured directly, but it can be measured by a set of observed variables. The core concept of SEM analysis is the covariance of variables. One is to use the covariance matrix between variables to observe the relationship between multiple continuous variables. This is the descriptive function of SEM; the other is to reflect the full range of theoretical models. The difference between the covariance and the covariance of the actual collected data is a confirmatory function.

A complete SEM model includes two parts: a measurement model and a structural model. The former refers to the relationship between actual measured variables and latent traits, while the latter describes the relationship between latent variables.

3.2 Theoretical Assumptions

Latent variables are variables that cannot be directly observed. In this study, independent innovation input capacity, internal environmental support, external environmental support, knowledge management capabilities, and independent innovation output capabilities are taken as five potential variables. According to research conducted by experts and scholars at home and abroad, independent innovation input capacity, internal environmental support, external environmental support, and knowledge management capabilities all have an impact on independent innovation capabilities. Increased investment in independent innovation, internal and external environmental support, and good innovation knowledge management capabilities can all enhance the innovation capabilities of enterprises, accelerate the flow and creation of knowledge resources in enterprises, and create a large number of independent innovation results for enterprises and bring huge economic benefits benefit. The quantity and quality of an enterprise's independent innovation achievements and the number of patents can reflect the enterprise's independent innovation ability. Therefore, we make the following assumptions:

Hypothesis H1: Independent innovation input capacity will have a positive impact on independent innovation output capacity.

Hypothesis H2: The support of the internal environment will have a positive impact on the output capacity of independent innovation.

Hypothesis H3: The supporting force of the external environment will have a positive impact on the output capacity of independent innovation.

Hypothesis H4: Knowledge management ability will have a positive impact on independent innovation output ability.

Among them, the four indicators of independent innovation input capability, internal environmental support, external environmental support, and knowledge management capability also have a certain impact on each other. Increasing the investment in independent innovation of enterprises is inseparable from the support of internal and external environments. At the same time, the ability of human capital to digest and absorb new technologies is an important way to improve the independent research and development of enterprises and accelerate the transmission and diffusion of knowledge. A positive enterprise innovation atmosphere, Appropriate incentive system and national policy guarantee are conducive to creating a good knowledge sharing atmosphere, promoting the accumulation of enterprise knowledge and the dissemination of knowledge within the enterprise, and the cooperation and competition between innovators can improve the overall innovation level of the enterprise:

Hypothesis H5: Internal environmental support will have a positive impact on knowledge management capabilities.

Hypothesis H6: The support of the external environment will have a positive impact on knowledge management capabilities.

Hypothesis H7: The ability to invest in independent innovation will have a positive impact on knowledge management capabilities.

Based on the above assumptions, the interaction between the potential variables of the independent innovation capability of new energy equipment manufacturing enterprises can be obtained, as shown in Fig. 1.

3.3 Data Analysis

Based on the 7 hypotheses put forward, this research uses AMOS software to establish a structural equation model to verify the theoretical model.

Confirmatory Factor Analysis. We tested the fit level of the model, and the absolute fit index CMIN/DF was 1.299. The significance level of the model is 0.027, which is less than 0.05, rejecting the null hypothesis. At this time, the sample covariance matrix S is not close to the matrix implicit in the hypothetical theoretical model, indicating that the theoretical model has a general degree of adaptation.

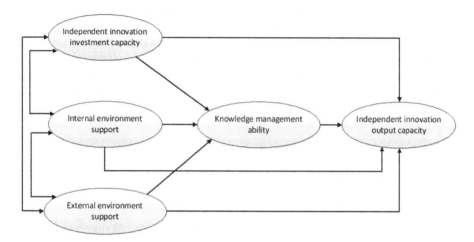

Fig. 1. Hypothetical relationship diagram of latent variables of independent innovation capability.

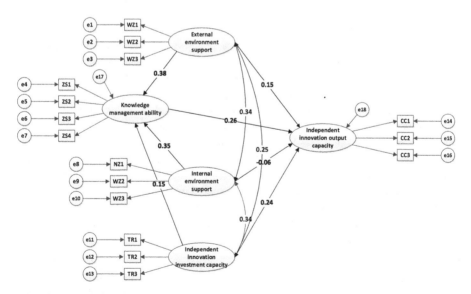

Fig. 2. The original structural equation model of the independent innovation capability of new energy equipment manufacturing enterprises.

Figure 2 and Table 3 show the standardized path coefficients and the theoretical hypothesis testing structure of the structural relationship between the various latent variables. The standardized path coefficients of the two paths did not pass the significance test. They are internal environmental support -> independent innovation output capacity (standard factor load coefficient is −0.06, t value is 3.319), and external environmental support -> knowledge management ability (labeling factor loading coefficient is 0.38, t value is −0.398), the former result shows a negative correlation, and the latter result shows that the relationship between the two is weak. At the same time, the significance test result of the structural equation model shows that the model rejects the null hypothesis, indicating that the model established based on the previous research experience of experts and scholars on the driving factors of independent innovation is not completely applicable to the new energy equipment manufacturing industry, so we use the MI table The data modifies the model.

Table 3. Hypothesis test result.

ID	Assumption	Factor loading	t	Whether to support the null hypothesis
H1	TR -> CC	0.24	3.619	Yes
H2	NZ -> CC	−0.06	3.319	No
H3	WZ -> CC	0.15	1.287	Yes
H4	ZS -> CC	0.26	1.542	Yes
H5	NZ -> ZS	0.35	1.344	Yes
H6	WZ -> ZS	0.38	−0.398	No
H7	TR -> ZS	0.15	1.051	Yes

Figure 2 and Table 3 show the standardized path coefficients and the theoretical hypothesis testing structure of the structural relationship between the various latent variables. The standardized path coefficients of the two paths did not pass the significance test. They are internal environmental support -> independent innovation output capacity (standard factor load coefficient is −0.06, t value is 3.319), and external environmental support-> Knowledge management ability (labeling factor loading coefficient is 0.38, t value is −0.398), the former result shows a negative correlation, and the latter result shows that the relationship between the two is weak. At the same time, the significance test result of the structural equation model shows that the model rejects the null hypothesis, indicating that the model established based on the previous research experience of experts and scholars on the driving factors of independent innovation is not completely applicable to the new energy equipment manufacturing industry, so we use the MI table The data modifies the model.

Modified Model. Figure 3 shows the revised structural equation model of the independent innovation capability of new energy equipment manufacturing enterprises. Tables 4 and 5 show that the revised model significance probability value $p = 0.363 > 0.05$, accepting the null hypothesis, and the chi-square degree of freedom ratio CMIN/DF = 1.156, indicating that the theoretical model can be adapted to the observed data. In addition, the overall model fit RMSEA value = 0.017 < 0.050, the values of GFI, IFI, TLI, and CFI are all greater than 0.900, and the values of AGFI, NFI, and RFI are close to 0.900, indicating that the model fits well.

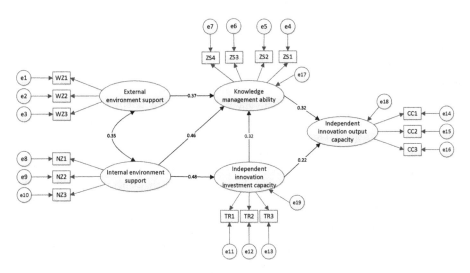

Fig. 3. Modified model.

Table 4. Confirmatory factor analysis results.

Variable		Null hypothesis	Path coefficient estimates	P	Test result
Knowledge management ability	←—	External environment support	0.374	***	Significantly affected
Knowledge management ability	←—	Internal environment support	0.459	***	Significantly affected
Independent innovation investment capacity	←—	Internal environment support	0.465	***	Significantly affected
Independent innovation output capacity	←—	Knowledge management ability	0.318	0.004	Significantly affected
Independent innovation output capacity	←—	Independent innovation investment capacity	0.220	0.082	Not significantly affected

Note: ***Indicates that the P value is less than 0.001.

Table 5. Model fit metrics.

CMIN/DF	GFI	AGFI	NFI Delta1	RFI Rho1	IFI Delta2	TLI Rho2	CFI	RMSEA
1.156	0.920	0.887	0.865	0.831	0.979	0.973	0.979	0.032

4   Conclusions and Recommendations

This study uses the knowledge of structural equation modeling to study the driving factors of the independent innovation capability of the new energy equipment manufacturing industry, collects data through questionnaires, and uses principal component analysis to extract five factors that affect the independent innovation capability of the new energy equipment manufacturing industry. The dimensions are independent innovation input capability, external environmental support, internal environmental support, knowledge management capability, and independent innovation output capability. Relevant assumptions were verified by constructing a structural equation model, and the model was revised based on the empirical analysis results, and the structural equation model and driving path of the driving factors of the independent innovation capability of the new energy equipment manufacturing industry were obtained.

From the hypothesis test results, it can be seen that the P value of external environmental support to knowledge management ability, internal environmental support to knowledge management ability, and internal environmental support to independent innovation input ability are all less than 0.001, indicating the external environmental support and internal environmental support Each has a positive impact on knowledge management capabilities, and the impact is significant. Hypotheses H5 and H6 have been verified; internal environmental support has a positive impact on independent innovation input capabilities, and the impact is significant. This conclusion is based on the hypothesis test results of the original model. New conclusions obtained after revision. The P value of knowledge management ability on independent innovation output ability is 0.004, which is less than 0.05, indicating that knowledge management ability has a positive influence on independent innovation output ability, and the hypothesis H4 is verified. The P value of independent innovation input capacity to independent innovation output capacity is 0.082, indicating that independent innovation input capacity has a positive impact on independent innovation output capacity, but the effect is not significant. Hypothesis H1 is verified. As for the hypotheses H2, H3, and H7, it can be seen from the verification results of the null hypothesis model that none of the hypotheses are valid.

From the structural equation correction model of the driving factors of independent innovation ability of new energy equipment manufacturing enterprises, it can be seen that both knowledge management ability and independent innovation input ability can directly affect the independent innovation output ability. The impact of knowledge management ability on independent innovation output ability is more direct and significant. Most literatures believe that the independent innovation input ability (including R&D capital investment, R&D human resource input, etc.) has a very significant impact on the independent innovation output ability, and is even one of the most important influencing factors. However, for new energy equipment manufacturing enterprises, the development of new energy technology is the driving force for the continuous expansion and development of enterprises. The investment of resources can promote the innovation behavior of enterprises, but the acquisition and absorption of knowledge are more decisive for the results of innovation.

The external environment support force and the internal environment support force do not directly affect the output capability of independent innovation, but affect the output capability of independent innovation by affecting the knowledge management capability; At the same time, the support of the internal environment also has a significant impact on the ability to invest in independent innovation. The awareness and quality of leaders, the enthusiasm and creativity of employees affect the knowledge management atmosphere of the enterprise. An organization that is good at communication often spreads information faster, and is better at acquiring knowledge and transforming it into the productivity of the enterprise. Both competition and cooperation factors in the external environment have an impact on the knowledge management of enterprises. The cooperation between enterprises and schools, R&D institutions, etc., is more conducive to enterprises to acquire new knowledge and create new products.

References

1. Lüthje, B.: Platform capitalism 'Made in China'? Intelligent manufacturing, Taobao Villages and the restructuring of work. Sci. Technol. Soc. **24**(2), 199–217 (2019)
2. Qu, C., Jun, S., Zhonghua, C.: Can embedding in global value chain drive green growth in China's manufacturing industry? J. Clean. Prod. **268**, 121962 (2020)
3. Fakhri, A.B., et al.: Industry 4.0: architecture and equipment revolution. Comput. Mater. Continua **66**(2), 1175–1194 (2021)
4. Wang, X., et al.: China's rare earths production forecasting and sustainable development policy implications. Sustainability **9**(6), 1003 (2017)
5. Lewis, J.I., Ryan, H.W.: Fostering a renewable energy technology industry: an international comparison of wind industry policy support mechanisms. Energy Policy **35**(3), 1844–1857 (2007)
6. Lee, K., Chaisung, L.: Technological regimes, catching-up and leapfrogging: findings from the Korean industries. Res. Policy **30**(3), 459–483 (2001)
7. Mattis, J.: Summary of the 2018 national defense strategy of the United States of America. Department of Defense Washington United States (2018)
8. Iyapparaja, M.: Fogqsym: an industry 4.0 analytical model for fog applications. Comput. Mater. Continua **69**(3), 3163–3178 (2021)
9. Du, H., et al.: Leader confirmation replication for millisecond consensus in private chains. IEEE Internet Things J. (2021). https://doi.org/10.1109/JIOT.2021.3113835
10. Chao, L., et al.: Comparison of modernization paths between China and Japan. China Economist **11**(2), 51 (2016)

A Cross-Platform Instant Messaging User Association Method Based on Spatio-temporal Trajectory

Pei Zhou[1,2] , Xiangyang Luo[1,2(✉)], Shaoyong Du[2,3], Lingling Li[4],
Yang Yang[5], and Fenlin Liu[2]

[1] School of Cyber Science and Engineering, Zhengzhou University,
Zhengzhou 450000, China
luoxy_ieu@sina.com
[2] State Key Laboratory of Mathematical Engineering and Advanced Computing,
Zhengzhou 450000, China
[3] State Key Laboratory of Information Security, Institute of Information
Engineering, Chinese Academy of Sciences, Beijing 100093, China
[4] School of Intelligent Engineering, Zhengzhou University of Aeronautics,
Zhengzhou 450000, China
[5] School of Computing and Information Systems, Singapore Management
University, Singapore 188065, Singapore

Abstract. The current research on cross-platform instant messaging user association is mainly divided into two categories: based on user attributes and based on user behavior. Methods based on user attributes mainly identify users through multiple attributes such as user name and multi-platform user information association based on cell phone number, but user association is not possible when multi-platform user information is inconsistent and users do not grant their address book permissions. Methods based on user behavior mainly calculate the similarity between user trajectories features such as geographic location frequency and co-occurrence, but this method lacks the user's information, which leads to the inability to fully excavate the sequential features of the trajectory and affects the accuracy of trajectory matching. In order to solve this problem, this paper proposes a cross-platform instant messaging user association algorithm based on temporal trajectories (CPTrajst). We firstly place probes in the area where the target may appear so as to obtain user information, gets user trajectory, then processes the trajectory and performs two trajectory matches, finally associate users of different platforms whose trajectories match, thus increasing the accuracy and reliability of cross-platform instant messaging user association. We conducts specific experiments for users of WeChat and Momo, the most commonly used instant messengers in China. The results show that we can achieve reliable association for these two types of instant messaging users and the user association accuracy can reach 99.5%, which is better than the existing user association algorithms based on trajectory matching.

Keywords: Instant messaging · Spatio-temporal trajectory · Trajectory matching · Cross-platform user association

X. Sun et al. (Eds.): ICAIS 2022, CCIS 1587, pp. 430–444, 2022.
https://doi.org/10.1007/978-3-031-06761-7_35

1 Introduction

With the rapid development of mobile Internet technology and wireless positioning technology and the rapid spread of mobile devices, mobile social networks have gradually emerged and profoundly changed people's lifestyles [1–3]. The combination of mobile devices and traditional social platforms has become a new trend, which has resulted in a variety of Location-Based Social Networks (LBSN) [4, 5], such as Twitter, WeChat [6], Momo, Foursquare, Weibo, etc. LBSN can use the location information of mobile devices to combine the virtual network with the real world, and providing people with more convenient social access and personalized services [7–9]. Location-Based Social Discovery (LBSD) in instant messaging applications allows common users to get nicknames, signatures, and gender information of other nearby users based on their current location, and to obtain distance information of nearby users. Typical examples of such services are WeChat "Nearby", Weibo "Nearby", and Momo "Nearby". Due to the different characteristics of instant messengers, there are some differences in obtained user behavior data. By matching and identifying the corresponding virtual accounts of the same user in multiple instant messengers, we can fully integrate multi-platform data sets and build complete user information. The research of cross-platform instant messaging user association technology is of great significance for locating malicious users.

The association method based on user attribute information mainly associates users through their attribute information, such as user name, cell phone number and other information, but this method cannot locate users with inconsistent user information and unopened address book permissions for multiple platforms. Therefore, it is necessary to use other identity characteristics of the user for correlation, such user's behavioral information. The existing user association methods based on trajectory features use frequency-based or co-occurrence-based methods to calculate the similarity between trajectories to determine whether users have a relationship. It is difficult to portray the temporal characteristics of user trajectories because the sequential characteristics of user trajectory locations are not considered enough, and the correlation between each geographical location is ignored.

To address the above problems, this paper proposes a cross-social platform instant messaging user trajectory matching method based on location access sequence and location distance. The method constitutes a collection of spatial-temporal trajectories of users through their location and time information; the matching is performed using a twice-matching algorithm, which improves the accuracy of user association. The experiments are conducted on public datasets and real instant messaging applications to verify the effectiveness of the proposed algorithm.

The main work of this paper is as follows:

- A new cross-platform instant messaging user association method is proposed. We consider the sequential access characteristics and distance characteristics of user trajectories, and increases the reliability and validity of cross-platform instant messaging association.
- We propose the TF-IWF weighted trajectory matching algorithm and the quadratic trajectory distance matching algorithm based on the nearest neighboring point.

The problems based on geographic location frequency and insufficient utilization of time information are fully solved, and the accuracy of cross-platform user trajectory matching is improved.

- We conduct data collection and processing and conduct specific experiments based on public datasets and the well-known domestic instant messaging applications WeChat and Momo. The results show that the effectiveness and efficiency of the proposed method are better than the existing methods.

The rest of this paper is organized as follows: Sect. 2 introduces the existing related work and analyzes the shortcomings; Sect. 3 we propose a cross-platform instant messaging user localization algorithm based on spatio-temporal trajectories and presents the key steps in details; In Sect. 4 we conduct experiments and analyze the experimental results based on existing public datasets and real instant messaging applications; Sect. 5 concludes the whole paper.

2   Background and Related Work

With the application of privacy protection technology for of LBSD users' location information, LBSD services gradually use distance segments to advertise the distance between users. Wazirali et al. in their paper [10] proposed a review on privacy preservation of location-based services in internet of things. To this end, scholars have proposed different solutions. In their paper [11], Yuan et al. proposed a trilateral measurement localization method based on reported distance segments to achieve the localization and tracking of WeChat users. Nguyen et al. in their paper [12] exploit the property of some instant messengers to rank nearby users from near to far by constructing virtual users to find the target The upper and lower bounds of the actual distance between the user and the probe are used to determine the ring region containing the target user; then the distance segment-based localization algorithm is used to locate the target. the iterative trilateral measurement-based localization algorithm of Li et al. in paper [13] utilizes the classical trilateral measurement localization idea. By generating three probe locations and using least squares [14] to calculate the centroid of the overlapping part of the ring region determined by the three probes; then, the probes are deployed at the intermediate positioning results and the probe locations for the next round of positioning are determined by evaluation, thus iteratively approximating the user's true location. To break the minimum reported distance limitation of LBSD service, Pang et al. proposed a spatial division-based localization algorithm in the paper [15]. This algorithm investigates the localization of the target user when the target user is located within the minimum reporting distance of the probe. In paper [16], based on the paper [15], the target reporting distance and its corresponding actual distance range are selected by analyzing the statistical characteristics of the distribution of the actual distance range corresponding to the reporting distance, and the probes are deployed based on a step-by-step strategy to improve the accuracy of spatial delineation to achieve the localization of the target user. Zhang et al. in their paper [17] proposed a street-level ip geolocation algorithm based on landmarks clustering. Cross-platform user association aims to identify the real user identity behind the account in the absence of a unified user identity, and to associate accounts belonging to the same real user in multiple platforms, providing a feasible solution for integrating multi-platform data and expanding the range of instant messaging location users. Wang et al. in their paper [18] proposed a association of mobile social network users privacy information based on big data analysis.

Cross-Platform User Association Based on User Attributes. The cross-platform user association based on user attributes is mainly associates with users through multiple information such as cell phone number, user name, home address, Tel, Email, personality signature, etc. The paper [20] uses user attributes such as username, user avatar, and geographic location for identification and is trained using supervised classification models such as decision tree and SVM for cross-platform user association. Malhotra et al. in paper [21] used Jaro distance and Wordnet ontology dictionary to calculate the similarity of attribute values by training a plain Bayesian classifier to achieve in [24], Guo et al. realize the association between "people nearby" users and cell phone numbers and then fuse the user information of multiple instant messengers.

Cross-Platform User Association Based on User Behavior Characteristics. Cross-platform user association based on user behavioral features mainly associates users through their behavioral features such as activity trajectories, friendships and other information. Chen et al. in paper [19] defined a new similarity function to measure the degree of connectivity between trajectories and query locations while considering the spatial distance and order constraints, and analyzes the feasibility of using a generic spatial index based on the simple incremental k-NN algorithm to achieve efficient k-BCT search. Hao et al. in paper [22] used the Term Frequency-Inverse Document Frequency. In [23], Chen et al. propose a cross-domain trajectory to vector algorithm based on Paragraph2vec. Chen et al. proposed a method based on Kernel Density Estimation in paper [25] that improves the accuracy by improving the data sparsity problem in user similarity measurement. Fang et al. proposed an RNN-based algorithm for spatio-temporal sequence prediction in the paper [26]. In [27], E. Felemban et al. propose a deep trajectory classification model for congestion detection in human crowds. Niu et al. in their paper [28] proposed a real-time recognition and location of indoor objects.

In cross-platform user association, when using user's attributes for an association, the user's attributes change over time and the data set is too large to affect the association results. At the same time, when using users' trajectory information for an association, the correlation between each geographic location is ignored, and the sequential characteristics of each geographic location in the trajectory are not fully explored. For this reason, this paper proposes a cross-platform instant messaging user association method based on spatio-temporal trajectories.

3   Cross-Platform Instant Messaging User Association Based on Spatio-temporal Trajectory

This section specifies the process of cross-platform instant messaging user association method based on temporal trajectory. We start by arranging probes, running each instant messenger, and automatically and accurately acquiring user information through the automatic information acquisition method of elemental precision finding. We use the reported distance information and time information of other users obtained to get the user trajectory. The method grids and vectorizes the trajectories separately and weights the processing results; it performs secondary user trajectory matching to achieve cross-platform user association. The general framework of the method is shown in Fig. 1.

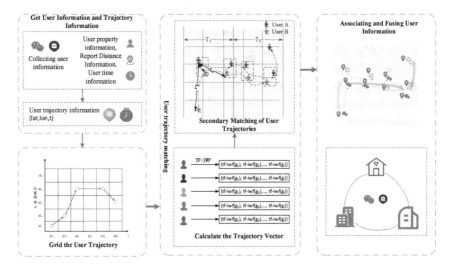

Fig. 1. An algorithmic framework for cross-platform instant messaging user association based on spatio-temporal trajectories.

The main steps of the method are as follows:

1. **Get user information and trajectory information.** We deploy probes (virtual instant messaging users) within a certain geographic area according to a specific strategy to query nearby users searched by the "People Nearby". We read the probe information at regular intervals and store the searched user attributes with the reported distance information to the local computer. For different types of instant messengers, we use the corresponding positioning algorithm to locate the user and obtain the latitude and longitude information of the user (lat, lon). Combined with the time of appearance of the user, we represent the user's trajectory as a spatio-temporal location point (lat, lon, t)

2. **Grid the user trajectory.** We divide the target user's activity area into appropriate grids and indicate the user's location by grid number. At the same time, the time is

divided into appropriate time intervals, and the interval number is used to indicate the time of user's appearance. In this way, the user's temporal trajectory points can be represented as (id, t).

3. **Calculate the trajectory vector.** Based on the TF-IWF model, the weights of each grid in the trajectory are calculated and adjusted, and finally, the TF-IWF values of each grid are integrated to calculate the user trajectory vector.

4. **Secondary matching of user trajectories.** Based on the distance of nearest neighboring points, we calculate the distance between matching points in turn for secondary matching of user trajectories.

5. **Associating and fusing user information.** Associating users of different platforms with matching trajectories to improve user trajectory information and increase the number of locatable users.

3.1   Get User Information and Trajectory Information

To enable the probe to collect information about all users using the "People Nearby" feature within the instant messaging software's range of activity, we modify the location of the Android emulator to run the instant messaging tool according to specific rules and build the corresponding probe to sense the users using "People Nearby" within the coverage area. We modify the location of the Android emulator according to specific rules so that it runs the instant messenger and builds the corresponding probes to sense users using "People Nearby" in the coverage area. Users enter the preset probe locations to sense nearby users for information collection.

User trajectory is defined as the set of geospatial points of the user over time, represented by $T = [l_1, l_2, \ldots, l_n]$. Each of these points l_i is composed of three dimensions $lat_u, lon_u, t, (lat_u, lon_u)$ represents the latitude and longitude information of the point, and t is the offline time of the user using the instant messenger. The acquisition of user trajectory is done by two steps, the first step is to get the user's location information based on the reported distance, and the second step is to get the user's offline time.

Get the User's Location Information Based on the Reported Distance. With the improvement of user location information protection policy, instant messaging tools no longer display the location of nearby users directly to that user, but return the distance between the probe and the user to the probe in the form of distance segments, so the reported distance of the probe from the target user can be used to locate the user. The final localization results obtained are stored in latitude and longitude (lat_u, lon_u).

Get User Offline Time. To obtain the time attribute, we can use the time promptly in the "Nearby" interface. Most instant messenger "Nearby" interfaces will display the nearby users with the time interval "n minutes ago" in the upper right corner of the user, and the record the current time is t_N then the time corresponding to the location $t = t_N - n$ in the trajectory. Some instant messengers with strict privacy protection policy do not mark the time interval of users' offline. When users use the "nearby people" function, the backend server will display multiple users near the user who have been offline for no more than Δt in the form of a list, and then the time corresponding to the location $t = t \pm \Delta t$.

The set of spatio-temporal points (lat_u, lon_u, t) obtained based on the user's change over time is the user's travel trajectory $T = [l_1, l_2, \ldots, l_n]$ using instant messenger during this time.

3.2   Grid User's Trajectory

The points in the user-generated trajectory are found to be relatively sparse in the initial experiments, which is mainly due to the error in the localization algorithm. When users use instant messengers in the same location, the error will lead to inconsistent local-ization results expressed in latitude and longitude, thus causing the problem of sparse samples and affecting the matching results. Therefore, we consider dividing the area into some small grids according to appropriate accuracy within the geographical range where the user appears, and using the small grids to replace the user positioning results, which not only avoids the sample sparsity problem, but also reflects the user geo-graphical location more intuitively and facilitates the calculation of the similarity of trajectories.

The process of trajectory meshing is divided into two main steps.

Step1. Represent the user's geographic locations in the trajectory as a grid. Firstly, a rectangular user activity area is determined based on the latitude and longitude coordinates of the geographic locations that appear in the user's trajectory, which contains all the geographic locations in the user's trajectory. The user activity area corresponds to a latitude range of (lat_1, lat_2) and a longitude range of (lon_1, lon_2). Then the side length of the grid is set according to the positioning error, which determines the number of rows l and the number of columns r of the grid. Finally, the coordinates of all geographic locations in the trajectory are expressed by transforming Eqs. (1) to (3) into the grid ordinate g_i. Where (lat, lon) denotes the coordinate point of any geo-graphic location in the trajectory, g_x denotes the row number where the grid is located, and g_y denotes the column number where the grid is located.

$$g_x = \left\lfloor \left| \frac{(lat - lat_1)*l}{lat_2 - lat_1} \right| \right\rfloor \tag{1}$$

$$g_y = \left\lfloor \left| \frac{(lon - lon_1)*r}{(lon_2 - lon_1)} \right| \right\rfloor \tag{2}$$

$$g_i = (r*(g_x - 1) + g_y) \tag{3}$$

Step2. Represents the temporal points in the user's trajectory as a grid. Firstly, we divide the day into 24-time segments according to the time interval. Then we combine the user's geographic location grid with the time interval to form the user's trajectory grid. The user trajectory is represented as $T = \{h_{t_1}^{g_1}, h_{t_2}^{g_2}, \ldots h_{t_n}^{g_i}\}$, where $g_1, g_2, \ldots, g_i$ denotes the number of the geolocation grid in the trajectory, $t_1, t_2, \ldots, t_n$ denotes the time point when the user appears in the g_i grid, and $h_{t_n}^{g_i}$ denotes the temporal point of the user.

3.3   Calculate the Trajectory Vector

Since the users' preferences and usage habits for different instant messaging tools are different, which leads to the possibility of differences in the trajectory information of the same users collected from different platforms, it is difficult to directly determine whether users have an association relationship by the grid representation of their trajectories. To this end, a user trajectory calculation method based on the word inverse frequency approach to calculate weighting (TF-IWF) is proposed, which calculates the weight of the grid for each spatio-temporal point and evaluates the importance of each spatio-temporal point in the trajectory.

The trajectory vector calculation method based on the TF-IWF model is shown in Algorithm 1 and is divided into the following three steps.

Step1. Calculate the frequency value TF for the ith grid in trajectory j. TF is defined as:

$$TF_{i,j} = \frac{n_{i,j}}{\sum_k n_{k,j}} \tag{4}$$

where $n_{i,j}$ denotes the number of times grid g_i appears in trajectory T_j and the denominator part denotes the sum of the frequencies of all grids in trajectory T_j. The TF value can be used to indicate the weight of grid g_i in the trajectory.

Step2. Calculate the co-occurrence frequency value IWF of the grid in the two trajectories. IWF is defined as:

$$IWF_i = \log \left(\frac{nt_i}{\sum_{i=1}^{m} nt_i} \right) \tag{5}$$

The numerator part of which is expressed as the number of occurrences of grid g_i in the combined spatio-temporal domain set of the two trajectories and the denominator part is expressed as the sum of all grid frequencies in the combined spatio-temporal domain set. This weighting method improves the influence of co-occurring grids in two trajectories on the weight of trajectory similarity and expresses more precisely the importance of this grid in the trajectory matching.

Step3. Calculate the TF-IWF value for each grid in the trajectory T_j. We compose the trajectory vector $v(T_j)$ by TF-IWF value, which is defined as:

$$v(T_j) = \left\{ tf - iwf_{(g_1)}, tf - iwf_{(g_2)}, \ldots, tf - iwf_{(g_n)} \right\} \tag{6}$$

Normalize this vector to:

$$v * (T_j) = \frac{v(T_j)}{\|v * (T_j)\|} \tag{7}$$

$v * (T_j)$ as user trajectory vector for similarity calculation (Table 1).

Table 1. TF-IWF based user trajectory vector generation algorithm.

algorithm 1 TF-IWF-based user trajectory vector generation
Input: $T_a = \{h_{t_1}^{g_1}, h_{t_2}^{g_2}, \dots, h_{t_n}^{g_i}\}$, $T_b = \{h_{t_1}^{g_1}, h_{t_2}^{g_2}, \dots, h_{t_n}^{g_i}\}$
Output: $v * (T_a)$, $v * (T_b)$
1    $S_V = \{T_a, T_b\}$;
2   **for each** $h_{t_n}^{g_i}$ **in the set** S_V **do:**
3        $TF = \frac{n_{i,j}}{\sum_k n_{k,j}}$
4        $IWF_i = (\frac{nt_i}{\sum_{i=1}^m nt_i})$
5        $TF - IWF = TF * IWF$
6   **end for**
7    $v(T_a) = \{tf - iwf(g_1), tf - iwf(g_2), \dots, tf - iwf(g_i)\}$
8   **for each** $h_{t_n}^{g_i}$ **in the set** S_V **do:**
9        $TF = \frac{n_{i,j}}{\sum_k n_{k,j}}$
10        $IWF_i = (\frac{nt_i}{\sum_{i=1}^m nt_i})$
11        $TF - IWF = TF * IWF$
12   **end for**
13    $v(T_a) = \{tf - iwf(g_1), tf - iwf(g_2), \dots, tf - iwf(g_i)\}$
14    $v * (T_a) = \frac{v(T_a)}{\|v(T_a)\|}$;
15    $v * (T_b) = \frac{v(T_b)}{\|v(T_b)\|}$

The TF-IWF model is used to calculate the user trajectory vectors, and the weighting method by two frequency calculations not only increases the weight of the high-frequency grid in the trajectory but also increases the weight of the co-occurring grid in the group of trajectories to be compared, which more accurately expresses the importance of the co-occurring high-frequency grid in the trajectory matching. In this section, the user trajectory vectors containing the sequence of grids are finally derived by calculating the weights of the grids and adjusting them, and the similarity between the user trajectory vectors is calculated to determine whether two users have an association. Calculating the vector similarity can be achieved by the cosine similarity of two trajectory vectors.

$$sim(T_i, T_j) = \cos(v * (T_i), v * (T_j)) \tag{8}$$

If the cosine similarity of the users' trajectories is greater than the threshold α, it is initially determined that these two users are related.

3.4   Secondary Matching User Trajectory

Due to the protection of user location information by instant messaging tools, errors will inevitably occur when trilateral positioning and spatial division positioning based on statistical features are performed on users. When there is no co-occurrence grid in all positions of the user's trajectory, it is difficult to perform weighted analysis through statistical co-occurrence grids. Therefore, we propose to perform secondary matching of the user trajectory based on the distance of the nearest neighbor to the user trajectory, as shown in Fig. 2. The distances *L1, L2, L3*... between the position point in one trajectory and the position point in another trajectory are calculated sequentially in the same time period *T1*. Find the nearest set of points of the two trajectories in the same time period *(L2 < L3 < L1)*, that is, a set of points connected by *L2*. In this way, we calculate the distance between each group of points after this group to get the set of user trajectory distance and carry out the secondary matching of user trajectory.

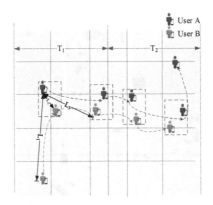

Fig. 2. User trajectory secondary matching.

Step1. Define the maximum distance between each set of matching points of two matching trajectories is less than the small grid edge length *g*.

Step2. Calculate the first set of points with similar distances in the first period of two trajectories and record the distance between these two points as d_1. Calculate and record the distance between each set of points after the first set of points in the trajectory as d_2, d_3, d_4... in turn.

Step3. Obtain the set of distances between two trajectory points close to the trajectory as follows. $Dis(d_1, d_2, d_3, d_4...)$

Step4. Statistical calculation of trajectory point distance set and the maximum matching distance *g* secondary matching user trajectory matching degree.

3.5 Associating and Fusing User Information

The similarity of user trajectory vector determines that users have association relationships, which can realize effective cross-platform association. After associating users with matching relationships, user trajectories obtained from different platforms are fused to improve user trajectory information, and location information from multiple platforms is used to supplement user positioning and improve the scale of locatable users (Table 2).

Table 2. Secondary matching algorithm for user trajectories.

algorithm 2 Secondary matching user trajectory algorithm

Input: $T_a = \{g_a^1, g_a^2, \dots, g_a^i\}$, $T_b = \{g_b^1, g_b^2, \dots, g_b^i\}$
Output: $Dis(d_1, d_2, d_3 \dots)$
1    $i = 1$;
2    $l_t = len(T_a)$;
3   Initialization $TDis, Dis$;
4   **for** $i = 0 \rightarrow l_t$ **do:**
5   **for** $k = 0 \rightarrow l_t$ **do:**
6        $d = g_a^i - g_b^k$;
7        $TDis. append(d)$;
8   **end for**
9   **end for**
10   $index = min(TDis)$;
11   **for** $j = 0 \rightarrow l_t$ **do:**
12   **if** $j \geq index$:
13       $d = g_a^i - g_b^j$
14       $Dis. append(d)$;
15   **end if**
16   **end for**
17   **return** Dis;

4 Experiments

4.1 Experimental Dataset and Evaluation Criteria

In this paper, the proposed algorithm is validated on the public dataset GeoLife project [29] and real instant messaging application-based dataset from Microsoft Research Asia. Since real multi-source user trajectory data are difficult to obtain, in the dataset Geolife, this paper divides the single spatio-temporal dataset into two parts and then uses these two parts for trajectory matching. When splitting each user trajectory, each segment of user trajectory is cross-sectioned into two parts and in turn, as shown in Fig. 3.

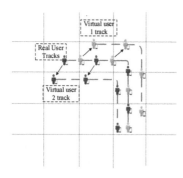

Fig. 3. Spatio-temporal dataset partitioning methods.

In the process of real experimental data acquisition, user information was obtained by running two instant messaging tools, WeChat and Momo, on the Yeshen Simulator every 10 min. Respectively read the user information that appears on the "Nearby People" interface of Momo and WeChat, save the information on the local computer, and set the Android emulator to the next probe location to continue collecting user information after the information collection is complete. The specific data set information is shown in Table 3.

Table 3. Experimental data set information.

Data source	Geolife		Real user experiment	
Divide the data set	D_{Geo1}	D_{Geo2}	D_{LBSD1}	D_{LBSD2}
Number of user trajectory	181	181	215	215
Coordinate Points	11312	11584	4261	4185
Range of grids	lat:39–41 lon:115–117	lat:39–41 lon:115–117	lat: 34.652–34.87 lon: 113.53–113.96	lat: 34.652–34.87 lon: 113.53–113.96
Time Range	2007.4–2012.8	2007.4–2012.8	2021.7–2021.8	2021.7–2021.8

This section uses Precision, Recall and *F1* Score as criteria to evaluate the performance of the algorithm, defined as follows:

$$precision = \frac{\sum_{i\epsilon[1,N]}TP_i}{\sum_{i\epsilon[1,N]}TP_i + \sum_{i\epsilon[1,N]}FP_i} \tag{9}$$

$$recall = \frac{\sum_{i\epsilon[1,N]}TP_i}{\sum_{i\epsilon[1,N]}TP_i + \sum_{i\epsilon[1,N]}FN_i} \tag{10}$$

$$F1 = \frac{2*precision*recall}{precision+recall} \tag{11}$$

where TP_i is the number of pairs of trajectories judged as matching and actually matched, FP_i is the number of pairs of trajectories judged as matching but actually mismatched by the algorithm, and FN_i is the number of pairs of trajectories judged as mismatched but actually matched by the algorithm. The *F1* value is the summed average of the accuracy rate and recall rate, which is a comprehensive evaluation index of the performance of the algorithm, and when the *F1* value of the algorithm is high, it means the algorithm is more effective.

4.2   Experimental Setup

The experimental parameters are set as shown in Table 4. Most of the positioning errors of WeChat and Momo users are in the range of [60 m, 80 m], so the side length of the mini-grid is set to 100 m, which makes it possible for users to locate in the grid at maximum. The number of rows and columns of the mini-grid is based on the latitude and longitude range of the user's activity area, which is calculated by the edge length of the mini-grid. The time information division threshold in the trajectory is 1 h, and the trajectory similarity threshold is 0.9. Since this paper is a cross-platform user association based on instant messaging, the experiments on the Geolife dataset are also conducted according to the above parameters (Fig. 4).

Table 4. Parameter meaning and setting.

Variable	Value	Illustrate
g	100 m	Side length of the grid
R_G	2224	The number of rows of the grid in Geolife
C_G	1728	The number of columns of the grid in Geolife
R_Z	418	The number of rows of the real user experiment grid
C_Z	571	The number of columns of the real user experiment grid
Δt	1 h	Threshold of trajectory time information division
α	0.9	Trajectory vector similarity determination threshold

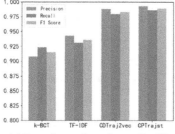 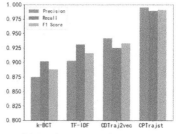

(a) Experimental results on Geolife   (b) Real user experiment results

Fig. 4. Experimental results.

5   Conclusion

In this paper, we aim to correlate the information of different instant-messaging platforms by matching the trajectories of users of different instant messaging tools. In the process of trajectory matching, we not only consider the similarity between sets based on frequency or co-occurrence but also consider the sequential characteristics of user trajectory locations and the distance characteristics of user trajectory locations, and this method will improve the accuracy of locating users while associating different instant messengers, and also increase the number of locatable users. The trajectory matching experiments carried out based on WeChat and Momo proved that the algorithm improved the accuracy of user association compared with existing algorithms. In future work, we will focus on more accurate localization of target users based on the relationship between reported distance and actual distance, as well as accurate association based on richer user information. This topic hopes to provide time-sensitive technical support for malicious social network instant messaging users.

Funding Statement. This work was supported by the National Natural Science Foundation of China (No. U1804263, 61872448, 62172435, and 62002386) and the Zhongyuan Science and Technology Innovation Leading Talent Project (No. 214200 510019).

Conflicts of Interest. The authors declare that they have no conflicts of interest to report regarding the present study.

References

1. China Internet Network Information Center. The 47th China Statistical Report on Internet Development (2021)
2. Li, J., Yan, H.Y., Liu, Z.L., Chen, X.F., Huang, X.Y.: Location-sharing systems with enhanced privacy in mobile online social networks. IEEE Syst. J. **11**(2), 439–448 (2017)
3. Wang, H.D., Li, Y., Chen, Y., Jin, D.P.: Co-Location social networks: linking the physical world and cyberspace. IEEE Trans. Mob. Comput. **18**(5), 1028–1041 (2019)
4. Yuan, F.J., Guo, G.B., Jose, J., Chen, L., et al.: Joint Geo-Spatial Preference and Pairwise Ranking for Point-of-Interest Recommendation, pp. 46–53. ICTAI, San Jose (2016)
5. Wang, R., Xue, M., Liu, K., Qian, H.: Data-driven privacy analytics: a we chat case study in location-based social networks. In: Xu, K., Zhu, H. (eds.) WASA 2015. LNCS, vol. 9204, pp. 561–570. Springer, Cham (2015). https://doi.org/10.1007/978-3-319-21837-3_55
6. Number of monthly active WeChat users from 2nd quarter 2011 to 2nd quarter 2021. https://www.statista.com/statistics/255778/number-of-active-wechat-messenger-accounts
7. Kim, J., Lee, J.G., Lee, B.S., Liu, J.J.: Geosocial co-clustering: a novel framework for geosocial community detection. ACM Trans. Intell. Syst. Technol. **11**(4), 1–26 (2020)
8. Xie, R., Chen, Y., Lin, S.H., Zhang, T.Y., et al.: Understanding Skout Users' Mobility Patterns on a Global Scale: A Data-Driven Study. World Wide Web, vol. 22, no. 11 (2018)
9. Nurgaliev, I., Qu, Q., Bamakan, S.M.H., Muzammal, M.: Matching user identities across social networks with limited profile data. Front. Comp. Sci. **16**(4), 1–14 (2020)
10. Wazirali, R.: A review on privacy preservation of location-based services in internet of things. Intell. Autom. Soft Comput. **31**(2), 767–779 (2022)
11. Ding, Y., Peddinti, S.T., Ross, K.W.: Stalking Beijing from Timbuktu: A Generic Measurement Approach for Exploiting Location-Based Social Discovery, pp. 75–80. ACM CCS, Arizona (2014)
12. Hoang, N.P., Asaon, Y., Yoshikawa, M.: Your Neighbors Are My Spies: Location and Other Privacy Concerns in Dating Apps, pp. 715–721. ICACT, JAN (2016)
13. Li, M.Y., Zhu, H.J., Gao, Z.Y., Chen, S., et al.: All Your Location Are Belong to Us: Breaking Mobile Social Networks for Automated User Location Tracking, pp. 43–52. MobiHoc, Philadelphia (2014)
14. Liu, J., Zhang, Y., Zhao, F.: Robust Distributed Node Localization with Error Management, pp. 250–261. MobiHoc (2006)
15. Ding, Y., Peddinti, S.T., Ross, K.W.: Location Prediction: Communities Speak Louder than Friends, pp. 43–52. COSN, California (2015)
16. Kim, J., Lee, J.G., Lee, B.S., Liu, J.J.: Geolocating a WeChat user based on the relation between reported and actual distance. Int. J. Distrib. Sens. Netw. **14**(4) (2018)
17. Zhang, F., Liu, F., Xu, R., Luo, X., Ding, S., et al.: Street-level IP geolocation algorithm based on landmarks clustering. Comput. Mater. Continua **66**(3), 3345–3361 (2021)

18. Wang, P., Wang, Z., Ma, Q.: Research on the association of mobile social network users privacy information based on big data analysis. J. Inf. Hiding Privacy Protect. **1**(1), 35–42 (2019)
19. Chen, Z.B., Shen, H.T., Zhou, X.F., Xie, X.: Searching Trajectories by Locations – An Efficiency Study, pp. 225–266. SIGMOD, Indianapolis (2010)
20. Goga, O., Perito, D., Lei, H.: Large-scale Correlation of Accounts Across Social Networks. Ph.D. dissertation, Université Pierre et Marie Curie, France (2013)
21. Malhotia, A., Totti, L., Meira, W., et al.: Studying User Footprints in Different Online Social Networks, pp. 1065–1070. ASONAM (2013)
22. Hao, T.Y., Zhou, J.B., Cheng, Y.S., Huang, L.B., Wu, S.H.: User Identification in Cyber-Physical Space: A Case Study on Mobile Query Logs and Trajectories. SIGSPATIAL, California (2016)
23. Chen, H.C., Xu, Q., Huang, R.Y., et al.: A cross-social network user identity recognition algorithm based on user trajectory. J. Electron. Inf. Technol. **40**(11) (2018)
24. Guo, J.D., Xu, R., Shi, W.Q., Luo, X.Y., Zhou, P.: Instant messaging user geolocating method based on multi-source information association. Int. J. Sens. Netw. **35**(2), 99–110 (2021)
25. Chen, W., Yin, H.Z., Wang, W.Q., Zhao, L., Zhou, X.F.: I effective and efficient user account linkage across location based social networks. In: IEEE International Conference on Data Engineering, pp. 1085–1096 (2018)
26. Fang, W., Chen, Y.P., Xue, Q.Y.: Survey on research of RNN-based spatio-temporal sequence prediction algorithms. J. Big Data **3**(3), 97–110 (2021)
27. Felemban, E., Khan, S.D., Naseer, A., Rehman, F.U., Basalamah, S.: Deep trajectory classification model for congestion detection in human crowds. Comput. Mater. Continua **68**(1), 705–725 (2021)
28. Niu, J., Hu, Q., Niu, Y., Zhang, T., Jha, S.K.: Real-time recognition and location of indoor objects. Comput. Mater. Continua **68**(2), 2221–2229 (2021)
29. Zheng, Y., Xing, X., Ma, W.Y.: GeoLife: a collaborative social networking service among user, location and trajectory. Bull. Tech. Commit. Data Eng. **33**(2), 32–39 (2010)

An Improved DNN Algorithm in Sorting Optimization of Intelligent Parcel Cabinets

Yang Yang[✉], Yi Wang, and Jianmin Zhang

China University of Mining and Technology (Beijing) School of Management,
Beijing 100083, China
bwu_yangyang@126.com

Abstract. In high-density residential areas, intelligent express delivery is often used to solve a large number of express parcels that need to be delivered in a short time. It effectively improves the efficiency of parcel delivery by means of information technology. However, with the continuous development of e-commerce, the logistics demand of the last kilometer delivery is constantly changing, and the problems of intelligent parcel cabinets are also exposed. For example, the express cabinet for parcel delivery is far away from the consignee, and when there are many parcels to be picked up, the consignee takes multiple express routes circuitously, and the inability to pick up all express shipments at one time causes the consignee to pick up the parcels in time and occupy the express cabinet for a long time, which affects the delivery of parcels. The article is clustered based on two main factors: the volume of express delivery and the walking distance to the delivery point. Take the area with a large logistics delivery volume as the center point. Based on the adaptive K-means algorithm, the best combination of package sorting is constructed so that multiple packages of the same address are stored in the same area of the smart express cabinet as much as possible. After determining the best possible delivery location of express parcels, a dynamic optimization model of the parcel delivery location is constructed based on the deep neural network (DNN) algorithm. When the logistics demand fluctuates sharply, it can still effectively allocate massive express parcels to the optimal delivery Click in. In this paper, an empirical study is conducted with the Beijing Mining Community as an example. The results show that the improved DNN algorithm can effectively improve the efficiency of parcel delivery based on smart express cabinets.

Keywords: High-density residential area · Intelligent parcel cabinet · Package sorting · K-means clustering algorithm · DNN

1 Introduction

With the vigorous development of e-commerce, the "last kilometer" problem of logistics is increasingly exposed. According to the data of the Ministry of Commerce of China in the first half of 2021, the turnover of e-commerce in China reached 37.1 trillion in 2020, an increase of 4.5% compared with 3.4 billion in 2019. With the exponential growth of orders today, if the sorting/distribution problem within the last kilometer can be optimized, the service cost/efficiency of the logistics industry will be

X. Sun et al. (Eds.): ICAIS 2022, CCIS 1587, pp. 445–462, 2022.
https://doi.org/10.1007/978-3-031-06761-7_36

further greatly improved in the future. If a courier needs to travel 100 km, a courier cost of 6 yuan will be incurred, of which 30% will be concentrated in the last 100 m.

An intelligent parcel cabinet is developed and designed to solve the delivery problem in the last kilometer of logistics. Its appearance brings great convenience to people, and at the same time, it also strengthens the connection between the receiver and the courier, effectively improves the delivery efficiency of the courier and enhances the shopping experience of consumers. The last kilometer of logistics is the core factor that affects the development speed of e-commerce. The growth chart of intelligent parcel cabinets in the first five years obtained from the statistics of the logistics industry in 2020 shows that the number of intelligent parcel cabinets reached more than 400,000 groups at the end of 2019. As the equipment of the logistics industry, it can be used in the terminal distribution stage, which can realize the automatic sending and receiving of express parcels, remote inquiry and control, save energy and protect the environment. It meets the development needs of the current era, solves the distribution problem of the last kilometer of express delivery to a certain extent, and alleviates the phenomenon of express backlog and poor service quality in schools, office buildings and some high-density residential areas of the same type to a certain extent.

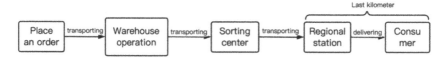

Fig. 1. Schematic diagram of terminal logistics.

With the intelligent parcel cabinet constantly occupying the market, the corresponding problems are increasingly exposed. The area set by the intelligent parcel cabinet is precisely the area with high population density and large express delivery volume. Faced with a large number of express parcels that need to be delivered in a short time, if users cannot pick up the parcels in time, the express mail will be "stored" in the express cabinet, which will lead to distributors and other users not being able to use the express cabinet normally, wasting resources and so on. Taking the university campus as an example, a large number of college students, teachers and their families live in the campus area. With the development of e-commerce, a large number of express parcels will be produced. Because of the characteristics of these express parcels, such as irregular receiving and delivery time, huge quantity, and irregular size and specifications of express parcels, if they are not delivered in time, they will accumulate in a large number, which will affect the normal teaching work of colleges and universities and the life of families. The way of letting couriers randomly put parcels into the intelligent parcel cabinet will result in users' roundabout pickup paths, poor customer experience, unwillingness to pick up parcels as soon as possible, and slow or even stagnant dispatch speeds. The scattered delivery mode of terminal logistics based on intelligent parcel cabinets will also lead to low delivery efficiency and success rates. Therefore, it is urgent to solve the optimization problem of express parcel delivery position of intelligent parcel cabinets.

According to the existing research, E-Logistics is the main method to solve the problem of campus express service promotion. Ren Dayong [4] (2013) and others put forwards the campus express service mode of self-organization and self-management for college students. Zhang Bingcheng [10] (2018) and others put forwards a solution to the "last kilometer" problem of campus express delivery based on the WeChat official account and the intelligent innovative service mode of intelligent parcel cabinets. Wang Chuang [16] (2019) and others believe that information technology should be further introduced into the campus express delivery mode, and the delivery mode should be continuously optimized and improved to improve the delivery efficiency by relying on the corresponding power platform. On the site selection of intelligent parcel cabinets, Shi Shu Biao [5] (2015) established a general mathematical model to solve the usage pattern of intelligent parcel cabinets on campus and took Dalian Maritime University as an example to select the best location of intelligent parcel cabinets in colleges and universities. Liu Rennin [7] (2015) and others took the logistics services of many universities in Wuhan as the research object, analysed the supply and demand status of campus express service in Wuhan universities, found some problems on campus, such as unreasonable pickup time, lack of door-to-door service, lack of diversity of service and too many agents, and put forwards some suggestions, such as integrating campus express logistics market, paying attention to network layout, and improving and expanding campus express service business. Wang Haihua [11] (2018) and others built a campus intelligent parcel cabinet using a model considering the service radius and solved it based on lingo software and concluded that express cabinets should be built in a suitable location and quantity so that they can meet all needs with a small service radius and construction cost. Lei Wenli [12] (2018) and other studies show that express delivery in colleges and universities in China has high cost and low intelligence. It is proposed that the use of intelligent parcel cabinets in campus express delivery can reduce costs and increase efficiency, and efforts should be made to promote the use of intelligent parcel cabinets in terms of putting into use the external environment and cultivating user habits. Zeng Zhicong [13] (2019) and others, based on the actual geographical conditions and market conditions of Wuyi University, used the Dijkstra algorithm to solve the data and obtained the best distribution points within the campus. Tang Yunfeng [15] (2019) proposed a comprehensive site selection method based on the gravity center method and analytic hierarchy process for campus express intelligent cabinets; that is, first, the gravity center method was used to determine the alternative locations of intelligent parcel cabinets, and then the optimal site selection was determined from the alternative locations by combining with the analytic hierarchy process. An empirical study was conducted in a university in Guangzhou.

To sum up, the existing studies have taken campus as an example to solve the last kilometer problem of logistics in areas with high residential density, focusing on the optimization of mode and the innovation and integration of single technology, without applying mode innovation and new technology to frontier problems, and then forming a set of novel solutions. In this paper, first, the parcel delivery cabinet classification algorithm based on adaptive K-means is used, and then the shortest distance model based on the improved DNN algorithm is constructed. Then, the solution of sorting/distribution efficiency optimization in the last kilometer of high-density residential area based on intelligent express delivery is put forwards, and an empirical analysis is made with a campus as an example.

2 System Model

An intelligent parcel cabinet provides a better solution to the "last kilometer" problem of express delivery, which not only facilitates the delivery and pick-up of goods but also greatly relieves the pressure of collecting and storing express delivery in residential property management areas, as shown in Fig. 1. The courier only needs to temporarily store the courier package in the courier cabinet and send the delivery information to the recipient by SMS, etc., and the recipient can enjoy the 24-h self-service pickup service, which is safe and reliable and helps to protect personal privacy. E-commerce and express delivery companies not only reduce the work pressure of couriers and ensure the timeliness of parcel delivery but also play an important supporting role in improving the logistics level of all e-commerce. In areas with high living density and large express delivery volume, it becomes the key to improving delivery efficiency if express parcels are sorted reasonably.

Definition of high-density residential area: This article explains the high-density residential area based on the definition in geography, that is, population density is the number of people per unit of land area. It is the main indicator used to measure the degree of land density. This article chooses person/square kilometer as the unit of measurement.

Population density in high-density residential areas: population density (people/km^2) = population (people)/area (km^2).

In communities with high living density and large express delivery volume, there are three points that affect the sorting efficiency of intelligent parcel cabinet packages: (1) The location of the container makes the picking path of some mails detour, and customers do not take the initiative to pick up the goods. (2) Because of the unreasonable place of picking up goods, customers do not take the initiative to pick up goods, occupying too many container resources. (3) Sorting efficiency Due to the lack of traditional operation mode and technology, the accuracy and efficiency of sorting are relatively low. In this paper. Therefore, this research first proposes an adaptive K-means parcel delivery cabinet classification algorithm; second, it proposes an optimized parcel delivery cabinet classification algorithm based on a machine learning model (Fig. 2).

The package delivery optimization objectives of the intelligent parcel cabinet are as follows: (1) Shorten the delivery time. According to actual research, under the traditional mode, limited by manual sorting and delivery, the delivery time of a single piece is often 4–12 h, including the long stay time of delivery, so shortening the stay time of parcels can reduce the occupation of express cabinets, meet the greater express demand and improve the efficiency of logistics dispatch. (2) Improve the accuracy of logistics dispatch. In the past, dispatchers themselves will fail and lag in delivery due to their own experience, objective conditions and other factors, and the rate of defective parts will reach 10% or more at the level of 100 pieces. Therefore, optimizing parcel express

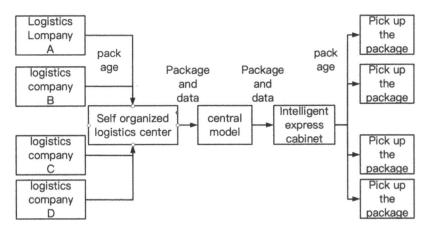

Fig. 2. Schematic diagram of the package delivery process based on an intelligent parcel cabinet.

delivery aims to reduce the rate of defective parts and improve the user experience. (3) Reduce the cost of express delivery. In the traditional mode, objective data show that the terminal delivery cost is high, and the single piece cost ranges from 5–8 yuan. Therefore, the package delivery classification optimization of intelligent parcel cabinets aims to reduce the delivery cost of each package.

3   Proposed Algorithm

3.1   Classification Algorithm Based on Adaptive K-means

In some studies, to optimize the location of the distribution center, traffic congestion, geographical location, population, logistics demand and other factors need to be considered. However, in densely populated areas, the space of express stations that can be used by us is limited, the location is relatively fixed, and there is little traffic flow in schools or residential areas, so there is almost no traffic jam. In such an area, the location of the intelligent parcel cabinet mainly considers the express delivery volume and the walking distance to the distribution point. In this paper, based on the two main factors of express delivery volume and walking distance to the distribution point, the clustering center is selected as the center point in the area with a large logistics delivery volume, and then the requirements of the shortest walking distance and the fastest aging time to the distribution point are considered. Cluster analysis is used to create suitable classification targets for subsequent artificial network sorting.

The K-Means algorithm means that given a number k, the data set can be divided into k "clusters" $C = \{C_1, C_2, ...C_k\}$, that is, k ethnic groups (clusters of buildings in this paper), regardless of whether this classification is reasonable or meaningful. The algorithm needs to minimize the square error; see formula (1):

$$E = \sum_{i=1}^{k} \sum_{x \in C_I} |\|x - u_i\||^2 \tag{1}$$

$u_i = \frac{1}{|C_i|} \sum_{x \in C_i} x$ the mean vector of cluster C_i, or centroid;

$\|x - u_i\|^2$: the distance from each sample point to the mean point, and the Minkowski distance (P norm) is used for distance measurement:

$$dist_{mk}(x_i, x_j) = (\sum_{u=1}^{n} |x_{iu} - x_{ju}|^p)^{\frac{1}{p}} \tag{2}$$

In this paper, let p = 2, that is, the norm is 2, and the distance is Euclidean distance, so that the distance between the distribution center and each demand point can be obtained.

Enter the data set D, the number of clusters K, and the classification algorithm flow of parcel delivery cabinet based on adaptive K-means is as follows:

(1) randomly select k sample points from a sample as an initial mean vector; $\{u_1, u_2, \ldots, u_k\}$;

(2) Loop the following steps until the optimal distance is found:

Step 1: Order $C_i = \emptyset (1 \le i \le k)$.

Step 2: Calculate the distance between them and k mean vectors for all sample points (that is, the distance between each building and the distribution center), take the mark of the mean vector with the shortest distance as the cluster mark of the point, and then add the point to the corresponding cluster C_i.

Step 3: Calculate their new mean vector for each cluster $u_i = \frac{1}{|C_i|} \sum_{X \in C_I} x$. If there is any change compared with the previous vector, update it as a new mean vector, and if there is no change, it will remain unchanged.

The research object of this paper is set in the campus area, so a multiconstraint logistics distribution location model is constructed according to the distance and demand of the distribution centre, in which the demand is evenly distributed in each office building and dormitory building in the school, and the demand is clustered by these two main factors. Then, the central point of a large number of demand points, that is, the clustering centre, is selected so that the requirements of the shortest distance and the fastest timeliness can be achieved.

3.2 Dynamic Optimization Algorithm Based on an Improved DNN

Based on the adaptive K-means algorithm, the best parcel cabinet for parcel sorting is constructed in this paper so that multiple parcels with the same address can be stored in the same area of the intelligent parcel cabinet as much as possible. However, when the logistics demand fluctuates drastically, the best delivery position of express parcels will change with the distribution demand. In this paper, a dynamic optimization model of parcel delivery location based on a deep neural network (DNN) algorithm is built to ensure that the mass express can still be effectively allocated to the optimal delivery point when the logistics demand fluctuates drastically.

There are many types of artificial neural networks, such as convolutional neural network CNN, circular neural network RNN for natural language processing, and DNN depth full link network applied in this paper. In this study, the DNN model is adopted because the data are simple, there are specific learning results, and there is no need for circular learning. Based on the above model, the random demand can be constrained according to certain requirements to form several specific distribution center points, and the direction of express mail flow is determined. The DNN model established can effectively distribute massive express mail to specific points to operate efficiently, aiming at solving the problem of low rate and accuracy of traditional sorting. With DNN, a large number of express mail can be sorted instantly without time and effort when they arrive, and the accuracy is extremely high. The complete model is divided into different levels, namely, the input level, the hidden level and the output level. The input level, that is, the input data, is divided into a training data set and the final predicted data set. The data should be cleaned according to the model structure and marked with data. The hidden layer is the training layer. There can be many hidden layers, depending on the data and results. Generally, the more hidden layers there are, the better the training results and the higher the accuracy. The output layer is the result obtained through training (Fig. 3).

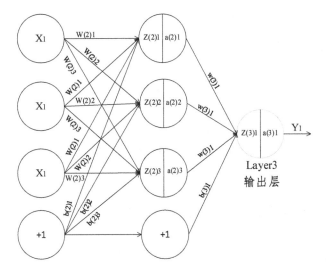

Fig. 3. Calculation diagram of the ANN model.

If a complete ANN model is to be established, the corresponding mathematical basis and the rules that the model should abide by are essential, among which there are three main items to be understood:

(1) Forwards propagation. The output of the previous layer is taken as the input of the next layer, and the output of the next layer is calculated until the operation reaches the output layer.

For the three outputs of Layer 2:

$$a_1^{(2)} = \sigma(z_1^{(2)}) = \sigma(w_{11}^{(2)}x_1 + w_{12}^{(2)}x_2 + w_{13}^{(2)}x_3 + b_1^{(2)}) \tag{3}$$

$$a_2^{(2)} = \sigma(z_2^{(2)}) = \sigma(w_{21}^{(2)}x_1 + w_{22}^{(2)}x_2 + w_{23}^{(2)}x_3 + b_2^{(2)}) \tag{4}$$

$$a_3^{(2)} = \sigma(z_3^{(2)}) = \sigma(w_{31}^{(2)}x_1 + w_{32}^{(2)}x_2 + w_{33}^{(2)}x_3 + b_3^{(2)}) \tag{5}$$

For the three outputs of Layer 3:

Output of the same layer2. From the above formula, it can be seen that it is more complicated to use the algebraic method to represent output individually, while it is simpler to use the matrix method. Therefore, the above formula is simplified to matrix form:

$$Z^{(1)} = W^{(1)}a^{l-1} + b^{(1)} \tag{6}$$

$$a^{(1)} = \sigma(z^{(1)}) \tag{7}$$

where σ is the activation function; here, the sigmoid function is selected in this paper (the effect is better when the feature difference is complex).

(2) Chain rule. Here, the chain rule in calculus is used to calculate the derivative of the compound function. Let x be a real number, and let f and g be functions mapped from real numbers to real numbers. Suppose $y = g(x)$ and $z = f(g(x)) = f(y)$. Then, the chain rule is $\frac{dz}{dx} = \frac{dz}{dy}\frac{dy}{dx}$.

(3) Back propagation (BP algorithm). This algorithm is the abbreviation of "error back propagation", which allows the information from the cost function to flow backwards through the network to calculate the gradient. Back propagation calculates the gradient of the loss function for all weights in the network. This gradient will be fed back to the optimization method to update the weight (W in Fig. 1) to minimize the loss function.

(4) Algorithm flow. Input: total number of layers 3, number of neurons in each hidden layer and output layer, activation function, loss function, iteration step a, maximum number of iterations Max and stop iteration threshold §, input n training samples $((x_1, y_1), (x_2, y_2), \ldots, (x_m, y_m))_\circ$

① Back propagation algorithm calculation for l = L − 1 to 2

$$\delta^{(1)} = (W^{(1)})^T \delta^{(l+1)} \odot \delta'(z^{(1)}) \tag{8}$$

② Update w, b. The values of and bias B of weight W are updated by the gradient descent algorithm, and a is the learning rate, where $a \in (0,1]$

$$w^{(1)} = w^{(1)} - a\frac{\partial C(w, b)}{\partial w^{(l)}} \tag{9}$$

$$b^{(1)} = b^{(1)} - a\frac{\partial C(w,b)}{\partial b^{(l)}} \tag{10}$$

③ If the change values of all W and B are less than the stop iteration threshold §, the iteration cycle will jump out.

④ Output the linear relation coefficient matrix W and offset B of each hidden layer and output layer.

(5) Data stream processing. Simplify the order data. Make the data conform to the requirements of the model, that is, clear the unnecessary data in the order, and sort the order into the corresponding integrated express cabinets 0, 1 and 2 according to the building number). After that, the open source machine learning library TensorFlow 2.0 is used to establish a machine learning core engine to sort thousands of data. As shown in the figure, considering that the DNN model has specific coding format requirements for data, the building number is converted into data in picture format, that is, considering that the express sorting is not just digital sorting in reality, the model is converted to identify, and then the identified numbers are pushed into the intelligent parcel cabinet 100% by using the loop structure (Fig. 4).

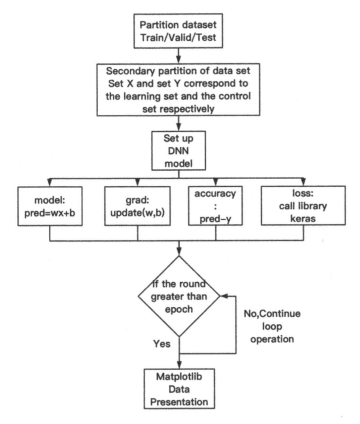

Fig. 4. DNN network modelling steps

4 Simulation Results

4.1 Data Processing

According to the latest official school website data, Beijing Mining University Community is located at No. 11. Xueyuan Road Ding, Haidian District, Beijing, China. There are 3 buildings for families of mining universities and 6 buildings for dormitories of mining university students in the community. The community covers an area of 0.24 square kilometers and has a population of approximately 10,000 people. The available population density is approximately 41,666.7 people/square kilometer, which is a typical high-density area. In this empirical study, this community is taken as an example to carry out empirical research, and the research conclusions must be representative and universal (Fig. 5).

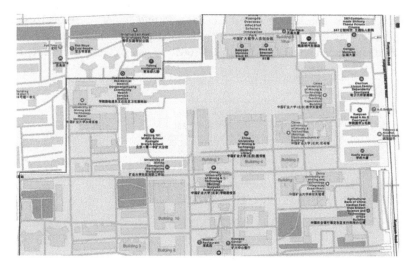

Fig. 5. Regional map of China University of Mining and Technology (Beijing).

According to the actual investigation, the calculation and analysis are carried out based on the single-day data volume. The maximum order quantity per day is 1,000 pieces, and the existing express cabinet resources of the school are 500 pieces. In this paper, the sample data are enlarged to 3000 items. If the data processing is successful, it can be considered that the general express quantity can run smoothly.

The method of generating e-commerce orders is as follows. This paper uses this step to generate massive data that meet the requirements of the data simulation format.

$$C = AB = \begin{pmatrix} A & B \\ C & D \end{pmatrix} \begin{pmatrix} D & C \\ B & A \end{pmatrix} \tag{11}$$

In formula (11), A is a 2×2 matrix, B is a 2×2 matrix, and the product C of A and B is a 2×2 matrix. An element of c is expressed as formula (12):

$$c_{i,j} = a_{i,1}b_{1,j} + a_{i,2}b_{2,j} + \cdots\cdots + a_{i,n}b_{n,j} = \sum_{r=1}^{n} a_{i,r}b_{r,j} \tag{12}$$

Write the product matrix c as formula (13).

$$\begin{pmatrix} AD + BB & AC + BA \\ CD + DB & CC + DA \end{pmatrix} \tag{13}$$

In this paper, the main name a and product b are taken as the 1×1 matrix, and the data main orders $a^T b$ are obtained by matrix operation. Call the random library to generate random numbers between (0,9) as order building number, phone number and order time, where the number 1 in order time is the express mail arriving in the morning, 2 in the afternoon and 3 in the evening. In the order number, the numbers are evenly distributed with the same probability. Assuming that the scenarios are all e-commerce, the payment methods are all online banking. In the order status, the unfinished ones do not involve the follow-up process, so all orders are in the completed status. Table 1 is an excerpt from more than 3,000 pieces of data.

Table 1. Data table of virtual order part.

(full) name	Commodity list	Order address	telephone number	Payment information	Order status	Order number	Order time
Peng Wanli	Printed napkin	Building 2	13226723929	Online Pay	complete	844368	2
Gaodashan	Hand companion	Building 3	15996360818	Online Pay	complete	343367	3
Xie Dahai	Printed napkin	Building 4	13385800774	Online Pay	complete	637801	2
Cheng xiaoxian	cleansing cream	Building 3	18755825195	Online Pay	complete	005638	3
Jie Zhenguo	Computer stand	Building 8	13515561107	Online Pay	complete	673260	1

Clean the data in Table 2, and use the map interface of a platform to clean all the order addresses into (X,Y) map coordinate format, where XY is the latitude and longitude that meets the general map standard, which is convenient for calculating the Euclidean distance and cluster analysis. The order data are integrated according to the coordinate points, in which 1, 2, 3, 4, 5, 7, and 8 are in one-to-one correspondence with the actual building label, 6 represents Yihai Building, and 9 represents the actual 10th building. The data are brought into the program for operation, and the iteration distance steps are 40 m, 60 m, 80 m and 100 m according to the actual distance.

4.2   Discussion

Selection of Delivery Area. For cluster analysis, the virtual order data are processed into standardized data, as shown in Table 2. According to the analysis of the data results, when the step size is less than 40 m, each building is an independent demand point, and intelligent parcel cabinets should be set up. When the step length (the distance from the cluster sample point to the center) is 60 m, the demand of Building 1 and Building 2 is clustered, and that of Building 8 and Building 10 is clustered, and the rest are independent demand points, so corresponding express cabinets should be set according to the demand. When the step size is 80 m, the requirements are integrated into 3 points. When the step size is 100 m, the other demand points will be merged together except for the far-end Yihai Building. The setting of express cabinets should be selected according to the actual situation of different high-density gathering areas. Considering the solution and actual situation in the following article, there is no classification problem if there are too many machine learning categories, and there is no need for classification if there are too few. Therefore, the demand integration points should not be too scattered or integrated. Therefore, in the following study, the clustering results with a step size of 80 m will be taken as the standard for discussion and research. Set the integration demand points such as Building 1 as code 0, the demand points of Yihai Building as code 1, and the integration demand points such as Building 8 as code 2. The same number in the cluster analysis results is the same cluster, as shown in Table 2.

Table 2. Cluster analysis data table.

Address	Quantity	X	Y	Steps = 40	Steps = 60	Steps = 80	Steps = 100
Building 1	334	116.357045	40.003848	0	0	0	0
Building 2	308	116.357045	40.003848	1	0	0	0
Building 4	369	116.355455	40.003882	2	1	0	0
Building 5	319	116.35501	40.003591	3	1	0	0
Building 6 (on behalf of Yihai Building)	344	116.356308	40.005882	4	2	1	1
Building 7	330	116.356173	40.003782	5	3	0	0
Building 8	351	116.354242	40.002338	6	4	2	0
Building 10	332	116.354264	40.002732	7	4	2	0
Building 3	349	116.353416	40.002324	8	5	2	0

Note: X and Y are coordinates after latitude and longitude are converted in standard map format; Steps are in meters

The cluster analysis results of different step sizes are shown in Fig. 6. The ordinate is the latitude in the geographic map coordinates in the international common format, and the abscissa is the longitude in the geographic map coordinates. According to the incremental iteration of the clustering step size, the results of Figures a, b, c and d appear, in which the step lengths of a, b, c, and d are 40 m, 60 m, 80 m, and 100 m, respectively. The map below shows the cluster analysis results more intuitively. The results of the two extreme cases with step sizes of 0 m and 100 m are very intuitive, so here, only the results of heatmaps with clustering step sizes of 60 m and 80 m are shown in turn.

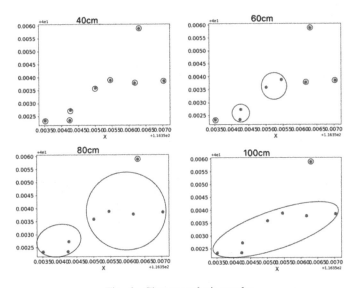

Fig. 6. Cluster analysis results.

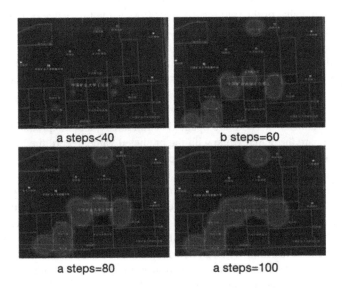

Fig. 7. Cluster analysis heatmap.

The clustering results are based on the results with a step length of 80 m, which will be the precondition in the later empirical analysis (Fig. 8).

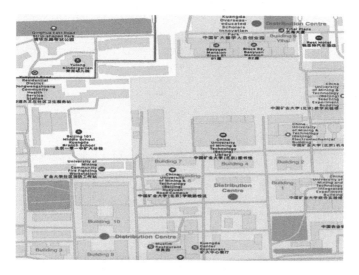

Fig. 8. Clustering results.

Dynamic Optimization of Parcel Delivery Area. As shown in the data results in Table 3, epoch is the training round, train_ Loss is the loss value of the training set (unlabelled data, continuous learning, and then compared with labelled data) _ acc is the true accuracy value of the training set; val_ Loss is the loss value of the control set, that is, the real data with labels, which can directly see the learning results, val_ acc is the true accuracy value of the control set.

The introduction of this model will greatly improve the problems of a low success rate and slow express speed in the end logistics sorting process. Bring the data into the DNN model established in Chapter 3. The training process is shown in Fig. 3 in Chapter 3.4. The values of w and b are preset by the pred function. After the training set enters, the values of w and b are updated continuously, and the predicted values are recorded. Compare the actual value with the predicted value, record the loss value, and then continuously use the for loop structure to dynamically adjust w and b until more accurate w and b values are obtained at the end of the training round. When the model in this chapter runs, set the epoch round to 20 rounds, the learning rate to 0.001, the single batch data size to 50, and the total step size to step = int (train_num/batch_size. Read the picture into the pixel mode of 28 * 28, normalize all the numbers according to the steps of the standardized formula, and then encode the reference set one hot with a depth of 10 to start learning. The update coefficient is selected by the random gradient descent algorithm, and the activation function is the SIGMOD function selected by 80% of the model in machine learning. The results are shown in Fig. 7. It shows that the learning accuracy can reach 91.1% by 20 rounds, and the accuracy can be recognized (Figs. 8 and 9).

Table 3. Data of DNN simulation results.

Training round (epoch)	Training set loss value (train_loss)	True accuracy value of training set (train_acc)	Control set loss value (val_loss)	Comparison set true accuracy value (val_acc)
1	1.6464	0.6870	1.5358	0.7032
2	1.0325	0.7907	0.9629	0.8044
3	0.8100	0.8316	0.7637	0.8428
4	0.6917	0.8534	0.6594	0.8613
5	0.6152	0.8664	0.5938	0.8717
6	0.561	0.8754	0.5477	0.8798
7	0.5208	0.8820	0.5144	0.8859
8	0.4894	0.8868	0.4884	0.8902
9	0.4643	0.8909	0.4675	0.8950
10	0.4436	0.8941	0.4503	0.8984
11	0.4262	0.8972	0.4358	0.9014
12	0.4112	0.8997	0.4234	0.9033
13	0.3982	0.9024	0.4127	0.9038
14	0.3868	0.9046	0.4035	0.9054
15	0.3766	0.9066	0.3954	0.9060
16	0.3674	0.9082	0.3881	0.9079
17	0.3592	0.9098	0.3815	0.9091
18	0.3518	0.9108	0.3756	0.9094
19	0.345	0.9123	0.3703	0.9107
20	0.3387	0.9132	0.3654	0.9115

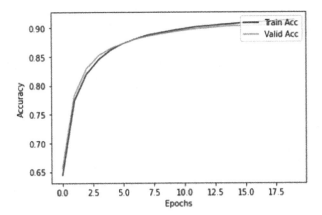

Fig. 9. DNN network simulation result diagram.

4.3   Effectiveness

Shorten the Delivery Time. According to the actual investigation, the traditional mode is limited by manual sorting and delivery, and the delivery time of a single piece is usually 4–12 h. After optimizing the parcel delivery location based on the improved DNN, the delivery efficiency is greatly improved. Assuming that the express delivery is divided into three time periods of 0, 1 and 2 on the same day, and a short message is sent at the moment when the express delivery is put into the express cabinet, the recipient will have a chance to take the express delivery, and then designing an appropriate punishment mechanism for the delay in picking up the express delivery can greatly shorten the pick-up efficiency of users, and the pick-up time is 0–4 h.

Improve the Accuracy. After optimizing the parcel delivery location based on the improved DNN, the stagnation of parcel delivery is reduced, and the bad parts rate is reduced from 10% to 9%.

Reduce the Single Delivery Cost. After optimizing the parcel delivery location based on the improved DNN, taking 500 pieces of intelligent parcel cabinets as an example, the price is approximately 500,000 pieces, and the average daily express delivery is approximately 400 pieces. Assuming that the service life of the equipment is only 10 years, then the single piece cost is controlled below 0.5 yuan. Considering that the use of intelligent parcel cabinets does not need service center personnel, only one or two people need to maintain irregularly or organize themselves in the region, and the single piece delivery cost is only approximately 1 yuan at the end (Table 4).

Table 4. Data comparison table.

	Delivery duration	Spoilage	Unit cost	Full time operation staff
Tradition	4–12 h	10%	5–8 yuan	More than 5 people
Post-reconstruction	0–4 h	9%	1 yuan	0 people

5   Conclusion

Based on adaptive K-means clustering and a deep neural network (DNN), this paper studies the last kilometer problem in high-density gathering areas and conducts an empirical analysis by taking the Beijing Mining University community as an example. The research shows that the efficiency of express delivery in the last kilometer can be improved by selecting an intelligent parcel cabinet and dynamically optimizing the parcel data in the sorting area when the number of express shipments is large and the living density is high. The research shows that the efficiency of express delivery in the last kilometer can be improved by selecting an intelligent parcel cabinet and dynamically optimizing the parcel data in the sorting area when the number of express shipments is large and the living density is high. The conclusions of this paper are also applicable to the last kilometer efficiency optimization of high-density areas such as urban office buildings and high-density residential areas. The possible innovations of this paper are as follows: (1) The clustering algorithm in machine learning is applied to parcel distribution. In high-density residential communities, when there is a large amount of logistics distribution, the parcel placement position is optimized, and the detour of the customer pickup route caused by the random investment position of parcels is reduced, which improves customer experience and distribution efficiency. (2) When the distribution demand in the community fluctuates drastically, a dynamic optimization model of parcel delivery location based on the deep neural network (DNN) algorithm is built to ensure that the optimal delivery location of express parcels will change with the distribution demand.

Acknowledgement. Fund Project: Key project of Beijing Social Science Foundation (19yja001); China University of mining and Technology (Beijing) Yueqi young scholars project (2602021rc17); Special fund for graduate students of basic scientific research business expenses of Central Universities (2021yjsgl02); Project supported by the special fund for Social Sciences of basic scientific research business expenses of Central Universities (2021 skgl01); National undergraduate scientific research topic selection training program (c202105030).

References

1. Li, Z., Guo, Q., Yang, S.: Research on the information sharing strategy of e-commerce platform under the competitive environment of suppliers. Soft Sci. **34**(5), 108–114 (2020). https://doi.org/10.13956/J.SS.1001-8409.2020.05.17
2. Zhu, H., Wang, S., Lu, X.: Discussion on the new mode of campus express delivery in colleges and universities-taking Jiangnan University as an example. Mark. Weekly (Theoret. Res.) **7**, 111–114 (2009)
3. Zhang, X.: Joint distribution mode and decision-making path of terminal logistics-supply and demand analysis based on e-commerce logistics and community service. Res. Financ. Issues **3**, 123–129 (2013)
4. Ren, D.: Research on the new mode of campus express delivery under autonomous management. Logist. Technol. **33**(11), 71–73 (2014)
5. Shi, S., Huang, Y., Yan, W.: Research on the application of smart cabinet in campus express delivery. Comput. Simulat. **32**(9), 421–424 (2015)
6. Wang, J., Zou, E.: Application analysis of online shopping terminal logistics based on intelligent parcel cabinet mode. Logist. Technol. **34**(05), 58–60 (2015)
7. Liu, R., He, Z., Wang, Q.: Investigation and analysis of the present situation of campus express service in Wuhan universities. Logist. Eng. Manag. **37**(03), 145–150 (2015)
8. Ruan, H., Geng, L., Xiao, R.: Research on flexible distribution strategy of e-commerce terminal logistics based on extremum-ant colony algorithm. Ind. Eng. **19**(01), 51–60 (2016)
9. Wang, C.: The development experience of overseas urban terminal logistics distribution and its reference. Logist. Eng. Manag. **39**(07), 16–19 (2017)
10. Zhang, B., Wang, Y.: Research on the "last kilometer" service mode of campus express. J. Zhejiang Wanli Univ. **31**(06), 18–22 (2018)
11. Wang, H., Wu, Y., Liu, X.: Study on the location of campus intelligent parcel cabinet considering service radius. Logist. Eng. Manag. **40**(08), 91–92 (2018)
12. Lei, W., Feng, C.: Development status and prospect of smart lockers in smart campus. Mod. Econ. Inf. **15**, 313–314 (2018)

13. Zeng, Z., Li, X., Wen, S., Liu, L.: Study on the location of campus express service concentration area based on Dijkstra shortest path algorithm-taking Wuyi University as an example. Mod. Bus. **05**, 174–175 (2019)

14. Li, W., Yang, Y., Liu, H., Liu, Y.: Research on optimization of logistics distribution path in urban terminal. Railw. Freight Transp. **37**(03), 5–10 (2019)

15. Tang, Y.: Research on the location and layout of intelligent parcel cabinets in colleges and universities based on gravity center method and analytic hierarchy process. Shandong Sci. **32**(03), 65–72 (2019)

16. Wang, C., Yu, Y., Wang, Q., Shi, X., Fei, C., Liu, X.: Research on campus express delivery mode with the help of platform. Mod. Market. (Bus. Edn.) **2020**(02), 154–155 (2020)

17. Liu, X., Wang, W.: Talent selection system based on fuzzy neural network. Soft Sci. **33**(6), 117–120 (2019)

18. Perboli, G., Rosano, M., Saint-Guillain, M., et al.: Simulation–optimization framework for City Logistics: an application on multimodal last-mile delivery. IET Intel. Transp. Syst. **12**(4), 262–269 (2018)

19. Wang, Y., Zhang, D., Liu, Q., et al.: Towards enhancing the last-mile delivery: an effective crowd-tasking model with scalable solutions. Transp. Res. Part E Logs Transp. Rev. **93**, 279–293 (2016)

20. Qi, W., Li, L., Liu, S., et al.: Shared mobility for last-mile delivery: design, operational prescriptions and environmental impact. Social Ence Electronic Publishing (2016)

21. Kervenoael, R.D., Schwob, A., Chandra, C.: E-retailers and the engagement of delivery workers in urban last-mile delivery for sustainable logistics value creation: leveraging legiti mate concerns under time-based marketing promise. PostPrint (2020)

22. Cui, Y.: Application of particle swarm optimization algorithm in port ship logistics. J. Coastal Res. **115**, 226 (2020)

23. Intisar, M., Khan, M.M., Islam, M.R., Masud, M.: Computer vision based robotic arm controlled using interactive GUI. Intell. Autom. Soft Comput. **27**(2), 533–550 (2021)

24. Ahmed, S., Khan, M.M., Alroobaea, R., Masud, M.: Development of a multi-feature web-based physIoTherapy service system. Intell. Autom. Soft Comput. **29**(1), 43–54 (2021)

25. Uddin, M., Memon, M.S., Memon, I., Ali, I., Memon, J.: Hyperledger fabric blockchain: secure and efficient solution for electronic health records. Comput. Mater. Continua **68**(2), 2377–2397 (2021)

26. Gepreel, K.A., Mohamed, M.S., Alotaibi, H.A.: Dynamical behaviors of nonlinear coronavirus (covid-19) model with numerical studies. Comput. Mater. Continua **67**(1), 675–686 (2021)

27. Ghazal, T.M., Hussain, M.Z., Said, R.A., Nadeem, A., Hasan, M.K.: Performances of k-means clustering algorithm with different distance metrics. Intell. Autom. Soft Comput. **30**(2), 735–742 (2021)

Design of Storage System Based on RFID and Intelligent Recommendation

Nijiachen Han[1], Yihui Fu[1], Yingnan Zhao[1(✉)], and S. K. Jha[2]

[1] Nanjing University of Information Science and Technology,
Nanjing 210044, China
zh_yingnan@126.com
[2] IT Fundamentals and Education Technologies Applications, University
of Information Technology and Management in Rzeszow, 100031 Rzeszow,
Voivodeship, Poland

Abstract. Practical warehouse system design can effectively improve warehouse management efficiency. Based on the characteristics of the modern warehouse system, it designs an intelligent warehouse system using Radio Frequency Identification (RFID) tag technology and an intelligent recommendation algorithm. The system includes an RFID-based warehouse management module, an intelligent recommendation module comprising a hybrid recommendation algorithm, and a database module. The hybrid intelligent recommendation algorithm consists of K-means clustering analysis, cosine similarity algorithm, and Markov chain algorithm. Firstly, K-means determines the cluster centroid and then recommends the shelf strategy according to the cosine similarity between the goods. After reaching a specific base, the intelligent recommendation algorithm based on Markov chain will analyze the warehousing habits and rules to deal with the instability caused by the frequent change of mass center after the increasing number of samples. Further, the system allows multi-platform operation of web client and WeChat Mini Programs and it shows the superiority of the system.

Keywords: Intelligent warehouse · RFID tag · Hybrid recommendation algorithm · Cosine similarity · Clustering analysis · Markov chain

1 Introduction

The rapid development of information technology brought severe challenges to many traditional industries, such as manufacturing, the surgical and medical industries [1], and the Warehousing industry. The intelligent storage system is a development trend of warehousing logistics, effectively saving labor and land costs and improving logistics efficiency. Therefore, intelligent storage system is applied in many industries, such as automobile manufacturing, aviation, harbor, Furniture Customization industry [2], mining industry [3], ceramic industry [4], and so on. The mainstream intelligent storage system is a ubiquitous network based on mobile technology and IoT. For example, in document [5], the warehouse management system of portable laser scanning intelligent terminal was established by using barcode identification technology, mobile Internet of things technology, wireless communication technology, and computer information technology; Reference [6] studied the collaborative optimization algorithm of intelligent storage location planning and automated guided vehicle (AGV) path planning in the intelligent storage system; In reference [7], the intelligent three-dimensional warehouse built by Dongguan Jianhui Paper Industry Co., Ltd. is composed of three-dimensional shelves, stacker, information identification system, inbound and outbound transportation system, warehouse control system software (WCS), and warehouse management system (WMS). Therefore, the intelligent storage system belongs to the ubiquitous network and synthesizes multi-disciplinary fields; It involves architecture design, network communication, computing technology, intelligent control technology, and many other aspects [8].

Radio Frequency Identification (RFID) is a kind of automatic identification technology in this paper. In the 1950s, the improvement and application of radar gave birth to RFID technology. The principle is that after scanning the tag, receiving the RF signal from the reader, and storing the physical information of the inventory products through the built-in inductive coupling electronic tag of the passive RFID reading and writing mechanism. The energy transmission mechanism is established by acquiring the magnetic field information (induced current) the wireless communication unit sends. The reader reads and decodes the data and sends it to the central information system for relevant data processing.

The project's design also combines the intelligent warehousing technology, the warehousing strategy based on intelligent recommendation. At present, the intelligent recommendation algorithms in warehouse systems usually have the following categories:

1. Content-based recommendation algorithm: in this algorithm, the characteristics of users and items are represented by explicit tags. According to the feedback information of users when they login to the system, users' interests or item features are collected, and the correlation vectors about the two are constructed by using the obtained user tags and item tags combined with their attribute features, through cosine similarity and Pearson similarity, the top-N items with high similarity are received to complete the recommendation. The content-based recommendation system can provide users with personalized recommendations and adapt to the cold start problem, but the accuracy rate is not high [9].

2. Collaborative filtering algorithm: the recommendation system based on this algorithm is the most widely used and can accurately recommend to users. Its performance in the global e-commerce field is outstanding. For example, Amazon search engine, about 35% of the sales on its website come from its personalized recommendation based on a collaborative filtering algorithm [10]. The algorithm does not rely on the relevant content information of items. However, the method's core is still based on historical data, which needs to be supported by user behavior data, so there is a "cold start" problem for new items and new users. Suppose the data in the database is sparse, or there is no data. In that case, there will not be enough information for the algorithm to analyze the user behavior, which will lead to poor recommendation quality and poor effectiveness of the recommendation results.

3. Hybrid recommendation algorithm: in practical applications, various recommendation methods are usually used simultaneously, which is the hybrid recommendation algorithm [11]. Taking the above two algorithms as an example, the collaborative filtering algorithm will show the problems of cold start and data sparseness when new users or items are added, which will reduce the effectiveness of recommendations. Therefore, the combination of similarity calculation in collaborative filtering algorithm and content recommendation can alleviate the cold start problem of items to a certain extent. Since the content-based recommendation algorithm only considers the characteristics of items and has nothing to do with user behavior, it can also alleviate the problem of data sparsity [12]. This paper also uses a hybrid recommendation method that combines the cosine similarity algorithm based on cargo attributes and the Markov chain algorithm.

In this paper, the system's overall architecture, the design of the database, and the recommendation algorithm are given. The main contributions of this paper are as follows:

1. In the recommendation algorithm, a hybrid recommendation algorithm is proposed based on the change of warehousing habits and the attributes of goods. On this basis, the shelf strategy of the warehousing system is given, which can improve the efficiency of warehousing and save a lot of time and labor costs.
2. In the system description part, combined with RFID technology, the overall design scheme of the intelligent storage system is given, and the workflow and implementation scheme of multi-platform interaction is introduced, which has specific reference significance for the development of intelligent storage systems.
3. The structure of the rest of the paper is as follows: the database design part describes the database tables involved in each stage of warehouse work and the corresponding function modules of each table. The relationship between objects and their related attributes is given in the E-R diagram. It realizes the functions of goods in and out warehouse management, staff management, supplier supply, goods information management, and inventory functions. The conclusion summarizes the positions of all the above modules and the advantages and disadvantages corresponding to each module and puts forward the future research direction and improvement direction.

2   System Description

The core application of the intelligent warehouse software system includes the background intelligent warehouse management system (WMS) client, the central database, and the front-end WeChat applet of RFID electronic tag technology, which interact with each other to realize the functions of strategy algorithm and transaction reservation. The architecture of the system is shown in Fig. 1. Different operation permissions are set for additional personnel to ensure system security. External access to cargo information and warehouse information through RFID tags and surveillance cameras. WMS and RFID realize the safe visualization and more detailed processing of a series of warehouse operations from storage to warehouse out. Through barcode technology and intelligent recommendation algorithm, WMS and RFID can realize the security visualization and more detailed processing of a series of operations; It can realize the functions of goods automatic storage, automatic allocation storage, automatic inventory, and warehousing habit analysis. Compared with the traditional warehouse, the intelligent warehouse management system mainly includes the automatic operation function. The automated stereoscopic warehouse can realize the automatic operation when the materials are put in and out of the warehouse. Second, the background software scheduling algorithm and location strategy can learn FIFO, improve efficiency, and reduce staff operation complexity, saving a lot of time and labor. In addition, informatization is also an essential part of constructing an intelligent warehouse. The information system of intelligent warehouse includes a warehouse control system (WCS), a warehouse operation app, and interfaces with other business systems. WMS is responsible for managing the warehousing business and inventory, and WCs is responsible for the mobilization and control of automation equipment. The warehouse app realizes the mobile operation of receiving and delivering operations and warehouse operations. At the same time, the interface part learns the data interaction and business linkage between warehouse management and other systems. The four subsystems complement each other to realize the automation of warehousing materials, warehouse operation, and business management.

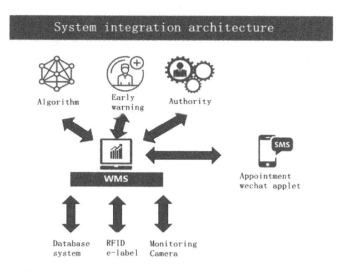

Fig. 1. The overall architecture of the intelligent storage system.

3   Database Design

The system database design aims to meet the essential data storage and query functions and optimize the database structure. The data redundancy is reduced to the minimum to improve the system's overall performance [13]. Considering the association between users with different authorities and the characteristics of the warehousing industry, its Entity-Relationship Diagram should revolve around a set of inbound and outbound processes. Figure 2 shows the Entity-Relationship Diagram of this system.

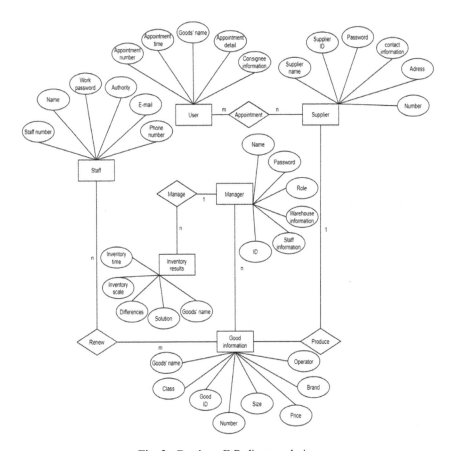

Fig. 2. Database E-R diagram design.

As shown in the figure, for example, the supplier entity contains the basic information of the supplier: supplier name, supplier account number, password, contact information, address, number, and so on. Other entities and their attributes are also included. The attributes of entities are mainly stored in the form of tables. According to the above analysis and diagram, we can conclude that we need to create these database tables: employee information table, user reservation table, administrator information table, supplier information table, warehouse information table, and goods inventory table.

At the same time, the basic workflow of the system can be seen through the E-R diagram. The system users fill in the reservation form and pass it to the supplier. The supplier provides the goods, and the employees fill in the relevant information for warehousing. At the same time, the results of periodic inventory will be sent to the administrator to deal with the inventory differences. Table 1 below shows several tables required by the system and their content descriptions.

Table 1. Database table and function description.

Employee information sheet	Store employee-related information
Administrator information table	Store administrator information
Supplier information table	Store supplier-related information
Warehouse information table	Store relevant information of the warehouse
User reservation table	Store information related to the appointment submitted by the user
Inventory list	Store regular inventory results
Cargo information table	Store specific information of all goods in the warehouse

4 Hybrid Intelligent Recommendation Algorithm

In the design of system intelligent recommendation algorithm, considering that only one attribute of goods in the warehouse cannot make good use of other attribute information of goods, and the result of division is too broad, this system uses K-means clustering algorithm to divide the warehouse area. On this basis, a content-based recommendation algorithm is adopted. Cosine similarity is widely used in information retrieval by comparing sentence similarity with the dimension given by terms. Also, the attributes of goods in warehouse system can be given parameters by some of their properties, which are similar to the dimension of terms mentioned above. The similarity between goods can be compared by the parameters that represent the attributes of goods [14]. Then, the division area into which the goods enter is determined by the similarity. Furthermore, considering that different industries have different demands for goods, it is thought that personalized warehousing habits can be analyzed when goods are put into storage. The change of warehousing habits of goods in different periods can be captured by using Markov chains to achieve the effect that the warehouse is ready for warehousing when goods are not put into storage. So the system can provide processing time and space for possible special situations in the future.

4.1 Cosine Similarity Algorithm Based on Goods Attributes

The algorithm is specified in the system, that is, the goods information is collected and integrated by RFID, and the high-dimensional vector which can fully describe the goods attributes is formed by assigning values to each detail. The similarity between two goods can be compared by calculating the included angle of attribute vector in high-dimensional positive space:

$$\cos(\theta)\frac{A \cdot B}{|A| \cdot |B|} \frac{\sum_{i=1}^{n}(A_i \cdot B_i)}{\sqrt{\sum_{i=1}^{n}(A_i^2)} \cdot \sqrt{\sum_{i=1}^{n}(B_i^2)}} \tag{1}$$

The vector in the existing system represents the properties of goods. When the size, category, and price of goods are given certain weights, a high-dimensional vector is created too. In formula (1), A, B represent two vectors, A_i, B_i for each component of the vector. The closer the calculation result is to 1, the more similar they are. The classification result with the highest similarity is determined by sorting the results.

4.2 K-means Clustering Algorithm

K-means is a method of clustering. The constant is determined in advance, and the constant means the final number of clustering categories. As shown in Fig. 3, the initial point is randomly selected as the centroid of the same kind of goods. Then the sample points are divided into the most similar categories by calculating the cosine similarity between each sample and the centroid. Then the centroid of each category is recalculated. Repeat this process until the centroid no longer changes, and finally determine the category to which each sample belongs and the centroid of each category, as shown in Fig. 3. The core idea is to find a partition scheme of clusters through iteration. The average value of clusters can be used to represent the corresponding samples with the slightest overall error. The elements in clusters should be as compact as possible, and the clusters should be separated as much as possible. Conform to the warehouse shelving strategy of compact stacking similar goods and separation of heterogeneous goods. That is, for warehousing, it is equivalent to allocating areas to warehouses, taking the first batch of goods as the primary samples. The initial cluster is found through the above method, and the warehouse occupied by each big classification is also divided into areas [15]. Formula (2) represents the cosine similarity sum of the object to its cluster centroid, and the following incoming goods are compared with the existing cluster centroid by similarity. The most suitable shelving area is recommended for employees by ranking the similarity. At the same time, update the primary sample and then update the centroid with each warehousing.

$$\sum_{i=1}^{K}\sum_{x \in C_i}\cos(C_i, x) \tag{2}$$

This formula represents the sum of cosine similarity between the object and C_i, the centroid of its cluster. The maximum result is the optimal result. Cosine similarity is used to measure the distance, and the cluster's centroid is its mean value, so all dimensions of the vector can be averaged.

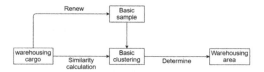

Fig. 3. K-means clustering algorithm.

4.3 Markov Chain Algorithm

Through some investigations, it is found that the system, to some extent, has Hearst statistical properties [16]. It reflects the results of a long list of related events. For example, two kinds of related goods are likely to be warehoused in the same batch, and the same kind of goods may be purchased many times, that is, warehousing habits can be studied and learned during a long warehousing process. The warehousing habit constantly changes with time, and this algorithm uses Markov chain to simulate this change. The algorithm can predict the subsequent actions by investigating the recent actions of users [17]. Markov's data structure allows the system to extend the existing data [18].

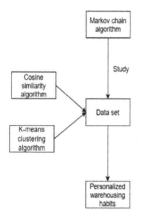

Fig. 4. Schematic diagram of hybrid recommendation algorithm

This method needs data sets for reference, and after clustering division of K-means algorithm and initial warehousing of the above content-based recommendation algorithm, a batch of data sets can be obtained for the latter to learn at the initial stage, as shown in Fig. 4, that is, after the data sets are accumulated for a period of time through the recommendation of the former algorithm at the initial stage, the warehousing habit is studied by this algorithm. Recommend a more adaptable strategy based on warehousing habits. In addition, this algorithm allows users and employees to know the forecast of incoming goods based on previous warehousing habits during the gap period without warehousing and make preparations on the corresponding shelves with this as a reference.

5 Concluding Remarks

The intelligent warehouse system designed in this paper includes a warehouse management module, an intelligent recommendation module, and a database module. By designing the practical database to avoid data redundancy and proposing a hybrid intelligent recommendation algorithm for warehousing strategy, the system makes warehouse management convenient and logical. In general, multi-platform operation and the use of RFID electronic tags, refined and relatively complete database design, intelligent recommendation algorithm with specific advanced characteristics, including its subsequent application, can effectively make up for the shortcomings of the traditional warehouse industry. At the same time, it is in line with the rapidly developing trend of the intelligent warehousing industry. To some extent, the innovation part of the system can provide some information for the current industry development trend as a reference.

In the follow-up research, we will further develop the warehousing field into networked and integrated services by extending the industrial service chain. Among them, for the recommendation algorithm based on Markov chain, the potential of its common use with multilayer neural network modeling will be explored in the future [19], and a more personalized recommendation algorithm that can follow the change of warehousing habits will be formed. Meanwhile, the prediction performance of the algorithm is further improved. During the design process, we found that the algorithm has its potential in the future, and its application value and methods of use need to be further developed. However, one thing is for sure that the improvement of the algorithm will bring further optimization improvements to the system, which can make it more advanced to an extent.

Acknowledgement. This paper is sported by undergraduate training program for innovation and entrepreneurship of NUIST(XJDC202110300242).

References

1. Zhang, X., Sun, X., Sun, W., et al.: Deformation expression of soft tissue based on bp neural network. Intell. Autom. Soft Comput. **32**(2), 1041–1053 (2022)
2. Guo, C.Y., Song, J., Lin, X.Y.: Demand analysis and development status of intelligent warehouse system for panel custom furniture enterprises. Forest Prod. Ind. **57**(10), 36–40 (2020)
3. Wu, J.S.: Design and application of intelligent warehouse and express service system in mines based on Internet of Things. China Mining **29**(5), 72–75 (2020)
4. Wu, X.R., Hu, B.: Design of intelligent storage system in ceramic park based on industrial Internet of Things technology. J. Ceram. **41**(5), 741–749 (2020)
5. Gao, N., Yang, Y.F., Gu, L.: Construction of mobile intelligent warehouse system based on barcode recognition and Internet of Things. Comput. Appl. **39**(S1), 228–234 (2019)
6. Lin, Y.S., Li, Q.S., Lu, P.H.: Collaborative optimization algorithm of intelligent warehouse location planning and AGV path planning. J. Softw. **31**(9), 2770–2784 (2020)
7. Han, Z.J., Liang, X.X.: Analysis of precise positioning and closed-loop algorithm of stacker. Zhonghua Paper **41**(14), 40–46 (2020)

8. Zhang, P., Miao, J., Hu, Z.: Overview of ubiquitous network research. J. Beijing Univ. Posts Telecommun. **33**(5), 1–6 (2010)

9. Li, X.T., Yang, S., Dilichati, I.: Application research of hybrid recommendation algorithm integrating content and collaborative filtering. Comput. Technol. Dev. **31**(10), 24–29 (2021)

10. Liu, J., Yang, J., Song, S.S.: Collaborative filtering recommendation algorithm based on users' willingness to buy. J. Jilin Univ. (Sci. Edn.) **59**(06), 1432–1438 (2021)

11. Wang, Y.G., He, H.J., Gao, J.: Recommendation algorithm of second-hand products on campus based on mixed recommendation model. Inf. Technol. Inf. **09**, 106–108 (2021)

12. Ma, M.X., Wang, G.Z.: Hybrid recommendation algorithm combined with item attribute weight. Intell. Comput. Appl. **11**(09), 161–164 (2021)

13. Rudniy, A.: Data warehouse design for big data in academia. Comput. Mater. Cont. **71**(1), 979–992 (2022)

14. Agarwal, A.K., Badal, N.: A novel approach for intelligent distribution of data warehouses. Egypt. Inform. J. **17**, 147–159 (2016)

15. Luo, X., Ouyang, Y.X., Xiong, Z.: Optimizing collaborative filtering algorithm based on K-nearest neighbor by similarity support. Chin. J. Comput. **33**(08), 1437–1445 (2010)

16. Zhang, X., Sun, X., Sun, W.: Robust reversible audio watermarking scheme for telemedicine and privacy protection. Comput. Mater. Cont. **71**(2), 3035–3050 (2022)

17. Palaniappan, L., Selvaraj, K.: Profile and rating similarity analysis for recommendation systems using deep learning. Comput. Syst. Sci. Eng. **41**(3), 903–917 (2022)

18. Zhao, X., Keikhosrokiani, P.: Sales prediction and product recommendation model through user behavior analytics. Comput. Mater. Cont. **70**(2), 3855–3874 (2022)

19. Xu, J.X., He, X.B., He, Q.Y.: Research on personalized recommendation algorithm based on user group interest change. J. China West Normal Univ. (Nat. Sci. Edn.) 1–8 (2021)

Visual Research and Predictive Analysis of Land Resource Use Type Change

YuDan Zhao[1], Wu Zeng[1(⊠)], YingGe Zhang[1], RuoChen Tan[2],
Jie Li[1], and DaChang Chen[1]

[1] Wuhan Polytechnic University, Wuhan 430023, Hubei, China
zengwu@whpu.edu.cn
[2] University of Miami, Miami, FL 33124, USA

Abstract. Land cover change is a hot topic in the interdisciplinary research of global change and land science. The existing spatial visualization methods based on remote sensing images have the advantages of wide detection range, strong timeliness and objective reflection of land surface changes. However, the data display mode is single and the interaction is weak, the reading threshold is high, and the visual analysis of land use statistics data is insufficient. This paper collects and collates land change data and social and economic data from 2009 to 2016 in China. Firstly, Echarts and other tools are used to achieve visual representation of data. Then the impact of social and economic development needs on land resource utilization is studied. Finally, a prediction model of land use data change is established. In conclusion, this paper presents an effective visual data analysis method according to the characteristics of land use data, which can assist land managers to understand and analyze data and provide scientific basis for their decision-making activities of land use.

Keywords: Data visualization · Land use type · National land change data

1 Introduction

In recent years, the problems of ecological balance and environmental protection have become increasingly serious, and the relationship between human beings and land use has been deteriorating. Land use and land cover Change (LUCC) is an important part of global environmental change and sustainability research. To study land use change and its impact on ecosystem due to the interaction between human activities and natural system, has gradually become the global change and land science cross cutting edge research at the core of the problem.

A great deal of research has been done on land use and land cover change at home and abroad. Camacho et al. [1] used remote sensing technology to analyze the changes of coastal landscape in South Sinaloa from 2000 to 2010, to connect the changes of wetland space with the economic value provided by ecosystem services, with the purpose of studying the impact of land use change on the value of coastal wetland ecosystem services. Tian et al. [2] reconstructed the main driving forces of land use change and land conversion in India during 1880–2010 based on high-resolution remote sensing image data sets and historical data. Based on remote sensing images and CLUE-S model, Niu Yafang [3] simulated and predicted the spatial distribution and pattern of land use in Changzhi City. Dai Chenguang [4] developed a real-time visualization algorithm for terrain data by studying terrain data and using data visual analysis technology. Ni Xingguo [5] designed and implemented the agricultural statistical data visualization platform and explored the visualization of agricultural statistical data. Aiming at the problems of multiple sources and heterogeneity of agricultural statistical data, single display mode of agricultural data and non-sharing of agricultural data, a system [6] with agricultural data collection, data filtering and integration, data visualization, system management and other functional modules was constructed to realize the diversified display of data and dynamic interaction of charts.

Most studies on land use/land cover use remote sensing image data with different precision, which has high openness, accuracy and integrity, and static charts drawn through remote sensing data analysis have visual effects. However, its data display mode is single and its interactive ability is weak. Through visualization, complex data can be understood and revealed with more intuitive color graphics. The way of data visualization analysis facilitates people's understanding of land resource change information, encourages people to explore the relationship between more information, and has good man-machine interaction.

In this paper, the visualization [7] method is used to analyze the data of land change and study the change of land resource utilization. Firstly, the area distribution information of all provinces and cities in China and the spatio-temporal dynamic evolution of land use change statistical data were presented from the perspective of time series and space [8], enabling people to quickly understand land use change information and encouraging users to explore and even manipulate data to discover other potential data features. Then the correlation between economic factors and land use data is analyzed to explore the correlation between economic factors and the change of farmland and land for transportation area. Finally, the grey prediction model is constructed to predict and analyze the trend of land change in the future.

2 Data Collection and Processing

The data in this paper mainly come from the authoritative data of the Ministry of Land and Resources [9] and the social and economic data of the National Bureau of Statistics [10]. At the same time, it also manually obtains data from online platforms such as the official website of the Institute of Geographic Sciences and Natural Resources Research of the Chinese Academy of Sciences to strive for data integrity and accuracy.

First, the crawler framework of Python scrapy was used to crawl the data. Then, the land use data of various provinces and cities in China were preprocessed and reclassified by tools such as Excel and Python. Finally, clear abnormal data, modify format errors, and add 0 for data vacancy values in Hong Kong, Macao special Administrative Region and Taiwan Province, so as to make data preparation for the following data visualization and model simulation prediction.

3   Visual Analysis of Land Use Data

This study collected information on land resource use types of provinces and cities in China from 2009 to 2016. The land use types are classified into 8 first-level categories: arable land, garden, woodland, grassland, towns and villages and industrial and mining land, land for transportation, land for water area and water conservancy facilities, and other land. As shown in Table 1, 36 secondary classifications are subdivided on the basis of the primary classifications.

Table 1. Eight types of land use and their secondary classification.

Land use types	Containing types
Arable land	Paddy field, irrigated land and dry land
Garden	Orchards, tea gardens and other gardens
Woodland	There are woodlands, shrub woodlands and other woodlands
Grassland	Natural pasture, artificial pasture and other grasslands
Towns, villages, industrial and mining land	Cities, towns, villages and mining land
Land for transportation	Land for railways, roads, rural roads, airports, ports and wharfs
Land for water area and water conservancy facilities	River water surface, lake water surface, reservoir water surface, pit water surface, coastal beach, inland beach, ditch, hydraulic structure, glacier and permanent snow
Other land	Facility agricultural land, ridge, saline alkali land, swamp and sandy land

Table 1 above is the first-level and second-level classification of land. In order to help managers better understand the relationship between different categories, a classification diagram is made to more clearly show the relationship between various categories. See Fig. 1.

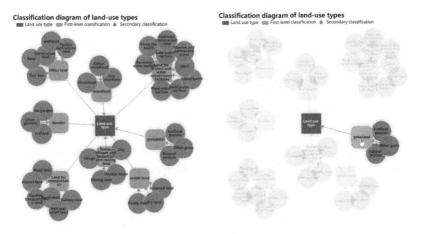

Fig. 1. Land type relationship diagram.

In this classification diagram, managers can control the highlighting of a certain category and its subordinate categories by controlling the mouse to better understand the relationship between various land types. An example is shown in Fig. 1, when the mouse moves to the primary category of "grassland", the "grassland" and its secondary classification will be highlighted at the same time. There are three categories of "Natural pasture", "Artificial pasture" and "Other grassland".

According to the data structure of land resource change data, the sunburst chart is also made, as shown in Fig. 2. Realize diversified display of data and dynamic interaction of charts, and create a more practical interactive graphical user interface (GUI) [11]. Through highly customizable land use data visualization services, assist land resource managers can understand and analyze data, and provide reliable data basis for their decision-making activities.

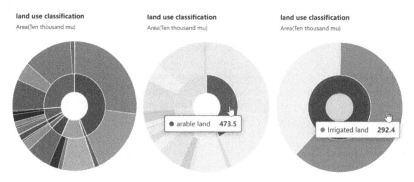

Fig. 2. Interactive sunburst map shows the information of Zhengzhou city, Henan Province in 2016.

The sunburst map in Fig. 2 shows the information of various regions in Zhengzhou, Henan province in 2016. The sunburst map can present the area proportion of the first and second classes to users, and allow managers to display more or less data details through interactive control [12]. For example, after clicking "arable land" in Fig. 2, only arable land and its secondary land class data can be displayed.

3.1 Spatial Distribution Dimension

China has a vast territory with a wide latitude span from north to south, spanning five temperature belts from south to north. Different climate makes obvious differences and distinctive characteristics of natural environment in different regions [13], which of course leads to strong spatial distribution characteristics of statistical data of land use types. In the system, land managers can select the type of land and year they want to observe through a cascade selector, as shown in Fig. 3.

Fig. 3. A diagram of a cascading selector.

In the cascade selector shown in Fig. 3, select the year 2009 and woodland options. The three-dimensional earth is taken as the carrier in Fig. 4, highlighting and various provinces in China, and use the height of the blue 3D pillars to represent the area value of provincial woodland, after moving the mouse pointer to the pillars corresponding to a province, the suspension prompt box will display the value of woodland area of the corresponding province. In addition, a one-button button to switch the "China perspective" is added to facilitate land managers to quickly focus on the view center.

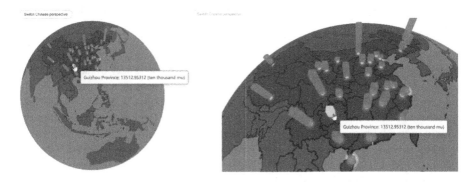

Fig. 4. Woodland distribution in China in 2009: 3D global perspective and China perspective.

On the basis of better regional awareness given by 3D earth, 2D histogram is used to realize the dynamic rotation of woodland data in each province (similarly, column height represents the value of woodland area in each province), so as to better compare the differences of certain year and certain land type in each province from the data perspective. Figure 5 shows the area ranking of woodland in all provinces of China in 2009, and dynamic rotation of data in 31 provinces, autonomous regions and municipalities except Hong Kong, Macao SAR and Taiwan Province.

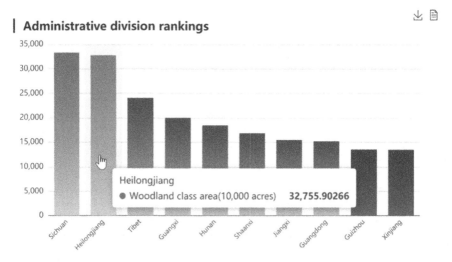

Fig. 5. 2D bar chart shows the distribution of woodland in each province of China in 2009.

The above method of visualizing the data by combining 3D earth with 2D histogram is not only more beautiful, but also makes it easier for managers to associate the actual spatial distribution. By setting cascade selectors, managers can always master their position in the whole data space [14]. In addition, multiple views are used to display different attributes of data, and data association is realized at the same time, so that data can be observed from different angles and in different display modes.

3.2   Time Series Dimension

The change and development of land use type are related to a variety of factors, such as government macro-control [15], climate change [16, 17], natural resources and environment [18, 19], etc. Under the joint action of these factors, the statistical data of land use type will show regular time series characteristics [20]. Click the 3D column or the column in the 2D histogram of Guizhou province in the system 3D Earth to display the year-by-year changes of the eight land types in the province from 2009 to 2016. As shown in Fig. 6, the graph shows the change of total land area of eight land types in Guizhou province from 2009 to 2016.

In Fig. 6, managers can select certain data they want to observe through a legend, using the filtering effects [21] like this to display more data in a limited space, increased the visual view of richness and understandability [22]. For example, the national land for transportation area shown in Fig. 6 continued to grow from 2009 to 2016. China's transportation has developed rapidly, and the convenience of transportation has greatly improved the fluidity of the national logistics network, which is one of the important supports of social and economic activities. Next, we will study the correlation between social economy and land use change.

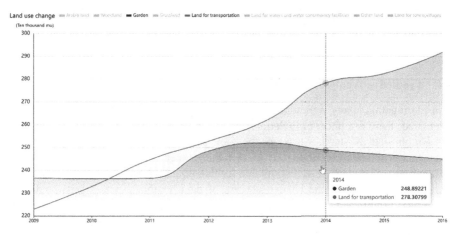

Fig. 6. Total land area changes of eight land types in Guizhou Province from 2009 to 2016.

3.3 Correlation Analysis Between Socio-economic Factors and Land Use Data

Through the above analysis, there may be a certain correlation between human social and economic activities and land use change.

Next, the relationship between economy and land use change will be analyzed.

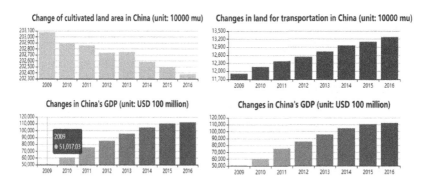

Fig. 7. Comparison of GDP change and area change of arable land and land for transportation from 2009 to 2016.

Through Fig. 7, the annual GDP is taken as the indicator to measure social and economic activities, and the annual changes of the arable land area and land for transportation area in China are compared vertically. It can be seen that from 2009 to 2016, with the rapid development of social economy, the area of land for transportation increased rapidly, while at the same time, the area of arable land in China decreased sharply. The continuous decrease of arable land resources is a direct threat to national food security, so its quantity and quality determine the sustainable development of social economy of a country or region. Therefore, it is necessary to take some measures of sustainable economic development to promote the coordinated development of economic development and arable land resources.

3.4   Predictive Analysis of Land Use Type Data

Considering that many agricultural data in this paper are difficult to be accurately calculated, there are uncertain relationships among various factors in the system, and the sample data is small, we adopt the grey prediction model [23], which is most consistent with data conditions, to predict the change of arable land area within a certain range. GM (1, 1) model is suitable for the sequence with strong exponential law and is used to describe the change process of data. In this paper, a grey prediction model was established for the change of arable land area from 2009 to 2016, and the grey model GM (1, 1) was used for quantitative analysis to predict the change of arable land area from 2009 to 2021. The predicted values are obtained by the following steps.

First, we know the element sequence data as formula (1):

$$x^{(0)} = \left(X^{(0)}(1), X^{(0)}(2), \cdots, X^{(0)}(n) \right) \tag{1}$$

Do a cumulative generation (1-AGO) sequence, and then be able to generate sequence close to the mean as shown in formula (2):

$$z^{(1)}(k) = 0.5x^{(1)}(k) + 0.5x^{(1)}(k-1) \tag{2}$$

Then, the grey differential equation model of GM(1, 1) is established as:

$$x(k) + az^{(1)}(k) = b \tag{3}$$

where, a is the development coefficient and b is the grey action.

Let $\hat{a}$ the parameter vector to be estimated, then we have:

$$\hat{a} = (a, b)^T \tag{4}$$

Then the least square estimation parameter column of the grey differential equation satisfies:

$$\hat{a} = \left(B^T B \right)^{-1} B^T Y_n \tag{5}$$

Among them:

$$B = \begin{pmatrix} -z^{(1)}(2), 1 \\ -z^{(1)}(3), 1 \\ \cdots, \cdots \\ -z^{(1)}(n), 1 \end{pmatrix}, \ Y_n = \begin{pmatrix} x^{(0)}(2), \\ x^{(0)}(3), \\ \cdots, \cdots \\ x^{(0)}(n), \end{pmatrix} \tag{6}$$

After, the whitening equation of grey differential equation is established:

$$\frac{dx^{(1)}}{dt} + ax^{(1)} = b \tag{7}$$

And the solution of the whitening equation is:

$$\hat{x}^{(1)}(t) = \left(\hat{x}^{(1)}(0) - \frac{b}{a}\right)e^{-at} + \frac{b}{a} \tag{8}$$

And finally, we take:

$$x^{(1)}(0) = x^{(0)}(1) \tag{9}$$

Then the time response sequence of the corresponding GM(1, 1) grey differential equation can be reduced and obtained:

$$\hat{x}^{(1)}(k+1) = \hat{x}^{(1)}(k+1) - \hat{x}^{(1)}(k) = \left[x^{(0)}(1) - \frac{b}{a}\right](1 - e^a)e^{-ak}, \quad k = 1, \ldots n - 1 \tag{10}$$

Formula (10) is the prediction equation, from which we can get the predicted value we need.

Based on the arable land area change data obtained from 2009 to 2016, GM (1, 1) model can be used to predict the arable land area change from 2009 to 2021. The algorithm steps involved are as follows:

1. Grade test and feasibility analysis of data.
2. Data transformation processing.
3. The GM (1, 1) model is established to calculate the predicted value column.
4. Test the predicted value.
5. Use the model for prediction.

After obtaining the predicted value data, a visual image is drawn based on Echarts [24, 25], as shown in Fig. 8, which is convenient for us to compare and analyze the predicted value and the actual value. Figure 8 shows the development trend of predicted value and actual value respectively by scatter diagram and line graph, in which solid red dot represents predicted value and hollow red dot represents actual value.

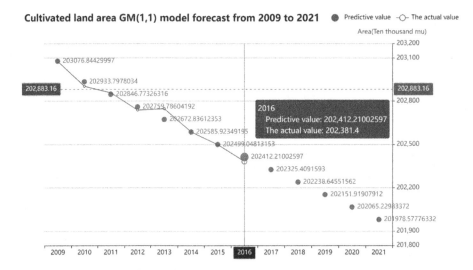

Fig. 8. Prediction results of GM (1, 1) model for arable land area from 2009 to 2021.

From Fig. 8, we can conclude that the arable land area decreases year by year with the increase of years, and the decrease rate has been flat since 2013, which is consistent with the change trend of China's GDP shown in Fig. 7. The prediction model shows that the arable land area continues to decline, which reminds us to take certain measures to protect the resources of arable land.

4   Conclusion

This paper mainly studies the process of land use change in a certain period through data collation, the setting of various evaluation indicators and the establishment of mathematical models. Through the analysis of spatial distribution characteristics, time series characteristics, correlation analysis of social and economic factors, model prediction and other aspects of land use change data visualization display, and realize the induction and summary of visual analysis results of land use change, in order to assist land managers to understand and analyze data. And provide scientific basis for the decision-making activities of land use.

References

1. Camacho-Valdez, V., Ruiz-Luna, A.: Effects of land use changes on the ecosystem service values of coastal wetland. Environ. Manage. **54**(4), 52–64 (2014)
2. Tian, H.: History of land use in India during 1880–2010: large-scale land transformations reconstructed from satellite data and historical archives. Global Planet. Change **121**, 78–88 (2014)

3. Niu, Y.: The study of dynamic change of land use and forecast analysis in Changzhi city from 2000 to 2020. Taiyuan University of Technology (2016)
4. Dai, C., Deng, X., et al.: An algorithm for real-time visualization of massive terrain dataset. J. Comput. Aided Des. Comput. Graph. **16**(11), 1603–1607 (2004)
5. Ni, X.: Design and realization of visualization system of agricultural statistical data. Hebei Agricultural University (2018)
6. Jin, Y., Zhu, Y.: Design and implementation of forestry statistical data visualization system —taking the forest product output data as an example. J. Fujian Forest. Sci. Technol. **47**(03), 51–55 (2020)
7. Xia, J., Li, J., et al.: A survey on interdisciplinary research of visualization and artificial intelligence. SCIENTIA SINICA Informationis **51**(11), 1777–1801 (2021)
8. Fisher, N.I., et al.: Graphical methods for data analysis. Biometrics **40**(2), 567 (1984)
9. Sharing Application Service Platform for Land Survey Results in the People's Republic of China (2020). https://tddc.mnr.gov.cn/
10. National Bureau of Statistics of the People's Republic of China (2020). https://data.stats.gov.cn/
11. Kovalerchuk, B.: Interpretable knowledge discovery reinforced by visual methods. In: Proceedings of the 25th ACM SIGKDD International Conference on Knowledge Discovery & Data Mining, pp. 3219–3220 (2019)
12. Ren, L.,Yi, D., et al.: Visual analytics towards big data. J. Softw. **25**(09), 1909–1936 (2014)
13. Bhagabati, N.K., Ricketts, T., et al.: Ecosystem services reinforce Sumatran tiger conservation in land use plans. Biol. Cons. **169**, 147–156 (2014)
14. Yang, Y., Liu, B., et al.: Review of information visualization. J. Hebei Univ. Sci. Technol. **35**(01), 91–102 (2014)
15. Qasim, M., Hubacek, K., et al.: Underlying and proximate driving causes of land use change in district Swat, Pakistan. Land Use Policy **34**, 146–157 (2013)
16. Kalnay, E., et al.: Impact of urbanization and land-use change on climate. Nature **423**(6939), 528 (2003)
17. Clarke, K.C., Hoppen, S.: A self-modifying cellular automaton model of historical urbanization in the San Francisco Bay area. Environ. Plann. B. Plann. Des. **24**(2), 247–261 (1997)
18. Lu, W., Yuan, G., Yang, H.: Visualization of reactor core based on triangular mesh method. Intell. Autom. Soft Comput. **29**(3), 689–699 (2021)
19. Sun, G., Li, F., Jiang, W.: Brief talk about big data graph analysis and visualization. J. Big Data **1**(1), 14 (2019)
20. Jiang, W., Wu, J., Sun, G.: A survey of time series data visualization methods. J. Quant. Comput. **2**(2), 13 (2020)
21. Sheng, Y., Chen, W., Wen, H.: Visualization research and application of water quality monitoring data based on Echarts. J. Big Data **2**(1), 1–8 (2020)
22. Cai, Y., Song, Z., Sun, G.: On visualization analysis of stock data. J. Big Data **1**(3), 135 (2019)
23. Jiao, J.: Brief introduction of grey system theory. Hydrogeol. Eng. Geol. **03**, 61 (1987)
24. Wang, Z., Zhang, C.: Design and implementation of data visualization analysis component based on ECharts. Inf. Microcomput. Appl. **35**(14), 46–48 (2016)
25. Hong, M., Wu, H., et al.: Design of dynamic data display front end using ECharts and HTML. Comput. Era **08**, 27–28+32 (2018)

A Research on Comprehensive Training Platform on Android for Software Engineering in Qinghai Minzu University

Chunhua Pan[(✉)]

Key Laboratory of Artificial Intelligence Application Technology State Ethnic Affairs Commission, Qinghai Minzu University, Xining 810007, China
155091145@qq.com

Abstract. With respect to the training program of software engineering specialty, this paper puts forward the comprehensive training platform of Chinese character dictation competition based on Android, and clarifies the purpose and main contents of the comprehensive training platform. Based on the hardware and software facilities of the campus, the C / S model training platform, the use of Android integrated training platform to achieve the Chinese character writing, clearing, timing and other functions, managers of the entire process of the game management, including the participating teams and players, the administrator can simultaneously obtain the client input Chinese characters, and display on the big screen, the judges then give the results after the score and statistical display. The whole integrated training platform is light and practical.

Keywords: Chinese character dictation integrated training platform · C/S · Server · Client APP

1 Introduction

Software is applied in many aspects in modern society. Almost all industries have computer software applications, such as manufacturing, agriculture, banking, aviation, government agencies [1]. Modern life is almost inseparable from mobile phone. Mobile applications are deployed in an incredible pace. These applications not only promote economic and social growth, but also improve the efficiency of work and life in general. The mainstream mobile phone operating systems include Android, IOS and, WP [2]. With the building of training platform on Android system, software engineering professionals would cultivate their software analysis, design, development and maintenance capabilities, as well as skills in project organization & management, teamwork, technological innovation & market development. This provides good experimental teaching innovation in practical environment, and reform new ideas in the process.

© The Author(s), under exclusive license to Springer Nature Switzerland AG 2022
X. Sun et al. (Eds.): ICAIS 2022, CCIS 1587, pp. 484–493, 2022.
https://doi.org/10.1007/978-3-031-06761-7_39

2 Skilled Required for Software Engineering Professionals

Software engineering professionals need to drive the theory, practice, network and experimental teaching as a whole, and complete the three-dimensional teaching as a complete teaching organization model [3].

The comprehensive training platform is based on software engineering development practice.

To build a unified mainstream software technology, the standard is based on the C/S architecture of the integrated training platform.

Android-based APP is to imitate the training platform of the CCTV Chinese character dictation competition. The specific function is to provide students a Chinese characters interface to write and to submit the results [4]. The server side allows the administrator to record the student's message and question, correct and send the answers, and summarize personal performance and team results, and finally show the result rankings.

3 Android-Based Training Platform

3.1 Training Platform System Design

The integrated training platform hardware requirement: a desktop computer installed with Windows and a Tablet PC installed Android system [5]. This setup is simple and easy to operate, with a strong practical and promotional value. Software development system requires Java programming JDK and a variety of IDE (Eclipse or Netbeans environment), and database software (such as the commonly used Excel and access database, SQL Server 2018). The software for the entire training platform is common, easy to use, and reliable.

3.2 Training Platform Architectural Framework

Modern computer science mathematical based graph theory, research shows that the structure determines the nature [6]. The architecture of the training platform is also a hierarchical structure of the tree. Based on the C/S model two-tier model: the client +server (server program+database program). Results also shows, by the training platform architecture allows students to fully grasp software engineering's required skills.

The client uses the countdown display control and input pen to write the required Chinese characters, complete the writing and modify the Chinese characters, submit the result, and then wait for the server to judge. as shown in Fig. 2.

Server-side manages the entire process of the competition: record the team and team members information, access client input Chinese characters and display on the big screen, server controls the time of competition, show the correct answer after the client completed the submission. The judges give the points and calculate the result of the competition. The structure is shown in Fig. 3.

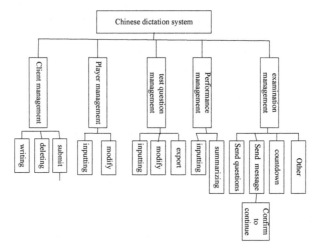

Fig. 1. Structure diagram of the software.

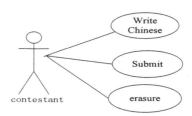

Fig. 2. Client-side structure.

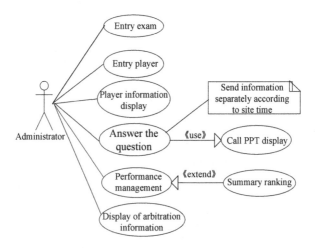

Fig. 3. Server-side structure.

The Client Input. students input words on the grid, complete the deletion of the whole word or erase a stroke, confirm the submission.

Player Information. Enter the modified unit, name information.

Test Results Management. Use ACCESSS database and Excel as a database with statistical support. Complete the entry, modify the questions and perform statistic functions.

Test Management. Send the beginning of the test information, questions, time information, arbitration information, send the arbitration officer.

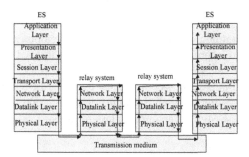

Fig. 4. Network OSI reference model.

Network communication concept and skillset is a weakness for many software engineering students. Understand and master the network architecture and communication model is the key to address this problem [7]. This is the core part of the training platform. The end system in Fig. 4 is the PC, mobile phones and other entities in the communication application process. The relay system is a router with routing and packet forwarding function. The development of network communication process based on Android system needs to have a bridge-like abstract unit connected to the application process [8]. In the Android system, we can use the existing Socket class to complete, and the interface Socket in the TCP / IP architecture is located in the Application Layer and Transport Layer, as shown in Fig. 5. From the figure if there is no interface, the entire communication will not be able to proceed; it is like we cannot send mail without postman. To understand the network structure specifically, students need to start from the horizontal peer-to-peer communication and the vertical direction of the actual data transfer. Understanding both the horizontal and the vertical levels of communication is difficult. The system training platform uses the TCP connection and socket interface to complete the underlying communication, achieving the correct timing and answer transmission with the send and receive functions. Students through the Android based training platform can experience a specific communication process.

A particular communication process: the Server first starts the service, the establishment of SOCKET and begins to listen to the state and waits to connect, and start the service [9]. The Client press the start button, set the client writing time and other display information. The Client enters into the connection state, the Client answers. After entering the answer and establish a connection with the Server, the answer is sent to the Server-side.

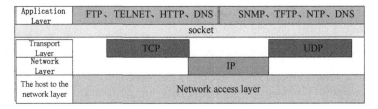

Fig. 5. TCP/IP architecture.

4 Complete Class Diagram of the Integrated Training Platform Design

The comprehensive training platform design and development uses the currently popular object-oriented approach. The design of the class and the various types of functional methods are: the boot interface Start, write interface class HztxView, write control class Hztx, and internal class (answer list class DatiListener, end of the answer list class JieshuListener, timing class MyCount), writing action classes MyAction and subclasses (writing class MyPath and erase class MyEraser), as shown in Fig. 6.

Fig. 6. TCP/IP architecture.

5 Timing Statistics Function

When the PC server sends a start entering command, the Android client counts down based on the received time and displays the correct answer at the end of the time for the judges and the audience to end the competition. The server can view all teams and player scores and rankings, and to send the required information to the client.

6 The System Implementation

6.1 The Control Functions

The interface of the control terminal is shown in Fig. 7. Firstly, click Start service. The PC starts TCP monitoring using Socket. When a client is connected, the IP address of the connection is displayed and the connection is established. Then, initialize the information of the contest, including the time and correct answer, etc. After setting, click start to answer, and then send the message to the client.

Fig. 7. The interface of the control terminal.

6.2 The Client Functions

The function of the client is to provide an answer board for players. When the client starts to answer, it will send a connection request to the control terminal and establish a connection, and enter the answer interface, under which operations such as writing, modifying, clearing and erasing Chinese characters can be performed. Meanwhile, the timer can countdown according to the time set by the control terminal. At the end of the time, the prompt to stop answering, and display the correct answer for the judges to judge. The client interface is shown in Fig. 8. The client answer interface is shown in Fig. 9.

Fig. 8. The interface of client.

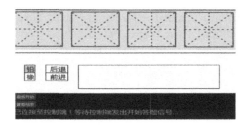

Fig. 9. The interface of client answer.

7 The System Test

The system in the real environment as android 4 and above version test results as shown in Fig. 10–12. First, the control end is set as shown in the Fig. 10.

Then, the client receives the signal to start answering, namely the voice prompt, and can start answering. If the answer is finished in advance, click the end of answering button to finish. The control terminal receives the correct answer sent by the control terminal and displays it in the answer box, which can be displayed on the big screen for the judges to judge. The answer interface is shown in Fig. 11.

When the remaining 5 s are left, the countdown will start and the end prompt box will pop up. The answer is finished, as shown in Fig. 12.

Fig. 10. Control terminal setting interface.

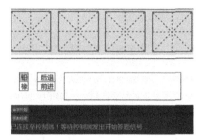

Fig. 11. Answer the interface.

Fig. 12. Answer end interface.

Click OK, and the correct answer will be displayed in the answer box, as shown in Fig. 13.

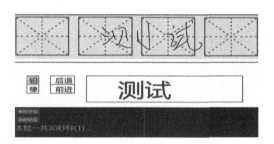

Fig. 13. Display result interface.

This is the end of a round of answer the questions.

8   Conclusion

Writing Chinese characters is the transmission of Chinese civilization, enhance the understanding of Chinese culture, and increase the love of our country. The development of the integrated training platform for writing Chinese characters provides a good platform with good social benefits. The comprehensive training platform for Chinese character dictation competition exceeds the basic requirements of school Chinese characters. To process information and the final score and display on the big screen for the judges and the audience in public places for judgments meets the requirement of fairness for the competition [10]. Through the training platform to create a way for students to take the initiative, self-learning environment, students can systematically master the basic knowledge of software engineering and software development of the whole process, train software engineering students other comprehensive ability, easy to use, functional software for the professional, to provide a complete, actual, open and simulated training integrated network platform.

Acknowledgement. Qinghai Provincial Department of Science and Technology Key Research and Development and Transformation Program, Qinghai Intangible Cultural Heritage Handicraft Digital Traceability System Development (No. 2020-GX-113) project support.

References

1. Xue, Y., Jiao, X., Wang, C., Chen, H., Aloqaily, M.: Analysis and design of university teaching equipment management information system. J. Cyber Secur. **3**(3), 177–185 (2021)
2. Mahmood, S.: Review of Internet of Things in different sectors: recent advance, technologies, and challenges. Journal of Internet of Things **1**(3), 19–26 (2021)
3. Dai, Y., Luo, Z.: Review of unsupervised person re-identification. J. New Media **4**(3), 129–136 (2021)
4. Chinese Character Dictation Contest Homepage. http://www.tingxie.cntv.cn/. Accessed 30 Sept 2020
5. Yang, X., Yu, X., Xie, L., Xue, H., Zhou, M.: Sleep apnea monitoring system based on commodity wifi devices. Comput. Mater. Cont. **2**(69), 2793–2806 (2021)
6. Abbas, S., Alhwaiti, Y., Fatima, A., Khan, M.A., Khan, M.A.: Convolutional neural network based intelligent handwritten document recognition. Comput. Mater. Cont. **3**(70), 4563–4581 (2022)
7. Li, J.: Android comprehensive training platform analysis and development. Lanzhou Jiaotong University master's degree thesis (2014)
8. Zhang, S.: Based on Google Android platform application development and research. Comput. Knowl. Technol. **28**, 31–32 (2009)
9. Yang, F.: Android application development Secret, pp. 40–52. Machinery Industry Press, Beijing (2011)
10. He, B.: From the fixed Internet to the mobile Internet. Inf. Commun. Technol. **4**, 54–58 (2010)
11. Yuan, Q.: Research on training optimization method of deep. Neural Netw. South China Univ. Technol. **5**(3), 118–121 (2020)

12. Xin, J., Jing, G.E., Zhu, S.: Research on iterative repair method of dam safety monitoring data missing based on partial least squares regression. Water Resour. Plann. Des. **11**, 100–104 (2021)
13. Zhang, J., Yang, Y., Qian, F.: Research on GNSS/INS error feedback correction based on Kalman filter-neural network prediction. Electron. Des. Eng. **23**(10), 103–105 (2015)
14. Wang, Y.: Behavior recognition algorithm based on deep neural network. Comput. Knowl. Technol **17**(03), 17–18 (2021)
15. Tan, E., Chong, Y., Anbar, M.F.: Flow management mechanism in software-defined network. Comput. Mater. Cont. **1**(70), 1437–1459 (2022)

Link Prediction with Mixed Structure Attribute of Network

Minghu Tang[1,2(✉)]

[1] Key Laboratory of Artificial Intelligence Application Technology State Ethnic Affairs Commission, Qinghai Minzu University, Xining 810007, China
mhtang@tju.edu.cn
[2] School of Computer Science, Qinghai Minzu University, Xining 810007, China

Abstract. Link prediction aim is to use known information of network to infer missing edges, identify spurious interactions, evaluate network evolving mechanisms, and so on. Currently, with the development of deep learning technology, many neural network-based link prediction algorithms have emerged. However, these existing algorithms, due to the introduction of many parameters, are too computationally expensive to efficiently process large-scale network data. In fact, based on the belief that network nodes with a great number of common neighbors are more likely to be connected, many similarity indices have achieved considerable accuracy and efficiency. Moreover, the method based on structural similarity, simple and applicable, low computing cost, and high prediction accuracy, can quickly process large-scale data. Inspired by the idea, in this paper through the analysis of the network structure index shows that the clustering and assortative coefficients can reflect the similarity between nodes. To this end, this paper integrates the two to form a new link prediction algorithm based on the overall characteristics of the network structure, which realizes the fast and efficient prediction of the missing links in the network. Experiments on 10 real-world networks show that the method is highly accurate and robust compared with baseline.

Keywords: Link prediction · Clustering coefficient · Assortative coefficient

1 Introduction

Link prediction is recognized as a critical research problem in the field of complex networks. It aimed to infer the missing links between two nodes in the light of available network information, or predict the possibility of links being generated in the future [1–3]. Link prediction has become a widely popular spot for researchers due to its important application to exploring system evolution mechanism [4, 5], community discovery [6–8], smashing criminal gangs [9, 10], and so on. Especially in recent years, with the development of big data technology, these research results of link prediction have been widely used in social, economic, and industrial fields such as combating terrorists [11, 12], stock prediction [13, 14], supporting recommended systems [15–17] and identification hidden key services on complex networks [18].

X. Sun et al. (Eds.): ICAIS 2022, CCIS 1587, pp. 494–508, 2022.
https://doi.org/10.1007/978-3-031-06761-7_40

Generally speaking, the existing algorithm of link prediction can be divided into two classes: unsupervised and supervised method. the supervised method models the link through its generation mechanism to realize the task of link prediction in the network [19, 20]. This kind of methods involve a wide range of fields in practice, such as based on probabilistic model [21], machine learning [22, 23], and network embedding [24–27]. However, these algorithms, due to the introduction of many parameters, are too computationally expensive to efficiently process large-scale network data.

The unsupervised methods which are mainly based on the structural similarity of a network design a metric to calculate a score of the similarity between any two nodes in the network. Then judging the possibility of existing a link between nodes according to the score. In present, these unsupervised methods such as common neighbor (CN), preferentially connected (PA), Adamic-Adar index (AA), resource allocation index (RA), local path index (LP), etc. are used commonly similarity indices [1]. In this paper, we only focus on similarity-based methods using topology structural information. The basic assumption for this kind of link prediction methods is that two nodes are more likely to have a link if they are similar to each other. Therefore, the key problem is to define proper similarity measures between nodes. Some methods combine many factors to define the similarity between nodes, such as attributes of nodes and links and structural information. However, these methods are based solely on the network local structure. Their idea mainly is that the link information of common-neighbors of target node is useful but still noisy. And the global structural properties of the network are ignored.

Although the above methods can attain better results than most Node-Neighborhood-based methods, they are hard to be applied to large networks. Nevertheless, the high cost and complexity make it almost impossible to build a complete network frame. This prompts us to consider new methods how to exploit the information of overall network structure to predict the potential links. Though, some literature considers the effect of clustering coefficient for link prediction problem [28]. Few but people consider the role of degree heterogeneity and assortative coefficients.

In this paper, we present a new structure similarity index, MSI (Mixed similarity index for Link Prediction), which employs more local and global link structure information than other index, but costs less computational time. The key idea of our method is to exploit the value of clustering coefficient, degree heterogeneity and assortative coefficient of common-neighbors. The experimental results on 10 real-world networks from five various fields show that our new method performs better and is more efficient.

2 Preliminaries

2.1 Problem Description

Given an undirected unweighted network is denoted by G (V, E), where $V = \{v_1, v_2, \cdots v_n\}$ is the set of nodes and $E = \{(v_i, v_j), 1 \leq i \text{ and } j \geq n, i \neq j\}$ is the set of edges in the network. In this problem definition, links can have different meanings in different networks. Moreover, self-loops and multi-edges are not allowed in the networks. The interaction relation between nodes is formally marked as an adjacency matrix $A_{n \times n}$ in network with n vertices. The element of the ith row and the jth column in the matrix correspond to the link between node i and j in the network, where $A_{ij} = 1$ if there is a link from i to j and $A_{ij} = 0$ otherwise. Set U contains all possible links in the networks, which is represented by $|U| = \frac{|V||V-1|}{2}$, where $|V|$ is the number of nodes in the network. Hence, the non-existing or non-observed link set can be denoted by N = U − E. In regards to the link prediction problem, we assume there are some missing links (or links that will appear in the future) in the set N; thus, our task is to identify those missing links using the network we observed. That is, the problem of link prediction is inferring the probability of an existent link between nodes i and j based on known information in the network, and the probability is expressed as score P_{ij}. The score can be viewed as the similarity of nodes i and j. The higher P_{ij} is, the more similar i is to j. According to the score, all non-existent links in the network can be sorted in descending order. The links at the top are the most likely to exist.

2.2   Division of the Datasets and Evaluation Metrics

Generally, we do not know which links are the missing or future links, otherwise we do not need to do prediction. Therefore, to obtain the accuracy of the prediction algorithm, we must perform tests on the real-world network we have built. In general, the observed links, E, is randomly divided into two parts: the training set, E^T, is treated as known information, and is not allowed to be exploited by the algorithm; while the probe set (i.e., validation subset), E^P, is used for testing and no information in this set is allowed to be used for prediction. Clearly, $E^T \cup E^P = E$ and $E^T \cap E^P = \emptyset$. The advantage of this random subsampling validation is that the proportion of the training split is not dependent on the number of iterations. But with this method some links may not be selected in the probe set, whereas others may be selected many times. The proportion of links in these two parts ranges from 90% to 20%. Thus, when the training set consists of 90% of links, the remaining 10% of links constitute the test set. In this paper, we conducted the experiments 100 times for each individual network independently to reduce random bias, and selected the average precision. Ten percent of the links from the original network are randomly removed to build the probe set E^P, while the connectivity of the remaining training network E^T is guaranteed.

Like many existing prediction studies [1–3], in our work adopts also the most frequently-used metrics AUC (*area under the receiver operating characteristic curve*) to measure the performance of link prediction. This metric is viewed as a robust measure in the presence of data imbalance. By obtaining the rankings of the non-observed links, we exploit AUC to evaluate effect. The AUC score is the probability that a randomly selected missing link $e \in E^P$ is assigned a higher score than a randomly selected nonexistent link (i.e., a link in U − E). In the implementation, if we perform n independent comparisons, there are n' times when the missing link score is higher than the nonexistent link score, and n'' times when they will be the same. The AUC value is then calculated using Eq. (1):

$$AUC = \frac{n' + 0.5n''}{n}. \tag{1}$$

In addition, we have adopted the Precision metric, which is also one of the most popular indexes of evaluation link prediction [1–3]. Given the ranking of the non-observed links in decreasing order according to their scores. The precision is defined as the ratio of relevant items selected to the number of items selected. That is to say, if we take the top-L links as the predicted ones, among which ℓ links are right, then,

$$\text{Precision} = \frac{\ell}{L}. \tag{2}$$

Clearly, a higher value of precision means a higher prediction accuracy.

Although the computing result is not unique through taking different L values for a single algorithm, in order to ensure the fairness for all comparison algorithms, the same value can be taken for L. This value does not affect the final comparison. Therefore, in our work, for the convenience of comparison, all the algorithms are unified to take the value of $L = 100$.

2.3 Baseline and Comparison Methods

We will provide the definitions and motivations of four well-known common-neighbour based algorithms. All these methods utilize the simplest link prediction framework, in which each pair of nodes is assigned a similarity score, and links with higher scores are expected to have a higher probability of existence.

Common Neighbours (CN). For a node x, let $\Gamma(x)$ denote the set of neighbours of x. In common sense, two nodes, x and y, are more likely to have a link if they have many common neighbours. The simplest measure of this neighbourhood overlap is the directed count, namely

$$S_{xy}^{CN} = |\Gamma(x) \cap \Gamma(y)|. \tag{3}$$

Here, $\Gamma(x)$ denotes the number of neighbors of node x.

Adamic-Adar Index (AA). This index refines the simple counting of common neighbors by assigning the less connected neighbors more weights, and is defined as

$$S_{xy}^{AA} = \sum_{z \in \Gamma(x) \cap \Gamma(y)} log \frac{1}{k_z} \tag{4}$$

Resource Allocation Index (RA). This index is motivated by the resource allocation dynamics on complex networks. Consider a pair of nodes, x and y, which are not directly connected. The node x can send some resource to y, with their common neighbors playing the role of transmitters. In the simplest case, we assume that each transmitter has a unit of resource, and will equally distribute it to all its neighbors. The similarity between x and y can be defined as the amount of resource y received from x, which is

$$S_{xy}^{RA} = \sum_{z \in \Gamma(x) \cap \Gamma(y)} \frac{1}{k_z} \qquad (5)$$

Preferential Attachment Index (PA)

$$S_{xy}^{PA} = |\Gamma(x)| \cdot |\Gamma(y)| \qquad (6)$$

where $\Gamma(x)$ denotes the set of neighbors of node x and $|A|$ is the number of elements in set A.

CAR Index (CAR). It is presented based on the assumption that the link existence between two nodes is more likely if their common neighbors are members of local community paradigm. More details can be referred to literature [29].

$$S_{xy}^{CAR} = S_{xy}^{CN} \times \sum_{z \in \Gamma(x) \cap \Gamma(y)} \frac{|\gamma(z)|}{2} \qquad (7)$$

where $\gamma(z)$ is the subset of neighbors of node z that are also common neighbors of x and y.

Katz Index (Katz). This index can be considered as a variant of the shortest path metric. It directly aggregates over all the paths between x and y and dumps exponentially for longer paths to penalize them. It can be expressed mathematically as

$$S_{xy}^{Katz} = \sum_{l=1}^{\infty} \beta^l \left| paths_{x,y}^{\langle l \rangle} \right| = \sum_{l=1}^{\infty} \beta^l (A^l)_{x,y} \qquad (8)$$

where, $paths_{x,y}^{\langle l \rangle}$ is considered as the set of total l length paths between x and y, β is a damping factor that controls the path weights and A is the adjacency matrix. The similarity between all pairs of nodes can be directly computed using the closed-form. Katz score for each pair of nodes in the network is calculated by finding the similarity matrix as

$$S_{xy}^{Katz} = \left((I - \beta A)^{-1} - I \right)_{xy} \qquad (9)$$

where β takes the default value 0.1, and I is the identity matrix.

Local Path Index (LP). With the intent to furnish a good trade-off between accuracy and computational complexity of local and global approaches, quasi-local methods are introduced.

$$S_{xy}^{LP} = A^2 + \varepsilon A^3 \qquad (10)$$

where ε represents a free parameter.

Jaccard Coefficient (JC). The JC is defined as the probability of selection of common neighbors of pairwise vertices from all the neighbors of either vertex.

$$S_{xy}^{JC} = \frac{|\Gamma(x) \cap \Gamma(y)|}{|\Gamma(x) \cup \Gamma(y)|} \tag{11}$$

Node2vec Index (N2V). This is an embedding technique where it learns a low dimensional continuous representation of nodes in a graph with the objective of preserving the neighborhood structure. It considers biased random walk as sampling strategy with four arguments. All these parameters are set to their default values as in the original paper [30].

Structural Perturbation Method (SPM). In [31], the structural perturbation method is proposed in quantum mechanics to reflect the link predictability without any prior knowledge of network organization. SPM does not use the similarity of two nodes to make prediction, but recovers the missing links by perturbing the network with another set of known links.

3 Methods

Generally, the networks we obtained in practice are incomplete because of the missing links; thus, the clustering coefficient calculated according the current network structure is inaccurate. And there are few literatures comprehensively considering the network properties influence on prediction precision. In this article, we explore the relationship between the statistic characteristics on network and the classic algorithm of link prediction. Then, we further put forward a new mixed similarity index for link prediction problem.

3.1 Correlation Analysis

The classical link prediction algorithm achieves very good prediction accuracy. However, few literatures can analyze whether there is a strong association between these algorithms and the statistical properties of the network. In fact, in the experiments, we find that the statistical properties of the network structure, such as clustering, assortative, and degree heterogeneity, have a very important influence on the prediction accuracy of the algorithm. In literature [32], a regression analysis was done between the network structure properties and AUC value of algorithm AA. And a linear relationship was also found as follows.

$$AA_{AUC} = 0.76 + 0.48C - 0.32H^{-2} - R^2 \tag{12}$$

where C, H, R is clustering coefficient, degree heterogeneity and assortative coefficient on complex networks respectively. AA_{AUC} is accuracy value of predictor AA using AUC evaluation index on the real network.

From the Eq. (12), The effect predicted by the structural similarity index, AA, is very closely related to the topological properties of the network. Moreover, in the experiments, we also found that other structural similarity metrics, such as RA, PA, CN, etc., share the same correlation. This shows that it is of great significance how to reasonably integrate degree heterogeneity, clustering coefficient, and assortative coefficient when designing a new link prediction algorithm.

According to the relevant literature of link prediction [1–3], in fact, there are many indicators to depict the statistical characteristics of complex network structure. In this paper, we focus on the contribution of the three indicators of degree heterogeneity, clustering coefficient, and assortative coefficient to the performance of the link prediction algorithm. They are calculated exactly as follows.

Degree Heterogeneity

$$H = \frac{\langle k^2 \rangle}{\langle k \rangle^2} \tag{13}$$

where k is the degree of node, $<k>$ denotes the average degree.

Assortative Coefficient

$$R = \frac{M^{-1} \sum_{e \in \{e_{ij}\}} k_i k_j - \left[M^{-1} \sum_{e \in \{e_{ij}\}} \frac{1}{2} (k_i + k_j) \right]^2}{M^{-1} \sum_{e \in \{e_{ij}\}} \frac{1}{2} (k_i^2 + k_j^2) - \left[M^{-1} \sum_{e \in \{e_{ij}\}} \frac{1}{2} (k_i + k_j) \right]^2} \tag{14}$$

where e_{ij} indicates the link between node v_i and v_j, k_i is the degree of node v_i, M is the total number of edges present in the network. According to the Eq. (14), the $R \in [-1, 1]$. If the value is greater than 0, it means that the nodes with large degree tend to be connected to the nodes with large degree in the networks. At this time, the network is positively correlated, so it is called the homogeneity network, the greater the value of R, the stronger the homogeneity of the network. If the value is less than 0, it indicates that the large degree nodes in the network prefer to connect with the nodes with small degrees, when the network is negatively correlated and is called a heterogeneity network. Moreover, the smaller the value of R, the stronger the heterogeneity of the network. In fact, Assortative coefficient is the Pearson correlation coefficient of degrees based on pairs of linked nodes. For clustering coefficient, the computing formula in Eq. (16).

The effect of networks with different statistical properties on the prediction performance will be particularly evident. To reflect the extent of this effect, we selected 31 classical structural similarity link prediction algorithms from the literature and performed experiments on multiple datasets. Figure 1 show the experimental results on the datasets USAir and Jazz. In the field of link prediction, these two datasets are often used as network objects to evaluate the performance of the proposed algorithms. It appears from Fig. 1 that the prediction performance of these 31 classical algorithms shows a very large contrast on the two datasets. If we judge the merits of the new algorithm without considering the statistical characteristics of the network, it will cause misleading conclusions.

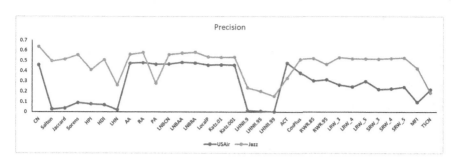

Fig. 1. Analysis of the association between network statistical properties and prediction model.

In the analysed datasets, USAir and Jazz, the difference is not obvious in their statistical characteristics, but like PA and Jaccard etc., the prediction result on them contrasts greatly. Regardless of the design principle and accuracy of the prediction algorithm itself, this relatively huge contrast effect can only prove that the network statistical characteristics have a very strong impact on the performance of the prediction algorithm. The differences of the statistical properties of the network will be the key to determine the stability or quality of the prediction algorithm. Further analysis of the statistical properties of the two datasets found reversed only on the assortative coefficient. That is to say, one is the compatibility, the other is the hetero-compatibility. From Fig. 1, it is clearly that the six algorithms starting from type 2 on the two datasets, together with the PA algorithm, have very large fluctuations in the prediction performance. This shows that these several algorithms are relatively sensitive to network heterogeneity, and that their predictive effect may decline. In addition, the assortative coefficient of the network has an obvious impact on the algorithm performance evaluation. On the other hand, can this influence be considered in the designed link prediction algorithm?

To further verify whether the assortative coefficient had a significant effect on the prediction result, Celegans and Yeast with almost similar measures were selected from the network dataset. Following the above analysis, the predicted effects of the 31 similarity algorithms selected in this paper should remain essentially consistent trend fluctuations on these two datasets. Figure 2 show the analytical results and verify our conjecture. As can be seen from the figure, on the two datasets with assortative coefficient, the fluctuations on results of the algorithm predicted is consistent. In particular, the six algorithms started from Salton data are even more obvious. This shows that they are more sensitive to heterogeneity and have an almost proportional relationship with network heterogeneity. This also suggests that there is a strong correlation between the network statistical properties and the algorithm performance.

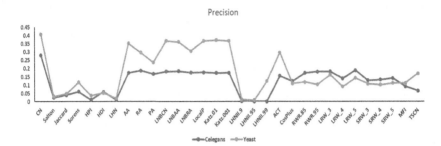

Fig. 2. Comparison of the prediction performance of different structural similarity algorithms on in networks with approximate assortative coefficient.

In conclusion, it is reliable to fully integrate the statistical characteristic indicators of the network structure, including clustering coefficients, assortative coefficient, and degree heterogeneity, and then to design a novel link prediction algorithm. Moreover, this kind of algorithms inherit the characteristics of the classical structural similarity indicators, such as the simple model, the low time complexity of the algorithm, have good robustness, and are easy to extend to large-scale networks.

3.2 Mixed Similarity Index Based on Statistical Characteristic

We find that three values of network attribute, clustering coefficient, degree hetero-geneity and assortative coefficient, are important effect on prediction accuracy of AUC evaluation index from the above results of regression analysis. It suggests we focus on these features of complex networks in the design similarity index of link prediction.

We consider this kind of information in our method by employing three attributes of statistical characteristic on network topology structure, because they can reflect the likelihood of the existence of a link between two nodes within a local and global network environment. The definition is given in Eq. (15),

$$S_{xy}^{MSI} = \sum_{z \in \Gamma(x) \cap \Gamma(y)} C(k_z)(k_z)^{\delta R} + \lambda \frac{k_x k_y}{k_x^2 + k_y^2} \tag{15}$$

where k_z is the degree of node z and $C(k_z)$ is the average clustering coefficient of a node with a degree of k_z; δ is the assortative-penalizing parameter that penalizes the effect of assortative coefficient; λ is the parameter that penalizes according to degree heterogeneity. the clustering coefficient is defined in Eq. (16).

$$C_i = \frac{2t_i}{k_i(k_i - 1)} \tag{16}$$

Here, t_i is the number of triangles containing node i, and k_i is the degree of node i. High clustering coefficient means high level of node aggregation in a network.

Of course, in the form of Eq. (15), it does not seem to reflect the effect of degree heterogeneity H. But we perform the analysis and mathematical transformation through the calculation formula for the degree heterogeneity H. Meanwhile, combined with many experimental tests, the second term of Eq. (15) was finally formed. And the parameter λ is used as a constraint to make the prediction effect better. This was also confirmed in the later experiments.

4 Experimental Results and Analysis

4.1 Datasets Description

In this paper, 10 well-known networks drawn from various fields were used to study the performance of new index. These datasets can be downloaded from the web sites [33, 34].

Dolphin. A social network of bottlenose dolphins living in Doubtful Sound, a fjord in New Zealand.

Small Griffith and Descendants (SmaGri). Citations to Small Griffith and Descendants.

USAir. A network representing the air transportation system in the US.

Yeast. A protein–protein interaction network of yeast.

Metabolic. A metabolic network of C.elegans.

Email. List of edges in a network of e-mail interchanges between members of the University Rovirai Virgili (Tarragona).

Political Blog (PB). A network of US political blogs. we process these as undirected graphs.

NetScience. A co-authorship network of scientists working on network theory and experiments.

C Elegans (CE). A neural network of the nematode worm C.elegans.

Jazz. A musician social network.

The topological features of all networks are listed in Table 1.

Table 1. The basic topological features of 10 networks.

Net	N	M	<k>	<d>	C	R	H
Dolphin	62	159	5.1290	3.3570	0.3088	−0.0436	1.3268
SmaGri	1059	4916	9.2842	2.7875	0.0942	−0.0872	4.0825
USAir	332	2126	12.8072	2.7381	0.656	−0.2072	3.4639
Yeast	2361	6646	5.63	2.3512	0.13	−0.099	2.944
Metabolic	453	2025	8.940	2.664	0.647	−0.226	4.4850
Email	1133	5451	9.622	3.5997	0.22	0.078	1.942
PB	1490	16715	22.436	2.7375	0.263	−0.221	3.622
NetScience	198	2742	27.6970	2.2350	0.5203	0.0306	1.3951
C.elegans	297	2148	14.466	2.4553	0.296	−0.163	1.801
Jazz	198	2742	27.698	2.243	0.618	0.02	1.395

Where, N is the number of nodes, and M is the total number of links. $<k>$ denotes the average degree. $<d>$ is the average distance between nodes. C and R are the global clustering coefficient and assortative coefficient respectively. H is the degree heterogeneity, which is defined as $H = <k^2>/<k>^2$.

4.2   Results and Analysis

To verify the effectiveness of the proposed method, we select the similarity measures of several common-neighbor-based similarity indices, which can reflect the role of the clustering coefficients. At the same time, in order to further compare the prediction accuracy of the proposed algorithm, several heuristic algorithms based on the structural similarity principle are adopted in this paper. According to literature records which these methods have a better predictive effect when solving the prediction of missing edges in the network.

The AUC score values for all these algorithms on the 10 real-networks are given in Table 2. These results are the mean value after 100 independent cross-validation. Although in the experiments, we adjusted the network partition ratio from between 90% and 10%, we only give the results under the 90% partitioning in Table 2. In addition, after extensive experimental validation, the parameter δ in the algorithm takes an optimal value of 0.1. For the parameter λ, takes values 0 and 0.12, respectively. The corresponding method names of λ at different values are indicated by MSI0 and MSI1, respectively. Clearly, the network statistical feature H does not play a role in the prediction when $\lambda = 0$. At this point, only the network statistical properties C and R interact. The prediction effect was improved by adjusting the clustering degree of nodes in real time based on the common neighbor by the statistical feature R. The predicted effects of all the methods are shown in Fig. 3 and 4. In fact, it can be seen from Fig. 3 and 4 that the proposed method predicts better overall results on 10 networks when the statistical feature H works. IN the experiment, the λ value was taken at 0.12. Notably, in each experiment, when the network is divided into the training and test sets, it corresponds to a different value of C, H, and R.

Table 2. Accuracy measured by AUC score.

Net	CN	AA	RA	PA	CAR	Katz	LP	N2V	JC	SPM	MSI0	MSI1
Dolphin	0.7839	0.7937	0.7986	0.6999	0.5021	0.7562	0.7891	0.7743	0.7697	0.773	0.8215	0.8315
SmaGri	0.8555	0.8587	0.8610	0.8536	0.4443	0.8692	0.8916	0.7452	0.7905	0.8847	0.8974	0.8982
USAir	0.9449	0.9567	0.9629	0.9547	0.8027	0.8902	0.9269	0.9238	0.9060	0.94	0.9552	0.9732
Yeast	0.9149	0.9153	0.9154	0.8643	0.8349	0.9103	0.9708	0.8986	0.8231	0.969	0.9270	0.9618
Metabolic	0.9230	0.9555	0.9602	0.8201	0.8530	0.8845	0.9233	0.9105	0.8510	0.931	0.9633	0.9650
Email	0.8559	0.8580	0.8578	0.8047	0.7030	0.7889	0.9176	0.8895	0.9004	0.899	0.8522	0.9162
PB	0.9299	0.9294	0.9291	0.9220	0.7902	0.9466	0.9386	0.8666	0.9079	0.926	0.9657	0.9663
NetScience	0.9570	0.9530	0.9652	0.6862	0.5328	0.9262	0.9416	0.9165	0.9506	0.969	0.9566	0.9541
C.elegans	0.8314	0.8512	0.8684	0.7451	0.6706	0.8796	0.8709	0.7956	0.7927	0.894	0.9018	0.9134
Jazz	0.9530	0.9588	0.9711	0.7895	0.9432	0.9357	0.9468	0.9118	0.9504	0.976	0.9709	0.9817

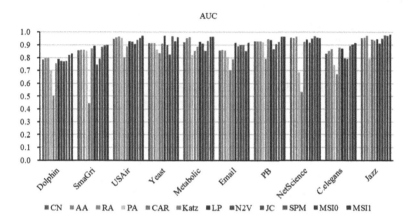

Fig. 3. Algorithm performance measured by AUC score.

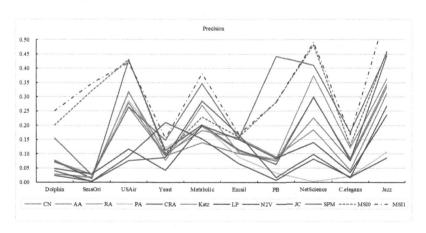

Fig. 4. Algorithm performance measured by Precision score.

5   Conclusion and Discussion

Inspired by the formula of regression analysis on the key index of network attributes, clustering coefficient, degree heterogeneity and assortative coefficient, we proposed a mixed measure index (MSI) to formalize our idea into a similarity method. This method assigns a clustering ability value to each local path, penalizes assortative index to increase their contribution, and calculates the fusion of clustering coefficient, degree heterogeneity and assortative coefficient. In this study, experiments on 10 real-world networks demonstrate that using the mixed index, MSI, outperforms other baseline methods in both accuracy and precision.

The results of numerous experiments show that the proposed similarity index has very good research potential in exploiting the structural statistical properties of the network to improve the link prediction performance. At the same time, from the perspective of mining structural properties, the method presented here can also be used to study the topological evolution patterns of the network. Moreover, on large-scale networks, especially with extremely sparse network structure, the method, which analyzes local interaction relations from macroscopic structural properties, has some inspiration in fields such as network reconstruction.

The mixed similarity index provides a broader space for research on link prediction and facilitates promising new applications in the future.

References

1. Martinez, V., Berzal, F., Cubero, J.C.: A survey of link prediction in complex networks. ACM Comput. Surv. **49**(4), 69–102 (2017)
2. Haghani, S., Keyvanpour, M.R.: A systemic analysis of link prediction in social network. Artif. Intell. Rev. **52**(3), 1961–1995 (2017). https://doi.org/10.1007/s10462-017-9590-2
3. Rossi, A., Barbosa, D., Firmani, D.: Knowledge graph embedding for link prediction: a comparative analysis. ACM Trans. Knowl. Discov. Data **15**(2), 1–49 (2021)
4. Zhang, Q.M.: Measuring multiple evolution mechanisms of complex networks. Sci. Rep. **5**(1), 10350 (2015)
5. Brandt, C., Leskovec, J.: Status and friendship: mechanisms of social network evolution. In: Proceedings of the 23rd International World Wide Web Conferences Steering Committee (2014)
6. Mei, P., Ding, G., Jin, Q., Zhang, F., Chen, Y.: Reconstruction and optimization of complex network community structure under deep learning and quantum ant colony optimization algorithm. Intell. Autom. Soft Comput. **27**(1), 159–171 (2021)
7. He, H., Zhao, Z., Luo, W., Zhang, J.: Community detection in aviation network based on k-means and complex network. Comput. Syst. Sci. Eng. **39**(2), 251–264 (2021)
8. Guo, W., Jia, R., Zhang, Y.: Semantic link network based knowledge graph representation and construction. J. Artif. Intell. **3**(2), 73–79 (2021)
9. Assouli, N., Benahmed, K., Gasbaoui, B.: How to predict crime - informatics-inspired approach from link prediction. Physica A **570**(15), 125795 (2021)

10. Tayebi, M.A., Glässer, U.: Social Network Analysis in Predictive Policing: Concepts, Models and Methods, pp. 7–14. Springer, Cham (2016). https://doi.org/10.1007/978-3-319-41492-8_2

11. Fellman, P.V.: Modeling terrorist networks: the second decade. In: Fellman, P.V., Bar-Yam, Y., Minai, A.A. (eds.) Conflict and Complexity. UCS, pp. 3–34. Springer, New York (2015). https://doi.org/10.1007/978-1-4939-1705-1_1

12. Alghamdi, H., Selamat, A.: Techniques to detect terrorists/extremists on the dark web: a review. Data Technologies and Applications (2022)

13. Awan, M.J., Shafry, M., Nobanee, H., Munawar, A., Yasin, A.: Social media and stock market prediction: a big data approach. Comput. Mater. Continua **67**(2), 2569–2583 (2021)

14. Agrawal, M., Shukla, P.K., Nair, R., Nayyar, A., Masud, M.: Stock prediction based on technical indicators using deep learning model. Comput. Mater. Continua **70**(1), 287–304 (2022)

15. Su, Z., Zheng, X., Ai, J.: Link prediction in recommender systems based on vector similarity. Physica A **560**, 125154 (2020)

16. Feng, J.: RBPR: a hybrid model for the new user cold start problem in recommender systems. Knowl.-Based Syst. **214**(6), 106732 (2021)

17. Li, S., Song, X., Lu, H.: Friend recommendation for cross marketing in online brand community based on intelligent attention allocation link prediction algorithm. Expert Syst. Appl. **139**, 112839 (2020)

18. Alharbi, A., Faizan, M., Alosaimi, W., Alyami, H., Nadeem, M.: A link analysis algorithm for identification of key hidden services. Comput. Mater. Continua **68**(1), 877–886 (2021)

19. Nasiri, E.: A novel link prediction algorithm for protein-protein interaction networks by attributed graph embedding. Comput. Biol. Med. **137**, 104772 (2021)

20. Berahmand, K., Nasiri, E., Rostami, M., Forouzandeh, S.: A modified DeepWalk method for link prediction in attributed social network. Computing **103**(10), 2227–2249 (2021). https://doi.org/10.1007/s00607-021-00982-2

21. Zhang, H.F.: Predicting missing links in complex networks via an extended local naïve Bayes model. Europhys. Lett. **130**(3), 38002–38002 (2020)

22. Cai, L.: Line graph neural networks for link prediction. IEEE Trans. Pattern Anal. Mach. Intell. (2021). https://doi.org/10.1109/TPAMI.2021.3080635

23. Kosasih, E., Elson, A.: Brintrup: a machine learning approach for predicting hidden links in supply chain with graph neural networks. Int. J. Prod. Res. **2021**, 1–14 (2021)

24. Cao, X., Chen, H., Wang, X.: Neural link prediction over aligned networks. In: Thirty-Second AAAI Conference on Artificial Intelligence, pp. 249–256 (2018)

25. Zhang, Q., Wang, R., Yang, J.: Knowledge graph embedding by translating in time domain space for link prediction. Knowl.-Based Syst. **212**(5), 106564 (2021)

26. Goyal, P., Ferrara, E.: Graph embedding techniques, applications, and performance: a survey. Knowl.-Based Syst. **151**(1), 78–94 (2018)

27. Zhou, J., Liu, L., Wei, W., Fan, J.: Network representation learning: from preprocessing, feature extraction to node embedding. arXiv preprint arXiv:2110.07582 (2021)

28. Wu, Z., Lin, Y., Wang, J., Gregory, S.: Link prediction with node clustering coefficient. Physica A **452**, 1–8 (2016)

29. Cannistraci, C.V., Alanis-Lobato, G., Ravasi, T.: From link-prediction in brain connectomes and protein interactomes to the local-community-paradigm in complex networks. Sci. Rep. **3**, 1613 (2013)

30. Grover, A., Leskovec, J.: Node2vec: scalable feature learning for networks. In: Proceedings of the 22nd ACM SIGKDD International Conference on Knowledge Discovery and Data Mining, pp. 855–864 (2016)

31. Lv, L., Pan, L., Zhou, T., Zhang, Y.C., Stanley, H.E.: Toward link predictability of complex networks. Proc. Natl. Acad. Sci **112**(8), 2325–2330 (2015)
32. Tang, M., Wang, W.: Analysis similarity index of link prediction based on multivariate statistics. Int. J. Mod. Phys. B **32**(28), 1850316 (2018)
33. Data Homepage. http://snap.stanford.edu/data/. Accessed 19 Jan 2022
34. Network Data Sources. http://vladowiki.fmf.uni-lj.si/doku.php?id=pajek:data:urls:index. Accessed 19 Jan 2022

Analysis of the Relationship Between the Passenger Flow and Surrounding Land Use Types at the Subway Stations of the Batong Subway Line of Beijing Based on Remote Sensing Images

Xuting Duan[1(✉)], Chen Sun[1], Daxin Tian[1], Shudong Xia[2],
Xuejun Ran[2], Xu Han[1,3], and Yafu Sun[2]

[1] School of Transportation Science and Engineering, Beihang University,
Beiijng 102206, China
duanxuting@buaa.edu.cn
[2] China TransInfo Co. Ltd., Beijing 100085, China
[3] Department of Engineering and Design, University of Sussex, Brighton BN1
9RH, United Kingdom

Abstract. Taking the Batong Line of Beijing subway as our research object, it includes nine stations, such as Communication Univ. of China Station, Shuang Qiao Station and soon on. The attraction range of passenger flow of the subway station is a circle which takes 800 m as the radius. The surrounding land use types of the subway station and its corresponding area within its attraction limit are determined based on the remote sensing images of each site. The prediction model of the passenger flow of each subway station and the area of different land use types surrounding it is established by using regression analysis. It is found that the average daily passenger flow on weekdays and the average daily passenger flow on weekends of each subway station are positively correlated with its surrounding total land use area. The passenger flow in and out of the subway station at different time periods has different relationship with the surrounding land use types and their corresponding area. Therefore, the average daily passenger flow and passenger flow in different time periods of the subway station can be predicted by its surrounding different land use types.

Keywords: Passenger flow prediction · Liner regression analysis · Land use types · Remote sensing images

1 Introduction

With the development of society and economy, the advancement of the urbanization process is continuous, and a series of urban traffic problems such as traffic congestion and environmental pollution are caused by the excessive rise of motorization level. Giving priority to the development of public transportation is considered as an important measure to alleviate urban traffic problems, thus it is extremely necessary for us to form the scientific and reasonable planning and construction of the public transportation stations.

© The Author(s), under exclusive license to Springer Nature Switzerland AG 2022
X. Sun et al. (Eds.): ICAIS 2022, CCIS 1587, pp. 509–523, 2022.
https://doi.org/10.1007/978-3-031-06761-7_41

On the one hand, city spatial morphology and land use characteristics are of important guiding significance for the layout of the subway station. On the other hand, the development and utilization of surrounding land of the site can be promoted by new traffic flow induced by its location advantage, which can direct a more perfect city function. Therefore, it is completely important to take the concept that is public transit-oriented development (TOD) into consideration for urban planning and transport planning [1–3].

At present, a lot of research on the relationship between the passenger flow of the station and its surrounding land use has been done by domestic and foreign scholars. Chakraborty, A., et al. [4] explores that the passenger flow of public transport stations under the concept of TOD has a good relationship with the surrounding land use. J. Choi, J., et al. [5] studies the influencing factors of subway passenger flow in the area of Seoul, and determines the important impact of built environment on subway rider-flow demand, including population and employment related variables. Yang, Z, Q., et al. [6] studies the passenger flow prediction method of urban rail stations based on land use, and builds a prediction model of passenger flow in and out of stations based on the K-nearest neighbor nonparametric regression prediction method. Zhang, N., et al. [7] studies the impact of land use on the passenger flow of railway stations, and predicts the rail passenger flow by taking the potential passenger flow per unit of the station within the scope of its influence and the average daily passenger flow on and off produced by per unit of construction area as indicators. Kong, X, F., et al. [8] analyzes passenger flow of railway stations from the perspective of land use and establishes nonlinear regression function based on direct estimation to provide ideas for passenger flow prediction of railway stations. He, Z, K. [9] proposes a passenger flow prediction method which is suitable for the concept of TOD by analyzing the passenger flow characteristics of rail stations and determining the influence of land use on the passenger flow. Zhu, J., et al. [10] analyzes the correlation between the land use along the railway station and its passenger flow characteristics, and studies the relationship between the passenger flow of the station and the plot ratio of land development around the station in the range of 800 m. Besides, with the development of satellite technology, the land use type can be classified by remote sensing images. Liu, X, C., et al. [11] proposes a new classification algorithm based on remote sensing image, in which the different texture features of remote sensing images and extreme learning machine are combined. Xu, H., et al. [12] proposes an unsupervised classification algorithm based on the terrain point cloud data through remote sensing, and then the recurrent gated graph convolutional network for classification is proposed. Islam, S, U., et al. [13] uses the remote sensing applications of Environment for Visualising Images (ENVI) and Geographic Information System (GIS) for the classification and image processing. Thamizhazhagan, P., et al. [14] presents an artificial intelligence based parallel autoencoder for the traffic flow prediction.

This paper takes the Batong Subway Line of Beijing as the research object, and selects nine stations, including Communication Univ. of China Station, Shuang Qiao Station, Guanzhuang Station, Bali Qiao Station, Tongzhou Beiyuan Station, Guoyuan Station, Jiukeshu Station, Liyuan Station and Linheli Station. Based on the remote sensing images in Baidu Map, QGIS is used to obtain different land use types and their corresponding area data within the 800 m attraction range of each station site. Eviews is used to build a regression prediction model based on the passenger flow data of the station and the area data of different land use types. The relationship between the passenger flow around the station and the land use type area is analyzed, so as to put forward reasonable suggestions for the planning and construction of the subway station and the development of its surrounding land use.

The technology roadmap for this article is shown in Fig. 1:

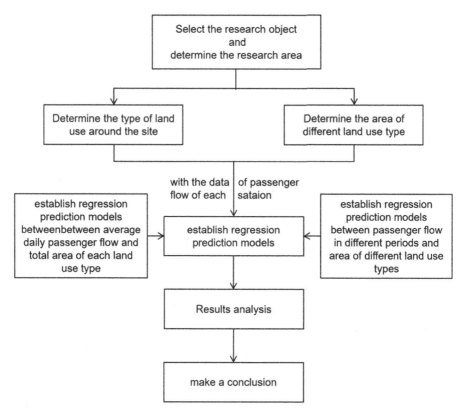

Fig. 1. Technology roadmap.

2 Data Source

This paper takes nine stations of Beijing Batong Subway Line as the research objects. The original data of Batong Subway Line is from April 1 to April 30, 2018. In order to reflect the changing characteristics of actual passenger flow and avoid interference from external factors, the passenger flow data of one week from April 17 to April 21, which is not affected by external factors, is selected for analysis.

The land use around the station site comes from the remote sensing image of Baidu Map. Based on the remote sensing image, QGIS is used to obtain the area data of different land use types within the attraction range of 800 m of the station. The obtained area data and the passenger flow data of these 9 stations within the attraction range are used to study. The passenger flow data of each station is shown in Table 1 below:

Table 1. Passenger flow data of each station of batong subway line.

Beijing Batong Subway Line Station	Weekdays average daily passenger flow (per person)	Weekends average daily passenger flow (per person)	Morning peak inbound passenger flow (per person)	Morning peak outbound passenger flow (per person)	Morning peak inbound and outbound passenger flow (per person)	Evening peak inbound passenger flow (per person)	Evening peak outbound passenger flow (per person)	Evening peak inbound and outbound passenger flow (per person)
Communication Univ. of China Station	37302	31996	7072	1844	8916	2428	4957	7385
Shuang Qiao Station	56712	35515	9067	3534	12601	3646	6705	10351
Guan Zhuang Station	35381	24843	8126	1555	9681	1750	4965	6715
Bali Qiao Station	11631	6898	3309	405	3714	398	1725	2123
Tongzhou Beiyuan Station	42200	41600	7500	2900	10400	3500	10100	13600
Guoyuan Station	31200	22700	6400	1600	8000	1200	8019	9219
Jiukeshu Station	22610	19600	4780	1068	5848	2380	5233	7613
Liyuan Station	50500	42680	9318	1527	10845	2356	12629	14985
Linheli Station	30000	26000	5000	500	5500	550	5200	5750

3 Current Situation of Land Use Around the Subway Station

3.1 Target Research Area

The scope of nine stations on Beijing Batong Subway Line is taken as the research range, and remote sensing images of these area are obtained from the Baidu Map which is shown in Fig. 2. From left to right, followed by Communication Univ. of China Station, Shuang Qiao Station, Guan Zhuang Station, Bali Qiao Station, Tongzhou Beiyuan Station, Guoyuan Station, Jiukeshu Station, Liyuan Station and Linheli Station.

Fig. 2. Remote sensing image of the target research area of batong subway line.

3.2   Obtain the Area of Land Use Type Around the Station Based on Remote Sensing Images

This article considers using 800 m radius as the passenger flow attractive radiation limits of each station, for the overlappingly attracting area of the adjacent stations, equal partition strategy is adopted to divide the overlapping scope. In this strategy, each overlapping region is firstly divided into two parts with equal area, and then the principle of proximity is adopted. The land use type in the divided part which is close to the station is regarded as the land use type within the attraction range of the corresponding station. In the target range of the Batong Subway Line, from left to right, the four stations from Communication Univ. of China Station to Bali Qiao Station have no overlapping area, while the five stations from Tongzhou Beiyuan Station to Linheli Station have overlapping area. The QGIS is used to determine the attracting range of passenger flow of each station and obtain the land use types around each station. The results are shown in Fig. 3:

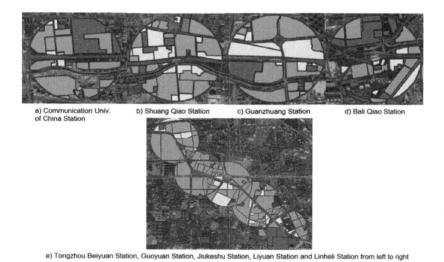

a) Communication Univ.   b) Shuang Qiao Station   c) Guanzhuang Station   d) Bali Qiao Station
of China Station

e) Tongzhou Beiyuan Station, Guoyuan Station, Jiukeshu Station, Liyuan Station and Linheli Station from left to right

Fig. 3.   Attracting range of passenger flow and surrounding land use types of each station.

As shown in Fig. 3, the bright red wire frame represents the attraction range of passenger flow of the site, the dark red represents the land for public administration and public service, the green represents the residential land, the yellow represents the commercial land, and the purple represents the industrial land.

QGIS is used to calculate the area of different land use types within the attraction range of each station, and then make statistical summary about the obtained area data, which is shown in Table 2:

Table 2. Area data of different land use types around each station.

Beijing Batong Subway Line Station	The residential land (square meters)	The commercial land (square meters)	The public administ-ration and public service land (square meters)	The industrial land (square meters)	The total area (square meters)
Communication Univ. of China Station	836346.992	62649.906	385706.844	0.000	1284703.742
Shuang Qiao Station	895070.126	411056.637	117486.869	34417.108	1458030.740
Guan Zhuang Station	810744.762	442390.172	172697.084	2238.788	1428070.806
Bali Qiao Station	440465.207	164177.475	310764.188	0.000	915406.870
Tongzhou Beiyuan Station	1368728.434	205024.391	51621.513	0.000	1625374.338
Guoyuan Station	1229363.598	10508.547	133127.306	0.000	1372999.451
Jiukeshu Station	904924.862	335256.719	25040.925	9432.517	1274655.023
Liyuan Station	1195389.954	127790.902	77874.123	0.000	1401054.979
Linheli Station	519907.606	103467.971	503266.812	67240.599	1193882.988

The proportions of different land use types around each station can be obtained through summary statistics as shown in Table 3:

Table 3. The proportion of different land use types around each station.

Beijing Batong Subway Line Station	The residential land (square meters)	The commercial land (square meters)	The public administration and public service land (square meters)	The industrial land (square meters)	The total area (square meters)
Communication Univ. of China Station	65.10%	4.88%	30.02%	0.00%	65.10%
Shuang Qiao Station	61.39%	28.19%	8.06%	2.36%	61.39%
Guan Zhuang Station	56.77%	30.98%	12.09%	0.16%	56.77%
Bali Qiao Station	48.12%	17.93%	33.95%	0.00%	48.12%
Tongzhou Beiyuan Station	84.21%	12.61%	3.18%	0.00%	84.21%
Guoyuan Station	89.54%	0.77%	9.70%	0.00%	89.54%
Jiukeshu Station	70.99%	26.30%	1.96%	0.74%	70.99%
Liyuan Station	85.32%	9.12%	5.56%	0.00%	85.32%
Linheli Station	43.55%	8.67%	42.15%	5.63%	43.55%

The graph is drawn by Excel software as shown in Fig. 4:

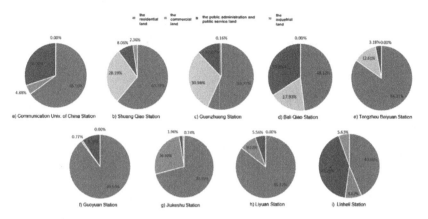

Fig. 4. The proportion of land use types around each station.

From Fig. 4, it suggests that most land use type around nine stations of Beijing Batong Subway Line within the attracting scope is residential land. The proportion of the residential land type surrounded the station can be as high as 80%, such as Tongzhou Beiyuan Station, Guoyuan Station, Liyuan Station. More than half of the stations where the proportion of the surrounding industrial land type is almost 0% within the corresponding range, indicating that the industrial land plays almost no impact on the passenger flow of these target stations.

Therefore, we mainly study the relationship between passenger flow of the station and three types of land use including the residential land, the commercial land and the public administration and public services land. And the regression prediction model is established based on the data of station passenger flow and the corresponding area of three types of land use around stations obtained by remoting sensing images within their attracting range.

4 Relationship Between Passenger Flow and Land Use of the Station

4.1 Relationship Between Average Daily Passenger Flow and Total Area of Each Land Use Type

This paper studies the relationship between the passenger flow of the station on Beijing Batong Subway Line and its surrounding development situation of the land use based on the remote sensing image. A regression prediction model is established to predict the passenger flow of the station using the area data of different types of land use. Taking 800 m radius of subway station within the target research area as the passenger flow attracting range, QGIS is used to obtain the area of different land use types around the nine stations based on the corresponding remote sensing images. Excel software is used to draw the distribution between the average daily passenger flow of different stations and the total land use area, as shown in Fig. 5:

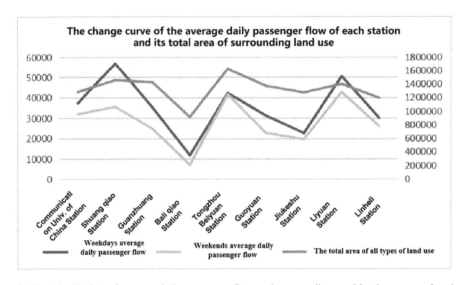

Fig. 5. Distribution of average daily passenger flow and surrounding total land use area of each station.

It can be seen that with the increase of the area of different land use types around the station, that is, the greater intensity of development and utilization of the land, the average daily passenger flow volume on weekdays and weekends of the station also presents an upward trend. Therefore, there is a positive correlation between the degree of land use around the station and passenger flow of the station. The linear regression prediction models between the intensity of development and utilization of land use and the average daily passenger flow on weekdays and weekends are respectively established as shown in Formula (1) and Formula (2):

$$lnY_1 = c_1 + \alpha_1 lnX \tag{1}$$

$$lnY_2 = c_2 + \alpha_2 lnX \tag{2}$$

Y_1 represents the average daily passenger flow of the station on weekdays, Y_2 represents the average daily passenger flow of the station on weekends, X represents the total area of different land use types of the station, c_1 and c_2 represent constant terms, α_1 and α_2 represent regression parameters.

Eviews is used for the parameter solution of the linear regression calculation, results are shown in Fig. 6:

Dependent Variable: LOG(Y1) Method: Least Squares Date: 02/05/21 Time: 19:32 Sample: 1 9 Included observations: 9				
Variable	Coefficient	Std. Error	t-Statistic	Prob.
C	-25.38978	7.666049	-3.303359	0.0131
LOG(X)	2.539367	0.545529	4.654670	0.0023
R-squared	0.756824	Mean dependent var		10.38568
Adjusted R-squared	0.720941	S.D. dependent var		0.473671
S.E. of regression	0.250169	Akaike info criterion		0.259767
Sum squared resid	0.438090	Schwarz criterion		0.303595
Log likelihood	0.831049	Hannan-Quinn criter.		0.165187
F-statistic	21.66781	Durbin-Watson stat		1.320345
Prob(F-statistic)	0.002329			

Dependent Variable: LOG(Y2) Method: Least Squares Date: 02/05/21 Time: 19:45 Sample: 1 9 Included observations: 9				
Variable	Coefficient	Std. Error	t-Statistic	Prob.
C	-32.60152	8.394400	-3.883722	0.0060
LOG(X)	3.033248	0.595805	5.091004	0.0014
R-squared	0.787352	Mean dependent var		10.13189
Adjusted R-squared	0.756974	S.D. dependent var		0.554234
S.E. of regression	0.273224	Akaike info criterion		0.436083
Sum squared resid	0.522561	Schwarz criterion		0.479910
Log likelihood	0.037628	Hannan-Quinn criter.		0.341503
F-statistic	25.91832	Durbin-Watson stat		0.821022
Prob(F-statistic)	0.001414			

a) Calculation results of parameters between Y_1 and X   b) Calculation results of parameters between Y_2 and X

Fig. 6. Calculation results of parameters of the liner regression prediction models.

Therefore, the relationship between the average daily passenger flow on weekdays and weekends and the total area of different land use types around the station is as follows:

$$lnY_1 = -25.340 + 2.539lnX \tag{3}$$

$$lnY_2 = 32.602 + 3.033lnX \tag{4}$$

By the Formula (3) and Formula (4) can be seen that the linear positive correlation is existed between the amount of average daily passenger flow and the area of different land use types around the station. in our study, the area of surrounding different land use types plays a greater effect on the amount of passenger flow on weekends than that on weekdays. Therefore, the average daily passenger flow of the subway station can be predicted according to the total area of different land use types around the station.

4.2 Relationship Between Passenger Flow in Different Periods and Area of Different Land Use Types

As mentioned in Sect. 3.2, the linear regression prediction models is established to describe the relationship between the area of the residential land, the commercial land, the public administration and public service land and the passenger flow of the corresponding station during weekdays within the attracting scope of the station. The passenger flow in different periods of the station can be subdivided into morning peak inbound passenger flow, morning peak outbound passenger flow, evening peak inbound passenger flow and evening peak outbound passenger flow. The distribution of weekday passenger flow in different periods of each station is shown in Fig. 7:

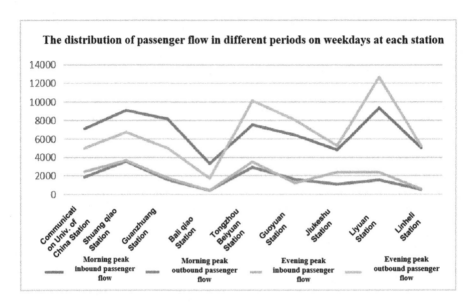

Fig. 7. The distribution of passenger flow on weekdays in different periods of each station.

The scatter diagrams are drawn by Eviews to show the relationship between the passenger flow of nine stations during different periods and the area of the three surrounding land use types, which are shown in Fig. 8:

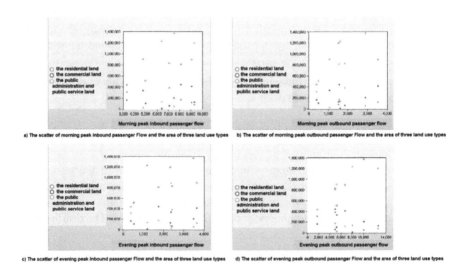

Fig. 8. The scatter diagrams of passenger flow during different periods and area of three land use types of stations.

For further quantitative analysis, the area of the residential land, the commercial land, and the public administration and public service land are taken as independent variables, and the passenger flow in different periods is taken as dependent variables. The regression prediction models of Formula (5), Formula (6), Formula (7), and Formula (8) are established respectively:

$$lnY_3 = c_3 + \beta_1 lnX_1 + \beta_2 lnX_2 + \beta_3 lnX_3 \tag{5}$$

$$lnY_4 = c_4 + \gamma_1 lnX_1 + \gamma_2 lnX_2 + \gamma_3 lnX_3 \tag{6}$$

$$lnY_5 = c_5 + \lambda_1 lnX_1 + \lambda_2 lnX_2 + \lambda_3 lnX_3 \tag{7}$$

$$lnY_6 = c_6 + \theta_1 lnX_1 + \theta_2 lnX_2 + \theta_3 lnX_3 \tag{8}$$

Y_3, Y_4, Y_5 and Y_6 represent the morning peak inbound passenger flow, morning peak outbound passenger flow, evening peak inbound passenger flow and evening peak outbound passenger flow of the subway station. X_1, X_2 and X_3 represent the area of the residential land, the commercial land, and the public administration and public service land within the attracting range of the station. c_3, c_4, c_5, and c_6 represent constant terms, and β_1, β_2, β_3, γ_1, γ_2, γ_3, λ_1, λ_2, λ_3, θ_1, θ_2, and θ_3 all represent regression parameters.

Eviews is used for linear regression analysis, and the corresponding regression parameters are solved and calculated as shown in Fig. 9:

Dependent Variable: LOG(Y3)
Method: Least Squares
Date: 02/05/21 Time: 21:10
Sample: 1 9
Included observations: 9

Variable	Coefficient	Std. Error	t-Statistic	Prob.
C	-15.56196	4.018716	-3.872372	0.0117
LOG(X1)	1.324610	0.206028	6.429266	0.0014
LOG(X2)	0.196817	0.052660	3.719218	0.0137
LOG(X3)	0.330969	0.082364	4.017640	0.0101

R-squared	0.898095	Mean dependent var	8.766592
Adjusted R-squared	0.836952	S.D. dependent var	0.342015
S.E. of regression	0.138103	Akaike info criterion	-0.820532
Sum squared resid	0.095362	Schwarz criterion	-0.732877
Log likelihood	7.692395	Hannan-Quinn criter.	-1.009692
F-statistic	14.68845	Durbin-Watson stat	1.671963
Prob(F-statistic)	0.006502		

a) The calculation result of the inbound passenger flow in the morning peak for the dependent variable

Dependent Variable: LOG(Y4)
Method: Least Squares
Date: 02/05/21 Time: 21:11
Sample: 1 9
Included observations: 9

Variable	Coefficient	Std. Error	t-Statistic	Prob.
C	-35.06172	10.59647	-3.309125	0.0213
LOG(X1)	2.446008	0.543200	4.501122	0.0054
LOG(X2)	0.325610	0.138813	2.345669	0.0659
LOG(X3)	0.424192	0.217208	1.952934	0.1083

R-squared	0.840758	Mean dependent var	7.212492
Adjusted R-squared	0.745212	S.D. dependent var	0.721351
S.E. of regression	0.364113	Akaike info criterion	1.118395
Sum squared resid	0.662890	Schwarz criterion	1.206051
Log likelihood	-1.032779	Hannan-Quinn criter.	0.929235
F-statistic	8.799556	Durbin-Watson stat	1.703692
Prob(F-statistic)	0.019403		

b) The calculation result of the outbound passenger flow in the morning peak for the dependent variable

Dependent Variable: LOG(Y5)
Method: Least Squares
Date: 02/05/21 Time: 21:11
Sample: 1 9
Included observations: 9

Variable	Coefficient	Std. Error	t-Statistic	Prob.
C	-30.16086	11.03673	-2.732772	0.0411
LOG(X1)	2.226766	0.565822	3.935454	0.0110
LOG(X2)	0.389526	0.144595	2.693919	0.0431
LOG(X3)	0.213310	0.226263	0.942792	0.3891

R-squared	0.854306	Mean dependent var	7.394468
Adjusted R-squared	0.766890	S.D. dependent var	0.785552
S.E. of regression	0.379277	Akaike info criterion	1.200000
Sum squared resid	0.719254	Schwarz criterion	1.287655
Log likelihood	-1.400000	Hannan-Quinn criter.	1.010840
F-statistic	9.772836	Durbin-Watson stat	1.211152
Prob(F-statistic)	0.015621		

c) The calculation result of the inbound passenger flow in the evening peak for the dependent variable

Dependent Variable: LOG(Y6)
Method: Least Squares
Date: 02/05/21 Time: 21:12
Sample: 1 9
Included observations: 9

Variable	Coefficient	Std. Error	t-Statistic	Prob.
C	-15.78916	9.644153	-1.637173	0.1625
LOG(X1)	1.602198	0.494429	3.240502	0.0229
LOG(X2)	0.062944	0.125350	0.498169	0.6395
LOG(X3)	0.154487	0.197706	0.781398	0.4699

R-squared	0.787172	Mean dependent var	8.672787
Adjusted R-squared	0.659475	S.D. dependent var	0.567944
S.E. of regression	0.331421	Akaike info criterion	0.930249
Sum squared resid	0.549200	Schwarz criterion	1.017904
Log likelihood	-0.186119	Hannan-Quinn criter.	0.741089
F-statistic	6.164375	Durbin-Watson stat	0.564680
Prob(F-statistic)	0.039187		

d) The calculation result of the outbound passenger flow in the evening peak for the dependent variable

Fig. 9. The calculation results of regression parameters.

The confidence is set to 0.05 in this linear regression fitting, that is, the variables greater than 0.05 are eliminated, and the linear regression parameters are statistically summarized as shown in Table 4:

Table 4. The summarized table of estimated linear regression parameters.

	The residential land (lnX_1)	The commercial land (lnX_2)	The public administration and public service land (lnX_3)	Constant terms
Morning peak inbound passenger flow (lnY_3)	1.325	0.196	0.331	−15.562
Morning peak outbound passenger flow (lnY_4)	2.445	/	/	−35.062
Evening peak inbound passenger flow (lnY_5)	2.227	0.340	/	−30.161
Evening peak outbound passenger flow (lnY_6)	1.602	/	/	−15.789

The relationship between the passenger flow inbound and outbound during different periods on weekdays and the total area of the three different land use types including the residential land, the commercial land, the public administration and public service land within the attracting range of the station is shown as follows:

$$lnY_3 = -15.562 + 1.325lnX_1 + 0.196lnX_2 + 0.331lnX_3 \tag{9}$$

$$lnY_4 = -35.062 + 2.445lnX_1 \tag{10}$$

$$lnY_5 = -30.161 + 2.227lnX_1 + 0.340lnX_2 \tag{11}$$

$$lnY_6 = -15.789 + 1.602lnX_1 \tag{12}$$

Therefore, it can be seen that there is a different linear relationship between the inbound and outbound passenger flow of the subway station at different time periods and the area of the residential land, the commercial land, and the public administration and public service land within the scope of attraction. The passenger flow inbound and outbound of the station at different time periods can be predicted by the area of different kinds of land use.

5 Result Analysis

The data of the area of different land use types within their attracting range, which is obtained from remote sensing images of subway stations along Beijing Batong Subway Line through QGIS software, and the data of its passenger flow are studied and analyzed to find out their relationship, and the following conclusions can be drawn from the liner regression prediction fitting results:

1. Different kinds of land use are identified based on the remote sensing images of subway stations within their passenger flow attracting range, and the area of the corresponding types of land use is calculated by using QGIS software. Then, the situation of the proportion of the surrounding different land use types of the stations is counted to determine what kind of land use is the dominant type for the station. the goal of the research object in this article is the subway station whose dominant land use type is the residential land and the proportion of the industrial land is tiny, so the industrial land has little influence on the passenger flow of the targeted subway station.

2. According to weekdays average daily passenger flow and the weekends average daily passenger flow of subway station and the total area of surrounding different land use types, the linear regression analysis is applied to discover the relationship between them through Eviews software. we can see that there exists positive correlation between weekdays average daily passenger flow as well as weekends average daily passenger flow and the area of different types of surrounding land use. And the total land use area has a greater impact on weekends passenger flow. Therefore, the regression prediction models for the average daily passenger of subway station on weekdays and weekends and the total area of different land use types around the station are established respectively.

3. Since the proportion of the industrial land in the study area is very small, we mainly study the relationship between the area of three types of land use including the residential land, the commercial land and the public administration and public service land and the corresponding passenger flow of the subway station during different time periods in this paper, which is in order to predict the morning and evening peak inbound and outbound passenger flow according to different land use conditions of stations. Through linear regression analysis by using Eviews software, the regression prediction models between the morning peak inbound passenger flow, morning peak outbound passenger flow, evening peak inbound passenger flow, evening peak outbound passenger flow and the area of three land use types are established respectively.

4. There is a significant positive linear correlation between weekdays morning peak station intake passenger flow and the area of the residential land, the commercial land and the public administration and public service land. Both the morning peak outbound passenger flow and the evening peak outbound passenger flow on weekdays have a positive linear correlation with the area of the surrounding residential land, while have no significant linear relationship with the area of the commercial land and the public administration and public service land. Weekdays evening peak inbound passenger flow has a remarkable linear correlation with the

area of the residential land and the commercial land, while has no significant linear correlation with public administration and public service land. Therefore, it can be seen that passenger flow in different peak periods of the subway stations has different relationships with the surrounding land use types.

6 Conclusion

This paper takes nine stations along Beijing Batong Subway Line as the research objects. First of all, the area of different types of surrounding land use within the attracting range of stations is obtained by QGIS software based on the remote sensing image. And then calculate the proportion of different land use types, which indicates that the type of land use of the station along the subway line is mainly dominant by the residential land. Secondly, based on the data of passenger flow and the data of area of different land use types of the station within the attracting scope, linear regression analysis is applied by Eviews software, and we find out that the average daily passenger flow is associated with the total intensity of the development of the surrounding land use, that there exists a linear positive correlation between total area of different types of land use and average daily passenger flow. Thus, the regression prediction models between the average daily passenger flow and its surrounding land use types are established, as well as passenger flow during different periods of the station and its surrounding land use types.

Based on the research results of this paper on the passenger flow of the station on Batong Subway Line and the different land use types within its attracting range, it can provide some guidance for the site selection and layout of the subway station in the future. By using the degree of development of the land use around the station target alternative area in the future, the average daily passenger flow and the peak inbound and outbound passenger flow in the region can be predicted, which can provide suggestions for the layout of subway stations and the planning and construction of station.

Acknowledgement. This research was supported by the National Key Research and Development Program of China (2018YFB1601300).

References

1. Zhou, J., Wang, H., Sun, D., Xu, S., Lv, M., et al.: Optimization scheme of large passenger flow in Huoying Station, line 13 of Beijing subway system. Comput. Mater. Continua **63**(3), 1387–1398 (2020)
2. Li, Z.T., Xiao, F., Wang, S.G., Pei, T.R., Li, J.: Achievable rate maximization for cognitive hybrid satellite-terrestrial networks with AF-relays. IEEE J. Sel. Areas Commun. **26**(2), 304–313 (2018)
3. Xiao, F., Liu, W., Li, Z,T., Chen, L., Wang, R.C.: Noise-tolerant wireless sensor networks localization via multi-norms regularized matrix completion. IEEE Trans. Veh. Technol. **67**(3), 2409–2419 (2018)

4. Chakraborty, A., Mishra, S.: Land use and transit ridership connections: implications for state-level planning agencies. Land Use Policy **30**(1), 458–469 (2013)

5. Choi, J., Yong, J.L., Kim, T., Sohn, K.: An analysis of metro ridership at the station-to-station level in Seoul. Transportation **39**, 705–722 (2012)

6. Yang, Z.Q., Shi, F.S., Huang, J.D., He, J.T.: Passenger flow forecast of new urban rail transit stations based on land use. Urban Rapid Rail Transit **33**(2), 70–74 (2020)

7. Zhang, N., Ye, X.F., Liu, J.F.: The impact of land use on demand of urban rail transit. Urban Transp. China **8**(3), 23–27 (2010)

8. Kong, X.F., Yang, J.W.: A new method for forecasting station-level transit ridership from land-use perspective: the case of Shenzhen city. Scientia Geographica Sinica **38**(12), 2074–2083 (2018)

9. He, Z.K.: TOD community land use intensity research based on the rail transit station. M.S. dissertation, Southwest Jiaotong University (2012)

10. Zhu, J., Hong, F., Liu, J.: Correlation analysis between the land use and the demand of urban rail transport. Traffic Transp. **36**(1), 88–91 (2020)

11. Liu, X.C., Yu, W., Song, W., Zhang, X.P., Zhao, L.Z., et al.: Remote sensing image classification algorithm based on texture feature and extreme learning machine. Comput. Mater. Continua **65**(2), 1385–1395 (2020)

12. Xu, H., Yang, H.J., Shen, Q.F., Yang, J.T., Liang, H.H., et al.: Automatic terrain debris recognition network based on 3d remote sensing data. Comput. Mater. Continua **65**(1), 579–596 (2020)

13. Islam, S.U., Jan, S., Waheed, A., Mehmood, G., Zareei, M., et al.: Land-cover classification and its impact on peshawar's land surface temperature using remote sensing. Comput. Mater. Continua **70**(2), 4123–4145 (2022)

14. Thamizhazhagan, P., Sujatha, M., Umadevi, S., Priyadarshini, K., Parvathy, V.S., et al.: AI based traffic flow prediction model for connected and autonomous electric vehicles. Comput. Mater. Continua **70**(2), 3333–3347 (2022)

Cloud Computing and Security

SCESP: An Edge Server Placement Method Based on Spectral Clustering in Mobile Edge Computing

Lijuan Wang[1,2,3], Yingya Guo[1,2,3(✉)], Jiangyuan Yao[4], and Siyu Zhou[5]

[1] College of Computer and Data Science, Fuzhou University, Fuzhou 350000, China
`guoyy@fzu.edu.cn`
[2] Fujian Key Laboratory of Network Computing and Intelligent Information Processing, Fuzhou University, Fuzhou 350000, China
[3] Key Laboratory of Spatial Data Mining and Information Sharing, Ministry of Education, Fuzhou 350003, China
[4] School of Computer Science and Cyberspace Security, Hainan University, Haikou 570228, China
[5] Tandon School of Engineering, New York University, New York 10012, USA

Abstract. With the rapid development of Internet of Things (IoT) and 5G, mobile edge computing is gaining popularity for its low computation latency, bandwidth costs and energy consumption. In mobile edge computing, the placement of edge servers is one of the most significant problems and attracts worldwide attention. However, two major problems of edge server placement: high access delay and unbalanced workload of edge servers, have not been completely solved yet. To better solve these two problems, this paper proposes a new Spectral-Clustering-based Edge Server Placement (SCESP) algorithm, which can effectively reduce the access delay and make the workload of each edge server more balanced. In the evaluation, we use the Shanghai Telecom's base station dataset to test the performance of SCESP and extensive experiments demonstrate the superior performance of SCESP in reducing the access delay and balancing the edge server workload.

Keywords: Edge server placement · Spectral clustering · Access delay · Workload balancing

1 Introduction

With the rapid development of IoT and 5G [14,18], the number of network edge devices and the traffic volume have grown exponentially. According to IDC (Internet Data Center) predictions [16], the total amount of global data will exceed 40ZB (Zetta Byte) by 2020, and 45% of the traffic data generated by the IoT will be processed at the edge of the network. In this situation, the centralized processing model centered on the cloud computing model [20] will not be able to efficiently process the massive datum generated by network edge devices.

© The Author(s), under exclusive license to Springer Nature Switzerland AG 2022
X. Sun et al. (Eds.): ICAIS 2022, CCIS 1587, pp. 527–539, 2022.
https://doi.org/10.1007/978-3-031-06761-7_42

The cloud computing model has many shortcomings, which is mainly reflected in the following aspects: longer network delay, data security, high bandwidth costs, large energy consumption. In order to solve the above problems, facing the massive datum calculation generated by the edge devices in the network, the edge computing come into being [12,15]. The edge computing model and the cloud computing model are not a superseding relationship, but a complementary relationship. Edge computing requires the cloud computing center to provide strong computing power and mass storage ability. At the same time, the cloud computing center also needs protection of the massive private data and fast service response in the edge computing. Mobile Edge Computing (MEC) networks can provide edge devices with real-time response services and privacy data protection through a small network bandwidth.

In MEC network [10,19,22], edge computing services are mainly implemented and guaranteed by edge servers. The placement of the edge server has a significant impact on the access delay of edge devices and the workload of the server. The location of the edge server is related to the real-time calculation of all edge devices in the IoT and the protection of important private data. Many experts and scholars have conducted research on this problem and proposed corresponding solutions. However, the placement of edge servers is not only to choose location, but more importantly, to ensure a high-quality service. In the large scale construction of smart cities, the number of edge devices has sharply increased [1], and users have put forward higher requirements for the network response speed and processing capabilities of edge services. In the smart cities made up of hundreds or thousands of base stations, edge services still have problems such as prolonged network response time [22] and serious imbalance in the workload of edge servers. Due to the uneven distribution and discrete distribution of edge devices [3], different edge server placement will lead to different network delays and unbalanced workload of base stations.

In order to better reduce access delays and balance the computing pressure of edge devices, we propose a novel Spectral-Clustering-based Edge Server Placement (SCESP) algorithm to solve the above problem in this paper. Using SCESP algorithm to cluster base station dataset, we can get lower access delay and more balanced workload. It is confirmed that the problem of edge server placement in MEC network is an NP-hard problem [22]. Since the geographical locations of base stations are discretely distributed, before clustering, we first pre-process the base station dataset and classify the base stations into two parts: normal set and abnormal set. For the normal set of base station, we leverage the Spectral Clustering (SC) [8] method for clustering, and for the abnormal set of base station, we use a single base station as a cluster to place edge server. Through extensive experiments, the clustering results of the normal set of base station and the abnormal set of base station jointly determine the placement of the edge server. The main contributions of this paper are shown as follows:

1 Before clustering, we first pre-process the base station dataset. We divide all base stations into two parts: normal set and abnormal set.

2 We propose a new Spectral-Clustering-based Edge Server Placement algorithm to achieve the lowest access delay and a more balanced workload in edge computing. Compared to the other placement algorithms, our proposed algorithm can greatly reduce the access delay and better balance the workload of edge servers.

3 Experimental results based on Shanghai Telecom's base station dataset show that our edge server placement algorithm outperforms other algorithms.

The rest of this paper is organized as follows. In Sect. 2, we briefly summarize the related work. In Sect. 3, we introduce our system model and define the problem. In Sect. 4, we propose a new edge server placement algorithm: SCESP. In Sect. 5, we show experimental results based on a real dataset and evaluate the performance of different algorithms. Finally, we draw a conclusion of the paper in Sect. 6.

2 Related Work

Regarding the placement problem, many scientific researchers have done a lot of research work on the cloudlet placement [2,4,6,9,13,23,25]. Mobile edge devices generate more and more computation intensive tasks. Xu et al. [25] proposed to offload the computation intensive tasks to remote cloud computing centers for processing and storage. Fajardo et al. [7] proposed a solution based on the placement of processing and storage capabilities close to the remote units, which is especially well suited for the deployment of clusters of small cells. Chen et al. [5] adopted a game theoretic method in a distributed manner and formulated the distributed computation offloading decision making problem among mobile device users as a multi-user computation offloading game. Zhang et al. [26] applied the CA (Covering Algorithm) to adaptively cluster the mobile devices based on their geographical locations. In [4,22,25], the placement problem was expressed as an integer linear programming problem. In the process of cloudlet placement, uneven distribution of mobile computing tasks is prone to occur. Dashti et al. [6] proposed to modify particle swarm optimization to redistribute migrated virtual machines among overloaded hosts, and dynamically integrate under-loaded hosts. If the amount of computing tasks for mobile edge users can be predicted, the placement of cloud servers can be better optimized. Mark et al. [13] proposed an evolutionary optimal virtual machine placement (EOVMP) algorithm with a demand forecaster.

In MEC network, users offload computationally intensive tasks to edge servers at base stations [9,17,24]. The placement of the edge server is similar to the location problem of the cloudlet in fact [9,25]. Wang et al. [22] formulated the placement problem as a multi-objective constraint optimization problem, and adopted mixed integer programming to find the optimal. Lee et al. [10] modeled MEC server placement as a capacitated clustering problem, and proposed a greedy-based heuristics algorithm, called LowMEP. Finally, they demonstrated that LowMEP required the minimum number of MEC servers to assure a certain latency budget to realize. In addition, there are some research work focused on placing k edge servers in MEC network, which is similar to placing k cloudlets in the network [9,25]. The above-mentioned experiments and research are very effective, but the experimental results still are not satisfactory. With the inspiration of the above research, we are the first to apply the algorithm of spectral clustering [1,8] to the placement of edge server for achieving the lowest access latency and make the workload of each edge server more balanced.

3   Problem Formulation

In this section, we present the system model of the placement of edge server in 5G network. Then, we model it as a location-based clustering problem. Finally, we introduce SCESP algorithm and we will adopt it to achieve the lowest access delay and a more balanced workload of the edge server. Related notations are summarized in details in Table 1.

Table 1. Notations

Symbol	Definition
G	Mobile edge computing network
K	Number of edge servers
B	Set of all base station in the network
S	Set of all edge servers that will be placed
E	Set of links between a base station and an edge server at a location in S
W_b	Workload of base station b and $b \in B$
W_s	Workload of edge server s and $s \in S$
l_b	Location of base station b and $b \in B$
l_s	Location of edge server s and $s \in S$
B_s	Set of base stations that are in control of edge server s and $s \in S$
d	Access delay between base station and edge server
D_{s_i}	Access delay of i-th edge server s_i
avg_W	Average workload of all edge servers
SD_W	Standard deviation of workload

3.1   System Model

Edge server will be placed in the base station. The terminals of IoT are connected to various terminal devices. The network communications of the IoT are connected through base stations. We model the network that needs to put into the edge server as an undirected graph G = (V, E), where V is composed of all base stations (the k base station location is where the edge server will be placed) and E is the undirected link between the base station and the edge server.

B and S represent the set of base stations and the set of edge servers respectively. l_b and l_s represent the location of base stations and the location of edge servers respectively. d represents the distance between the base station and the edge server. In the network, the access delay is directly proportional to the distance, wherefore we can equivalently express the distance between the base station and the edge server as the network access delay when users link to the base station and access the edge server. B_s represents a set of base stations within the same edge server. The number of users connected to a base station affects the workload of this base station. W_b represents the workload of base station. The sum of W_b of base stations within the same edge server is the workload of this edge server, denoted as W_s. In the performance evaluation of the algorithm, we compute the standard deviation of W_s obtained by each algorithm and then compare them. We assume that k edge servers will be placed in the 5G IoT, and these k edge servers have the same sufficient computing and storage resources to provide services for edge devices. The edge devices can access the edge server by linking to base station, and the edge server can provide services for all edge devices in its coverage area, including real-time computing and data storage and so on. In a specific time, each edge device can only be connected to one base station. At the same time, each base station only exists in the coverage area of one edge server. We constantly adjust the location of edge servers to achieve the minimum access delay, which is our optimization goal.

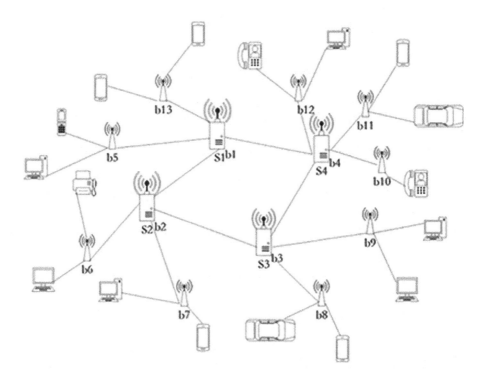

Fig. 1. A scene of edge server placement in the network

From Fig. 1, we can see that there are 13 base stations and many edge devices in the local network, such as smart phones, laptops, smart vehicles, fax equipments and so on. Four edge servers s_1, s_2, s_3, s_4 are placed at the location of base stations b_1, b_2, b_3, b_4. At the same time, we can also see that the workload of the edge server s_1 is the sum of the edge devices linked to the base station b_5 and the base station b_{13}. Through calculation we can get the following result: W_{s_1} is 4, and W_{s_2} is 4, and W_{s_3} is 4, and W_{s_4} is 5.

3.2   Problem Model

In this paper, we first make some assumptions: each edge server has the same and limited computing resources to handle some tasks from edge devices. In other words, in this paper, the attributes of each edge server are exactly the same. Besides, the edge server placed at the base station can be accessed all edge devices linked to this base stations in the same cluster. This also requires that the edge server must be placed in certain base stations. The placement of edge server is actually a distance-based clustering problem. The result of clustering accomplishes two main goals. One is to achieve the minimum access delay of the edge server, and the other is to achieve the balanced workload of the edge server. We formulate this placement problem as follows:

$$D(L) = \min \max d(l_b, l_s), s \in S, b \in B \tag{1}$$

$$W(L) = \min \max(W_i - W_j), i \in S, j \in S \tag{2}$$

L is the optimal solution of the placement plan, and $d(l_b, l_s)$ is the distance between base station (b) and edge server (s). At this time, we do not consider the distance between the edge device and the base station, because this is not the focus of our research and the edge device has characteristics such as mobility. Assume that during network communication, the network is always unimpeded and there is no network congestion. In the communication of the IoT, we use the distance between the edge server and the base station to measure the access delay between them. The goal of the experiment is to reduce the value of d by continuously optimizing the plan of placement, as shown in Eq. (1). When we measure whether the workload of the edge server is balanced, the difference between the workload of any two edge servers is computed. In order to achieve a more balanced workload of edge servers, we should minimize the difference between the workloads of any two edge servers, as shown in Eq. (2).

$$E_i \cap E_j = \emptyset \tag{3}$$

$$\cup E_s = B, s \in S \tag{4}$$

Each base station can only be subordinate to the one edge server, as shown in Eq. (3). The sum of the base stations linked to the edge server should be the total number of base stations, as shown in Eq. (4).

$$W_s = \sum W_b, b \in E_s \tag{5}$$

The sum of users' online time is the workload of the base station that users link to. The workload of edge server is the sum of the workload of all base stations subjected to this edge server, as shown in Eq. (5). That means all edge devices linked to these base stations can access the edge server.

$$\min(D(L) + W(L)) \tag{6}$$

Through the above five Eq. (1)–(5), we can conclude that the edge server placement problem is a multi-objective optimization problem [22], as shown in Eq. (6).

4 Algorithm Description

An overview of SCESP algorithm is shown in Fig. 2. Before clustering, we first pre-process the base station dataset and filter out the abnormal set of base station and the normal set of that. Secondly we leverage the Spectral Clustering [8] algorithm only for the normal set of base station to obtain the clustering result. With the clustering result obtained, we calculate the center point of each cluster and get the placement of edge server. Finally, we measure the access latency of the edge server and the workload of that, and get the optimal placement of edge server by conducting extensive experiments.

To effectively cluster base stations and reduce the access latency of the edge server, the dataset needs to be preprocessed, that is:

- **Preprocessing 1**: Separate the locations of effective base station from Shanghai Telecom's base station dataset.
- **Preprocessing 2**: By comparing with the results of k-means clustering, the base station dataset is divided into two parts: abnormal set and normal set. (line 1)

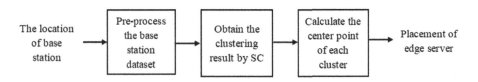

Fig. 2. An overview of SCESP algorithm

The SC algorithm is used for the normal set to obtain the clustering result. The abnormal set is clustered separately into the single cluster. The results of two sets jointly constitute the final clustering result. The SC algorithm is a clustering algorithm that can handle large-scale dataset. In this paper, we adopted a mixed selection strategy of random selection and k-means to select the initial center points of clustering, which greatly improves the effectiveness of SCESP algorithm. Next, we construct the sparse affinity sub-matrix, and interpret it as a bipartite graph. Finally, we can obtain the clustering result of the normal set. At this time, we have not got the center point of each cluster. At this time, we need to perform the next step of the algorithm to find the center point of all the clusters. In the dataset, the location of the base station is represented by longitude and latitude. Therefore, when we determine the center point of the cluster, we need to compute the spherical distance. When determining the center point of each cluster, we use two steps to complete, that is:

- **Step 1**: For each base station in the cluster, calculate its spherical distance from other base stations in the same cluster and record. (line 4)
- **Step 2**: Select the base station with the smallest distance in the cluster as the cluster center point, which is the location of the edge server. (line 5)

In step 1, we calculate the distance between each base station and other base stations in the same cluster, as shown in Eq. (7).

$$\min D_{s_i} = \sum d(b_m, b_n), b_m \in E_{s_i}, b_n \in E_{s_i} \tag{7}$$

$$avg\_W = \frac{\sum W_{s_i}}{k}, i = 1, 2, 3, ..., k \tag{8}$$

$$SD\_W = \sqrt{\frac{\sum(avg\_W - W_{s_i})^2}{k}}, i = 1, 2, 3, ..., k \tag{9}$$

The location of the base station with the smallest distance in the cluster is the potential location of the edge server. We use D_{s_i} to represent the access delay of i-th edge server. In the abnormal point set, the location of each base station is the potential location of the edge server. After getting the placement location of edge server, we can calculate the workload of each edge server and the average load of k edge servers, as shown in Eq. (8). For clearly judging whether the workload of edge server is balanced, we need to calculate the standard deviation of the workload, as shown in Eq. (9).

5   Evaluation

In this section, we first describe the Shanghai Telecom's base station dataset. Then, we will evaluate the performance of SCESP under the different number of base station and edge server. The experiments are carried out on a personal computer with five Intel cores of 3.00 GHz and 8.00 GB memory.

5.1   Dataset Description

During the experiment, we leverage the Shanghai Telecom's base station dataset [11,22], which includes Internet information of 3042 effective base stations. The base station dataset includes the longitude and latitude of each base station, the

Algorithm 1. SCESP: Spectral-Clustering-based Edge Server Placement

---

Input:

    location(x_b, y_b), $b \in B$

Output:

    $L(l_{b_1}, l_{b_2}, l_{b_3}, ..., l_{b_k})$, SD_W

1: Filter (x_b, y_b) as center point set and abnormal point set according to k-means
2: $SC(x_b, y_b)$, $b \in Bcps$
3: Get the set of label, which indicates the clustering result of the base station
4: Calculate D_{s_i} as the access delay, $i = 1, 2, 3, ..., k$
5: Find $L(l_{b_1}, l_{b_2}, l_{b_3}, ..., l_{b_k}) \longleftarrow \min(D_{s_i})$
6: $W_{s_i} = \sum W_{b_i}, b_i \in B_s, i = 1, 2, 3, ..., k$
7: $avg\_W = \frac{\sum W_{s_i}}{k}, i = 1, 2, 3, ..., k$
8: $SD\_W = \sqrt{\frac{\sum (avg\_W - W_{s_i})^2}{k}}, i = 1, 2, 3, ..., k$
9: **return** $L(l_{b_1}, l_{b_2}, l_{b_3}, ..., l_{b_k})$, SD_W

---

number of users linked to the base station. Part of the dataset information is shown in Table 2. It can be seen from Table 2 that the workload of each base station is different. In a densely populated and smart city like Shanghai, the placement of edge server will greatly affect the user's experience of accessing the Internet. Our experiment achieves the workload balance of each server as much as possible while achieving the lowest access delay.

Table 2. Detailed information of some base stations in the Shanghai Telecom's base station dataset

Base station ID	1	2	3
User number	247	73	273
Longitude/latitude	31.237872/121.470259	31.246946/121.513919	31.232877/121.48753

5.2 Experiment

We compare the method proposed in this paper with the current mainstream algorithms in terms of access latency and workload. In order to better show performance of the algorithm, we leverage real dataset called Shanghai Telecom's base station dataset to test the performance of algorithms. For the placement of edge servers, the current mainstream algorithms include K-means [21], Top-k, Random, and the newly proposed MIP [22] algorithm. K-means algorithm randomly selects k clustering centers in the initial clustering, and then continuously refines the clustering to adjust the clustering centers, and finally outputs the best clustering results based on the current initial clustering centers. The Top-k algorithm is a placement algorithm based on sorting. First this approach sorts the workload of all base stations in the network in descending order, and then select the position of the Top-k base stations as the placement of the edge server.

Random algorithm randomly selects the location of k base stations as the placement of the edge server in the network. Based on mixed integer programming [4,22,25], Wang et al. [22] proposed a MIP placement algorithm, whose main goal is to achieve load balancing of edge servers.

In this paper, we compute the distance between the edge server and the base stations in the same cluster to be equivalently evaluated as the access delay, and the number of all edge devices linked to all base stations in the same cluster is recorded as the workload of edge server. First, we consider placing different numbers of edge servers in a network with a fixed number of base stations. Specifically, a range of 200 to 600 edge servers will be placed in the 3000 base stations. Each experiment is carried out with an increment of 50 edge servers, as shown in Fig. 3.

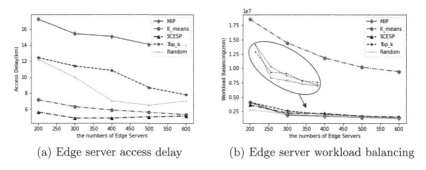

(a) Edge server access delay   (b) Edge server workload balancing

Fig. 3. The influence of the number of edge servers on the placement algorithm under the fixed number of base stations

It can be seen from Fig. 3 that the SCESP algorithm shows outstanding performance effects in terms of access latency and workload. The SCESP algorithm is significantly better than other algorithms in general, not only achieving the lowest access latency of edge devices, but also achieving workload balancing of edge servers. It can be seen from Fig. 3(a) that the SCESP-line is at the bottom of the figure, which shows that our method has a smaller access delay than other algorithms. As can be seen from Fig. 3(b), all the lines are falling. We can know that the workload of the edge servers is becoming more and more balanced by placing more edge servers.

Next, we consider placing edge servers in networks with different numbers of base stations. At this time, we keep the ratio of the number of edge servers to the number of base stations at 0.1 unchanged. We conduct extensive experiments and evaluate the performance of algorithms, as shown in Fig. 4. From Fig. 4, we can see that the SCESP algorithm has more obvious advantages. It can be seen from Fig. 4(a) that the SCESP-curve never exceeds the k-means-curve. When the number of base stations is 1600, the two points are very close. It can be clearly seen from Fig. 4(b) that the SCESP-curve is gradually decreasing. However the overall change of the k-means-curve is not obvious, and the other

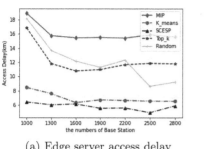
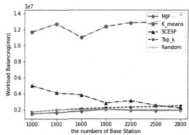

(a) Edge server access delay   (b) Edge server workload balancing

Fig. 4. Performance evaluation when keeping the ratio of the number of edge servers to the number of base stations at 0.1

three curves have a slight increase, which shows that in the dynamic change scenario, workload of edge server in SCESP method is steadily becoming more and more balanced.

Table 3. The average access latency determined by SCESP algorithm method and other placement algorithms

Placement algorithms	MIP	Top-k	Random	K-means	SCESP
Average access latency	15.151312	10.220413	8.537814	6.049215	5.092494
Placement algorithms	MIP	Top-k	Random	K-means	SCESP
Average access latency	16.057783	12.241326	12.194410	6.989984	5.800903

For the performance of access latency, we conduct a quantitative performance analysis. We calculate the average access latency of each placement algorithm in Fig. 3(a) and Fig. 4(a), as shown in Table 3. From the second row of data in Table 3, the performance of the SCESP algorithm is improved by approximately 66% compared to the MIP algorithm, and by approximately 50% compared to Top-k, and by approximately 40% compared to Random, and by approximately 16% compared to K-means. From the fourth row of data in Table 3, the performance of the SCESP algorithm is improved by approximately 64% compared to the MIP algorithm, and by approximately 53% compared to Top-k, and by approximately 52% compared to Random, and by approximately 17% compared to K-means.

6   Conclusion

This paper studies the problem of edge server placement under the requirements of massive data and low access latency. We propose a new placement algorithm, called SCESP algorithm. Before clustering all the base stations in the network, we first pre-process the base station dataset and classify them into a normal set and an abnormal set. The distance between the base stations is proportional to the access delay, so the access delay between the base stations can be equivalently obtained by calculating the distance between the base stations. The spectral clustering algorithm is used to cluster the normal set of base station. After obtaining the clustering results, we calculate the access delay between the base stations in the same cluster and think of the base station with the minimal access delay as the center point of the cluster, whose location is the potential location of the edge server. Finally, we calculate the workload of each edge server based on the placement of the edge server. The extensive experiments are carried out using the base station dataset of Shanghai Telecom. The experiment results demonstrate the superior performance of SCESP in reducing the access delay and balance the workload of edge servers.

The edge server placement is just the first step in MEC network. In the future, we will concentrate on the energy consumption problem of edge servers and service profits related issues from the perspective of service providers. Therefore, how to design a low-cost and high-profit edge computing network is a key issue for our future work.

Acknowledgements. This work is partially supported by National Natural Science Foundation of China under Grant No.62002064, and the Natural Science Foundation of Fujian Province under Grant 2020J05110.

References

1. Abas, A.R., Mahdy, M.G., Mahmoud, T.M.: Adaptive landmark-based spectral clustering for big datasets. IEEE Access **9**, 88291–88300 (2021)
2. Almutairi, J., Aldossary, M.: Investigating and modelling of task offloading latency in edge-cloud environment. Comput. Mater. Continua **68**, 4143–4160 (2021)
3. Bouet, M., Conan, V.: Mobile edge computing resources optimization: a geo-clustering approach. IEEE Trans. Netw. Serv. Manag. **15**(2), 787–796 (2018)
4. Ceselli, A., Premoli, M., Secci, S.: Cloudlet network design optimization. In: Kacimi, R., Mammeri, Z. (eds.) Proceedings of the 14th IFIP Networking Conference, Networking 2015, Toulouse, France, 20–22 May 2015, pp. 1–9. IEEE Computer Society (2015)
5. Chen, X., Jiao, L., Li, W., Fu, X.: Efficient multi-user computation offloading for mobile-edge cloud computing. IEEE/ACM Trans. Netw. **24**(5), 2795–2808 (2016)
6. Dashti, S.E., Rahmani, A.M.: Dynamic VMS placement for energy efficiency by PSO in cloud computing. J. Exp. Theor. Artif. Intell. **28**(1–2), 97–112 (2016)
7. Fajardo, J.O., et al.: Introducing mobile edge computing capabilities through distributed 5G cloud enabled small cells. Mob. Networks Appl. **21**(4), 564–574 (2016)
8. Huang, D., Wang, C., Wu, J., Lai, J., Kwoh, C.: Ultra-scalable spectral clustering and ensemble clustering. IEEE Trans. Knowl. Data Eng. **32**(6), 1212–1226 (2020)
9. Jia, M., Cao, J., Liang, W.: Optimal cloudlet placement and user to cloudlet allocation in wireless metropolitan area networks. IEEE Trans. Cloud Comput. **5**(4), 725–737 (2017)

10. Lee, S., Lee, S., Shin, M.: Low cost MEC server placement and association in 5G networks. In: 2019 International Conference on Information and Communication Technology Convergence, ICTC 2019, Jeju Island, Korea (South), 16–18 October 2019, pp. 879–882. IEEE (2019)

11. Li, Y., Wang, S.: An energy-aware edge server placement algorithm in mobile edge computing. In: 2018 IEEE International Conference on Edge Computing, EDGE 2018, San Francisco, CA, USA, 2–7 July 2018, pp. 66–73. IEEE Computer Society (2018)

12. Mach, P., Becvar, Z.: Mobile edge computing: a survey on architecture and computation offloading. IEEE Commun. Surv. Tutorials **19**(3), 1628–1656 (2017)

13. Mark, C.C.T., Niyato, D., Tham, C.: Evolutionary optimal virtual machine placement and demand forecaster for cloud computing. In: 25th IEEE International Conference on Advanced Information Networking and Applications, AINA 2011, Biopolis, Singapore, 22–25 March 2011, pp. 348–355. IEEE Computer Society (2011)

14. Math, S., Tam, P., Kim, S.: Intelligent real-time IoT traffic steering in 5G edge networks. Comput. Mater. Continua **67**(3), 3433–3450 (2021)

15. Shi, W., Cao, J., Zhang, Q., Li, Y., Xu, L.: Edge computing: vision and challenges. IEEE Internet Things J. **3**(5), 637–646 (2016)

16. Shi, W., Pallis, G., Xu, Z.: Edge computing [scanning the issue]. Proc. IEEE **107**(8), 1474–1481 (2019)

17. Siew, M., Guo, K., Cai, D.W.H., Li, L., Quek, T.Q.S.: Let's share VMS: optimal placement and pricing across base stations in MEC systems. CoRR abs/2101.06129 (2021)

18. Sreekanth, G., Ahmed, S., Sarac, M., Strumberger, I., Bacanin, N., Zivkovic, M.: Mobile fog computing by using SDN/NFV on 5G edge nodes. Comput. Syst. Sci. Eng. **41**(2), 751–765 (2022)

19. Sun, S., Zhou, J., Wen, J., Wei, Y., Wang, X.: A DQN-based cache strategy for mobile edge networks. CMC-Comput. Mater. Continua **71**(2), 3277–3291 (2022)

20. Varghese, B., Reaño, C., Silla, F.: Accelerator virtualization in fog computing: moving from the cloud to the edge. IEEE Cloud Comput. **5**(6), 28–37 (2018)

21. Wang, G., Zhao, Y., Huang, J., Duan, Q., Li, J.: A K-means-based network partition algorithm for controller placement in software defined network. In: 2016 IEEE International Conference on Communications, ICC 2016, Kuala Lumpur, Malaysia, 22–27 May 2016, pp. 1–6. IEEE (2016)

22. Wang, S., Zhao, Y., Xu, J., Yuan, J., Hsu, C.: Edge server placement in mobile edge computing. J. Parallel Distributed Comput. **127**, 160–168 (2019)

23. Xiang, H., et al.: An adaptive cloudlet placement method for mobile applications over GPS big data. In: 2016 IEEE Global Communications Conference, GLOBECOM 2016, Washington, DC, USA, 4–8 December 2016, pp. 1–6. IEEE (2016)

24. Xiong, A., et al.: An energy aware algorithm for edge task offloading. Intell. Automat. Soft Comput. **31**(3), 1641–1654 (2022)

25. Xu, Z., Liang, W., Xu, W., Jia, M., Guo, S.: Efficient algorithms for capacitated cloudlet placements. IEEE Trans. Parallel Distributed Syst. **27**(10), 2866–2880 (2016)

26. Zhang, Y., Wang, K., Zhou, Y., He, Q.: Enhanced adaptive cloudlet placement approach for mobile application on spark. Secur. Commun. Netw. **2018**, 1937670:1–1937670:12 (2018)

PTAC: Privacy-Preserving Time and Attribute Factors Combined Cloud Data Access Control with Computation Outsourcing

Rui Luo, Yuanzhi Yao[✉], Weihai Li, and Nenghai Yu

School of Cyber Science and Technology, University of Science
and Technology of China, Hefei 230027, China
yaoyz@ustc.edu.cn

Abstract. Cloud storage service has significant advantages on both cost reduction and convenient data sharing. It frees data owners from technical management. However, it poses new challenges on privacy and security protection. To protect data confidentiality and privacy of users against malicious entities in the cloud, fine-grained data access control in cloud storage has become a challenging issue and draws considerable investigation. Ciphertext-policy attribute-based encryption (CP-ABE) is a promising cryptographic technique to address the above issue. In many scenarios, access policies are associated with privacy and sensitive information of users which needs to be preserved from disclosure. However, existing schemes cannot simultaneously support time-sensitive data publishing and attribute information preservation. In this paper, we propose a privacy-preserving time and attribute factors combined cloud data access control with computation outsourcing scheme (named PTAC). To preserve attribute privacy, we design a dual access policy tree mechanism where one access policy tree is public and another is sensitive and hidden. Moreover, time-sensitive data publishing can be achieved by combining CP-ABE with timed-release encryption. By using edge computing and cloud computing, we also outsource partitive computational cost of encryption and decryption to third parties. Extensive security and performance analysis demonstrate the security and efficiency of our proposed scheme in cloud storage. As a result, valuable attribute information in the access policy can be preserved in case of disclosing to unauthorized recipients.

Keywords: Cloud storage · Attribute-based encryption · Privacy preservation · Time-sensitive data · Computation outsourcing

1 Introduction

The growing adoption and development of cloud storage service has led to a new paradigm of outsourcing data to the cloud. There are several advantages

X. Sun et al. (Eds.): ICAIS 2022, CCIS 1587, pp. 540–555, 2022.
https://doi.org/10.1007/978-3-031-06761-7_43

of cloud storage service including efficient management over data and reduction of cost. However, outsourcing data to the cloud will pose many new challenges on privacy and security protection of user data [1]. Data owners will lose the physical control of their data if they choose to use cloud storage service. Hence, secure and privacy-preserving access control has become a challenging problem in public cloud storage service.

Ciphertext-policy attribute-based encryption (CP-ABE) [2,3] is a useful cryptographic approach for data access control in cloud storage. It enables data owners to realize fine-grained and flexible access control on their own data. As an important access control technique, many scholars have published a lot of studies on CP-ABE, such as large universe CP-ABE [4] and traceable CP-ABE [5]. Nevertheless, most schemes based on CP-ABE determine access privilege of users only depend on their inherent attributes without any other critical factors, such as the time factor which is very important in time-sensitive data sharing. In fact, the time factor usually plays a very important role in managing time-sensitive data. For example, time is an essential factor to be considered in exposing the future business plan of a company. In many scenarios, both fine-grained access control function and the approach of access control privilege timed releasing need to be taken into account together.

Another thing worth noting in traditional CP-ABE scheme is that the access policy should be published with the encrypted data to notify data users whether their attribute sets satisfy the access policy related to ciphertext or not. Nevertheless, the privacy information corresponding to the encrypted data will be exposed in this way. Therefore, this feature is not suitable for many scenarios, especially the medical treatment and financial fields which pay much attention to the privacy of user information. Lai et al. [6] designed a CP-ABE scheme based on LSSS which realized hidden access policy. Based on Lai's scheme, Cui et al. [7] introduced their work using prime order groups. However, all the hidden access policy schemes above do not pay much attention to time-sensitive data and time factor.

To achieve both fine-grained access control and timed-release mechanism in cloud storage, taking the time factor as an ordinary attribute is an obvious approach. However, unbearable number of time-related keys required for each user at all predefined time points which brings heavy cost on both communication and computation in this way. Hong et al. [8] proposed a data access control scheme for outsourcing time-sensitive data. Their scheme retained the feature of timed-release function from Timed-Release Encryption (TRE) [9] as well as realized fine-grained access control mechanism. However, the access policy must be revealed in their work which will lead to privacy disclosure. Meng et al. [10] proposed a policy partly hidden CP-ABE based scheme, but they do not support timed-release function for time-sensitive data.

In the existing CP-ABE schemes such as work of [8], the number of pairing and exponentiation operations for encryption of sharing data is linear with the complexity of access policy. It means that the computation overhead of users is very expensive. To reduce the computational burden of users, some operations in cryptography with heavy computational overhead can be outsourced to third-party entities like edge nodes. In fact, edge computing [11,12] is able to provide fast and convenient computing resources for data owners and users. To sum up, privacy-preserving and fine-grained access control which supports computation outsourcing and time-sensitive data should be sought.

In this paper, we propose a privacy-preserving time and attribute factors combined cloud data access control with computation outsourcing scheme named PTAC. Following are the key contributions of this paper:

1) The proposed PTAC improves the access structure of fundamental CP-ABE to support any potential timed-release access policy and protects the privacy information of data users by using dual access policy tree mechanism.
2) By using the edge computing, the computational overhead of data owner generating the part of ciphertext which is corresponding to the public access policy tree can be outsourced to the edge nodes. Besides, most computational overhead of decryption is shifted from data user to the cloud service provider. The data owner only needs to do a constant number of operations to decrypt the ciphertext. Therefore, PTAC can reduce computational burden of data owners and data users.
3) Furthermore, we present an evaluation of security and performance for our proposed scheme. All experimental results indicate that our proposed PTAC is secure and efficient.

The rest of this paper is organized as follows. We introduce system and security model in Sect. 2. Following the technical preliminaries explained in Sect. 3, we carefully introduce the detailed construction of our proposed PTAC in Sect. 4. We give the security and performance analysis results in Sect. 5. Finally, the conclusion of our work is provided in Sect. 6.

2   System and Security Model

2.1   System Model

Our system consists of six entities: *attribute authority*, *time server*, *cloud service provider*, *data owner*, *data user* and *edge node*. Figure 1 shows the organization of all above entities and implementation of PTAC.

- *Attribute authority (AA)* is responsible to manage the security parameters of the whole system. It needs to generate system parameters for data sharing and distribute security keys to each user. The security parameters for time server to publish time token are controlled by **AA**, too.
- *Time server (TS)* has the ability to get the exact time and generate time token with the help of **AA**. It needs to distribute time token to **CSP** after a certain time point. In other words, **TS** acts as a time agent to maintain the timed-release function.

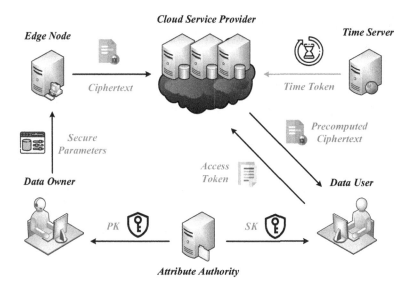

Fig. 1. System Model and operations of our proposed PTAC.

- **Cloud service provider (CSP)** manages the uploaded data and provides access services for data users. The **CSP** owns huge computing resource as well as storage capacity. It has ability to provide computing and storage service for data owner and data user. Especially, **CSP** can accomplish a part of computational overhead in decryption process of data user.
- **Data owner (DO)** defines the access policies and one or more releasing time points for the data. Then **DO** encrypts the data under the decided policies by public key prior to uploads it with moving some computing burden to edge nodes.
- **Data user (DU)** is able to decrypt the ciphertext by private key only if both of the following two conditions are satisfied: 1) The current access time is later than the releasing time defined by **DO**; 2) The attribute set of **DU** satisfies the access policy of cloud data.
- **Edge Node (EN)** can help **DO** to accomplish the encryption of message. Some computational overheads of **DO** in encryption process can be outsourced to **EN**.

2.2   Security Assumption

We assume that the **AA** and **TS** are fully trusted, while **DU** could be malicious. The **AA** is responsible for key generating and distribution. The **TS** receives time token from **AA** in secure way and publish it to **CSP** at a specific time point. A malicious **DU** may try to decrypt ciphertext to obtain unauthorized data by any possible method including colluding with other malicious users. In our proposed PTAC, **CSP** and **EN** are honest but curious entities. They correctly execute every computation mission for other entities but also are curious about the sensitive information of ciphertext and trapdoors for their own benefits. Our proposed PTAC is considered to be compromised if either of the following two types of users can correctly decrypt the ciphertext: 1) a user whose attribute set does not satisfy the dual access policy tree linked to a corresponding ciphertext; 2) a user owns satisfied attribute set but specific time point has not been reached.

3   Technical Preliminaries

3.1   Access Structure

Let $\{P_1, P_2, \cdots, P_n\}$ be a set of parties. A collection $\mathbb{L} \subseteq 2^{\{P_1, P_2, \cdots, P_n\}}$ is monotone if $\forall M, N$: if $M \in \mathbb{L}$ and $M \subseteq N$ then $N \in \mathbb{L}$. An access structure (respectively, monotone access structure) is a collection (respectively, monotone collection) $\mathbb{L}$ of non-empty subsets of $\{P_1, P_2, \cdots, P_n\}$, i.e., $\mathbb{L} \subseteq 2^{\{P_1, P_2, \cdots, P_n\}} \setminus \{\emptyset\}$. The sets in $\mathbb{L}$ are called the authorized sets, and the sets not in $\mathbb{L}$ are called the unauthorized sets.

3.2   Bilinear Map

We consider $\mathbb{G}_1$ and $\mathbb{G}_2$ that are two multiplicative cyclic groups of prime order p. If $e : \mathbb{G}_1 \times \mathbb{G}_1 \to \mathbb{G}_2$ satisfies the following properties:

1) *Bilinearity.* For all $m, n \in \mathbb{G}_1$ and $a, b \in Z_p$, we have $e\left(m^a, n^b\right) = e\left(m, n\right)^{ab}$;
2) *Non-degeneracy.* If g is a generator of $\mathbb{G}_1$, then $e\left(g, g\right)$ is also a generator of $\mathbb{G}_2$;
3) *Computability.* There is an efficient algorithm to compute $e\left(m, n\right) \in \mathbb{G}_2$, for any $m, n \in \mathbb{G}_1$.

Then we call it a bilinear map [13].

4   Construction of Our Scheme

In this section, we present the concrete construction of our scheme. In order to realize function of privacy protection and timed-release, we design a dual access policy tree mechanism. The general idea of our scheme is to build access structure in a new form. As shown in Fig. 2, different from many existing CP-ABE based schemes, access structure of PTAC is composed of dual access policy tree that one is public and another is secret. The secret access policy tree is hidden and contains one or more time trapdoors, each of which is related to a time point. Inspired by the TRE mechanism, time trapdoor of PTAC can be placed upon any node in the access structure. By using time trapdoor, we can define releasing time point of access privilege for **DU**. Both of accessing time and attribute set determine whether the user satisfies access policy or not. Note that, in secret access policy tree, the information of attributes corresponding to the leaf nodes are fully hidden which means only the index of these nodes are revealed.

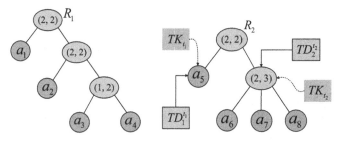

(a) Public access policy tree.   (b) Secret access policy tree.

Fig. 2. Example of dual access policy tree mechanism.

In general, **DO** sets the dual access policy tree to encrypt the shared data by the help of edge computing. Especially, the time trapdoors related to the secret access policy tree are generated according to a time point $t \in T_f$. T_f is the time format set by the access control system just like "mm/dd/yyyy". For example, "October 12, 2021" in T_f is equal to "10/12/2021". The granularity of timed-release function can be controlled by the time format T_f, e.g., monthly, daily or hourly. Moreover, we have introduced a less tight time synchronization mechanism to realize an approximate time consistency. It means that all the other entities in our system synchronize with the time server which can provide time synchronization service and send time token to the cloud service provider.

PTAC is composed of nine algorithms. The details of these algorithms are described as follows. Without loss of generality, we suppose there are at most n possible attributes and $S = \{a_1, a_2, \ldots, a_n\}$ is the set of all possible attributes.

4.1 Setup

After setting the security parameter λ and the set of all possible attributes S, **AA** conduct the following procedures. **AA** generates $I = \{p, \mathbb{G}_1, \mathbb{G}_2, g, e, H_1, H_2, T_f\}$, where $e : \mathbb{G}_1 \times \mathbb{G}_1 = \mathbb{G}_2$ denotes a bilinear map, $\mathbb{G}_1$ and $\mathbb{G}_2$ are cyclic multiplicative groups of a prime order p, g is a generator of $\mathbb{G}_1$, $H_1 : \{0,1\}^* \to \mathbb{Z}_p^*$, $H_2 : \mathbb{G}_2^* \to \mathbb{Z}_p^*$, $H_3 : \{0,1\}^* \to \mathbb{G}_1^*$ and T_f is the time format. Then **AA** randomly chooses $\alpha, \beta, \gamma \in \mathbb{Z}_p^*$ and $h \in \mathbb{G}_1$. For each attribute $a_j \in S$, **AA** picks $r_j, r_j' \in \mathbb{Z}_p$ randomly. The public key PK is generated as

$$PK = \left\{ \begin{array}{l} I, h, g^\alpha, g^\gamma, e(g,g)^\beta, e(g,h)^\beta; \\ \forall a_j \in S : g^{r_j}, h^{r_j}, g^{r_j'}, h^{r_j'} \end{array} \right\} \tag{1}$$

and the master key is generated as

$$MK = \left\{ \alpha, \beta, \gamma, \{\forall a_j \in S : r_j, r_j'\} \right\} \tag{2}$$

which implicitly exists in the system. In fact, MK should not be obtained by any other entity. In addition, γ and g^γ are used for timed-release function.

4.2 Key Generation

For each user U_j with attribute set S_j, **AA** first randomly chooses $u_j, u_j' \in Z_p^*$ for U_j. Then **AA** computes the user's security key as

$$SK_j = \left\{ \begin{array}{l} g^{\beta+\alpha u_j}, h^{\beta+\alpha u_j}, g^{\alpha u_j} h^{u_j'}, h^{\alpha u_j + u_j'}, g^{u_j'}; \\ \forall a_j \in S_j : g^{\alpha u_j/r_j}, h^{\alpha u_j/r_j}, g^{\alpha u_j/r_j'}, h^{\alpha u_j/r_j'} \end{array} \right\}. \tag{3}$$

When this procedure is finished, the security key SK_j is sent to U_j in a secure way. Note that, the attributes of user U_j can be divided into two parts: public attribute set S_j' and private attribute set S_j''. We suppose that $S_j = \{S_j', S_j''\}$.

4.3 Encryption

At first, the data owner randomly chooses a key $\kappa \in \mathbb{G}_2$ to encrypt the data m using a symmetric cryptography like AES. Then, it encrypts κ with the help of **EN** as follows: **EN** gets T_1 from the **DO**. Then **EN** randomly picks a polynomial q_x of T_1 from the root node R_1 in a top-down manner. For each node x of T_1, the degree of q_x is $d_x = k_x - 1$ where k_x is the threshold value of x. Beginning with root node R_1, the **EN** randomly chooses $s_1 \in \mathbb{Z}_p^*$ and sets $q_{R_1}(0) = s_1$. According to structure of T_1, the **EN** chooses a polynomial q_x whose degree is $d_x = k_x - 1$ and $q_x(0) = q_{parent(x)}(index(x))$ for each non-leaf node x. For each child node y with a unique index $index(y)$ of x, **EN** sets $q_y(0) = q_x(index(y))$.

For a leaf node x of T_1 which is corresponding to attribute a_j, **EN** computes:

$$C_x = \left\{ \forall a_j \in S_j' : C_1' = g^{r_j q_x(0)}, C_2' = h^{r_j q_x(0)} \right\}. \tag{4}$$

Then **EN** generates the CT_1' as

$$CT_1' = \{T_1, g^{s_1}, h^{s_1}, C_x\}. \tag{5}$$

Note that, S_j' denotes a set of attributes which is corresponding to all leaf nodes in T_1. Moreover, T_1 is stored in CT_1' in the form of plaintext which means the privacy of the access policy represented by T_1 is exposed.

DO randomly chooses $s_2 \in Z_p^*$ and sends g^{s_2}, h^{s_2}, $e(g,h)^{\beta s_2}$ to **EN**. Then **EN** computes CT_1 as

$$CT_1 = \left\{ g^{s_2}, h^{s_2}, e(g,h)^{\beta s_2}, CT_1' \right\}. \tag{6}$$

DO randomly chooses $s_3, s_4 \in Z_p^*$ and generates the ciphertext CT_2 corresponding to the T_2. To support timed-release function in our PTAC, we set three secret parameters q_x^0, q_x^1 and t_x^μ associated with each node x in the T_2. In our scheme, q_x^0 is shared with its parent node, q_x^1 is shared with its child node and t_x^μ is a time-related parameter. Specifically, $q_{R_2}^0$ is the base secret of T_2 if x is the root R_2. The parameter assigning is in a top-down manner, starting from the root R_2 as follows:

If node x is R_2, **DO** sets $q_{R_2}^0 = s_3$. For each node x with q_x^0, the parameter $t_x^\mu \in Z_p^*$ is randomly chosen for the time trapdoor. The other value q_x^1 is computed as:

$$\begin{cases} q_x^1 = q_x^0 + t_x^\mu & x \text{ is related to a time trapdoor} \\ q_x^1 = q_x^0 & \text{otherwise} \end{cases} \tag{7}$$

For each non-leaf node x with q_x^1, **DO** chooses a polynomial q_x whose degree is $d_x = k_x - 1$ and $q_x(0) = q_x^1$. For each child node y with a unique index $index(y)$ of x, **DO** sets $q_y^0 = q_{parent(y)}(index(y)) = q_x(index(y))$.

To generate a time trapdoor TD_x^t related to a releasing time $t \in T_f$ and a secret parameter t_x^μ, **DO** picks a random $l_\mu \in Z_p^*$ to compute TD_x^t as follows:

$$TD_x^t = \left\{ D_x = g^{l_\mu}, D_x' = t_x^\mu + H_2(e(H_3(t), g^\gamma)^{l_\mu}) \right\}. \tag{8}$$

For a leaf node y with q_y^1 and related to attribute a_j, **DO** computes C_y as:

$$C_y = \left\{ \begin{array}{c} \forall a_j \in S_j'' : C_1'' = g^{r_j'(q_y^1 - s_2)}, C_2'' = h^{r_j'(q_y^1 - s_2)}, \\ C_3'' = g^{q_y^1}, C_4'' = h^{q_y^1}, C_5'' = e(g,h)^{\beta q_y^1} \end{array} \right\}. \tag{9}$$

Then **DO** can compute CT_2' and CT_2 as follows:

$$CT_2' = \left\{ T_2', g^{s_3}, h^{s_3}, C_y; \forall TD_x^t \in T_2' : TD_x^t = (D_x, D_x') \right\} \tag{10}$$

and

$$CT_2 = \{ g^{s_4}, h^{s_4}, CT_2' \}. \tag{11}$$

Note that, S_j'' is a set of all leaf nodes in T_2 and T_2' is defined the same as T_2 except that the attribute name and its value in the T_2' are fully hidden. In this way, the privacy of T_2 can be preserved by our PTAC. Finally, **DO** chooses a secure symmetric cryptography to encrypt the message m with the key κ. Specifically, **DO** computes $C = \kappa e(g,g)^{\beta(s_2+s_4)}$ and sends $Enc(\kappa, m)$, C, CT_2 to **EN** which generates and uploads the final ciphertext CT to the **CSP**, where

$$CT = \{ T_1, T_2', Enc(\kappa, m), C, CT_1, CT_2 \}. \tag{12}$$

4.4   Time Token Generation

At each time point $t \in T_f$, **TS** generates and sends a time token TK_t to **CSP**.

$$TK_t = H_3(t)^\gamma \tag{13}$$

4.5   Time Trapdoor Exposure

When arriving at the releasing time point t related to TD_x^t, **CSP** can obtain a corresponding token TK_t from **AA**. Then, **CSP** executes the following procedure to expose the trapdoor.

When **CSP** gets TK_t, it queries all trapdoors associated with t in all access structures associated with the stored files on it. For each trapdoor $TD_x^t = (D_x, D_x')$, **CSP** computes the exposed trapdoors as

$$TD_x' = D_x' - H_2(e(TK_t, D_x)). \tag{14}$$

We can get $TD_x' = t_x^\mu$ if the procedure is implemented. Then **CSP** can replace TD_x^t with TD_x' in each related CT whose time trapdoor can be removed and access privilege in the CT is transferred to be only determined by the attribute set.

4.6 Access Token Generation

In this procedure, **DU** randomly chooses $a', b', c', \theta \in \mathbb{Z}_p^*$ and computes the attribute index $H_j = H_1(\theta \parallel j)$ for each $a_j \in S_j''$. Then, **DU** U_j generates the following access token TK_a using its SK_j as

$$TK_a = \left\{ \begin{array}{l} N = a' + b', A_1 = h^{(\alpha u_j + u_j')(a'+b')+c'}, A_2 = g^{u_j'(a'+b')+c'}, \\ A_3 = g^{(\beta + \alpha u_j)a'}, A_4 = h^{(\beta + \alpha u_j)b'}, A_5 = g^{\alpha u_j a'} h^{u_j' a'}, \\ A_6 = g^{u_j' a'}; \forall a_j \in S_j' : B_1 = g^{\alpha u_j a'/r_j}, B_2 = h^{\alpha u_j b'/r_j}; \\ \forall a_j \in S_j'' : B_1' = g^{\alpha u_j a'/r_j'}, B_2' = h^{\alpha u_j b'/r_j'}, H_j \end{array} \right\}. \tag{15}$$

In our proposed PTAC, **DU** U_j keeps a', θ secret and sends TK_a to **CSP**.

4.7 Attributes Verification

After receiving the access token TK_a from **DU** U_j, the **CSP** runs a recursive algorithm in a bottom-up manner as follows:

For a leaf node x from $\mathcal{T}_1$, we suppose that a_j is the corresponding attribute of node x. If $a_j \in S_j'$, the **CSP** computes

$$\begin{aligned} F_x &= e(C_2', B_1) \cdot e(C_1', B_2) \\ &= e(h^{r_j q_x(0)}, g^{\alpha u_j a'/r_j}) \cdot e(g^{r_j q_x(0)}, h^{\alpha u_j b'/r_j}) \\ &= e(h, g)^{\alpha u_j q_x(0)a'} \cdot e(g, h)^{\alpha u_j q_x(0)b'} \\ &= e(g, h)^{\alpha u_j q_x(0)(a'+b')}. \end{aligned} \tag{16}$$

If $a_j \notin S_j'$, then $F_x = \perp$.

If x is a non-leaf node, let S_x be an arbitrary k_x-size set of its child nodes and $F_z \not\subset \perp$ for each $z \in S_x$. If such S_x exists, then **DU** U_j calculates

$$\begin{aligned} F_x &= \prod_{z \in S_x} F_z^{\Delta_{i, S_x'}(0)} \\ &= \prod_{z \in S_x} \left(e(g, h)^{\alpha u_j (a'+b') q_{parent(z)} index(z)} \right)^{\Delta_{i, S_x'}(0)} \\ &= e(g, h)^{\alpha u_j q_x(0)(a'+b')} \end{aligned} \tag{17}$$

where $i = index(b)$ and $S'_x = \{\forall b \in S_x : index(b)\}$. Then we have

$$\Delta_{i,S'_x}(0) = \prod_{b \in S_x, b \neq z} \frac{index(b)}{index(b) - index(z)}. \tag{18}$$

Otherwise, F_x returns $\perp$.

For the root node R_1 of $\mathcal{T}_1$, if $F_{R_1} \neq \perp$, **CSP** can get $F_{R_1} = e(g,h)^{\alpha u_j s_1(a'+b')}$. Then, **CSP** computes E as

$$
\begin{aligned}
E &= \frac{e(A_1, g^{s_1+s_2})}{F_{R_1} \cdot e(A_2, h^{s_1+s_2})} \\
&= \frac{e(h^{(\alpha u_j + u'_j)(a'+b')}, g^{s_1+s_2})}{F_{R_1} \cdot e(g^{u'_j(a'+b')+c'}, h^{s_1+s_2})} \\
&= \frac{e(h^{(\alpha u_j + u'_j)(a'+b')}, g^{s_1+s_2})}{e(g,h)^{\alpha u_j s_1(a'+b')} \cdot e(g^{u'_j(a'+b')+c'}, h^{s_1+s_2})} \\
&= e(g,h)^{\alpha u_j s_2(a'+b')}.
\end{aligned} \tag{19}
$$

As $TD'_y = t^\mu_y$, for each node y of $\mathcal{T}'_2$, we can have

$$
\begin{cases}
t^\mu_y = TD'_y & y \text{ is related to an exposed time trapdoor} \\
t^\mu_y = 0 & \text{no time trapdoor is set related to } y
\end{cases} \tag{20}
$$

If all time trapdoors related to $\mathcal{T}'_2$ have been removed, then **CSP** defines

$$
\begin{aligned}
F_{H_j} &= e(C''_1, B'_2) \cdot e(C''_2, B'_1) \\
&= e(g^{r'_j(q^1_y - s_2)}, h^{\alpha u_j b'/r'_j}) \cdot e(h^{r'_j(q^1_y - s_2)}, g^{\alpha u_j a'/r'_j}) \\
&= e(g,h)^{\alpha u_j(q^1_y - s_2)(a'+b')}
\end{aligned} \tag{21}
$$

for each leaf node $y \in \mathcal{T}'_2$. **CSP** needs to check whether there exists a H_j in TK_a such that

$$C''^N_5 \cdot F_{H_j} \cdot E = e(A_3, C''_4) \cdot e(A_4, C''_3). \tag{22}$$

Equation(22) means that, for a **DU** U_j, if S'_j satisfies $\mathcal{T}_1$ and there exists a H_j such that a_j is the corresponding attribute of leaf node y, then we have

$$
\begin{aligned}
C''^N_5 \cdot F_{H_j} \cdot E &= e(g,h)^{\beta q^1_y(a'+b')} \cdot e(g,h)^{\alpha u_j q^1_y(a'+b')} \\
&= e(g,h)^{(\beta + \alpha u_j)q^1_y(a'+b')} \\
&= e(g^{(\beta + \alpha u_j)a'}, h^{q^1_y}) \cdot e(h^{(\beta + \alpha u_j)b'}, g^{q^1_y}) \\
&= e(A_3, C''_4) \cdot e(A_4, C''_3).
\end{aligned} \tag{23}
$$

In the procedure above, **CSP** can find out whether this U_j has the attribute corresponding to each leaf node of $\mathcal{T}'_2$. If S'_j satisfies $\mathcal{T}_1$ and S''_j satisfies $\mathcal{T}'_2$, CT is accessible to **DU** U_j.

4.8 Ciphertext Precomputation

If CT is accessible, **CSP** can generate the precomputed ciphertext as follows:
If x is a leaf node of T_1 and its related attribute $a_j \in S'_j$, **CSP** computes

$$
\begin{aligned}
P_x &= e\left(C'_1, B_1\right) \\
&= e\left(g^{r_j q_x(0)}, g^{\alpha u_j a'/r_j}\right) \\
&= e\left(g, g\right)^{\alpha u_j q_x(0)a'}.
\end{aligned}
\tag{24}
$$

If $a_j \notin S'_j$, $P_x = \perp$.

If x is a non-leaf node, **CSP** runs the following algorithm recursively for all child nodes z of x. Let S_x be an arbitrary k_x-size set of its child nodes satisfying $P_z \neq \perp$. If such S_x do not exist, we set $P_x = \perp$. Otherwise, **CSP** calculates

$$
\begin{aligned}
P_x &= \prod_{z \in S_x} P_z^{\Delta_{i,S'_x}(0)} \\
&= \prod_{z \in S_x} \left(e(g,g)^{\alpha u_j a' q_{parent(z)}(index(z))}\right)^{\Delta_{i,S'_x}(0)} \\
&= e(g,g)^{\alpha u_j q_x(0)a'}
\end{aligned}
\tag{25}
$$

where $i = index(b)$ and $S'_x = \{\forall b \in S_x : index(b)\}$. After runing the recursive algorithm above, **CSP** gets $P_{R_1} = e(g,g)^{\alpha u_j s_1 a'}$ and computes

$$
\begin{aligned}
J' &= \frac{P_{R_1} \cdot e(A_6, h^{s_1+s_2})}{e(A_5, g^{s_1+s_2})} \\
&= \frac{e(g,g)^{\alpha u_j s_1 a'} \cdot e(g^{u'_j}, h^{s_1+s_2})}{e(g^{\alpha u_j a'} h^{u'_j a'}, g^{s_1+s_2})} \\
&= e(g,g)^{\alpha u_j s_2 a'}.
\end{aligned}
\tag{26}
$$

Then **CSP** can generate

$$
\begin{aligned}
J &= \frac{e(A_3, g^{s_2})}{J'} \\
&= \frac{e(g^{(\beta+\alpha u_j)a'}, g^{s_2})}{e(g,g)^{\alpha u_j s_2 a'}} \\
&= e(g,g)^{\beta s_2 a'}.
\end{aligned}
\tag{27}
$$

If S''_j satisfies T'_2, for each leaf node y of T'_2, **CSP** computes

$$
\begin{aligned}
P_y &= e(g^{r'_j(q_y(0)-s_2)}, g^{\alpha u_j a'/u'_j}) \cdot J \\
&= e(g,g)^{\alpha u_j q_y(0)a'}.
\end{aligned}
\tag{28}
$$

Then **CSP** can generate $P_{R_2} = e(g,g)^{\alpha u_j s_3 a'}$ in a bottom-up manner.

Finally, **CSP** computes the precomputed ciphertext $\overline{CT}$ and sends it to **DU** U_j.

$$\overline{CT} = \left\{ Enc(\kappa, m), J, \grave{C}, C \right\} \tag{29}$$

$$
\begin{aligned}
\grave{C} &= \frac{e(A_3, g^{s_4}) \cdot e(A_5, g^{s_3+s_4})}{P_{R_2} \cdot e(A_6, h^{s_3+s_4})} \\
&= \frac{e(g^{(\beta+\alpha u_j)a'}, g^{s_4}) \cdot e(g^{\alpha u_j a'} h^{u'_j a'}, g^{s_3+s_4})}{e(g,g)^{\alpha u_j s_3 a'} \cdot e(g^{u'_j a'}, h^{s_3+s_4})} \\
&= e(g,g)^{\beta s_4 a'}
\end{aligned}
\tag{30}
$$

4.9   Decryption

If S_j of **DU** U_j satisfies $\mathcal{T}_1$ and $\mathcal{T}'_2$, U_j will receive correct precomputed ciphertext $\overline{CT}$ from **CSP**. Otherwise, $\overline{CT} = \perp$. U_j can generate the symmetric secret key κ' as follows:

$$
\begin{aligned}
\kappa' &= \frac{C}{(J\grave{C})^{\frac{1}{a'}}} \\
&= \frac{\kappa e(g,g)^{\beta(s_2+s_4)}}{e(g,g)^{\beta(s_2+s_4)}} \\
&= \kappa.
\end{aligned}
\tag{31}
$$

Then U_j can decrypt $Enc(\kappa, m)$ by using symmetric key κ and get data m.

5   Security and Performance Analysis

5.1   Security Analysis

Security analysis of PTAC can be summarized as follows.

1) Security against Collusion Attack: The security key SK_j corresponding to attribute set of each user is blinded based on secure random parameters $u_j, u'_j \in \mathbb{Z}^*_p$ in PTAC. In this way, different security keys can not be combined to compute a new security key corresponding to a disparate attribute set which belongs to other users. Hence, collusion attack like this will not bring more advantages to the adversary.

2) Data Confidentiality: To analyse the data confidentiality of our proposed PTAC, we classify all adversaries into two categories. 1) Adversaries without a satisfied attribute set for dual access policy tree $\mathcal{T}_1$ and $\mathcal{T}'_2$, though arriving at stated releasing time point; 2) adversaries with satisfied attribute set for $\mathcal{T}_1$ and $\mathcal{T}'_2$, but the stated releasing time point has not arrived yet. Apart from the above two categories, the rest of adversaries are those neither after the specific releasing time point, nor have the satisfied attribute set. For this condition, we can generate some security keys which contain additional attributes or time tokens for them. In this way, the adversaries can be classified to the above two categories. Appended information at least will not diminish the advantage of adversaries. The further analysis only focus on the above two categories.

In order to realize dual access policy tree mechanism and computation outsourcing, PTAC makes necessary modifications towards CP-ABE. These modifications have not change the structure of CP-ABE algorithm, therefore PTAC holds the same property of data confidentiality against the first category of adversaries as scheme in [2] and [10].

In PTAC, the generation and exposure of time trapdoors implements *Identity-based Encryption* scheme just like [14] and [15]. Therefore, the security of token can be proved security in random oracle model. Moreover, without a correct time token to expose a time trapdoor, the reconstructed P_{R_2} will become a random element belongs to $\mathbb{G}_2$. In this way, the adversary who belongs to the second category is unable to compromise PTAC. From the above analysis, we can conclude that PTAC performs well in data confidentiality.

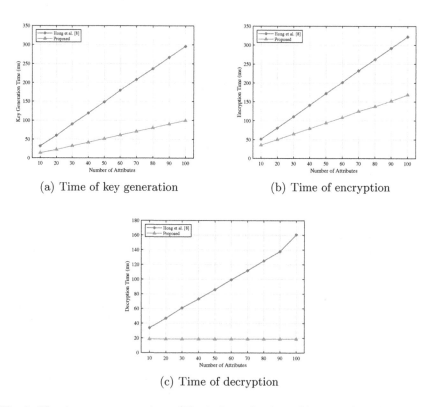

(a) Time of key generation

(b) Time of encryption

(c) Time of decryption

Fig. 3. The time cost comparison. (The independent variable is number of attributes)

Table 1. Comparisons of different CP-ABE based access control schemes

Schemes	Policy hidden	Computation outsourced	Timed releasing
Li et al. [16]	Partially hidden	○	○
Lweko et al. [17]	Fully hidden	○	○
Lai et al. [6]	Partially hidden	○	○
Zhang et al. [18]	Partially hidden	○	○
Cui et al. [7]	Partially hidden	○	○
Khan et al. [19]	Fully hidden	○	○
Hong et al. [8]	No	○	●
Michalevsky et al. [20]	Fully hidden	○	○
Ours	Secret policy is fully hidden	●	●

5.2 Performance Analysis

In order to intuitively evaluate the performance of PTAC, we compare it with the related scheme which is Hong et al. [8]. We have implemented both two framework prototypes using Charm [21], which is a extensible Python-based framework for rapidly prototyping advanced cryptography systems. The following simulation results are compiled using Python on the 64-bit Ubuntu 16.04 system with the AMD Ryzen5 4600H CPU processor at 3.00 GHz and 2.00 GB of RAM. We compare the time overhead of key generation, encryption and decryption algorithms on the basis of elliptic curve SS512. Figure 3 shows that computational cost of PTAC is less than the scheme in [8]. With the help of computation outsourcing mechanism, our proposed PTAC shows its superiority on time cost reduction of **DO** and **DU**. Moreover, the time of decryption is free from influence of the attributes number because partially computational overhead of data users is outsourced to cloud service provider. We summarize the comparisons of some other CP-ABE based schemes with our proposed PTAC in Table 1.

6   Conclusion

In this paper, we have proposed an integrated framework for privacy-preserving attribute-based access control to protect time-sensitive data which is outsourced to cloud. The proposed approach supports fine-grained access control of time-sensitive data outsourced to a cloud storage and privacy protection. The proposed framework also supports computation outsourcing which means the computational overheads of encryption and decryption can be partially shifted to edge nodes and cloud server respectively. Therefore, our proposed scheme is friendly to some resourced-limited mobile devices. Our scheme simultaneously achieves both flexible timed-release and fine granularity with lightweight overhead. With a suit of proposed methods, this scheme provides data owner with ability to release the access privilege to different users at different time point flexibly according to a well-defined dual access policy tree mechanism over attributes and release time. The security and performance analysis of PTAC shows that it is secure and efficient.

Acknowledgements. This work was supported in part by the National Key Research and Development Program of China under Grant 2018YFB0804102, in part by the National Natural Science Foundation of China under Grant 61802357, and in part by the Fundamental Research Funds for the Central Universities under Grant WK3480000009.

References

1. Tabrizchi, H., Kuchaki Rafsanjani, M.: A survey on security challenges in cloud computing: issues, threats, and solutions. J. Supercomput. **76**(12), 9493–9532 (2020). https://doi.org/10.1007/s11227-020-03213-1
2. Bethencourt, J., Sahai, A., Waters, B.: Ciphertext-policy attribute-based encryption. In: 2007 IEEE symposium on security and privacy (SP 2007), pp. 321–334. IEEE (2007)
3. Wang, S., et al.: A fast CP-ABE system for cyber-physical security and privacy in mobile healthcare network. IEEE Trans. Ind. Appl. **56**(4), 4467–4477 (2020)
4. Zhang, Z., Zeng, P., Pan, B., Choo, K.K.R.: Large-universe attribute-based encryption with public traceability for cloud storage. IEEE Internet Things J. **7**(10), 10314–10323 (2020)
5. Sethi, K., Pradhan, A., Bera, P.: Practical traceable multi-authority CP-ABE with outsourcing decryption and access policy updation. J. Inf. Secur. Applicat. **51**, 102435 (2020)
6. Lai, J., Deng, R.H., Li, Y.: Expressive CP-ABE with partially hidden access structures. In: Proceedings of the 7th ACM Symposium on Information, Computer and Communications Security, pp. 18–19 (2012)
7. Cui, H., Deng, R.H., Wu, G., Lai, J.: An efficient and expressive ciphertext-policy attribute-based encryption scheme with partially hidden access structures. In: Chen, L., Han, J. (eds.) ProvSec 2016. LNCS, vol. 10005, pp. 19–38. Springer, Cham (2016). https://doi.org/10.1007/978-3-319-47422-9_2
8. Hong, J., et al.: TAFC: time and attribute factors combined access control for time-sensitive data in public cloud. IEEE Trans. Serv. Comput. **13**(1), 158–171 (2017)
9. Fan, C.I., Huang, S.Y.: Timed-release predicate encryption and its extensions in cloud computing. J. Internet Technol. **15**(3), 413–425 (2014)
10. Meng, F., Cheng, L., Wang, M.: Ciphertext-policy attribute-based encryption with hidden sensitive policy from keyword search techniques in smart city. EURASIP J. Wirel. Commun. Netw. **2021**(1), 1–22 (2021). https://doi.org/10.1186/s13638-020-01875-2
11. Shi, W., Cao, J., Zhang, Q., Li, Y., Xu, L.: Edge computing: vision and challenges. IEEE Internet Things J. **3**(5), 637–646 (2016)
12. Qian, C., Li, X., Sun, N., Tian, Y.: Data security defense and algorithm for edge computing based on mean field game. J. Cybersecur. **2**(2), 97 (2020)
13. Zhang, P., Chen, Z., Liu, J.K., Liang, K., Liu, H.: An efficient access control scheme with outsourcing capability and attribute update for fog computing. Futur. Gener. Comput. Syst. **78**, 753–762 (2018)

14. Boneh, D., Franklin, M.: Identity-based encryption from the Weil pairing. In: Kilian, J. (ed.) CRYPTO 2001. LNCS, vol. 2139, pp. 213–229. Springer, Heidelberg (2001). https://doi.org/10.1007/3-540-44647-8_13

15. Xue, Y., Hong, J., Li, W., Xue, K., Hong, P.: LABAC: a location-aware attribute-based access control scheme for cloud storage. In: 2016 IEEE Global Communications Conference (GLOBECOM), pp. 1–6. IEEE (2016)

16. Li, J., Ren, K., Zhu, B., Wan, Z.: Privacy-aware attribute-based encryption with user accountability. In: Samarati, P., Yung, M., Martinelli, F., Ardagna, C.A. (eds.) ISC 2009. LNCS, vol. 5735, pp. 347–362. Springer, Heidelberg (2009). https://doi.org/10.1007/978-3-642-04474-8_28

17. Lewko, A., Okamoto, T., Sahai, A., Takashima, K., Waters, B.: Fully secure functional encryption: attribute-based encryption and (hierarchical) inner product encryption. In: Gilbert, H. (ed.) EUROCRYPT 2010. LNCS, vol. 6110, pp. 62–91. Springer, Heidelberg (2010). https://doi.org/10.1007/978-3-642-13190-5_4

18. Zhang, Y., Chen, X., Li, J., Wong, D.S., Li, H.: Anonymous attribute-based encryption supporting efficient decryption test. In: Proceedings of the 8th ACM SIGSAC Symposium on Information, Computer and Communications Security, pp. 511–516 (2013)

19. Khan, F., Li, H., Zhang, L., Shen, J.: An expressive hidden access policy CP-ABE. In: 2017 IEEE Second International Conference on Data Science in Cyberspace (DSC), pp. 178–186. IEEE (2017)

20. Michalevsky, Y., Joye, M.: Decentralized policy-hiding ABE with receiver privacy. In: Lopez, J., Zhou, J., Soriano, M. (eds.) ESORICS 2018. LNCS, vol. 11099, pp. 548–567. Springer, Cham (2018). https://doi.org/10.1007/978-3-319-98989-1_27

21. Akinyele, J.A., et al.: Charm: a framework for rapidly prototyping cryptosystems. J. Cryptogr. Eng. **3**(2), 111–128 (2013)

A Novel Evaluation Model of Data Security Protection Capability in Edge Computing Environment

Caiyun Liu[1], Yan Sun[1], Jun Li[1(✉)], Mo Wang[1], and Tao Wang[2]

[1] China Industrial Control Systems Cyber Emergency Response Team,
Beijing 100040, China
dqw_1982@126.com
[2] University of Leicester, Leicester LE1 7RH, UK

Abstract. With the rapid development and wide application of 5G networks, artificial intelligence, and big data, traditional cloud computing cannot handle the massive data generated by edge terminals. Edge computing has gradually been widely used as a computing method close to objects. However, due to the open features of edge computing, such as content perception, real-time computing, and parallel processing, the data security issues that already exist in the cloud computing environment have become more prominent. Data security protection capability evaluation is an important part of the improvement of data security capabilities. However, current protection capability evaluations are mostly qualitative evaluations and lack quantitative evaluation models. Aiming at the edge computing network architecture, this paper proposes a data security protection capability evaluation model based on weight presets. By studying the edge architecture data security protection capability score and cost curve, the data security protection model is adaptively selected. Experiments show that the method can quantitatively calculate the data security protection capability in the edge computing environment, and can guide the construction of the protection model through the score-cost curve.

Keywords: Edge computing · Data security · Cost · Protection capabilities

1 Introduction

Currently, data resources are considered to have exceeded the value of oil. Data-driven innovation is expanding to various fields such as economic society, scientific research and development, changing the work and lifestyle of human beings, and becoming an important driving force for innovation and development. With the popularity of virtual reality, digital twins, logo analysis, and ultra-large bandwidth and ultra-high-speed mobile Internet, people, machines, objects, workflows, and educational streams have all become components of the digital process. The amount of data has increased exponentially. According to the "2017–2018 China Internet of Things Development Annual Report" released by China Economic Information Service in September 2018, the number of Internet of Things devices grew strongly in 2017, reaching 8.4 billion units, exceeding the global population for the first time Quantity. Accompanied by the rapid growth of data volume, data statistics company Statista predicts that by 2020, there will be approximately 31 billion IoT devices connected. At the same time, according to the Cisco Cloud Index, the total data traffic of cloud computing will reach 18.9ZB in 2021, an increase of 2.15 times compared to 6.0ZB in 2016. Mass data collection, intelligent analysis, and association mining will generate a large number of high-value data models and knowledge mechanisms, serving government affairs, finance, and other industries, while exerting huge revenue-generating benefits. At the same time, the centralized cloud computing model can no longer meet the data storage and processing requirements in scenarios with high real-time requirements, and cannot effectively solve the problems of cloud center load, transmission broadband, and data privacy protection. As a computing method close to objects, edge computing can realize the intelligent analysis and calculation of some data on the edge side and reduce the pressure on the cloud computing center [1], so it is gradually being widely used.

However, with the marginal processing and utilization of massive data, data security risks have also increased correspondingly. On the one hand, the edge computing infrastructure is located at the edge of the network, it lacks effective data encryption, backup, and recovery measures, and the edge data security protection capability is weak, so the risks are prominent. On the other hand, the data interaction between edge nodes, network terminals, and cloud computing centers is frequent, and the security protection requirements for data transmission links are higher. For example, in the edge computing scenario of the Internet of Things, the edge node saves data such as on-site temperature and humidity. Hackers can tamper with the data by attacking the edge node, causing production accidents and affecting the safety of life and property.

In addition, because the edge device obtains the user's original data, it can obtain a large amount of sensitive privacy data. For example, in a telecom operator's edge computing scenario, it is very easy for users of edge nodes to collect and snoop on the location information, service content, and frequency of use of other users. Compared with traditional cloud centers, edge nodes lack effective encryption or desensitization measures. Once they are attacked, sniffed and corroded by hackers, their stored household consumption, personal health information in the electronic medical system, road incident vehicle information would be leaked.

In this context, the issue of edge computing data security has gradually attracted attention. Enterprises deploy protection measures such as encryption and authentication at edge nodes, terminals and cloud computing centers to protect important data, personal information and sensitive data. As an important part of data security capacity building, data security protection capability assessment is indispensable in the life cycle of enterprise data security construction. However, most of the current data security assessment models are qualitative assessment models, which cannot quantitatively assess the corporate data security protection capabilities. Aiming at the edge computing network, this paper proposes a quantitative evaluation model of data security protection capabilities based on weight presets. The main arrangement of the article is as follows: The first part introduces the background of the protection capability evaluation, the second part introduces the related work, the third part introduces the quantitative evaluation model and the experimental analysis, and the fourth part summarizes the full text.

2 Related Work

Currently, edge computing data security protection is still in the exploratory stage. Jiale Zhang et al. [2] present a comprehensive analysis of the data security and privacy threats, protection technologies, and countermeasures inherent in edge computing. Chadwick D W et al. [3] propose a five-level trust model for a cloud-edge based data sharing infrastructure. The data owner can choose an appropriate trust level and cyber threat information data sanitization approach, ranging from plain text, through anonymization/pseudonymization to homomorphic encryption, in order to manipulate the cyber threat information data prior to sharing it for analysis. Liu D et al. [4] propose an efficient data integrity auditing scheme which can be used in enterprise multimedia security. Guan Y et al. [5] propose the unique data security and privacy design challenges presented by the fog layer and highlight the reasons why the data protection techniques in cloud computing cannot be directly applied in fog computing. Han W et al. [6] propose a Mapreduce-style algorithm, named Mapreduce-style Fast Non-Technical Loss Fraud Detection scheme (Mapreduce-style FNFD), to detect Non-Technical Loss fraud in Smart Grid. Guan Y et al. [7] discuss the design issues for data security and privacy in fog computing and present the unique data security and privacy design challenges presented by the fog layer. Puthal D et al. [8] propose a novel load balancing technique that enables EDC authentication as well as identification of idle EDCs for better load balancing and strengthen the security of the network by incorporating destination EDC authentication.

However, the above-mentioned related research mainly focuses on the application and improvement of one or a few security tools, and does not conduct data security protection for the overall network of the cloud and the edge, and lacks cost optimization considerations. Therefore, it is necessary to propose a data security model that takes into account both cost and protection effects to solve the data security problem of the edge and the cloud as a whole network. This paper proposes a data security protection capability evaluation model based on inspiration from papers [9–11].

3 Data Security Protection Evaluation Model

As user data gradually sinks, the original cloud-pipe-end model has gradually evolved into a cloud-edge-end model. A typical edge computing architecture is shown in Fig. 1. Under this architecture, the terminal device is the end of the architecture and is mainly responsible for display and interaction. As the first node of calculation and analysis, the edge node is responsible for processing and analyzing data near the terminal. Because the cloud computing center has the most computing and storage resources, it is responsible for processing resource-intensive computing analysis and storing data that needs to be stored for a long time. This architecture realizes intelligent data analysis and application through the close cooperation of cloud computing centers, edge nodes, and network terminals.

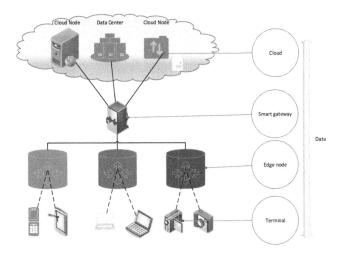

Fig. 1. Edge computing architecture.

Under the architecture in Fig. 1, the enterprise's network is divided into three layers, which are labeled as terminal (L1), edge (L2), and cloud (L3). After expert argumentation and research, the terminal layer needs to deploy a firewall to control the flow of data across different levels, and the edge needs to deploy a firewall, sensor trusted security monitoring system, identity authentication and access control, vulnerability scanning system, antivirus software, data identification and traceability System, the cloud needs to deploy firewalls, identity authentication and access control systems, vulnerability scanning systems, antivirus software, data identification and traceability systems, intrusion detection systems, data desensitization systems, data watermarking systems, and storage data encryption systems. Now use the following method in Table 1 to identify the required tools:

Table 1. Data security protection subsystem and its identification.

Label	Description
FW	Firewall
S	Sensor credible safety monitoring system
A	Identity authentication and access control system
V	Vulnerability Scanning System
I	anti-virus software
T	Data identification and traceability system
IDS	Intrusion detection system
DM	Data masking system
DW	Data Watermarking System
DE	Storage data encryption system

For tool set $\{FW, S, A, V, I, T, IDS, DM, DW, DE\}$, assuming that the data security score weights of each layer are W_1, W_2, and W_3 respectively, then the data security protection capability scores are:

$$score = W_1 \times score_{L1} + W_2 \times score_{L2} + W_3 \times score_{L3} \tag{1}$$

Each protective device of each layer of L1, L2, L3 needs to be preset with a weight according to the actual situation, forming the following weight matrix:

$$W = \begin{bmatrix} w_{00} & w_{01} & w_{02} & w_{03} & w_{04} & w_{05} & w_{06} & w_{07} & w_{08} & w_{09} \\ w_{10} & w_{11} & w_{12} & w_{13} & w_{14} & w_{15} & w_{16} & w_{17} & w_{18} & w_{19} \\ w_{20} & w_{21} & w_{22} & w_{23} & w_{24} & w_{25} & w_{26} & w_{27} & w_{28} & w_{29} \end{bmatrix} \tag{2}$$

Among them, $w_{ij} \in [0,1][0,1]$, $i = \{0,1,2\}$, $j = \{0,1,2,3,4,5,6,7,8,9\}$.

The deployment of equipment at each layer of L1, L2, and L3 can form the following matrix:

$$K = \begin{bmatrix} k_{00} & k_{01} & k_{02} & k_{03} & k_{04} & k_{05} & k_{06} & k_{07} & k_{08} & k_{09} \\ k_{10} & k_{11} & k_{12} & k_{13} & k_{14} & k_{15} & k_{16} & k_{17} & k_{18} & k_{19} \\ k_{20} & k_{21} & k_{22} & k_{23} & k_{24} & k_{25} & k_{26} & k_{27} & k_{28} & k_{29} \end{bmatrix} \tag{3}$$

Among them, $k_{ij} \in \{0,1\}$.0 means that the device has not been deployed, and 1 means that the device has been deployed. The sub-item score matrix of data security protection capability is denoted by C, the protection capability score of each layer of equipment is denoted by $score_{Lm}$, and the total protection capability score is denoted by score, and then,

$$C = W \cdot K \tag{4}$$

$$score_{L1} = \sum c_{0j} \tag{5}$$

$$score_{L2} = \sum c_{1j} \tag{6}$$

$$score_{L3} = \sum c_{2j} \tag{7}$$

$$score = W_1 \times score_{L1} + W_2 \times score_{L2} + W_3 \times score_{L3} = \sum \left(W_{i+1} \times \sum c_{ij} \right) \tag{8}$$

When constructing a data security protection model, in addition to the protection effect, the cost of the model needs to be considered. Generally speaking, the cost of the model consists of the fixed purchase cost of the equipment and the operating cost of the equipment. The operating cost of the equipment includes electricity and personnel maintenance costs. t represents, the operating cost is represented by $PW \times t$, the fixed purchase cost is represented by FC, and the model cost is represented by cost. Then the model cost score calculation formula is as follows:

$$\cos t = PW \times t + FC \qquad (9)$$

For an enterprise, the default matrix K is the full mark model.

$$K = \begin{bmatrix} 1 & 0 & 0 & 0 & 0 & 0 & 0 & 0 & 0 & 0 \\ 1 & 1 & 1 & 1 & 1 & 1 & 0 & 0 & 0 & 0 \\ 1 & 0 & 1 & 1 & 1 & 1 & 1 & 1 & 1 & 1 \end{bmatrix} \qquad (10)$$

The weight of each layer is set to [0.2 0.4 0.4], then the score weight matrix can be set as:

$$C = \begin{bmatrix} 0.2 & 0 & 0 & 0 & 0 & 0 & 0 & 0 & 0 & 0 \\ 0.1 & 0.04 & 0.06 & 0.05 & 0.05 & 0.1 & 0 & 0 & 0 & 0 \\ 0.04 & 0 & 0.06 & 0.03 & 0.03 & 0.05 & 0.01 & 0.05 & 0.05 & 0.05 \end{bmatrix} \qquad (11)$$

Assuming FC = [1 2 0.2 0.5 0.5 8 10 0.6 4], PW = [0.01 0.01 0.01 0.01 0.01 0.01 0.01 0.01 0.01 0.01 0.01].

Then the corresponding protection cost scores are as follows:

$$\begin{aligned} cost = [1 + 0.01t \times 2 + 0.01t \times 0.2 + 0.01t \times 0.5 + 0.01t \times 0.5 + 0.01t \\ \times 8 + 0.01t \times 10 + 0.01t \times 0.6 + 0.01t \times 4 + 0.01t] \end{aligned} \qquad (12)$$

Then the protection ability score-cost score may be:

Table 2. Protection ability-cost score

score	cost
0.8	33.4 + 0.15t
0.4	12.2 + 0.06t
0.34	3 + 0.03t
0.3	2 + 0.02t
0.27	3.5 + 0.03t
0.24	3 + 0.02t
0.21	22.6 + 0.05t
0.2	1 + 0.01t
0.16	2.2 + 0.04t
0.15	1 + 0.02t
0.08	1 + 0.02t
0	0

Therefore, the protection score-cost curve is shown in the Fig. 2, 3, 4, 5, 6 and Fig. 7.

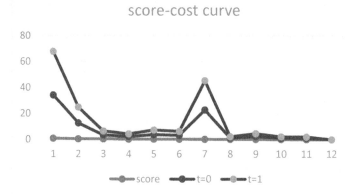

Fig. 2. Score-cost curve when t = 0 and t = 1.

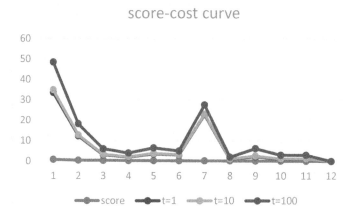

Fig. 3. Score-cost curve when t = 1, t = 10 and t = 100.

During the experiment, it was discovered that the same protection effect of a certain evaluation model may adopt different equipment deployment methods, and the cost of models with different methods may be very large. Therefore, the minimum cost under the same protection capability score can be obtained first according to the evaluation model, and then the strongest protection effect at the same cost will be got. It can be seen that as the t value changes, the trend of the curve is basically the same from Fig. 2, 3, 4, 5, 6 and Fig. 7. Therefore, in the actual data security model deployment process,

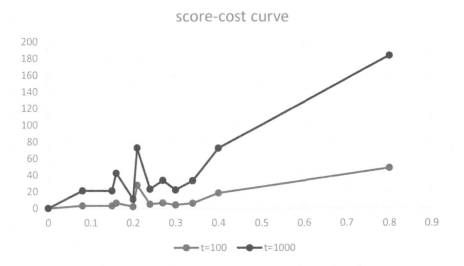

Fig. 4. Score-cost curve when t = 100 and t = 1000.

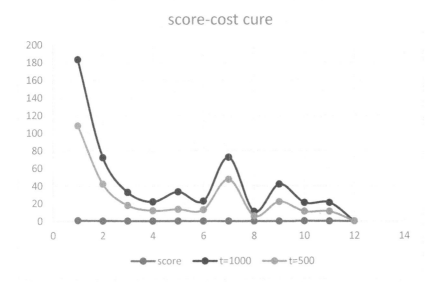

Fig. 5. Score-cost curve when t = 500 and t = 1000.

when the running time is short, the time factor has relatively weak influence on the results. The optimal data security protection model can be determined by considering the balance of equipment purchase costs and protection capability scores. However, when the running time is long enough, the score-cost curve tends to be flat. At this

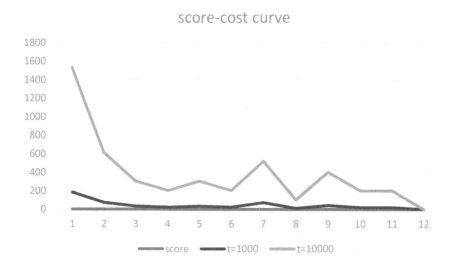

Fig. 6. Score-cost curve when t = 1000 and t = 10000.

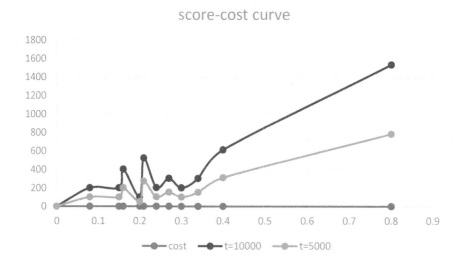

Fig. 7. Score-cost curve when t = 5000 and t = 10000.

time, the time factor accounts for a large proportion of the cost factor. No matter how the data security protection model is selected, the cost difference will be small, and the cost can be ignored at this time, but only consider the data security protection effect to choose the data security protection model.

4 Conclusion

This paper proposes a data security protection capability evaluation model based on weight presets for edge computing architecture, which quantitatively evaluates data security protection capabilities by setting the weight of protection equipment. Compared with the traditional qualitative evaluation model, it has a more intuitive effect. Besides, the model proposed in this paper takes into account the two factors of data security protection effect and cost at the same time, and realizes the optimal data security protection model judgment method by using the protection capability score-cost curve, which plays an important role in the evaluation of data security protection capability.

Conflicts of Interest. The authors declare that they have no conflicts of interest to report regarding the present study.

References

1. Shi, W., Cao, J., Zhang, Q., et al.: Edge computing: vision and challenges. Internet Things J. **3**(5), 637–646 (2016)
2. Zhang, J., Chen, B., Zhao, Y., et al.: Data security and privacy-preserving in edge computing paradigm: survey and open issues. IEEE Access 18209–18237 (2018)
3. Chadwick, D.W., Fan, W., Constantino, G., et al.: A cloud-edge based data security architecture for sharing and analysing cyber threat information. Future Generat. Comput. Syst. **102**, 710–722 (2020)
4. Liu, D., Shen, J., Vijayakumar, P., Wang, A., Zhou, T.: Efficient data integrity auditing with corrupted data recovery for edge computing in enterprise multimedia security. Multimedia Tools Applicat. **79**(15–16), 10851–10870 (2020). https://doi.org/10.1007/s11042-019-08558-1
5. Guan, Y., Shao, J., Wei, G., et al.: Data security and privacy in fog computing. IEEE Netw. **32**(5), 106–111 (2018)
6. Han, W., Xiao, Y.: Big data security analytic for smart grid with fog nodes. In: International Conference on Security. Springer, Cham (2016). https://doi.org/10.1007/978-3-319-49148-6_6
7. Guan, Y., Shao, J., Wei, G., et al.: Data security and privacy in fog computing. IEEE Netw. 106–111 (2018)
8. Puthal, D., Ranjan, R., Nanda, A., et al.: Secure authentication and load balancing of distributed edge datacenters. J. Parallel Distribut. Comput. **124**, 60–69 (2019)
9. Mahmoud, S., Salman, A.: Cost estimate and input energy of floor systems in low seismic regions. Comput. Mater. Continua **71**(2), 2159–2173 (2022)
10. Attaallah, A., Khan, R.A.: Estimating usable-security through hesitant fuzzy linguistic term sets based technique. Comput. Mater. Continua **70**(3), 5683–5705 (2022)
11. Aydi, W., Alduais, F.S.: Estimating weibull parameters using least squares and multilayer perceptron vs. Bayes estimation. Comput. Mater. Continua **71**(2), 4033–4050 (2022)

Research on Technical System for Cyberspace Surveying and Mapping

Wanli Kou[(⊠)], Lin Ni, and Jia Du

School of Information and Communication,
National University of Defense Technology, Xi'an 710106, China
56282618@qq.com

Abstract. With the rapid development of the network, various businesses continue to appear, and the number of cyberspace protection targets is increasing exponentially. How to find out the family background, recognize the risks, find out the loopholes and perceive the network security situation is an urgent problem to be solved. This paper briefly introduces the related concepts of cyberspace and cyberspace surveying and mapping, then analyzes the technical system of cyberspace surveying and mapping, and puts forward the iterative evolution technical framework of five links: target classification, collaborative detection, fusion analysis, visual mapping and system application. Among them, target classification is the basis of cyberspace surveying and mapping, and collaborative detection and fusion analysis are the key of Surveying and mapping, Visual mapping is the efficiency presentation of Surveying and mapping, and system application is the final surveying and mapping goal. Several stages of cyclic evolution make the surveying and mapping ability of cyberspace rise spirally. The purpose of this paper is to quickly and accurately find all kinds of asset targets in the network, timely perceive asset risk, and lay the foundation for the research progress of cyberspace mapping.

Keywords: Cyberspace surveying and mapping technology system ·
Cyberspace · Virtualization · Network security · Target classification ·
Cooperative detection

1 Introduction

With the application of IPv6, artificial intelligence, cloud computing and other new information technologies, computer network has been closely coupled with politics, economy, military and culture, and has become an indispensable part of our life and work [1–3]. However, while the computer network brings us convenience, hundreds of millions of assets and equipment are exposed to unknown threats every day, and the security risk has doubled exponentially. Without network security, there is no national security. How to timely perceive threats, identify and locate assets and accurately perceive the security situation in cyberspace before the outbreak of network threats has become an important part of the digital twin era. Compared with the real world, cyberspace confrontation also needs the help of maps to find out where important resources and assets in cyberspace are distributed, how they are related and whether

X. Sun et al. (Eds.): ICAIS 2022, CCIS 1587, pp. 566–574, 2022.
https://doi.org/10.1007/978-3-031-06761-7_45

there are risks. Cyberspace surveying and mapping technology came into being. Studying cyberspace surveying and mapping technology and comprehensively mastering cyberspace characteristics and resource distribution have very important theoretical significance and practical value for ensuring national security.

2 Concepts Related to Cyberspace Surveying and Mapping

The rapid development and popularization of network technology has bound the computer terminals related to human life and work to the Internet. The rapid rise of Internet of things, 5g and other related technologies has enabled more and more intelligent devices to access the Internet, and the era of "interconnection of all things" has come. Therefore, cyberspace is not only limited to computer network, but also has more extensive connotation and extension.

2.1 Cyberspace

The concept of cyberspace was first mentioned in the science fiction novel "neural Rover" in 1984. Since then, official institutions and many scholars at home and abroad have expounded cyberspace from different angles. Sterling et al. [4] believes that cyberspace depends on hardware, software equipment and other material bases. Adams et al. [5] believes that cyberspace is a space generated by the combination of Internet technology and social behavior. Fang et al. [6] further divided the constituent elements of cyberspace into four types: carrier, information, subject and operation. In the official documents, the national military strategy for cyberspace of the US military in 2006, the network security strategy of the UK in 2009, the network security strategy of Germany in 2011 and the network security strategic concept of Russia in 2014 all define cyberspace from different angles.

With the development and wide application of network technology, cyberspace has become the "second living space" of human production and life, and its connotation and extension are also changing. Combined with the understanding and understanding of cyberspace by scholars at home and abroad, the following definition of cyberspace is given. Cyberspace is an interactive network composed of Internet, communication system, network equipment, computer system and key industrial facilities. It uses electronic means to generate, store, transmit, process and apply information data to realize the control of the physical world and the impact on social activities. It can be seen that cyberspace is a special cosmic space covering material and social attributes.

2.2 Cyberspace Surveying and Mapping

The term "Surveying and mapping" originated from the discipline of geography. It refers to the measurement and collection of the shape, size, spatial location and attributes of natural geographical elements or surface artificial facilities within the scope of geospatial space, and the drawing of paper or electronic maps that meet the requirements. Since the 21st century, with the rapid development of network technology and network infrastructure, real geospatial and virtual cyberspace complement each other.

Geospatial carries cyberspace, and cyberspace expands geospatial infinitely. At present, it has reached the realm of "you have me, I have you".

China is in a critical period of rapid development of network and information technology, and cyberspace is facing more and more security threats. On April 19, 2016, in his speech at the Symposium on network security and informatization, President Xi stressed that "perceiving the network security situation is the most basic and basic work. We should comprehensively strengthen the network security inspection, find out the family background, recognize the risks, find out the loopholes, report the results and urge rectification". For cyberspace protection, finding out the family background and recognizing the risk means comprehensively finding out the number, status, type, distribution and relationship of cyberspace protection targets, so as to form the dynamic perception, accurate portrait and rapid positioning ability of cyberspace protection, so as to provide data support for situation early warning, information control and defense confrontation. Therefore, with the main purpose of network entity resource measurement and positioning, virtual resource detection and early warning, virtual and real mapping between cyberspace and geospatial, cyberspace surveying and mapping has gradually attracted the attention of scholars in the fields of Surveying and mapping and network.

As an interdisciplinary emerging technology, cyberspace surveying and mapping has no authoritative definition at present. In combination with the surveying and mapping objects, basic technologies and expected objectives of cyberspace surveying and mapping, cyberspace surveying and mapping can be defined as taking cyberspace protection objectives as the object, taking computer science, network science, surveying and Mapping Science and information science as the basis, and adopting network detection, network analysis, entity positioning, geographic surveying and mapping and other related technologies, The theory and technology of detecting the node distribution and network relationship index in Internet space, mapping it to geographic space, drawing its coordinates, topology, surrounding environment and other information in the form of map or other visual forms, showing the relevant situation, and carrying out spatial analysis and application based on it [7].

3 Technical System of Cyberspace Surveying and Mapping

Cyberspace mapping is a cyclic iterative process of collaborative detection, fusion analysis, visual mapping and system application based on the classification of protection targets (see Fig. 1). Collaborative detection and fusion analysis are the basis and key of cyberspace surveying and mapping. Visual mapping is the efficiency presentation of Surveying and mapping, and system application is the final surveying and mapping goal. Several stages of cyclic evolution make the ability of cyberspace surveying and mapping spiral.

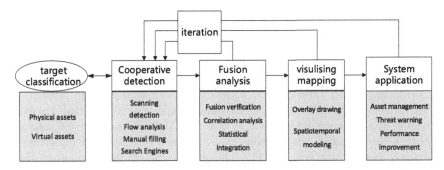

Fig. 1. Technical system of cyberspace surveying and mapping.

3.1 Target Classification

In a broad sense, cyberspace resources are the organic integration of various elements such as "carrier", "information", "subject" and "operation". Based on this, the goal of cyberspace surveying and mapping is to obtain comprehensive and complete information of various elements in cyberspace. The protection goal in cyberspace mapping is the network assets for security protection and strategic reinforcement in the network, including not only physical assets such as servers, routers and terminal equipment, but also virtual assets such as users, services, IP and ports (see Fig. 2).

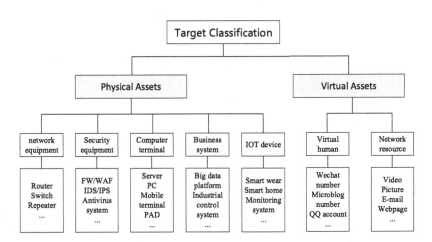

Fig. 2. The classification framework of Cyberspace assets.

Physical assets refer to the actual network elements that can be seen and touched, including network devices such as routers and switches, security devices such as firewalls and IDS, computer terminals such as servers and PCs, business systems such as big data platform and industrial control system, intelligent wear, monitoring system and other Internet of things devices. The mapping of physical resources in cyberspace is mainly to identify and map the attribute information, geographical location and associated topological relationship of physical resources. The geographic location, topological relationship and attribute information of physical assets are mapped among geographic space, cyberspace and social space to lay the foundation for later analysis and drawing.

Virtual assets refer to images, sounds and text information stored in cyberspace in electronic form. Compared with physical assets, its existence form is intangible, mainly including virtual human information such as WeChat, QQ number and microblog number, video resources, image resources, E-main and other network resources. The mapping of virtual assets is mainly through data extraction of the basic information of the target account and its website content information and account friend relationship, and association through identity information in the technology of data extraction, so as to avoid various gullies caused by virtual identity in the virtual cyberspace and carry out visual rendering in the later stage.

3.2   Cooperative Detection

The target detection and acquisition of cyberspace mapping is the basis and key of cyberspace mapping. At present, there are many classification methods. For example, according to the detection content, it can be divided into traffic detection, topology detection and performance detection [8]. According to the adopted protocol, it can be divided into detection based on BGP, TCP/IP, SNMP and other protocols. In order to realize the detection of large-scale, complex and diverse cyberspace resources, the detection of cyberspace resources needs to carry out all-round collaborative detection by means of active scanning, traffic analysis, search engine and manual filling (see Fig. 3).

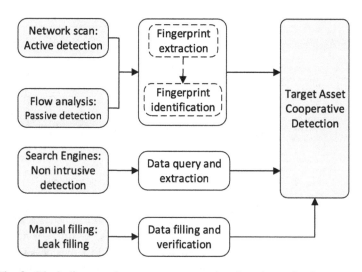

Fig. 3. Block diagram of target asset cooperative detection technology system.

Active scanning detection obtains the fingerprint information of the target asset by first constructing a specific data packet locally and sending it to the target host, and then extracting and collecting information according to the data packet returned from the target host (mainly including the protocol data packet of the transport layer and application layer and the retransmission waiting time of the packet). Then match the detected target results with the local fingerprint database of the system to identify the fingerprint information such as the code language type of the asset, the asset operating system type, the service and application type, and the open port range of the asset. Common scanning detection technologies include host detection technology based on TCP or ICMP, port detection technology based on TCP flag bit and UDP, server detection technology based on open port and banner return judgment, operating system detection technology based on Ping and protocol stack fingerprint identification judgment, fingerprint identification methods based on TCP/IP protocol lifetime and service type Fingerprint identification method based on application layer protocol, service identification and file characteristics. Active scanning can also be assisted by LAN detection suite, which, as an extension of the client, mainly solves the problem of blocking detection by protective equipment such as firewall.

Flow analysis is a passive detection technology. It needs to deploy probes in the network to monitor and continuously monitor and analyze the traffic on the network. According to the different characteristics of data packets of different protocols, comprehensively analyze the special fields in each protocol (mainly the fields containing relevant information of target assets) to obtain the relevant information of the target host. In traffic monitoring, sniff and analyze the data packets of mainstream protocols such as HTTP, SMTP, telnet and FTP, and extract and analyze the fingerprint characteristics of special fields such as banner or TCP triple handshake data packets and DHCP protocol data packets, so as to obtain the identification and collection of effective information such as host operating system, port, service and application of the target asset. Traffic analysis needs to be supplemented by topology restoration technology based on fusion analysis. By fusing multi class and multi-layer network protocol packets, the link attributes are described from multiple angles and levels, so as to improve the accuracy and integrity of the results of network analysis. Through the mutual verification of multi-source traffic data from external systems, the accuracy of network traffic analysis is further improved.

Search engine technology has experienced four generations of development. At present, the mainstream is to understand the needs of users and focus on providing personalized content results for different users. By using AI intelligent technology, adopting strategies such as feature extraction and text intelligence, and combining with manual intervention, the personalized search and query ability and search efficiency are enhanced. In addition to the full development and application of mainstream general search engines such as Google, Bing and Baidu, a number of search engines dedicated to cyberspace exploration (such as Shodan and zoomeye) have also been greatly developed, which provides a foundation for the implementation of search engine network asset detection system.

In addition, it is also necessary to check the loopholes and fill in the deficiencies under the constraints and incentives of the system and mechanism, and complete the target collection through manual registration, mainly to solve the problems of incomplete and inaccurate detection of defense targets. In this way, resource detection is carried out through active scanning combined with LAN suite, information is obtained through passive and manual methods, and then such information is further detected in cyberspace through active methods, so as to obtain more and more comprehensive results.

3.3   Fusion Analysis

Data analysis extracts resources and their related attributes from the detection results, and carries out the process of analysis, modeling and association mapping, so as to realize the high-precision panoramic portrait of cyberspace protection targets. However, the types and attributes of cyberspace protection targets are rich and diverse. The amount of data obtained through collaborative detection is huge and the relationship is complex, which is a certain distance from the requirements for resource data in the next visual rendering and even system application. Therefore, the collected resource data needs to be processed by cross verification based on multi-class resource fusion and association mapping based on multi-source data fusion. Through data fusion, data verification and data analysis, the depth and accurate analysis of protection targets can be realized; Through the aggregation, fusion and verification of protection target information, the data from different sources are standardized, sorted and stored to form a diversified protection target information base.

In the analysis of network topology fusion, based on the results of multi-source data fusion, the network topology map is presented from the multi-dimensional aspects of network space location, protection target entity attribute, virtual attribute and management attribute. Traceroute technology, UDP based topology detection technology and TCMP based detection technology are often used in topology analysis. They all send different detection packets to the target host and record the TTL value to comprehensively analyze the network path and topology.

The fusion analysis of important network assets is generally based on the combination of knowledge map, association analysis, similar target clustering and other means. The convolution neural network method is used to infer and mine the missing attributes of network assets [9]. The website fingerprint is constructed and identified by self-encoder and various deep neural networks to construct the relationship map between cyberspace and physical space, Obtain the organizational structure, key persons, IP address, device details, open port/service details, vulnerability information and other information of network assets.

In view of the huge amount of data and the inability of a single data source to include cyberspace resource objects and complex data types, in order to achieve accurate resource analysis, it is necessary to use the relationship between various resource features for cross verification and association mapping, comprehensively process multi-source information, and iteratively feedback the problems found in the fusion process to the collaborative detection stage, Realize the accurate description of cyberspace resources and their attributes.

3.4 Visual Mapping

The traditional network map only presents the topology of the network structure and visualizes the information flow of network nodes. It ignores the space-time coordinate mapping relationship between the real geographical space and the virtual network space, resulting in unclear space-time relationship and not very consistent with human visual thinking. Therefore, it is difficult to further mine and utilize network information with the help of the traditional network map.

The visual presentation in cyberspace surveying and mapping needs to integrate the theories and technologies of computer science, geography, surveying and mapping and other related fields. On the basis of collaborative detection and fusion analysis of cyberspace, multi-dimensional cyberspace resources and their relationships are mapped to the visual space, and a visualization system of network resource elements is constructed Overlay the network spatial mapping results on the cross-scale spatio-temporal map to realize the visual expression, situation analysis and deduction of geographic network spatial information [10].

In terms of rendering technology, research teams at home and abroad have proposed telecommunications network analysis methods of cyberspace geographic images, some rules of cyberspace landscape mapping, topology visualization and other methods, which can visualize the relationship between geospatial and physical network topology. The scholar Guo Li team proposed the methods of overlay rendering of multi class resources in cyberspace and spatio-temporal modeling of geospatial and cyberspace, which can draw high-dimensional and dynamic virtual resources. After the visual presentation and even the actual system is completed, it is necessary to continuously feed back to the collaborative detection iteration and repeatedly optimize to obtain the optimal cyberspace mapping effect [11].

4 Conclusion

With the rapid advancement and development of virtualization, big data, deep learning and other technologies, cyberspace mapping has made some progress in threat early warning and emergency response, asset management, exposure analysis and network performance improvement. However, due to the complexity of cyberspace assets and the dynamics of network assets, the accuracy and real-time of asset identification, asset positioning and threat judgment need to be improved. This requires continuous iterative optimization and improvement in target classification, collaborative detection, fusion analysis, visual mapping, system application and other links, so as to comprehensively find out the family background and recognize the risks [12, 13].

References

1. Sood, I., Sharma, V.: Computational intelligent techniques to detect DDOS attacks: a survey. J. Cyber Secur. 3(2), 89–106 (2021)

2. Bautista-Villalpando, L., Abran, A.: A data security framework for cloud computing services. Comput. Syst. Sci. Eng. **37**(2), 203–218 (2021)
3. Alzahrani, F.A.: Estimating security risk of healthcare web applications: a design perspective. Comput. Mater. Continua **67**(1), 187–209 (2021)
4. Vinciguerra, S., Frenken, K., Valente, M.: The geography of the internet infrastructure: a simulation approach based on the Barabasi-Albert model. Evol. Econ. Geogr. **63**(1), 19–37 (2010)
5. Adams, P.C.: A taxonomy for communication geography. Prog. Hum. Geogr. **35**(1), 37–57 (2011)
6. Fang, B.X.: Define cyberspace security. J. Netw. Inf. Secur. **4**(1), 1–5 (2018)
7. Zhou, Y., Xu, Q., Luo, X.Y., Liu, F.L., Zhang, L., Hu, X.F.: Research on the concept and technical system of cyberspace surveying and mapping. Comput. Sci. **45**(05), 1–7 (2018)
8. Motamedi, R., Rejaie, R., Willinger, W.: A survey of techniques for Internet topology discovery. IEEE Commun. Surv. Tut. **17**(2), 1044–1065 (2015)
9. Cao, Y.N., Wang, S., Li, X.X., Cao, C., Liu, Y.B., Tan, J.L.: Inferring social network user's interest based on convolutional neural network. In: Proceedings of the International Conference on Neural Information Processing, pp. 657–666 (2017)
10. Fang, B.X., Zou, P., Zhu, S.B.: Research on cyberspace sovereignty. Eng. Sci. **18**(6), 1–7 (2016)
11. Guo, L., et al.: Mapping of cyberspace resources: concepts and technologies. J. Inf. Secur. **3**(4), 1–14 (2018)
12. Li, T., Hu, Y., Ju, A., Hu, Z.: Adversarial active learning for named entity recognition in cybersecurity. Comput. Mater. Continua **66**(1), 407–420 (2021)
13. Alsharif, M., Mishra, S., AlShehri, M.: Impact of human vulnerabilities on cybersecurity. Comput. Syst. Sci. Eng. **40**(3), 1153–1166 (2022)

Software-Defined Industrial Internet of Things (SD-IIoT) Oriented for Industry 4.0

Pengfei Hu[1,2(✉)] ⓘ, Chunming He[3], and Yan Sun[4]

[1] Research Institute of HollySys Group Co., Ltd., Beijing 100176, China
hupengfei@hollysys.com
[2] Beijing HollySys Co., Ltd., Beijing 100176, China
[3] HollySys Group Co., Ltd., Beijing 100176, China
[4] China Industrial Control Systems Cyber Emergency Response Team,
Beijing 100040, China

Abstract. The Industrial Internet of Things (IIoT) enables interconnection and intelligent collaboration among basic industrial production factors which include human, machine, thing, method and environment. In the current IIoT applications, it is difficult for collaborative optimization and unified management and control of industrial production factors. Applications and industrial production factors are tightly coupled, so that many industrial software applications generally have the problems such as high degree of customization and difficult replication and promotion. In this paper, focusing on the most basic industrial production factors, we propose the solution and system architecture of software-defined Industrial Internet of Things (SD-IIoT) based on the ideas and technologies of software definition and Cyber-Physical System (CPS). The principle of SD-IIoT is introduced from the perspective of cyber-physical space mapping. On basis of the digital twin models of industrial production factors, the system architecture of SD-IIoT is designed, which decouples upper-level industrial applications from the underlying industrial production factors. Furthermore, the software definition mechanism based on industrial information model is proposed to abstract and describe industrial production factors with semantic technology to implement the virtualized modeling. The SD-IIoT paradigm can maximize the utilization of resources, and achieve the modular management, on-demand reusing, dynamic reconfigurability and efficient collaboration of industrial production factors, thus improving overall service capability of IIoT.

Keywords: Industrial Internet of Things (IIoT) · Cyber-Physical System (CPS) · Industrial production factor · Software definition · Industrial information model

1 Introduction

The development of information and communication technologies, Internet of Things (IoT), Cyber-Physical System (CPS) and embedded systems is promoting and driving the industrial upgrading and evolution. The current industrial mode is moving towards the Industry 4.0 era [1]. In this context, operational technology (OT), information technology (IT) and communication technology (CT) are integrated into OICT, and cyber space and physical space are also converged into CPS. The characteristics of "integration", "collaboration" and "intelligence" enable the adjustment and change of overall system architecture of Industrial Internet [2].

In Industry 4.0 context, the bottom production units are fully interconnected and intercommunicated to realize data closed-loop and promote end-to-end data circulation and integration [3]. The organizational boundaries and information islands are broken. Through the decoupling between software and hardware and the deconstruction of process flow, the mapping relationship between physical space and cyber space is established to form a virtual industrial panorama and intelligent knowledge graph. Industrial enterprises will accelerate the construction of a new industrial production system with data driven, software definition, virtual-real mapping and intelligence [4].

As the core and key technology of Industry 4.0, the Industrial Internet of Things (IIoT) implements the interconnection and intercommunication among industrial production factors (i.e., human, machine, thing, method and environment) [5]. These production factors are the most basic elements of industry. Almost all industrial applications are developed and operated on the basis of them. Therefore, the unified management and control, collaborative optimization and integration analysis for industrial production factors are the core tasks of IIoT [6].

In the current industrial applications, applications and industrial production factors are tightly coupled. Software and hardware are also tightly coupled, and resources are bound with applications. This is a hardware-defined mode, which lacks flexibility. Due to the lack of top-level design, many software applications generally have problems such as high degree of customization and difficult replication and promotion. Furthermore, there are a large number of chimney-style industrial applications. This results in the piecemeal "information island", "data island" and "application island". Although industrial enterprises have massive data, they encounter difficulties in data management, operation and integration, and cannot really create core value for enterprises.

Therefore, it is necessary that a more flexible IIoT architecture with the ability to carry out effective information exchange should be designed to enhance the reliability and scalability of complex industrial applications [7]. Currently, there are some IIoT platforms designed from the perspective of industry 4.0. For example, MindSphere of SIEMENS, Predix of GE, ABB Ability, and so on. They adopt IIoT, cloud computing, artificial intelligence (AI) and other advanced technologies to support the agile development and deployment of industrial applications. These platforms implement the interconnection of industrial equipments, the intelligent analysis and decision of big data, and the construction of core capability and basic development environment. However, they pay less attention to the most basic industrial production factors at the bottom. And they rarely virtualize and digitize the bottom production unit completely. It is difficult to construct a highly flexible and reconfigurable industrial operating system.

In this paper, based on the ideas and technologies of software definition and CPS, we propose the solution and system architecture of software-defined Industrial Internet of Things (SD-IIoT). Different from the other existing software definition objects (e.g., software-defined networking (SDN), software-defined data center (SDDC), etc.), we take the human, machine, thing, method and environment in industry scenario as research objects. Starting from the most basic industrial elements, we can build a unified IIoT platform based on digital twins to meet the new application demands of Industry 4.0.

The principle of SD-IIoT is proposed from the perspective of cyber-physical space mapping. The human, machine, thing, method and environment are respectively abstracted and virtualized into digital twin models by industrial information model technology to realize the mapping from the physical space to the cyber space. It decouples the hardware and software. The control and management functions are separated from physical industrial objects, and running it as software instead. The programmers of industrial applications do not need to worry about the details of underlying physical objects. Through the software definition mechanism, the on-demand management and dynamic reconfiguration of industrial production factors can be realized.

The system architecture of SD-IIoT is designed. Different from traditional IIoT system architecture, our proposed scheme is based on the digital twin models of industrial production factors. The proposed SD-IIoT platform downward manage all kinds of industrial production factors through the virtualization modeling technology, and upward provide various resources and public services for various IIoT applications through programmable functions of management. Furthermore, the software definition mechanism based on industrial information model is proposed to abstract and describe industrial production factors. The semantic technology are adopted to implement the virtualized description modeling. The SD-IIoT paradigm focuses on implementing a dynamic and reconfigurable smart IIoT system. The various industrial product factors can be flexibly managed, on-demand reused, maximumly utilized and efficiently collaborated to improve overall service capability of IIoT.

The rest of this paper is organized as follows. Section 2 presents the overview of SD-IIoT. Section 3 proposes the system architecture of SD-IIoT. Section 4 proposes software definition mechanism based on industrial information model for SD-IIoT. Section 5 draws a conclusion.

2   The Overview of SD-IIoT Based on Cyber-Physical Space Mapping

The paradigm of software definition is proposed to manage the hardware infrastructure in a flexible, dynamic and reconfigurable way [8]. It decouples the original highly coupled and integrated hardware into different components through standardization and virtualization. Then a virtualized software layer is established for these basic hardware [9]. By providing application programming interface (API) for the virtualized software layer, the controllable part of hardware is exposed to realize the functions provided by original hardware. Finally, through the management and control software, the hardware system is automatically deployed, optimized and managed to provide open, flexible and intelligent services [10]. Software definition technology can realize the maximum utilization and efficient collaboration of resources [11].

The core of software definition is hardware resource virtualization and programmable management function. The essence is to expose the controllable components of hardware through virtualization and its APIs, so as to realize the on-demand management of hardware. Specifically, it abstracts basic hardware resources (such as computing, storage and network) into virtualized resources, which are managed and called by system software. On this basis, users can develop applications and access the services provided by resources, so as to change the behavior of resources and meet the diverse needs of applications for resources [12].

In the industrial scenario, the basic production factors is composed of human, machine, thing, method and environment. The IIoT implements the interconnection and intercommunication among these production factors. By introducing the idea and technology of software definition into IIoT, we propose the SD-IIoT paradigm from the perspective of cyber-physical mapping in this article. It extends the concepts of software definition and virtualization modeling to the various production factors. The software definition mechanism realizes the flexible management, on-demand reusing, dynamic reconfiguration, modular combination and efficient collaboration of them.

The idea of SD-IIoT is consistent with cyber-physical space mapping in CPS. Figure 1 presents the cyber-physical mapping processes of SD-IIoT paradigm.

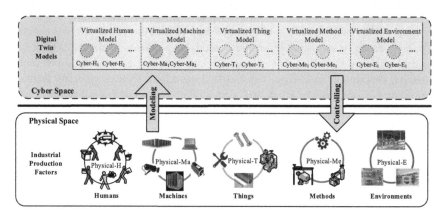

Fig. 1. Cyber-physical mapping processes of SD-IIoT paradigm.

The processes mainly involve mapping in two directions:

The Mapping from Physical Space to Cyber Space. This is a modeling process. The human, machine, thing, method and environment in industry scenario are connected to cyber space through various ways. The raw data of their identifier (ID), attributes, behaviors and events are obtained from physical space. By analyzing and processing these raw data and related history data, further in-depth information and knowledge can be abstracted and extracted. Combined with industrial information model technology, the virtual digital mapping model (also known as digital twin model) is constructed. These models are the unique and comprehensive digital counterpart or digital clone of corresponding industrial production factors. The relationship between virtual model and industrial production factor is a one-to-one correspondence. They always keep in synchronization throughout their lifecycle.

The Mapping from Cyber Space to Physical Space. This is a controlling process. Based on the digital twin models of industrial production factors, flexible and intelligent services can be provided to support various industrial applications. Upper industrial applications interact directly with these models. They can obtain data and resources on demand through models. The results of industrial applications will be fed back to the model first. Then the objects in physical space are controlled through the state synchronization mechanism between model and physical production factor.

SD-IIoT realizes the maximum utilization of various production factors and improves the information interaction through software definition mechanism. In addition, it also achieves the decoupling and separation between upper industrial applications and lower production factors. The control and management functions are separated from physical objects, and running it as software instead. The application developers and programmers do not need to worry about the details of underlying physical objects.

Based on the software definition mechanism for IIoT, each manufacturing unit can automatically exchange information, trigger action and realize control independently in the whole product life cycle, so as to transform the industry mode to intelligence. The goal of SD-IIoT is to establish a highly flexible and digital production and service mode, and realize the independent information interaction and collaboration among various production factors.

3   The System Architecture of SD-IIoT

For the demands of unified management and control, collaborative optimization and integration analysis of industrial production factors in the context of Industry 4.0, a flexible and open IIoT system architecture need to be designed. Figure 2 shows the system architecture of SD-IIoT. Compared with the traditional industrial Internet architecture, it is a hierarchical decoupling architecture, and adds the SD-IIoT platform to achieve software definition and virtualization modeling for all the industrial production factors.

In essence, the SD-IIoT platform is a cloud-based open industrial operating system. Its function is similar to Windows, Android or iOS in the field of information technology. Downward, SD-IIoT platform manages all kinds of industrial production factors through the virtualized modeling technology. Upward, SD-IIoT platform provides model data, resources and public services to support the development and deployment of various IIoT applications through programmable functions of management. In this way, the decoupling and separation between upper applications and lower production factors are realized. The upper applications don't need to pay too much attention to the details of the lower layer. This reduces the difficulty of application development.

In this system architecture, all the industrial production factors are connected into the SD-IIoT platform in various ways. They are uniformly managed and scheduled through the SD-IIoT platform.

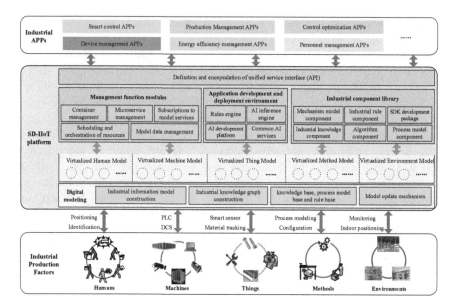

Fig. 2. System architecture of SD-IIoT.

The functions of every layer in the SD-IIoT platform are as follows.

Digital Modeling. The digital modeling for industrial production factors is the basis and core of the overall software definition mechanism. It abstracts and maps the human, machine, thing, method and environment into the virtual digital twin models from the physical space to the cyber space. This will support that various production factors can be understood, discovered, shared, and scheduled by multiple IIoT applications.

All the objects connected into platform need to be assigned a unique identifier (ID) to facilitate the discovery and addressing of object, data and service capability. Usually, there are two main types of IIoT identification methods, which include investitive identification and natural attribute-based identification. The former is artificially assigned, and usually composed of numbers, letters and symbols according to the corresponding coding rules. The latter is based on unique identity features of natural attributes, for example, face, fingerprint, physical unclonable function properties, etc. The object identity resolution is a process which the ID is recognized and resolved to obtain the related information of objects. Based on IIoT identification and resolution, all the industrial production factors and their model data can be managed and discovered quickly and exactly [13].

The industrial information model technologies based on semantic are adopted to realize the semantic intercommunication [14]. In addition, the domain specific knowledge base, process model base and rule base are constructed to present how these industrial production factors should be combined and cooperate with each other to solve some practical problems.

In SDD-IIoT paradigm, there is a one-to-one relationship between virtual twin model and production factor. Therefore, the automatic update mechanism of models needs to be considered and deployed to ensure the consistency between production factors and digital twin models. It includes the changes of object properties, relationship, technological process, and so on.

Virtual Twin Model Library. The digital twin models need to be transformed into the data expression form that can be understood and processed by machines. Then the virtual twin model library is responsible for managing and storing the formal twin models and data of all industrial production factor throughout their lifecycle. The virtual twin model library includes virtualized human, machine, thing, method and environment models. Some programmable interfaces are defined to handle and operated models data. Furthermore, when the object in physical space changes, the corresponding virtual twin model in library need to be updated and adjusted synchronously.

Platform Basic Capabilities. The platform basic capabilities mainly serve and support the upper IIoT applications. On the basis of digital twin models of production factors, the management function module, application development and deployment environment, and industrial component library are built respectively. They are defined and packaged into unified service interface (API) to support various smart industrial applications. These basic capabilities and algorithms enable efficient utilization of resources and intelligent collaboration of production factors.

The SDD-IIoT paradigm maximizes the utilization of resources, and achieves the uniform management, sharing and reusing, dynamic reconfigurability of industrial production factors. Through the SDD-IIoT platform, the data of OT system and IT system are collected and modeled uniformly and form a data source. Based on the uniform data source, industrial applications are developed and deployed by model analysis. Moreover, industrial applications can schedule and control physical resources in turn. In this way, a complete closed loop of CPS is implemented in Industry 4.0 context.

Through the SDD-IIoT paradigm, the breeding and rise of a number of new modes and new business formats is promoted in industry. Some typical industrial application modes will be presented, for example, platform-based design, intelligent manufacturing, networked collaboration, personalized customization, service-oriented extension, and digital management.

4 Software Definition Mechanism Based on Industrial Information Model for SD-IIoT

Industrial information model is a standard digital description and modeling for the various industrial production factors in IIoT at the semantic level. It is an abstracted description of objects with a group of simplified information according to specific rules. The purpose is to realize the standardized expression of information among industrial constituent elements. It provides a language that can be understood by all participants for the interaction and cooperation among industrial objects. It builds a bridge of mutual mapping, interconnection, intercommunication and interoperability between physical space and cyber space [15, 16].

In this paper, we adopt the industrial information model technology based on semantic to describe and model industrial production factors. This is the basis and core of the overall software definition mechanism for SD-IIoT paradigm. The basic framework of model consists of ID, class and attribute. Moreover, the class can contain ID, subclass and attribute, and the subclass can also contain ID, subclass and attribute. In this framework, the ID, class and attribute can be extended according to the practical demands of information interaction. Figure 3 shows the illustrative information model of industrial motor.

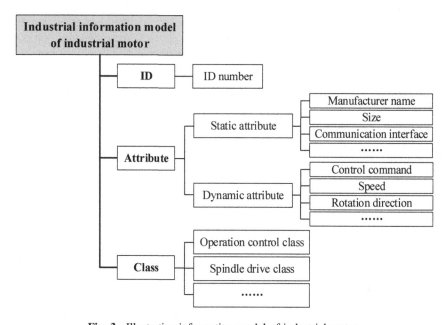

Fig. 3. Illustrative information model of industrial motor.

ID. ID mainly realizes the marking and identification of information model. It runs through the whole life cycle of information model as a unique mark. ID can be composed of meaningless strings, which is only used for the uniqueness mark of the information model. It can also be composed of meaningful strings. For example, the ID coding and resolution based on data dictionary can describe the information model on the premise of meeting the uniqueness mark.

Class. Class is the abstraction of information with common characteristics expressed or represented by the information model. It includes industry class, product class, collection class, communication class, engineering class, configuration class, alarm and event class, network security class, control class, service class, etc. For example, a service class refers to the specific services that can be implemented, which is used to describe the modular business function combination of an object. The service class can be composed of attributes, commands and events. Attributes refer to the status data collected by objects. Commands are operations or methods performed by objects. Events refer to the behavior and configuration parameters of data actively reported by objects [17].

Attribute. The attribute part covers the various attribute information of industrial objects, including data, interface, status, relationship, etc. It reflects the professional description of object knowledge. Attributes can be divided into static attribute and dynamic attribute. Static attribute is a general description of the static properties and relationships of objects. It is generally related to the description of object entities, such as shape, size, etc. Dynamic attribute is a description of the dynamic properties and relationships of objects. It is generally related to environment and business description, such as temperature, speed, etc.

In order to enable the computer and upper application program to understand the abstract model information, the Resource Description Framework (RDF) language is adopted to formalize the model description. It converts them into a semantic language form that the machines can understand.

The industrial information model implements standard digital description and expression for the industrial production factors from three dimensions of ID, class and attribute. The disordered attribute data of various industrial objects can be defined, organized, correlated and stored into their digital twin models in an orderly form, so as to be cognized, understood and processed by industrial service and applications. This forms the basis of software definition mechanism for SD-IIoT.

5   Conclusion

In this paper, we focus on the most basic industrial production factors (namely human, machine, thing, method and environment), and have proposed the solution and system architecture of SD-IIoT. By introducing the ideas and technologies of software definition and CPS into IIoT area, we have proposed the principle of SD-IIoT paradigm from the perspective of cyber-physical space mapping. Based on the digital twin models of production factors, the system architecture of SD-IIoT has also designed. The proposed SD-IIoT platform can be regarded as a cloud-based open industrial operating system. It downward manages all kinds of industrial production factors through the virtualization modeling, and upward provides various resources and public services for various IIoT applications through programmable functions of management. Furthermore, the software definition mechanism based on industrial information model has been proposed to abstract and describe production factors by adopting the semantic technology. The proposed SD-IIoT scheme can maximize the utilization of resources, achieve the modular management, on-demand reusing, dynamic reconfigurability and efficient collaboration of industrial production factors, and improve overall service capability of IIoT. This provides a new mode and technology framework for the IIoT applications in the context of Industrial 4.0.

Acknowledgement. This work was supported by the National Key R&D Program of China (No. 2019YFB1705100).

References

1. Aazam, M., Zeadally, S., Harras, K.A.: Deploying fog computing in industrial Internet of Things and Industry 4.0. IEEE Trans. Industr. Inform. **14**(10), 4674–4682 (2018)
2. Leitão, P., Karnouskos, S., Ribeiro, L., Lee, J., Strasser, T., Colombo, A.W.: Smart agents in industrial cyber–physical systems. Proc. IEEE **104**(5), 1086–1101 (2016)
3. Fakhri, A.B., Mohammed, S.L., Khan, I., Sadiq, A.S., Alkazemi, B.: Industry 4.0: architecture and equipment revolution. Comput. Mater. Contin. **66**(2), 1175–1194 (2021)
4. Bajic, B., Rikalovic, A., Suzic, N., Piuri, V.: Industry 4.0 implementation challenges and opportunities: a managerial perspective. IEEE Syst. J. **15**(1), 546–559 (2021)
5. Kaur, K., Garg, S., Aujla, G.S., Kumar, N., Rodrigues, J., Guizani, M.: Edge computing in the industrial internet of things environment: software-defined-networks-based edge-cloud interplay. IEEE Commun. Mag. **56**(2), 44–51 (2018)
6. Karmakar, A., Dey, N., Baral, T., Chowdhury, M., Rehan, M.: Industrial Internet of Things: a review. In: 2019 International Conference on Opto-Electronics and Applied Optics (Optronix), pp. 1–6. IEEE (2019)
7. Delfino, L.R., Garcia, A.S., Moura, R.L.: Industrial Internet of Things: digital twins. In: 2019 SBMO/IEEE MTT-S International Microwave and Optoelectronics Conference (IMOC), pp. 1–3. IEEE (2019)
8. Mei, H.: Understanding "software-defined" from an OS perspective: technical challenges and research issues. Sci. China Inf. Sci. **60**, 271–273 (2017)
9. Nunes, B.A.A., Mendonca, M., Nguyen, X.N., Obraczka, K., Turletti, T.: A survey of software-defined networking: past, present, and future of programmable networks. IEEE Commun. Surv. Tutor. **16**(3), 1617–1634 (2014)
10. Kreutz, D., Ramos, F.M.V., Veríssimo, P.E., Rothenberg, C.E., Azodolmolky, S., Uhlig, S.: Software-defined networking: a comprehensive survey. Proc. IEEE **103**(1), 14–76 (2015)
11. Jararweh, Y., Al-Ayyoub, M., Darabseh, A., Benkhelifa, E., Vouk, M., Rindos, A.: SDIoT: a software defined based Internet of Things framework. J. Ambient. Intell. Humaniz. Comput. **6**(4), 453–461 (2015)
12. Hu, P., Chen, W., He, C., Li, Y., Ning, H.: Software-defined edge computing (SDEC): principle, open IoT system architecture, applications, and challenges. IEEE Internet Things J. **7**(7), 5934–5945 (2020)
13. Hu, P., Ning, H., Qiu, T., Zhang, Y., Luo, X.: Fog computing based face identification and resolution scheme in Internet of Things. IEEE Trans. Industr. Inf. **13**(4), 1910–1920 (2017)
14. Shi, F., Li, Q., Zhu, T., Ning, H.: A survey of data semantization in Internet of Things. Sensors **18**(1), 313–332 (2018)
15. Li, Y., Cheng, T., Pan, L.: Research and application of information model of industrial robot welding system based on OPC UA. In: 2021 IEEE 2nd International Conference on Big Data, Artificial Intelligence and Internet of Things Engineering (ICBAIE), pp. 1084–1087. IEEE (2021)
16. Schmied, S., Großmann, D., Mathias, S.G., Mueller, R.K.: An approach for an industrial information model management. In: 2020 IEEE Conference on Industrial Cyberphysical Systems (ICPS), pp. 402–405. IEEE (2020)
17. Jamil, S., Noor, S., Ahmed, I., Gohar, N., Fouzia: Semantic modeling of events using linked open data. Intell. Autom. Soft Comput. **29**(2), 511–524 (2021)

Task Scheduling Based on Improved Particle Swarm Optimization for Cloud Computing

Qiming Zhang[2], Xiaolan Xie[1,2(✉)], and Jiaming Wang[2]

[1] Guangxi Key Laboratory of Embedded Technology and Intelligent System,
Guilin 541006, Guangxi, China
237290696@qq.com
[2] School of Information Science and Engineering, Guilin University
of Technology, Guilin 541006, Guangxi, China

Abstract. Particle Swarm Optimization (PSO) algorithm is widely used in cloud computing task scheduling. As PSO algorithm tends to fall into local optimum and has poor convergence accuracy in the later stage, as a result, in this paper i integrates Simulated Annealing algorithm (SA) into PSO algorithm and adopts a strategy of mixing random and nonlinear decreasing inertia weight. At the same time, the idea of "accept the bad solution with a certain probability" in simulated annealing is used to improve the global search ability of the algorithm. Finally, the chaotic disturbance strategy is added to make the algorithm search for a better solution as far as possible, so as to improve the convergence accuracy of the algorithm in the later stage. The improved PSOSA algorithm and the standard particle swarm optimization algorithm are applied to the task scheduling test in the cloud environment through the Cloudsim simulation platform. The results show that the improved algorithm can achieve better scheduling results and faster convergence speed.

Keywords: Cloud computing · PSO · Task scheduling · Simulated annealing

1 Introduction

Resources in cloud computing are shared between cloud clients through the concept of virtualization. Virtualization technology is one of the main features of cloud data centers, enabling cloud customers to dynamically share physical resources. It allows multiple applications, or tasks, to run on different platforms called virtual machines in a physical server. Generally speaking, cloud computing gathers software resources or hardware resources together to form a resource pool that can be configured. For all these resources, people can access them at any time or anywhere through the network [1], which is both safe and convenient. These resources are provided to users in the form of services, reducing service costs and improving operation and maintenance efficiency. In the Internet before has not developed to like now, due to network users, Internet data are limited, and the data related computing tasks are not heavy, but in the data after the "big bang", the data volume growth with blowout, followed then cause the computing tasks related to data processing become very heavy. Cloud computing from thought is how to efficiently handle these huge data, in a computer resources are insufficient to computing task within the allotted time, composed of a large number of hardware and software resources common resource pool has super computing ability, the computing task allocation to the resource pool is able to efficiently handle the computing tasks, therefore, people hand over computing tasks to resource pools to obtain results, which are provided to users through the network in the form of services [2]. In the cloud environment, users use services provided by cloud providers in the form of rent. The basic principle of cloud computing is to use the Internet to decompose large and difficult tasks into smaller tasks and send them to the server for distributed calculation, analysis and summary [3].

How to efficiently and reasonably schedule the task set to the virtual machine in the resource pool is task scheduling, which is an NP-complete problem [4] and also the priority among the key technologies of cloud computing. Particle swarm optimization has been applied to cloud computing task scheduling by many scholars due to its few parameters for modification and fast convergence in early stage. In reference [5], genetic algorithm and particle swarm optimization algorithm are integrated, and the linear weight dynamic allocation strategy is introduced into the fitness evaluation function modeling of the algorithm, and three factors including completion time, completion cost and quality of service are also taken into account. Reference [6] used the clustering strategy to divide the population, introduced the reverse learning mechanism and reproduction mechanism, and proposed a reverse learning behavior particle optimization swarm algorithm. Reference [7] added the improved dynamic inertia weight strategy to the particle swarm optimization algorithm, and improved the convergence speed and search accuracy of the algorithm through external disturbance. Reference [8] adaptively searched for the optimal solution based on particle swarm fitness to dynamically adjust the inertia weight coefficient. Reference [9] proposed an improved PSOGA algorithm integrating particle swarm optimization and genetic algorithm. By taking advantage of the crossover and variation characteristics of genetic algorithm, the GENETIC algorithm was mixed with particle swarm optimization to improve the accuracy of PSOGA search. Reference [10] proposed a particle swarm optimization algorithm of chaotic search and population crossover based on logical self-mapping function. These scholars usually combine PSO with other algorithms to achieve the balance of global search and local search.

In this paper, on the basis of the standard particle swarm algorithm using a mixture of random and nonlinear decreasing inertia weight strategy, every certain number of iterations, determine if the fitness value of the current iteration is much better than the former one iteration of fitness value, though, there was a big probability sharply decreasing inertia weight value, so as to accelerate the algorithm convergence speed, at the same time, the thought of using simulated annealing, If the optimization effect of two iterations is not obvious, there is a certain probability to increase the inertia weight and expand the search range, which is helpful to jump out of the local optimal solution. Finally, chaotic perturbation strategy is added to find a better solution as far as possible.

2 Task Scheduling Problem Description

There are two types of scheduling related to cloud computing, one is resource scheduling and the other is task scheduling. Resource scheduling is to rationally allocate and use physical resources to maximize resource utilization. Task scheduling refers to the task to be assigned to the appropriate computer resources, so that the task to complete the shortest time or meet some other conditions. With the increasing number of cloud users, the service experience of users has gradually become the primary consideration, so task scheduling becomes very important. The stages of task scheduling in cloud computing services are shown in Fig. 1.

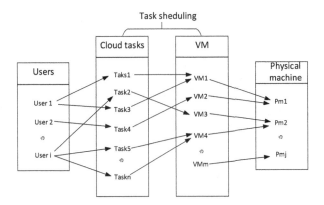

Fig. 1. Task scheduling phase.

In the Cloud System, there are N_{pm} Physical machines, and each Physical machine contains N_{vm} Visual machines. Cloud system CS can be expressed as vector CS = $\{P_{m1}, P_{m2}..., P_{mi}, ..., P_{mNpm}\}$, where P_{mi} (I = 1...,N_{pm}) can be expressed as the vector Pmi = $\{VM_1, VM_2... VM_j, ..., VM_{Nvm}\}$, VM_j is the jth virtual machine, Nvm is the number of virtual machines, VM_j (j = 1, ..., Nvm) contains two attributes, which can be expressed as VM_j = $\{SIDV_j, MIPS_j\}$, where $SIDV_j$ stands for the SERIAL number of the VM and $MIPS_j$ stands for the data processing speed of the VM. Task set T can be expressed as vector T = $\{Task_1, Task_2..., Task_q, ..., Task_{Ntsk}\}$, Ntsk is the number of tasks submitted by the user, and Taskq is the q task in the task queue, which can be expressed as $Task_q$ = $\{SIDT_q, task\_length_q, ECT_q\}$, where $SIDT_q$ is the serial number of the task. Task_length$_q$ specifies the command length of the q task. ECT_q is the estimated completion time matrix of the Q task on each VM. The estimated completion time matrix of the total task is as follows:

$$ECT = \begin{bmatrix} ECT_{11} & ECT_{12} & ... & ECT_{1N_{vm}} \\ ECT_{21} & ECT_{22} & ... & ECT_{2N_{vm}} \\ ... & ... & ... & ... \\ ECT_{N_{tsk}1} & ECT_{N_{tsk}2} & ... & ECT_{Nt_{sk}N_{vm}} \end{bmatrix} \quad (1)$$

$ECT_{NtskNvm}$ indicates the expected completion time of the N_{tsk} task on the N_{vm} VM. $ECT_{NtskNvm} = task\_length_{Ntsk}/MIPS_{Nvm}$ The main purpose of task scheduling is to reduce the task completion time. Because VMS use distributed computing, the task completion time is determined by the vm that takes the longest to complete the task. Task completion time $FTime = Max(\sum_1^{Nvm} ECT_{qj})$, q is the task running on virtual machine j, j = 1, 2... N_{vm}.

3   Relevant Algorithms

3.1   Standard Particle Swarm Optimization

The PSO algorithm simulates the foraging behavior of birds, with particles and particle swarm acting as birds and flocks respectively. The algorithm provides swarm intelligence search through information sharing among particles in the swarm. All particles in a swarm contain two properties, the position of the particle and the velocity of the particle, and each particle is an independent individual [11]. Particle individuals will own information and group, comparing the feedback information in keeping the following tend to be under the principle of optimal solution, through the comprehensive analysis of constantly dynamically adjust their position and speed, will be updated after the new particles as the new generation into the fitness function, according to the fitness function value to judge the merits of the solution, Finally, the optimal solution is found in the solution space through iteration. In the process of iteration, each particle will be recorded in the optimal solution in the process of iteration, the history of individual optimal solution is also called individual extreme value pbest, and particle swarm namely populations in the iteration process of the optimal solution is called the global optimal solution gbest, each particle in under the influence of gbest and pbest eventually find extremum constantly update location and speed. The two basic properties of a particle position and velocity are determined by two formulas.

$$v_i^{t+1} = v_i^t + c_1 r \, and \, 1(pbest_i^t - x_i^t) + c_2 r \, and \, 2(gbest^t - x_i^t) \tag{2}$$

$$x_i^{t+1} = x_i^t + v_i^{t+1} \tag{3}$$

In Eq. (2) and Eq. (3), assuming N particles search for the optimal solution in the D-dimensional space, the current position of the ith particle can be expressed as vector $x_i = (x_{i1}, x_{i2}, \cdots, x_{iD})$, x_i^t represents the position of the ith particle after t times of iteration during the operation of the algorithm, x_i^{t+1} represents the position of the ith particle after t + 1 times of iteration during the operation of the algorithm. The velocity of the ith particle can be expressed as the vector $v_i = (v_{i1}, v_{i2}, \cdots, v_{iD})$, v_i^t represents the velocity of the ith particle after t iterations, and v_i^{t+1} represents the velocity of the ith particle after t + 1 iterations. Particle velocities range between plus and minus V_{max}. c1 and c2 are usually taken as 2, both of which are acceleration constants. Their values determine the influence degree of the historical optimal solution pbest of the particle itself and the global optimal solution gbest of the particle swarm on the current particle velocity. To ensure the diversity of particle directions, rand1 and rand2 are random numbers ranging from 0 to 1 to increase the random uncertainty of particle optimization and prevent premature convergence.

Equation (1) and Eq. (3) are basic particle swarm optimization algorithms, which have a constant dependence on the velocity of particles in the last iteration and lack flexibility. In reference [12], Shi Y introduced inertial weight for the first time to enhance the optimization capability of the algorithm, known as the standard particle swarm optimization algorithm, as shown in Eq. (4).

$$v_i^{t+1} = \omega v_i^t + c_1 r \, and \, 1(pbest_i^t - x_i^t) + c_2 r \, and \, 2(gbest^t - x_i^t) \tag{4}$$

In the formula, ω is the inertia weight, and its value is similar to the acceleration constants C1 and C2 in the basic particle swarm optimization algorithm, and represents the reference specific gravity of the particle's speed in the next iteration to the particle's current speed. If ω is large, the particle's speed is also large, and it can span a longer distance and has strong exploration ability. However, it may lead to the particle always drifting outside the range of global optimal solution, resulting in slow convergence rate. If ω is small, it means that the algorithm has strong local optimization ability, but it is easy to keep searching in the same solution region and fall into the local optimal solution. The standard PSO algorithm is the special case of $\omega = 1$ in Eq. (4).

3.2 Simulated Annealing Algorithm

Simulated annealing algorithm is often used in local search, which can be regarded as an extension of local search. Because of the jump ability of simulated annealing algorithm, it can be used to jump out of the local optimal solution and tend to the optimal solution with a certain probability under certain conditions. In practical application, the internal energy E is replaced by fitness function value, the temperature T is replaced by control parameter, and the reserved solution is selected from the new and old solutions according to the acceptance criterion. When the new solution is better than the old one, the poor solution is allowed to be accepted with a certain probability, so as to avoid the algorithm falling into the local optimal solution prematurely. After several iterations, the relative optimal solution of the optimization problem can be obtained when the control parameters approach 0 and there is no new state that can be updated or the threshold value is reached.

4   Cloud Computing Task Scheduling Based on PSOSA

4.1   Particle Coding and Fitness Function

When particle swarm optimization algorithm is applied to task scheduling in the cloud environment, since the sub-tasks to be assigned are usually discrete values, it is necessary to encode particles, which contain two attributes of position and speed. Task scheduling is combined with particle position and speed through coding [4]. In cloud computing, the tasks are discrete values, so the particles are encoded by natural numbers. If n tasks are assigned to M virtual machines, particle population size is NP, and the position of each particle is represented by vector P, then the ith particle can be encoded as the N-dimensional vector shown in Eq. (5):

$$P_i = \{p_{i1}, p_{i2}, \ldots, p_{ij}, \ldots, p_{in}\} \tag{5}$$

In Eq. (5), $1 \leq p_{ij} \leq m$, each one-dimensional component represents the virtual machine assigned to this task. For example, if the optimal solution is (1, 4, 2..., m, ...)., indicates that VM1 accepts task1, VM4 accepts task2, and VM2 accepts task3. During initialization, the value of p_{ij} is a random integer ranging from 0 to M + 1. The particle velocity is represented by vector V, and the velocity of the ith particle is expressed as:

$$v_i = \{v_{i1}, v_{i2}, \ldots, v_{ij}, \ldots, v_{in}\} \tag{6}$$

In Eq. (6), $-m \leq v_{ij} \leq m$, v_{ij} is a random number between -m and m when initialized. Define two n * m matrices Time and S, as shown below.

$$S = \begin{bmatrix} S_{11} & S_{12} & \cdots & S_{1m} \\ S_{21} & S_{22} & \cdots & S_{2m} \\ \cdots & \cdots & \cdots & \cdots \\ S_{n1} & S_{n2} & \cdots & S_{nm} \end{bmatrix} \quad Time = \begin{bmatrix} Time_{11} & Time_{12} & \cdots & Time_{1m} \\ Time_{21} & Time_{22} & \cdots & Time_{2m} \\ \cdots & \cdots & \cdots & \cdots \\ Time_{n1} & Time_{n2} & \cdots & Time_{nm} \end{bmatrix}$$

The relationship between the corresponding task and the corresponding VM is represented by the value of the corresponding column and column in the matrix S. S_{ij} indicates whether task i is executed on VM_j. If S_{ij} is 0, task i is not executed on VM_j; otherwise, it is 1. Where, $Time_{ij}$ represents the time taken by VM_j to complete task i. $Time_{ij}$ is equal to the ratio of the length of task i to the execution speed of VM_j. The execution time on VM_j can be obtained as follows:

$$Time_j = \sum_{i \in S_j} Time_{ij}, j \in \{1, 2, 3, \ldots, m\} \tag{7}$$

Set the time for all VMS to complete all tasks to FTime. The task scheduling evaluation standard is FTime, which is the maximum time for each VM to complete a task, as shown in Eq. (8).

$$FTime = Max(Time_j = \sum_{i \in S_j} Time_{ij}), j \in \{1, 2, 3, \ldots, m\} \tag{8}$$

The fitness function in this paper is FTime. The smaller FTime is, the faster the task is completed and the better the algorithm performance is. In practical applications, task scheduling is a multi-objective optimization problem, which needs to be considered not only the total task completion time, but also computing cost, bandwidth, energy consumption and other factors.

4.2   Improved Dynamic Inertia Weight Strategy

Considering the global and local search capability of the algorithm and the convergence speed of the algorithm comprehensively, this paper adopts the inertia weight strategy of mixing random and nonlinear decreasing, that is, the random inertia weight is inserted in the process of nonlinear decreasing inertia weight, the randomness is not really random value. By referring to the idea of simulated annealing, the results of random selection can be divided into two types: sharply increasing or decreasing inertia weight, which will lead to two completely different effects. The former greatly enhances the global search ability and searches for better solutions as far as possible, which is conducive to jumping out of the local optimum, while the latter greatly enhances the local search ability and speeds up the convergence of the algorithm.

During algorithm iteration, the current fitness value of particle $FTime_i^t$ and the previous fitness value of particle $FTime_i^{t-1}$ were obtained every 5 iterations. Assume the probability value P, and the value formula of P is as follows:

$$p = \begin{cases} 1 & FTime_i^{t-1} \leq FTime_i^t \\ \exp\left(-\frac{FTime_i^{t-1}-FTime_i^t}{temp}\right) & FTime_i^{t-1} > FTime_i^t \end{cases} \tag{9}$$

$$temp = \frac{averageFTime_i^t}{pbestFTime_i^t} - 1 \tag{10}$$

In Eq. (10), $averageFTime_i^t$ represents the average fitness value of particle i to t iterations, and $pbestFTime_i^t$ represents the fitness value of the optimal solution of particle i to T iterations. The formula of inertia weight for every 5 iterations is as follows:

$$\omega = \begin{cases} \omega_s + random/2 & p \geq random \\ random/2 & p < random \end{cases} \tag{11}$$

The value formula of inertia weight in ordinary iterations is as follows:

$$\omega = \omega_s - (\omega_s - \omega_e)\left|\sqrt{\frac{t}{T_{max}}}\right| \tag{12}$$

In Eq. (10), random is a random number whose value is between 0 and 1. In Eq. (11), t is the current iteration number, and T_{max} is the maximum iteration number. When t = 0, ω is ω_s, when t = Tmax, ω is ω_e, in most cases ω_s is 0.9, ω_e is 0.4, T_{max} is 1000. Equations (10) and (11) constitute a new dynamic inertia weight strategy. When t is 0, ω is ω_s, and when t is T_{max}, ω is ω_e.

With the iteration, the inertia weight as a whole decreases from 0.9 to 0.4, which solves the problem of fast convergence in the early stage and slow convergence in the late stage. Every 5 times during the iteration, if current fitness value of particles is also is a task completion time is greater than the previous iteration fitness value, the greater the inertia weight, improve the search scope, if the current particle fitness value is less than the last iteration of the fitness value, according to certain probability choose increasing or decreasing inertia weight, the former expand the search scope, It is helpful to jump out of local optimum to find a better solution, which greatly speeds up the convergence rate.

4.3   Chaos Disturbance

Chaotic perturbation is sensitive to the initial value of a particle and acts as a constant random and regular search around a given initial particle. In the process of algorithm iteration, the fitness value of a few particles is much better than that of other particles. These extremely excellent particles will affect the particles around them and make the particles cluster together, which may lead to the algorithm falling into local optimum prematurely [7]. At this time, only changing the inertia weight is not enough to jump out of the local optimum solution. To solve this problem, this paper adopts the chaotic sequence generated by Logistic mapping, whose equation is:

$$z_{k+1} = \mu z_k (1 - z_k) \tag{13}$$

When the particle population iterates for A certain number of times, the global optimal value will remain unchanged. At this time, the particles corresponding to the global optimal value are disturbed by chaotic sequence. Each dimension of the global optimal particle is mapped to the interval $(0, 1)$, and A new vector $A = (a1, a2..., an)$, and the value range of each one-dimensional component in vector A is $(0, 1)$. Then, vector A is substituted into Eq. (13) as the initial value to generate A new sequence Z1, which is substituted into the fitness function to calculate and compare with the fitness value of the global optimal solution. If it is better than the current optimal solution, z1 is updated as the global optimal solution.

4.4   Location and Speed Updates

Each iteration, the velocity of the particles according to the Eq. (3) and Eq. (8) to (11) is updated, since the task scheduling is discrete problems, this paper USES a natural number coding, according to the Eq. (2) after the update will become a floating point number, some dimensions of the component may be beyond the scope of regulation, in this paper, the floating point Numbers, in turn, take the absolute value, rounded down, take more, formula is as follows:

$$
x_i^t = \begin{cases} \lfloor |x_i^t| \rfloor & |x_i^t| \in (0, m] \\ 1 & x_i^t = 0 \\ \lfloor |x_i^t| \rfloor \% m & |x_i^t| > m \end{cases} \tag{14}
$$

Updated particle velocity can be beyond the scope of particles fly out feasible range, so the particles set maximum speed V_{max}, if $|v_{ij}| > V_{max}$, $v_{ij} = V_{max}/2$.

4.5 Improved Algorithm Description

The improved PSOSA algorithm is applied to cloud computing task scheduling, and the algorithm implementation process is shown as follows.

Step 1: Randomly generate NP particle size population, initialize particle position and speed, set algorithm parameters, particle initial position $X_i \sim U(0, m + 1)$, particle initialization speed $v_i \sim U(-m, m)$, m is the number of virtual machines. The individual historical optimal solution pbest is determined by the initial position of each particle, while the global optimal solution gbest is calculated and compared by Eq. (7).

Step 2: Dynamically update the inertia weight according to Eq. (8)–(11), and then substitute it into Eq. (2)–(3) to update the particle position and velocity;

Step 3: Calculate the fitness function value of each new particle and update the individual optimal value and global optimal value;

Step 4: When the population iteration times t > 50 if the global optimal location is not updated for 15 consecutive times, go to Step 5. Otherwise, go to Step 7.

Step 5: The global optimal position is disturbed by chaos to generate new particles;

Step 6: Calculate the fitness value of the new particle generated after chaos disturbance, namely the task completion time. If the task completion time is smaller than that corresponding to the global optimal particle, the position of the new particle is updated to the global optimal position;

Step 7: Judge whether the current iteration times t is greater than Tmax, if T > Tmax, perform step 8; otherwise, perform step 2;

Step 8: Output the optimal solution, and the execution of the task scheduling algorithm ends.

The algorithm realization flow chart is shown in Fig. 2.

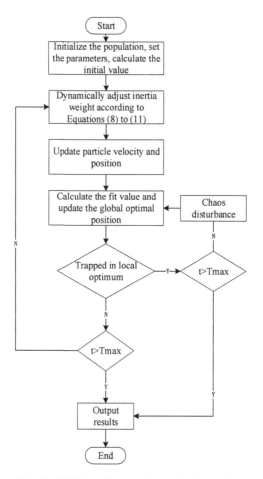

Fig. 2. PSOSA task scheduling algorithm flow.

5   Simulation Experiment and Analysis

In order to verify the superiority of the improved PSOSA algorithm, which combines random and nonlinear decreasing inertia weight strategy, based on the idea of simulated annealing and adding chaos disturbance, this paper selects the test experiment of task scheduling algorithm in simulated cloud environment on the Simulation platform Cloudsim-4.0. Under the same experimental conditions, It is compared with the standard PSO algorithm. In the experiment, only the processing speed of the virtual machine and the length of tasks to be processed were considered, so the total completion time of all tasks was taken as the evaluation index.

In the experiment, the task to be assigned to virtual machines is generated by data set HPC2N-2002-2.1-CLN from Swedish high performance Computing Center HPC2N, and the population size is set to 30. The main parameter Settings of the algorithm are shown in Table 1.

In the experiment, when the number of tasks is 100, 300, 500 and 700, and the number of iterations is 500, the time required to complete the task according to the two different algorithms is tested respectively.

Table 1. The main parameters of the algorithm.

Parameter	Values
NP	30
m	6
n	100, 300, 500, 700
$\omega_s \omega_s$	0.9, 0.4
c1	2
c2	2

The comparison of experimental results is shown in Figs. 3, 4, 5 and 6.

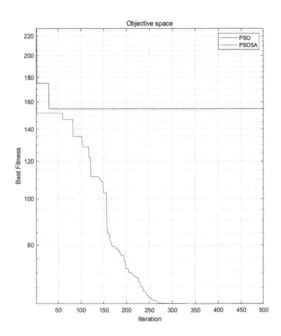

Fig. 3. Total time to complete 100 tasks.

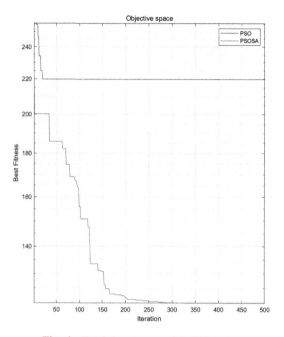

Fig. 4. Total time to complete 300 tasks.

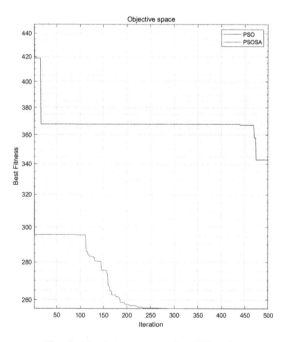

Fig. 5. Total time to complete 500 tasks.

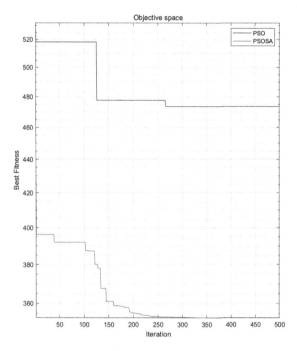

Fig. 6. Total time to complete 700 tasks.

The convergence result of the improved PSOSA is obviously better. When the number of tasks is 100, an extreme value is found when the number of iterations is close to 275, and the extreme value does not change in a long time. Under the influence of chaotic disturbance strategy, the current optimal solution is jumped out and a new extreme value is found when the number of iterations is close to 55. The shortest task completion time is 60.7 s, which is shorter than the task completion time obtained by PSO algorithm. Similarly, the task completion time was much shorter than the task completion time obtained by PSO in other environments.

From the analysis of the above experimental results, it can be seen that the improved particle swarm optimization algorithm PSOSA has strong global development ability in task scheduling. It constantly explores the global optimal solution in the early stage of the algorithm, and has good local exploration ability in the later stage. Due to the addition of chaotic perturbation strategy, the position information of particles is constantly randomly changed, so that the algorithm can jump out of the local optimal solution as far as possible, so that the final convergence result is better. However, the standard particle swarm optimization algorithm has a longer step length in the process of developing the optimal solution, and the particles are easy to stride over the better solution space in the iterative process. Therefore, the improved particle swarm optimization (PSOSA) algorithm proposed in this paper is superior to PSO in cloud environment task scheduling.

6 Summary

In this paper, the inertia weight of standard particle swarm optimization algorithm combined with simulated annealing is improved, and the hybrid perturbation strategy is added. Experimental results show that compared with the standard particle swarm optimization algorithm, the improved particle swarm optimization algorithm not only has faster convergence speed, but also has better convergence results in cloud computing task scheduling. Due to the demand of the user task scheduling each are not identical, is not a simple pursuit of task completion time as short as possible, in the practical application of bandwidth, computational cost, energy consumption is generally need factors into account, and this paper on the task of total completion time to make a improvement on the particle swarm algorithm, according to the different needs of users, how to realize the multi-objective optimization needs further research.

References

1. Kumar, M., et al.: Hybrid cuckoo search algorithm for scheduling in cloud computing. Comput. Mater. Contin. **71**(01), 1641–1660 (2022)
2. Ganesan, S., et al.: A multi-objective secure optimal VM placement in energy-efficient server of cloud computing. Intell. Autom. Soft Comput. **30**(02), 387–401 (2021)
3. Aldossary, M.: A review of dynamic resource management in cloud computing environments. Comput. Syst. Sci. Eng. **36**(03), 461–476 (2021)
4. Hamed, A.Y., Alkinani, M.H.: Task scheduling optimization in cloud computing based on genetic algorithms. Comput. Mater. Contin. **69**(03), 3289–3301 (2021)
5. Sun, M., Chen, Z.X., Lu, W.R.: Task scheduling algorithm based on DO-GAPSO in cloud environment. Comput. Sci. **45**(S1), 300–303 (2018)
6. Lai, Z.L., Femg, X., Yu, H.Q.: Large-scale task scheduling in cloud computing based on inverse learning behavioral particle swarm optimization. J. East China Univ. Sci. Technol. **46**(02), 259–268 (2020)
7. Xu, X.Y., Zhang, F.L.: Task scheduling based on chaotic disturbance particle swarm optimization algorithm in cloud computing. Inf. Technol. Netw. Secur. **37**(08), 27–30 (2018)
8. Hou, H.H.: Adaptive dynamic adjustment of particle swarm optimization for cloud computing task scheduling. Comput. Appl. Softw. **36**(09), 46–51 (2019)
9. Wang, B., Zhang, X.L.: Task scheduling algorithm based on particle swarm optimization genetic algorithms in cloud computing environment. Comput. Eng. Appl. **51**(6), 84–88 (2015)
10. Yang, S.P., Li, Z.Y., Chen, Z.Y.: Particle swarm optimization algorithm based on chaotic searching and people crossover operator. Comput. Simul. **33**(06), 218–222 (2016)
11. Xue, Y., Aouari, A., Mansour, R.F., Su, S.: A hybrid algorithm based on PSO and GA for feature selection. J. Cyber Secur. **3**(02), 117–124 (2021)
12. Shi, Y., et al.: A modified particle swarm optimizer. In: IEEE International Conference of Evolutionary Computation, Anchorage, Alaska (1998)

Optimization Design of Privacy Protection System Based on Cloud Native

Yifan Zhang, Shuli Zhang, Chengyun Guo, Luogang Zhang,
Yinggang Sun$^{(\boxtimes)}$, and Hai Huang

Harbin University of Science and Technology, Harbin 150040, China
syg15688708938@163.com

Abstract. In order to meet the needs of group enterprises for data privacy protection processing in the internal private network environment, this paper proposes an optimization design method of Privacy Protection System (PPS) based on
cloud native. The main goal of this method is to transform structured data using
data anonymization techniques to mitigate attacks that could lead to privacy
breaches. From the perspective of logical architecture, this method supports the
anonymization of data using the privacy protection model and related parameters
selected by the user. First, the identifiers are removed from the dataset to be
processed, and constraints are imposed on the quasi-identifiers. Further, the
algorithms for protecting sensitive properties that require certain assumptions
about the attacker's goals and background knowledge are also supported. In
particular, in the process of anonymization, the scheme introduces the methods of
utility analysis and risk analysis, so that the anonymization results can be accurately evaluated. Finally, the proposed method allows users to iteratively update
the privacy-preserving model and related parameters according to the results of the
anonymization evaluation. From the perspective of technical architecture, the
proposed method uses Spring Boot as the back-end framework and MyBatis as the
persistence layer framework. At the same time, in order to ensure system security
requirements, Json Web Token is also used for user authentication. Finally, when
designing the system deployment scheme, cloud native technology is introduced
to encapsulate system functions into microservice containers, and cluster management tools are used to dynamically manage microservice containers to ensure
high availability of the system.

Keywords: Privacy protection · Anonymization · Cloud native · Microservice

1 Introduction

With the advent of the Internet Web2.0 era, technologies such as big data and cloud
computing have developed rapidly. Ordinary users are no longer just information
viewers and receivers, but information producers and participants. From mobile payment to personal travel, since almost all users connected to the Internet in the world are
generating information anytime and anywhere, the total amount of information on the
Internet has shown an explosive growth trend. Such a huge amount of data has brought
huge benefits to various enterprises, and has also made significant contributions to
important fields such as scientific research, medical treatment, and health. It can be said

that the arrival of the big data era has brought earth-shaking changes to human society. But at the same time, we should not ignore the issue of personal privacy protection, which is now that all kinds of information can be more easily obtained and widely disseminated. On the one hand, the Internet records people's social conditions, living habits, reading habits, consumption habits, lifestyles and other information. Once leaked, it may be maliciously tampered with and cause serious consequences. On the other hand, once all kinds of data are completely fixed, many scientific research and economic activities cannot be carried out. Therefore, it is necessary to explore a solution that supports data processing in the intranet environment of group enterprises to reduce the risk of possible privacy leakage.

Data release anonymity protection technology is the basic means and core key technology to achieve big data security and privacy protection [1]. The concept of anonymity was proposed by Samarati [2]. Data anonymization refers to the deletion or modification of the data owner's personal information, sensitive attributes, and identifiers through certain technologies and methods during the data release stage. It is impossible to identify individuals through data.

Currently, some tools for anonymization are Toolkit [3], TIAMAT [4], Anamnesia [5] and SECRETA [6]. These tools are capable of automating user-specified privacy-preserving models, but typically only support a limited set of privacy models, making them more limited. There are also privacy models such as sdcMicro [7] and μ-Argus [8] that implement more flexible anonymization methods, but their capabilities for risk measurement are still lacking. Moreover, the above tools are all desktop applications and do not adopt a more flexible B/S architecture. In addition, the laws and regulations of many countries now have strict regulations on the use of data, and some data are not even allowed to be uploaded to the server. For example, some group companies have high data sensitivity and can only be used in the intranet environment, and there are also a lot of demands for data privacy protection during the use process.

In order to solve the above-mentioned problem of data privacy protection of group enterprises in the internal private network environment, this paper proposes a PPS based on cloud native, which adopts a more flexible B/S architecture. In terms of system functions, it supports more diverse privacy protection models and more flexible data anonymization methods. And it can automatically identify various types of attributes in the data set, which is more friendly to data publishers who are not familiar with the anonymization process. In addition, through cloud native technology, the system encapsulates each functional module into microservices, deploys using docker containers, and maintains continuous and rapid updates. This solves the problem that the desktop program of the traditional C/S architecture cannot be updated in real time, and can quickly add, modify or update system functions anytime and anywhere, bringing a better experience to users. The second part of this article focuses on the system framework, including the functional division of the system and the overall technical framework of the system. The third part introduces the rule base constructed by this system according to different standards, laws and regulations. The fourth part introduces the main technologies used in this system, including asynchronous call technology, Devops, adaptive capacity expansion, CI/CD, etc. The fifth part is a summary of the whole system.

2 Related Work

In order to combat privacy attacks, Seweney first proposed the K-anonymity model, and later Seweney proposed an improved version of the K-anonymity privacy protection model based on generalization and concealment technology on the basis of the K-anonymity model [9]. Machanavajjhala [10] proposed the L-diversity model to solve the problem of K-anonymity model attribute leakage. Li Z D [11] proposed the (k, l)-anonymity model, which solved the problem of low flexibility of L-diversity, and at the same time improved the ability of personalized protection of anonymous data. Li N H [12] further proposed the T-Closeness model for the lack of L-diversity model. Erlingsson [13] described an algorithm whose privacy cost is the logarithm of the number of user value changes. The privacy cost of this algorithm is lower in the central model of differential privacy. Lalit Garg [14] designed and proposed a new privacy and anonymity IoT model, which makes it easy to identify clusters of infected contacts while protecting personal privacy. Deng Jinsong [15] aimed at the issue of privacy leakage caused by trajectory and non-sensitive information when data is released, and proposed a trajectory data privacy protection publishing algorithm (TP-NSA) based on non-sensitive information analysis to realize the trajectory data set k-anonymity. Liu Xiangyu [16] proposed a personalized privacy protection model (p, q, ε) for spatiotemporal data-anonymity and a personalized spatiotemporal data privacy protection algorithm based on this model, so as to personalize the privacy of users. Data (location privacy, sign-in data privacy, and track privacy) are protected. Meanwhile, in [17–19], we use the privacy protection method in cloud computing for reference, and have a more in-depth understanding of the application of privacy protection.

3 Optimization Design of Architecture for PPS

3.1 The Logical Framework of PPS

The main challenge of anonymization technology is to achieve a balance between utility and risk of anonymized data, Therefore, in the process of anonymization, this system allows users to iteratively update initial parameters based on the results of data utility and risk analysis to obtain optimal anonymized data.

Figure 1 shows the relationship diagram of the various functional modules of the system, which also includes the basic processing flow of data. First, the user needs to import the original data, which will be pre-processed in the pre-analysis module. The preprocessing module is responsible for parsing the basic parameter information of each attribute of the original data and passing the information to the parameter configuration module. In the parameter configuration module, users define conversion rules and privacy models according to their needs. After that, the system starts to anonymize the original data based on user-defined parameters and calculate the solution space for the anonymization. In the solution space module, all possible solutions will be displayed and the optimal solution will be found. The optimal solution will be transmitted to the utility analysis and risk analysis modules, which are combined to judge whether the anonymous data achieves the balance between utility and risk. These two modules are combined to determine whether the anonymized data has reached a balance between utility and risk. If the anonymized data does not reach the balance between utility and risk, the user can reconfigure the parameters until the optimal result is obtained.

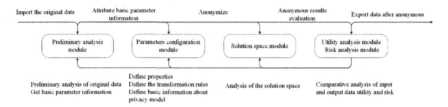

Fig. 1. The relationship diagram of system function modules.

The pre-analysis module is mainly used to upload the original data, and through operations such as semantic analysis and field value matching on the raw data, it can identify the characteristics of the attributes of each column in the data. The specific functions have the following two points: (1) Identify the data level of the attribute. Data levels are divided into levels 1 to 5, and the importance is gradually increasing. For different levels of data, the system will adopt different strategies to process the data; (2) Identify whether the attribute is an identifier attribute, a quasi-identifier attribute or a sensitive attribute. For different attributes, the algorithm used by the system will be different. The system provides an interface for the user to input the matching degree threshold in the pre-analysis module, and the user inputs a threshold to set the correct rate of the desired result. During calculation, the pre-analysis module will change the calculation strategy according to the threshold to meet user requirements. At the same time, users can also set the standards that the original data to be anonymized need to follow to quickly and accurately obtain the corresponding attribute analysis results. After the pre-analysis is over, all the analysis results will be transmitted to the parameter configuration module for the work of the parameter configuration module.

The parameter configuration module is mainly divided into three parts. The first part is to configure the attribute parameters of the original data, the second part is to configure the privacy model, and the third part is to configure the global parameters. To configure the attributes of the original data, the system parses the original data and lists each attribute separately, and then configures each attribute separately. The main content of the configuration is: (1) Set the data type of the attribute; (2) Set whether it is the target variable. When combined with an appropriate data quality model, the system will try to minimize the impact of the structural relationship between the alignment mark variable and the specified target variable; (3) Set the hierarchy. The hierarchical structure is a generalization level defined according to each attribute. For different types of data, the system provides a variety of methods to set the hierarchy. The most important method is to import the configuration file of the hierarchy. This method is applicable to all types of data; (4) Setting the data Conversion method. The conversion method provides users with three choices, namely generalization, clustering and micro-aggregation. For these three conversion methods, the configured parameters are also different. Generalization needs to configure minimum generalization and maximum generalization, and clustering and micro-aggregation need to configure corresponding aggregation functions; (5) Set weights. Users can set weights for corresponding attributes according to their needs. This system will reduce the loss of information for attributes with higher weights. Privacy model configuration is a process in which users select a privacy model for processing based on the original data set. These privacy models can be combined according to the actual situation to achieve the best anonymization effect.

The global configuration part includes: (1) Set the suppression limit. This parameter is used to set the proportion of suppressed records. If a record cannot meet the requirements of the corresponding privacy model algorithm, it needs to be completely suppressed; (2) Setting is used To quantify the data quality model, the model will be used as an optimization function in the anonymization process; (3) Set up heuristic search. The user can choose whether to perform a heuristic search. This function will significantly improve the efficiency of anonymization, but at the same time, the corresponding accuracy rate will also decrease to a certain extent.

After configuring all the parameters, all the parameters will be stored in the database. Through the version list, you can find the parameters corresponding to the version. The system will begin to anonymize the original data and calculate the solution space.

The solution space module is used to output all possible solutions of the anonymization process. These solutions are displayed as Hass diagrams of generalized lattices in the form of nodes. The figure shows every possible output, and each node represents a possible solution. In addition to the Hass diagram, the corresponding list section explains in detail the transformation vector of the nodes of the structure diagram, the explanation of the nodes, and the basic information about the currently selected transformation. This module is used to analyze the solution space to obtain the optimal node. The anonymized results obtained by this node will be added to the utility analysis and risk analysis process.

Both the utility analysis module and the risk analysis module are used to evaluate the anonymized data to ensure that the final data obtained can meet the needs of users.

Among them, the utility analysis module is divided into two parts, the left side is the input data part, and the right side is the output data part. The results of the two parts are juxtaposed to form a visual comparison of input data and output data. The part of the input data is to analyze the original data through various utility analysis methods, and calculate all the values of the data utility of the original data. The output data is the same calculation on the anonymized data, so the two can be clearly compared. The utility analysis module has direct comparison of input and output data, as well as comparison of information such as classification performance, data quality model, summary statistics, experience distribution, contingency, and equivalence. Through this information, users can clearly get the size of the utility of the anonymized data set.

Like the utility analysis module, the risk analysis module also displays a comparative analysis of input data and output data. In this module, the risk distribution section shows the distribution of re-identified risks in the data set record. Calculate distributions for input and output data in the form of histograms. In the quasi-identifier part, the combination of attributes can be used to analyze the risks associated with re-identification. This view provides information about the degree to which the combination of variables separates the records from each other and the degree to which the variables make the records different. The attacker model part is an overview of several metrics for re-identifying risks, including the prosecutor scenario, the reporter scenario, and the marketer scenario. In the section of population uniqueness, the results of comparing different methods under the assumption of different sampling scores are shown.

The results of utility analysis and risk analysis will be used as the basis for evaluating whether the data after anonymization meets the standard. If all the evaluation results do not meet the user's needs, the user needs to reconfigure the parameters for processing.

3.2   Technical Framework of PPS

In the cloud native theory, the cloud native application architecture should be service-oriented, deployment should be simple and fast, and the infrastructure should be scalable and flexible on demand, which requires the use of container technology.

The system adopts front-end and back-end separation technology for architecture. The separation of front and back ends realizes high cohesion and low coupling of the system, reduces the pressure on the back end, reduces maintenance costs, and enhances code refactoring and maintainability. The front end mainly uses React as the development framework and TypeScript as the main development language. React is fast, compatible across browsers, and makes code modular, making it easier to reuse code. TypeScript is a superset of JavaScript, providing a type system and support for ES6, increasing the readability and maintainability of the code. This system uses Vite as the front-end construction tool. Compared with webpack, it is faster and greatly reduces the startup time of the development server.

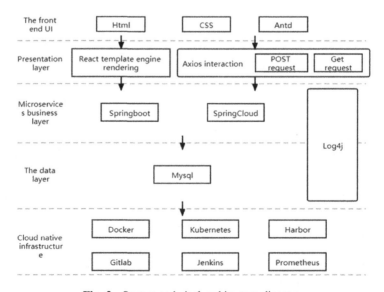

Fig. 2. System technical architecture diagram.

The back-end mainly uses Spring Boot as the framework and Java language as the main development language. Spring Boot can quickly build projects, which can run independently, and provide runtime application monitoring. It also greatly improves the efficiency of development and deployment, and is naturally integrated with cloud computing. This system uses MySQL as the database. It is an open source database with small size, high speed, low total cost of ownership, and supports multiple operating systems. The back-end uses MyBatis as a persistent framework, which can be well integrated with Spring, and MyBatis is quite flexible, and will not impose any impact on the existing design of the application or database. In terms of user authority, this system adopts JWT authentication technology to ensure the safety of users when using this system.

System deployment adopts docker container and Kubernetes cluster management solution. Docker allows developers to quickly build a standard development environment using images. After the development is completed, testing and operation and maintenance personnel can directly use the exact same environment to deploy code. As long as the code is developed and tested, it can be guaranteed to run seamlessly in the production environment. Docker can quickly create and delete containers, achieve rapid iteration, and save a lot of time in development, testing, and deployment. Kubernetes has complete cluster management capabilities. Including multi-level security protection and access mechanisms, multi-tenant application support capabilities, transparent service registration and service discovery mechanisms, built-in smart load balancers, powerful fault detection and self-repair Capabilities, rolling service upgrades and online expansion capabilities, scalable automatic resource scheduling mechanism, and multi-granularity resource quota management capabilities.

Micro-service Infrastructure Framework

In the early stage of enterprise development, the general company's website traffic is relatively small and only needs one application. Therefore, a single application architecture is generally adopted. All the functional codes are packaged into a service, which can be deployed on the server to support the company's business. This can also reduce the cost of development, deployment and maintenance. However, it will cause the modules of the project to be too coupled before. If there is a problem with one module, the entire project will be unavailable, and it will not be possible to improve the performance of a specific module. With the development of the Internet, the business of Internet companies is also developing rapidly, which in turn leads to continuous changes in the architecture of the system. In this context, a new type of technical architecture with microservices as the core has emerged. Microservices embodies the decentralization and natural distribution. To solve the problems of system flexibility and scalability, agile iteration, and technology-driven business innovation faced by enterprises during rapid business development and innovation (Fig. 3).

The system also uses microservice architecture in functional development. The microservice architecture divides the single application into multiple small services with high cohesion and low coupling according to the business domain. Each service runs in an independent process and is developed and maintained by different teams. A lightweight communication mechanism is adopted between services. For example, HTTP RESTful API, independent and automatic deployment, can use different

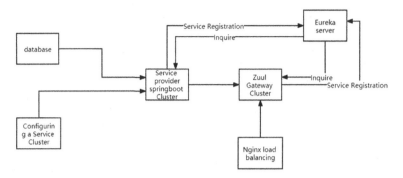

Fig. 3. The basic framework of microservices

languages and storage methods. This paper designs a microservice basic framework that provides registry, service gateway, authentication service, and service invocation functions, and can be fault-tolerant, current-limiting, and load-balancing. It can be reused as a basic framework in subsequent development projects.

Containerization and Containerization Management Schemes

Containers are the best implementation carrier for microservices and cloud-native architecture. Microservices and containers are almost a perfect match. Monolithic architecture (Monolithic) becomes microservice architecture (Microservices), which is equivalent to turning an all-round type into N specialized types. Each specialized type is assigned an isolated container, which gives the greatest degree of flexibility. We choose to use Docker to create the service container we need. Docker is an open source application container engine that allows developers to package their applications and dependencies into a portable container, and then publish it to any popular Linux machine. Virtualization can also be achieved (Fig. 4).

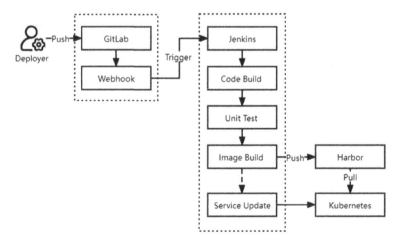

Fig. 4. Containerized management flow chart

Running a container on a single machine cannot maximize its effectiveness. Only by forming a cluster can the advantages of container isolation, resource allocation, and orchestration management be maximized. Therefore, a management system is needed to perform more advanced and flexible management of Docker and containers. According to the wishes of users and the rules of the entire system, the various relationships between containers are completely automated. We choose Kubernetes to orchestrate containers. Kubernetes is a new leading solution for distributed architecture based on container technology. It is an open source version of Borg [20], Google's secret weapon that has been kept strictly confidential for more than ten years. It is based on container technology and aims to automate resource management and maximize resource utilization across multiple data centers. Our system design follows the Kubernetes design philosophy, so the underlying code or functional modules that have little to do with the business in the traditional system architecture can disappear from our sight immediately. We don't have to worry about the selection and selection of load balancers. For deployment and implementation issues, you no longer need to consider introducing or developing a complex service governance framework yourself, and you no longer have to worry about the development of service monitoring and fault handling modules. In short, using the solution provided by Kubernetes, we not only saved no less than 30% of development costs, but also can focus more on the business itself, and because Kubernetes provides a powerful automation mechanism, the later operation and maintenance of the system is difficult and difficult. Operation and maintenance costs are greatly reduced.

Continuous Integration and Continuous Delivery
In the traditional development model, team work efficiency is low, and manual operations will inevitably lead to errors, causing some long-existing errors to be ignored. In order to reduce or avoid these problems, it is necessary to understand and implement continuous integration and continuous delivery.

Continuous integration is the continuous integration of the code being written by developers, which can be verified through automated testing to ensure that problems are discovered and resolved this morning. Continuous delivery is to minimize deployment, which can be deployed continuously, and can also ensure that the code is checked. The best practice of continuous delivery further extends continuous integration to ensure that the software review is in the main program and can be deployed to users to ensure that the actual deployment process can be very fast [21]. It can be implemented using Jenkins and GitLab or Travis CI.

As shown in Fig. 2, first split the microservices, and try to ensure that the table connection operations on the microservices are in the same microservice. The developer will submit it to the local branch of Git and generate an environment for testing. Later, docker images are automatically built through Travis CI, continuously integrated into Docker Cloud, and services are automatically created or updated on the cloud server (Fig. 5).

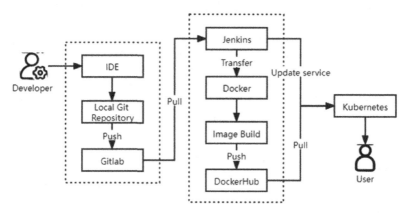

Fig. 5. Detailed process of continuous integration and continuous deployment

3.3 DevOps

In daily development, due to the inability to closely collaborate between the development team and the operation and maintenance team, there will be a large communication cost in the implementation process, and DevOps was born. Through DevOps, the software delivery process can be accelerated, collaboration can be expanded, and development, testing, operation and maintenance, and users can be in a business production line, so as to eliminate obstacles to organizational communication and management. It can also balance software development speed, cost, quality, and risk, and automate the software delivery process to eliminate waste of manpower and resources and delays in construction schedules. At the same time, the customer feedback time can be reduced and the user feedback circle can be expanded so that the product quality can be continuously improved. DevOps is a culture that promotes communication and closed-loop collaboration between R&D, testing, and operation and maintenance to jointly achieve business goals; at the same time, DevOps is also a continuous iterative delivery process that connects development, construction, testing, deployment, operation and maintenance, and repair In addition, DevOps is a tool chain, including Git, Jenkins, Docker, etc., among which automated testing tools are the key. Compared with CI/CD, which focuses on tools that emphasize automation in the software life cycle, DevOps focuses on the cultural role of responsiveness.

4   Optimization Design of Preanalysis Modules

Pre-analysis is mainly to understand user requirements, accept data, determine tasks, classify and check data according to the rules in the rule base, and generate data that can be used in the next step through operations such as data integration and cleaning. This step is to analyze the column name and field content according to the selected data standard, and automatically mark the data level, identifier, quasi-identifier, and sensitive attributes.

The following is the detailed procedure. After obtaining the data passed by the user, the data is processed first. It is not simply a combination of data, but a form of field name + field value that can be recognized by the system. In this process, in order to prevent the deviation between the processed data and the original data from being too large, it is necessary to remove the obviously wrong data in the data set and the processing of the missing data. The mean value interpolation is used here. After the preprocessing is completed, filter according to the selected rule library (here the default is the bank's standard), first judge the field name, and compare through the strong match of the string, if they are exactly the same, the result in the library is directly output. Otherwise, for the sake of safety, we also perform regular expression matching on the corresponding field value under the field name to further increase the accuracy. Usually we will perform these two comparisons, and label different data according to the results, to show the accuracy of data judgment more clearly, and it is convenient for users to modify. If there are too many field values, some data attributes will have no effect on the task. The addition of these data will greatly increase the processing time, reduce efficiency, and may even cause deviations in the results. Therefore, appropriately reducing the data scale can shorten the time. Reduce the user's waiting, get the result faster and proceed to the next step. The user makes repeated comparisons by setting the field value and the percentage of strong matching with the data in the library, and finds the data that the user thinks are satisfactory.

The two libraries, the Chinese library and the English library, need to be written in accordance with the existing financial standards as templates. By reading and storing in the database, it can achieve the function of supporting configurable and replaceable standards. Among them, Table 1 defines Algorithm 1 to find the corresponding Chinese and English libraries by passing in a standard name.

Table 1. Standard name

Algorithm 1 Get the Chinese and English library by standard name
Input: *I*: Standard name
Output: Modify uses the Chinese and English library name
Begin
1: ret← *select * from b_standard_file where standard_name*
2: payload← *Array for storage results*
3: **for** *result in ret* **do**
4:     *payload ← result*
5: **end for**
6: **Return** Array containing the name of the Chinese and English library

In addition, Table 2 defines Algorithm 2 by passing in a standard name and the Chinese library and English library corresponding to this standard, and storing it in the database as a standard.

Table 2. Add standard.

Algorithm 1 Add data standard
Input: *I*: Standard name, Chinese library name, English library name
Output: True or False
Begin
1: ret← *select ∗ from b_standard_file where standard_name*
2: payload← *Array for storage results*
3: name ← Standard name
4: s1 ← Chinese library name
5: s2 ← English library name
6: **for** *result in ret* **do**
7:     payload ← *result*
8: **end for**
9: **if** *payload exists* **then**
10:    **Return** false
11: **end if**
12: standardData1 ← *Insert name s1 s2 into the database*
13: Add to the database and submit
14: **Return** true

In order to expand the scope of data processed by this system and enable users to get a better experience, the rule base here can be constructed or modified according to different standards or laws and regulations. It can support multiple rule bases without modifying the code, and you can choose different rule base predictions to reduce errors. If the data forecast does not meet the expectations of individuals or companies, it can also be modified and confirmed artificially to adjust to the effect that users are satisfied with. In addition, the system also adds tags to each piece of data, and sorts them according to the tags, putting the low-recognition ones to the front, so that users must modify these parts to make the data more accurate.

5   Optimization Design of Utility Analysis Modules

This system provides a variety of utility analysis methods. The most basic, this system provides basic data information summary statistics function. For attributes with ordinal proportions, the median, minimum, and maximum parameters will be calculated; for attributes with interval scales, the arithmetic mean, sample variance, population variance, standard deviation, range, kurtosis will be calculated; with proportions For the attribute of the scale, its geometric mean will be calculated. Secondly, the system will calculate the frequency distribution of the attribute values in the data set. At the same time, the contingency between any two adjacent attributes in the data set is also calculated. The system expects comparable data visualization of the attributes of the original data set and the transformed data set. To this end, the system uses information from attribute data types and the relationship between their values to generate empirical distribution histograms and contingency views. Finally, the system will calculate the equivalence class to obtain the minimum, maximum, and average size of the equivalence class, the number of classes, and the number of suppressed and remaining records.

The system also applies a variety of utility analysis models and standards to accurately calculate the utility of the output data under these models and standards. These utility analysis models and standards include different levels of metrics. The first is the quality of the attribute level, that is, the quality estimation related to a single quasi-identifier, which specifically includes the granularity\loss, accuracy, nonuniform entropy, variance, etc. of the calculated attribute. The second is the quality of the data set level, that is, the quality estimation of the quasi-identifier set in the data set, which specifically includes calculating the average equivalence class, identifiability, ambiguity, entropy of the quasi-identifier set. In addition to the above-mentioned utility analysis methods, this system also provides methods based on machine learning. The system has three classification models: logistic regression, naive Bayes, and random forest. The system can compare the performance of the three types of models trained on the original input data and anonymous output data for utility analysis.

5.1 Asynchronous Communication Technology

When designing a distributed software architecture, it is an important task to define the way services exchange messages, because decoupling components in asynchronous communication use cases can simplify expansion, reduce the impact of updates, and make the release of new features more convenient. Easily, the system adopts the asynchronous call integrated by springboot + websocket to realize the message subscription service. As shown in Fig. 6, the client sends a message to the server through a websocket connection, and opens a channel to send a message to server A. Regardless of whether server A receives the message or not, it also opens a channel to send a message to server C asynchronously, and the server receives the message. Later, the websocket server replies to the client to achieve asynchronous message communication. http is a half-duplex mode, which cannot achieve two-way communication between the client and the server, while websocket provides a full-duplex communication mechanism between the web application client and the server (note that it is the client-server). Websocket is a supplement to the http protocol. It borrows the http protocol to complete a part of the handshake. Only need to go through an HTTP request, you can achieve a steady stream of information transmission and better asynchronous calls.

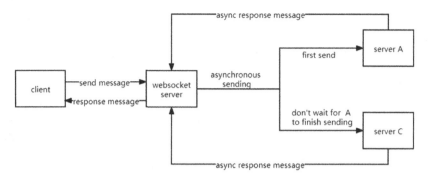

Fig. 6. Asynchronous communication process diagram.

All of the above are performed on a local stand-alone demonstration. If deployed to a server, the websocket connection may be automatically disconnected sometimes. When deploying nginx, you need to pay attention to the http upgrade configuration. In addition to reverse proxying, you must increase the time for automatic shutdown when there is no data interaction. Adjust it according to actual needs. You can also choose the conventional heartbeat packet sending mechanism. When the web application traffic is too large, we need to do load balancing to distribute requests for the same domain name to different servers. nginx can do it. It can load balance the back-end servers in multiple ways such as polling and weighting. But after being distributed to different machines, if the request is stateful, for example, some pages need to be accessed after the user logs in, we need to ensure that a single user request falls on one machine or realizes session sharing between multiple machines. Only then can you stay logged in. Since this system is a k8s cluster deployment environment, docker can realize decoupling between applications, so it is deployed to the server through docker port mapping, and the k8s management system can manage docker and containers more advanced and flexible. Better complete the message subscription mechanism in microservices.

5.2   Auto-scaling

In actual production systems, we often encounter scenarios where a service needs to be expanded, and may also encounter scenarios where the number of service instances needs to be reduced due to resource shortage or reduced workload. At this time, you can use the Scale mechanism of Deployment/RC to complete these tasks. Kubernetes provides manual and automatic modes for Pod expansion and contraction operations. In manual mode, you can set the number of Pod copies for a Deployment/RC by executing the kubectl scale command or setting the number of Pod copies for a Deployment/RC through the RESTful API. Obviously, this cannot be done in the face of real online traffic. We hope that the scheduling platform can intelligently adjust the scale according to the load of the service, and perform elastic scaling. At this time, it is the turn of AutoScaler in k8s to play.

Kubernetes divides elastic scaling into two categories:

- Resource dimensions: Ensure that the size of the cluster resource pool meets the overall plan. When the resources in the cluster are not enough to support the production of new pods, the boundary will be triggered to expand.
- Application dimension: To ensure that the load of the application is within the expected capacity plan.

Two corresponding scaling strategies:

- Horizontal scaling: automatically adjust the number of Pod replica sets
- Vertical scaling: automatically adjust the resource allocation of the application (increase/decrease the CPU and memory usage of the pod)

By reading relevant information, we choose the most mature and commonly used scaling strategy-HPA (Horizontal Pod Scaling). According to the description of the official document, HPA uses the control loop mechanism to collect the usage of Pod resources. The default collection interval is 15 s, and you can use the –horizontal-pod-autoscaler of the Controller Manager (a process on the Master node) -sync-period parameter to manually control.

At present, the implementation of HPA's default collection index is Heapster, which mainly collects the CPU usage rate. Therefore, it can be simply considered that HPA uses the CPU usage rate as the monitoring index. After collecting the CPU indicators, k8s uses the following formula to determine how many pods need to be expanded. DesiredRepli = ceil[currentReplica * (currentMetricValue / desiredMetricValue)]. Among them, ceil means round up.

Of course, the above indicators are not absolutely accurate. First of all, k8s will make the indicators as close as possible to the expected value instead of being completely equal. Secondly, HPA sets up a tolerance concept, allowing the indicator to deviate from the expected value within a certain range. The default is 0.1, which means that if you set the scheduling policy to 50% of the expected CPU usage, the actual scheduling policy will be less than 45% or greater than 55% for scaling, HPA will try to control the index within this range (Tolerance can be adjusted by –horizontal-pod-autoscaler-tolerance).

There are two other details that need to be explained. The first is the interval at which k8s makes decisions. It does not continuously perform expansion and contraction actions, but there is a certain cd. Currently, the cd for the expansion action is 3 min, and the reduction is 5 min; Secondly, k8s sets a maximum limit for expansion, and the number of pods for each expansion will not be more than twice the current number of copies.

6 Conclusion

In the past, the processing procedures of PPS in the intranet environment of group-type enterprises were mostly not perfect, and often only one or several privacy models could be applied, so the limitations were relatively large. And due to the rapid iterative update of privacy protection technology, the PPS needs to be able to add, change the privacy model or other functions at any time. However, these previous systems all adopted the C/S architecture, so it was impossible to update the corresponding privacy model in real time. Therefore, a PPS with a more flexible B/S architecture is required. Therefore, the PPS based on cloud native described in this paper uses B/S architecture and cloud-native technology to deploy and integrate each module in the form of micro-services, which not only strengthens the fault-tolerant mechanism and flexibility of the system, but also enables the system to Fast iterative updates of features.

Acknowledgements. The authors would like to acknowledge the helpful feedback of the anonymous reviewers, which significantly improved this paper.

Funding Statement. Project supported by the National Natural Science Foundation, China (No. 62172123), the Fundamental Research Foundation for of Heilongjiang Province, China (No. 2019KYYWF0214), the Postdoctoral Science Foundation of Hei-longjiang Province, China (No. LBH-Z19067), the special projects for the central government to guide the development of local science and technology, China (No. ZY20B11), the Heilongjiang Provincial Natural Science Foundation of China, China (No. YQ2019F010).

References

1. Zhang, X.: Research on key technologies of big data security and privacy protection. Modern Commer. Trade Ind. **40**(32), 146–147 (2019)
2. Samarati, P., Sweeney, L.: Generalizing data to provide anonymity when disclosing information. In: Proceedings of The Seventeenth ACM SIGACT-SIGMOD-SIGART Symposium on Principles of Database Systems, p. 188 (1998)
3. Cornell Database Group: Cornell Anonymization Toolkit (2014). Https://Sourceforge. Net/Projects/Anony-Toolkit/
4. Dai, C., Ghinita, G., Bertino, E., Byun, J.W., Ninghui, L.: TIAMAT: a tool for interactive analysis of microdata anonymization techniques. Proc. VLDB Endow. **2**(2), 1618–1621 (2009)
5. Openaire, A.: (2019). https://amnesia.openaire.eu/index.html
6. Giorgos, P., Aris, G.D., Grigorios, L., Spiros, S., Tryfonopoulos, C.: SECRETA: a system for evaluating and comparing relational and transaction anonymization algorithms. In: Proceeding of The 17th International Conference on Extending Database Technology, pp. 620–623 (2014)
7. Templ, M.: Statistical Disclosure Control for Microdata: Methods and Applications. Springer, Cham (2017). https://doi.org/10.1007/978-3-319-50272-4
8. Hundpoola, W.: ARGUS: software packages for statistical disclosure control. In: Payner, G. (ed.) COMPSTAT, pp. 341–345. Physica, Heidelberg (1996)
9. Sweeney, L., Anonymity, K.: A model for protecting privacy. Int. J. Uncertain. Fuzziness Knowledge-Based Syst. **10**(05), 557–570 (2002)
10. Machanavajjhala, A., Gehrke, J., Kifer, D.: L-Diversity: privacy beyond k-anonymity. In: Proceeding of the 22nd Internaional Conference on Data Engineering, pp. 24–35. IEEE Computer Society (2006)
11. Li, Z., Zhan, G., Ye, X.: Towards an anti-inference (k, ℓ)-anonymity model with value association rules. In: Bressan, S., Küng, J., Wagner, R. (eds.) DEXA 2006. LNCS, vol. 4080, pp. 883–893. Springer, Heidelberg (2006). https://doi.org/10.1007/11827405_86

12. Li, N., Li, T., Venkatasubramanian, S.: t-closeness: privacy beyond k-anonymity and l-diversity. In: 2007 IEEE 23rd International Conference on Data Engineering, pp. 106–115. IEEE (2007)
13. Erlingsson, Ú., Feldman, V., Mironov, I.: Amplification by shuffling: from local to central differential privacy via anonymity. In: Proceedings of the Thirtieth Annual ACM-SIAM Symposium on Discrete Algorithms, pp. 2468–2479. Society for Industrial and Applied Mathematics (2019)
14. Garg, L., Chukwu, E., Nasser, N., Chakraborty, C., Garg, G.: Anonymity preserving IoT based COVID-19 and other infectious disease contact tracing model. IEEE Access 08, 159402–159414 (2020)
15. Deng, J., Luo, Y., Yu, Q., Chen, F.: Privacy-preserving trajectory data publishing based on non-sensitive information analysis. J. Comput. Appl. 318(02), 488–493 (2017)
16. Liu, X., Xia, G., Xia, X., Zong, C., et al.: Personalized privacy protection for spatio-temporal data. J. Comput. Appl. 367(03), 643–650 (2021)
17. Li, Q., Qian, Y., Ren, Y., Ren, J.: Privacy-preserving recommendation based on kernel method in cloud computing. Comput. Mater. Continua 66(1), 779–791 (2021)
18. Xia, X., Wang, L., Zhang, Z., Qin, X., Sun, K., Ren, K.: A privacy-preserving and copy-deterrence content-based image retrieval scheme in cloud computing. IEEE Trans. Inf. Forensics Secur. 11(11), 2594–2608 (2016)
19. Xia, Y., Zhu, X., Sun, Z., Qin, K.: Towards privacy-preserving content-based image retrieval in cloud computing. IEEE Trans. Cloud Comput. 6, 276–286 (2018)
20. Verma, A.: Large-scale cluster management at google with Borg. In: Proceedings of the Tenth European Conference on Computer Systems (2015)
21. Booch, G.: Object Oriented Design with Applications. Benjamin-Cummings Publishing Co., Inc., Redwood City (1990)

Autoperman: Automatic Network Traffic Anomaly Detection with Ensemble Learning

Shangbin Han[1], Qianhong Wu[1], Han Zhang[2(✉)], Bo Qin[3], Jiangyuan Yao[4], and Willy Susilo[5]

[1] School of Cyber Science and Technology, Beihang University, Beijing, China
[2] INSC&BNRist, Tsinghua University, Beijing, China
zhhan@tsinghua.edu.cn
[3] School of Information, Renmin University of China, Beijing, China
[4] School of Computer Science and Technology, Hainan University, Haikou, China
[5] School of Computing and Information Technology, University of Wollongong, Wollongong, Australia

Abstract. Network traffic, which records users' behaviors, is valuable data resources for diagnosing the health of the network. Mining anomaly in network is essential for network defense. Although traditional machine learning approaches have good performance, their dependence on huge training data set with expensive labels make them impractical. Furthermore, after complex hyperparameters tuning, the detection model may not work. Facing these challenges, in this paper, we propose Autoperman through supervised learning. In Autoperman, machine learning algorithms with fixed hyperparameters as feature extractors are integrated, which utilize a small amount of training data to be initialized. Then Random Forest is selected as the anomaly classifier and achieves automatic parameters tuning via well studied online optimization theory. We compare the performance of Autoperman against traditional anomaly detection algorithms using public traffic datasets. The results demonstrate that Autoperman can perform about 6.9%, 34.2%, 4.3%, 2.2%, 37.6 % better than L-SVM, NL-SVM, LR, MLP, K-means, respectively.

Keywords: Anomaly detection · Autoperman · Ensemble learning

1 Introduction

The interconnected network has an unprecedented impact on economies and societies around the globe. By January 2021, the number of Internet users accounts for 59.5% of the global population [1]. The network presents users' convenience, which could not be achieved previously. However, it faces severe security issues, such as DDoS attack and malware.

Anomaly detection [2,4,6,20] plays an important role in timely response to stop service failures. In the past, manual anomaly detection was a natural solution to this problem. The IT operators define a regular expression to match

X. Sun et al. (Eds.): ICAIS 2022, CCIS 1587, pp. 616–628, 2022.
https://doi.org/10.1007/978-3-031-06761-7_49

anomalies. However, the rapid growth of traffic volume has imposed great challenges for manual monitoring methods. The manual anomaly detection cannot cope with large-scale traffic efficiently.

As a result, there is a huge demand in designing an automated anomaly detection framework. To this end, machine learning technologies (SVM [9], MLP [19]) is progressively being used in the anomaly detection area. However, we find that they have the following **limitations**: First, the definition of anomaly is limited. All anomalies are defined strictly at the data level. The anomalies that do not exist in the training data cannot be classified. Second, the traditional machine learning methods need huge training data with expensive labels to drive an optimal detection model. Third, it is hard to tune hyperparameters of a detection model in an offline manner. Even the trained model with optimal hyperparameters may be unable to work in the future due to the fast changing network behavior over time. Facing these challenges, in this paper, we make the following **contributions**:

First, we find that traditional machine learning anomaly detection algorithms will reduce their performance when training data is not enough and may not work over time.

Second, we propose an anomaly detection framework named Autoperman. It needs a small amount of training data to initialize model parameters. Autoperman uses popular detectors with fixed hyperparameters to extract features, and uses the dynamic labels defined by the application layer (feedback of IT operators) for further automatic update of classification model over time.

Third, we compare the performance of Autoperman against traditional anomaly detection algorithms using three public traffic datasets (i.e., CICIDS2017 [26]). The results show that Autoperman can produce competitive performance, which performs about 6.9%, 34.2%, 4.3%, 2.2%, 37.6 % better than L-SVM [13], NL-SVM [9], LR [23], MLP [19], K-means [15], respectively.

2   Background and Motivation

Traditional data-driven anomaly detection framework usually comprises three components: traffic collection, feature generation and anomaly detection. Traffic collection captures the traffic and sends it to the designated analysis equipment. Feature generation is the stage of feature extraction and labeling. Finally, the trained module predicts whether the current traffic is abnormal or not.

In reality, the data-driven anomaly detection needs huge training data to drive an optimal model. We take SVM and the public CICIDS2017 data set [26] as the example to illustrate this point. As shown in Fig. 1(a), the performance of the detection model is improved with the increase of training data. It means that more expensive labels are needed to derive an optimal model.

Besides, model training is time-consuming. Tuning hyperparameters of SVM is impractical for the data on Tuesday of CICIDS2017 with about half-a-million instances. In our experiment setting, $\frac{1}{9}$ of the data are randomly selected, and 12

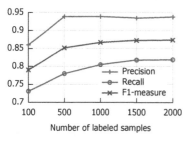 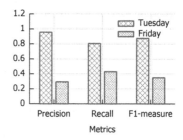

(a) SVM needs more training data to derive a satisfactory model.

(b) SVM may not work over time after turning hyperparametrs.

Fig. 1. Limitations of SVM.

groups of hyperparameter combinations of SVM are tuned through grid search and cross-validation. The time cost is as high as 3.5 h. Unfortunately, they may not work over time. We use the traffic on Tuesday and Friday of CICIDS2017 to show the problem. As shown in Fig. 1(b), the model is trained with data on Tuesday, and the corresponding detection shows good performance. However, when the well trained model is used for detecting traffic on Friday, the resulting performance is poor. All the metrics are lower than 0.5. The reason for this is that new attacks emerge over time, which affects the data pattern.

3   The Autoperman Framework

In this section, we present the Autoperman framework: the feature generation and the anomaly detection algorithm. The traffic collector is omitted here, since it is not the focus of this work.

3.1   Overview

Autoperman is an anomaly detection framework without tuning hyperparameters manually, designed for automatic and efficient abnormal traffic detection

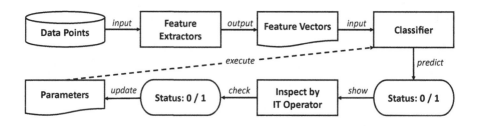

Fig. 2. Autoperman contains feature generation and automatic classifier update.

in large scale network. It proceeds by detecting anomalous traffic in an online fashion through supervised machine learning.

Instead of the heavy labeling workload, we leverage the feedback of IT operators to achieve the supervised learning. Figure 2 shows the process. First, network traffic is expressed in the form of value vector, which is a point on the hyperplane. We call them data points. Second, the existing machine learning algorithms (e.g., SVM) with different fixed hyperparameters are used as feature extractors to generate the feature vectors. Before the execution, all the feature extractors are initialized by small amount of training data. Third, random forest is adopted as the classifier to derive current status, whose function is to select the feature extractors. Fourth, IT operators feedback the labels for model update only when false alarm happens. That is, if the positive report shows an error, the real status is revealed. While for the negative report, IT operators selectively review and provide feedback when there is an error. Finally, the difference between the predicted status and real status are used to automatically update parameters of classifier. This online iterative parameter updating method continuously optimizes the classification model to achieve the optimal detection performance.

The advantages of Autoperman are that it can save most of the work of expert labeling, the time consuming of repetitive parameter tuning and realize automatic and efficient anomaly detection over time. Next, we give the design details for the feature generation and parameter update of classifier.

3.2   Feature Generation

Many learning based anomaly detectors have been used to detect anomalies. We model the detector as a mapping function: $\phi(\mathbf{x}) \rightarrow score \in [0, 1]$, where $\mathbf{x}$ is a data point, and the *score* represents the severity of anomaly. The *score* is a metric of the anomaly which can be seen as a feature.

The *score* is derived from the well-trained model. To avoid time-consuming hyperparameters tuning, we sample the hyperparameters of each detector to form different detectors. The *scores* predicted by all the detectors are concatenated to generate the feature vectors. Next, we introduce the selected anomaly detectors that implemented in scikit-learn [24] and corresponding hyperparameters combination.

1) **K-means.** It groups similar items with the number of clusters represented by the variable K. The algorithm works iteratively to assign each data point to one of the K clusters based on the features that are provided. We select the parameter $K = 2$, since anomaly detection is a binary classification problem.

2) **Logistic Regression.** It uses a *sigmoid function* to map any real values to probabilities. We consider linear logistic regression with different regular terms. We select the parameters from set {0.1, 0.3, 0.5, 0.7, 0.9, 1.1, 1.3, 1.5, 1.7, 1.9} for l_1-regularization and l_2-regularization, respectively.

3) **Decision Tree.** It is a tree structure for classification. The key hyperparameters of decision tree we consider are the criterion that split data points and the maximum depth of the decision tree. For the criterion, we can choose 'gini'

or 'entropy'. Additionally, for the tree depth, we can choose from the set {3, 5, 7, 9, 11, 13, 15, 17, 19} and do not set the maximum depth.

4) **SVM.** It aims to create the best decision boundary to classify n-dimensional feature space into groups. We employ two kinds of SVM: linear SVM and non-linear SVM. For the linear SVM, we need to sample the parameters of regularization term and corresponding coefficient. The regularization term has two options $\{l_1, l_2\}$, and the coefficient can be selected from {0.2, 0.4, 0.6, 0.8, 1.0, 1.2, 1.4, 1.6, 1.8, 2.0}. For the non-linear SVM, we have two parameters to sample, i.e., kernel function and the degree of a polynomial kernel function. We consider three kernel functions, such as *poly*, *rbf* and *sigmoid*. If the kernel function is *poly*, we sample its degree from the set {1, 2, 3, 4, 5}, otherwise we ignore the parameter.

5) **MLP.** MLP is a feed-forward artificial neural network model that maps multiple inputs to a set of outputs. In this paper, we fixed two hyperparameters. For the number of hidden layers, we get the value from the set {0, 1, 2, 3}. The neurons number of each layer can be chosen from {32, 64, 128, 256, 512}.

Finally, considering all the hyperparameters combination of each detector, we can get total 88 features.

3.3   Classifier

In this paper, we select random forest as the classifier due to its randomness.

Random Forest. Random forest consists of a large number of individual decision trees. Each tree in the random forest will make a class probability prediction, and the average prediction taken over all individual trees will be the final prediction of the model [24].

The final result is obtained via equal weight distribution of each decision tree. However, the characteristics of network traffic will change over time. Hence the equal weight should be adjusted *automatically* according to the network environment. Next, we describe how to update weight by leveraging online optimization.

Automatic Update of Weight. As noted in Fig. 2, the prediction status is set before the real status is revealed (findings of IT operator). Therefore the prediction can be cast as an online convex optimization (OCO) problem [11].

The metric of *regret* commonly used in the machine learning literature is introduced to measure the performance of online algorithms. $Regret_T$ is the accumulated difference of losses between *weight* (vector $\mathbf{w}$) and an offline *optimal weight* (a vector $\mathbf{w}^*$) called the optimal static policy, which is taken when the entire data is known in hindsight. Specifically, the worst-case static regret constructed in a horizon T-iterations repeated game is defined as follow:

$$Regret_T = \max_{\mathcal{F}} \left\{ \sum_{t=1}^{T} f_t(\mathbf{w}_t) - \min_{W^* \in \mathcal{S}} \sum_{t=1}^{T} f_t(\mathbf{w}^*) \right\} \tag{1}$$

Let the concatenated probability values predicted by decision trees in Random Forest be vector $\mathbf{v}_t$, the prediction of Random Forest be $\hat{y}_t$, the IT operator's feedback be y_t, and the loss function be f_t. We hope that when the prediction is accurate ($\hat{y}_t = y_t$), the loss can be small, while the wrong prediction has the opposite effect. Therefore, we would like to use the following convex loss function of $\mathbf{w}_t$ over any convex vector set $\mathcal{S}$:

$$f_t(\mathbf{w}_t) = -y_t \log p_t - (1 - y_t) \log(1 - p_t) \tag{2}$$

where p_t is a discrete anomaly probability distribution: $p_t = \frac{1}{1+exp(-\mathbf{w}_t \cdot \mathbf{v}_t)}$. If $p_t > 0.5$, then the prediction $\hat{y}_t = 1$, otherwise $\hat{y}_t = 0$. Therefore, when IT operator returns a feedback $\hat{y}_t = 1$, the loss will decrease with increasing p_t, and when the feedback $\hat{y}_t = 0$, the situation is reversed as expected. Next we can give the details of weight update.

Follow the regularized leader (FTRL) is an excellent algorithm for OCO framework. To derive the best *weight* $\mathbf{w}_t$ at current t, any vector that has minimal loss on all past rounds is preferred:

$$\mathbf{w}_{t+1} = \arg \min_{\mathbf{w}} \sum_{i=1}^{t} f_i(\mathbf{w}) + R(\mathbf{w}) \tag{3}$$

where $R(\mathbf{w})$ is a L_2 regularized function which can stabilize the update of weight $\mathbf{w}$. We set the regularization term $R(\mathbf{w})$ as: $R(\mathbf{w}) = \frac{1}{2\eta}||\mathbf{w}||_2^2$, where η is the learning rate. According to KKT condition [8], we can obtain the solution by setting the derivative of (3) to be 0. Therefore, we can obtain the update policy of best weight as follows: $\mathbf{w}_{t+1} = \mathbf{w}_t - \eta \nabla f_t(\mathbf{w}_t)$, where $\nabla f_t(\mathbf{w}_t)$ is the gradient of f_t at $\mathbf{w}_t$: $\nabla f_t(\mathbf{w}_t) = (p_t - y_t)\mathbf{x}_t$.

Finally, Algorithm 1 shows the proposed Online FTRL for updating weight (OFUW) algorithm. Algorithm 1 takes initial weight $\mathbf{w}$ and learning rate η_t as input. After receiving a probability value vector $\mathbf{v}_t$ (Line 2), it uses the current weight $\mathbf{w}_t$ to predict anomaly (Line 3). Subsequently, the true status of network is observed by IT operators (Line 4). At last, $\mathbf{w}_t$ is updated with the loss function (Line 5–6).

Algorithm 1: Online FTRL for updating weight (OFUW)

Input: $\mathbf{w}_1 \in \mathcal{S}$, learning rate η
1 **for** $t \in T$ **do**
2 $\quad$ Get vector $\mathbf{v}_t$ from Random Forest;
3 $\quad$ Predict the status $\hat{y}_t$ with p_t;
4 $\quad$ IT operator returns the real status $y_t \in \{0, 1\}$ if $\hat{y}_t$ is wrong;
5 $\quad$ $\nabla f_t(\mathbf{w}_t) = (p_t - y_t)\mathbf{v}_t$;
6 $\quad$ $\mathbf{w}_{t+1} = \mathbf{w}_t - \eta \nabla f_t(\mathbf{w}_t)$;

In theory [25], given an appropriate choice of $\eta = \psi(\frac{1}{\sqrt{t}})$, the FTRL algorithm can derive a theoretical guarantees of upper bound of regret, which is a sublinear function of T, i.e., $o(\sqrt{T})$. This shows Autoperman with OFUW has no regret as T goes to infinity.

4   Evaluation

In this section, we evaluate the performance of Autoperman with public traffic data sets.

4.1   Data Sets

In our evaluation, three public network traffic data sets are used to examine the performance of Autoperman:

1. **Kitsune network attack data set.** It is generated on an IoT network [17], which contains Denial of Service (SSDP Flood, SYN DoS), Botnet Malware (Mirai), etc. Each attack data set is labeled as malicious or not.
2. **UNSW-NB15 data set.** It is a traffic data set mixed with normal real modern network behaviors and synthetic contemporary attacks [18]. The data set has totally 49 features with the class label (0 or 1).
3. **CICIDS2017 data set.** It is generated from a proposed B-Profile system [26]. The data set is captured from July 3, 2017 (Monday) to July 7, 2017 (Friday). The normal instances are labeled with "BENIGN" while the remaining with common attacks.

4.2   Experiment Setup

We conduct all our experiment on a Linux server, which is configured with 32G memory, 9T hard disk and 16 Intel Xeon E5-2630 CPUs. All the feature extractors in Autoperman are implemented from scikit-learn [24] and they are all initialized with default hyperparameters using small training samples, e.g., 500 samples. For classifier Random Forest, the number of trees is set to 100, the depth of each tree is considered no maximum. For algorithm OFUW, we set the default value of learning rate η to $\frac{1}{\sqrt{t}}$, where t is the iteration times. To simulate the feedback of IT operators, Autoperman uses the labels of public traffic data set only when false alarm happens.

4.3   Baselines

We compare the performance with five methods: one classical unsupervised learning methods K-means [15], three classical supervised learning methods linear SVM (L-SVM) [13], non-linear SVM (NL-SVM) [9] and Logistic regression (LR) [23], one neural network method Multi-layer Perceptron (MLP) [19].

We use the following metrics to evaluate the performance:

1. Precision: It calculates the proportion of predicted positive instance that are actually positive instance. It is expressed as: Precision $= \frac{TP}{TP+FP}$, where TP denotes True Positives and FP denotes False Positives.

2. Recall: It is the ability of a detection model to identify positive instance, which is defined as: Recall $= \frac{TP}{TP+FN}$, where FN denotes False Negatives.

3. F1-measure: It considers both Precision and Recall, and is defined as the harmonic average of the two metric: F1-measure $= \frac{2*Precision*Recall}{Precision+Recall}$.

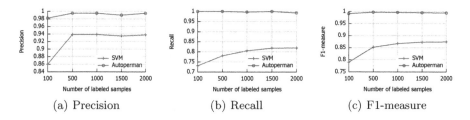

(a) Precision   (b) Recall   (c) F1-measure

Fig. 3. Autoperman can maintain good performance with a small amount of labels.

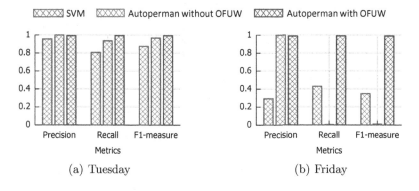

(a) Tuesday   (b) Friday

Fig. 4. Autoperman can automatically adapt to the network over time.

4.4 Revisiting the Motivating Example

In this section, we will revisiting the motivating example to verify the effectiveness of Autoperman. All the parameters are set with default value. We also plot the results of SVM to make comparisons.

First, we use the same traffic trace to investigate the performance impact of training samples number for Autoperman. The results are illustrated in Fig. 3. From this figure, we can see that the performance of Autoperman fluctuates very little w.r.t. different number of training samples. Additionally, SVM needs more data to perform better. When the amount of training data is 100, the precision of Autoperman can reach up to 0.98, while SVM is lower than 0.9. Therefore, the detection performance of Autoperman is much better than that of SVM. This is because Autoperman can use feedback from IT operators to improve performance. Autoperman uses less labels to produce comparable performance, which has less labeling cost.

Second, we investigate the adaptability of Autoperman. We also paint the SVM and Autoperman without OFUW for comparison. Subsequently, Fig. 4 shows the results. We use the data on Tuesday to train detection models and use the trained models to detect anomalies on Tuesday and Friday. Specifically, Fig. 4(a) shows the performance comparison for SVM and Autoperman on Tuesday. We can see that both SVM and Autoperman can achieve satisfactory performance. However, as Fig. 4(b) shown, SVM has poor detection accuracy. Although the precision of Autoperman without OFUW is high, the Recall and F1-measure are almost zero. In contrast, Autoperman with OFUW can work very well in this case. The reason is that Autoperman can update parameters to adapt to changes in the network. This means that Autoperman can automatically adapt to the dynamic network environment without repetitive and time-consuming hyperparameters tuning.

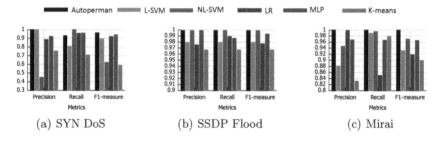

(a) SYN DoS   (b) SSDP Flood   (c) Mirai

Fig. 5. Detection accuracy under Kitsune network attack data set.

4.5   Performance Comparison

In this part, we compare the performance of Autoperman with baseline methods on the three public traffic data sets. Figure 5 shows the results on Kitsune network attack data set. On the whole, Autoperman shows the best performance. Take SYN DoS (Fig. 5(a)) for example, in terms of F1-measure metric, Autoperman performs about 6.9%, 34.2%, 4.3%, 2.2%, 37.6% better than L-SVM, NL-SVM, LR, MLP, K-means, respectively. The reason for this is that Autoperman can use feedback of IT operator to automatically update to adapt to the dynamic characteristics of network data.

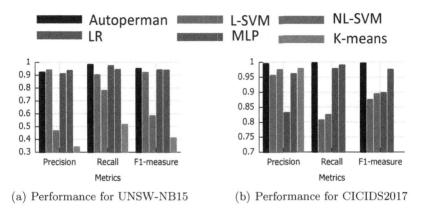

Fig. 6. Detection accuracy under UNSW-NB15 and CICIDS2017 data sets.

Figure 6(a) shows the performance for UNSW-NB15 data set. The results are basically the same as Fig. 5. We can see that Autoperman can improve the detection accuracy by up to 50%. Figure 6(b) shows the performance under CICIDS2017 data set. We can see that Autoperman is obviously better than other algorithms. Although K-means has high precision, the other two metrics are basically 0, which are not painted here. This means the detection model cannot find anomalies. Generally, Autoperman shows better performance, and it only needs a small amount of labels to get competitive accuracy.

5   Related Work

Anomaly detection is an important component in the field of network security. A much more convincing line of research has been proposed.

Supervised machine learning is widely used in the anomaly detection domain. Shubhra et al. [9] optimized the SVM algorithm to improve the detection accuracy. Kasim et al. [13] employed SVM as the classifier to identify anomalies from features processed by autoencoder. Sultana et al. [23] used logistic regression for anomaly detection in smart power grids. Mao et al. [16] applied the decision tree to selected feature vectors for anomaly detection.

Ahmed et al. [3] used the decision tree and rule-based models to construct different anomaly detectors. They have high detection accuracy. Unfortunately, these methods rely heavily on huge labels.

Besides supervised learning methods, many unsupervised learning methods have been proposed. Yang et al. [15] evaluated different clustering methods, K-means, Canopy, FarthestFirst for network traffic classification, and K-means shows the better performance in accuracy. Keval et al. [7] used K-means clustering to identify anomalies in traffic videos. Sahil et al. [10] optimized DBSCAN (Density-Based Spatial Clustering of Applications with Noise) algorithm to achieve clustering of abnormal Internet of things data. Ning et al. [12] proposed a multi-kernel clustering based anomaly detection methods to make up the absent traffic characteristics. These approaches have the advantage of not using labels. However, the detection accuracy is reduced.

The recent popular deep learning approaches [22] were also applied to detect anomalies in network traffic. Teoh et al. [19,29] proposed advanced deep learning techniques MLP to detect malicious traffic. Vinod et al. [14] evaluated different machine learning algorithms for anomaly detection, including MLP, decision tree, etc. [17,21,28] proposed autoencoder based anomaly detection methods. [5,27] adopted the recurrent neural network LSTM as the anomaly detector. These methods have strong learning ability and perform very well. However, they require a massive amount of training data combined with significant computational resources.

6   Conclusion

In this paper, we proposed an Autoperman framework to solve the limitations of traditional network traffic anomaly detection based on machine learning algorithms. Autoperman framework contains feature generation and online anomaly detection. Autoperman consumes a small amount of training data to initialize the detection model and automatically tune parameters through online optimization theory, which has less labeling cost and does not need time-consuming parameter tuning. We conducted experiments to show that Autoperman has better performance than traditional methods on two representative public traffic datasets.

Acknowledgements. This paper is supported by the National Key R&D Program of China through project 2020YFB1005600, the Beijing Natural Science Foundation through project M21031, the Natural Science Foundation of China through projects U21A20467, 61932011 and 61972019.

References

1. Digital 2021: Global overview report. https://datareportal.com/reports/digital-2021-global-overview-report
2. Afzal, R., Murugesan, R.K.: Rule-based anomaly detection model with stateful correlation enhancing mobile network security. Intell. Autom. Soft Comput. **31**(3), 1825–1841 (2022)
3. Ahmim, A., Maglaras, L., Ferrag, M.A., Derdour, M., Janicke, H.: A novel hierarchical intrusion detection system based on decision tree and rules-based models. In: 2019 15th International Conference on Distributed Computing in Sensor Systems (DCOSS), pp. 228–233. IEEE (2019)
4. Assiri, A.: Anomaly classification using genetic algorithm-based random forest model for network attack detection. CMC-Comput. Mater. Continua **66**(1), 767–778 (2021)
5. Chastikova, V., Sotnikov, V.: Method of analyzing computer traffic based on recurrent neural networks. J. Phys. Conf. Ser. **1353**, 012133 (2019)
6. Dong, Z., Han, J., et al.: Deep learning anomaly detection based on hierarchical status-connection features in networked control systems (2021)

7. Doshi, K., Yilmaz, Y.: Fast unsupervised anomaly detection in traffic videos. In: Proceedings of the IEEE/CVF Conference on Computer Vision and Pattern Recognition Workshops, pp. 624–625 (2020)

8. Dreves, A., Facchinei, F., Kanzow, C., Sagratella, S.: On the solution of the KKT conditions of generalized Nash equilibrium problems. SIAM J. Optim. **21**(3), 1082–1108 (2011)

9. Dwivedi, S., Vardhan, M., Tripathi, S.: Building an efficient intrusion detection system using grasshopper optimization algorithm for anomaly detection. Clust. Comput. **24**(3), 1881–1900 (2021). https://doi.org/10.1007/s10586-020-03229-5

10. Garg, S., Kaur, K., Batra, S., Kaddoum, G., Kumar, N., Boukerche, A.: A multi-stage anomaly detection scheme for augmenting the security in IoT-enabled applications. Futur. Gener. Comput. Syst. **104**, 105–118 (2020)

11. Hazan, E., et al.: Introduction to online convex optimization. Found. Trends® Optim. **2**(3–4), 157–325 (2016)

12. Hu, N., Tian, Z., Lu, H., Du, X., Guizani, M.: A multiple-kernel clustering based intrusion detection scheme for 5G and IoT networks. Int. J. Mach. Learn. Cybernet. **12**, 1–16 (2021)

13. Kasim, Ö.: An efficient and robust deep learning based network anomaly detection against distributed denial of service attacks. Comput. Netw. **180**, 107390 (2020)

14. Kumar, V., Choudhary, V., Sahrawat, V., Kumar, V.: Detecting intrusions and attacks in the network traffic using anomaly based techniques. In: 2020 5th International Conference on Communication and Electronics Systems (ICCES), pp. 554–560. IEEE (2020)

15. Liu, Y., Xue, H., Wei, G., Wu, L., Wang, Yu.: A comparative study on network traffic clustering. In: Liu, J.K., Huang, X. (eds.) NSS 2019. LNCS, vol. 11928, pp. 443–455. Springer, Cham (2019). https://doi.org/10.1007/978-3-030-36938-5_27

16. Mao, J., Hu, Y., Jiang, D., Wei, T., Shen, F.: CBFS: a clustering-based feature selection mechanism for network anomaly detection. IEEE Access **8**, 116216–116225 (2020)

17. Mirsky, Y., Doitshman, T., Elovici, Y., Shabtai, A.: Kitsune: an ensemble of autoencoders for online network intrusion detection. arXiv preprint arXiv:1802.09089 (2018)

18. Moustafa, N., Slay, J.: UNSW-NB15: a comprehensive data set for network intrusion detection systems (UNSW-NB15 network data set). In: 2015 Military Communications and Information Systems Conference (MilCIS), pp. 1–6. IEEE (2015)

19. MR, G.R., Somu, N., Mathur, A.: A multilayer perceptron model for anomaly detection in water treatment plants. Int. J. Crit. Infrastruct. Prot. **31**, 100393 (2020)

20. Muneer, A., Taib, S.M., Fati, S.M., Balogun, A.O., Aziz, I.A.: A hybrid deep learning-based unsupervised anomaly detection in high dimensional data. Comput. Mater. Contin **71**, 6073–6088 (2021)

21. Neuschmied, H., Winter, M., Hofer-Schmitz, K., Stojanovic, B., Kleb, U.: Two stage anomaly detection for network intrusion detection. In: Proceedings of the ICISSP (2021)

22. Nkenyereye, L., Tama, B.A., Lim, S.: A stacking-based deep neural network approach for effective network anomaly detection. CMC-Comput. Mater. Continua **66**(2), 2217–2227 (2021)

23. Noureen, S.S., Bayne, S.B., Shaffer, E., Porschet, D., Berman, M.: Anomaly detection in cyber-physical system using logistic regression analysis. In: 2019 IEEE Texas Power and Energy Conference (TPEC), pp. 1–6. IEEE (2019)

24. Pedregosa, F., et al.: Scikit-learn: machine learning in python. J. Mach. Learn. Res. **12**, 2825–2830 (2011)

25. Shalev-Shwartz, S., et al.: Online learning and online convex optimization. Found. Trends Mach. Learn. **4**(2), 107–194 (2011)

26. Sharafaldin, I., Lashkari, A.H., Ghorbani, A.A.: Toward generating a new intrusion detection dataset and intrusion traffic characterization. In: ICISSp, pp. 108–116 (2018)

27. Shi, Z., Li, J., Wu, C., Li, J.: DeepWindow: an efficient method for online network traffic anomaly detection. In: 2019 IEEE 21st International Conference on High Performance Computing and Communications; IEEE 17th International Conference on Smart City; IEEE 5th International Conference on Data Science and Systems (HPCC/SmartCity/DSS), pp. 2403–2408. IEEE (2019)

28. Siddiqui, A.J., Boukerche, A.: Adaptive ensembles of autoencoders for unsupervised IoT network intrusion detection. Computing **103**, 1–24 (2021)

29. Teoh, T., Chiew, G., Franco, E.J., Ng, P., Benjamin, M., Goh, Y.: Anomaly detection in cyber security attacks on networks using MLP deep learning. In: 2018 International Conference on Smart Computing and Electronic Enterprise (ICSCEE), pp. 1–5. IEEE (2018)

Emotion Features Research
for Internet-of-Emotions

Demeng Wu[1], Zhongjie Li[1], Xingqun Tang[1], Wenbo Wu[2],
and Huiping Jiang[1(✉)]

[1] Brain Cognitive Computing Lab, School of Information Engineering,
Minzu University of China, Beijing 100081, China
jianghp@muc.edu.cn
[2] Case Western Reserve University, Cleveland, USA

Abstract. Recent advancements in human-computer interaction research of Internet-of-Emotion have led to the possibility of emotional communication via the human-computer interface for a user with neuropsychiatric disorders or disabilities. There are several ways of recording psychophysiology data from humans, and in this paper, we focus on emotion detection using electroencephalogram (EEG). Various emotion extraction techniques can be used on the recorded EEG data to classify emotional states. Band energy (E), frequency band energy ratio (REE), the logarithm of the frequency band energy ratio (LREE), and differential entropy (DE) of band energy ratio is some emotion features that previously have been used to classify EEG data in various emotional states. Four different emotion features were analyzed in this paper, classifying EEG data associated with specific emotional states. The results showed that DE is the best choice in Wavelet Transform-Support Vector Machine (WT-SVM) model during the period of training an SVM classifier to be accurate over the whole data sets (16 subjects), and the whole accuracy up to 86.5%, while DE's classification results are between 73.81% to 97.62%. This phenomenon shows that it is difficult to find features that are generally working well over each subject, and there is also the possibility that the pictures of the International Affective Picture System (IAPS) did not induce strong enough emotions on some subjects making it difficult to classify some emotional states. Based on the result, we only conclude that DE is the optimal choice for the WT-SVM model, and the individual factors will be considered as one of the influencing factors of the emotion classification system in future work.

Keywords: Pattern recognition · Emotion computing · Feature extraction · DE

1 Introduction

Embedded Internet-of-Things (IoT) devices get progressively smarter and more connected, running software intelligence near the point where the data is being generated within a network. And having memory and compute capabilities at the IoT solves multiple conundrums related to connectivity, bandwidth, latencies, and privacy/security, meanwhile, there existed many problems to be considered for IoT's applications [1–4].

© The Author(s), under exclusive license to Springer Nature Switzerland AG 2022
X. Sun et al. (Eds.): ICAIS 2022, CCIS 1587, pp. 629–641, 2022.
https://doi.org/10.1007/978-3-031-06761-7_50

With advances in technology requirements for the design of machines and products must have a deep humanistic concern, it should be to enhance human-computer interaction, to create harmony in line with the real needs of the user interaction products. Due to the diversification of multi-user demand for massive heterogeneous IoT information, the IoT technology needs to add intelligent elements, and change from "perception" to "cognition". The highest realm of IoT devices is to connect emotions, which will be the trend of IoT. And emotion recognition is also possible to develop an HCI-based cloud-assisted platform that can improve individualization services for the user of IoT.

Since it is necessary for HCI equipment to be able to recognize human emotions automatically, there existed much successful research on emotion recognition using facial expressions, text, speech, or gestures as stimuli [5–11]. In addition, cerebral signals, EEG, have received much attention, which is expected to contain the comprehensive information of emotion in that recognition of emotions from Electroencephalogram (EEG) signals have the benefit of being more passive and less intrusive for the human than facial expressions or vocal intonation [12–14].

Recently, electroencephalography (EEG) has played a key role in HCI systems. EEG reflects the electrical activities of the brain and provides a subjective emotional response based on the subject's own experience [15]. Soleymani [16] used face videos, audio signals, eye gaze data, and peripheral/central nervous system physiological signals to build a multimodal database recorded in response to affective stimuli with the goal of emotion recognition and implicit tagging research. And the result for single modality and modality fusion shows the potential uses of the recorded modalities and the significance of the emotion elicitation protocol. They proposed an emotion recognition system using multimodal bi-potential signals.

An emotion recognition system is developed based on valence/arousal model using electroencephalography (EEG) signals [17], in which EEG signals are decomposed into the gamma, beta, alpha, and theta frequency bands using discrete wavelet transform (DWT), and spectral features are extracted from each frequency band. Support vector machine (SVM), K-nearest neighbor (KNN), and artificial neural network (ANN) are used to classify emotional states.

Koelstra and Patras [18] also used EEG signals to distinguish different emotions in response to music videos. EEG signal is a non-stationary time series signal with strong randomness. It has the characteristics of weak intensity and strong background noise. It needs some processing techniques to extract its characteristics. Feature extraction means to minimize the most important loss in the original signal, and simplify the huge original data set, so the goal of feature extraction is to minimize the complexity of the application, to reduce the consumption of information processing. There are many methods to extract EEG features, such as time-frequency distribution, fast Fourier transform, wavelet transform, autoregressive method, etc. [19, 20].

EEG classification is a pattern recognition problem, linear discriminant analysis, support vector machine (SVM), and deep learning model are commonly used [21, 22]. Deep learning models such as auto-encoder (AE), deep belief networks (DBN), convolutional neural networks (CNN), and recurrent neural networks (RNN) are widely used in emotion computing [23, 24]. However, EEG contains a lot of time-frequency information, which means that deep learning may be more effective if it can make targeted use of the timing of EEG signals. The traditional RNN model may appear gradient vanishing or gradient explosion in the training process. Hochreiter&Schimidhuber [25] improved the RNN model and proposed a long short-term memory network (LSTM) with long-term memory function, and it is much faster and more accurate than both standard Recurrent Neural Nets (RNNs) and time-windowed Multilayer Perceptron (MLPs). These results support that BLSTM is an effective architecture in text, speech recognition.

Some common ones that previously have been used for EEG data associated with affective or emotional states are K-Nearest Neighbor, Bayesian Network, Support Vector Machine (SVM), and Deep Learning. Rani et al. [26] strongly support SVM based on a comparative study of four machine learning methods - K-nearest neighbor, regression tree (RT), Bayesian network, and support vector machine (SVM), and similar claims are also supported [27–29].

Most of existed work mainly focused on an acceptable accuracy for some specific emotion recognition system based on EEG, so it is difficult to compare the results between different studies due to different experiment environments, preprocessing techniques, feature selection, etc. However, studies have shown that various factors such as data acquisition and emotion feature extraction techniques can strongly affect the accuracy of results. Even if several methods have successfully been used to develop emotion classifiers from physiological indices, it is still important to select an appropriate feature extraction method for the classification of EEG data to attain uniformity in various aspects of emotion selection.

In consideration of the fact that SVM was used in most of the empirical studies, we have found and were suitable for the classification of EEG data associated with specific affective/emotional states based on the achieved classification accuracy. And the important features of EEG signal patterns within specific frequency bands vary slightly according to the condition of each subject, therefore, this manuscript will analyze the variations for the methods of emotion feature extraction in the time-frequency domains under the classification framework of WT-SVM, which seemed to be the most common ones among the classifiers with the highest attained accuracy.

In this paper, we analyze the accuracy of four emotion features commonly used in WT-SVM. In Sect. 2, we will introduce the acquisition of EEG data. Section 3 presents data feature extraction based on WT. The emotion classification results are analyzed in Sect. 4. Discussion and Conclusions are in Sect. 5.

2 Materials and EEG Data Acquire

The goal of the experiments was to collect EEG signals that arise by the various emotional states in subjects as they look at different pictures that are inducing strong emotions. Presenting emotional pictures to subjects is a common way to evoke these states. International affective picture systems (IAPS) and China affective picture systems (CAPS) are standard picture databases specially designed for experiments in emotions with normative values for valence, arousal, and dominance [30, 31]. To ensure the emotions were distinct, two affective states were selected: low valence–high arousal (LV_HA) and high valence–high arousal (HV_HA), 70 positive and 70 negative pictures were selected from

IAPS and CAPS. A total of 16 subjects (6 men and 10 women) participated in the experiment. All subjects were students of the Minzu University of China and aged from 19 to 23 years. The subjects were from different cultural backgrounds and fields of study. The EEG signals were captured from left and right frontal, central, anterior temporal, and parietal regions according to the 10–20 system and referenced to Cz.

During the experiments, EEG data for each subject was recorded using the Neuroscan 4.5 system. This device has a maximum of 64 electrodes and collects 250 samples every second. We used all electrodes to record the neural activity of the brain. Previous studies have shown that each brain region has a different simultaneous emotional response [32], so we decided to record all EEG channels.

Each subject took approximately 18 min individually to complete an experiment. Based on these findings, the experiment was executed as described as follows and shown in Fig. 1.

(1) EPRIME2.0 was applied for the automated projection of emotion-related pictures.
(2) 140 IAPS pictures (70 pictures for each emotion cluster as positive arousing/calm, negative arousing/calm) were displayed randomly for 3 s with a gap of a black screen between 3 s. The purpose of the black screen duration was to reset the emotional state of subjects offering them the time to relax having no emotional content. A cross shape projection was displayed for 1 s before each picture to attract the attention of the subject. This process was repeated for every picture.
(3) A subject may feel an emotion that differs from the one expected. Therefore, each subject was asked to report his/her emotion on a Self-Assessment Manikin. Each subject rated their level of emotion on a five-point scale.
(4) During the whole process, subjects were directed to stay quiet and still with a few eye blinks as possible to get rid of other artifacts.

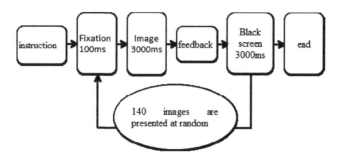

Fig. 1. Presentation of stimuli.

After the recorded EEG data of each subject were verified, the raw EEG signals were be preprocessed. The main preprocessing steps consisted of artifact rejection, filtering, and epoch selection using the software of Scan4.5. And this study protocol was approved by the institutional review boards (ECMUC2019008CO) at the Minzu University of China. All participants provided IRB-approved written informed consent after they were explained the experimental procedure.

3   Related Work of Emotion Feature Based on Wavelet Transform

Power spectra of the EEG were often assessed in five distinct frequency bands, which are delta (δ: 1–3 Hz), theta (θ: 4–7 Hz), alpha (α: 8–13 Hz), beta (β: 14–30 Hz), and gamma (γ: 31–50 Hz), to examine their features accompanied by the different emotional states. The alpha and beta bands have been shown to contain useful features [33, 34], and it is also known that the distribution of the power spectrum in brain wave patterns changes [35] when the subject is stimulated by an emotional picture.

Wavelet Transform (WT) is a commonly used time-frequency transform method, which can decompose the signal into different frequency ranges and save the time information of the signal. It is often used to extract EEG features in affective computing [36].

Each WT has a mother wavelet and a parent wavelet namely a scaling function. Assumed that is a square-integrable function, which means. If the Fourier transform satisfies the Eq. (1), then could be used as a mother wavelet.

$$\int_{-\infty}^{+\infty} \frac{|\psi(t)|^2}{|\omega|} d\omega < +\infty \tag{1}$$

All wavelet series of WT can be obtained by the translation and scaling of the mother wavelet and the father wavelet. The scaling multiple is an integer power of 2, and the magnitude of the translation is related to the scaling multiple. Wavelet series are standard orthogonal, that is, they are not only two orthogonal, but also must be normalized. The complete WT is described as Eq. (2)

$$f(t) = \sum_{-\infty}^{+\infty} c_k \phi(t-k) + \sum_{k=-\infty}^{+\infty} \sum_{j=0}^{+\infty} d_{j,k} \psi(2^j t - k) \tag{2}$$

In which, $\phi(x)$ is the father wavelet, $\psi(x)$ is the mother wavelet. And the parameters c and D can be calculated by choosing suitable $\phi(x)$ and $\psi(x)$. The approximate wavelet expansion is shown in Eq. (3).

$$f(t) = \sum_k \sum_j a_{j,k} \psi_{j,k}^*(t) \tag{3}$$

The signal is decomposed into a series of wavelet bases and scale functions, and the solution is Eq. (4).

$$WT_f(a,b) = \frac{1}{\sqrt{a}} \int_R f(t) \psi^* \left(\frac{t-b}{a} \right) dt, a > 0 \tag{4}$$

In which, $f(t) \in L^2(R)$. Carry out 5-scale wavelet transform (as shown in Fig. 2) on the data after down-sampling, and decompose the low-frequency band in each layer. After wavelet decomposition, the wavelet coefficients of six frequency bands can be obtained. We keep the coefficients of the lower five frequency bands (the coefficients of the lowest five frequency bands roughly correspond to the five bands of EEG), and the wavelet coefficients of the frequency band corresponding to δ wave are approximate coefficients, and the wavelet coefficients of θ band, α band, β band, and γ band are detail coefficients.

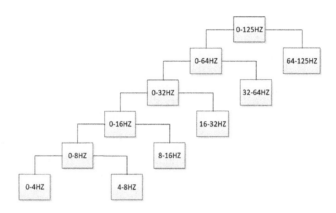

Fig. 2. Schematic diagram of EEG signal decomposition.

The decomposition results of the wavelet transform are shown in Table 1.

Table 1. Comparison of WT with the bands of EEG

Wavelet coefficients	EEG bands	Wavelet coefficients bands
CD1	Noise	64–125
CD2	γ	32–64
CD3	β	16–32
CD4	α	8–16
CD5	θ	4–8
CA5	δ	0–4

3.1   The Selection of Mother Wavelet

Choosing the right mother wavelet is very important to extract EEG features effectively. MATLAB can finish the WT based on fifteen kinds of mother wavelets, and there is no uniform standard for the selection of the mother wavelet, which is mainly based on the accuracy of classification and the effect of Sym8 is better than another mother wavelet, so we choose Sym8 wavelet as the mother wavelet in this study. Compared with dbN wavelet, symN has better symmetry, which can reduce the phase distortion of signal analysis and reconstruction to some extent. Figure 3 shows the comparison between the db8 mother wavelet function and Sym8 mother wavelet function.

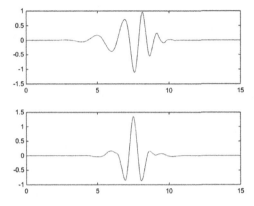

Fig. 3. db8 mother wavelet(top) and sym8 mother wavelet(bottom).

The difference in the symmetry between the sym8 and db8 can be found. Meanwhile, they are consistent in support length, continuity, and filter length. Taking the Fz channel of EEG as an example, the preprocessed signal is shown in Fig. 4, after the 5-layer wavelet transform, the result of Sym8 wavelet transform is shown in Fig. 5.

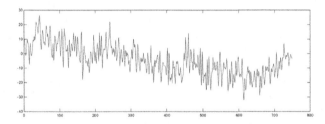

Fig. 4. EEG signal preprocessed by FZ channel of a sample.

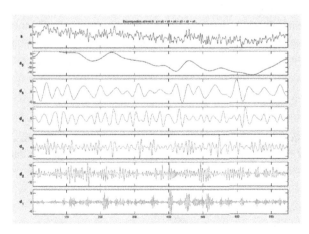

Fig. 5. EEG signals of each frequency band after FZ 5-layer wavelet transform.

In which a5 is the decomposed 0–4 Hz signal, d5 is the decomposed 4–8 Hz signal, d4 is the decomposed 8–16 Hz EEG signal, d3 is the decomposed 16–32 Hz EEG signal, d2 is the decomposed 32–64 Hz signal, d1 is the decomposed 64–125 Hz signal and d1 is high-frequency noise. The signal is restored with 5 low-frequency bands, and the results are shown in Fig. 6.

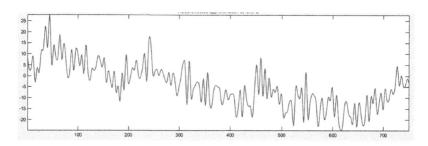

Fig. 6. The restore result of Fz.

Compared with Fig. 4 and Fig. 6, it is found that the reduced EEG signal is very consistent with the original EEG signal by using Sym8 wavelet base, and the signal becomes more stable due to the removal of high-frequency noise. The wavelet coefficients of each frequency band are calculated after the WT for the EEG signal. And we need to further process to extract EEG features from the wavelet coefficients.

Commonly used emotional features include band energy, band energy ratio, logarithm, and differential entropy of band energy ratio based on WT. Band energy is the energy of each band after WT. It is obtained by summing the square of the coefficients of each band. The formula is Eq. (5).

$$E_i = \sum_{j=1}^{n_i} d_{ij}^2 \tag{5}$$

In which, E_i is the energy of the i-th band, n_i is the number of decomposition coefficients for the i-th layer, d_{ij} is the j-th coefficient of wavelet for the i-th layer. The frequency band energy ratio is the energy ratio of each frequency band in the total energy. Its solution is Eq. (6).

$$REE_i = \frac{E_i}{\sum_{j=1}^{n} E_j} \tag{6}$$

In which REE_i is the ratio of the ith band, n is the number of bands. The logarithm of the frequency band energy ratio is the logarithm of the frequency band energy ratio of each frequency band. The solution formula is as follows Eq. (7):

$$LREE_i = \log_{10} REE_i \tag{7}$$

In which *LREE$_i$* is the logarithm for the i-th REE. If the distribution of the signal is different, the solution of differential entropy is not the same. Assuming that the collected EEG signal x obeys the Gaussian distribution in Eq. (8):

$$p(x) = \frac{1}{\sqrt{2\pi\sigma^2}} e^{-\frac{(x-m)^2}{2\sigma^2}}, -\infty < x < \infty \tag{8}$$

In which,

$$m = E(x) = \int_{-\infty}^{\infty} xp(x)dx \tag{9}$$

$$\sigma^2 = E\left[(x-m)^2\right] = \int_{-\infty}^{\infty} (x-m)^2 p(x)dx \tag{10}$$

And the solution formula of differential entropy is as Eq. (11):

$$h(x) = -\int_{-\infty}^{\infty} p(x)logp(x)dx = \frac{1}{2}log\left(2\pi e\sigma^2\right) \tag{11}$$

It can be seen from the above formula that the key to solving the differential entropy is to find the variance of the EEG signal. The variance of the EEG signal is approximately the same as the average value of EEG energy in each frequency band. In practical application, the logarithm of band energy ratio is often used instead of differential entropy. The simplified formula of differential entropy is as Eq. (12):

$$DE_i = \log_{10} E_i \tag{12}$$

4   Research of Four Emotion Features Based on WT-SVM

Support vector machine (SVM) is the most common classifier in pattern recognition. It performs well in solving small samples, nonlinear and high-dimensional pattern recognition. Support vector machine is a two-class classification model. It mainly classifies data by finding the hyperplane with the largest classification interval. If the samples cannot be classified effectively in the current dimension, it can map the samples to the high-dimensional space through the kernel function, and then find the optimal classification hyperplane.

There are many kinds of kernel functions, such as polynomial kernel function, sigmoid kernel function, linear kernel function, Gaussian radial basis function, and so on. On the one hand, the parameters of the Gaussian radial basis function are less than that of a polynomial function, on the other hand, the selection of parameters of sigmoid kernel function is too complicated, so the SVM classification algorithm in this paper chooses Gaussian radial basis function as the kernel function.

Next, we use the method of control variables to study the four emotional features of the wavelet transform based on Sym8, that is, after determining the structure of the SVM classifier, we classify the four emotional features based on Sym8 respectively, and use the classification results to determine which emotional features are the best, to find the most relevant EEG features. Six subjects were selected randomly to calculate the classification results of their four emotional characteristics for each subject, as shown in Table 2.

Table 2. Emotion classification results of WT-SVM model of six subjects.

	Subiect1	Subject2	Subject3	Subject4	Subject5	Subject6
E	54.76%	50.00%	97.62%	78.57%	80.95%	90.48%
REE	38.10%	92.86%	78.57%	61.90%	76.19%	80.95%
DE	78.57%	90.48%	97.62%	73.81%	85.71%	92.86%
LE	35.71%	95.24%	92.86%	64.29%	61.90%	88.10%

In addition, we calculated the whole classification results of four emotional characteristics of all subjects, and the average classification accuracy and variance statistics are shown in Table 3.

Table 3. Mean and variance of classification results of four emotional features based on WT-SVM model

Feature	Average accuracy	The variance of accuracy
E	75.40%	0.036659108
REE	71.43%	0.036507937
DE	86.51%	0.00808768
LE	73.02%	0.054119426

To facilitate intuitive observation, we made a line chart to mark the data according to the data in Table 3, as shown in Fig. 7. The vertical axis represents the average accuracy of emotion classification, and the vertical axis represents the variance of the accuracy of emotion classification.

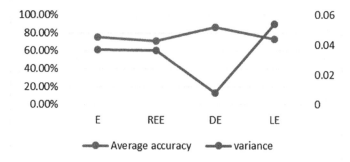

Fig. 7. Mean and variance of Four Feature Classification Results Based on WT-SVM Model.

From Fig. 7, we can see that when wavelet entropy is selected as the feature, not only the average accuracy of classification is the highest, but also the variance value is the smallest, which shows that when wavelet entropy is selected as the feature classification, it not only has high accuracy but also has good stability among different subjects, which is also reflected in Table 3. From the data of S1 in Table 3, it can be found that when the accuracy of the other three features is very low or even less than 50%, the accuracy of wavelet entropy as feature classification is still 78.57%. Based on the above analysis results, it is not difficult to see that wavelet entropy is the best choice for feature classification in the WT-SVM model, and the average accuracy of classification is 86.51%.

5   Discussion and Conclusion

As Rani et al. discuss the feature selection is a key challenge in affective computing due to phenomena of person stereotype [21]. The main purpose of our research work is to analyze different emotion features, and in this paper, taking four emotion features extracted by sym8 as an example. From our results, we can conclude that it is not trivial to process and classify data to be accurate over many subjects. The results from all 16 participants were in the best case 86.5% using DE as emotion feature, meanwhile, its variance is as low as 0.008, which shows that DE is very prominent in the WT-SVM classification model.

When dividing the subjects separately, take 6 subjects, for instance, the number of emotion feature with the accuracy of more than 90% is 9, in which DE is 3, E and LE are 2, and REE is 1. Although the classification accuracy of DE ranges from 73.81% to 97.62%, and the fluctuation range is relatively large, the classification effect of DE is more obvious than other emotional characteristics. The conclusion could be concluded that DE extracted by Sym8 is more suitable for the SVM classification algorithm. As for whether DE is the optimal representation of EEG emotional characteristics, the result in this paper is not enough to give a positive answer.

According to the classification results for this research, it can be found that a single subject has a greater impact on classification accuracy. From the perspective of subject 6, the classification accuracy of its four emotional features is higher than the other subjects, meanwhile, the four emotion recognition rates of subject 1 were lower than the average level of each emotion feature. This phenomenon shows that it is not enough to improve the accuracy of emotion classification from the perspective of emotion feature extraction and classification algorithm design.

In the future, we would be interested in using more features and different combinations of them to see how it affects the accuracy over many subjects. To improve the overall emotion recognition, the individual factors will be considered as one of the influencing factors of the emotion classification system.

Acknowledgement. The author thanks all subjects who participated in this research and the technical support from FISTAR Technology Inc.

Funding Statement This work was supported by the National Nature Science Foundation of China (No. 61503423, H. P. Jiang). The URL is http://www.nsfc.gov.cn/
.

Conflicts of Interest The authors declare that they have no conflicts of interest to report regarding the present study.

References

1. Niyato, D., Lu, X., Wang, P., Kim, D.I., Han, Z.: Economics of Internet of Things: an information market approach. IEEE Wirel. Commun. **23**(4), 136–145 (2016)
2. Jia, M., Yin, Z.S., Li, D.B., Guo, Q., Gu, X.M.: Toward improved offloading efficiency of data transmission in the iot-cloud by leveraging secure truncating OFDM. IEEE Internet Things J. **6**(3), 4252–4261 (2019)
3. Deng, L., Wang, X., Jiang, F., Doss, R.: EEG-based emotion recognition via capsule network with channel-wise attention and LSTM models. CCF Trans. Pervas. Comput. Interact. **3**(4), 425–435 (2021)
4. Jia, M., Gao, Z., Guo, Q., Lin, Y., Gu, X.: Sparse feature learning for correlation filter tracking toward 5g-enabled tactile internet. IEEE Trans. Indust. Inf. **16**(3), 1904–1913 (2020)
5. Kwon, J., Kim, L.: Emotion recognition using a glasses-type wearable device via multi-channel facial responses. IEEE Access **1**, 146392–146403 (2021)
6. Gunes, H., Piccardi, M.: Bi-modal emotion recognition from expressive face and body gestures. J. Netw. Comput. Appl. **30**(4), 1334–1345 (2007)
7. Zhang, J., Qi, X., Myint, S.H., Wen, Z.: Deep-learning-empowered 3d reconstruction for dehazed images in iot-enhanced smart cities. Comput. Mater. Continua **68**(2), 2807–2824 (2021)
8. Byoung, K.: A brief review of facial emotion recognition based on visual information. Sensors **18**(2), 401 (2018)
9. Hao, X., Meng, X., Zhang, Y., Xue, J., Xia, J.: Conveyor belt detection based on deep convolution gans. Intell. Autom. Soft Comput. **30**(2), 601–613 (2021)
10. Calvo, R.A., D'Mello, S.: Affect detection: an interdisciplinary review of models, methods, and their applications. IEEE Trans. Affect. Comput. **1**(1), 18–37 (2010)
11. Pushpa, C., Priya, M.M.: A review on deep learning algorithms for speech and facial emotion recognition. Int. J. Control Theory Appl. **9**(24), 183–204 (2016)
12. Atkinson, J., Campos, D.: Improving BCI-based emotion recognition by combining EEG feature selection and kernel classifiers. Expert Systems with Applications **47**(C), 35–41 (2015)
13. Yue, Q., Li, X., Li, D.: Chinese relation extraction on forestry knowledge graph construction. Comput. Syst. Sci. Eng. **37**(3), 423–442 (2021)
14. Sourina, O., Liu, Y., Nguyen, M.K.: Real-time EEG-based emotion recognition for music therapy. J. Multimod. User Interfaces **5**(1–2), 27–35 (2012)
15. Huang, Y., Yang, J., Liao, P., Pan, J.: Fusion of facial expressions and EEG for multimodal emotion recognition. Comput. Intell. Neurosci. **2017**(1), 2107451 (2017)
16. Soleymani, M.: A multimodal database for affect recognition and implicit tagging. IEEE Trans. Affect. Comput. **3**(1), 42–55 (2012)

17. Bazgir, O., Mohammadi, Z., Habibi, S.: Emotion recognition with machine learning using EEG signals. Statistics (2019)
18. Koelstra, S., Patras, I.: Fusion of facial expressions and EEG for implicit affective tagging. Image Vis. Comput. **31**(2), 164–174 (2013)
19. Upadhyay, D.: Classification of EEG signals under different mental tasks using wavelet trans- form and neural network with one step secant algorithm. Int. J. Sci. Eng. Technol. **2** (4), 256–259 (2013)
20. Kim, B.K., Lee, E.C., Suhng, B.M., Ryu, D.Y., Lee, W.H.: Feature extraction using FFT for banknotes recognition in a variety of lighting conditions. In: 2013 13th International Conference on Control, Automation and Systems (ICCAS 2013) (2013)
21. Gupta, A., Agrawal, R.K., Kaur, B.: Performance enhancement of mental task classification using EEG signal: a study of multivariate feature selection methods. Soft. Comput. **19**(10), 2799–2812 (2014)
22. Subasi, A., Gursoy, M.I.: Comparison of PCA, ICA and LDA in EEG signal classification using DWT and SVM. Expert Syst. Appl. **37**, 8659–8666 (2010)
23. Zhang, X., Wu, D.: On the vulnerability of CNN classifiers in EEG-based BCIs. IEEE Trans. Neural Syst. Rehabil. Eng. **27**(5), 814–825 (2019)
24. Zheng, W.L., Zhu, J.Y., Peng, Y., Lu, B.L.: EEG-based emotion classification using deep belief networks. In: IEEE International Conference on Multimedia & Expo (2014)
25. Graves, A., Schmidhuber, J.: Framewise phoneme classification with bidirectional LSTM and other neural network architectures. Neural Netw. J. Int. Neural Netw. Soc. **18**(5–6), 602–610 (2005)
26. Rani, P., Liu, C., Sarkar, N., Vanman, E.: An empirical study of machine learning techniques for affect recognition in human-robot interaction. Pattern Anal. Appl. **9**(1), 58–59 (2006)
27. Peng, X.J., Wang, Y.F.: A normal least squares support vector machine (NLS-SVM) and its learning algorithm. Neurocomputing **72**, 3734–3741 (2009)
28. Sun, W., Chen, X., Zhang, X., Dai, G., Chang, P.: A multi-feature learning model with enhanced local attention for vehicle re-identification. Comput. Mater. Continua **69**(3), 3549–3561 (2021)
29. Wu, Q., et al.: Classifying the multiplicity of the EEG source models using sphere-shaped support vector machines. IEEE Trans. Magn. **41**(5), 1912–1915 (2005)
30. Lang, P.J., Bradley, M.M., Cuthbert, B.N.: International affective picture system (IAPS): technical manual and affective ratings. In: NIMH Center for the Study of Emotion and Attention, pp. 39–58 (1997)
31. Bai, L., Ma, H., Huang, Y.X., Luo, Y.J.: The development of native Chinese affective picture system-A pretest in 46 college students. Chin. Ment. Health J. **19**(11), 719–722 (2005)
32. Teplan, M.: Fundamentals of EEG measurement. Measur. Sci. Rev. **2** (2002)
33. Du, R., Mehmood, R.M., Lee, H.J.: Alpha activity during emotional experience revealed by ERSP. J. Internet Technol. **15**(5), 775–782 (2018)
34. Nie, D., Wang, X.W., Shi, L.C., Lu, B.L.: EEG-based emotion recognition during watching movies. In: 2011 5th International IEEE/EMBS Conference on Neural Engineering (2011)
35. Oh, S.H., Lee, Y.R., Kim, H.N.: A novel EEG feature extraction method using Hjorth parameter. Int. J. Electron. Electric. Eng. **2**(2), 106–110 (2014)
36. Momennezhad, A.: EEG-based emotion recognition utilizing wavelet coefficients. Multim. Tools Appl. **77**(20), 27089–27106 (2018)

Computing Offloading Strategy Based on Improved Firework Algorithm

Yan Wang and Tao Wu[(⊠)]

Chengdu University of Information Technology, Chengdu 610000, China
`wut@cuit.cn`

Abstract. The emergence of mobile edge computing greatly alleviates the problem of insufficient computing power of mobile devices and does not support high-energy applications. As an important part of edge computing, computing offloading can greatly improve the quality of service through a reasonable computing offload scheme. For time delay sensitive tasks, the time delay of computational offloading under energy consumption constraints is too large, this paper introduces an improved fireworks algorithm based on grouping and classification (GCFA). The problem is modeled as the minimum delay problem under the constraint of energy consumption, and the offloading vector is calculated by GCFA, which transforms the task offloading into the process of fireworks particle optimization. Finally, through experiments, the genetic algorithm (GA) offloading strategy, standard fireworks algorithm (FA) offloading strategy, bat algorithm (BA) offloading strategy and mayfly optimization algorithm (MA) are compared, the average total system cost of GCFA is much lower than that of the other four. The total system cost of GCFA is 20% lower than that of the original. The experimental results show that GCFA has a good performance in reducing MEC time delay and balancing the load of MEC server.

Keywords: Edge computing · Computing offloading · Firework algorithm

1 Introduction

The emergence of many new services such as virtual reality, Internet of things, industrial Internet and Internet of vehicles puts forward higher and higher requirements for network transmission capacity, data distribution and other capabilities. At the same time, the development of related technologies has led to an explosive growth in global network traffic [1]. Facing the rapid growth of traffic and increasing user demand, the communication network will face more and more pressure. Although cloud computing solves the problem of insufficient computing power, it also brings a series of problems, such as data transmission cost, cloud storage cost and so on. In order to reduce the network load and improve the utilization of computing resources, the European Telecommunications Standards Institute (ETSI) proposed mobile edge computing (MEC) in 2014 [2, 3].

MEC has built a terminal-edge server-cloud server three-tier architecture, deployed computing resources to the edge of the network, provided services to users nearby, and effectively improved the network environment. As a key technology of edge

X. Sun et al. (Eds.): ICAIS 2022, CCIS 1587, pp. 642–655, 2022.
https://doi.org/10.1007/978-3-031-06761-7_51

computing, computing offload allows terminal equipment to offload tasks to MEC server for execution. With the help of high-performance MEC server, the purpose of reducing user equipment energy consumption and task processing time is realized [4].

Computing offload technology mainly includes offload decision and resource allocation. The offload decision is mainly concerned with whether the task should be offloaded, where to offload, and what to offload [5]. In order to solve the above problems, researchers have put forward feasible schemes from different angles in recent years.

The offloading decision mainly concerns whether the task should be offloaded, where to offload, and what to offload. In order to solve the above problems, researchers have put forward feasible schemes from different angles in recent years. Reference [6] offloads some tasks to the cloud server by introducing the assistance of cloud computing, which further reduces the time delay and energy consumption of the system. Reference [7] developed an offloading strategy based on Lyapunov optimization technology, which can dynamically offload tasks while detecting energy consumption and execution delay. Reference [8] proposed a MEC system with energy acquisition device based on Lyapunov optimization technology, which expanded the application range of MEC system. Reference [9] proposed an offloading scheme to optimize the energy with guaranteed delay. In this scheme, the link conditions of the forward network and the return network are considered at the same time, and the artificial fish swarm algorithm is used for global optimization. Reference [10] modeled the problem as a linear programming problem and proposed two optimization algorithms, including two-stage optimization algorithm and iterative improvement algorithm. For the partial offloading model, reference [11] proposed the influence of the dependencies between tasks on the offloading decision, and used the polynomial time algorithm to solve the optimal scheme of the offloading decision. Reference [12] combined with artificial intelligence, based on LSTM (Long Short Term Memory) network to predict computing tasks, proposed a computing offloading strategy based on task prediction, the combination of edge computing and artificial intelligence is also an important direction. Reference [13] studies the MEC offload problem in the case of single user and multiple base stations in ultra-dense wireless networks. For the scenario of multi-user and single MEC server, reference [14] introduces the Stackelberg Game theory to solve the problem of inconsistent goals between users and MEC server, so that users and MEC server can continuously game to reach the equilibrium state, and this method can effectively reduce the time delay. In reference [15], in view of the limited computing resources of a single cloud server, considering offloading computing tasks to multiple cloud servers, genetic-based decision algorithm for multisite computation offloading (GAMCO) is proposed to improve the performance of applications. Reference [16] proposes a new edge computing task scheduling scheme based on genetic algorithm.

Based on the above research on offloading problem, this paper mainly studies the minimum delay problem under energy consumption constraints, and proposes an offloading strategy based on improved fireworks algorithm (GCFA), the algorithm improves the offloading efficiency by more than 20%, which is much higher than the other four algorithms.

The rest of this paper is organized as follows. In the second section, we propose a system model and a solution based on GCFA. The third section makes an experimental analysis of the proposed method. Finally, the fourth section summarizes the full text.

2 System Models

MEC system is mainly used in scenarios that are sensitive to time delay and have a relatively large amount of task computation. The user mobile device is mainly responsible for the collection of task data and the computation of tasks with small amount of data, while MEC is responsible for the computation of large tasks. This paper considers a multi MEC server and multi-user application scenario. MEC server can provide users with the service of computing. User equipment can also perform simple computing tasks. Let the set of users be N = {n_1, n_2, ..., n_k}. Each user will specify a server or local to execute a task after it is generated. Each user has N + 1 options.

2.1 Time Delay

The execution delay of each task is different according to different task sizes generated by different devices and different servers selected for execution. If local execution is selected, the time delay can only be calculated locally. If the computation offloading is selected, the time delay includes transmission delay and MEC server computation delay. The transmission delay includes the delay that the mobile device transmits the task to the MEC server and the delay that the MEC server transmits the result back to the mobile device. Among them, the delay of the MEC server returning to the mobile device is very small, so it can be ignored. In the following tags, the subscript i represents the current user number, the subscript j represents the current MEC server number, u is the user equipment tag, and s is the server tag.

Local Computing Time

$$T_{local} = B_i * f_i * f_{u,i} \tag{1}$$

B_i represents the amount of data of the processing task, and f_i represents the clock cycle required to process each bit of data. $f_{u,i}$ represents the processor frequency of the local device.

MEC Transmission Time
According to Shannon's theorem, the transmission rate between mobile devices and MEC devices is:

$$r_{i,j} = W * \log_2\left(1 + \frac{S_i}{N}\right) \tag{2}$$

$$T_{i,j} = \frac{B_i * f_i}{r_{i,j}} \tag{3}$$

S_i represents the average signal power, and N represents the average noise power.

MEC Computation Time

$$T_{s,i} = \frac{B_i * f_i}{f_{s,i}} \tag{4}$$

$f_{s,i}$ represents the CPU clock frequency of the MEC server.

2.2 Energy Consumption Model

Local Execution

$$E_i = C_i * L^2 * f_{u,i} * B_i * f_i \tag{5}$$

Ci represents capacitance and L represents voltage.

MEC Server Execution

$$E_{i,j} = P_i * T_{i,j} \tag{6}$$

In MEC server execution, only the transmission energy consumption needs to be considered, in which the transmission time delay has been calculated.

2.3 Computational Model

A multi MEC server multi-user scenario is abstracted in the model. Due to the limitations of mobile devices, it is necessary to ensure that the energy consumption of each mobile device is less than the maximum energy consumption. Therefore, the practical problem is the minimum time delay problem under the constraint of maximum energy consumption.

The total time delay for uninstalling to MEC server to complete the task is, and the delay for transferring to MEC is

$$T_i = T_{i,j} + T_{s,i} \tag{7}$$

The time delay for local execution is

$$T_i = T_{local} \tag{8}$$

Taking minimizing the time delay as the goal, the minimum delay optimization expression can be obtained as

$$P1 : \min_{V_i} \sum_{i=1}^{n} \sum_{j=1}^{k} T_i \tag{9}$$

Constraints are as follows:

$$E_i < E_{\max} \tag{10}$$

$$f_{u,i} \leq f_{u,\max} \tag{11}$$

$$f_{s,i} \leq f_{s,\max'} \tag{12}$$

$$P_i \leq P_{\max} \tag{13}$$

The constraints are as follows, where Eq. 10 represents the energy consumption constraint, and the energy consumption for each task execution needs to be less than the maximum energy consumption. Equation 11 indicates that the CPU clock frequency of MEC server is less than the maximum clock frequency. Equation 12 indicates that the CPU frequency of the local device is less than the maximum frequency. Equation 13 indicates that the transmission frequency of local equipment shall be less than the maximum transmission frequency.

For the implementation of energy consumption constraint, the penalty function is selected to increase the total system cost of the current offloading vector, so as to avoid the situation that some MEC servers have strong computing power, so that a large number of tasks are offloaded to the MEC server, resulting in excessive energy consumption of the server exceeding the maximum energy consumption limit. The purpose of adding penalty item is to balance energy consumption and time delay.

Penalty function:

$$penalty(V) = g * \sum_{j=1}^{k} \sum_{i=1}^{n} (E_i - E_{\max}) \tag{14}$$

Therefore, P1 is converted to problem P2

$$P2 : \min_{V_i} \sum_{i=1}^{n} \sum_{j=1}^{k} T_i + penalty(V) \tag{15}$$

Constraint:

$$P_i \leq P_{\max} \tag{16}$$

$$f_{s,i} \leq f_{s,\max'} \tag{17}$$

$$f_{u,i} \leq f_{u,\max} \tag{18}$$

$P_{\max}$ represents the maximum transmission power of the mobile device, $f_{s,\max'}$ represents the maximum clock frequency of the server CPU, and $f_{u,\max}$ represents the maximum CPU clock frequency of the local device.

3 Offloading Decision Based on GCFA

3.1 Firework Algorithm

Fireworks algorithm [17] is a swarm intelligence algorithm based on the phenomenon that fireworks explosion produces sparks. The basic components are explosion operator, mutation operator, mapping rules and selection strategy. The basic process is shown in Fig. 1.

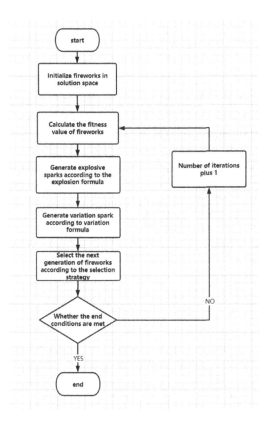

Fig. 1. Flow chart of fireworks algorithm.

3.2   Fireworks Particle Coding

Assuming that the user size is N, K represents the number of MEC servers. The task set generated by all users is {m1, m2, m3, ..., mn}.

Each firework represents an offloading decision vector, and the dimension of fireworks is consistent with the number of tasks. Suppose there is a task set {m_1, m_2, m_3, m_4}. If there is a firework, the code is {v_1, v_2, v_3, v_4}. The value of v_i must be guaranteed from 0 to K. $v_i = 0$, which means that the task is executed on the user's device. If $v_i = n$ ($1 \leq n \leq K$), it means that the task is offloaded to server n to execute.

3.3   Fitness Function Design

The fitness value of fireworks represents the total system cost generated by the implementation of all task assignments, so the computation formula is:

$$Fitness(V) = \sum_{i=1}^{n} \sum_{j=1}^{k} T_i + g * \sum_{j=1}^{k} \sum_{i=1}^{n} (E_i - E_{max}) \tag{19}$$

3.4   Improvement

When solving the problems in the model proposed in this paper, the fireworks algorithm needs to be improved to meet the requirements of this paper. Firstly, the solution of the ordinary fireworks algorithm is continuous, and the model proposed in this paper needs to be adapted to the integer solution. Secondly, aiming at the problem that it is difficult to determine the explosion parameters in the explosion operator of fireworks algorithm and the explosion amplitude of the best fireworks is too small, so that the utilization rate of the best fireworks is not enough, a classification and grouping explosion algorithm is proposed to better solve this problem. Finally, in order to solve the problem that the traditional fireworks algorithm can not guarantee the fireworks selection quality and the selection speed is too slow, an improved tournament selection algorithm is adopted.

Reverse Learning Initialization. The accuracy of the fireworks algorithm is affected by the initial population. In order to improve the quality of the initial fireworks population and improve the convergence speed, this paper uses reverse learning to initialize the fireworks population.

Definition 1. Reverse point: if x is a point in the solution space, then the reverse point X of X in the solution space is: X = LB + UB − x.

Reverse learning is to initialize a group of solutions randomly and obtain the reverse solutions of the group of solutions. Let f be the fitness function of the minimization problem. If f (X) < f (x), X replaces x to form a new set of solutions.

Classification and Grouping Explosion Operator. In the traditional fireworks algorithm, the explosion radius and explosion number are determined by the fitness value of each fireworks. The better the fitness value, the smaller the explosion radius, while the worse the fitness value, the larger the explosion radius. That is, the better the fireworks, the more local search, and the worse the fireworks, the more global search. In this way, the explosion range of the best fireworks will be very small, and its local search ability will be very poor or even lost.

In order to improve the above problems, this paper uses the fitness value of fireworks to divide fireworks into three categories: in the minimum value problem, the fitness values of all fireworks are sorted from small to large, and the one with the smallest fitness value is the best fireworks. This kind of fireworks disturbs itself with a certain probability or produces explosive sparks in a global random position. The second to fourth fireworks are good fireworks, which learn from the best fireworks with a certain probability or generate explosive sparks at their own random position. The remaining fireworks are ordinary fireworks. In order to maintain the diversity of fireworks population, this kind of fireworks is divided into n groups with m fireworks in each group. Each group of fireworks learns from the group of optimal fireworks with a certain probability to produce explosive sparks, or carries out random disturbance in the global solution space.

$$\begin{cases} Spark_i = F_{best} * N(0,1), & R_1 > Pd_1 \\ Spark_i = LB + (UB - LB) * rand(1,d); & others \end{cases} \tag{20}$$

LB and UB represent the upper and lower bounds of each dimension of the solution, respectively. R_1 represents a random number from 0 to 1. Pd_1 is used to control the probability of Gaussian disturbance of the best fireworks, which is generally set to 0.2. F_{best} stands for the best firework.

$$\begin{cases} Spark_i = F_{mid}^i + (Fbest - F_{mid}^i) * N(0,1), & R_2 > Pd_2 \\ Spark_i = LB + (UB - LB) * rand(1,d); & others \end{cases} \tag{21}$$

F_{mid}^i indicates good fireworks. Pd_2 is used to control the probability of the fireworks moving to the best fireworks.

$$\begin{cases} Spark_j^i = F_j^i + (F_{normal}^j - F_j^i) * N(0,1) & i != bestfire_j \\ Spark_j^i = F_j^i * N(0,1) & i = best \end{cases} \tag{22}$$

F_j^i represents the ith firework in group j. F_{normal}^j represents the best fireworks in group j, and *bestfire_j* represents the number of the best firework in group j.

Simulated Annealing Operator. The traditional fireworks algorithm is easy to fall into local optimization, and the addition of simulated annealing operator enhances the ability of the algorithm to jump out of local optimum. Each time the optimal individual of the previous generation of fireworks is simulated annealing, according to the Metropolis criterion in the simulated annealing algorithm, accept the suboptimal optimum with a certain probability to jump out of the local optimum. Each time, Gaussian perturbation is applied to the original optimal solution to generate a new solution.

The specific pseudo code of the operator is as follows:

Simulated Annealing Operator

```
    optimal individual p
    while Tem>Tmin
      for Markov chain length
        newp=p*g
        mapped into feasible region according to the mapping rules
        Δf=f(newp)-f(p)
          if Δf<0
            p=newp;
          else
            Decide whether to accept the new solution according to Me-
tropolis guidelines
          end if
      end for
        Tem=Tem*alpha;
      end while
```

The output result is a better or suboptimal solution of the current optimal solution after simulated annealing operator.

Tem is the initial temperature, Tmin is the minimum temperature, and alpha is the temperature decay rate.

Mapping Strategy. In the algorithm, mapping rules are used to avoid the problem that a dimension of sparks generated in simulated annealing operator, explosion operator and guidance operator exceeds the upper and lower bounds. Random mapping rules are used to map the excess dimensions to the feasible domain. The formula is:

$$x_i^k = LB + rand * UB; \tag{23}$$

x_i^k represents the k-th dimension of the solution, LB represents the lower bound of the feasible region, and UB represents the upper bound of the feasible region. *rand* represents a random value of 0–1.

Selection Strategy. The traditional fireworks algorithm adopts the roulette algorithm based on distance. Although this method can ensure the randomness of the population, because its method is time-consuming and easy to make the optimal individual unavailable, a selection algorithm of elite tournament is adopted. In each generation, the best individuals in the fireworks, explosive sparks population are put into the next generation, and then the remaining fireworks are selected in the championship. Select multiple individuals randomly from the population, put the best one into the next generation, and put the rest back into the population, and then repeat the process until the population size reaches the requirements.

GCFA Technological Process. As shown in Fig. 2, GCFA is mainly composed of four parts. Firstly, initialize the initial value of fireworks according to the fitness function, and then enter the cycle of a certain number of iterations. The first step in the cycle is to simulate annealing the current last fireworks, and the second step is to generate more spark particles according to the improved explosion operator. Finally, the next generation of fireworks population is selected by the improved selection operator to enter the next iteration.

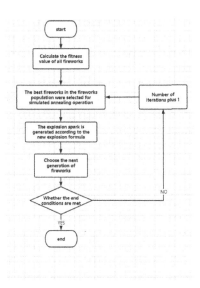

Fig. 2. Flow chart of GCFA.

4 Experiment and Analysis

4.1 Experimental Parameter Setting

The fireworks population size is 100, the maximum number of explosive sparks is 150, the maximum number of iterations is 60, and the feasible region of the solution is [0, 10]. The initial temperature is 2000 and the minimum temperature is 1e−8.

4.2 Simulation Results and Analysis

In order to comprehensively compare the advantages and disadvantages of the modified algorithm, the convergence accuracy, convergence speed and stability are compared between the basic particle swarm optimization algorithm and the basic fireworks algorithm. The parameter settings of other compared algorithms are consistent with the original algorithm. Each algorithm runs independently for 20 times, and the dimension of algorithm problem is d = 50. Figure 3 shows the convergence analysis of five algorithm.

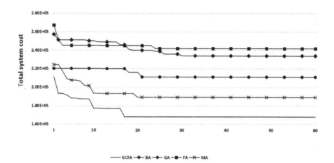

Fig. 3. Convergence analysis.

As can be seen from Fig. 3, GCFA has the fastest convergence speed among the five algorithms, and the global optimum solution is found in the 17th iteration. Moreover, GCFA is also ahead of the other four algorithms in optimization effect. After the algorithm optimization, the total cost of the system is reduced by more than 20%, far more than the other four algorithms.

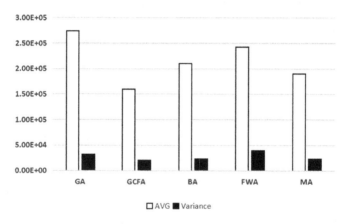

Fig. 4. Stability analysis.

Figure 4 shows the comparison of the average total system cost of different offloading strategies. Each offloading strategy runs 100 times respectively. Set the number of user k = 50 and the number of MEC servers n = 10. It can be seen that in terms of convergence accuracy, GCFA is far ahead of the other four algorithms, and the accuracy of GA is the worst. In the stability of the algorithm, GCFA is not much different from MA, but it still leads by a small margin.

In order to evaluate GCFA, this paper selects BA offloading strategy, FWA offloading strategy, GA algorithm offloading strategy and MA offloading strategy, and compares the optimization effect under different task size. Each offloading strategy operates independently for 100 times.

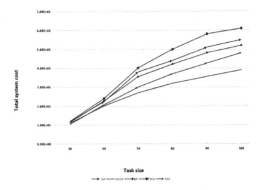

Fig. 5. Number of devices vs. total system cost.

Figure 5 is a comparison of the total system costs obtained by different offloading schemes under different number of user. For the sake of fairness, the initial parameters of various schemes are set to the same case. As can be seen from the figure, the increase in the number of tasks leads to the increase in the total cost of the system. Meanwhile, among the four schemes, the growth rate of GCFA is the most gentle. As the number of users increases, the interval between this scheme and the total cost curve of the other three systems also increases, because this scheme has better ability to balance energy consumption and delay when the number of users increases than the other three schemes.

5 Conclusion

Random offloading strategy or local offloading strategy will cause too high time delay in practical application. Aiming at the delay optimization problem in MEC network, this paper proposes a offloading strategy based on GCFA to balance the balance between energy consumption and time delay This strategy transforms the actual computational offloading problem into a multi-dimensional particle optimization problem in solution space. In this paper, the total cost of the system is reduced by about 20% by GCFA offloading strategy. At the same time, according to the experimental results, although GA, FA, BA and MA can play a certain optimization effect to a certain extent, but with the increase of task size, it is easy to fall into local optimal and GCFA is better than the other four algorithms in terms of optimization effect and algorithm stability.

Acknowledgement. On the occasion of the completion of this paper, I would like to express my heartfelt thanks to my mentor, Mr. Wu, who not only gave me a lot of help in life and study, but also put forward a lot of suggestions for this paper. At the same time, I want to thank my family for always supporting me behind my back. In words, there are too many people who have helped me. I sincerely thank all those who care and help me. I thank them for giving me the strength to constantly surpass myself. Thank you.

Funding Statement. This research was funded by the National Key Research number 2018 YFC15007005 and Key R & D projects in Sichuan Province 2020YFG0189. Authors should describe sources of funding that have supported their work, including specific grant numbers, initials of authors who received the grant, and the URLs to sponsors' websites. If there is no funding support, please write "The author(s) received no specific funding for this study." this research was funded by the National Key Research number 2018YFC15007005 and Key R & D projects in Sichuan Province 2020YFG0189.

Conflicts of Interest. The authors declare that they have no conflicts of interest to report regarding the present study.

References

1. Simiscuka, A.A., Bezbradica, M., Muntean, G.M.: Performance analysis of the quality of service-aware networking scheme for smart internet of things gateways. In: Proceedings of IWCMC, pp. 1370–1374 (2017)
2. Hu, Y.C., Patel, M., Sabella, D.: Mobile edge computing a key technology towards 5G. ETSI White Paper 11(11), 1–16 (2015)
3. European Telecommunications Standards Institute (ETSI), Mobile-edge computing-Introductory Technical White Paper (2014)
4. Flores, H., Hui, P., Tarkoma, S.: Mobile code offloading: from concept to practice and beyond. IEEE Commun. Mag. 53(3), 80–88 (2015)
5. Xie, R., Lian, X., Jia, Q., et al.: Survey oncomputation offloading in mobile edge computing. J. Commun. 39(11), 42–159 (2018)
6. Wang, Y., Ge, H.B., Feng, A.Q.: Computation offloading strategy in cloud-assisted mobile edge computing. Comput. Eng. 46(8), 27–34 (2020)
7. Guang, L., Zhang, W.Q.: Energy-delay tradeoff for dynamic offloading in mobile-edge computing system with energy harvesting devices. IEEE Trans. Industr. Inf. 14, 4642–4655 (2018)
8. Mao, Y., Zhang, J., Letaief, K.B.: Dynamic computation offloading for mobile-edge computing with energy harvesting devices. IEEE J. Sel. Areas Commun. 34(12), 3590–3605 (2016)
9. Zhang, H., Guo, J., Yang, L., Li, X., Ji, H.: Computation offloading considering fronthaul and backhaul in small-cell networks integrated with MEC. In: 2017 IEEE Conference on Computer Communications Workshops (INFOCOM WKSHPS), pp. 115–120. IEEE (2017)
10. Wang, W., Zhou, W.: Computational offloading with delay and capacity constraints in mobile edge. In: 2017 IEEE International Conference on Communications (ICC), pp. 1–6. IEEE (2017)
11. Kao, Y.H., Krishnamachari, B., Ra, M.R., Bai, F.: Hermes: latency optimal task assignment for resource-constrained mobile computing. IEEE Trans. Mob. Comput. 16(11), 3056–3069 (2017)
12. Miao, Y., Wu, G., Li, M., Ghoneim, A., Al-Rakhami, M., Hossain, M.S.: Intelligent task prediction and computation offloading based on mobile-edge cloud computing. Futur. Gener. Comput. Syst. 102, 925–931 (2020)
13. Chen, X., Zhang, H., Wu, C., Mao, S., Ji, Y., Bennis, M.: Optimized computation offloading performance in virtual edge computing systems via deep reinforcement learning. IEEE Internet Things J. 6(3), 4005–4018 (2019)

14. Wang, C., Yu, F.R., Liang, C., Chen, Q., Tang, L.: Joint computation offloading and interference management in wireless cellular networks with mobile edge computing. IEEE Trans. Veh. Technol. **66**(8), 7432–7445 (2017)
15. Goudarzi, M., Zamani, M., Toroghi Haghighat, A.: A genetic-based decision algorithm for multisite computation offloading in mobile cloud computing. Int. J. Commun. Syst. **30**(10), e3241 (2017)
16. Nan, Z., Wen, L., Zhu, L., Zhi, L., Yu, L.: A new task scheduling scheme based on genetic algorithm for edge computing. Comput. Mater. Contin. **71**(1), 843–854 (2022)
17. Tan, Y., Zhu, Y.: Fireworks algorithm for optimization. In: Tan, Y., Shi, Y., Tan, K.C. (eds.) ICSI 2010. LNCS, vol. 6145, pp. 355–364. Springer, Heidelberg (2010). https://doi.org/10.1007/978-3-642-13495-1_44

Privacy-Preserving Neural Networks with Decentralized Multi-client Functional Encryption

Changji Wang$^{(\boxtimes)}$, Xinyu Zhou, Panpan Li, and Ning Liu

School of Information Science and Technology, Guangdong University of Foreign Studies, Guangzhou 510006, China
wchangji@126.com

Abstract. Emerging machine learning methods have become a powerful driving force to revolutionize many industries nowadays, such as banking, healthcare services, retail, manufacturing, transportation. Meanwhile, privacy has emerged as a big concern in this machine learning-based artificial intelligence era. Functional encryption is a new type of encryption primitive in which a secret functional-key allows one to compute a specific function of plaintext from the ciphertext, making it very suitable for privacy protection machine learning scenarios. In this paper, we apply the concepts of decentralized multi-client function encryption to explore a new solution to the privacy-preserving convolutional neural network. The results of the experiment show that our scheme is feasible, and the accuracy of the final model on the test set is 92.1%, which is close to 93.2% of the convolution network connected to plain text.

Keywords: Privacy-preserving machine learning · Convolutional neural network · Functional encryption · Decentralized multi-client functional encryption

1 Introduction

As a front-runner in modern technological advancement, machine learning methods have become a strong driving force to revolutionize a wide range of industries, such as financial technology, smart healthcare, and intelligent transportation systems. In machine learning, analytic models are used to make informed predictions on the provided data set. In most cases, due to privacy concerns, the data set is prohibited to access. For example, access to medical data sets is an infringement of patient privacy.

To tackle serious privacy concerns in machine learning based applications, recent significant research efforts have focused on developing privacy-preserving machine learning approaches by integrating emerging privacy protection cryptographic techniques (such as secure multiparty computation [1], homomorphic encryption [2] and functional encryption [3]) into machine learning pipeline.

Homomorphic encryption is a form of encryption that allows computation on ciphertexts, generating an encrypted result which, when decrypted, matches

X. Sun et al. (Eds.): ICAIS 2022, CCIS 1587, pp. 656–667, 2022.
https://doi.org/10.1007/978-3-031-06761-7_52

the result of the operations as if they had been performed on the plaintext. Homomorphic encryption can be used for privacy-preserving outsourced storage and computation. Wu et al. [4] used the Paillier cryptosystem and used polynomials to approximate the logistic function. Some research workers used an additively homomorphic encryption scheme to summarize some intermediate statistics. Others had good performance in training small logistic regression models, but this solution only allowed to calculate data with very few characteristics. However, these schemes all required expensive computational costs. Moreover, the computations of homomorphic encryption are slow, and only a finite number of operations can be performed on the encrypted data.

The secure multiparty computation may be defined as the problem of n players to compute jointly on an agreed function securely on the inputs without revealing them. Intuitively, the secure multiparty computation makes it possible to replace the ideal situation, where everyone would transmit their data to a trusted third party and the latter would perform the calculation to return only the result, by an interactive protocol between the participants only. Unlike the use of a trusted third party, whose ability to protect data and exchanges is essential, the secure multiparty computation does not require any trust in anyone. Nikolaenko et al. [5] presented a system for privacy-preserving ridge regression by combining both homomorphic encryption and Yao garbled circuits to achieve the best performance. The main limitations of secure multiparty computation are the computational overhead and high communication costs.

Traditional public-key encryption provides an all-or-nothing approach to data access: given a ciphertext encrypting m, a receiver either decrypts and recovers the entire message m, or learns nothing about the encrypted message. To overcome the all-or-nothing barriers of existing public-key encryption, a new public-key encryption paradigm called functional encryption was proposed. Functional encryption emerged from a series of refinements of public-key encryption, identity-based encryption [6], attribute-based encryption [7–10] and predicate encryption [11], allowing users to finely control the amount of information that can be recovered from a ciphertext by a given receiver. Specifically, functional encryption allows for a receiver to recover a function $f(m)$ of the encrypted message m, without revealing anything else about m. Loosely speaking, functional encryption may be seen as the non-interactive dual of multi-party computation. Functional encryption has numerous applications in the field of privacy-preserving computation, including privacy-preserving machine learning and private statistical analysis.

In this paper, we apply the idea of decentralized multi-client function encryption scheme (DMCFE) to the convolutional neural network and propose a privacy-preserving neural network framework called (DMCFE-CNN). In DMCFE-CNN framework, pictures are converted to vectors and scattered across multiple clients, we use the decentralized multi-client function encryption output as a value for the convolutional layer. In addition, this picture and the convolution kernel are two-dimensional tensors. Therefore, to complete the filling of the convolutional layer in the CNN training process, we first convert the two-dimensional convolution kernel into a vector, directly expand and retain the position and run the DMCFE scheme uniformly to get the decryption output, which is an element of the convolutional layer, and finally, the filling of the convolutional layer is completed through multiple iterations. In addition, the data in the first layer of the convolution kernel update action needs to be protected. Unlike a fully connected deep neural network, its calculation error requires direct access to the plain text. As we all know, the error calculation method in CNN is still convolution. Therefore, we update the convolution kernel in the same way as filling the convolutional layer. In this process, we realized the training of the neural network model and data protection at the same time.

The rest of this paper is organized as follows. In Sect. 2, we introduce some technical preliminaries such as inner-product functional encryption scheme (IP-FE), DMCFE scheme, and convolutional neural network. In Sect. 3, we propose the architecture and training algorithm of the DMCFE-CNN. In Sect. 4, we present results from the experimental evaluation. Finally, we draw our conclusions in Sect. 5.

2   Preliminaries

2.1   Functional Encryption

Functional encryption (FE) is a new paradigm formalized by Dan Boneh, et al. [3] and a powerful cryptographic tool that overcomes all-or-nothing data access approach of traditional public-key encryption that can control the exposed information of plaintexts by supporting computation on encrypted data. FE facilitates fine-grained access control to encrypted data in a non-interactive way. In FE, a user creates ciphertext for a plaintext m using a public key pk, and an entity who possesses the secret key sk_f for a function $f(\cdot)$ issued by a trusted authority can obtain $f(x)$ by decrypting the ciphertext.

Abdalla et al. [12] proposed the first single-input inner-product functional encryption scheme. Subsequently, Abdalla et al. [13] extends single-input functional encryption scheme to multi-client functional encryption scheme (MCFE). Next, Chotard et al. [14] introduced the concept of decentralized MCFE scheme, and propose a concrete construction of DMCFE scheme for inner-product function. A DMCFE scheme for inner-product function with a set of n clients C_i, for $i = 1, \ldots, n$ is described as follows.

- SetUp(1^λ): The initialization of common parameters is completed between clients C_i by the protocol, and eventually generate their own secret keys sk_i and encryption keys ek_i and the public parameters mpk, as well as $\mathbf{T}_i$ for private stream aggregation.
- Encrypt(ek_i, x_i, ℓ): Each client uses an encryption key ek_i and a label ℓ to encrypt its own plaintext x_i and outputs the ciphertext $ct_{\ell,i}$.
- DKeyGenShare($sk_i, \vec{y}$): Each client uses its own private key component sk_i and vector $\vec{y}$ to generate the decryption key component $dk_{\vec{y},i}$ locally.
- DKeyComb($dk_{\vec{y},i}, \ell$): Decryption client C_i aggregate function decryption key $dk_{\vec{y},j}$ from other clients C_j, which have the same label ℓ, and get the complete function decryption key $dk_{\vec{y}}$.

– Decrypt($dk_{\vec{y}}, \ell, \vec{ct}$): The client C_i uses the decryption key $dk_{\vec{y}}$ to decrypt the ciphertext $\vec{ct}$ gathered from other clients C_j, and finally obtains the function result $f(x) = \langle \vec{x}, \vec{y} \rangle$.

2.2 Convolutional Neural Network

Convolutional Neural Network (CNN) is a deep neural network with convolution operation, which is constructed by mimicking biological vision mechanisms. It can perform supervised learning and unsupervised learning and is widely used in computer vision, graphics processing and natural language processing [15–17]. As shown in Fig. 1, the input layer of CNN usually connects the convolutional layer, which can extract textures and can also reduce the size of the picture and subsequent computations.

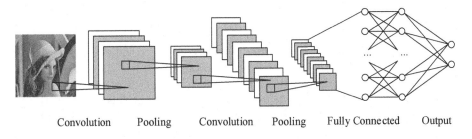

Convolution   Pooling   Convolution   Pooling   Fully Connected   Output

Fig. 1. Convolutional neural network.

The convolutional layer is obtained by stepping the input data through a convolution kernel or filter, as shown in the Fig. 2, where the convolution core moves in turn to complete the convolutional layer. If we convert a two-dimensional tensor into a one-dimensional vector, we can convert the convolution operation into an inner product operation. Remember, the position cannot go wrong between the corresponding pair of elements.

The convolutional layer is the first layer of a convolutional network. While convolutional layers can be followed by additional convolutional layers or pooling layers, the fully-connected layer is the final layer. As the image data progresses through the layers of the CNN, it finally identifies the intended object. During the learning phase, model errors will be updated by the back-propagation algorithm to the convolutional layer. In the forward propagation algorithm, the convolutional layer is calculated as follows:

$$z(W, b)^l = a^{l-1} \cdot W^l + b^l$$

where a is the output of the previous layer, W is the convolution kernel, b is the offset, and l represents the layer. We will not consider the activation function

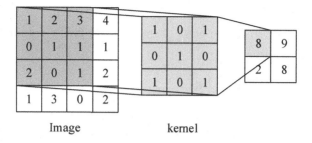

Fig. 2. Convolution calculation.

for the time being. Thus, we can write the loss of convolutional layer according to the back-propagation algorithm.

$$\frac{\partial \text{loss}_{\text{net}}}{\partial W^l} = a^{l-1} * \sigma^l$$

where σ is the loss propagated to this layer according to the chain rule. And σ is also a matrix, in two-dimensional convolution, which has the same shape as the output of the convolutional layer. loss_{net} is the output of the loss function of the network. If we observe the details of the formula at this time, where p, q corresponds to the row index and column index of the kernel, we will find that the calculation method of convolution loss is still convolution.

$$\frac{\partial \text{loss}_{\text{net}}}{\partial W_{pq}^l} = \sum_i \sum_j (\sigma_{ij}^l \times a_{i+p-1,j+q-1}^{l-1})$$

3 DMCFE-CNN Framework

Consider a scenario where a hospital, for a well-trained deep neural network, usually needs as many medical images as possible. However, hospitals are unwilling and unable to disclose their raw medical image data due to patient privacy concerns and legal and regulatory constraints. This leads to a conflict between medical image data sharing requirements and medical data security and patient privacy. This conflict is easily resolved if there is a trusted authority. In the real world, however, it is hard to find such a trusted authority. How to realize the sharing of medical images under the premise of ensuring the security of medical images and patient privacy without the trusted authority is a challenge. In response to this challenge, we propose a privacy-preserving convolutional neural network framework by applying decentralized multi-client functional encryption scheme. Figure 3 illustrates the DMCFE-CNN framework, which can perform CNN training in a decentralized environment. This training method can realize neural network training without directly accessing the original data.

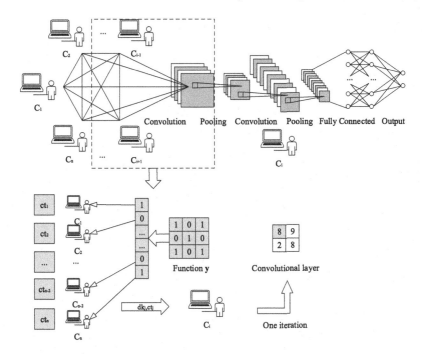

Fig. 3. DMCFE-CNN scheme.

The medical image is mapped into a vector $\vec{x} = [x_1, x_2, ..., x_n]$, and each client C_i holds only a vector component x_i. Note that one component x_i is not enough to expose the entire image $\vec{x}$. It is worth noting that the location index i for each client C_i and image vector elements x_i are bound and visible to all clients, that is, a client C_i knows that data x_j is in the hands of client C_j. For datasets in supervised learning mode, we also make the data labels public in the settings. In this context, we design our scheme so that each client C_i can eventually train their private model and the pictures will not be leaked. The proposed framework allows clients to access a decentralized multi-client environment with only a few modifications. The hyperparameters settings of the local model are designed by the corresponding clients themselves, such as the number and shape of convolution cores, learning rate, and so on.

As shown in the Fig. 3, there are n clients in the proposed framework. The client C_i trains private CNN by filling the convolutional layer first, and the convolutional layer is obtained by multiple convolution operations between convolution kernel and data. At this time, the parameters of the convolution kernel are equivalent to the function $\vec{y}$ in the DMCFE scheme. We don't care whether the expansion rule of convolution kernel is based on row or column, as long as the transmitted location index is consistent. Then C_i uses $dk_{\vec{y}}$ and $\vec{ct}$ from other clients to calculate the value of one convolution operation, which is the same as in the figure.

The above process is iterated in turn, and finally, the complete convolutional layer is obtained. One can directly use the above methods when updating the convolution kernel. The following algorithm illustrates the details of the training stage of DMCFE-CNN framework.

Algorithm 1: Training Algorithm for DMCFE-CNN

Input: dataset $\mathbf{D} = \{X_1, X_2, \ldots, X_i\}$, where $i \in \mathbf{Z}$

Output: model $\mathbf{M}$

	Function SecConv($\mathbf{I}$):
(1) Setup(1^λ):	All parties execute interactively to complete the initial parameter construction. Finally, it outputs $(mpk, ek_i, sk_i, \ell, \vec{y})$, where $\vec{y}$ was made public together parameter mpk, ℓ is the label.
(2) Encrypt(ek_i, x_i, ℓ):	Client C_i encrypts x_i with an encryption key ek_i and a label ℓ, and outputs outputs the ciphertext $ct_{\ell,i}$.
(3) DKeyGenShare($sk_i, \vec{y}$):	Client C_i generates the decryption key component $dk_{\vec{y},i}$ with private key sk_i and vector $\vec{y}$.
(4) DKeyComb($\{dk_{\vec{y},i}\}, \ell_{\vec{y}}$):	The client aggregates decryption key component $dk_{\vec{y},j}$ from other clients with the same label $\ell_{\vec{y}}$, and gets the complete function decryption key $dk_{\vec{y}}$.
(5) Decrypt($dk_{\vec{y}}, \ell_{\vec{y}}, \vec{ct}$):	The client gets $\langle \vec{x}, \vec{y} \rangle$ by using aggregated function decryption key $dk_{\vec{y}}$ and ciphertext $\vec{ct}$.
	Function SecOnceTrain($\vec{x}, \vec{y}$):
(1) SecConv($\mathbf{I}$):	The convolutional layer output is obtained by recursively calling SecConv($\cdot$) and continues with the subsequent NN forward propagation.
(2) Forward($\cdot$):	Forward propagation obtains the loss value through the remaining network.
(3) Backward($\cdot$):	The backward propagation algorithm propagates the loss to the first convolutional layer.
(4) SecConv($\mathbf{I}$):	Loop call SecConv($\cdot$) to get the loss update matrix, and then update the convolution kernel.
	Function SecCNNTrain($\mathbf{D}$):
(1) Init($\mathbf{D}$):	Data distribution.
(2) FindClientSet($\vec{y}$):	Find the user group $\mathbf{P}$ corresponding to the vector $\vec{y}$ and output the user group index set.
(3) SecOnceTrain($\mathbf{X}, \vec{y}$):	$\mathbf{X} \in \mathbf{D}$. Loop call SecOnceTrain($\cdot$) until the accuracy converges. Finally output $\mathbf{M}$.

The function SecConv($\cdot$) is used to connect the local neural network to the decentralized environment. The client C_i's x_i will exist in the whole decentralized environment in the form of ct_i during training. The training process of a deep neural network is mainly divided into two stages: forward propagation and backward propagation.

In the forward propagation phase, the first thing to do is to complete the padding of the first layer of the convolution. The padding method is to convolve the image data $\vec{x}$ with a convolution kernel $\vec{y}$. To achieve this goal in a decentralized environment, C_i first maps the convolution kernel from two-dimensional data (or higher dimensions) to a one-dimensional vector. Like $\vec{y}$ in Fig. 4, we use $\vec{y}$ to represent the convolution kernel here. As mentioned earlier, the location relationship between C_j and x_j is bound and public. Therefore, C_i can know which clients will interact with itself, and bind y_j with C_j, that is, C_i will also know which y_j they need to use for calculation. After the preparation, all clients in the client set $\mathbf{J}$ jointly establish a DMCFE. At this time, the padding of the CNN convolutional layer began. Readers who understand CNN will notice that C_i is not required to participate in the calculation of convolutional layer elements every time, but C_i must participate in each DMCFE mode in the process of padding C_i's convolutional layer, otherwise C_i cannot obtain the results of a certain time she is not involved. In order to solve this problem, we make a slight change to the convolution kernel $\vec{y}$, that is

$$\vec{y} = \begin{cases} \vec{y} & i \in \mathbf{J} \\ \vec{y} + y_i & i \notin \mathbf{J} \end{cases}$$

Using this method, C_i will participate in each time relevant DMCFE mode. When C_i gets the client set required for this operation, it exposes the convolution kernel $\vec{y}$ in this DMCFE network. Then, the other C_j obtains its own corresponding y_j according to $\vec{y}$ and calculates the ciphertext ct_j and the function decryption secret key $dk_{\vec{y},j}$. The client C_i collects $dk_{\vec{y},j}$ and ct_j from other C_j to obtain $dk_{\vec{y}}$ and $\vec{ct}$, and then obtains the convolution operation result $\langle \vec{x}, \vec{y} \rangle$ to complete the calculation of a convolutional layer element. After that, C_i calls SecConv($\cdot$) to fill the convolutional layer. The propagation method of the layer after the convolutional layer is consistent with the local CNN model. At the end of forward propagation, the loss function of the model is calculated, and then the second stage is carried out.

In the backward propagation stage, the model performs parameter updates. Our focus is still on the update of the parameters of the convolution kernel of the first layer. The update of the convolution kernel of the convolutional neural network needs to first calculate the convolution kernel error matrix. As we mentioned in Sect. 2, the convolution kernel error matrix is still obtained through the convolution operation. Therefore, the updated matrix of the convolution kernel can also be calculated in the same way as the convolution layer.

The above two stages are implemented in the SecOnceTrain($\cdot$). Finally, each client can train its own private model under the condition that the image information is not leaked using the SecCNNTrain($\cdot$).

4   Experimental Performance Evaluation

The experimental platform uses Corei7 personal computer, 8G memory and no GPU. The ECC Library of rust is used for encryption, and the security parameters are set to 256 bits. The neural network is built on Python 3.9. We use the neural network library pytorch. The data set MINST is used, which contains 60000 training data and 10000 test data. The size of each picture is 1 * 28 * 28. The Convolutional Neural Network uses the variant of lenet-5.

In the experiment, we set the convolution kernel size to (5×5), the step is 2, and the padding use 0. The first convolutional layer output channel is 1, the second convolution kernel output channel is 32, and the cross entropy loss function is used as the loss function.

Since floating-point numbers cannot be used in the encryption model, the convolution kernel and loss update matrix only retain the integer part, and we normalize the picture to $(0, 10)$. As shown in Fig. 5, the accuracy convergence of the first 25 batches is shown. As shown in Table 1, the accuracy of our model (92.1%) is approximate to that of CNN (93.2%) with the same parameters.

Table 2 shows the relationship between the time consumption and the data boundary when the number of clients $n = 25$. Although the time-consuming of the model is very expensive, the model training is actually parallel for each client in the model. Therefore, we can train multiple local NN at the same time through the way that each client performs locally.

Like other distributed models, collusion attack will cause non negligible damage to system security. Of course, this problem will weaken with the increase of the number of participating users, like blockchain. This is another weakness in the inner product function encryption model. Attackers can construct a query matrix, which is composed of a series of $\vec{y}$, and solve $\vec{x}$ by solving algebraic equations [3]. Therefore, we have to check the legitimacy of function $\vec{y}$, that is, a set of submitted functions $\mathbf{Y}$ form a matrix, which is irreversible. The last one is the time consumption of the model. It can be seen from the previous experiments that the ciphertext calculation in the model will take a lot of time.

Table 1. Scheme performance.

	Accuracy	Time-cost
DMCFE-CNN	92.1%	93.75 h
CNN	93.2%	6.5 s

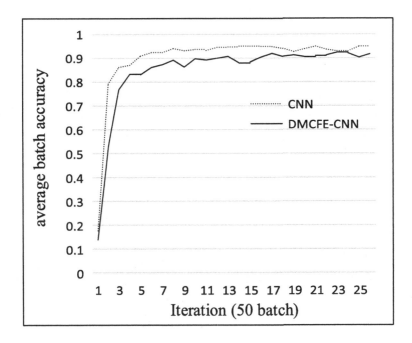

Fig. 4. Model convergence.

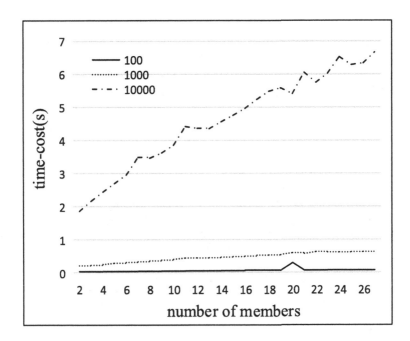

Fig. 5. Time cost of encryption algorithm.

Table 2. Encryption time cost.

Number of clients	N = 25		
Bound	100	1000	10000
Time	0.0683 s	0.615 s	6.288 s

5 Conclusions

In this paper, we apply the concept of decentralized multi-client functional encryption to explore a new solution for privacy-preserving convolutional neural network (DMCFE-CNN), which can help multiple users to train through a distributed secure method their neural network models without revealing their private data. The proposed DMCFE-CNN is trained on MINST to achieve an accuracy similar to that of the same kind of network in a non-encrypted environment. In future work, we will increase the protection of data labels and look for a more efficient distributed encryption algorithm or hardware acceleration support. In addition, we will use obfuscation to increase the invisibility of a client's local model to other clients, while protecting data and models.

Acknowledgements. This research is funded by scientific research project of Guangdong University of Foreign Studies under Grant No. 299-GK20CQ34.

References

1. Goldreich, O., Micali, S., Wigderson, A.: How to play any mental game. In: Proceedings of the Nineteenth Annual ACM Symposium on Theory of Computing (STOC 1987), pp. 218–229 (1987)
2. Gentry, C.: Fully homomorphic encryption using ideal lattices. In: Proceedings of the Forty-First Annual ACM Symposium on Theory of Computing (STOC 2009), pp. 169–178 (2009)
3. Boneh, D., Sahai, A., Waters, B.: Functional encryption: definitions and challenges. In: Ishai, Y. (ed.) TCC 2011. LNCS, vol. 6597, pp. 253–273. Springer, Heidelberg (2011). https://doi.org/10.1007/978-3-642-19571-6_16
4. Wu, S., et al.: Privacy-preservation for stochastic gradient descent application to secure logistic regression. In: The 27th Annual Conference of the Japanese Society for Artificial Intelligence, pp. 1–4 (2013)
5. Nikolaenko, V., Weinsberg, U., Ioannidis, S., et al.: Privacy-preserving ridge regression on hundreds of millions of records. In: IEEE Symposium on Security and Privacy, pp. 334–348 (2013)
6. Boneh, D., Franklin, M.: Identity-based encryption from the Weil pairing. In: Kilian, J. (ed.) CRYPTO 2001. LNCS, vol. 2139, pp. 213–229. Springer, Heidelberg (2001). https://doi.org/10.1007/3-540-44647-8_13
7. Sahai, A., Waters, B.: Fuzzy identity-based encryption. In: Cramer, R. (ed.) EUROCRYPT 2005. LNCS, vol. 3494, pp. 457–473. Springer, Heidelberg (2005). https://doi.org/10.1007/11426639_27

8. Goyal, V., Pandey, O., Sahai, A., Waters, B.: Attribute based encryption for fine-grained access control of encrypted data. In: ACM Conference on Computer and Communications Security, pp. 89–98 (2006)

9. Bethencourt, J., Sahai, A., Waters, B.: Ciphertext-policy attribute-based encryption. IEEE Symposium on Security and Privacy, pp. 321–334. IEEE Press (2007)

10. Waters, B.: Ciphertext-policy attribute-based encryption: an expressive, efficient, and provably secure realization. In: Catalano, D., Fazio, N., Gennaro, R., Nicolosi, A. (eds.) PKC 2011. LNCS, vol. 6571, pp. 53–70. Springer, Heidelberg (2011). https://doi.org/10.1007/978-3-642-19379-8_4

11. Katz, J., Sahai, A., Waters, B.: Predicate encryption supporting disjunctions, polynomial equations, and inner products. J. Cryptol. **26**, 191–224 (2013)

12. Abdalla, M., Bourse, F., De Caro, A., Pointcheval, D.: Simple functional encryption schemes for inner products. In: Katz, J. (ed.) PKC 2015. LNCS, vol. 9020, pp. 733–751. Springer, Heidelberg (2015). https://doi.org/10.1007/978-3-662-46447-2_33

13. Abdalla, M., Gay, R., Raykova, M., Wee, H.: Multi-input inner-product functional encryption from pairings. In: Coron, J.-S., Nielsen, J.B. (eds.) EUROCRYPT 2017. LNCS, vol. 10210, pp. 601–626. Springer, Cham (2017). https://doi.org/10.1007/978-3-319-56620-7_21

14. Chotard, J., Dufour Sans, E., Gay, R., Phan, D.H., Pointcheval, D.: Decentralized multi-client functional encryption for inner product. In: Peyrin, T., Galbraith, S. (eds.) ASIACRYPT 2018. LNCS, vol. 11273, pp. 703–732. Springer, Cham (2018). https://doi.org/10.1007/978-3-030-03329-3_24

15. Gu, J., et al.: Recent advances in convolutional neural networks. Pattern Recogn. **77**, 354–377 (2018)

16. Rawat, W., Wang, Z.: Deep convolutional neural networks for image classification: a comprehensive review. Neural Comput. **29**(9), 2352–2449 (2017)

17. Jmour, N., Zayen, S., Abdelkrim, A.: Convolutional neural networks for image classification. In: 2018 International Conference on Advanced Systems and Electric Technologies (IC_ASET), pp. 397–402 (2018)

Optimization of Space Information Network Topology Based on Spanning Tree Algorithm

Peng Yang[1] , Ming Zhuo[2] , Zhiwen Tian[2] , Leyuan Liu[2(✉)] ,
and Qiuhao Hu[3]

[1] School of Mathematical Sciences, University of Electronic Science
and Technology of China, Chengdu 611731, People's Republic of China
[2] School of Information and Software Engineering, University of Electronic
Science and Technology of China, Chengdu 610054, People's Republic of China
leyuanliu@uestc.edu.cn
[3] Huawei Technologies Co., Ltd., Chengdu 611730, People's Republic of China

Abstract. Space information networks (SINs) has the advantages of low power consumption and high data transmission rate in the process of network information transmission. It is a good solution to realize the systematic application of space information. The establishment of SINs need to generate network topology, and optimize and improve the invulnerability of SINs on this basis. In order to optimize the distributed minimum spanning tree algorithm (DMST) algorithm, an improved approximation algorithm, degree-guarantee minimum spanning tree algorithm (DGMST) algorithm, is proposed. DGMST algorithm adopts advanced data structure, which greatly reduces the time complexity. On the basis of fully considering the limit of satellite node link degree, generating the minimum average edge weight of subgraph and the requirements of topology invulnerability, DGMST algorithm further considers some boundary conditions to ensure the successful generation of the generated subgraph. Finally, it also reduces the average edge weight of the generated subgraph as much as possible, so that the dynamic network structure has better invulnerability and security.

Keywords: Space information network (SIN) · Network topology ·
Invulnerability

1 Introduction

Space information networks is a network system that uses space platform as the carrier to acquire, transmit and process space information in real time. Satellite networks is an important part of space information network, processing and forwarding information. Space information networks originates from traditional network, but it is different from traditional network [1]. Most of the existing satellite network protocols do not fully consider the survivability of satellite networks, and satellite nodes may fail due to attacks [2]. The failure of one or more nodes in the network may lead to the loss of communication ability of the network. Scientists believe that the future space information network will develop into a self-organized system without human intervention, so as to realize the independent establishment of links and the independent configuration of network topology [3, 4].

The early spatial information network structure is relatively simple, and the research and optimization objectives of spatial information network topology at home and abroad are mainly to improve the link communication performance [5, 6]. With the deepening of research, the scale of satellite nodes in spatial information network system is expanding day by day. It is no longer a single-layer structure, but a multi-layer structure. The topology of spatial information network changes rapidly. The topology generation method of single-layer structure is not suitable for multi-layer spatial information network with dynamics and complexity [7].

It is essential to develop a tracking network that is still effective in resource-constrained environments [8]. In recent research, the construction idea of minimum spanning tree has been applied to the generation of spatial information network topology. In order to build a free space optical (FSO) network, Literature [9] proposed a distributed bottom-up algorithm (BUA), which can make the degree of nodes in the built spanning tree as large as possible, that is, the connectivity as high as possible, but the BUA algorithm does not consider the problem of resource consumption, it is one of the most important problems in spatial information network. Literature [4] proposed a DMST algorithm for optical satellite networks and a connectivity guarantee (CG) algorithm to construct a robust topology, the tree is introduced into optical satellite networks to avoid bridge loops or routing loops.

Based on DMST algorithm, an improved DGMST algorithm is proposed to minimize the average edge weight on the premise of meeting the requirements of point connectivity and graph connectivity [10]. The algorithm uses advanced data structure to greatly reduce the time complexity, considers some boundary conditions to ensure the successful generation of the generated subgraph, and finally reduces the average edge weight of the generated subgraph as much as possible, so as to obtain a dynamic spatial information network topology with better survivability.

The article in this paper is organized as follows. Firstly, the topology of the spatial information network and its optimization are briefly introduced. Secondly, Sect. 2 presents the related work on topology optimization. Then, Sect. 3 proposes the degree-guarantee minimum spanning tree algorithm after that, Sect. 4 conducts experiments on the dataset. Finally, Sect. 5 concludes and summarizes the whole paper.

2 Related Work

In graph theory, spanning tree T is a connected subgraph <V, E> of undirected graph G with n nodes, where the size of nodes set V is n, that is, set V contains all nodes of undirected graph G, and the size of edge set E is n−1, that is, the connected subgraph is acyclic. If the edges in undirected graph G are weighted, the edges of spanning tree are also weighted. Spanning tree with minimum average edge weight is called minimum spanning tree or minimum average edge weight spanning tree. As shown in Fig. 1, the yellow dot represents the node of undirected graph G, the line represents the edge of G, the thick line represents the edge in the spanning tree, and the number on each edge represents the weight of the edge. The spanning tree in figure (a) is an ordinary spanning tree with an average edge weight of 5.4, The spanning tree in figure (b) is the minimum spanning tree with an average edge weight of 3.8.

The construction idea of minimum spanning tree has been applied to the generation of space information networks topology. Space information networks is abstracted from the perspective of graph theory and regarded as undirected weighted graph$G(V, E)$, where the nodes set $V = \{v_1, v_2, \ldots, v_n\}$ is a finite node set abstracted from n satellites in a network, and the finite edge set E represents the potential links that can be established between satellite nodes in a network. The spanning subtree generated by the spanning tree step in degree-guarantee minimum spanning tree algorithm and the spanning subgraph after meeting the node connectivity limit are the spatial information network topology.

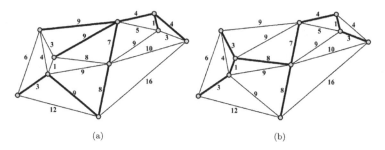

Fig. 1. Spanning tree and minimum spanning tree.

The status of satellite nodes in the network and the position relationship between satellite nodes change with time, so the generated space information network topology also changes with time. In order to reduce the impact of this complex dynamic topology relationship with time on topology generation, the satellite network cycle is divided into several time periods with very small length [8, 9]. In such a period of time, the state of satellite nodes and the mutual position relationship of satellite nodes will not change, which is fixed, that is, the spatial information network topology is fixed. This satellite topology is called snapshot, and the degree guarantee minimum spanning tree algorithm is designed on this basis. Each satellite node is equipped with a certain number of optical receivers to establish links with other satellite nodes, which limits the maximum number of links established by satellite nodes. At the same time, each satellite node also undertakes transmission responsibilities to varying degrees. They have their own connectivity task requirements, which makes the number of inter satellite links established by satellite nodes have a lower limit. The state of the link established between satellite nodes is described by visual matrix, also known as adjacency matrix, and edge weight matrix.

Define the visibility matrix A, where the element a_{ij} represents the visibility of the ith satellite node and the jth satellite node in the nodes set V. If and only if two satellite nodes are visible to each other, $a_{ij} = 1$, otherwise $a_{ij} = 0$. In particular, diagonal elements have values of 0. It is not difficult to find that matrix A is a symmetric 01 matrix, and the diagonals are zero elements, indicating that there is no self-loop in undirected graph G.

The weight matrix W is defined, where the element w_{ij} represents the cost of establishing the inter satellite link between the ith satellite node and the jth satellite node in the nodes set V. If and only if the two satellite nodes are visible to each other, i.e. a = 1, $w_{ij} > 0$, otherwise $w_{ij} = 0$. For a potential inter satellite link e_{ij}, defining r_{ij} is the square of Euclidean distance between two satellite nodes. If we do not consider the influence of other satellite nodes and objects on the two satellite nodes, we can simply regard the square of Euclidean as edge weight.

As mentioned above, the topology of space information networks also changes with time, r_{ij} is a variable that changes with time. We can calculate the cost of establishing the link w_{ij} through the following formula. Definition t_{ij} means that the satellite i node and the satellite j node is visible to each other and have the possible duration of establishing inter satellite links. Definition t_{thr} is the observable threshold within the duration. If $t_{thr} \leq t_{ij} < \infty$, then $w_{ij} = \frac{\int r_{ij}(t)dt}{t_{ij}}$, if $t_{ij} = \infty$, then $w_{ij} = r_{ij}(t)$, if $t_{ij} \leq t_{thr}$, then $w_{ij} = \infty$. Where ∞ means that two satellite nodes are running in the same orbit. Because the positional relationship between them is fixed, they are either always visible or never visible. If the length of the time period is set to 1 s, the influence of t_{thr} can be ignored, and $r_{ij}(t)$ is fixed in this time period.

Define the topology matrix X, where element x_{ij} represents whether the ith satellite node and the jth satellite node in the spatial information network topology generated by the algorithm have established a link. This matrix is the result matrix output by the algorithm. And only if two satellite nodes have established a link, $x_{ij} = 1$, otherwise $x_{ij} = 0$. Determinant of the matrix is closely related to spanning tree or spanning sub-graph. $\lambda_2(X)$ represents the absolute value of the second smallest determinant of matrix X. if $\lambda_2(X) > 0$, it means that the graph represented by the matrix is a connected graph and also indicates the number of spanning trees of the graph. If $\lambda_2(X) = 1$, it means that the graph is a tree. And if $\lambda_2(X) = 0$, it means that the graph is not connected.

3 Degree-Guarantee Minimum Spanning Tree Algorithm

The DGMST algorithm proposed in this paper is based on the DMST algorithm. DGMST has three main steps. Firstly, a spanning tree is established to ensure the connectivity of the graph. DMST algorithm can't ensure the connectivity of the graph in very few cases. The improved DGMST algorithm is optimized in this step to ensure the correctness of the spanning tree algorithm. Second, replacing edges reduces the average cost. DGMST algorithm greatly optimizes the time complexity by coloring the spanning tree, which is the main gap between DGMST algorithm and DMST algorithm. Finally, add edges. After the above two steps are completed, the lower limit of the degree of nodes may not be satisfied, so an edge needs to be added to meet the degree limit. DMST algorithm greedily sorts the potential connection costs and then adds edges. In some cases, the degree does not meet the conditions. DGMST algorithm improves this deficiency by global sorting.

3.1   Build Spanning Tree

Firstly, any spanning tree is generated to ensure the connectivity of each satellite node. As long as the undirected graph G is connected, we can find a legal spanning tree without degree limit. However, the degree of nodes in satellite topology is limited, so when the number n of nodes is large, it is difficult to solve this problem in linear time complexity. The DMST algorithm tries to use distributed to reduce the time complexity of the algorithm when building the spanning tree, but when one or two endpoints of the inter satellite link reach the degree limit and can't continue to establish the inter satellite link, it may lead to the failure of building the spanning tree. In order to solve this problem, the BUA algorithm improves this step and tries to find replacement edges in each subtree in the generated forest, so that the degrees of these points can be reduced when they can still remain connected and there is no self-loop, then the inter satellite link that has not been established due to the degree limit will be reestablished. However, the complexity of this process is very high. Each time you reduce the degree of a point, you need to traverse all the inter satellite chains that can be established by all satellite nodes in a subtree.

The space information network is no longer single-layer but multi-layer. The links that can be established and the degree limit of satellite nodes in the same orbit on the same layer are very similar. Therefore, the satellite nodes in the same orbit are preferentially connected, and then try to connect the satellite nodes in other orbits or other layers. This method not only reduces the complexity of the algorithm, but also improves the success rate of building spanning tree. Through this step, we will get a spanning tree and the degree of each node is less than or equal to its upper limit of degree, but the spanning tree is random and its average edge weight is not as small as possible.

3.2   Replace Edge

The goal of this step is to reduce the average edge weight and obtain an approximate degree constrained minimum spanning tree with the lowest average edge weight on the premise of ensuring connectivity and degree constraints. The optimization problem can be expressed by the following mathematical formula:

$$\min \frac{1}{|E|} \sum_{(i,j)|e_{ij} \in E} w_{ij} \tag{1}$$

$$s.t. \lambda_2(X) > 0 \tag{2}$$

$$1^T X 1 = 2(N - 1) \tag{3}$$

$$\sum_j x_{ij} \leq d_i \tag{4}$$

$$X \leq A \tag{5}$$

$$x_{ij} \le \{0,1\} \tag{6}$$

Equation (1) is the optimization objective, representing the minimum average edge weight. Equation (2) is the second small row column of the topological matrix. When its value is positive, it means that after the link is established according to the topological matrix, the abstract undirected graph of the spatial information network is connected. Equation (3) shows that the non-zero elements in the topology matrix are twice the number of satellite nodes minus one, which shows that it is just necessary to establish $n - 1$ inter satellite links, which is also the minimum value to make the graph connected, and the resulting spanning subgraph is a spanning tree. Equation (4) represents the upper limit of the degree of satellite nodes, which is the upper limit of the number of inter satellite links that can be established by satellite nodes; Eq. (5) represents that the established inter satellite links are all qualified and potentially settable; Eq. (6) indicates that the topology matrix is 01 matrix, and each element represents whether two satellite nodes establish inter satellite links or not.

For the edge (i,j) in each spanning tree, we need to get its replacement edge set $R_{(i,j)}$, and then select the edge with the smallest edge weight in $R_{(i,j)}$ to replace edge (i,j), so that the average edge weight decreases the fastest. There are many ways to obtain the replacement edge set $R_{(i,j)}$, but the time complexity of the algorithm is relatively high. This paper introduces a coloring array col. When we look for the replacement edge set $R_{(i,j)}$, we can first delete edge (i,j) from the tree. At this time, the tree is divided into two connected blocks, and the satellite node i and the satellite node j are in these two connected blocks respectively. Mark all the nodes x coloring arrays in the same connected block as the satellite node i as $col[x] = i$, and the other node y coloring arrays as $col[y] = j$. Enumerate each non-tree edge, and then judge whether this edge is a legal potential edge and whether the coloring array values of the two endpoints of this edge are different, so as to judge whether this edge is in the replacement edge set. The time complexity of coloring is $O(N)$, and the time complexity of enumeration is $O(|E|)$, so the time complexity of finding the replacement edge set of an edge after optimization through the coloring array is $O(N + |E|) \sim O(|E|)$, which is acceptable. It should be noted that after each edge replacement, the replacement edge set of most points has changed greatly due to this replacement, that is, the replacement edge set R needs to be retrieved after each improved replacement.

3.3   Add Edge

In the first two steps, we have obtained an approximate minimum spanning tree satisfying the upper limit of degree. Now we only need to add some edges to make the minimum spanning tree a spanning subgraph satisfying the lower limit of degree, so as to make the average edge weight of this spanning subgraph as small as possible. The optimization problem can be expressed by the following mathematical formula:

$$\min \frac{1}{|E'|} \sum_{(i,j)|e_{ij} \in E'} w_{ij} \tag{7}$$

$$s.t.\lambda_2(\mathbf{X'}) > 0 \tag{8}$$

$$c_i \leq \sum_j x'_{ij} \leq d_i \tag{9}$$

$$X \leq X' \leq A \tag{10}$$

$$x'_{ij} \leq \{0,1\} \tag{11}$$

Equation (7) is the optimization objective, representing the minimum average edge weight. Equation (8) is the second small row column of the topological matrix. When the value is positive, it means that the abstract undirected graph of the spatial information network is connected after the link is established according to the topological matrix. In Eq. (9), c_i represents the lower limit degree of satellite node i, which means that the satellite node has corresponding connectivity requirements. d_i represents the upper limit of satellite node degree. Equation (10) indicates that the new topology matrix is generated on the basis of the original topology matrix. Equation (11) indicates that the topology matrix is 01 matrix, and each element indicates whether two satellite nodes establish inter satellite links.

After constructing the minimum degree restricted spanning tree, DMST algorithm uses the connectivity guarantee (CG) algorithm to increase the edges. This method ignores the dynamics and complexity of the graph in the process of edge increase. Specifically, the adjacency queue of each satellite node may change after the primary edge increases, so the first $c[i] - deg[i]$ candidate node set with the lowest cost among the satellite nodes that the satellite node needs to try to establish the inter satellite link will change, It may cause the addition of redundant edges or the graph that should meet the conditions is judged to be unable to generate a topology that fully meets the degree limit.

Define the candidate node set P and adjacency queue Q. The adjacency queue $Q[i]$ stores the potential inter satellite link nodes of satellite node i, which are stored in ascending order according to the cost of establishing inter satellite link. Consider the following situations: $Q[1] = \{2,3,4,5\}, Q[2] = Q[3] = Q[4] = Q[5] = \{1\}[5] = \{1\}$. Regardless of the upper degree limit of each satellite node, node 1 needs to successfully establish inter satellite links with at least three nodes to meet the lower degree limit, while node 3, node 4 and node 5 need to successfully establish inter satellite links with at least one node to meet the lower degree limit, but node 2 does not need to establish any additional inter satellite links. CG algorithm will make $P[1] = \{2,3,4\}$, and the addition of edges to node 5 will make all four inter satellite links (1,2), (1,3), (1,4) and (1,5) established. Obviously, the establishment of (1,3) is unnecessary. We find that the phenomenon of adding redundant edges occurs because node y outside the candidate node set P of a node x establishes an inter satellite link with the node x, resulting in that the last node z in the set P does not need to establish an inter satellite link with node x, but the cost of establishing a link between node x and node y is greater than that with node z, which is a phenomenon of large impact small.

DGMST introduces a new potential edge set ES, which contains all inter satellite links that each node attempts to establish with the nodes in its candidate node set. It can be represented by the position of triplet $<i,j$, The position of j in $[i]$. This set is sorted in descending order of the third dimension. If we don't reach the lower limit of degree in advance or large influence small, we just need to add all the edges in the potential edge set ES into the generated subgraph. Otherwise, after each edge addition, the corresponding P and ES will be updated. Since each non-tree edge may be added to the ES, each edge in the ES may be added to the generated subgraph, and the ES needs to be updated every time an edge is added to the generated subgraph, so the time complexity of this step is $O(E^2)$. If we consider using data structures such as priority queue or heap, we can reduce the time complexity of updating ES from $O(E)$ to sharing complexity $O(ElogE)$, because the number of times each edge is added to and removed from ES is limited.

3.4 Algorithm Analysis

The time complexity of generating topology by DMST + CG algorithm is $O(N^2) + O(NE^2) + O(NElogN)$, while the time complexity of DGMST algorithm is $(N^2)/O(T) + O(E^2) + O(E^2)/O(ElogE)$. The first part of DGMST algorithm consists of two parts: directly enumerating edges to build spanning tree and trying to reduce the degree with the improved algorithm in BUA. The time complexity is $O(N^2)$ and $O(T) \sim O(NE)$ respectively. Generally speaking, the random spanning tree is easy to get in a given satellite network. In the second part of the algorithm, the time complexity is greatly reduced compared with DMST algorithm through the idea of spanning tree coloring, and the worst-case complexity is determined by the number of edge replacement. In the step of adding edges, the dynamics and complexity of adjacent queues are considered, and the time complexity is sacrificed for correctness and better optimization effect. If you try to use data structure optimization, the time complexity of the third step can be greatly reduced. In a word, the average time complexity of DGMST is $O(E^2)$, which is quite improved compared with the average time complexity $O(NE^2)$ of the DMST algorithm.

4 Experimental Simulation and Result Analysis

4.1 Data Sets

This paper uses two data sets. The first kind of data set comes from locally constructed random data. The random data set consists of two parts: one is a group of satellite networks with 10 satellites in a single time period after artificial construction and random data; The second is 10000 groups of satellite networks in a single time period. Compared with the first group of data, in addition to the random visual matrix and weight matrix, the degree is limited from 20 to 150. Two sets of random data are mainly used to verify the success rate and operation efficiency of DGMST algorithm in constructing spanning tree and generating subgraph. The second kind of data sets have large differences in network inclination, appropriate number of orbits and a large number of satellites. The networks are commonly used in the research, and the data sets can cover most cases. The dataset contains multiple parts. (1) The Iridium-like network with an altitude of 780 km above the ground has 6 orbits, and each orbit has 11 satellites with an inclination of 87.5°. (2) The DSS network with an altitude of 35786 km above the ground has 10 orbits, and each orbit has 10 satellites with an inclination of 1.2°. (3) The MEO1 network with an altitude of 20000 km above the ground has three orbits, and each orbit has eight satellites with an inclination of 30°. (4) The MEO2 network with an altitude of 10000 km above the ground has three orbits and four satellites with an inclination of 45° in each orbit. (5) A hybrid network composed of two networks (1) and (2) (Table 1).

Table 1. Satellite network information.

Constellation	Iridium-like	DSS	MEO1	MEO2
Number of orbits	6	10	3	3
Number of satellites in each orbit	11	10	8	4
Height (km)	780	35786	20000	10000
Inclination (°)	87.5	1.2	30	45

Table 2. Success rate of building spanning tree.

Degree limit Algorithm	D = 3	D = 4	D = 5	Unlimited D
DMST	80.3%	87.2%	97.7%	100%
DGMST	95.6%	98.5%	100%	100%
Enumeration	100%	100%	100%	100%

Table 3. Average running time.

Number of nodes Algorithm	N = 20	N = 50	N = 100	N = 150
DGMST	0 ms	30 ms	237 ms	562 ms
DMST	0 ms	60 ms	722 ms	3198 ms

Table 4. Minimum average edge weight of generated subgraphs of Iridium-like networks.

Degree limit Algorithm	D = 3	D = 4	D = 5
DGMST	3092 km	2985 km	2917 km
DMST	3228 km	3177 km	3101 km

Table 5. Minimum average edge weight of generated subgraphs of DSS networks.

Degree limit Algorithm	D = 3	D = 4	D = 5
DGMST	4820 km	4235 km	3627 km
DMST	5011 km	4389 km	3773 km

Table 6. Minimum average edge weight of generated subgraphs of hybrid networks.

Degree limit Algorithm	D = 3	D = 4	D = 5
DGMST	5318 km	5148 km	4986 km
DMST	5629 km	5466 km	5210 km

4.2   Simulation Analysis Results

The success rate of building a spanning tree that meets the degree limit is shown in Table 2. The success rate of constructing spanning tree by DGMST algorithm is obviously better than DMST algorithm, but this is under the condition of random satellite network and strict degree limit. In practice, there is a certain gap in the success rate of constructing spanning tree between the two, but it is not as obvious as that in random cases, which has little impact on the subsequent generation subgraphs of reducing the average edge weight and constructing the minimum average edge weight.

The average running time of the data in a single time period, as shown in Table 3. The theoretical time complexity of the DGMST algorithm is significantly better than that of the DMST algorithm. However, the gap in actual operation is also very obvious but not as large as in the theoretical analysis. Considering that DGMST uses some data structures and additional skills, this is also reasonable. When the number of nodes N of the undirected graph is relatively small, since the computer cannot calculate a smaller time interval, the running time is 0 ms or 30 ms or greater 60 ms.

As shown in Tables 4, 5 and 6, the difference of the minimum average edge weight of the network topology constructed by DGMST algorithm and DMST algorithm is not large, and even the results on DSS network are quite close. This is because the distribution of satellite nodes in DSS network is relatively uniform and regular, so that satellite nodes can establish inter satellite links with other satellite nodes according to a fixed law to generate a space information network topology that meets the conditions and has better survivability. In hybrid networks or individual Iridium-like networks, the network topology constructed by DGMST algorithm is better than that of DMST algorithm. The process of adding edges in DGMST algorithm eliminates some problems caused by degree limitation by considering the global state.

In general, compared with DMST, the DGMDT algorithm is excellent in time complexity, and its ability to build a generated subgraph with minimum average edge weight is improved.

5   Conclusion

DGMST algorithm has great advantages in operation efficiency and building a more survivable network topology. Like DMST, DGMST is also a greedy approximation algorithm. The main disadvantage of DGMST algorithm is that the edge addition process in the third step still can't fully ensure the generation of legal topology, which may turn the original solution into no solution. The optimization problem in the third step is very similar to the problem that can be solved by the network flow algorithm with minimum cost and maximum flow, so we can consider using the network flow related algorithm to solve this problem. When there is no solution, you can find a chain formed by an edge, such as $a_1 a_2 a_3 \ldots a_n$. If the inter satellite link previously established is $(a_1, a_2)(a_3, a_4) \ldots (a_{n-2}, a_{n-1})$, you can modify the inter satellite link to $(a_2, a_3)(a_4, a_5) \ldots (a_{n-1}, a_n)$. In this way, the degree of node a_1 is successfully transferred to node a_n, and node a_1 can try to establish inter satellite links with other nodes, which is also similar to the way of finding augmented paths in network flow algorithm. Whether this approach can make the edge weight as small as possible remains to be discussed.

Acknowledgement. The authors are grateful to the editor and anonymous reviewers for their suggestions in improving the quality of the paper.

Funding Statement This paper is supported by: 1. Major Science and Technology Special Project of Sichuan Province, P.R. China (Grant no. 2018GZDZX0006). 2. Major Science and Technology Special Project of Sichuan Province, P.R. China (Grant no. 2018GZDZX0007).

Conflicts of Interest The authors declare that they have no conflicts of interest to report regarding the present study.

References

1. Asokan, A., Anitha, J., Patrut, B., Danciulescu, D., Hemanth, D.J.: Deep feature extraction and feature fusion for bi-temporal satellite image classification. Comput. Mater. Continua **66** (1), 373–388 (2021)

2. Hao, X.W.: Research on Survivalbility Routing and Anti-Attack Technology in Space Information Networks. Xidian University, Xi'an (2013)
3. Zheng, Y., Zhao, S., Liu, Y., Tan, Q., Li, Y., Jiang, Y.: Topology control in self-organized optical satellite networks based on minimum weight spanning tree. Aerosp. Sci. Technol. **69**, 449–457 (2017)
4. Liu, X., Chen, X., Yang, L., Chen, Q., Guo, J., Wu, S.: Dynamic topology control in optical satellite networks based on algebraic connectivity. Acta Astronaut. **165**, 287–297 (2019)
5. Li, Y., Xie, J., Xia, M., Li, Q., Li, M.: Dynamic resource pricing and allocation in multilayer satellite network. Comput. Mater. Continua **69**(3), 3619–3628 (2021)
6. Jwo, D., Wu, J., Ho, K.: Support vector machine assisted gps navigation in limited satellite visibility. Comput. Mater. Continua **69**(1), 555–574 (2021)
7. Zhuo, M., Liu, L., Zhou, S.: Survey on security issues of routing and anomaly detection for space information networks. Sci. Rep. **11**, 22261 (2021)
8. Wu, Z., Zhou, S., Liu, Q.: Review on object tracking methods for restricted computing resources. Comput. Eng. Appl. **57**(21), 24–40 (2021)
9. Liu, F., Vishkin, U., Milner, S.: Bootstrapping free-space optical networks. IEEE J. Sel. Areas Commun. **24**(12), 13–22 (2006)
10. Peter, S.J.: Minimum spanning tree based clustering for outlier detection. J. Discrete Math. Sci. Cryptogr. **14**(2), 149–166 (2011)

Tibetan Language Model Based on Language Characteristics

Kuntharrgyal Khysru[1][✉], Yangzom[1], and Jianguo Wei[1,2]

[1] Key Laboratory of Artificial Intelligence Application Technology State Ethnic Affairs Commission, Qinghai Minzu University, Xining 810007, China
{gtj186,jianguo}@tju.edu.cn
[2] Tianjin Key Laboratory of Cognitive Computing and Application, Tianjin University, Tianjin 300072, China

Abstract. Most of existing language models function by predicting next candidate words based on previous words or contextual statistics. However, they ignore the characteristics of the language itself, such as morpheme including words prefixes, roots, suffixes, etc. which play a significant role in understanding. Tibetan is a language whose complete meaning relies on its functional words such as the suffix of their front adjacent words, where some functions expresses by the radicals, the parts of the Tibetan characters. To utilize the characteristics of Tibetan in a language model, we proposed a novel language model which considers the functional words, especially free-functional words and suffixes of their preceding words. We first construct a Tibetan language model by utilizing the relationship between functional words and the ten explicit Tibetan suffixes, referred to as Tibetan Radical Suffix Unit-Explicitly (TRSU-E). To taking into account of the free-functional words, we improve the TRSU-E model to address the implicit relationship between free-functional words and their front suffix words, which denotes as Tibetan Radical Suffix Unit-ALL (TRSU-ALL). A standard Tibetan corpus is constructed and used for comprehensive analyses and evaluations. Experimental results show that TRSU-E achieves 16.29% and 10.65% relative perplexity reduction compared with two state-of-the-art methods, i.e. RNNLM and Tibetan Radicals Unit (TRU) respectively.

Keywords: Tibetan language model · Functional words · Tibetan radical suffix

1 Introduction

Today's society is an information age, and information exchange and transmission are of great significance for accelerating regional economic and social development. As a carrier of information transmission, language plays an important role in the development of information. Language model plays an important role in many fields, such as speech recognition, machine translation, information retrieval, and text generation [1–3,38,39]. There are many methods for language

X. Sun et al. (Eds.): ICAIS 2022, CCIS 1587, pp. 680–695, 2022.
https://doi.org/10.1007/978-3-031-06761-7_54

model research, such as n-gram, RNN, etc., which are basically English-oriented Rich language. For the low resource language research, on the other hand, it is basically the application of existing methods and cross-language information [3–5,40], without considering the characteristics of the language itself. As a minority language, Tibetan is also a low resource language. At present, the Tibetan population in the world is about 10 million, and about 7 million (2016) in China use Tibetan. The study of Tibetan language models can promote the progress of Tibetan machine translation, Tibetan speech recognition accelerate the economic development of Tibetan areas, facilitate the convenient communication, and so on. It has important application to the Tibetan people.

For the Tibetan language model, previous approaches are largely based on the character-level [6] Ngram method. A recent study of the Tibetan language model found that in order to obtain more useful information in a limited corpus, Shen et al. constructed a method combining the combination of character and radical [7]. We found that this method works well over traditional methods. However, in reality not all Tibetan radicals have an impact on the next character [8]. Although this method has achieved good results, it has problems in the judgment of functional words. We find that the judgment error of the words in the sentence has an influence on the semantics of this sentence.

Although the [7] method supplements the deficiencies of Tibetan corpus, the semantic influence of the Functional Words on the sentence is very important, and the key to the judgment of the Functional Words is suffix. Because in the Tibetan grammar, there is a theory of virtual lexical theory for character suffix. Therefore, we propose a Tibetan Radical Suffix Unit-Explicit (TRSU-E) method for judging the Functional Words, which solves the problem that the explicit suffix is not correct in the sentence.

In order to verify the validity of our method, we proposed the Tibetan News Corpus (i.e. TNC) with reference to the study of [12]. TNC is a corpus extracted from the Internet, including News, Education, Law, Buddhism, Culture, Literature and Wiki themes. In addition, in order to deal with web page tag noise, we also preprocessed the which will be introduced in experiments.

The rest of paper is organized as follows. Section 2 reviews some important concepts and previous work on language modeling. Section 3 describes the role of Tibetan suffix and the meaning of functional words to sentences. Section 4 introduces the method of processing suffix features and the fusion of suffix features in the Tibetan language model. Section 5 discusses the methods of data preprocessing and model comparisons and Sect. 6 conclude this paper.

2   Related Work

For morphologically rich languages, the goal is to study the internal structural formation of words [13–16]. Take English morphology for example, the goal is to study the relationship between the compositions of words, and sort out the rules of its composition. However, in their studies,syntax and semantic information have been largely ignored. Language models can apply such type of information to get word sequence with acceptable accuracy.

With the development of deep learning, many kinds of deep neural networks have been used for language modelling. Neural Network Language Model (NNLM) was introduced by [17], which puts several historical words together as input and places the cur-rent word in the output layer as the target. Although NNLM can solve the problem of high dimensionality of dictionaries by utilizing the mapping layer to reduce the dimension of input, it cannot address more contextual information. Recurrent Neural Network Based Language Model (RNNLM) can address sequence modeling and capture long distance information [12,18–22,42]. RNNLM exacts the history of words into a state and reduce the number of input dimensions. Besides, for the problem of huge output dimension, RNNLM also applies matrix factorization to cluster the words in the output layer, reducing the computational complexity. The proposed methods have been applied to tasks such as speech recognition [12,20,23–25].

Since words are the smallest language units that can be used independently, most of those language models of RNNLMs employ a word as a processing unit. In order to deal with such a problem, [3] proposed a character embedding level based model. They built a deeper network to improve the traditional word embedding level to character embedding level [27] by a technique of highway network, which avoids the problem of large-scale embedding computation. Furthermore, [28,29,41] also present the model which combines RNN and the character embedding level-based CNN.

To obtain more information from different levels, some researchers put forward many language models combining word-level and character-level information. Among them, [30] proposed a new model mixing the word embed-ding level and character embedding level model knowledge, which applies a gating mechanism of selecting the word embedding level or character embedding level to obtain a word vector. The model not only makes use of the information of the words in the dictionary, but also utilizes the information of low-frequency and unknown words by the character embedding. In fact, this model also includes other level information, such as etyma, prefix, suffix, well as the internal structural formation including the word-level and character-level information.

Tibetan, as a morphologically rich language [31], also has intrinsically structural information, in which a character has up to seven radicals [8]. The radicals of prefix and the root have great influence on the meaning of the character or the word, and the suffix affects the functional word, enriching the grammatical rules and semantic information in Tibetan sentences [9–11].

3   Effect and Significance of Tibetan Suffix on Functional Words

Each language has its own grammatical system. Tibetan is an alphabetic writing language with its own spelling rules. It has some differences in word-formation compared with English. English uses space to partition the words, while Tibetan needs to do word segmentation. In this paper, the Tibetan word needs to be segmented, and the character refers to each unit in which the Tibetan separator is separated, and the radical is the component that constitutes the character. Since so far there is no existing standard for segmentation in Tibetan language, we use character as a unit. Tibetan has a set of its own grammatical systems [9–11]. The most common sentences in Tibetan are inseparable from functional words, which are used to connect word to word or phrase to phrase to express semantics.

3.1 Structure of Tibetan Characters

Fig. 1. The most components of a word in Tibetan are prefix, root (This is to show that the components of a word in Tibetan often includes prefix, root (vowel, superscript and subscript)) and suffix (farther suffix).

Writing language of Tibetan is composed of Tibetan characters, which are spelled by several radicals. A Tibetan character is generally composed of one to seven radicals. Figure 1 shows the position and the name for each radical of a Tibetan character. The root (bottom left in the figure) is the indispensable part, while the other parts are depending on the individual characters. In general, the characters are independent from each another. The suffix, however, is related to the following functional words, where the combination of the suffix and the functional words affect the semantic meaning of the sentence. The suffix may contain farther suffix, which has higher priority than suffix.

The suffix mainly has an effect on the functional words, playing the role of connection and, expressing different ideas according to the different context environment. While functional words do not have independent ideographic functions, they can express the special semantic function by connecting the words nearby. Functional words are added according to different suffixes in Tibetan characters (i.e. the suffix appearing in the front of the functional words). There are two forms of suffix in Tibetan, i.e. the suffix and farther suffix, which are both included in the suffix ("ga", "nga", "da", "na", "ba", "ma", "v", "ra", "la", "sa") [32].

3.2 Effects of the Suffix on Functional Word

Tibetan suffix connects functional words (phrad), and induces different meanings based on the combination. Tibetan functional words themselves do not have independent ideographic functions, and they expresses special semantic meaning by nearby characters [9–11]. Functional words can be divided into free-functional words

(rang dbang can) and non-free-functional words (gzhan dbang can).

Non-free-functional words determine the function of the connected relation based on the suffix or farther suffix of the preceding character. For completing character (a class of functional words) "go","ngo","do","no","bo","mo" ,"vo" ,"ro","lo","so","to", the suffix of the character must be the same as the root of the functional words, (so that the character and functional words can be connected). For genitive character (another class of functional words) "gi", "kyi","gyi","vi","yi", they determine functional words according to the continuation rule ("da", "ba","sa","kyi", "ga","nga","gi","na","ma", "ra","la","gyi"), [32]. In other words, it is a continuation relationship with certain grammatical rules.

Free-functional words include the suffix "v" and implicit suffix. When there is no suffix, we regard "v" and "da" as implicit suffix. However, they are not fixed. For example, compared with non-free-functional words, "dang","nas", "las", "ma","mi","ni" has relatively free combination. They select functional words according to the structure of the sentence. So it is worth noting that, the functional words mentioned above are not complete, but simply a part of the functional words reported in [9,11,33].

4 Tibetan Language Model Considering Suffix

The study of neural network language model is a popular research trend at present. As one of the minority language, Tibetan is quoted and referenced in some resource rich languages, such as English, French, and Chinese. In our study, we found that each language has its own characteristics due to the differences in the language. The feature of a language can be integrated into the language model, to more accurately determine the next character or word.

4.1 Conventional RNNLM

A statistical language model gives a sequence of words and then predicts a possible sentence by its probability value. For instance RNNLM uses the temporal information to save the context to obtain the hidden layer information. Here x_t denotes the input layer of time t, which encodes the present character w_t using the one-hot vector whose size is V_{word}. The hidden layer, denoted by h_t, preserves the remaining context information by using the activation function. The output layer of RNNLM is o_t, which is the probability of each character at time $t+1$ in vocabulary given the history character sequence $< w_t \cdots w_1 >$, produced by a softmax function. The input layer, hidden layer and output layer in the propagation process of RNNLM can be computed as follows:

$$h_t = f(W_{IH}x_t + W_{HH}h_{t-1}) \tag{1}$$

$$o_t = g(W_{HO}h_t) \tag{2}$$

$$P_{RNN}(x_{t+1} = k|x_t, h_{t-1}) = o_{t,k} \tag{3}$$

$$f(z) = \frac{1}{1 + e^{-z}} \tag{4}$$

$$g(z_m) = \frac{e^{z_m}}{\sum_k e^{z_k}} \tag{5}$$

Beyond the RNNLM structure, the idea is to make full use of sequence information in the implicit character information about the loop, so that it can simulate any long span of information. But in practice, it is limited to the first few characters. However, we need to modify the RNNLM and interpolation of the multiple-mode functionality, (i.e., some structural information and morphological features) to enrich sentences.

4.2   Tibetan Suffix Feature Fusion

Based on the theory of "Suncupa" in Tibetan Grammar [9,11,33], this paper presents the suffix feature Tibetan language model. We present a Tibetan linguistic model for Tibetan Radical Suffix Unit-Explicitly (i.e.TRSU-E) and Tibetan Radical Suffix Unit-Implicit (i.e.TRSU-I). TRSU-E adds suffix type features explicitly, fusing ten suffix ("ga","nga","da","na","ba","ma","v","ra","la", "sa") (and farther suffix) features into the model, improving the connecting effect and semantic expression for the explicit suffix when connecting with the next functional words. Using the suffix "sa" as a suffix feature, TRSU-I adds the implicit relationship to the model after adding the suffix "v". Since the Tibetan language will not normally write implicit suffix "v", in the procession, TRSU-E mainly aims at explicit suffix, and TRSU-I also takes implicit suffix into consideration.

As showed in Fig. 2, we add the feature information extracted from suffix when using RNN to calculate the probability of characters, and then predict the latent semantics while solving the continuation problem of the functional words in the sequence. Here c_t, h_t, o_t are the input, hidden and output activations at time step t. The probability produced by the language model can be used to predict character at time $t + 1$. The input layer, hidden layer and output layer in RNNLM calculation process are as follows:

$$c_t = f(W_{IC}x_t + W_{SC}s_t) \tag{6}$$

$$h_t = f(W_{CH}c_t + W_{HH}h_{t-1}) \tag{7}$$

$$o_t = g(W_{HO}h_t) \tag{8}$$

In Eq. (6), W_{IC} represents the character weight, W_{SC} represents the suffix feature weight, and the activation function input character probability and suffix feature weight fusion. Among them, W_{SC} is used to process suffix information in Tibetan grammar. The information of suffix will have a connection meaning

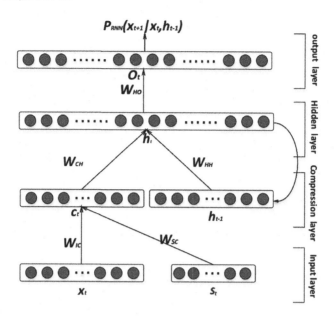

Fig. 2. Tibetan language model considering the semantic relation of the functional words of suffix.

to the functional words, so that sentences can express semantics accurately. Equation (7) is the hidden layer h_t, with the activation function on the input layer c_t time W_{CH} weight and hidden layer h_{t-1} time W_{HH} weight add, with the activation function to retain the context information, and finally output.

In the language model based on grammar, because the grammar affects the sentence in Tibetan, the suffix determines the continuation of the functional words. By analyzing the Tibetan grammatical relationship, the suffix information in the character will be obtained, and then the functional words will be judged according to the continuation relationship of the Tibetan grammar. This kind of functional words plays an important role in the semantics of the sentence, so solving the continuation relationship of the Tibetan functional words can further optimize the representation of Tibetan sentences.

5   Experiments

In this section, we first introduce data processing and distribution, then extract suffix features and apply RNN method in language model. We choose perplexity (PPL) as the evaluation criteria, the smaller the PPL, the better the predictive ability of the language model. Finally, we compare the latest methods for dealing with Tibetan language models as baselines [7]. The previous method aims to obtain the structural information inside the character to supplement the low resource language problem, without considering the characteristics of the language itself.

Table 1. Statistics of tibetantext data

Data		# Token	%OOV
Char vocabulary	–	2472	–
Training set	News	1.5m	1.08
	Education	1.2 m	1.28
	Law	1.1 m	1.35
	Buddhism	1.4 m	1.61
	Culture	1.2 m	1.15
	Literature	3.8 m	1.35
	Wiki	11.1 m	2.55
	ALL	21.3 m	1.48
Valid set		125k	1.12
Test set		126k	1.11

5.1 Data Processing

As a minority language in China, Tibetan language only circulates in Tibetan areas, and the official language is Chinese. Therefore, the corpus collected on the Internet is relatively limited, and the research personnel are relatively rare. As a result, little progress has been made in this filed in the current study.

Referring to the study by Mikolov *et al.*, we designed Tibetan News Corpus (TNC) to extract and post-process Tibetan news corpora from the Internet, including the genres of News, Education, Law, Buddhism, Culture, Literature and Wiki [3,12,20]. The wiki data was collected through the wiki website, while the other types of data were obtained through different genres on the domestic Tibetan website. According to the Tibetan vocabulary frequency characteristics, the amount of vocabulary is 2,472, and other character which are not in the vocabulary are replaced out of vocabulary (OOV).

In addition to removing the noise from the online label, we segment the crawled data in to sentences using Tibetan sentences segmentation symbol ("—"). We replaced the character segmentation symbol ("tsheg",) in the Tibetan language with space. After the denoising process the corpus is divided into 25 section (10:1:1). Section 0–20 are the training set, section 21–22 and 23–24 are for a valid set and a test set, respectively.

In Tibetan language, the suffix feature is very important to the Tibetan word function, and the functional words have the functions of changing semantics. Using statistical methods, we analyze the data, as shown in Fig. 3 (A). Here, the proportion of their respective functional words is 28%, which fully illustrates the importance of the functional words.

In order to have a better understanding of the functional words, which contain both the free-functional words and non-free-functional words, we obtained the proportion of each kind. From the B chart of Fig. 3 we can see that free-functional words occupy a larger proportion (70%), that is, our task contains how to handle

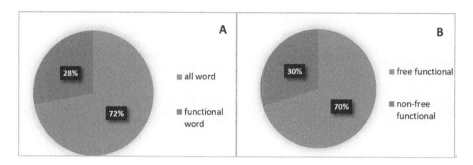

Fig. 3. (A) Shows the proportion of the functional words in the corpus, (B) the proportion of free-functional words and non-free-functional words

the successively relation of not only the specific grammatical rules, but also no specific successively relationship. It is worth noting that the non-free-functional successive relationship is relatively fixed, which can be judged according to the suffix. For free-functional words, on the other hand, they are more flexible and there is no fixed successive relationship. We can learn the suffix features from corpus to generate some successively relationships.

5.2   Results and Analysis

Results. This paper presents Tibetan Radical Suffix Unit (TRSU), a language model method of Tibetan radical Suffix Unit-Explicitly (TRSU-E) and Tibetan Radical Suffix Unit-Implicit (TRSU-I). In the experiment, we compared the traditional methods of applying the language model with the latest methods of Tibetan language model research. Parameter settings are based on the CUED-RNNLM method [34–37]. Since the test set in our dataset is related to News, we experimented with datasets on the same genres, different genres, and all genres in the experiment to verify the effectiveness of our approach.

On Datasets with the Same Genres: Because the test set is News-themed, we need to validate our approach on the same genres in our experiments. In Table 2, we divide the experiment into three parts. The first part is the method of the existing language model research (the traditional method and some new methods), the second part is the latest method of the Tibetan language model research, and the last is our proposed method. We first compare the existing method with our method. It can be seen that our method relative decreases perplexity (PPL) by about 7.4% compared with the existing language model. Compared with the latest methods for studying Tibetan language models, our method relative decreases PPL by 4.8%. This shows that the proposed method solves the problem of functional words error.

In order to verify the effectiveness of our proposed method, we not only compare our method with other methods, but also compare our proposed TRSU-E and TRSU-I. TRSU-E solves the continuation of non-free words, but there

Table 2. The previous method and our method compare ppl on the genres

Model	News
N-gram(Mikolov et al. 2012)	55.2
RNNLM(Mikolov et al. 2012)	62.9
CUED_RNNLM(Xie Chen et al. 2016)	58.4
CUED_RNNLM(LSTM)(Xie Chen et al. 2016)	55.9
CharCNN (Kim et al. 2016)	55.2
_TRU(Shen et al. 2017)	57.6
_TRD(Shen et al. 2017)	54.3
_TRC(Shen et al. 2017)	53.8
TRSU-E	**52.7**
TRSU-I	**51.2**

are some suffix in Tibetan that are implicit. These implicit suffix will affect the connection of free words. Therefore, we proposed TRSU-I to solve such problems. The experimental results show that the PPL of TRSU-I is about 3% lower than TRSU-E. This also verifies that the implicit suffix method we proposed can capture the implicit relationship of the suffix.

Table 3. Comparison of previous research methods and our methods on different genres

Model	Edu	Law	Bud	Cul	Lit	Wiki
N-gram(Mikolov et al. 2012)	122.3	**288.8**	**497.5**	170.4	132.9	254.1
RNNLM(Mikolov et al. 2012)	147.9	374.1	698.9	196.2	155.9	218.7
CUED_RNNLM(Xie Chen et al. 2016)	139.8	367.8	655.1	179.3	123.2	189.9
CUED_RNNLM(LSTM)(Xie Chen et al. 2016)	127.2	364.1	618.4	169.8	118.2	160.2
CharCNN (Kim et al. 2016)	123.7	366.5	602.4	168.1	116.5	159.8
_TRU(Shen et al. 2017)	131.2	364.4	702.3	171.1	118.1	162.8
_TRD(Shen et al. 2017)	125.8	367.4	596.3	167.9	113.8	157.2
_TRC(Shen et al. 2017)	122.3	356.6	590.4	175.1	114.9	155.7
TRSU-E	118.5	358.9	562.8	165.8	110.4	152.4
TRSU-I	**117.6**	354.1	549.9	**165.2**	**109.8**	**152.1**

On Datasets with the Different Genres: Similarly, the results on other genres are shown in Table 3. It can be seen that our method is still more accurate than the traditional in this case. In education, culture, and literature genres our approach decreases PPL by 18.6% to 22.2%. Compared to the latest Tibetan language model approach, our approach decreases PPL by 3.8% to 10.4% in education, culture and literary, respectively.

Table 3 also shows that the value of PPL varies from one genre to another. There is no traditional n-gram method on religious and legal-themed data, indicating that our test sets differ greatly from such data genres. Although there is a certain improvement from the context and structure information, no n-gram method is effective.

On Datasets with the All Genres: Table 4 summarizes the PPL-values across all genres. On the entire fusion dataset, our method decreases PPL by 1.9%–16.2% compared with the traditional method, and by 4.7%–6.4% compared with the latest Tibetan language model method. This again shows the effectiveness of our method.

Table 4. Results on topical best data and on all data

Model	ALL
N-gram(Mikolov et al. 2012)	98.6
RNNLM(Mikolov et al. 2012)	92.5
CUED_RNNLM(Xie Chen et al. 2016)	89.2
LSTM(Xie Chen et al. 2016)	84.1
CharCNN (Kim et al. 2016)	98.1
_TRU(Shen et al. 2017)	88.1
_TRD(Shen et al. 2017)	87.5
_TRC(Shen et al. 2017)	86.7
TRSU-E	**84.5**
TRSU-I	**82.6**

As can be seen from the results in Table 3. The overall PPL value on the news data set is lower, which indicates that the theme of our test set is biased towards news, so it has achieved good results on this data set. All genres is the integration of data for each genre, which will cause noise that is not a news genre to affect the outcome. Table 4 shows that our method also achieves the best results on the whole data set including all the genres, demonstrating that our method is effective for the Tibetan language model.

Due to the insufficient amount of data, in order to compare our methods and the previous method fairly, we applied the n-gram method to interpolate all models on the dataset of each genre. We use a linear interpolation method, where λ is the proportion interpolation weights model. In order to verify the range of λ, we set the hidden layer as 700 and λ from 0 to 1, and compare the interpolation results of RNNLM, CUED_RNNLM, LSTM, Char(CNN), TRU, TRD, TRC, TRSU-E, TRSU-I, and tri-gram. When $\lambda = 0$, we take RNN model, and when $\lambda = 1$, trigram model N-gram with N=3 is used.

Figure 4 shows that the optimal λ is obtained when the method and n-gram are interpolate, We set the hidden layer to 700 to interpolate each method. It

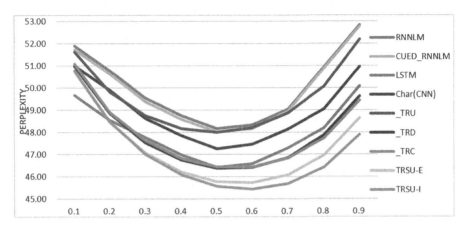

Fig. 4. When the hidden layer is 700, RNNLM, CUED_RNNLM, LSTM, Char(CNN), TRU, TRD, TRC, TRSU-E, TRSU-I model and trigram interpolation

can be seen from Fig. 4 that our method works best when taking 0.5 or 0.6. In this article, we set $\lambda = 0.5$.

Table 5 makes interpolation RNNLM, CUED_RNNLM, LSTM, Char(CNN), TRU, TRD, TRC, TRSU-E, TRSU-I, and trigram, where the lambda takes 0.5. From the results we can see that our method still achieved good results on the dataset of each genre after interpolation. In Table 3 we can see that our method does not perform as well as the n-gram method on the law and Buddhism datasets. However, after interpolation our approach decreases PPL by 3% to 16.8% over traditional methods, especially on law and Buddhism datasets. From this, we can see that interpolation indeed improves the accuracy of our method.

Table 5. The results of RNNLM, CUED_RNNLM, LSTM, Char(CNN), TRU, TRD, TRC, TRSU-E, TRSU-I with trigram interpolation

Model	News + ngram	Edu+ ngram	Law+ ngram	Bud+ ngram	Cul+ ngram	Lit+ ngram	Wiki+ ngram
N-gram(Mikolov et al. 2012)	55.2	122.3	288.8	497.7	170.4	132.9	254.1
RNNLM(Mikolov et al. 2012)	48.2	116.5	277.5	456.5	161.5	123.4	169.5
CUED_RNNLM(Xie Chen et al. 2016)	48.0	110.4	272.5	427.2	153.2	112.6	151.2
LSTM(Xie Chen et al. 2016)	46.4	107.3	274.8	419.5	143.3	107.8	139.1
CharCNN (Kim et al. 2016)	47.3	103.8	276.5	410.4	143.0	104.7	138.8
_TRU(Shen et al. 2017)	47.9	102.7	251.2	419.3	140.8	103.9	138.5
_TRD(Shen et al. 2017)	47.0	101.8	250.8	402.6	141.4	103.5	136.2
_TRC(Shen et al. 2017)	46.9	99.9	249.2	396.7	141.2	102.9	135.8
TRSU-E	45.7	98.1	249.1	387.3	139.8	102.0	134.5
TRSU-I	**45.1**	**97.3**	**247.1**	**383.1**	**137.9**	**100.4**	**133.9**

Discussion. As the baseline, TRU joins Tibetan character in each radical as a feature to RNN. The problem is that not every radical has meaning and not every radical, can catch the syntax information. The method proposed in this paper aims to accurately enrich the successive relationship and express sentence semantics for the functional words.

The TRSU-E method is to extract the suffix in the Tibetan language and then add the further suffix after the addition, as a feature to join the RNN. This method can be extracted from the suffix to judge the continuation of the functional words, solving the problem of free-functional words and non-free-functional words. However, the TRSU-E method has a problem that it is unable to solve the implicit after the character "v" and "da". Based on this problem, we propose a TRSU-I method which not only solves the successive relationship between suffix and functional words, but also learns the implicit relation of implicit suffix "v" and "da". This can effectively solve the relationship between the non-free-functional words and free-functional words, and enrich predict the sentence semantic expression.

Table 6. The influence of Functional Words on sentence semantics

Method	Sentence
Original	ཁོང་ གིས་ ཐབས་ འདི་ ལ་ བརྟེན་ ནས་ རིག་ གཞུང་ ཐད་ དུ་ བསམ་ བློ་ བརྗེ་ རེས་ བྱས་ པ་ དང་
	Khong gis thabs vdi la brten nas rig gzhung thad du bsam blo brje res byas ba dng
n-gram	ཁོང་ གི་ ཐབས་ འདི་ ལ་ བརྟེན་ ནས་ རིག་ གཞུང་ ཐད་ འདུག་ བསམ་ བློ་ བརྗེ་ རེས་ བྱེད་ པ་ དང་
	Khong gi thabs vdi la brten nas rig gzhung thad vdug bsam blo brje res byas ba dng
RNNLM	ཁོང་ གི་ ཐག་ དེ་ ལ་ བརྟེན་ ནས་ རིག་ གཞུང་ ཐད་ དུ་ བསམ་ བློ་ བརྗེ་ རེས་ བྱེད་ པ་ དང་
	Khong gi thag de la brten nas rig gzhung thad du bsam blo brje res byas ba dng
Ours	ཁོང་ གིས་ ཐབས་ འདི་ ལ་ བརྟེན་ ནས་ རིག་ གཞུང་ ཐད་ དུ་ བསམ་ བློ་ བརྗེ་ རེས་ བྱེད་ པ་ དང་
	Khong gis thabs vdi la brten nas rig gzhung thad du bsam blo brje res byas ba dng

In Table 6 refers to the original sentence, where the sentence was arbitrarily selected from the test set. The original sentence means "he uses this method for academic communication." It can be seen that the error of the functional words in the "thad vdug" sentence produced by the n-gram method leads to unclear semantics. The RNNLM method also causes errors in the "khong gi" functional words, leading to the change of both the following character as well as the semantics. From the expression of the sentence, "apply some kind of academic exchange" can be used to determine this kind of misrepresentation. The method we proposed solves this problem very well and thus can clearly express the semantics of the sentence.

6   Conclusion and Future Work

In this paper, we presented a Tibetan language linguistic model based on suffix features, which aims to predict the next character in corpus. By introducing suffix information, the proposed model can 1) consider the successive relation of the functional words from the sequence of sentences, 2) judge the corresponding functional words of the suffix accurately, and 3) distinguish the two meanings of the character in the sentence. Here, the functional words in the Tibetan is judged according to the connection and context. The method proposed in this paper not only considers the regular functional words, but also utilizes the irregular functional words effectively. Empirical results show that this method has a good auxiliary effect on the Tibetan language model, and the perplexity (PPL) is 10% lower than the best baseline. To better illustrate the validity of suffix method, we also compare the Tibetan radical unit (TRU) method with the proposed approach. We find that the radical information indeed improves the effectiveness of the proposed method. Moreover, after the trigram interpolation, the proposed method has obtained the best results, and the PPL is about 5% lower than the TRU interpolation which performs the second best.

The Tibetan language model, which is based on the suffix feature fusion, is used to support the continuation of the Tibetan functional words, and can solve the semantic relation of the sentence in the sequence. There are some future works. 1) The dataset we built have a related small size, thus in the future we will run our method on a larger dataset. 2) Due to considering only character-level information, the new Tibetan language model mixes the character-level, word-level, phrase-level as well as sentence-level information together. In practical tasks, we can achieve better results on Automatic Speech Recognition (ASR). Although this article has involved some, but we still need more research in order to standardize its grammatical and semantic effect. We hope that in the future Tibetan natural language processing can also perform better in other relative fields based on this research.

Acknowledgments. This work was supported by the Regional Innovation Cooperation Project of Sichuan Province (Grant No. 22QYCX0082).

References

1. Michiel, H., Schrauwen, B.: Training and analysing deep recurrent neural networks. In: Advances in Neural Information Processing Systems, pp. 190–198 (2013)
2. Kyuyeon, H., Sung, W.: Character-level language modeling with hierarchical recurrent neural networks. In: Acoustics, Speech and Signal Processing (ICASSP), pp. 5720–5724 (2017)
3. Yoon, K., Jernite, Y., Sontag, D., Rush, A.M.: Character-aware neural language models. In: AAAI, pp. 2741–2749 (2016)
4. Dalmia, S., Li, X., Metze, F., Black, A.W.: Domain robust feature extraction for rapid low resource ASR development. In: 2018 IEEE Spoken Language Technology Workshop (SLT), pp. 258–265 (2018)
5. Li, G.Y., Yu, H.Z.: Large-vocabulary continuous speech recognition of Lhasa Tibetan. Appl. Mech. Mater. **519**, 802–806 (2014)
6. Li, J., Wang, H., Wang, L., Dang, J., Khuru, K., Lobsang, G.: Exploring tonal information for Lhasa dialect acoustic modeling. In: 2016 10th International Symposium on Chinese Spoken Language Processing (ISCSLP), pp. 1–5 (2016)

7. Shen, T., Wang, L., Chen, X., Khysru, K., Dang, J.: Exploiting the Tibetan radicals in recurrent neural network for low-resource language models. In: International Conference on Neural Information Processing, pp. 266–275 (2017)

8. Yeh, E.T.: Tibet and the Problem of Radical Reductionism, pp. 983–1010. Wiley Online Library, Antipode (2009)

9. Tharrgyal, L.: A Study of Tibetan Grammar. Qinghai Nationalities Publishing House (In Tibetan), Qinghai (2008)

10. Tournadre, N.: The classical Tibetan cases and their transcategoriality: from sacred grammar to modern linguistics. Himalayan Linguist. **9**(2), 87–125 (2010)

11. Xiarong, T.: Detailed Explanation About Tibetan Grammar. Qinghai Nationalities Publishing House (In Tibetan), Qinghai (1954)

12. Mikolov, T., Karafiát, M., Burget, L., Černockỳ, J., Khudanpur, S.: Recurrent neural network based language model. In: Eleventh Annual Conference of the International Speech Communication Association (2010)

13. Hao, F., Ostendorf, M., Baumann, P., Pierrehumbert, J.: Exponential language modeling using morphological features and multi-task learning. IEEE/ACM Trans. Audio Speech Lang. Process. **23**, 2410–2421 (2015)

14. Lazaridou, A., Marelli, M., Zamparelli, R., Baroni, M.: Compositionally derived representations of morphologically complex words in distributional semantics. In: Proceedings of the 51st Annual Meeting of the Association for Computational Linguistics, vol. 1, pp. 1517–1526 (2013)

15. Luong, T., Socher, R., Manning, C.: Better word representations with recursive neural networks for morphology. In: Proceedings of the Seventeenth Conference on Computational Natural Language Learning, pp. 104–113 (2013)

16. Yildiz, E., Tirkaz, C., Sahin, H.B., Eren, M.T., Sonmez, O.: A morphology-aware network for morphological disambiguation. arXiv preprint arXiv:1702.03654 (2017)

17. Bengio, Y., Ducharme, R., Vincent, P., Jauvin, C.: A neural probabilistic language model. J. Mach. Learn. Res. **3**, 1137–1155 (2003)

18. Cho, E., Kumar, S.: A conversational neural language model for speech recognition in digital assistants. In: 2018 IEEE International Conference on Acoustics, Speech and Signal Processing (ICASSP), pp. 5784–5788 (2018)

19. Liu, X., Chen, X., Wang, Y., Gales, M., Woodland, P.: Two efficient lattice rescoring methods using recurrent neural network language models. IEEE/ACM Trans. Audio Speech Lang. Process. **24**, 1438–1449 (2016)

20. Mei, H., Bansal, M., Walter, M.R.: Coherent dialogue with attention-based language models. In: AAAI, pp. 3252–3258 (2017)

21. Mikolov, T.: Statistical language models based on neural networks. Presentation at Google, Mountain View, 2 April 2012

22. Mikolov, T., Kombrink, S., Burget, L., Cernocky, J.H., Khudanpur, S.: Extensions of recurrent neural network language model. In: IEEE International Conference on Acoustics (2011)

23. Irie, K., Lei, Z., Schlüter, R., Ney, H.: Prediction of LSTM-RNN full context states as a subtask for N-Gram feedforward language models. In: 2018 IEEE International Conference on Acoustics, Speech and Signal Processing (ICASSP), pp. 6104–6108 (2018)

24. Lee, K., Park, C., Kim, N., Lee, J.: Accelerating recurrent neural network language model based online speech recognition system. In: 2018 IEEE International Conference on Acoustics, Speech and Signal Processing (ICASSP), pp. 5904–5908 (2018)

25. Liu, S., et al.: Limited-memory BFGS optimization of recurrent neural network language models for speech recognition. In: 2018 IEEE International Conference on Acoustics, Speech and Signal Processing (ICASSP), pp. 6114–6118 (2018)
26. Pascanu, R., Mikolov, T., Bengio, Y.: On the difficulty of training recurrent neural networks. In: International Conference on Machine Learning, pp. 1310–1318 (2013)
27. Bojanowski, P., Joulin, A., Mikolov, T.: Alternative structures for character-level RNNs. arXiv preprint arXiv:1511.06303 (2015)
28. Chung, J., Gulcehre, C., Cho, K., Bengio, Y.: Empirical evaluation of gated recurrent neural networks on sequence modeling. arXiv preprint arXiv:1412.3555 (2014)
29. Jozefowicz, R., Vinyals, O., Schuster, M., Shazeer, N., Wu, Y.: Exploring the limits of language modeling. arXiv preprint arXiv:1602.02410 (2016)
30. Nuo, M., Liu, H., Ma, L., Wu, J., Ding, Z.: Automatic acquisition of Chinese-Tibetan multi-word equivalent pair from bilingual corpora. In: 2011 International Conference on Asian Language Processing, pp. 177–180 (2011)
31. Miyamoto, Y., Cho, K.: Gated word-character recurrent language model. arXiv preprint arXiv:1606.01700 (2016)
32. Zhabsdrung, T.: Sumrtags kyi bshadpa Thonmivi Zhallung, Kansua Zu Mirigs Dpeskrunkhang (In Tibetan), Qinghai (1989)
33. Luosang Tsechum Gyumsto, S.: Tibetan Grammatical Theories by Seduo. Nationalities Publishing House (In Tibetan), Qinghai (1957)
34. Chen, T., Caseiro, D., Rondon, P.: Entropy based pruning of Backoff Maxent Language Models with contextual features. In: 2018 IEEE International Conference on Acoustics, Speech and Signal Processing (ICASSP), pp. 6129–6133 (2018)
35. Chen, X., Liu, X., Gales, M., Woodland, P.: Improving the training and evaluation efficiency of recurrent neural network language models. In: 2015 IEEE International Conference on Acoustics, Speech and Signal Processing (ICASSP), pp. 5401–5405 (2015)
36. Chen, X., Liu, X., Gales, M., Woodland, P.: Recurrent neural network language model training with noise contrastive estimation for speech recognition. In: 2015 IEEE International Conference on Acoustics, Speech and Signal Processing (ICASSP), pp. 5411–5415 (2015)
37. Chen, X., Liu, X., Qian, Y., Gales, M.J.F., Woodland, P.C.: CUED-RNNLM-an open-source toolkit for efficient training and evaluation of recurrent neural network language models. In: 2016 IEEE International Conference on Acoustics, Speech and Signal Processing (ICASSP), pp. 6000–6004 (2016)
38. Changrampadi, M.H., Shahina, A., Narayanan, M.B., Khan, A.N.: End-to-end speech recognition of Tamil language. Intell. Autom. Soft Comput. 32, 1309–1323 (2022)
39. Zhao, Y., et al.: Tibetan multi-dialect speech recognition using latent regression Bayesian network and end-to-end mode. J. Internet Things 1(1), 17–23 (2019)
40. Jyoshna, G., Zia, M., Koteswararao, L.: An efficient reference free adaptive learning process for speech enhancement applications. Comput. Mater. Continua 3067–3080 (2022)
41. Lee, D., Park, H., Seo, S., Kim, C., Son, H., et al.: Language model using differentiable neural computer based on forget gate-based memory deallocation. Comput. Mater. Continua 680, 537–551 (2021)
42. Sun, Y., Chen, C., Chen, A., Zhao, X.: Tibetan question generation based on sequence to sequence model. Comput. Mater. Continua 68, 3203–3213 (2021)

Multimedia Forensics

Digital Forensics Study on Smart Watch and Wristband: Data Sniffing, Backup and Database Analyzing

Pu Chen[1,2,3], GuangJun Liang[1,2,3(✉)], Ziqi Ding[1,2,3], Zixiang Xu[1,2,3], and Mochi Zhang[1,2,3]

[1] Department of Computer Information and Cyber Security, Jiangsu Police Institute, Nanjing, China
lianggjun@126.com
[2] Jiangsu Province Electronic Data Forensics and Analysis Engineering Research Center, Nanjing, China
[3] Key Laboratory of Digital Forensics of Jiangsu Provincial Public Security Department, Nanjing, China

Abstract. With the technology advancing rapidly, it has become apparent that it is nearly impossible to go without a digital trace when committing a crime. Device such as Xiaomi wristband, keeps the record of a user's daily activities, heart rate, pressure value, step count, and sleep quality. Due to daily use, these messages are valuable for digital forensic investigators as it may serve as evidence and proofs to a crime, as well as revealing the motives of crime. This paper will demonstrate some useful examples to investigators about the methods to extract and analyze smart watch using Bluetooth tools like Ubertooth One. Experiments about wireless sniffing and wired transmission are given in this paper. We are making a tentative exploration and hoping to provide some useful experience and practice to investigators in the field of forensics.

Keywords: Smart watch and wristband · Digital forensics · Data sniffing

1 Introduction

With the advent of the era 'Internet of Things' and the general trend of modern intelligence, electronic forensics have already exceeded the traditional field of forensic [1]. Connected to our mobile phone, smart watches and wristbands are making records of our daily life, including our position [2], heart rate, steps and so on [3]. Therefore, the evidence collection of smart watch and wristband is of inestimable value to today's evidence-obsessed society. Forensic measures are adopted to extract data from smart watch and wristband. Scientific analysis and evaluation are carried out on the base of the extracted data to target the key value [4] which propels the progress of the case, providing comprehensive materials for case restoration.

Information stored in smart watch and wristband is just the beginning of a large amount of evidence smart watch and wristband can store, which represents a huge opportunity to electronic forensic investigators. On the basis of recent work and research in this area, there does not appear to be much work that has already taken

X. Sun et al. (Eds.): ICAIS 2022, CCIS 1587, pp. 699–711, 2022.
https://doi.org/10.1007/978-3-031-06761-7_55

place on smart watch and wristband. Feasible methods for data acquisition in Android based smart watch and wristband are discussable because of the complexity of obtaining data without modifying any state of the wearable bands. Researches show that a team has successfully recovered a swath of digital evidence directly from the watches compared to the data on the phone synchronized with the watches after gaining root access to them [5]. In a new system developed to aid emergency practices after earthquake, data of heart rate and movement of victims are also tracked and obtained to identify the critical rescue area in the shortest possible time. Another team analyzed the security infringement environment in a smart watch device and found out a hashing function to verify data integrity. Approaches to extract data depend on the level of intrusion and destruction. Regarding forensic reliability, the non-intrusive data extraction was applied. However, difficulty does exist as forensic challenges can either be technical, administrative or legislative and Anti-Forensic which add complexity in accessing evidence during a forensic investigation. In real-world scenarios, it hurdles forensic examiners from acquiring an image of evidences to continue with forensic examinations. Hence, more researches shall be done to seek for ways of reliable forensics on smart watch and wristband.

In our experiment, we first carry out experiments concerning wired transmission. We obtain data from an Android-based smart watch through Android Debug Bridge in the situation that the phone is not rooted [6]. Then we should conduct the same process on the watch when the phone is rooted to see whether more data is exposed after higher limits are acquired. It decides whether we are to root the criminals' phone in the reality [7]. After the experiments upon wired transmission achieves reliable results, we look into the methods of wireless sniffing, which involves skills in the use of tools and configuration of environment. We decide to use Ubertooth One to capture packets to identify what kind of packets we can make use of, to connect or to get control of the device. As we know, Bluetooth messages have unique description of their own, difference between them shall be told. After this process, we are to verify the security level of the smart watch and wristband in detail.

We have been convinced that the development of electronic forensics technology implies great research potential and provides great convenience for legal identification [8, 9]. Furthermore, the development of electronic forensic techniques will also promote the development of business to some degree. Viewing that the current society is a well-governed one ruled by a robust system of law, accurate proof and the defence of human rights are increasingly gaining focuses [10]. The development of electronic forensic techniques is bound to be beneficial to the implementation of fairness in legal concept, reinforcing the stability of public order and restraining the possibility of crime. After a period of study, we have conducted several experiments on smart watches of Android system [11] with tools like ADB.

This paper is organized as follows. Section 2 discusses the use of the tools and classifies the techniques into two types: the wireless and the wired. An overview of the whole experiment progressing in the techniques mentioned before is presented in Sect. 3. Section 4 is about the examples and experiment. Also, difficulty and trouble we met in the process will be included. In the last, conclusion and conceivable future are given in Sect. 5.

2 Tools Classification and Techniques Analysis

Generally, we get messages regarding work affairs simply through email or online chatting software, or sometimes from a portable device like the flash disk or SD card. The same way we get the data from the Bluetooth Smart. The most direct and efficient method is to do as it does, we intercept the data packets transmitting between these devices and receivers, trying to elicit something from the data though this way seem to be a little difficult and tough. And if permitted, with the right condition prepared, we get those data through wired methods.

2.1 Wireless Sniffing Through Ubertooth

Hardware Analysis: The evidence in smart watch and wristband cannot be obtained without tools. The use of tools allows us to better process data. However, all methods are exploited based on the tools. In our experiment, Ubertooth One and ADB are mainly used to collect evidence of intelligent devices.

Ubertooth One is the hardware platform of Project Ubertooth. It supersedes Ubertooth Zero and is currently the preferred platform. Reasons for the choice of this tool in experiment are as follows. Since Ubertooth One lists among the smallest stream-lined models, it enjoys a reputation for its superior performance in transmission and reception of RF signals up to 2.4 GHz. It includes radio, chassis and antenna in the whole kit. What's more, its software kit provides a direct usage guide and is open-sourced. The last factor we cannot neglect is that the device's micro controller is based on ARM Cortex-M3 which can be working at the full speed of USB. These are the advantages other tools do not possess.

Ubertooth One sniffs data packets and we use Wireshark to demonstrate the viewable results. After capturing packets, we use 'gatttool' to communicate with the Bluetooth lock of the BLE device to unlock the Bluetooth lock.

We use Ubertooth One to capture the signals sent from the Bluetooth devices, which effectively solves the problem of inability of extracting data by wire under inconvenient circumstances. It includes five parts:

RP-SMA RF connector, connects to test equipment, antenna, or dummy load.

CC2591 RF front end, a high-performance RF front end for low-power 2.4-GHz wireless application.

CC2400 wireless transceiver, a low-power single-chip 2.4 GHz ISM band transceiver with hardware features.

LPC175x ARM Cortex-M3 micro controller, it is equipped with Full-Speed USB 2. 0.

USB A plug, it connects to host computer running Kismet or other host code.

Environmental Prerequisites: Before running the hardware, we are to make some preparation for building libbtbb and Ubertooth tools. However, many of the prerequisites are available from the operating system's package repositories. Here we take Ubuntu 20. 04 for example (Figs. 1 and 2).

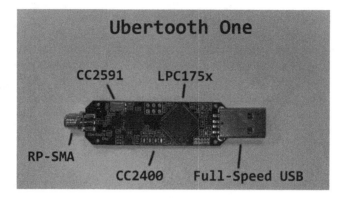

Fig. 1. Ubertooth introduction.

```
p46@ubuntu:~/Desktop$ sudo apt install cmake libusb-1.0-0-dev make gcc g++ libbluetooth-dev wget \
> pkg-config python3-numpy python3-qtpy python3-distutils python3-setuptools
```

Fig. 2. Packages to be installed.

These packages are required to guarantee the proper operation of the device. If you fail in installing some of them, you may refer to the Internet and correct it.

Next the Bluetooth baseband library (libbtbb) needs to be built for Ubertooth tools to decode Bluetooth packets (Fig. 3):

```
1   wget https://github.com/greatscottgadgets/libbtbb/archive/2020-12-R1.tar.gz -O libbtbb-2020-12-R1.tar.gz
2   tar -xf libbtbb-2020-12-R1.tar.gz
3   cd libbtbb-2020-12-R1
4   mkdir build
5   cd build
6   cmake ..
7   make
8   sudo make install
9   sudo ldconfig
```

Fig. 3. Libbtbb installation.

Ubertooth repository contains host code for sniffing Bluetooth packets, configuring Ubertooth and updating firmware. All three are built and installed by default using the following method (Fig. 4):

```
1   wget https://github.com/greatscottgadgets/ubertooth/releases/download/2020-12-R1/ubertooth-2020-12-R1.tar.xz
2   tar -xf ubertooth-2020-12-R1.tar.xz
3   cd ubertooth-2020-12-R1/host
4   mkdir build
5   cd build
6   cmake ..
7   make
8   sudo make install
9   sudo ldconfig
```

Fig. 4. Ubertooth packets installation.

When all these steps are over, do not forget to check your firmware version. You can run the command: **sudo Ubertooth-util −v** (Fig. 5).

```
cp48@ubuntu:/$ sudo ubertooth-util -v
[sudo] password for cp48:
Firmware version: 2020-12-R1 (API:1.07)
```

Fig. 5. Firmware version check.

If it is the first time for you to check the version and this command failed, run another command which manages the Dynamic Link Library: **sudo ldconfig**, and then run the previous command again.

Using Wireshark: The Wireshark BTBB and BR/EDR plugins allow Bluetooth baseband traffic that has been captured using Kismet to be analysed and directed within the Wireshark GUI. They are built separately from the rest of Ubertooth and libbtbb software (Fig. 6).

```
sudo apt-get install wireshark wireshark-dev libwireshark-dev cmake
cd libbtbb-2020-12-R1/wireshark/plugins/btbb
mkdir build
cd build
cmake -DCMAKE_INSTALL_LIBDIR=/usr/lib/x86_64-linux-gnu/wireshark/libwireshark3/plugins ..
make
sudo make install
```

Fig. 6. Wireshark installation.

Then repeat the BT BR/EDR plugin. When everything is ready, we are trying to capture some signals.

Replay Attack: A replay attack (also known as a repeat attack or playback attack) is a form of network attack in which valid data transmission is maliciously or fraudulently repeated or delayed. This is carried out either by the originator or by an adversary who intercepts the data and re-transmits it, possibly as part of a spoofing attack by IP packet substitution. This is one of the lower-tier versions of a man-in-the-middle attack. Replay attacks are usually passive in nature.

Another way of describing such an attack is: "an attack on a security protocol using a replay of messages from a different context into the intended (or original and expected) context, thereby fooling the honest participants into thinking they have successfully completed the protocol run."

In this case, we eavesdrop the packets transmitting between the Bluetooth Smart and the terminal (like a phone or a personal computer). Through this process, we can confirm the handle and value, thus come to a conclusion how the key is encrypted.

2.2   Wired Transmission

Android Debug Bridge: A versatile command line tool that lets you communicate with an emulator instance or connected Android-powered device. It is a client-server program that includes three components:

A client which runs on your development machine. You can invoke a client from a shell by issuing an ADB command. Other Android tools such as the ADT plugin and DDMS also create ADB clients. A server which runs as a background process on your development machine. The server manages communication between the client and the ADB daemon running on an emulator or device. A daemon which runs as a background process on each emulator or device instance.

Smart devices forensics dressing exquisite Bluetooth lock unlock, the data capture, different from the traditional forensics, intelligent dressing equipment of forensics with implanted with the most advanced encryption mechanism, also caused the difficulty of the forensics great influence, but despite this, smart wear equipment forensics will promote the forensics, evidence extraction.

However, for some devices they don't have an adapter interface but a charging port which by no means transmits data, like Xiaomi wristband. In this condition we check the data through a mobile phone. We ideally put the experimental environment into an Android terminal emulator on PC which to some extent restores a real mobile phone environment. It restores a Linux-like command terminal. We can get the data through ADB (Android Debug Bridge) orders quickly and discovered the key points in the database elicited from the Bluetooth Smart.

When we start an ADB client, the client first checks whether there is an ADB server process already running. If there isn't, it starts the server process. When the server starts, it binds to local TCP port 5037 and listens for commands sent from ADB clients —all ADB clients use port 5037 to communicate with the ADB server.

The server then sets up connections to all running emulator/device instances. It locates emulator/device instances by scanning odd-numbered ports in the range 5555 to 5585, the range used by emulators/devices. Where the server finds an ADB daemon, it sets up a connection to that port.

Once the server has set up connections to all emulator instances, you can use ADB commands to control and access those instances. Because the server manages connections to emulator/device instances and handles commands from multiple ADB clients, you can control any emulator/device instance from any client.

3   Methods Utilized in Research

Wireless Sniffing Section: In this part, we are going to depend on Ubertooth One to carry out our survey. First we plan to erect a tunnel like a pipe to capture signals through these ports. Because Uberooth One is able to work only in Linux environments, for it is easy to install all the packages needed. Moreover it is quite hard to set up a complete environment on Windows. So we conduct this experiment mainly on a Ubuntu virtual machine. Second, we are going to capture the signals from reliable bluetooth devices. They could be phones, headsets, PCs and wristbands and watches. We get to tell the difference between them and find the ones we need to contact and communicate with. The third step is that we have to follow these signals, by any form like MAC address or IP address and trace down to the device. We launch some attack messages and test how the device is going to respond. We judge its feasibility on every response we receive and then decide how to deal with the entrance defence mechanism.

After we have broken into the targeted watch, we are in total control of the device. Then we have to find some measure to search for the data stored in the watch itself. Finally, if possible we are going to find out how to make the device send back some data it recorded using command and orders.

Wired Transmission Section: Concerning Android-based watches and wristbands, we contact them through ADB, the debug bridge for transmission of computer and Android phone. We send commands to enter a Linux terminal environment. By then we look for data and installation packages of the application linked to the Bluetooth Smart in the interface of the whole Android system. Once we find the packages we can transfer them to the computer and make a deeper analysis of them, again, we use commands to do the transmission job. Via the two hardware, the ADB can reach a relatively high transmission speed.

In the backup file we have got we can find the corresponding messages using a forensics software, or we can count on the forensics software itself to read and automatically analyze the data. By this, the work of search may be easier. All we have to do is to look into the data and records and reach the final conclusion.

Last step, it is our task to summarize the data we collected into a right order and systematically simulate how the man wearing the device go with his life and style. Among the steps and experiences, we also have to elicit valuable and useful tips and information.

4 Smart Watch and Wristband Analyzing Examples

Upon previous theoretical study, we have had the idea how to fetch the data from the watch and wristband. Through experiment, we are more familiar and skillful with forensic process of smart watch and wristband.

4.1 Wireless Sniffing

When all the prerequisites have been settled, we can capture BLE in Wireshark with standard Wireshark builds.

1. Run the command: **mkfifo/tmp/pipe**

This step means open up a tunnel to listen in the signals captured by Ubertooth (Fig. 7).

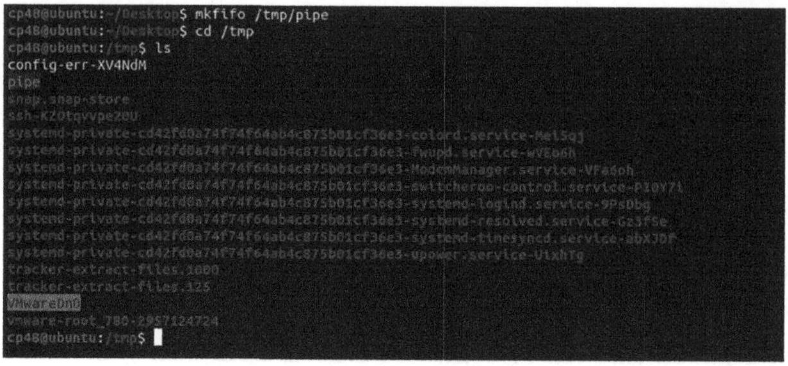

Fig. 7. Pipe set.

2. Open Wireshark in another terminal, click Capture -> Options
3. Click "Manage Interfaces" button on the right side of the window (Fig. 8).

Fig. 8. Operation guidance.

4. Click the "New" button, in the "Pipe" text box, type "**/tmp/pipe**" (Fig. 9).
5. Click Save, then click Close, back to the menu, click "Start".

Fig. 9. Operation guidance.

6. In a terminal, run Ubertooth-btle: **ubertooth-btle -f -c /tmp/pipe** (Fig. 10).

Fig. 10. Operation guidance.

In the Wireshark window you should see packets scrolling by (Fig. 11).

Fig. 11. The captured packets.

Packet Analysis: In the end of the process we have captured some packets with Info listed below:

ADV_IND, General broadcast

ADV_DIRECT_IND, Directional connection

ADV_NONCONN_IND, Unable to connect

ADV_SCAN_IND, Scannable device

SCAN_REQ, Active scanning request from the host

SCAN_RSP, Active scanning response from the guest

CONNECT_REQ, Connection request from the guest

…(and so many others like Unknown Direction Write Request, Handle: xxxx means request written in, and only with this request can we communicate with the smart devices.)

Problems Met: In these types only a few are available for qualified communication, and by no means can we anticipate how many of these are to be captured. In our study, no valid written-in request was received, so we had no choice but to stop researches with Ubertooth.

Replay Attack Simulate: As to the replay attack, we use a device that can capture signals, even a Bluetooth-ON mobile phone is adequate. Here we do with a smart phone. To analyze a Bluetooth log, we have to confirm the handle and value of a Bluetooth packet.

Authentication Mechanism: Smart band may be in two conditions: it is bonded to a phone, or not bonded. Through the phone, we can receive the Bluetooth log. As long as the smart watch is bonded, in the descriptor of the characteristic, we write in data in the descriptor handle. By then, the app on phone send back a Hexadecimal string to acquire a random digit. Then the wristband returns a corresponding string attached with the sixteen-bytes key to the app on the phone. Next, the app encrypts the key with the random digit, and send the string with encrypted data to the wristband. Here we come to the last step, wristband encrypts the key with the random digit in the same way. On contrast to the encrypted messages, if it compares the same, the wristband ought to return the specified string which means authentication passed. On the other hand, if it fails, it returns the string representing false.

Problems Met: Theory goes smoothly, however we have to mention it again that problems appear again. In our experimental mobile phone, we can see the descriptor in the characteristic, but we have no means to get response from it after we sent out the signals. After analysis we all think it should be the problem of limits of user or no entrance to a true developer mode. It is really a pity stopping here.

4.2   Wired Transmission

For it is hard to root a real Android phone these days and by using the emulator we can get to the same consequence. Data which is stored in one of the app on the phone can also be found on the app installed in the emulator as long as it has been synchronized. As we previously talk about, ADB is actually a C\S program run in the way of command. So we launch a terminal on Windows.

Connection: Enter the command: **adb devices**. This command will show all the devices available and try to complete the connection if you haven't connected the bridge to the emulator. For this is a emulator installed on computer, so right by the time the emulator turns on, the debug bridge has already been connected to the emulator by default (Fig. 12).

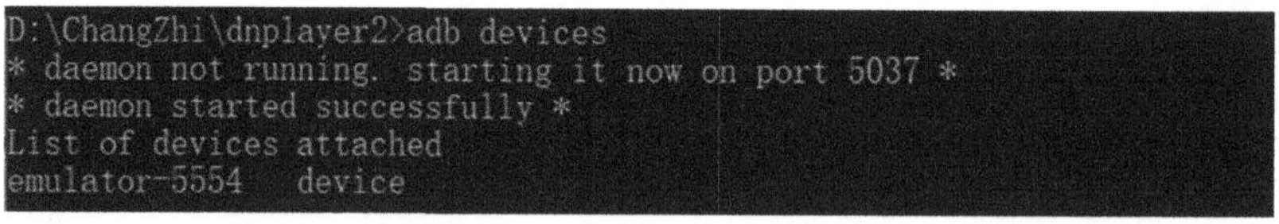

```
D:\ChangZhi\dnplayer2>adb devices
* daemon not running. starting it now on port 5037 *
* daemon started successfully *
List of devices attached
emulator-5554   device
```

Fig. 12. ADB devices listed.

If it is a real phone, we will have to know the phone's IP address. Connect the phone to the computer with a USB cable or some wire alike and then enter the command: **adb connect <host> [: <port>]**. 5037 is the default port of Android Debug Bridge.

Searching: After connected to the emulator, we are going to search for the relevant data stored in the packages. In order to provide a more familiar researching environment, enter the command: ADB **shell.**

By this we enter a interface like the terminal in Linux. It has been rooted by default. Enter the command: **pm list packages.**

In the packages we find one named *com.xiaomi.hm.health.* Enter the command: **cd /data/data/com.xiaomi.hm.health** and open it: **ls** (Fig. 13)

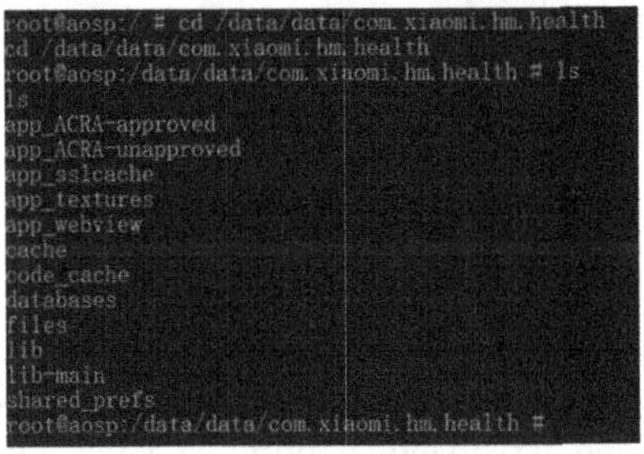

Fig. 13. Search of xiaomi health.

Transmission: We have to transmit the package to the computer. Exit the Linux shell interface. Enter the command: **adb pull/data/data/com.xiaomi.hm.health D:/** (Fig. 14).

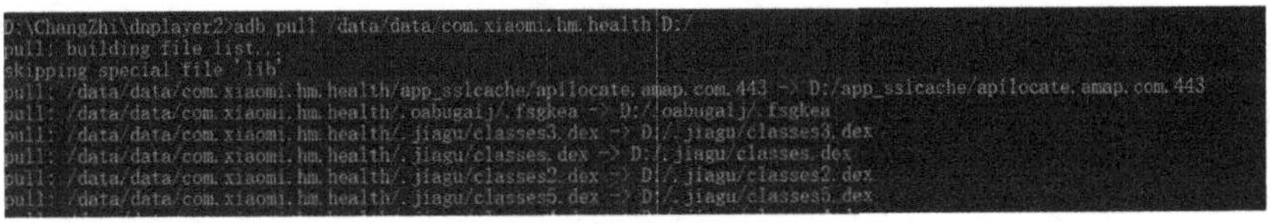

Fig. 14. Data transmission process.

And we can see file transmitted to the computer in a relatively short time.

Analysis: We have to find some crucial data from the database, especially with a suffix of.*db*. By use of Navicat Premium, we can observe some basic data like pressure and heart rate. Thus learning what condition the man wearing the device is in (Fig. 15).

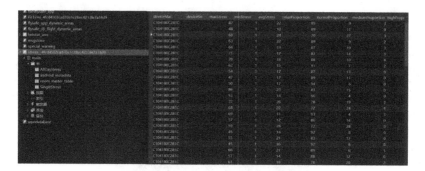

Fig. 15. Navicat database view.

5 Conclusion

The smart wearable device industry is in the ascendant, and its broad market potential is guaranteed as well as the prevalence rate in life. In this paper, through the forensics attempt of smart watch and wristband, it provides some help and reference for the future work of investigators. As the promising development of the market of the Bluetooth Smart, the forensic study about Bluetooth devices is bound to reach a new level of academic and practice.

Acknowledgement. The work is supported by 2020 Major Natural Science Research Project of Jiangsu Province Colleges and Universities: Research on Forensic Modeling and Analysis of the Internet of Things (20KJA520004), 2020 Open Project of National and Local Joint Engineering Laboratory of Radio Frequency Integration and Micro-assembly Technology: Research on the Security Performance of Radio Frequency Energy Collection Cooperative Communication Network (KFJJ20200201), 2021 Jiangsu Police Officer Academy Scientific Research Project: Research on D2D Cache Network Resource Optimization Based on Edge Computing Technology (2021SJYZK01), High-level Introduction of Talent Scientific Research Start-up Fund of Jiangsu Police Institute (JSPI19GKZL407).

References

1. Yuadi, I., Artaria, M.D., Asyhari, S., Asyhari, A.T.: Digital forensics for skulls classification in physical anthropology collection management. Comput. Mater. Continua **68**(3), 3979–3995 (2021)
2. Jones, G.M., Winster, S.G., Valarmathie, P.: Integrated approach to detect cyberbullying text: mobile device forensics data. Comput. Syst. Sci. Eng. **40**(3), 963–978 (2022)
3. Kazi, R.N.A., Kolhar, M., Rizwan, F.: Smart cardiowatch system for patients with cardiovascular diseases who live alone. Comput. Mater. Continua **66**(2), 1237–1250 (2021)
4. Almutairi, J., Aldossary, M.: Exploring and modelling IoT offloading policies in edge cloud environments. Comput. Syst. Sci. Eng. **41**(2), 611–624 (2022)
5. Oliver, S.G., Purusothaman, T.: Lightweight and secure mutual authentication scheme for IoT devices using CoAP protocol. Comput. Syst. Sci. Eng. **41**(2), 767–780 (2022)

6. Almogbil, A., Alghofaili, A., Deane, C., Leschke, T.: Digital forensic analysis of fitbit wearable technology: an investigator's guide. In: 2020 7th IEEE International Conference on Cyber Security and Cloud Computing (CSCloud)/2020 6th IEEE International Conference on Edge Computing and Scalable Cloud (EdgeCom), pp. 44–49. IEEE (2020)
7. Bulbul, H.I., Yavuzcan, H.G., Ozel, M.: Digital forensics: an analytical crime scene procedure model (ACSPM). Forensic Sci. Int. **233**(1–3), 244–256 (2013)
8. Akbal, E., Dogan, S.: Forensics image acquisition process of digital evidence. Int. J. Comput. Netw. Inf. Secur. **5**, 1–8 (2018). https://doi.org/10.5815/IJCNIS.2018.05.01
9. Chang, C.P., Chen, C.T., Lu, T.H., Lin, I.L., Huang, P., Lu, H.S.: Study on constructing forensic procedure of digital evidence on smart handheld device. In: 2013 International Conference on System Science and Engineering (ICSSE), pp. 223–228. IEEE (2013)
10. Marshall, A.M.: Digital forensic tool verification: an evaluation of options for establishing trustworthiness. Forensic Sci. Int. Digital Invest. **38**, 301181 (2021)
11. Lin, I.L., Chao, H.C., Peng, S.H.: Research of digital evidence forensics standard operating procedure with comparison and analysis based on smart phone. In: 2011 International Conference on Broadband and Wireless Computing, Communication and Applications, pp. 386–391. IEEE (2011)

Author Index

Printed in the United States
by Baker & Taylor Publisher Services